£5.00

ARISTOTLE

ARISTOTLE

New light on his life and on
some of his lost works

Volume I

*Some novel interpretations
of the man and his life*

Anton-Hermann Chroust

University of Notre Dame Press

American edition 1973
University of Notre Dame Press
Notre Dame, Indiana 46556

First published in 1973
by Routledge & Kegan Paul Ltd,
Broadway House, 68–74 Carter Lane
London EC4V 5EL
Printed in Great Britain by
Richard Clay (The Chaucer Press) Ltd, Bungay, Suffolk
© *1973 by Anton-Hermann Chroust*

Library of Congress Cataloging in Publication Data

Chroust, Anton-Hermann.
    Some novel interpretations of the man and his life.

    (His Aristotle: new light on his life and on some of his lost works,
v. 1)
    Includes bibliographical references.
    1. Aristoteles. I. Title. II. Series.
B481.C56 Vol. 1   185 [B]s   [185 [B]]   73-8892
ISBN 0–268–00517–6

To the Memory of
Roscoe Pound
Teacher, Friend, Scholar

Contents

CONTENTS

Volume II

Observations on some of Aristotle's lost works

Preface

This book, which consists of two distinct volumes, essentially is a collection of papers which I wrote between 1963 and 1968, when I became interested in the 'historical Aristotle'—the Aristotle revealed not merely in the highly problematic *Corpus Aristotelicum*, but also in the ancient biographical tradition and in the 'lost works' of the young Stagirite. Some of the papers collected and edited here owe their origin to classroom discussions and lectures which I offered while on leave from the Notre Dame Law School. They have previously been published in various journals, both in the United States and elsewhere. When re-editing these papers for this book, I made some far-reaching alterations, important additions, incisive corrections and, it is hoped, some worthwhile improvements.

But let the reader beware. This book, which is neither pro-Aristotelian nor anti-Aristotelian, reflects a predominantly historical attitude towards Aristotle and the essentially enigmatic 'Aristotelian problem.' Such an attitude might make it rather unpopular in certain quarters which, for reasons known only to the 'initiated,' insist on the timeless impersonality and absolute philosophic sovereignty of Aristotelian philosophy. The historical approach, which is opposed to all forms of emotional idolatry and uncritical dogmatism, however, should not make this book completely useless to those who for reasons of their own prefer 'Aristotelianism'—whatever that means—to Aristotle himself. Without an adequate grasp of Aristotle as a concrete historical phenomenon we may never gain an adequate understanding of his true position and concrete significance within the intellectual history of Western mankind. The particular human condition, being what it is, always was, and probably always will be, simply demands that man's deeds, from the most insignificant performance to the most exalted achievement, take place in a time continuum and, hence, in history. Timelessness and a-historicity always result in the deplorable loss of personality and individuality, and concomitantly, in the loss of

ix

real meaning. Dogmatic fervor, aside from impeding or retarding real scholarship, can never become an adequate substitute for historical facts.

Modern Aristotelian scholarship, which undoubtedly begins with Werner Jaeger, has brought about the realization that a more satisfactory and more adequate insight into Aristotle the philosopher requires a better understanding of Aristotle the man. Hence, we must know more about the historical personality called Aristotle and about the salient circumstances or events of his life. No attempt is made here, however, to write a coherent and exhaustive biography of the Stagirite. I limit myself to the scrutiny and discussion of several traditional biographies of Aristotle. Within the confines of these I further restrict myself to some significant incidents in his life and to certain characteristic traits of the man. Many of my discussions consist of 'educated guesses' and what appear to be reasonable conjectures or hypotheses intended to stimulate further investigations, rather than to offer definite or final answers. In brief, aside from attempting to supply some tentative answers, this book is also a deliberate search for additional suggestions, informed challenges and scholarly disagreements. Only in the dispassionate confrontation of conflicting scholarly views may we ever hope to obtain true insights into the significant incidents in the ntellectual history of mankind.

Since some of Aristotle's 'lost works,' at least those discussed here, apparently belong to the formative era of his philosophic thought, they would seem to reveal, as Werner Jaeger has pointed out, the main trends in Aristotle's intellectual development. Hence, Jaeger's views on matters relating to the evaluation of Aristotle's philosophic thought are considered as being of great importance. It is conceded, however, that as regards certain details and interpretations, subsequent scholarship has added, amplified, modified, corrected and even discarded some of Jaeger's notions. To list the names of all the scholars who, in one way or another, have contributed to the retrieval, reconstruction and interpretation of the 'lost works' would require a separate volume, especially if I had intended to discuss all their suggestions, theories and scholarly disagreements. Suffice it to say that their many and varied contributions are of the highest quality, always stimulating and certainly exciting. Their labors, hypotheses and even their errors have vitally contributed to the tentative solutions of the many almost insurmountable difficulties connected with Aristotle's 'lost works.'

Aside from supplying clues as to the general course of Aristotle's intellectual development, the 'lost works' of the Stagirite are in themselves of abiding interest to us. They are, in an unequivocal sense, an essential part of the philosophic literature of antiquity. As such they deserve our close attention, especially since they seem to have enjoyed much authority during the third, second, and early part of the first centuries B.C. When dealing with the 'lost works,' we must always proceed on the fair assumption that their identification, attribution, reconstruction and interpretation have, in the main, been successful. In the light of present Aristotelian scholarship, it must be conceded, however, that these identifications, attributions, reconstructions and interpretations are at best disciplined conjectures. This fact is only too well known to all those who have dealt with the many vexing problems connected with the 'lost works' of Aristotle.

Some, though by no means all, scholars are of the opinion that in certain vital aspects the 'lost works' of Aristotle seem to conflict with the philosophic views espoused in the traditional *Corpus Aristotelicum*. This, in turn, raises the further and far-reaching problem, not to be discussed here: whether the author of the 'lost works' and the author of at least some of the treatises included in the *Corpus Aristotelicum* are one and the same person. Valentin Rose, who already realized that the philosophic standpoint manifest in the 'lost works' is not always compatible with that expressed in the doctrinal treatises or *pragmateia*, simply declared the former *pseudepigrapha*. W. Jaeger attempted to overcome this impasse by claiming that in his progression from the early 'lost works' to the later doctrinal treatises collected in the *Corpus*, Aristotle underwent a noticeable philosophic conversion from an initial Platonism characteristic of his earlier years to a definite 'Aristotelianism' typical of his later years. Both Rose and Jaeger, it will be noted, never so much as questioned Aristotle's authorship of the *Corpus*. In 1952, Joseph Zürcher, in his *Aristoteles Werk und Geist—Aristotle's Work and Spirit*—(Paderborn, 1952), advanced or, more accurately, implied the startling thesis, subsequently rejected by almost all scholars,[1] that certain treatises incorporated in the *Corpus*, especially the *Metaphysics*, must in large part be credited to Theophrastus and to the Early Peripatus, although it is quite certain that some Aristotelian compositions actually came to be included in the *Corpus*. In this fashion, Zürcher in fact reversed, at least in part, the obviously traditionalist position taken by Rose and Jaeger. Perhaps the theses advocated by Zürcher, with certain far-reaching reservations and modifications, deserve further investigation. After all, the tradition concerning the transmission of Aristotle's doctrinal or 'intra-mural' writings lends some support to his views.[2] Presumably, at some future time, we might, whether we like it or not, be compelled to rename the present *Corpus*

Aristotelicum and call it more discriminatingly *Corpus Scriptorum Peripateticorum Veterum*, that is, a 'collection' of writings which not only includes authentic *Aristotelica*, but in all likelihood also contains authentic *Peripatetica*. In other words, in the light of Theophrastus' last will and testament (DL V. 52), this 'collection' might also contain compositions of the Early Peripatetics (down to approximately the year 287–86 B.C.). As regards present-day progressive Aristotelian scholarship, such a possibility, however, is highly problematic. Upon closer scrutiny, it might prove to be wholly abortive or, more likely, incapable of scientific proof.

Any scholarly undertaking which aims at renaming the traditional *Corpus Aristotelicum* by calling it *Corpus Scriptorum Peripateticorum Veterum* implies nothing less than the extremely involved and, in a way, very risky attempt to challenge the authenticity of at least certain parts of the *Corpus Aristotelicum*. Such an endeavor would, in all likelihood, have to proceed along the following four major lines of inquiry (two of which are discussed in the present book).

First, we must produce a more thorough, more detailed and more reliable account of the salient events in the life of Aristotle. The external circumstances surrounding as well as influencing the life of a scholar and author, as a rule, have a determining, if not decisive, influence on his scholarly and literary productivity. In the particular case of Aristotle, our main sources, that is, the extant ancient biographical reports or remarks, provided they contain reliable information, permit us to assume that during the greater part of his adult life he was vitally involved in some of King Philip's political operations and aspirations, which during a relatively short span of time transformed Macedonia, the homeland of Aristotle, into a world power. Thus it might be surmised that Aristotle's prolonged visit with Hermias of Atarneus (348–47 to 345–44 B.C.), for instance, was primarily a diplomatic mission in the service of King Philip rather than a purely 'philosophic excursion,' commonly referred to as the 'Assian period,' or, as some scholars would have it, a 'phase in his intellectual reorientation' spent in Assos in the company of Erastus and Coriscus. It may be possible that a different political mission preoccupied the time of Aristotle's second sojourn in Athens between 335–34 and 323 B.C., a period which traditionally has been referred to as his philosophic *Meisterjahre*—the years in which he is said to have produced his greatest systematic works on philosophy. The particular circumstances of his return to Athens in the year 335–34 B.C.; the general political and emotional atmosphere prevailing in Athens during his second stay; and the particular nature of his likely 'political mission' in Athens during these turbulent thirteen years—all these facts or factors, however, do not seem to have been particularly conducive to the production of great systematic works on philosophy.

Second, we must more thoroughly investigate the lost early works of Aristotle, the vast majority of which were probably composed before his departure from Athens and from the Platonic Academy in 348–47 B.C.[3] Since we possess only 'fragments' of these lost works, and since some of these fragments are of a very problematic nature, as is their proper assignment to a specific composition, such an investigation in itself is extremely hazardous. While some scholars maintain to have discovered distinct Platonisms in these early lost works (which as such are unquestionably authentic), other scholars emphatically deny this. Assuming that the Platonism of the lost early works can reliably be established, then the following three hypotheses might possibly be advanced: (I) The historical Aristotle was essentially a Platonist, although on some minor points as well as in the manner in which he presented his arguments he deviated from Plato; (II) after his departure from Athens and from the Platonic Academy in 348–47 B.C. he abandoned the 'philosophic life' in order to dedicate himself primarily to political and diplomatic activities on behalf of King Philip; and (III) the great systematic works or *pragmateia* of a later period are mainly the products of Theophrastus' school (the Early Peripatus) and of its 'systematizing tendencies,' although they probably contain some substantially Aristotelian elements.

Third, we would have to know more about the details concerning the transmission of the traditional *Corpus Aristotelicum* after 286 B.C. Perhaps the most significant, as well as most fateful, event in the whole history of this transmission is the passage contained in the last will and testament of Theophrastus, the scholarch of the Peripatus, probably drafted shortly before 287–86 B.C. and preserved by Diogenes Laertius (DL V. 52): 'And the library [of the Peripatus] I leave and bequeath to Neleus [of Scepsis].' This passage, which refers to the whole library of the Peripatus as it existed in *c.* 287–86 B.C., undoubtedly relates not only to the 'intra-mural' works of Aristotle, provided such 'intra-mural writings' ever existed, but also to the compositions of the Early Peripatetics (written after 323–22 B.C.). Neleus took the whole library to Scepsis (in North-Western Asia Minor), where after his death his heirs permitted it to deteriorate badly and to become partly lost or irreparably damaged. The long and confusing wanderings of this library, which lasted for more than two centuries, the several futile as well as inept attempts to recover and restore it, and the many capricious efforts to implement, correct and edit its essentially unidentifiable remnants, make it impossible for us to ascertain with any degree of certainty which parts, if any, of this Peripatetic library were authored by Aristotle, and which parts were composed by Theophrastus and by Theophrastus' associates and disciples. It is quite possible and, as a matter of fact, very likely that after its recovery (*c.* during the first decade of the first century B.C. by Apellicon of Teos, or *c.* the middle of the first century B.C. by Andronicus of Rhodes), this whole library simply came to be known as 'the works of Aristotle.' This might also explain, among other matters, why so few of the authentic compositions of the Early Peripatetics who, judging from the surviving ancient lists of their works, must have been rather prolific writers, are preserved under the name of their true authors. Whether or not some of the Aristotelian *pragmateia* ever reached Alexandria during the third and second centuries B.C., or whether some 'copies' of these *pragmateia* ever existed outside the Peripatus and, hence, escaped the tragic fate that befell the library of Neleus, is difficult to ascertain. The fact that these *pragmateia* seem generally to have remained unknown until about the middle of the first century B.C., apparently speaks against such an assumption.[4] In any event, the manner in which the library of the Peripatus (as it stood in *c.* 287–86 B.C.) was handled after Neleus had transported it to Scepsis, in all likelihood will defeat any effort to establish with any degree of certainty the true identity of those authors who, prior to the year 287–86 B.C., might have contributed to it.[5]

And, *fourth*, we might attempt to ascertain the Aristotelian authorship of the *Corpus Aristotelicum*, or of any part thereof, through the reliance on 'internal evidence,' that is, through the use of such criteria as literary style, linguistics, and technical terminology; as well as through the employment of such standards as methodology, systematics, modes of argumentation and proof, and the general philosophic tenor of the works incorporated in the *Corpus*. In view of the fact that we apparently lack any authoritative knowledge of Aristotle's authentic writings and, hence, do not possess any valid or reliable criteria to carry out such an investigation, this last approach, as the scholarly work of Joseph Zürcher has clearly shown, is an extremely difficult if not impossible undertaking, not to say an unrewarding and outright hazardous task.

It remains for some intrepid and unprejudiced scholar to explore these four proposed avenues of inquiry, and in doing so, to verify, particularize, modify, implement or reject the general suggestion that the traditional *Corpus Aristotelicum* might possibly and, perhaps, more appropriately be renamed *Corpus Scriptorum Peripateticorum Veterum*.[6] It is possible, therefore, that further investigations may, indeed, remove any and all reasonable doubts about the authenticity of the whole *Corpus Aristotelicum* and thus assuage our justifiable apprehension. But only in the restrained confrontation of conflicting views may we ever attain to scholarly truth; and only through competent and dispassionate investigation into the merits of each of these conflicting views may we ever resolve our unending quest for true knowledge.

Acknowledgments are gratefully made to the following learned journals or publications which permitted, in a substantially altered and often radically modified form, the re-publication of the articles or papers collected in this book: *Acta Antiqua Academiae Scientiarum Hungaricae* (Hungary); *Acta Classica* (South Africa); *Acta Orientalia* (Denmark); *Antiquité Classique* (Belgium); *Apeiron* (Australia); *Classical Folia* (U.S.A.); *Classical Philology* (U.S.A.); *Divus Thomas* (Italy); *Emerita* (Spain); *Greece and Rome* (Britain); *Hermes* (Germany); *Historia* (Germany); *Journal of the History of Philosophy* (U.S.A.); *Laval Théologique et Philosophique* (Canada); *Mnemosyne* (The Netherlands); *Modern Schoolman* (U.S.A.); *New Scholasticism* (U.S.A.); *Notre Dame Lawyer* (U.S.A.); *Review of Metaphysics* (U.S.A.); *Revue des Études Grecques* (France); *Rheinisches Museum für Philologie* (Germany); *Rivista Critica di Storia della Filosofia* (Italy); *Symbolae Osloenses* (Norway); *Tijdschrift voor Filosofie* (Belgium); and *Wiener Studien* (Austria).[7]

The major draft of the original manuscript had to be completed early in 1968. Hence, barring a few exceptions, the subsequent secondary literature could not be considered. In view of the fact that there exists an immense host of secondary works on Aristotle of greatly varying value and of frequently irreconcilable philolosophic or scholarly viewpoints, it was decided to forgo the task of adding a special bibliography. The reader will find ample references to the sources and to the secondary literature in the numerous footnotes.

I am deeply indebted to many persons: to my several assistants, who during the past years have aided me in many ways; to countless libraries and librarians, both in the United States and elsewhere, who were always ready to supply me with materials and valuable bits of information; to my many friends and colleagues in many universities, both in the United States and elsewhere, who not only counselled me wisely and generously, but also criticized some of my views as well as directed my attention to texts and publications which had escaped me; and to the many scholars, both past and present, whose tireless efforts and brilliant publications have been of immeasurable help to me. To all these friends, mentors and benefactors, whose encouragement, counsel and assistance was sorely needed and is sincerely appreciated, I express my deeply felt and everlasting gratitude.

Since I am under obligation to so many people, it is simply impossible to list all the individual names of those who have helped and assisted me. I wish, however, to mention my student assistants who unstintingly gave me much of their time as well as their devotion and ability in the writing, re-writing, editing, typing and proof-reading of the original manuscript or the original papers: Miss N. Deane (now Mrs Dennis W. Moran), Mr Ronald G. Brander and Mr Joseph A. Novak, all of the University of Notre Dame Graduate School; Mr John G. Hund and Mr Thomas Farrell, both of the Notre Dame Law School; Miss Aletta M. Fonte of the College of St Mary's; Mr Kelly Morris, Mr Daniel J. Burns, Mr Dudley Andrew, Mr Joseph Starshak, Mr Kevin Flynn, Mr Alfred J. Leotta, Mr Bernard M. Ryan, Mr Phillip R. Herndon, Mr Richard J. Wall, Jr. and Mr Glenn L. Smerillo, all students at the University of Notre Dame; and Mr. Michael E. Libonati, a student at the Yale Law School. It was both delightful and instructive to work with this splendid group of earnest young people who, although pursuing vastly different interests and studies, were enthusiastically collaborating with me in the spirit of that intellectual eagerness and curiosity which is the very soul of any true *universitas litterarum*. I also want to thank the University of Notre Dame, the Center of the Study of Man in Contemporary Society at the University of Notre Dame, and the Institute for International Studies at the University of Notre Dame for having assisted me with generous grants-in-aid and leaves of absence which enabled me to carry on scholarly investigations. Last, but not least, I am forever indebted to Mr Frank P. Mancino, a former student of mine, whose generosity made possible the publication of this book. For the errors which I have undoubtedly committed I assume full responsibility.

No simple words of acknowledgement, however, could possibly express my feelings of affection and gratitude towards the one to whose memory this book is dedicated: Roscoe Pound, who by his many accomplishments in the almost limitless realms of the human intellect has won for himself an everlasting place among scholars.

Abbreviations

DL   Diogenes Laertius, *The Lives and Opinions of Eminent Philosophers*

DH   Dionysius of Halicarnassus, *I Epistola ad Ammaeum*

VH   *Vita Aristotelis Hesychii* (*Vita Menagiana, Vita Menagii*)

VM   *Vita Aristotelis Marciana*

VV   *Vita Aristotelis Vulgata* (*Vita Pseudo-Ammoniana, Vita Pseudo-Elias*)

VL   *Vita Aristotelis Latina*

I VS   *I Vita Aristotelis Syriaca* (author unknown), Cod. Berol. Sachau 226

II VS   *II Vita Aristotelis Syriaca* (author unknown), Cod. Vat. Syriacus 158

I VA   *I Vita Aristotelis Arabica* (Ibn Abi Yaqub an-Nadim, *Kitab al-Fihrist*)

II VA   *II Vita Aristotelis Arabica* (Abu-l-Wafa al-Mubassir (or Mubashir) Ibn Fatik, *Kitab Mukhtar al-Hikam wa-Mahasin al-Kilam—The Book of Selections from Wisdom and Beautiful Sayings*)

III VA   *III Vita Aristotelis Arabica* (Al-Qifti Gamaladdin al-Qadi al-Akram, *Tabaqat al-Hukama—Schools of the Wise Men*)

IV VA   *IV Vita Aristotelis Arabica* (Ibn Abi Usaibia, *Uyun al-Anba fi Tabaqat al-Atibba—Book of Sources of Information About the Schools of Doctors*)

In the Arabic names and titles, the 'accents' have been omitted. The *Vitae Aristotelis* mentioned above have been compiled and are easily accessible in I. Düring, *Aristotle in the Ancient Biographical Tradition*, Studia Graeca et Latina Gothoburgensia, vol. 63, no. 2 (Göteborg, 1957).

Introduction

Aside from a more general and rather sweeping discussion of the several *Vitae Aristotelis* in Chapter I, only the *Vita* (or *Chronologia*) *Aristotelis* of Dionysius of Halicarnassus, the *Vita* of Diogenes Laertius and the *Vitae* of the Syriac and Arabic biographers are treated in this book with any detail. The *Vita Aristotelis Marciana*, which was recently edited by O. Gigon, the *Vita Hesychii* (*Vita Menagii* or *Vita Menagiana*), the *Vita Vulgata*, the *Vita Latina* and the brief biographical sketches found in the Neo-Platonic commentaries to the works of Aristotle, on the other hand, have not received special treatment, although frequent reference is made to them.[1] Chapter I also makes an attempt to re-construct the essential content of the lost *Vita Aristotelis* of Hermippus of Smyrna as well as that of the likewise lost *Vita Aristotelis* of Ptolemy (-el-Garib). These two *Vitae*, it is claimed, constitute the most important sources or intermediary authorities for the majority of the subsequent *Vitae*. Chapter II, which discusses the *Vita Aristotelis* of Dionysius of Halicarnassus, indicates that this *Vita* is actually a brief chronology which offers little detailed information, except some valuable and apparently accurate biographical data. The *Vita Aristotelis* of Diogenes Laertius, which is analyzed in Chapter III, poses many vexing problems, some of which are almost impossible to resolve. Especially difficult to determine are the sources used by Diogenes Laertius. There can be little doubt, however, that this *Vita*, as we shall see in Chapter I, draws heavily on the *Vita* of Hermippus. Chapter IV, again, presents a general survey and discussion of the Syriac and Arabic *Vitae Aristotelis* without entering into a detailed analysis of each individual *Vita*. This particular chapter is primarily an attempt to illustrate the peculiar biographical trend introduced (?) by the Neo-Platonic biographers and by Ptolemy (-el-Garib) in particular. Of necessity no less than by design, the expository and analytical discussions of all these *Vitae Aristotelis* are at times repetitious in that certain statements found in one *Vita* are referred to or restated again and again.

It may be contended that Chapters I–IV are actually part of a more general introduction to Chapters V–XVII. This is also indicated by the fact that Chapters V–XVII are prefaced by a lengthy 'Headnote.' Hence, a reader not wishing to be bored by acribic '*Quellenforschung*,' may safely ignore Chapters I–IV. More specifically, Chapters I–IV present and discuss the many and at times desperately involved problems connected with a more detailed analysis and evaluation of certain, though by no means all, biographical sources. The somewhat arbitrary selection of these biographical sources was made on the basis of the following considerations: The lost *Vita Aristotelis* of Hermippus and the lost *Vita Aristotelis* of Ptolemy (-el-Garib), it is widely and probably correctly held, constitute what appear to be the two main biographical trends. The *Vita* of Diogenes Laertius, in particular, to a fairly large extent, though not exclusively, relies on the *Vita* of Hermippus (as does the *Vita Aristotelis* of Hesychius) and, hence, at least in part, may be considered an 'epitome' or 'derivative' of the latter. The Syriac and Arabic *Vitae*, in turn, are primarily based on the *Vita* of Ptolemy (-el Garib)—as are the *Vita Marciana*, the *Vita Vulgata* and the *Vita Latina*—and, hence, may be called 'epitomes' or 'derivatives' of Ptolemy's biography. The *Vita Aristotelis* of Dionysius of Halicarnassus, which is largely based on what appear to be independent investigations, seems to follow a course of inquiry all its own.

The remainder of Volume I contains observations, at times of a highly speculative or conjectural nature, on some salient events in the life and experiences of Aristotle, including a tentative genealogy of Aristotle (Chapter V) as well as a discussion of his relationship to Callisthenes of Olynthus (Chapter VI). Of particular interest to the student of ancient philosophy and ancient history might be Chapter VII, which investigates Aristotle's entrance into the Platonic Academy in the year 367 B.C. and the particular circumstances surrounding this significant incident. This subject is touched upon again in Chapter XIII. Chapter VIII discusses Aristotle's first attempt at teaching rhetoric in the Academy. Chapter IX tries to shed some light on the likely reason or reasons for Aristotle's rather sudden withdrawal from Athens and the Academy in the year 348 B.C. This particular chapter denies that Plato's death was the cause of Aristotle's departure—a subject which is also discussed in Chapter XIII. Chapter X, which is highly conjectural, raises the question of whether Aristotle was in fact the preceptor or chief instructor of Alexander the Great. Chapter XI deals with some of the peculiar circumstances surrounding Aristotle's return to Athens in the year 335–34 B.C. Chapter XII, like Chapter XIII, attempts to shed some light on the likely causes of Aristotle's second flight from Athens in the year 323 B.C. Chapter XIII, which takes up again some of the problems and events discussed in Chapters VII, IX, XI and XII, essays to show that Aristotle might have been something more than just a withdrawn and unworldly philosopher—that he might have been actively involved in some of King Philip's political and diplomatic machinations. Chapter XIV attempts to disprove the story, apparently circulated in antiquity, that Aristotle committed suicide in the year 322 B.C. Chapter XV analyzes and evaluates the two extant major versions of Aristotle's last will and testament, one of the few surviving primary documents relating to the Stagirite. Chapters XVI and XVII contain attempts to sketch what appear to be some of Aristotle's main traits of character as they might be culled from his writings.

The general nature of this book as well as the particular mode in which certain topics are presented or argued make it almost necessary to repeat or restate certain statements, analyses and conjectures. Chapter XIII, for instance, reviews, in a slightly altered form and for a different purpose, topics, incidents and issues which are also discussed or prepared in Chapters VII, IX, XI and XII. In a book of this kind, such repetitions are apparently unavoidable and, perhaps, even necessary for the sake of clarity and persuasiveness.

It goes without saying that much of what is suggested especially in Chapters V–XVII is to some extent based on conjectures, educated guesses and informed speculations resting on the mastery and intelligent exploitation of all available sources. In the light of our frequently inadequate and often conflicting sources—the fact that many of these sources often manifest either an unmistakably encomiastic tendency or an outright defamatory and hostile attitude—such conjectures are now and then necessary, not to say unavoidable, provided they stay within the bounds of reason tempered by an adequate grasp and intelligent evaluation of all available information. It is not expected, however, that the reader accept any of the suggestions proffered in these chapters. But he might be stimulated to re-think and re-evaluate some of the conventional notions concerning certain crucial incidents in the life of Aristotle. In so doing he might also discover more satisfactory and persuasive answers to some of the many puzzling and so far unanswered or inadequately answered problems connected with the biographical tradition of Aristotle. In any event, a closer and perhaps more critical scrutiny of all the available biographical materials should divulge or at least suggest that the historical Aristotle was apparently a very complex person, having many interests and pursuing varied activities. It may also show that he probably played an active and, perhaps, important role in the political rise of Macedonia to a great power. Furthermore, such an examination might indicate that, in consequence of his political and diplomatic activities, Aristotle assisted in laying the foundation as well as in establishing the political pre-requisites for the far-flung conquests of Alexander the Great which ushered in a new and extremely fruitful epoch in the intellectual, political and cultural history of Western mankind. Together with the early but now lost works and the later doctrinal treatises of Aristotle, provided the latter are in their entirety by Aristotle, such a scrutiny also seems to indicate that Aristotle was possessed of a very attractive personality.

Shortly before the year 200 B.C., the Alexandrian grammarian Hermippus of Smyrna composed a *Collection of the Lives of the [Peripatetic] Philosophers* which also included a *Vita Aristotelis*. It is safe to assume that Hermippus made use of a *Collection* (of pertinent facts and documents pertaining to the lives and achievements of the first scholarchs of the Peripatus, including those of Aristotle) compiled by Ariston of Ceos, the successor (in 226 B.C.?) of Lycon in the Peripatetic scholarchate. Around the middle of the second century B.C., Apollodorus of Athens established what appears to be a fairly accurate 'chronology' of the main events in the life of the Stagirite. After the middle of the first century B.C., it seems, Andronicus of Rhodes, in connection with his edition of the *Corpus Aristotelicum*, composed a sort of brief *Vita Aristotelis*—a kind of outline recording the main events in the life of Aristotle. The thesis that Andronicus was the author of a *Vita Aristotelis*, however, has been rejected by some scholars.

All these *Vitae* are lost, but they seem to have survived, at least in part and certainly with some important changes, in later biographical accounts. Thus, the *Vita Aristotelis* (or *Chronologia Vitae Aristotelis*) of Dionysius of Halicarnassus, written during the first century B.C., to some extent might have been influenced by the *Chronology* or *Chronicle* of Apollodorus. During the third century A.D., Diogenes Laertius composed his *Vita Aristotelis*, which constitutes the first part of Book V of his *Vitae Philosophorum*. This particular *Vita*, it is widely held, relies rather indiscriminately and not always judiciously upon Ariston of Ceos, Apollodorus and, especially, on Hermippus, as well as on a host of other reporters. Probably in the course of the fourth century A.D., Ptolemy, who in all likelihood was a member of the Neo-Platonic school of Iamblichus, wrote a *Vita Aristotelis*. The sources or materials used by Ptolemy, whom the Arabs called Ptolemy-el-Garib (Ptolemy 'the Stranger'), are not known for certain, but it is reasonably safe to assume that he relied, at least to a limited extent (and perhaps indirectly), upon the *Vita* of Hermippus, the *Vita* of Andronicus of Rhodes and upon a number of other biographers and authors who can no longer be identified.

The original *Vita Aristotelis* of Ptolemy is lost, but during the fifth century A.D. an epitome of this *Vita* was made. This epitome became the basis of the following (surviving) *Vitae Aristotelis*: The *Vita Aristotelis Marciana*, the *Vita Aristotelis Vulgata* (which might date back to the Neo-Platonic school of Elias), the *Vita Aristotelis Latina* (which is a thirteenth-century Latin translation of a Greek epitome of Ptolemy's *Vita*), the two (anonymous) Syriac *Vitae Aristotelis*, and the four Arabic *Vitae Aristotelis*. The *Vita Marciana*, the *Vita Vulgata*, and the Greek original of the *Vita Latina*, in the main reflect the practice of the Neo-Platonic authors and teachers to preface their writings and lectures on Aristotle with some excursions on the life of Aristotle, based on an epitome of Ptolemy's *Vita Aristotelis*. Hence, they are the products of several generations of Neo-Platonic teachers and commentators. The four Arabic *Vitae Aristotelis*, on the other hand, are based on a Syriac (now lost) translation of an epitome of Ptolemy's original *Vita Aristotelis*, while the two Syriac *Vitae* are short *résumés* of this translation. The *Vita Aristotelis Hesychii*, also called the *Vita Menagiana* or *Vita Menagii*, was authored during the sixth century A.D. by the historian Hesychius of Miletus who made it a part of his *Onomatologon*. This *Vita* seems to have been influenced by the *Vita Aristotelis* of Hermippus or by sources which in part rely on Hermippus, including perhaps the *Vita* of Diogenes Laertius.

Some of these *Vitae Aristotelis* are discussed in greater detail in Chapters I–IV. Finally, there survives a number of short 'biographical introductions' to some of the Neo-Platonic commentaries to the doctrinal treatises of Aristotle. These 'biographical introductions,' which date back to the sixth century A.D., likewise were influenced by the *Vita Aristotelis* of Ptolemy.

Aside from the extant *Vitae Aristotelis*, our biographical knowledge of Aristotle is based on the following evidence: (a) autobiographical references or allusions contained in the preserved didactic or doctrinal treatises (*Corpus Aristotelicum*), provided the latter in their entirety are authentic; (b) autobiographical references and allusions found in the surviving fragments of the early lost works of Aristotle; (c) documentary evidence; (d) versifications of Aristotle; (e) letters of Aristotle, provided the latter are authentic; and (f) the reports and accounts of ancient authors, especially those of his contemporaries or of writers who lived one or two generations after Aristotle.

One of the striking features of the preserved *Corpus Aristotelicum* is the paucity of direct autobiographical references.[2] *Nicomachean Ethics* 1096 a 33 ff., for instance, contains an indirect and rather general allusion to Aristotle's close association with the Platonic Academy. *Nicomachean Ethics* 1172 b 15 ff., on the other hand, might contain a personal remark of Aristotle reflecting his admiration for Eudoxus' excellence of character. In the *Metaphysics* and *Nicomachean Ethics* we find some direct or indirect (and occasionally highly critical) references to Speusippus[3] and Xenocrates.[4] There are no indications of Aristotle's friendship with Hermias of Atarneus, although *Politics* 1267 a 31 ff. relates an episode in the life of Eubulus of Atarneus, the 'predecessor' of Hermias. Neither are we informed of the fact that there existed close ties of friendship between Aristotle and King Philip of Macedonia, although the assassination of Philip is mentioned in *Politics* 1311 b 1 ff. This almost complete lack of any autobiographical reports in the doctrinal treatises, even where such reports would be wholly appropriate, is in itself rather disturbing. As such, it might cast an ominous shadow on the authenticity of these treatises. The doctrinal treatises, provided they are authentic or, at least, in part authentic, however, permit certain indirect references or some valid assumptions as to the main traits of Aristotle's character and intellectual or moral outlook in general.[5]

The surviving fragments of Aristotle's lost works, on the other hand, seem to indicate that these early compositions contain some valuable bits of biographical information, such as Aristotle's close friendship with Eudemus of Cyprus,[6] his acquaintance (?) with Themison of Cyprus,[7] his personal relations with Alexander,[8] his religious convictions,[9] his personal views on 'nobility' of character and deportment[10] and his conception of true *paideia*,[11] pleasure[12] and wealth.[13] Moreover, according to weighty ancient evidence, the majority of Aristotle's early works, which are without doubt authentic, were written in the form of dialogues in which the author himself often appeared as the main interlocutor or leader of the discussion,[14] while the other interlocutors maintained a philosophic position frequently opposed to that held by Aristotle. Such a method, it will have to be conceded, not only permits but actually invites 'autobiographical' observations or self-revelations which would indicate Aristotle's basic outlook as well as his intellectual attitude towards other philosophers or philosophies.

As might be expected, the 'documentary evidence' concerning Aristotle is rather meager. It consists (a) of Aristotle's last will and testament, preserved in an abridged (and perhaps somewhat mutilated) form by Diogenes Laertius as well as by some of the Arabic biographers of Aristotle;[15] (b) of an 'inscription' by the Amphictionic League (probably of the year 329–28 B.C.) honoring Aristotle for certain services he had rendered the League;[16] and (c) of an honorific inscription by the city of Ephesus (probably of the year 318–17 B.C.) conferring the decree of *proxenia* on Nicanor, the nephew (or adopted son?) of Aristotle.[17] It may also be argued that the *Vita Aristotelis Marciana* 17, the *Vita Aristotelis Vulgata* 17 and the *Vita Aristotelis Latina* 17[18] contain what might be a reference to, or distinct echo of, an honorific decree (or decree of *proxenia*) which at one time was bestowed upon Aristotle by the city of Stagira. The same may hold true as regards the report contained in the *Vita Aristotelis Arabica* of Ibn Abi Usaibia 17–21, where we are informed that at one time the Athenians proposed (and perhaps erected) an honorific *stele* dedicated to Aristotle, commemorating his many beneficial services to the city of Athens.[19]

As far as we are still able to ascertain, the versifications of Aristotle consist of an *Elegy* in memory of Plato (or Eudemus?),[20] a *Hymn* to Eros(?) or to Helios(?),[21] an *Elegy* to Artemis,[22] an honorific inscription intended for a commemorative *stele* for Hermias of Atarneus in Delphi,[23] and a *Hymn* in memory as well as in honor of Hermias.[24]

The ancient biographers of Aristotle, as well as some other ancient authors, relate that the Stagirite wrote numerous letters to a great many people.[25] It is well-nigh impossible, however, to ascertain whether these letters, or at least some of them, are authentic, or whether they are naïve forgeries of a later date.[26] It is widely held, however, that the overwhelming majority of these letters are probably forgeries.

The ancient authors who supply certain biographical data concerning the life and the work of Aristotle, are constantly referred to throughout Chapters I–XVII. Hence, there is no need here to recite all their names, their individual contributions and their different attitudes towards Aristotle—attitudes which range all the way from uncritical but deliberate encomia bordering on near-deification, to spiteful and derogatory slander born of enmity, prejudice or plain ignorance. It must be borne in mind, however, that the earliest biographies of Aristotle coincide with the beginnings of Hellenistic biographical literature, that is, with a novel effort to report not merely the great achievements of a prominent man but also to record some of the minor details of his personal life and personal experiences. One might also speculate here whether the letters of Theophrastus addressed to Nicanor,[27] or the letters that were exchanged by Theophrastus and Eudemus of Rhodes,[28] contained accurate biographical data concerning Aristotle.

Whenever we rely on, or make use of, ancient biographers in general, we must always realize how little we actually know about the manner and method by which they worked. Some biographers might have employed whatever sources or materials were available to them, others might have relied primarily on memory or plain hearsay-tradition, and others, again, might have indulged in fanciful fabrications and *fabulae*. What is certain, however, is that these biographies of Aristotle are not always reliable. Hence, many justifiable and justified disagreements have arisen among scholars as regards the historical worth of these biographies. Not a few of these disagreements, it seems, may be attributed to the fact that some scholars are totally, or almost totally, committed to *Quellenforschung*, and nothing but *Quellenforschung*, as well as to endless, though not always productive, comparative studies of texts. Other scholars, again, stubbornly insist that unless we are in possession of explicit and presumably 'unchallengeable' historical evidence, we should refrain as much as possible from making any definite assertions whatever. Needless to say, this latter view, in the final analysis, would vitiate almost any form of ancient history or historiography. It has already been pointed out that perhaps the most acceptable procedure in this frustrating impasse, acceptable to at least some scholars, are reasonable and educated conjectures or hypotheses based upon all available evidence. An intelligent and imaginative interpretation of such fragmentary and, hence, inadequate, faulty and often contradictory evidence must be our alternative.[29] Moreover, we might also draw certain inferences from otherwise known facts, general circumstances and from the broader historical (or political) situations or incidents. Such a procedure, which most certainly will not be accepted by every scholar, might, after all, be the best as well as the most promising approach among all possible approaches to an almost hopeless historical problem. Otherwise we might as well resign ourselves, in a spirit of an abject and uncompromisingly defeatist 'give-it-all-up-philosophy,' to the Socratic dictum: 'All I know is that I know nothing.'

A Brief Account of the (Lost) *Vita Aristotelis* of Hermippus and of the (Lost) *Vita Aristotelis* of Ptolemy (-el-Garib)*

In recent years there has been a striking and most fruitful revival of historical studies of Aristotle and his philosophic work. W. Jaeger's brilliant 'evolutionary thesis,' first expounded in 1912[1] and further elaborated in 1923,[2] has stimulated and necessitated a veritable flood of important scholarly investigations of Aristotle's life and writings. These investigations are by no means concluded.[3] One of the most significant by-products of Jaeger's ageless work was a renewed interest in the so-called 'lost' or 'exoteric' compositions of the young Aristotle.[4] At the same time, it has been pointed out repeatedly and emphatically that in order to understand more adequately the development of Aristotle's philosophic thought, we must pay increased attention to the salient incidents in the life of the Stagirite and also to the ancient biographical tradition concerning Aristotle.[5] The following pages are an attempt to give a brief account or compressed overview of what may be called the 'traditional' *Vitae Aristotelis*, namely, the lost *Vita* authored by the Peripatetic Hermippus of Smyrna, and the lost *Vita* composed by the Neo-Platonist Ptolemy, whom the Arabic biographers call Ptolemy-el-Garib. These two *Vitae*, which have been compiled in antiquity, survive in one form or another only through their respective 'derivatives' or epitomes of which we still possess a fair number.

The more important biographies of Aristotle,[6] which have been handed down to us from antiquity, are: Diogenes Laertius, *The Lives and Opinions of Eminent Philosophers* V. 1–35;[7] the *Vita Aristotelis Hesychii*;[8] the *Pseudo-Hesychius*;[9] the *Vita Aristotelis Marciana*;[10] the *Vita Aristotelis Vulgata*;[11] the *Vita Lascaris*;[12] the *Vita Aristotelis Latina*;[13] the *Vita Aristotelis Syriaca I* (anonymous);[14] the *Vita Aristotelis Syriaca II* (anonymous);[15] the *Vita Aristotelis Arabica I* (by An-Nadim);[16] the *Vita Aristotelis Arabica II* (by Al-Mubashir or Mubassir);[17] the *Vita Aristotelis Arabica III* (by Al-Qifti);[18] and the *Vita Aristotelis Arabica IV* (by Usaibia).[19] All these *Vitae* in some ways are related to, or are more

1

or less accurate abridgments of, either the *Vita Aristotelis* of Hermippus or the *Vita Aristotelis* of Ptolemy-el-Garib. An attempt shall be made here to reconstruct the essential content or outline of these two basic *Vitae* with the help of their surviving 'derivatives' or epitomes. Such an undertaking, however, is a purely tentative effort based on much conjecture and many hypotheses.

According to C. A. Brandis, E. Zeller, F. Susemihl, E. Heitz, W. Christ, F. Littich, W. Jaeger, W. D. Ross, L. Robin, I. Düring and others,[20] Hermippus—the Peripatetic, the disciple of Callimachus and the justly famed librarian at Alexandria (towards the end of the third century B.C.)—must be considered the main, though by no means the sole, source for the biographical notes found in Diogenes Laertius. It has been claimed by some scholars that as a librarian at the Alexandrian Museum this Hermippus had at his disposal ample biographical materials about Aristotle. In the year 306 B.C., when all 'alien' or 'subversive' philosophers were threatened with banishment from Athens by the decree of Demetrius Poliorcetes,[21] Ptolemy Soter, the King of Egypt, invited Theophrastus to come to Egypt and also to transfer the Peripatetic School together with its library to Alexandria. Although Theophrastus declined this invitation, two of his disciples or colleagues in the Peripatus, Straton of Lampsacus and Demetrius of Phaleron, for a short period of time actually went to Egypt.[22] Undoubtedly, these two men brought to Alexandria some of the writings of the Peripatetics, including probably some of Aristotle's compositions or, at least, notes and excerpts from his works. It is also known that at the time of his death (288–87 or 287–86 B.C.) Theophrastus bequeathed the library of the Peripatus, including the writings of Aristotle, to Neleus of Scepsis.[23] Neleus (or his heirs) subsequently might have sold parts of this library or 'collection' to Ptolemy Philadelphus, the successor of Ptolemy Soter.[24]

All this would indicate that in the course of the third century B.C., Alexandria had become one of the great centers of Aristotelian and Peripatetic scholarship as well as the repository for many Aristotelian and Peripatetic works. Such a situation, in turn, enabled Hermippus to draw much reliable information concerning the life and works of Aristotle from the materials which had accumulated in Alexandria. Moreover, Hermippus himself was considered a painstakingly objective and conscientious scholar whose statements could unquestionably be taken at face value.

This highly idealized picture, which, among other matters, is based on the entirely unsupported presumption that many of Aristotle's writings had reached Alexandria and that Hermippus was a dispassionate as well as objective reporter, was shattered by I. Düring. On the strength of his detailed and searching studies, Düring, in opposition to many scholars, reached the well-founded conclusion that Hermippus' biographical reports were uncritical accounts, heavily slanted in favor of Aristotle.[25] In keeping with the general literary tendencies of the time (which were concerned primarily with entertaining and amusing one's readers), Hermippus, according to Düring, concocted a strange *mélange* of fact and fiction, history and anecdote, truth and gossip, praise and slander. To be sure, Hermippus' biography contains many items which are correct, or almost correct. In accord with a widespread Hellenistic trend, however, it is also replete with many fanciful stories devoid of all foundations in fact. Moreover, it is by no means certain that any of the intramural, 'esoteric' or doctrinal late writings of Aristotle, provided they were actually and *in toto* authored by the Stagirite, ever reached Alexandria during the fourth and third centuries B.C., although it will have to be admitted that some of his 'exoteric' early compositions were known there. According to tradition, after the death of Theophrastus (*c.* 286 B.C.) the 'esoteric' works were carried to Scepsis by Neleus of Scepsis, where they were gradually lost. Düring believes that Hermippus' most important contribution (and, perhaps, least credible addition) to the biographical tradition concerning Aristotle was his determined effort to present Aristotle as the true and sole founder of the Peripatetic school. Among the many and, in all likelihood, fanciful stories he invented, probably the most conspicuous was the legend, subsequently widely accepted (and widely exploited), that Aristotle seceded from the Academy and from Plato's basic teachings while Plato was still alive.[26] This story was invented and propagated by a Peripatetic, and intended to demonstrate the original philosophic genius of Aristotle which allegedly developed in complete independence of Plato and the Academy. Hermippus might have relied here on a report, also found in Aristoxenus and others, that a few brash young men (members of the Academy?) 'revolted' against Plato and, in a spirit of defiant antagonism, started a rival school of their own. Hermippus apparently identified these 'rebels' with Aristotle,[27] although there exists no evidence that the latter participated in this 'revolt' or that such a revolt ever took place. Such a substitution, however, seems to have suited Hermippus and his intent to depict the young Aristotle as a wholly independent and completely original philosopher who owed nothing to Plato and who already as a young man was able to establish an independent school of philosophy in Athens. It is also possible that some later authors or biographers misinterpreted or distorted the fact that during Plato's third sojourn in Syracuse in 361–60 B.C., Heracleides of Pontus, but not Aristotle, took Plato's place in the Academy by becoming the 'acting scholarch,' thus temporarily 'replacing' (or 'displacing') Plato.

When attempting to recast some of the main features of Hermippus' *Vita Aristotelis*, we must always bear in mind, however, that with the exception of the very complex *Vita Aristotelis* of Diogenes Laertius and some parts of the *Vita Hesychii*, all surviving *Vitae Aristotelis*, in the main, go back to Ptolemy (-el-Garib) rather than to Hermippus. It is more than likely, however, that Ptolemy (or his sources) to some extent is also influenced by Hermippus' *Vita*, although the degree of this influence can no longer be determined. Hence, it would appear that any attempt to reconstruct the basic contents of Hermippus' *Vita Aristotelis* will have to rely almost exclusively on Diogenes Laertius. Düring has suggested a tentative and conjectural sketch of the main features that were characteristic of the likely contents of Hermippus' original biography of Aristotle.[28] Implementing Düring's suggestions, it may be assumed, as some of the other *Vitae* of Diogenes Laertius indicate, that ancient biographies of philosophers seem to have followed a general pattern. They recite, (i) the name of the philosopher; (ii) the name of his father, but rarely that of his mother; (iii) sometimes the 'social position' and occupation of the father; (iv) the place of birth of the philosopher; (v) the time of his birth; (vi) sometimes the more remote ancestry of the father and occasionally that of the mother; (vii) the philosopher's schooling and his teacher or teachers; (viii) his 'intellectual qualities'; (ix) his physical appearance and physical peculiarities; (x) his travels; (xi) his 'social connections'; (xii) sometimes his 'family status'; (xiii) his public or political activities; (xiv) his scholarly activities and achievements; (xv) bits of general information; (xvi) some particular events in his life; (xvii) some particular honors bestowed upon him or some unusual misfortunes that befell him; (xviii) sometimes his last will and testament or his last sayings; (xix) his death; (xx) a list of the works he wrote; (xxi) his most distinguished pupils; and (xxii) a summary of his philosophic teachings. Naturally, not every ancient biography follows this pattern, mentions all the fact we have indicated or observes the order suggested above.

In keeping with this general pattern, it may be presumed that Hermippus' *Vita Aristotelis* probably contained the following bits of information: descent and family of Aristotle, including the name of his father (Nicomachus), that of his mother (Phaestis), that of his (younger?)

4

brother (Arimnestus) and that of his (older?) sister (Arimneste); the story that the father descended from the Homeric Asclepius, through Machaon and Machaon's son Nicomachus and perhaps through another Nicomachus (?), and that the mother, too, was an Asclepiade (DL V. 1);[29] that Aristotle's paternal ancestor originally came from the island of Andros, while those of the mother came from Chalcis on the island of Euboea: Aristotle's place of birth (Stagira) and the date of his birth (DL V. 1); an excursion into the flattering fact that the father, Nicomachus, was the personal physician as well as a close friend or intimate advisor of King Amyntas III of Macedonia, the father of King Philip and the grandfather of Alexander (DL V. 1);[30] Aristotle's general schooling as a young boy and his later training in philosophy, as well as his stay at the Academy under Plato's personal tutelage (DL V. 1–2);[31] the story that in keeping with his unsurpassed intellectual qualities, Aristotle was the 'most genuine' and most talented disciple of Plato (*ibid.*);[32] Aristotle's personal appearance (*ibid.*);[33] Aristotle's secession from the Academy during Plato's lifetime, demonstrating his intellectual originality (DL V. 2);[34] the metaphor about Aristotle's spurning Plato 'as colts kick their mother who bore them' (*ibid.*);[35] Aristotle's alleged ingratitude towards Plato;[36] Speusippus' rise as the new scholarch of the Academy after the death of Plato (DL V. 2);[37] Aristotle's rivalry with Isocrates (and Xenocrates), and the beginning of Aristotle's independent course of lectures on rhetoric and other systematic topics (DL V. 3);[38] Aristotle's departure from Athens (in 348–47 B.C.) to join Hermias of Atarneus (*ibid.*);[39] Aristotle's marriage to Pythias, the daughter or niece of Hermias, the birth of his daughter (Pythias) and his relations with Herpyllis, who bore him a son, Nicomachus (*ibid.*, derived in part from Timaeus or Timotheus?);[40] the death of Hermias (DL V. 6) and Callisthenes' encomium of Hermias[41] as well as Aristotle's hymn in honor of Hermias (DL V. 7);[42] Aristotle's epigram on Hermias (DL V. 6);[43] Aristotle's sojourn in Macedonia at the personal request of King Philip and his tutorship of Alexander (DL V. 4);[44] Aristotle's request that Philip (or Alexander) rebuild Stagira (*ibid.*);[45] Aristotle's composition of a code of laws for the restored city of Stagira (*ibid.*);[46] that for these services Aristotle was greatly honored by the people of Stagira;[47] that despite the fact that Aristotle was Plato's 'most genuine' disciple (DL V. 1), Xenocrates became scholarch of the Academy after the death of Speusippus and during Aristotle's absence in Macedonia as the Athenian envoy to King Philip (DL V. 2);[48] Aristotle's return to Athens, leaving behind his nephew Callisthenes as his 'successor' at the court of Alexander (DL V. 4–5);[49] that upon his return from Macedonia, Aristotle established his own independent school in the Lyceum because Xenocrates had been made the scholarch of the Academy (DL V. 2);[50] Aristotle's twelve (or thirteen) year sojourn in Athens as the head of his own school (DL V. 5);[51] Aristotle's indictment for impiety by Eurymedon and his flight to Chalcis (*ibid.*);[52] some bitter remarks by Aristotle on the occasion of his flight from Athens;[53] the several stories about the cause of his death in Chalcis (DL V. 6);[54] Aristotle's age (sixty-two or in his sixty-third year) at the time of his death, and his age (sixteen or in his seventeenth year) at the time of his entrance into the Academy (DL V. 9–10);[55] the story that he selected his successor (Theophrastus) in the Lyceum;[56] Theocritus' of Chios epigram on Aristotle (DL V. 11);[57] Timon's epigram on Aristotle (*ibid.*); Aristotle's last will and testament (DL V. 11–16);[58] some anecdotes about Aristotle credited to Lycon Pythagoraeus (DL V. 16);[59] a list of Aristotle's writings (DL V. 22–7);[60] and possibly some of the 'sayings' that were subsequently ascribed to Aristotle (DL V. 17–22). It will be noted that Hermippus apparently cited as his authorities Eumelus and Bryon (or Ambryon or Bryson?) from whom he quoted Theocritus of Chios, Timaeus, Timotheus (unless the latter two authors are one and the same person), Lycon and Timon. But we have no assurance whatever that he cites all the sources from which he derived his information, or even his main source,[61] or that he quotes them correctly and impartially.

This attempt at recapturing the main contents of Hermippus' *Vita Aristotelis* is purely tentative and highly conjectural. It is, as has been shown, a sort of proposal for a general 'table of contents' which does not necessarily follow the sequence observed by Hermippus. Neither does it purport to contain every bit of information relayed by Hermippus.

Despite O. Gigon's occasional and penetrating disagreements,[62] I. Düring's learned efforts to reconstruct the essential content of Hermippus' *Vita Aristotelis* must be considered in the main eminently successful. It might have been helpful, however, if Düring would have attempted to integrate into his reconstruction also Ptolemy's *Vita Aristotelis* (as transmitted to us by the *Vita Marciana*, the *Vita Latina* and the *Vita Vulgata*, as well as by the Syriac and Arabic *Vitae Aristotelis*).[63] The statement that Aristotle was instrumental in the restoration of Stagira[64] or that he was the lawgiver of Stagira (DL V. 4), for instance, can also be found in *Vita Marciana* 17, in *I Vita Syriaca* 7 (only that he was the lawgiver of Stagira), in *I Vita Arabica* (An-Nadim) 13, in

II Vita Arabica (Al-Mubashir) 27, and in *IV Vita Arabica* (Usaibia) 25. Hence, it is fair to assume that these statements had been contained in the *Vita* of Ptolemy. At this point one may wonder to what extent Ptolemy also relied on Hermippus. There exists evidence that he did so directly or, at least, that he made use of a source or sources which ultimately go back to Hermippus.[65]

In complete opposition to the general views held by the vast majority of scholars, P. Moraux vigorously advanced the far-reaching thesis that a *Vita Aristotelis* of Ariston of Ceos, the scholarch of the Peripatus towards the end of the third century B.C., rather than the biography of Hermippus, constitutes the main source of information used by Diogenes Laertius.[66] Moraux observed that in his biographical sketch of Straton of Lampsacus, who was the successor of Theophrastus in the scholarchate of the Peripatus, Diogenes Laertius expressly mentions Ariston as his source and authority.[67] As a matter of fact, Ariston is quoted here as the source from which Diogenes Laertius derives his information about the last will and testament of Straton of Lampsacus. Relying on Diogenes Laertius V. 64, Moraux also insisted[68] that Ariston of Ceos not only wrote a *History of the Peripatetic School*,[69] but also that he transmitted, perhaps in the form of a 'Collection,' the testaments of Aristotle, Theophrastus, Straton of Lampsacus and Lycon.[70] In the opinion of Moraux, these four testaments were not handed down separately but were part of a major *History of the Peripatetic School* (or *History of the Peripatetic Scholarchs*), which contained a great deal of biographical material concerning the members or scholarchs of the School, including a 'life' of Aristotle as well as lists or catalogues of their writings.[71] The fact that Diogenes Laertius' account of the Peripatetic school ends with Lycon is, according to Moraux, highly significant; it is a definite indication that the Alexandrian biographies, on which Diogenes Laertius relies, are under the spell of the *History of the Peripatetic School* by Ariston of Ceos, the successor of Lycon in the scholarchate (in 226–5 B.C.), who wrote an account of his predecessors.[72]

The theses advanced by P. Moraux were seriously challenged by I. Düring,[73] who reaffirmed the traditional view that Hermippus constitutes Diogenes Laertius' prime source of information concerning the life and writings of Aristotle. Düring made the following arguments in favor of Hermippus: (i) a considerable number of ancient authors credit Hermippus with having composed a biography of Aristotle, consisting of several books;[74] (ii) Hermippus authored the 'catalogue' of Theophrastus' writings (probably in his *Life of Theo-*

phrastus);[75] (iii) there are some ancient references to the differences between Hermippus' catalogue of Aristotelian writings and the catalogue of Andronicus of Rhodes.[76] This in itself would indicate that already in antiquity there existed at least two major catalogues, namely, the one by Hermippus and a later one by Andronicus. But Düring conceded that it is impossible to ascertain fully whether Hermippus is the original author of Diogenes Laertius' list of Aristotelian compositions. And (iv) the 'stichometric method'—the method of reporting the sum total of lines published by an author[77]—is definitely a method that must be traced back to the Alexandrian library (and Hermippus, though not Ariston of Ceos, was a librarian at Alexandria).[78] Since Diogenes Laertius uses this method in his accounts of Aristotle and Theophrastus (as well as of Speusippus and Xenocrates), his source must have been Hermippus rather than Ariston of Ceos, who probably never employed this particular method of stating the total literary output of an author.[79]

I. Düring, however, admitted the impossibility of establishing with certainty whether Hermippus was in fact the original source of information (and the main authority) used by Diogenes Laertius or, to be more exact, the source from which the latter derived his catalogue of Aristotelian writings and, for that matter, some of his biographical data about Aristotle. However, since Hermippus was practically a contemporary of Ariston of Ceos, and since Hermippus' biographical work in all likelihood was composed around the year 200 B.C., it is not impossible, Düring conjectured, that Hermippus used Ariston's biographies of the Peripatetic scholarchs (from Aristotle to Lycon), his '*Collection*' of their testaments,[80] as well as some of the anecdotes he (Ariston) had preserved.[81] But the bulk of Hermippus' (and, hence, Diogenes Laertius') information about Aristotle and his writings in all likelihood is based on materials that go back to the days of the Early Peripatus and, perhaps, to the times of Theophrastus himself.[82] These materials, it must be assumed, gradually were collected in the Alexandrian library.

By consensus, the extant *Vita Aristotelis Hesychii*[83] must be considered an abridged version of a more detailed biography which originally might have constituted a part of Hesychius' *Onomatologon*. Although it is extremely difficult to reconstruct with any degree of certitude the sources used by Hesychius of Miletus for his *Vita*—a difficulty which is compounded by the fact that we possess only an abridgment of this *Vita*—it is possible to establish some likely connections between the *Vita Hesychii* and other extant *Vitae*. Thus it seems

8

that Hesychius draws upon Hermippus (possibly through the intermediary of Diogenes Laertius); on Diogenes Laertius;[84] on some Neo-Platonic *Vitae Aristotelis* (including perhaps the *Vita Aristotelis* of Ptolemy)[85] or on some other Neo-Platonic biographical materials; perhaps on Theocritus of Chios;[86] on Timaeus (probably through Hermippus *via* Diogenes Laertius);[87] perhaps on Apollodorus' *Chronicle* for his chronology; and probably on Eumelus, as he is quoted in Diogenes Laertius.[88] Hesychius' 'catalogue' of Aristotle's writings has been discussed and analyzed in great detail by P. Moraux.[89] The first 139 titles seem to follow rather closely the list of Hermippus as it is preserved by Diogenes Laertius. The remainder of Hesychius' 'catalogue' is probably a compilation from a variety of sources that can no longer be accurately identified. It appears, however, that Hesychius did consult the list of Aristotelian writings originally compiled by Andronicus of Rhodes.

With the sole exception of Diogenes Laertius' and Hesychius' reports, all other extant biographies of Aristotle, whether Greek, Latin, Syriac or Arabic, are generally held to have their ultimate source in the *Vita Aristotelis* of Ptolemy. But, we possess no reliable information about this Ptolemy, who has been identified by many scholars with Ptolemy Chennos and whom the Arabic authors called Ptolemy-el-Garib, that is, Ptolemy 'the Stranger.'[90] Until quite recently this Ptolemy has also been considered a member of the Alexandrian School of Aristotelians (the 'Peripatus of the Early Roman Empire').[91] This view, which was advanced by W. Christ and others, has been vigorously attacked by P. Moraux, who flatly denied that Ptolemy Chennos and Ptolemy-el-Garib, the author of a *Vita Aristotelis*, were one and the same person.[92] I. Düring likewise objected to this identification. He pointed out that the *Vita Aristotelis* of Ptolemy is in essence a boundless and uncritical glorification of Aristotle. As such, it is undoubtedly Neo-Platonic in its character and tendency.[93] Our Ptolemy, Düring insisted, must have been a member of Porphyry's (232–33 to *c.* 310 A.D.) or Iamblichus' (a pupil of Porphyry) School of Neo-Platonists.[94] In brief, Düring insisted that we should discard the traditional but wholly unfounded identification of our Ptolemy with Ptolemy Chennos. Moreover, Düring stated that Ptolemy's *Vita Aristotelis* clearly indicates that its author was a Neo-Platonist; and that this Ptolemy wrote his *Vita Aristotelis* probably during the first half of the fourth century A.D.[95]

Dissenting to some extent from the views held by P. Moraux,[96] I. Düring also maintained[97] that of the Neo-Platonic *Vita Aristotelis* composed by Ptolemy, there exist three major Neo-Platonic abridgments or epitomes, namely, the *Vita Marciana*, the *Vita Vulgata* and the *Vita Latina*.[98] The two extant (anonymous) Syriac *Vitae Aristotelis*,[99] which likewise are abridgments of the *Vita* of Ptolemy, belong to approximately the same period. The four extant Arabic *Vitae Aristotelis*[100] ultimately go back to an Arabic translation of an earlier Syriac translation of an abridgment of Ptolemy's original biography.[101] Hence, all these nine *Vitae* have a single common source: Ptolemy's original *Vita Aristotelis* or, to be more exact, an epitome of Ptolemy's *Vita*. This is substantiated by the fact that the materials contained in these nine 'derivative' *Vitae*, on the whole, are fairly uniform in their general tenor and basic content, although on occasion they manifest some noticeable differences of detail.

The dominant characteristics, tendencies and peculiarities of Ptolemy's *Vita Aristotelis*, as they are clearly reflected in its nine 'derivatives,' may be seen in their boundless exaltation of Aristotle—a typical Neo-Platonic feature. According to Ptolemy, Aristotle was held in highest esteem by all people with whom he came in contact, be they kings, conquerors, scholars or just plain folk. In contrast with other biographers, Ptolemy also makes ample use of the so-called 'letters' of Aristotle,[102] probably relies on Hermippus' (or some other) chronology of Aristotle's life, and in all likelihood derives some of his detailed information from the self-same Hermippus[103] as well as from a number of other biographers, historians or authors who unfortunately can no longer be identified. On the whole, Ptolemy manifests an unquestionable proclivity for carrying on extensive scholarly investigations. Whenever he refutes stories about Aristotle that might be damaging to the latter's reputation or scholarly prestige, Ptolemy displays a certain critical acumen. But his boundless and uncritical admiration for Aristotle and his obviously encomiastic tendencies detract much from his reliability as a historical reporter. It appears, however, that, on the whole, his *Vita* is based on an adequate knowledge and mastery of the biographical materials that were available during the early part of the fourth century A.D.

In the opinion of the present author, barring perhaps a few minor details, I. Düring[104] has made what appears to be a most successful and most convincing attempt to piece together the likely content of Ptolemy's *Vita Aristotelis*. Düring has done this in the form of a 'collection of materials' culled from the nine *Vitae Aristotelis* which are ultimately based on this work of Ptolemy.[105]

The *Vita Aristotelis* of Ptolemy, it is safe to assume, contained Aristotle's name and possibly the etymology of his name,[106] his immediate family, that is, the name of his father (Nicomachus) as well as that of his mother (Phaestis),[107] his descent,[108] his birth place and the date of his birth.[109] His father, Nicomachus, was a physician and the court physician and close friend of King Amyntas III of Macedonia.[110] It probably continued with a biography of Aristotle: in his early youth, Aristotle received a 'liberal' and 'well-rounded' education (and perhaps some training in medicine).[111] After the death of his father, Aristotle was brought to Athens by his 'guardian' Proxenus of Atarneus to study, first under Isocrates[112] and then under Plato in the Academy.[113] This was done presumably on the advice of the Delphic oracle or perhaps because Plato and Proxenus were personal friends.[114]

Aristotle joined the Academy at the age of seventeen[115] (or in his seventeenth year), while Eudoxus of Cnidus was (acting) scholarch (προστάτης) during Plato's absence in Syracuse.[116] It is not true, as some have alleged, that he began the study of philosophy only at the age of thirty.[117] In the beginning he took up rhetoric.[118] After having completed his 'preliminary' or 'pre-philosophic' studies, he came under the personal tutelage of Plato. He stayed with Plato and the Academy for about twenty years.[119]

While Plato's pupil at the Academy, Aristotle studied ethics, politics, mathematics, physics and theology (metaphysics).[120] During all this time he was on excellent terms with Plato, who admiringly referred to him as 'the great reader' and 'the brain' (νοῦς) or 'the intellect.'[121] Because he made such a favorable impression on Plato, the latter insisted on instructing him personally, not wishing him to be taught by other (and lesser) teachers, as was the case with ordinary students.[122] When Plato departed on his third journey to Syracuse, out of respect and admiration for Aristotle's great learning and many intellectual achievements, he made him (acting) scholarch of the Academy during his absence.[123] Aristotle valiantly and successfully defended Platonic rhetoric when it came under serious attack from some outsiders (Isocrates?).[124] Aristotle also insisted upon the scholar's right (and duty) to write down and publish his philosophic conviction— a right he defended even against Plato.[125]

Then probably followed a description of Aristotle's intellectual and moral qualities,[126] as well as a report on his personal appearance.[127] He was an avid reader of books and a prodigious worker; he shunned empty talk,[128] weighing every word before answering a question.[129] He liked music (the liberal arts) and preferred the company of mathematicians and logicians.[130] He was a most eloquent man, a most distinguished author and, after Plato, the most eminent among Greek

philosophers.[131] At the same time he was a good man, practicing goodness with a zest and displaying a genuine interest in the problems of his
fellow men.[132] He was modest, unassuming and considerate;[133] and
he was moderate in his habits and restrained in his emotions.[134]
Aristotle was fair, a little bald-headed, of a good figure, and rather
bony. He had small bluish eyes, an aquiline nose, a small mouth, a
broad chest, and a thick (or sparse) beard.[135] He had two children, a girl
and a boy, who were still quite young at the time of his death.[136]

There were some ill-informed or slanderous persons who made it
their task to malign Aristotle. They invented a host of untrue stories
about his unpleasant relations with and his flagrant ingratitude towards
Plato.[137] Then, in Ptolemy's account probably followed detailed
refutations of some of these unpleasant stories. On the contrary,
Aristotle was a life-long admirer and friend of Plato's, as evidenced not
only by the fact that he dedicated and inscribed an altar in honored
memory of Plato,[138] but also by his letters in which he boasted of
having been a disciple of the 'kingly' Plato.[139] After the death of Plato,
Speusippus became the new scholarch of the Academy, although in the
opinion of many, Aristotle was the most outstanding disciple of Plato
and, hence, more than anyone else deserved to succeed him. After the
death of Speusippus, Xenocrates assumed the scholarchate because
Aristotle was absent from Athens.[140] Speusippus, aware of Aristotle's
matchless talents and qualifications, asked the latter to return to the
Academy and take charge of the school.[141]

After the death of Plato, Aristotle went to Hermias of Atarneus,[142]
and after the death of Hermias,[143] King Philip of Macedonia called him
to Macedonia and made him the tutor of Alexander.[144] He was held
in highest esteem at the Macedonian court, and many honors were
bestowed upon him by Philip and his wife Olympias.[145] When
Alexander became king, Aristotle disassociated himself from the
ruler.[146] He returned to Athens,[147] leaving Callisthenes with
Alexander.[148] Originally, he had intended to accompany Alexander
on his Persian venture,[149] but perturbed by unfavorable omens, he
desisted and tried to persuade Alexander to call off the whole undertaking.[150]

Aristotle returned to Athens after the conclusion of the Persian War
(after the start of the Persian War?; after the suppression of the
Athenian revolt in 335 B.C.?)[151] or after the death of Alexander
(Philip).[152] On his return, he rejoined the Academy[153] but soon left
it again in order to found his own independent school in the Lyceum,[154]
which was also called the 'Peripatetic school.'[155] There he had many

disciples, among them not only persons distinguished for their scholarly accomplishments, learning, philosophic ability and nobility of character as well as descent[156] but also kings and princes.[157] He wrote many books.[158] At the same time he devoted himself to the promotion of the Athenian commonweal[159] and to the promotion of happiness among men in general.[160] He corresponded a great deal with kings and leading statesmen[161] and had much influence among the great men of his time, not only with King Philip but also with other potentates. He was honored and respected by the mighty of this world. He carried on many diplomatic and statesmanlike negotiations with kings and rulers,[162] thereby promoting peace and contentment among peoples.[163] In particular he rendered many public services to the city of Athens.[164] He was also active as an *oicist*[165] and *nomothetes*,[166] not only of Stagira, but of other cities as well. Hence, upon Aristotle's death, the grateful people of Stagira brought his remains to Stagira[167] and named their council house after him.[168] Some Athenians likewise tried to honor him for the many public services he had rendered their city. They decreed that a *stele* with a commemorative inscription be set up in his honor on the Acropolis, but this action was foiled by the antagonism of some thoughtless people.[169]

After the death of Alexander and during the ensuing anti-Macedonian revolt in Athens, Aristotle was indicted by the hierophant Eurymedon for alleged impiety and for failing to worship the old gods.[170] Eurymedon's action was prompted primarily by jealousy and by an old (political) grudge against Aristotle.[171] When Aristotle learned about Eurymedon's indictment,[172] he left the city of his own accord before any official action was taken.[173] He did so because he feared that the Athenians might do to him what they had previously done to Socrates.[174] He also did not wish the Athenians to sin twice against philosophy.[175] In addition, he confessed (in a letter to Antipater?) that it was difficult and even dangerous for a stranger (alien) to live in Athens.[176] Quoting Homer's *Odyssey* VII. 120, he also maintained that the city of Athens was too crowded with sycophants (informers).[177] No one interfered with Aristotle's voluntary departure.[178] It is not true, however, that Aristotle wrote a detailed defense against the charges made by Eurymedon.[179]

Aristotle withdrew to Chalcis on the island of Euboea,[180] moving into the home he had inherited from his mother or maternal ancestors.[181] There he studied the flow of the Euripus[182] and wrote a book about this phenomenon.[183] It was in Chalcis that he died at[184] the age of sixty-two.[185] A swarm of bees was found around the urn containing his ashes,[186] an indication that he was a good and righteous man.[187]

This was probably followed by Aristotle's last will and testament,[188] and by a reference to his two children (Pythias and Nicomachus).[189] He left a large estate and numerous servants[190], and appointed Theophrastus not only to succeed him in the scholarchate of the Peripatus,[191] but also made him one of the executors of his will.[192] Then followed a list of his more prominent disciples[193] and probably some more statements to the effect that he was the friend and benefactor of many individuals,[194] of many cities,[195] of Athens and the Athenians in particular,[196] and of the whole of mankind.[197] For his many noble and unselfish deeds, he was esteemed, honored and loved by King Philip (and his wife Olympias),[198] by kings and princes in general,[199] and by many cities and communities.[200] After Plato, he was assuredly the greatest philosopher among the Greeks.[201]

The biography probably concluded with a (incomplete) list or catalogue of Aristotle's writings[202] and perhaps with a cursory (and in all likelihood not too accurate) summary of his main philosophic teachings.[203] There might also have been a general chronology of Aristotle's life, apparently taken from Hermippus.[204]

In the light of the surviving *Vitae Aristotelis*, which seem to depend to a large extent on Ptolemy's *Vita Aristotelis* or on some abridgment of Ptolemy's *Vita*, not much more can reasonably and safely be said about Ptolemy's biography. Ours is not a 'reconstruction' or collection of fragments, excerpts or doxographical reports in the traditional sense of the term. It is, at best, a kind of tentative and, in all likelihood, disorderly as well as overly optimistic 'table of probable main contents' of Ptolemy's *Vita Aristotelis*. Frequently it is based on conjectures lacking precision and ultimate confirmation. Such a tentative 'table of probable main contents,' which in all likelihood is neither exhaustive nor always accurate, must limit itself to some fairly vague statements. For, at this point, we cannot possibly know the precise and detailed content or the exact wording of Ptolemy's *Vita*, or even the particular order or sequence in which he originally presented his materials. One thing, however, stands out clearly: Ptolemy's *Vita*, no matter what one might think about its historical accuracy or scholarship, is without doubt a biography which apparently attempts, by its numerous encomia, to suppress, gloss over or refute any and all unfavorable views or reports concerning Aristotle. To what extent these encomiastic efforts affect the accuracy and, hence, the reliability of Ptolemy's account is not always easy to assess. Moreover, it seems to emphasize, at least by implication, the 'many political and public activities or involvements' of Aristotle, as well as the important role he played in the rise of Macedonia as a great power during the reign of King Philip (359–36 B.C.).

Chapter II

The *Vita Aristotelis* of Dionysius of Halicarnassus[*]

In his *Vita Aristotelis* (or *Chronologia Vitae Aristotelis*), which because of its brevity and alleged unimportance has been sadly neglected, Dionysius of Halicarnassus writes: 'Aristotle was the son of Nicomachus, who traced his ancestry and his profession to Machaon, the son of Asclepius. His mother, Phaestis, descended from one of the colonists who led the [Greek] settlers from Chalcis to Stagira. Aristotle was born in the 99th Olympiad, when Diotrephes was archon in Athens [384–83 B.C.]. Hence, he was three years older than Demosthenes. During the archonship of Polyzelus [367–66 B.C.], and after his father had died, he went to Athens, being then eighteen years of age. Having been introduced to the company of Plato, he spent a period of twenty years with the latter. On the death of Plato, during the archonship of Theophilus [348–47 B.C.], he went to Hermias, the tyrant of Atarneus. After spending three years with Hermias, during the archonship of Eubulus [345–44 B.C.], he repaired to Mytilene. From there he went to the court of Philip [of Macedonia] during the archonship of Pythodorus [343–42 B.C.], and spent eight years there as the tutor of Alexander. After the death of Philip [in 336 B.C.], during the archonship of Evaenetus [335–34 B.C.], he returned to Athens, where he taught in the Lyceum for a space of twelve years. In the thirteenth year [of his second stay in Athens], after the death of Alexander [in 323 B.C.] and during the archonship of Cephisodorus [323–22 B.C.], he retreated to Chalcis where he fell ill and died at the age of sixty-three.'[1]

In order to understand the particular *Vita Aristotelis* of Dionysius of Halicarnassus, which is contained in a letter addressed to Ammaeus, we must bear in mind that Dionysius is objecting here principally to certain allegations made by his friend, Ammaeus. This Ammaeus apparently had informed Dionysius that 'a certain Peripatetic philosopher, in his desire to honor and exalt Aristotle, the founder of the Peripatetic school, undertook to demonstrate that it was from Aristotle that Demosthenes had learned the rules of rhetoric which he subsequently applied to his own orations; and that it was through his adherence to the precepts laid down by Aristotle that he later became the foremost of all orators.'² 'My first impression,' Dionysius replies, 'was that this brash man [the "certain Peripatetic philosopher"] who made this statement [that Demosthenes was the pupil of Aristotle] was a person of no consequence. . . . But on learning his true name I found him to be a person whom I respect on account of his high personal qualities and literary merits. Hence, I did not know what to think, and after careful reflection I came to the conclusion that this matter needed more thorough discussion. For it is possible that I had failed to realize the true facts, and that this man had not uttered sheer nonsense. I wished, therefore, either to abandon my previous position on this matter if I could be convinced that the *Rhetoric* of Aristotle preceded the orations of Demosthenes, or to induce the person who had adopted this view and is about to put it into writing to change his opinion before submitting his treatise to the general public.'³

['In short, my dear Ammaeus,'] Dionysius continues, 'you have furnished me with a strong motive to search out the truth. You have challenged me to state the arguments by which I have convinced myself that it was not until Demosthenes had reached his peak, and had delivered his most celebrated orations, that Aristotle composed his *Rhetoric*. Furthermore, you seem to be right in advising me not to rest my case on mere "circumstantial evidence" and plain hypotheses or bits of extraneous evidence—for this sort of proof is never truly convincing or persuasive—but rather to call upon Aristotle himself to bear witness . . . as to the truth of my position. . . .'⁴ Dionysius then gives us a précis of his findings: 'The above mentioned story (namely, that Aristotle had a decisive influence on the rhetoric of Demosthenes), my dear Ammaeus, is simply not true. The *Rhetoric* of Aristotle, which was published at a fairly late date, did not influence the composition of Demosthenes' orations. These orations were indebted to other teachers. . . . I shall endeavor to demonstrate that at the time Aristotle wrote his *Rhetoric*, Demosthenes was already at the height of his public career and had delivered his most celebrated orations . . . and was famous throughout the Hellenic world for his eloquence. And perhaps I ought first of all to recite the facts I have gleaned from the current histories (κοιναὶ ἱστορίαι), which the compilers of biographies have bequeathed to us. . . .'⁵

The 'certain Peripatetic philosopher,' who apparently started the tradition that Demosthenes' rhetorical excellence had been decisively influenced by the precepts laid down by Aristotle, has been identified as Critolaus of Phaselis, a member of the Peripatetic school.[6] The theory advanced by Critolaus was propagated by others. It received renewed attention about the year 25 B.C., the approximate date of Dionysius' *First Epistle to Ammaeus*. In order to disprove this thesis, Dionysius attempts to demonstrate in his *Epistle*, first, that the Aristotelian *Rhetoric* was written at a fairly late stage of the Stagirite's literary activity;[7] and second, that the chronology of Aristotle's life simply precludes the possibility that he should have molded the rhetorical talents of Demosthenes. In short, Dionysius' *Vita Aristotelis* is meant to disprove the contentions of Critolaus and his followers by showing that these contentions involve a fatal anachronism.[8]

Although it is almost impossible to ascertain the source or sources used by Dionysius for his *Vita Aristotelis*—he refers rather indiscriminately to some 'current histories,'[9] to 'compilers of biographies'[10] and to 'biographers of Aristotle'[11]—it is probable that, like Diogenes Laertius centuries later,[12] he consulted the *Chronicle* of Apollodorus[13] or an even more remote source used by Apollodorus and then added some bits of information as well as some modifications of his own. (It has been claimed that the text of Dionysius is independent of the text cited in Diogenes Laertius (DL V. 9–10), and that both texts ultimately go back to Philochorus.)[14] After having recited the main data of Aristotle's life, Dionysius concludes: 'Such, then, are the historical facts as they have been transmitted to us by the biographers of this man (*scil.*, Aristotle).'[15]

Apollodorus' chronology of the life of Aristotle, which bears a close resemblance to Dionysius' chronology, reads as follows: 'Aristotle was born in the first year of the 99th Olympiad [384–83 B.C.]. He attached himself to Plato and remained in his company for twenty years, having become his pupil at the age of seventeen. He went to Mytilene during the archonship of Eubulus, that is, in the fourth year of the 108th Olympiad [345–44 B.C.]. When Plato died in the first year of that Olympiad, during the archonship of Theophilus [348–47 B.C.], he went to Hermias and stayed with him for three years. During the archonship of Pythodotus, that is, in the second year of the 109th Olympiad [343–42 B.C.], he journeyed to the court of Philip [of Macedonia], Alexander then being in his fifteenth year. He arrived in Athens during the second year of the 111th Olympiad [335–34 B.C.], and he taught in the Lyceum for thirteen years. He then retired to Chalcis in the third year of the 114th Olympiad [322–21 B.C.], and died there a natural death at the age of about sixty-three during the archonship of Philocles [322–21 B.C.], in the same year in which Demosthenes died in Calauria.'[16]

A comparison of Apollodorus' (Diogenes') text and that of Dionysius reveals some slight differences between these two chronicles. Apollodorus maintains that Aristotle was born in the first year of the 99th Olympiad (384–83 B.C.), while Dionysius relates that he was born in the 99th Olympiad, during the archonship of Diotrephes (384–83 B.C.), adding that 'he was therefore three years older than Demosthenes.' This latter addition, which in all likelihood is incorrect— Demosthenes was born probably in 384–83—is a personal observation of Dionysius and is in keeping with the main topic of his *Epistle*. While Apollodorus says that Aristotle was seventeen years of age when 'he attached himself to Plato,' he fails to mention the exact year in which this event took place. Dionysius, on the other hand, insists that this happened 'during the archonship of Polyzelus [367–66 B.C.], after the death of his father, when he was eighteen years old.' In the light of the generally accepted chronology of Aristotle's life, Dionysius would have done better to write, 'when he was in his eighteenth year.' Aristotle, it is commonly held, was born during the second half (July–September) of 384 B.C., that is, during the early part of Diotrephes' archonship (384–83 B.C.). He arrived in Athens in the year 367 B.C. Philochorus insists that he arrived during the latter part of Nausigenes' archonship (368–67 B.C.), that is, during the first half of the year 367 B.C.[17] Dionysius, on the other hand, reports that this happened during the early part of Polyzelus' archonship (367–66 B.C.). This latter report then, would indicate that he arrived about October 367 B.C. after he had celebrated his seventeenth birthday. Hence, according to Dionysius, Aristotle was in his eighteenth year—not eighteen years old—when he went to Athens, while according to Philochorus, whose dating is widely accepted, he was only sixteen years of age, that is, in his seventeenth year. The only discrepancy between Philochorus and Dionysius is whether Aristotle went to Athens before or after July–October of 367 B.C., that is, before or after the month of his birth.

Both Apollodorus (Diogenes Laertius) and Dionysius agree that Aristotle stayed with Plato for about twenty years (367–48–47 B.C.); that Plato died during the archonship of Theophilus (348–47 B.C.), in the first year of the 108th Olympiad (Apollodorus); and that, after Plato's death, Aristotle went to Hermias of Atarneus with whom he stayed three years. According to Dionysius, Aristotle repaired to Mytilene during the archonship of Eubulus (345–44 B.C.). For some unknown reason, Diogenes Laertius (Apollodorus?) mentions the journey to Mytilene, which he likewise places in the fourth year of the 108th Olympiad (345–44 B.C.), that is, during the archonship of

Eubulus, before he relates the death of Plato and Aristotle's sojourn in Atarneus. Apollodorus and Dionysius also concur that during the archonship of Pythodotus (343–42 B.C.)—Apollodorus adds, 'in the second year of the 109th Olympiad [343–42 B.C.]'—Aristotle proceeded to the court of King Philip of Macedonia. But while Dionysius records that he 'spent there eight years as the tutor of Alexander,' Apollodorus only reports that at the time of Aristotle's arrival in Macedonia 'Alexander [who was born in 356 B.C.] was in his fifteenth year.'[18] It will also be noted that Apollodorus does not mention the story that Aristotle became the tutor of Alexander.[19]

Dionysius claims that after the death of Philip (in the summer of 336 B.C.), Aristotle returned to Athens during the archonship of Evaenetus (335–34 B.C.), while Apollodorus insists that he did so during the second year of the 111th Olympiad (335–34 B.C.). Dionysius maintains that after his return to Athens, Aristotle taught in the Lyceum for twelve years, while Apollodorus (or Diogenes Laertius) speaks of thirteen years. This discrepancy can easily be explained: Apollodorus (or Diogenes Laertius) apparently includes in his calculation the year 323 B.C.—the year in which Aristotle fled from Athens. This figure would also indicate that Aristotle arrived in Athens late in 335 B.C., that is, after Athens had made its abject surrender to Alexander, following an abortive revolt in the summer of 335 B.C.

According to Dionysius, Aristotle retired to Chalcis 'in the thirteenth year [of his second sojourn in Athens—323 B.C.], during the archonship of Cephisodorus [323–22 B.C.]. There he fell ill and died at the age of sixty-three [that is, in his sixty-third year (322 B.C.)].' Apollodorus (Diogenes Laertius) relates that 'in the third year of the 114th Olympiad [322–21 B.C.], Aristotle retired to Chalcis and there he died a natural death at the age of about sixty-three, during the archonship of Philocles [322–21 B.C.].' Obviously, the reference to the third year of the 114th Olympiad and the archonship of Philocles (322–21 B.C.) does not refer to Aristotle's flight from Athens in 323 B.C.,[20] but rather to the date of his death in 322 B.C., which occurred during the early part of Philocles' archonship. In transcribing his source, Diogenes Laertius (or Apollodorus) probably committed an error.[21] All these dates indicate that Aristotle died during the latter half (July–October) of the year 322 B.C.

The major surviving biographies of Aristotle agree that he was the son of Nicomachus and his wife Phaestis,[22] although *I VS* 3 erroneously calls his mother Parysatis,[23] *IV VA* 3 calls her Phaestias, and *II VS* does not mention her at all. They also concur that he was born in Stagira.[24] Dionysius abridges the lineage of Nicomachus. It appears that Aristotle's father, Nicomachus, was the descendant of another Nicomachus, who was the son of Machaon (the famous physician), who in turn was the son of Asclepius.[25] His mother, Phaestis, Dionysius relates, 'was a descendant from one of the colonists who led the [Greek] settlers from Chalcis to Stagira.'[26] But Dionysius does not claim, as some of the other biographers do,[27] that she too was a descendant of Asclepius. Neither does Dionysius relate that the father, Nicomachus, was the personal physician, as well as the intimate friend and trusted advisor, of King Amyntas III of Macedonia.[28] He implies, however, that Nicomachus was a physician when he reports that this Nicomachus 'traced his ancestry and his profession to Machaon.'

The fact that Aristotle's father, Nicomachus, died while Aristotle was still rather young is also hinted at in *VM* 3, *VV* 2, *VL* 3 and *IV VA* 3; and the story that he went to Athens (or was brought to Athens by his 'guardian' Proxenus) when he was a young man can be found in all the other *Vitae Aristotelis*. Some of these *Vitae* insist, however, that he was then seventeen years of age.[29] Dionysius does not mention the story, found in *VM* 5, *VV* 4, *VL* 5 and *IV VA* 3, that he went to Athens and joined the school of Plato on the advice of the Pythian oracle.[30] Neither does Dionysius relate the unusual (and perhaps spurious) story, told only in *II VA* 3, that his father, Nicomachus, brought him to Athens when he was only eight years old, placing him 'in a school of poets, orators, and schoolmasters,' and that Aristotle stayed in this 'school' for nine years until, at the age of seventeen, he attached himself to Plato.[31] Like *VM* 5, *VV* 4, *VL* 5, *DL* V. 9, *I VS* 4, *I VA* 4, *II VA* 10, *III VA* and *IV VA* 3, Dionysius insists that Aristotle stayed with Plato twenty years.[32]

Dionysius notes that 'upon Plato's death ... Aristotle went to Hermias,' with whom he spent three years.[33] Aristotle's sojourn in Mytilene in 345–44 B.C., however, is mentioned only by Dionysius and Diogenes Laertius (Apollodorus).[34] While Dionysius refers only briefly to the fact that in the year 343–42 B.C. Aristotle proceeded to Macedonia where he spent eight years as the tutor of Alexander,[35] some of the other ancient biographers make a great deal of Aristotle's stay in Macedonia.[36] In this they apparently follow a Hellenistic tradition of connecting famous men with some important dynasty. Whether Aristotle was actually the preceptor of Alexander for a period of eight years is open to doubt.[37]

Dionysius, who seems to connect Aristotle's departure from Macedonia with the death of Philip (summer of 336 B.C.), insists that the Stagirite returned to Athens in 335–34 B.C.[38] The other biographers are a little more explicit. Thus DL V. 4-5, which also insinuates that the relations between Aristotle and Alexander had become somewhat strained, maintains that when Aristotle thought that he had stayed long enough with Alexander, he departed for Athens, 'leaving behind his nephew Callisthenes.' *II VA* 19 and *IV VA* 6 insist that he stayed with Alexander until the latter invaded Persia (in 334 B.C.). Some of the Arabic *Vitae Aristotelis*[39] once more try to explain Aristotle's departure by reporting that when Philip had died and Alexander had succeeded him to the throne of Macedonia, the latter soon marched off to Persia. Freed of all 'responsibilities,' Aristotle simply disassociated himself from the affairs of the king and thus was able to return to Athens.[40]

In Athens, according to Dionysius, Aristotle taught at the Lyceum for a period of twelve years. DL V. 5 remarks that, after leaving Macedonia, Aristotle came to Athens and was the head of his school for thirteen years.[41] *II VS* 6, *II VA* 3 and *IV VA* 34 relate that during these years he had many notable disciples; and *II VA* 35 also reports that during this particular period he wrote many books, about one hundred, on a great many philosophic subjects.[42] This is about all that the ancient biographers have to say about what traditionally have been considered the most important and productive years of Aristotle's life.

Dionysius concludes his account by stating that in the thirteenth year of his teaching in the Lyceum, that is, after the death of Alexander (June 13, 323 B.C.) and during the archonship of Cephisodorus (323-22 B.C.), Aristotle 'retired to Chalcis [on the island of Euboea] where he fell ill and died at the age of sixty-three' or, better, in his sixty-third year, thus making it appear that he died during the archonship of Cephisodorus rather than during the archonship of Philocles (322-21 B.C.), as it is commonly held. Dionysius neglects, however, to supply any reason for Aristotle's sudden retreat to Chalcis. On the strength of the available evidence found in some of the other ancient *Vitae Aristotelis*, the following might be cited as the real reason for Aristotle's rather hasty departure from Athens in the summer (or early fall) of 323 B.C.: his status as a 'Macedonian resident alien' and his close ties with the Macedonian royal house as well as with Antipater, the lieutenant of Alexander in Europe, made him immediately suspect in the eyes of the Athenians who considered him a philo-Macedonian, if not a Macedonian 'political agent' stationed in Athens to report on the political developments throughout Greece. When the news of Alexander's death reached Athens in the summer of 323, the city once again revolted against her Macedonian overlords and Aristotle no longer felt safe in Athens. Hence, it was actually on account of political pressure (as it had happened once before in the year 348 B.C.)[43] that he had to leave Athens.[44] DL V. 5, *II VA* 20 and *IV VA* 7 relate that the hierophant Eurymedon[45] formally charged Aristotle with impiety, and that Aristotle, in order to avoid the fate which befell Socrates in 399 B.C., fled to Chalcis.[46]

VM 43, *VL* 45–6, DL V. 6, V. 10 (Apollodorus), *I VS* 8, *II VS* 7, *I VA* 15, *II VA* 23, *III VA* and *IV VA* 11 imply that Aristotle died a natural death in Chalcis.[47] It is commonly held that Aristotle died at the age of sixty-two, that is, in his sixty-third year, although *I VS* 8 erroneously claims that he died at the age of sixty-seven, *II VS* 8, *II VA* 23, *III VA* and *IV VA* 11 that he died at the age of sixty-eight, and *I VA* 15 that he died at the age of sixty-six.[48]

The brief and not very informative *Vita Aristotelis* of Dionysius of Halicarnassus, it must be borne in mind, is primarily a 'chronology' rather than a detailed biography of Aristotle, compiled to disprove the allegation that Demosthenes owed his rhetorical prowess to Aristotle's *Rhetoric*. Hence, like Apollodorus in his *Chronicle* (DL V. 9–10), Dionysius was of the opinion that he could restrict himself to citing some of the essential dates in the life of Aristotle. Aside from this rather scanty bit of information, the *Vita Aristotelis* of Dionysius contains practically nothing that might shed additional light on the life and work of the Stagirite. The only novel piece of information furnished by Dionysius is the report that Aristotle's mother Phaestis was a descendant from the original colonists who led the Chalcidian settlers from Chalcis on the island of Euboea to Stagira. Of great importance and much assistance to us is also his effort to date, though in all likelihood not always accurately, certain key events in the life of Aristotle by referring to the respective archonships during which these events took place.

Despite its brevity, the *Vita Aristotelis* of Dionysius of Halicarnassus appears to be based on extensive research and what seems to be a fairly accurate grasp of the most relevant facts and dates in the life of the Stagirite. It was motivated by the desire to check and disprove the claims of certain Peripatetics who exalted and exaggerated beyond reason and historical fact the importance and influence of Aristotle upon the history of rhetoric in general and on the rhetoric of Demosthenes in particular. In so doing, Dionysius, like so many apologists, occasionally overstates his case and becomes guilty of some minor inaccuracies. What he did not know, and probably could not know, is that certain parts of the Aristotelian *Rhetoric*—the '*Urrhetorik*' according to W. Jaeger—may date back to the years 360–55 B.C., and that during the fifties of the fourth century B.C., Aristotle probably composed two works on rhetoric as well as taught a course of lectures on rhetoric.[49] Moreover, his manner of dating Aristotle's arrival in Athens in the year 367 B.C., that is, his insistence that Aristotle went there during the archonship of Polyzelus (367–66 B.C.), when he was eighteen years old (in his eighteenth year), is open to debate.[50] Most likely, Aristotle went to Athens during the latter part of Nausigenes' archonship (368–67 B.C., or the first year of the 103rd Olympiad), that is, in the late spring of 367 B.C. (after Plato had departed for Syracuse), when he was seventeen years old (in his seventeenth year), rather than in the summer or early fall of 367. Dionysius also seems to imply that Aristotle died during the archonship of Cephisodorus (323–22 B.C.), that is, during the first half of the year 322, rather than during the early part of Philocles' archonship (322–21 B.C.), that is, between July and October of 322 B.C.[51]

Chapter III

An Analysis of the *Vita Aristotelis* of Diogenes Laertius (DL V 1–16)*

Book V, sections 1–16, of Diogenes Laertius' *The Lives and Opinions of Eminent Philosophers*, also called *The Lives of the Philosophers* (Photius) or *The Lives of the Sophists* (Eusthatius),[1] contains a rather important, though at times confused (and confusing), account of the life of Aristotle.[2] In his *Vita*, which to a large extent relies rather heavily on a biography of Aristotle by Hermippus of Smyrna, Diogenes Laertius also employs a number of other divergent sources. Some of these sources are cited by name, others can be determined with a reasonable degree of certainty, while others cannot readily be identified. What is perhaps the most striking characteristic of Diogenes' biography, however, is that he constantly alternates his use of two distinct types of sources or biographical tendencies: the decidedly sympathetic, favorable and even encomiastic tradition; and the clearly unsympathetic, unfavorable and even hostile trend.[3] In this, Diogenes Laertius and his *Vita Aristotelis* differs from the majority of the extant biographies of Aristotle. The following is a tentative analysis of Diogenes' rather bewildering account in terms of these two types of sources or tendencies.

Diogenes Laertius V. 1 (subsequently cited as DL V. 1), down to μαθητῶν, is sympathetic, the remainder unsympathetic; DL V. 2, down to μετήρα, is unsympathetic, while the remainder is sympathetic or at least 'neutral'; DL V. 3, down to ἐπασκῶν, on the whole seems to be sympathetic, but beginning with ἔπειτα μέντοι (down to γέγραπται in DL V. 4) the text becomes distinctly unsympathetic; DL V. 4, beginning with ἐντεῦθεν (down to κατέστρεψεν in DL V. 5), is once more sympathetic, but beginning with ὁ δ'οὖν Ἀριστοτέλης (DL V. 5, down to Φιλοκλέους in DL V. 10) the account seems constantly to vacillate between sympathetic and unsympathetic sources; DL V. 10, beginning with λέγεται (down to ἀλεγεινῆς in DL V. 11), is unsympathetic; the last will and testament of Aristotle (DL V. 11–16) is obviously 'neutral' (though perhaps intended to be sympathetic); and

DL V. 16, beginning with λέγεται (down to διαπωλοῖτο and perhaps to ἐξέγροιτο), on the whole is once more unsympathetic.

Although Hermippus, the author of an *On Aristotle* or *The Life of Aristotle* (lost) and a decidedly sympathetic and even encomiastic biographer of the Stagirite, is doubtless the main source consulted by Diogenes Laertius for his *Vita Aristotelis*,[4] he is certainly not the only authority used by the latter. Frequently Diogenes Laertius also employs and occasionally names other sources, materials or authors, some of which are decidedly unsympathetic towards Aristotle. DL V. 1 (the genealogy of Aristotle), down to μαθητῶν, is in all likelihood derived from Hermippus, although Diogenes Laertius might also have found this information in some other source or sources. The description of Aristotle's external appearance is derived in part from Hermippus or, more likely, from Timotheus, and in part from some anonymous source or sources (Ariston of Ceos?). The remainder of DL V. 1 relies on Timaeus. DL V. 2, down to μητέρα, might be based on Ariston of Ceos, Aristoxenus or on some unknown source; the story of Aristotle's diplomatic mission and Xenocrates' taking over the Academy is probably based on Hermippus; and the etymology of the term 'Peripatus' in all likelihood relies on some unknown Hellenistic authority (perhaps Hermippus?). DL V. 3, down to ἐπασκῶν, is derived from an anonymous author;[5] Aristotle's stay with Hermias (DL V. 3) is probably taken from Hermippus (who in turn relies on, and probably modifies, some unsympathetic reports, such as the accounts of Theopompus and Theocritus of Chios); and some of the details connected with the Hermias episode (including the first part of DL V. 4), down to γέγραπται, go back to Demetrius of Magnesia, to the otherwise unknown author (Aristippus?) of Ἀρίστιππος ἢ Περὶ παλαιᾶς τρυφῆς (*Aristippus or On the Luxury of the Ancients*), probably to Theopompus (and Theocritus of Chios), and to some other (unknown) authors. DL V. 4, beginning with ἐντεῦθεν, is taken from Hermippus, as is DL V. 5 and V. 6 (including the epigram on Hermias), with the exception of a short reference (DL V. 6) to Demophilus (which is based on Favorinus) and the recital of Eumelus' (erroneous) account of Aristotle's death by suicide at the age of seventy. DL V. 7 and the first part of DL V. 8 (the hymn or paean in honor of Hermias) might contain the original Aristotelian paean (recorded by Hermippus), while the remainder of DL V. 8 is probably by Diogenes Laertius himself. DL V. 9–10 draws on Favorinus as well as on Apollodorus' *Chronicle*,[6] but the statement that Aristotle incurred Alexander's displeasure and that Alexander heaped honors and presents on Anaximenes[7] and

Xenocrates (DL V. 10) seems to go back to an anonymous authority or perhaps to Hermippus (?) who as a Peripatetic probably had a low opinion of Alexander on account of what the latter had done to Callisthenes. DL V. 11, which contains some unsympathetic remarks made by Theocritus of Chios (according to Ambryon's or, better, Bryon's or Bryson's work *On Theocritus*) and by Timon, is probably based on Hermippus who cites here some hostile accounts. Aristotle's last will and testament (DL V. 11-16) might have been taken from Hermippus or, more likely, from Ariston of Ceos.[8]

A study of the other *Vitae* of Diogenes Laertius, namely, those of (i) Theophrastus (DL V. 36-57), (ii) Straton of Lampsacus (DL V. 58-64), (iii) Lycon (DL V. 65-74), (iv) Demetrius of Phaleron (DL V. 75-85) and (v) Heracleides of Pontus (DL V. 86-94), divulges that in his biographical accounts Diogenes Laertius seems to have followed a definite pattern which can also be detected in his *Vita Aristotelis*: (a) the name, the father's name and the place of birth (i, ii, iii, iv and v); (b) the parents in general and the more remote ancestors (i and iv); (c) the teacher or teachers (i, iv and v); (d) the intellectual or philosophic qualifications or qualities (i, ii, iii and v); (e) the physical appearance (iii and v); (f) connections with some ruling dynasty or dynasties (i, ii, iii and v); (g) the death (i, ii, iii, iv and v); (h) epigrams by Diogenes Laertius on the individual philosophers (i, ii, iii, iv and v); (i) bits of chronological information (i, ii, iii and iv); (j) a list of writings (i, ii, iv and v); (k) the last will and testament (i, ii and iii); (l) some apophthegms (i and iv); and (m) homonyms (ii, iii, iv and v). Diogenes Laertius does not always observe this sequence, however.

In keeping with this general pattern, which is also followed by other ancient biographers,[9] Diogenes Laertius (DL V. 1) begins his *Vita Aristotelis* with a genealogy, relating the names of Aristotle's parents (Nicomachus and Phaestis),[10] as well as his place of birth, Stagira (Stagiros).[11] Referring to Hermippus' *On Aristotle* (or, *The Life of Aristotle*), Diogenes Laertius adds a rather detailed portrait of Aristotle's father, intended to be laudatory: the father, Nicomachus, is apparently the son (the descendant) of another Nicomachus (?) or 'Nicomachus the Elder' (?)—Diogenes Laertius does not actually say this—the descendant (grandson?) of Machaon, and the descendant (great-grandson?) of Asclepius.[12] Thus Aristotle is the descendant of the illustrious (legendary?) Asclepius, the famed and widely-honored physician of Homeric antiquity.[13] In order to further exalt Aristotle's father and, by implication, Aristotle himself, Diogenes Laertius (Hermippus) adds the remark that Nicomachus, Aristotle's father, was a physician at the Macedonian royal court. Moreover, he was not merely the court physician of King Amyntas III of Macedonia (c. 393 to 370–69), but was also—and Diogenes Laertius (Hermippus) makes a special point of this—the monarch's personal friend and confidant.[14] In so doing, Hermippus (and after him Diogenes Laertius) intends to emphasize the social and professional standing as well as the political importance of Aristotle's ancestry. Apparently he also wishes to introduce and justify the close connections between the Macedonian royal house and the family of Aristotle (including Aristotle himself).

Aristotle's mother, Phaestis, is referred to again in his last will and testament (DL V. 16) where the pious son provides that a 'likeness' of her should be dedicated to Demeter in Nemea.[15] The father, Nicomachus, is not mentioned again, however. Hence, it can be inferred that he as well as his wife Phaestis died while Aristotle was still rather young.[16] In his testament (DL V. 15), Aristotle also speaks of his brother Arimnestus but fails to name his sister Arimneste.[17]

Diogenes Laertius continues (DL V. 1): 'Aristotle was the most genuine disciple of Plato,' a remark which can also be found in Dionysius of Halicarnassus.[18] For some unknown reason this observation, which presumably goes back to Hermippus, is inserted between the account of Aristotle's genealogy and a description of his external appearance. Originally, this particular observation, in all likelihood, was connected with DL V. 2, where we are informed, on the authority of Hermippus, that on the death of Plato in 348–47 B.C., Speusippus became the new scholarch of the Academy, and that on the death of Speusippus in 339 B.C. (and while Aristotle supposedly was on a diplomatic mission to Macedonia on behalf of Athens), Xenocrates rather than Aristotle became the new scholarch (despite the fact that Aristotle rather than Speusippus or Xenocrates was 'the most genuine disciple of Plato').[19] According to Timotheus' Περὶ βίων, Aristotle 'spoke with a lisp' (DL V. 1).[20] Diogenes Laertius also relates that it is said (φασίν) that Aristotle's 'calves were slender, his eyes small (or, closely set, μικρόμματος), and that he was conspicuous by his attire, his rings and the cut of his hair' (DL V. 1).[21] The several accounts of Aristotle's external appearance in all likelihood were not based on Hermippus but on some other authority who, like Timotheus, is decidedly unsympathetic towards Aristotle.[22] It should also be noted that the expression μικρόμματος is probably used here in a distinctly derogatory sense. Μικρόμματος is said to be an indication of μικροψυχία (pettiness or meanness).[23] While it is difficult to assess the exact meaning, or the true implication, of the statement that Aristotle 'was conspicuous by his dress, his rings, and by the cut of his hair' (DL V. 1), there can be little doubt that it is derogatory in intent.[24] All this might indicate that the account in DL V. 1, beginning with τραυλὸς down to μητέρα (DL V. 2), is not based on Hermippus, but on some other (and hostile) source or sources, although this is by no means certain. Aelian, on his part, relates that serious tensions developed between Plato and Aristotle, and that Plato was repelled by Aristotle's fanciful attire, appearance and habits.[25] It is possible that Aelian uses here the same (derogatory) source which was also relied upon by Diogenes Laertius. But this particular source can no longer be identified (Epicurus?). Aristocles[26] mentions several stories according to which Aristotle in his youth had been a medical quack or peddler of drugs (φαρμακοπωλεῖν); that he had recklessly squandered his patrimony; that when totally destitute because of his riotous living, he had become a mercenary soldier;[27] that he had practiced medicine;[28] and that finally, when he had failed in everything else, he had entered Plato's school.[29] To counteract some of these unfavorable accounts, especially the report that in his youth Aristotle was a dissipated person of little or no education and refinement, some biographers probably invented the story that already as a very young man Aristotle wrote works on the Homeric poems,[30] that he was a dedicated student of the 'liberal arts,' and that he had seriously studied medicine (with his father?).

Diogenes Laertius, citing Timaeus, further narrates that Aristotle had a son by Herpyllis, his concubine, and that this son was called Nicomachus (DL V. 1).[31] This seems to be confirmed by Aristotle's last will and testament (DL V. 11–16) where Aristotle makes some rather generous provisions for Herpyllis (DL V. 13–14), although, under the existing (Athenian) laws, she was only his concubine[32] (unless he married her legally after the death of his first wife, Pythias, something which is extremely doubtful).[33] One may ask here why Hermippus, from whom Diogenes Laertius probably derived this information, should refer to Aristotle's concubine. The answer seems to be astonishingly simply: Although Herpyllis was a 'lowly person,' the magnanimous Aristotle treated her like his own wife; he lived with her until his death, and he provided for her in a most generous manner in his testament. These facts make Aristotle appear in a very favorable light. For some unknown reason, no mention is made here of Aristotle's legitimate wife, Pythias,[34] or of his only legitimate child by Pythias, a daughter named Pythias. The daughter[35] (and the mother),[36] however, are referred to in Aristotle's last will and testament.[37]

The statement that Aristotle 'seceded from the Academy while

Plato was still alive' (DL V. 2),[38] seems to contradict the earlier remark that he was Plato's 'most genuine disciple' (DL V. 1). Behind the rather cryptic statement that Aristotle 'seceded from the Academy while Plato was still alive,' we might detect one of the many unpleasant stories that were told by the detractors of Aristotle, and which referred to the alleged serious 'rifts' (personal as well as doctrinal) which supposedly marred the relations of these two men. This statement may also refer to the claim that Aristotle had begun to criticize some of Plato's philosophic teachings while the latter was still alive. Our story might also be based on the following (unsupported) tradition: according to Aristoxenus, some unnamed young and brash members of the Academy (or some 'outsiders') started their own rival school while Plato was absent in Syracuse in 361–60 B.C.[39] Later biographers (Hermippus?), wishing to demonstrate that already as a young man Aristotle was a 'wholly independent thinker,' simply may have substituted Aristotle's name. Our story might also be a misinterpretation and (deliberate?) distortion of the fact that during Plato's absence in 361–60 B.C. Heracleides of Pontus took the place of Plato by becoming the 'acting scholarch' of the Academy. By substituting the name of Aristotle for that of Heracleides, some biographers or authors made it appear that Aristotle established his own independent school while Plato was still alive.[40] Aelian relates the fanciful tale[41]—a story which ultimately might go back to Heracleides of Pontus (?)[42]—that a serious conflict or a kind of 'intellectual confrontation,' took place in the Academy. Aristotle and some of his young friends constantly harassed the ageing Plato by arguing with him and contradicting him on every point. At the time Xenocrates was away in Chalcedon, and Speusippus was gravely ill. Hence, neither of these two men could come to the succor of Plato. In desperation, the helpless and bewildered Plato withdrew to his private quarters, abandoning the school to the young rebels. Xenocrates, who might have been summoned by Speusippus,[43] suddenly returned and restored order within the Academy by putting the young rebels 'in their place.' But nowhere in the account of Aristoxenus is there any reference to a deliberate 'secession' from, or to a planned 'taking over' of, the Academy by Aristotle.[44] Aelian (or his source) probably related, or more likely, invented this whole story in order to explain as well as justify the fact that in 348–47 and again in 339–38 B.C., Aristotle was bypassed as a possible successor to the vacant scholarchate of the Academy: Aristotle's unconscionable deportment *vis-à-vis* the aged and venerable Plato, his teacher and benefactor, forever disqualified him from becoming the

scholarch of the Academy. This seems to be the ultimate meaning of
Aelian's account. Conversely, by his courageous and determined
handling of this sordid affair or crisis, Xenocrates had proved himself
not only the loyal friend and disciple of Plato as well as the 'saviour' of
the Academy, but also as the stalwart defender of the Academic
tradition—as the one man who was eminently qualified to become the
scholarch of the Academy at some future time. In short, this story,
perhaps in a fanciful and not altogether accurate form, also contains an
explanation of the reason why in 339–38 B.C. Xenocrates, rather than
Aristotle, became the new scholarch of the Academy.[45]

Perhaps in an effort to be impartial and in order to quote side by side
both favorable and unfavorable accounts concerning Aristotle,
Diogenes Laertius juxtaposes two conflicting stories (DL V. 1–2),
namely, that Aristotle was Plato's 'most genuine disciple,' and that he
'seceded from the Academy while Plato was still alive.' But the report
that Aristotle 'seceded from the Academy while Plato was still alive,'
may also imply, in an encomiastic spirit, that already at an early stage
of his philosophic development Aristotle displayed intellectual independence and scientific originality. Hence, this story might very well
go back to Hermippus who seems to have stressed the philosophic
originality of Aristotle. It might also be interesting to note here that
Diogenes Laertius tells a similar story of 'defection' about Chrysippus,
the Stoic, who 'seceded from Cleanthes' school' while the latter was
still alive (DL VII. 179).[46] Plato, we are told by Diogenes Laertius
(DL II. 2), reacted to Aristotle's alleged defection by quoting an
apophthegm (Cynic?): 'Aristotle spurns me as colts kick their mother
who bore them.'[47] Whether this account goes back to Aristoxenus,
the slanderer of Plato, or to some other detractor of Aristotle (and
Plato), cannot be determined.[48] In any event, ancient literature abounds
with stories, metaphors and analogies in which the attachment of
parents to their wayward offspring and the frequently encountered
ingratitude of children towards their devoted (and doting) parents is
illustrated with the help of examples borrowed from the animal
kingdom.

Diogenes Laertius next discusses the 'succession problem' connected
with the scholarchate of the Academy (DL V. 2). Quoting once more
from Hermippus, Diogenes Laertius maintains that when Speusippus
died (*c.* 339–38 B.C.), Aristotle (who at the time of Plato's death in
348–47 B.C. was passed over as a prospective scholarch) was at the royal
court of Macedonia engaged in a diplomatic mission on behalf of
Athens (?)[49] and, hence, absent from Athens. Diogenes Laertius also

relates that Xenocrates became the new scholarch in 339-38 B.C. Aristotle's alleged diplomatic mission to Macedonia in 339-38 B.C., that is, on the eve of the battle of Chaeronea (in 338 B.C.), raises a number of interesting problems: how it is possible that a Macedonian alien such as Aristotle should officially represent Athens at the Macedonian court, especially, since after 348 B.C., the year King Philip of Macedonia captured and sacked the city of Olynthus,[50] Macedonians in general were quite unpopular in Athens. Hence, it may be surmised that the story about Aristotle's diplomatic mission (DL V. 2) might have been an invention which Hermippus devised in order to magnify Aristotle and discredit Aristotle's 'rivals' as well as the Academy in general. But then, again, Aristotle, in one way or another, might have been connected with the diplomatic negotiations which were carried on between Athens and Macedonia prior to the battle of Chaeronea.[51] We may assume that in his *Vita Aristotelis* Hermippus wished to emphasize the flagrant ingratitude of the Academy (and, by implication, that of Athens) towards Aristotle: Aristotle, who is actually 'the most genuine disciple of Plato' (DL V. 1) and, hence, more than anyone else deserves to succeed Speusippus (and Plato), gives of himself in the interest of Athens and, concomitantly, in the interest of the Academy. However, his lesser 'colleagues' in the Academy, perhaps out of jealousy or because of an overriding prejudice, repay him with flagrant ingratitude—a clever and apparently effective *riposte* to the widely spread allegation that Aristotle had acted in an ungrateful manner towards Plato.[52] In short, the noble and unselfish Aristotle is contrasted here with his ignoble and selfish brethren in the Academy. Moreover, this story also implies that the Platonists utterly lacked good sense and sound judgment. This condemnation of the Platonists and the Academy, in turn, might suggest that Hermippus, a Peripatetic and a man inclined to depreciate the Platonists, after all is the author of the whole account.

Diogenes Laertius, however, does not specifically mention the particular events that took place on the death of Plato in 348-47 B.C., when Speusippus, presumably at the request of Plato, assumed the scholarchate of the Academy. DL V. 3 merely suggests that in 348-47 Aristotle departed from Athens and went to Hermias of Atarneus. When Plato 'appointed' Speusippus, the son of his sister, his successor in the scholarchate, he did so, we must surmise, for primarily 'legal reasons.' Under Athenian law, which did not recognize the legal fiction of the 'corporate personality,' the legal title to the school property of the Academy, including the grounds, the buildings, the library and the appurtenances, was vested in the scholarch and, hence, was his private property. On his approaching death, the scholarch, by a formal will, bequeathed this property to his intended successor in the scholarchate. This is also the reason why, for instance, the testaments of the Early Peripatetic scholarchs (Theophrastus, Straton of Lampsacus and Lycon) have been so carefully preserved: they establish and confirm the legitimacy of the successive Peripatetic scholarchs. It was also a basic policy of the Athenian law of succession to keep the estate of the deceased, in our case that of Plato which included the school property of the Academy, within his immediate family. Since Plato died without male issue, the existing laws or customs demanded that he should bequeath his estate and, hence, appoint as his successor to the scholarchate of the Academy, to his nearest male agnate which was Speusippus, the son of his sister Potone. The appointment of Speusippus to the scholarchate in 348–47 B.C., therefore, in all likelihood was a matter of 'legal policy' or 'legal necessity,' rather than the expression of a personal preference or, perhaps, an indication of Speusippus' scholarly excellence.[53] As a matter of fact, upon Speusippus' assumption of the scholarchate, Aristotle and Xenocrates are said to have left the Academy because they were disenchanted with his appointment, the more so since they had a rather low opinion of his character, personality and scholarly qualifications.[54]

Diogenes Laertius (DL V. 2), however, raises some additional and far-reaching questions as regards Aristotle's personal and professional relationship with Xenocrates, as well as regards his personal and 'official' connections with the Macedonian royal house. DL IV. 6 relates that Plato made the following caustic comparisons between Aristotle and Xenocrates: 'The one [*scil.*, Xenocrates] needed a spur, the other [*scil.*, Aristotle] a bridle.... Observe what an ass [*scil.*, Xenocrates] I am training, and what a steed [*scil.*, Aristotle] he has to race against.' Such invidious comparisons, even if not articulated by Plato himself, indicate a disparity of talent which, needless to say, must have aroused Xenocrates' resentment against Aristotle. From DL V. 10 we gather that after the outrageous murder of Aristotle's nephew Callisthenes of Olynthus at the instigation of Alexander (in 327 B.C.), the latter, 'in order to annoy Aristotle, sent presents to Xenocrates.' We are told that Aristotle mocked Xenocrates for his prudery,[55] a trait of character which is also stressed in DL IV. 7–8.[56] The personal and professional relations between Aristotle and Xenocrates, in the main, are difficult to assess, however. According to one tradition, these two men were close personal friends.[57] This may be inferred from the fact that both are said to have left the Academy together,[58] and to have jointly visited Hermias of Atarneus. According to another tradition, Aristotle and Xenocrates were committed rivals and even personal enemies. This latter tradition probably goes back to Hermippus. We know already that Hermippus attempted to show that Aristotle was an absolutely original thinker who owed nothing to Plato and the Academy,[59] and that there existed a bitter rivalry between Aristotle and Xenocrates. These two conflicting traditions, namely, that Aristotle and Xenocrates were friends or that they were rivals and even enemies, are also reflected in the several accounts of the circumstances surrounding the appointment of Xenocrates to the scholarchate of the Academy in 339–38 B.C. Those sources which attempt to play down any possible antagonism between Aristotle and Xenocrates [60] state that after the death of Speusippus both Aristotle and Xenocrates were called upon jointly to take charge of the Academy, the former as a teacher in the Lyceum, the latter as a teacher in the Academy. Philodemus, a reporter who is definitely hostile towards Xenocrates (and Aristotle), relates that Xenocrates was elected to the scholarchate by an over-whelming majority, and that the election took place while Aristotle was abroad (in Macedonia)[61] and, hence, had no influence on these proceedings.[62] But as a Macedonian 'resident alien' (*metic*), Aristotle, who might have been one of the 'candidates' for the vacant scholar-chate, had little if any chance of being elected, especially since in the year 339–38 B.C. the relations between Athens and Macedonia were strained because of King Philip's encroachment on the Chalcidian cities (and on Olynthus in particular) in 349–48 B.C. According to a third tradition, when about to die, Speusippus wrote a letter to Xenocrates (who at the time was in Chalcedon) urging him to return to Athens and take charge of the school, thus offering him the scholarchate.[63] Another source, however, maintains that 'when Plato had died, Speusippus, who was Plato's nephew, took charge of Plato's school. He [*scil.*, Speusippus] sent a message to Aristotle asking him to return and take charge of Plato's school.'[64] This report might contain a transfer of the events which actually took place in 339–38 B.C. to the year 348–47 B.C., and/or a confusion of Aristotle and Xenocrates.

Aristotle's official contacts or connections with the Macedonian royal house [65] to which Diogenes Laertius (DL V. 2) alludes here, raise a further problem. These official contacts, which are different from his personal connections with either King Philip, King Alexander or with Olympias, are stressed by Diogenes Laertius in order to emphasize and extol Aristotle's many statesmanlike achievements in general, as well as in order to glorify him as the true benefactor of Athens and of the Academy in particular. It has already been mentioned that, according to Diogenes Laertius (DL V. 2, who relies here on Hermippus), Aristotle was in Macedonia on an important diplomatic mission on behalf of Athens at the time of Xenocrates' appointment to the scholarchate of the Academy.[66] Thus, it would appear that Diogenes Laertius (or Hermippus) is also concerned with disproving the virulent charge that Aristotle was really an enemy of Athens or, at least, a philo-Macedonian partisan working against the true political interests of Athens and, especially, against the anti-Macedonian or patriotic party (Demosthenes) in Athens. In the year 306 B.C., for instance, Demochares, in support of Sophocles' motion to have all alien ('subversive') philosophers expelled from Athens, made a speech in which he also denounced Aristotle for allegedly having betrayed Stagira to King Philip, with having denounced the wealthiest Olynthians to Philip, and with having carried on 'treasonable correspondence' with Antipater, a correspondence which proved to be detrimental to Athens and her political interests and aspirations.[67] Hermippus (and Diogenes Laertius), who probably attempted to refute the charges made against Aristotle by Demochares and others—charges which make Aristotle appear to have been the 'great despoiler' of the Athenian commonweal—on the other hand made every effort to depict him as the genuine and devoted benefactor of Athens and the Athenians.[68]

The remainder of DL V. 2 and the first part of DL V. 3 present a complex and rather confusing (and confused) account in which Diogenes Laertius apparently attempts to summarize at least five bits of rather loosely related information. First, upon his return to Athens (in 335–34 B.C.) Aristotle discovered that Xenocrates had been made the scholarch of the Academy. Hence, he was compelled to 'choose the public walk in the Lyceum' as the locus of his own teaching. Second, in the Lyceum 'he [*scil.*, Aristotle] would walk up and down discussing philosophy with his disciples—and this is the origin of the name "Peripatetic."' Third, the name 'Peripatetic' was occasioned by the philosophic discussions between Aristotle and Alexander on therapeutic walks (in Mieza) during the latter's convalescence from a serious illness. Fourth, Aristotle initially taught while walking about, but later, when the number of his students had increased, he sat down to lecture on a specific topic (DL V. 3). And, fifth, Aristotle included rhetoric in his curriculum (*ibid.*).[69]

The report of Aristotle's 'separation' from Xenocrates (in 339–38 or, more likely, in 335–34 B.C.), and the subsequent choice of the Lyceum as the place where he wished to teach,[70] probably owes its origin to Hermippus. According to one tradition, represented, for instance, by Strabo,[71] Aristotle and Xenocrates were rather close friends and as such collaborated in carrying on the work of the Academy. Strabo relates that after the death of Plato, Hermias of Atarneus invited both Aristotle and Xenocrates to stay with him. *VM* 24, *VV* 18 and *VL* 24, as we have seen, maintain that after the death of Speusippus, the members of the Academy called back Aristotle and Xenocrates, and handed over to them the running of the Academy. For purely 'organizational reasons,' this joint supervision was carried out in the Academy (by Xenocrates) as well as in the Lyceum (by Aristotle). Hence, according to this particular tradition, which also seeks to deny the existence of any rifts or philosophic disagreements between Aristotle and Xenocrates or between Aristotle and the Academy, there did not exist in Athens in 339–38 or afterwards two distinct and mutually independent schools which rivalled one another: the Platonic Academy and the Aristotelian Lyceum. That such an harmonious 'co-existence' or collaboration of the Academy and the Lyceum would be welcomed and even propagated by the essentially syncretist Neo-Platonic philosophers, commentators, historians and biographers needs no special comment. Conversely, it should also be borne in mind that under the existing Athenian laws (which did not permit resident aliens to acquire real property in Athens or Attica), Aristotle, the resident Macedonian alien, could not have established or have owned his own independent school with its own grounds or buildings. But he could always make use of the Lyceum in order to meet his students. For the Lyceum was a 'public place' and, hence, accessible to practically everyone.

Of particular interest is the paraphrase of the verse from Euripides' *Philoctetes*[72] which, according to Diogenes Laertius (DL V. 3), allegedly was quoted by Aristotle when he parted company with Xenocrates in order to establish his own school in the Lyceum (in 335–34 B.C. ?): 'It would be a base thing to keep silent and let Xenocrates speak out.' Although the majority of scholars as well as some ancient commentators put the name of Isocrates in the place of that of Xenocrates,[73] it is quite possible that this paraphrase in fact named Xenocrates. Aristotle, indeed, might have justified his 'transfer' to, and independent teaching in, the Lyceum by publicly announcing in a rather pointed statement that it would be intolerable and unthinkable to abandon the teaching of philosophy just because Xenocrates was in control of, and was probably monopolizing, the Academy. Hermippus, who represents the tradition that Aristotle and Xenocrates were not on amicable terms, undoubtedly is the main source consulted here by Diogenes Laertius. Apparently, Hermippus had insisted (i) that Aristotle and Xenocrates were bitter rivals (and perhaps personal enemies); (ii) that Speusippus personally, and for personal reasons, engineered the appointment of Xenocrates to the scholarchate of the Academy by asking him to return from Chalcedon and take over the school; (iii) that the absence of Aristotle in Macedonia (and the ill-will of some members of the Academy towards Aristotle) made Xenocrates' appointment a foregone conclusion; and (iv) that this whole rather unpleasant incident, which was not of Aristotle's making, left the latter no choice but to establish his own independent school. It might be well to remember that one of the main themes of Hermippus' *Vita Aristotelis* is the deliberate effort to affirm (and justify) the philosophic originality as well as the institutional independence of the Peripatus by showing that Aristotle's secession from the Academy was an 'expulsion' rather than a voluntary withdrawal.

The second problem concerns the origin of the term 'Peripatetic'[74] (which, incidentally, did not come into general use until after the death of Theophrastus).[75] Περιπατεῖν, it will be noted, may signify a special kind of philosophic discussion, or it may refer to a type of physical or therapeutic (or hygienic) exercise.[76] Περίπατος originally meant simply the locale where certain activities of a perambulatory nature were performed, including philosophic or literary discussions. The passage from Diogenes Laertius (V. 2) touches, it appears, only on the locale (Lyceum) and on the therapeutic meaning of the term 'περιπατεῖν.'

Of some interest is the tradition, known to Diogenes Laertius (who probably derived it from Hermippus), which traces the etymology of the term περιπατεῖν to Aristotle's instruction of Alexander while the latter was recovering from an illness and, hence, required physical or therapeutic exercise. With this explanation, Diogenes Laertius and Plutarch (*Alexander* 7–8) seem essentially to agree. It is possible, however, that they both consulted a single source, which, unless it be Hermippus (?), can no longer be identified.[77] The *Vita Marciana* records that 'from his father, and in keeping with a family tradition, he [*scil.*, Aristotle] inherited an inclination towards the natural sciences and towards medicine.'[78] Perhaps this tradition, the ultimate source of which is unknown, is reflected in our story: Aristotle, the 'great healer' of both soul (mind) and body,[79] tries out his art on the person considered to have been his greatest 'patient' (and pupil), Alexander.

Moreover, we are told that Aristotle first taught while walking around, but that subsequently, when the numbers of his students or listeners increased, he sat down[80] to lecture on a set subject or theme.[81] This peculiar passage, which might well be a badly garbled summary of several conflicting bits of information or tradition, possibly touches also upon the not yet completely resolved exegetical problems raised by the distinction between the 'exoteric' and the 'esoteric' lectures of Aristotle[82]—between the early dialogues and the later 'acroatic' (or 'acroamatic') or doctrinal treatises of the Stagirite. It may also refer to the internal structure of the curriculum as well as to the kind of instruction which was offered at the Lyceum. The story that while addressing a large audience Aristotle sat down might possibly have been part of a tradition hostile to Aristotle: his teaching degenerates to lifeless and routinized lectures on a set subject.

Finally, we are informed (DL V. 3) that Aristotle included rhetoric among his formal 'lectures' or discussions. According to reliable tradition, Aristotle decided rather suddenly, perhaps on the strength of the success he had with his *Gryllus*, to compete with Isocrates and his school in the teaching of rhetoric—a decision he must have reached while Plato was still alive (and which probably had Plato's full approval).[83] In any event, one extant fragment of the $T\epsilon\chi\nu\hat{\omega}\nu$ $\Sigma\upsilon\nu\alpha\gamma\omega\gamma\acute{\eta}$,[84] which might have been connected with Aristotle's first course of lectures on rhetoric delivered in the Academy, contains a rather petulant remark on Isocrates. This would be an indication that the lectures on rhetoric were prompted by his desire to compete with Isocrates.[85] Interpreted in this sense, DL V. 3 and the paraphrase of Euripides' *Philoctetes* quoted by Diogenes Laertius might in fact refer to Isocrates rather than to Xenocrates, as most scholars would contend.[86]

The remainder of DL V. 3 (starting with $\check{\epsilon}\pi\epsilon\iota\tau\alpha$ $\mu\acute{\epsilon}\nu\tau o\iota$) relates only unsympathetic or derogatory reports about Aristotle.[87] They touch upon Aristotle's relationship with Hermias of Atarneus,[88] an association which elicited much criticism from a host of ancient authors.[89] These unsympathetic stories might be, among other things, the echoes of Theopompus' and Theocritus' vitriolic attacks on Hermias (and indirectly on Aristotle) which were widely circulated throughout the ancient Hellenic world.[90] Aside from Theopompus and Theocritus, who are not specifically mentioned (and who might have been only a remote influence), the main sources from which Diogenes Laertius derives his information concerning Hermias and Aristotle's connections with Hermias, are Demetrius of Magnesia (DL V. 3), the $\mathcal{A}\rho\acute{\iota}\sigma\tau\iota\pi\pi\sigma$ $\mathring{\eta}$ $\Pi\epsilon\rho\grave{\iota}$ $\pi\alpha\lambda\alpha\iota\hat{\alpha}s$ $\tau\rho\upsilon\phi\hat{\eta}s$ (DL V. 3-4), and at least one other unknown and unnamed author.[91]

38

The statement that Aristotle 'was on very affectionate terms with Hermias' (DL V. 3)—a remark which undoubtedly has homosexual implications—might also have been intended to counteract another (unfavorable) story, according to which Aristotle 'ran out' on Hermias when the Persians began to close in on the latter, thus permitting Hermias to be captured by Mentor and subsequently executed by the Persians in 341–40 B.C. It could persuasively be argued that, when touching upon the Hermias episode (which he could not possibly suppress in its entirety), Diogenes Laertius compiles and reproduces in a rather uncritical and indiscriminate manner several seriously conflicting reports without any attempt to reconcile these stories. These reports, the majority of which were strongly antagonistic to Aristotle, apparently contained the following bits of information (or deliberate slander): (i) there existed homosexual relations between Aristotle and Hermias;[92] (ii) Hermias made Aristotle his kinsman by giving him in marriage his daughter, niece, adopted daughter (Hermias allegedly was a eunuch) or sister, Pythias (Demetrius of Magnesia);[93] (iii) Hermias, the 'lowly Bithynian,' was originally the slave (or eunuch) of Eubulus, and Eubulus was a greedy and dishonest money changer; (iv) by murdering his master, Eubulus, Hermias assumed Eubulus' place (Demetrius of Magnesia);[94] (v) Aristotle fell in love with one of Hermias' concubines (Pythias? Herpyllis? some other woman?), and married her (Pythias) with Hermias' consent (Aristippus); (vi) Aristotle married Pythias out of compassion after the violent death of Hermias which left her without a protector (Aristocles);[95] and (vii), in an excess of delight, Aristotle sacrificed to his wife in a manner offensive to Greek religious feelings (Lycon Pythagoraeus? Aristippus?).[96] One of these sources (Lycon Pythagoraeus) relates that Aristotle sacrificed to Pythias in this offensive manner after her death, while another source (Aristippus?) states that he did so while she was still alive. Finally, there also exists the story that Aristotle composed an offensive or sacrilegious hymn as well as an offensive inscription (for a statue of Hermias in Delphi) in honor of Hermias. All these bits of information (and outright slander) are culled from a great variety of unrelated and frequently conflicting sources, among them probably Theopompus, Theocritus of Chios, Lycon Pythagoraeus, Timaeus, Alexinus, Eubulides, Cephisodorus, Demochares, Aristoxenus, Eumelus, Epicurus and many others. While some of these detractors are personally hostile towards Aristotle, others, such as Theopompus and Theocritus of Chios, are hostile towards Hermias and only incidentally towards Aristotle. Aristocles aptly has summed up these vilifications of Aristotle: 'From the persons who have reviled him [*scil.*, Aristotle] one might safely infer that all the things that have been said about him are untrue. This may also be inferred from the fact that these persons do not all make the same charges or accusations, but each says something of his own. If there were any truth in what they have been saying, he [*scil.*, Aristotle] would surely have deserved to have been put to death by his contemporaries not once, but ten thousand times.'[97]

Diogenes Laertius (DL V. 11) also quotes Theocritus of Chios (definitely a source hostile to Aristotle), who, according to Ambryon's (Bryon's or Bryson's) work, entitled *On Theocritus*, ridicules Aristotle in the following epigram: 'To Hermias the eunuch, the slave of Eubulus, an empty monument was raised by empty-witted Aristotle, who by constraint of a lawless appetite chose to dwell at the mouth of the Borborous [muddy river] rather than in the Academy.' This epigram, which has a pornographic connotation, is recorded by Plutarch, Areius Didymus, Aristocles and by Diogenes Laertius. This, in turn, would indicate that many unfavorable accounts concerning Aristotle and his deportment were widely circulated and believed, and that some of these stories originated already during the lifetime of Aristotle.[98] Theocritus' epigram and its pornographic connotations might possibly have originated the story that there existed unnatural or homosexual relationships between Aristotle and Hermias, and that these relationships were the basis for the close friendship between these two men.[99] The 'empty monument' mentioned in the epigram, on the other hand, probably refers to Aristotle's Delphic inscription in honor of Hermias[100] or, perhaps, to Aristotle's hymn commemorating Hermias' death.[101]

Judging from Areius Didymus,[102] Theopompus of Chios must have harbored an unrelenting hatred for Hermias of Atarneus, who in the eyes of Theopompus had betrayed Chios. Already in antiquity Theopompus had been notorious for his malicious and frequently groundless slanders.[103] His undisguised prejudices against Hermias (and, by implication, against Aristotle, the friend and kinsman of Hermias) are a matter of common knowledge.[104] The extreme viciousness of these polemics is simply striking and, as a matter of fact, so striking that it seriously affects the credibility of his statements. Theopompus (whose personal prejudices as well as general inclination to belittle and defame other people induced him to resort to deliberate distortions, clumsy misinterpretations and outright falsehoods) seems to have been the first representative of the unfavorable or slanderous tradition concerning Hermias (and Aristotle)—a tradition, which was to further develop and expand during the succeeding centuries. He hurled his probably groundless invectives against Hermias, denouncing him as a scoundrel of the worst sort. Thus Hermias is labelled a vile and villainous barbarian, a lowly and cunning slave, a eunuch, a cheap and dishonest money-lender, a vicious and unscrupulous person who came to power through the use of treachery, and a man driven by insatiable avarice.[105] Theopompus also insists that Hermias dealt savagely with friend and foe alike, and that he was in the habit of betraying his allies and benefactors.

Theocritus of Chios, who likewise harbored a boundless hatred for Hermias, denounced the latter in a most unrestrained and vicious manner. His deep resentment against Hermias (and, incidentally, against Aristotle) may have been caused by Hermias' interference in the political affairs of the island of Chios during the forties. Moreover, Theocritus was a rabid enemy of Macedonia and of King Philip in particular. Since at about that time Hermias apparently was pro-Macedonian and, perhaps, secretly allied with Macedonia (and since Aristotle himself was a Macedonian), it is not surprising that both Hermias and Aristotle should come under heavy attack by so violent an anti-Macedonian as Theocritus.[106]

The pronounced and, at times, vicious hostility of Theopompus and Theocritus towards Hermias is probably the origin of the unfavorable and even slanderous tradition concerning Hermias. This tradition, which also implicated Aristotle, soon became widespread and widely believed. It was effectively used to discredit and embarrass Aristotle, and it probably also contributed to Aristotle's enforced withdrawal from Athens in the year 323 B.C.[107] It might be possible, however, that both Theopompus and Theocritus transferred to Hermias some of the deeds as well as the 'special condition' of Hermotimus of Pedesa, who is said to have been a eunuch and a slave.[108] However, there also existed a distinctly favorable tradition concerning Hermias which, it may be surmised, goes back to Hermippus, a Peripatetic, and may have originated with Aristotle himself. In this connection, one should also bear in mind the following: when the barbaric and wanton murder of Callisthenes, the nephew or great-nephew of Aristotle,[109] by Alexander (in 327 B.C.) made it impossible for the Peripatetics to idealize Alexander or call him the 'ideal ruler,' they gradually came to regard Hermias, the friend and pupil of Aristotle, as the ideal philosophic ruler. This already becomes manifest in Aristotle's hymn (or paean) in honor of Hermias (and in the honorific inscription at Delphi dedicated by Aristotle to the memory of Hermias)[110] as well as in Callisthenes' *encomium* of Hermias.[111] The glorification of Hermias by the Peripatetics, in turn, prompted some of the critics or opponents of the Peripatus to denounce Hermias. By exposing, rightly or wrongly, Hermias, the 'hero' of the Peripatetics, as a scoundrel, these critics wished primarily to discredit, as much as possible, Aristotle and the Peripatetics. This might also explain, at least in part, the subsequent and widely held unfavorable views about Hermias which came to be a characteristic feature of Hellenistic literature: Hermias became one of the prime targets of anti-Aristotelian and anti-Peripatetic criticism which, by maligning Hermias, attempted to discredit Aristotle, at least indirectly.[112]

The author of the Ἀρίστιππος ἢ Περὶ παλαιᾶς τρυφῆς charges some of the great men of antiquity, among them Empedocles, Socrates, Xenophon, Plato, Theophrastus and Aristotle, with having had unnatural relationships with boys (παιδικὸς ἔρως). It also appears that this author intended to demonstrate the moral depravity of all those who accepted, or were interested in, the eros doctrine advanced (and advocated) in Plato's *Symposium*.[113] The story that there existed homosexual relations between Hermias of Atarneus and Aristotle probably originated with Theocritus of Chios, the passionate slanderer of Aristotle,[114] or perhaps with Eubulides,[115] but not likely with Theopompus, who had called Hermias a eunuch. This story was in part refuted by Himerius who stated: 'Now Hermias became a close friend of the philosopher from Stagira, and from the depths of his very being and by the practice of all manner of excellence this Hermias aroused in his preceptor a most genuine admiration. Many were the tokens of affection which Aristotle displayed, exercising him in [philosophic] debate, and training him in excellence of character. . . .'[116] Himerius wishes to create the impression that Aristotle's fondness for Hermias was based on his admiration for Hermias' intellectual as well as moral qualities, something which also becomes apparent in Aristotle's hymn or paean commemorating Hermias, or in the Delphic inscription which Aristotle dedicated to the honored memory of Hermias.[117] The author of the Ἀρίστιππος ἢ Περὶ παλαιᾶς τρυφῆς, in particular, accuses Aristotle outright with having fallen in love with a concubine of Hermias (Pythias? Herpyllis? some other woman?); of having married Pythias with Hermias' consent, noting that Hermias was a lowly slave, a murderer and a person of inferior moral standards; of 'having sacrificed, in an excess of delight, to a weak woman [Pythias] as the Athenians sacrificed to Demeter of Eleusis' (DL V. 4); and of having 'composed a hymn in honor of Hermias' in an outburst of gratitude for Hermias' 'generosity.'[118]

42

On the authority of Aristocles,[119] we know that Eubulides of Megara had criticized Aristotle for having fallen out with such great men as Plato and King Philip of Macedonia, while remaining the life-long intimate friend and defender of so great a scoundrel as Hermias. To prove his point, Eubulides quotes some panegyrics to Hermias which had allegedly been composed by Aristotle. This would, in turn, indicate that during the latter half of the fourth century B.C., and probably also during the third century, a number of hymns and poems in praise of Hermias, Herpyllis (?) and of Aristotle's wife, Pythias, were circulated in Aristotle's name. According to Lycon the Pythagorean,[120] on the death of Pythias, Aristotle sacrificed to her 'as the Athenians sacrificed to Demeter of Eleusis.' The author of Ἀρίστιππος ἢ Περὶ παλαιᾶς τρυφῆς apparently made use of this story. He gave it, however, a novel twist of his own by claiming that these sacrifices took place while Pythias was still alive.[121]

It is possible and, as a matter of fact, quite likely that on the death of Pythias—we do not know when or where she died—Aristotle did hold some elaborate funeral services.[122] We know, however, that on the death of Hermias in 341-40 B.C., Aristotle, assisted by Callisthenes, arranged what seems to have been impressive memorial celebrations.[123] According to Lucian, 'Aristotle, whose admiration for Hermias, the eunuch and tyrant of Atarneus, was excessive, [on the occasion of Hermias' death?] sacrificed to the latter in a manner befitting the gods.'[124] Lucian may allude here to the funeral or memorial services held by Aristotle (and Callisthenes) in honor of the deceased Hermias. Quoting from Demetrius of Magnesia, *Poets and Authors of the Same Name*, Diogenes Laertius (DL V. 3) relates that Aristotle 'was on very affectionate terms with Hermias.' The author of *Aristippus or On the Luxury of the Ancients* (DL V. 3-4),[125] on the other hand, insists that 'Aristotle was enamored of a mistress of Hermias and, with the latter's consent, married her'; and that, as has already been stated, 'in his delight he sacrificed to her [during her lifetime] as the Athenians sacrifice to Demeter of Eleusis.'

Some of these derogatory and slanderous accounts may in part transfer to Aristotle the actions of Harpalus who erected a temple in honor of his deceased mistress Pythionice, or they might refer to the honors which Harpalus bestowed upon his living mistress, Clycera.[126] It has already been pointed out that Aristotle, who seems to have been very fond of his wife Pythias, after her death may have held some elaborate services in her memory. He may also have dedicated a statue in her honor, and it is quite possible that this statue may have had some of the attributes of Demeter. We also know that in his last will and testament, Aristotle stipulated that a statue or 'likeness' of his mother, Phaestis, be dedicated to Demeter of Nemea.[127] This provision in Aristotle's will and the stories about Harpalus' mistresses which might subsequently have been transferred to Pythias (who in the meantime had also been degraded to Hermias' mistress by some detractors of Hermias and Aristotle), possibly were used by Aristotle's slanderers and enemies. The determined detractors of Aristotle probably also claimed that all these honorific as well as religious (sacrilegious) ceremonies or memorials were performed while Pythias was still alive, implying thereby that Aristotle was a totally depraved as well as wholly irreligious, nay, blasphemous person who had no respect for the religious feelings of his fellow-men. When some authors call Pythias the concubine of Hermias, they might confuse her with Herpyllis, who after the death of Pythias became Aristotle's mistress.

Diogenes Laertius does not refer to, or elaborate on, the story that Hermias had sent several invitations to Aristotle before and after the death of Plato urging him to come to Atarneus.[128] There even exists a report that Hermias came personally to Athens to attend the Academy (and perhaps to persuade Aristotle to visit him in Asia Minor).[129] Areius Didymus writes that Aristotle, Coriscus and Erastus (and for a while Xenocrates), frequently consulted with Hermias on matters of statecraft. These men persuaded Hermias to be less autocratic and tyrannical.[130] It may be presumed that Hermias made these men, especially Aristotle, his personal counsellors.[131] As a result of these consultations, Hermias' régime became less oppressive. He apparently won over some of the adjoining territories, including the city of Assos. According to Areius Didymus, Hermias acquired Assos by his moderate and intelligent government,[132] suggested perhaps by Aristotle. It has also been surmised that since Aristotle was in frequent and close consultations with Hermias, he must have lived in Atarneus rather than in Assos. Assos might have been 'assigned' to Aristotle not in the sense that the philosopher lived there permanently, but in the sense that the revenues of this city were given to Aristotle as a sort of compensation for his services to Hermias—a common practice in antiquity. All this, however, is not mentioned by Diogenes Laertius. It is impossible to determine whether or not Hermippus discussed in detail some of Aristotle's political (or diplomatic) activities in Atarneus.[133]

The remainder of DL V. 4 and the first part of DL V. 5 treat Aristotle's relations with the royal court of Macedonia or, to be more exact, his personal relations with King Philip and Alexander. The report of Diogenes Laertius, which seems to be partially derived from

Hermippus, relates three incidents in Aristotle's associations with the Macedonian royal house: first, Aristotle's accession as the preceptor of the young Alexander; second, his instrumental role in having his native town of Stagira rebuilt by Alexander or Philip, who had destroyed it originally in 349–48; and third, the tragic Callisthenes affair.

According to a widely accepted tradition,[134] Aristotle did go to Macedonia (in 343–42) and, at the request of King Philip, took charge of Alexander's education.[135] But surprisingly enough, neither Onesicritus the Cynic[136] nor Marsyas of Pella,[137] two contemporary reporters, ever mention the story that Aristotle was in fact Alexander's tutor.[138] Alexinus of Megara, likewise an early source, only knows that Alexander strongly protested when his father Philip suggested that he should be instructed by Aristotle.[139] There is also an interesting story according to which Xenocrates, the 'rival' of Aristotle, was Alexander's preceptor. This might be inferred from Plutarch, who quotes an early source which apparently insists that Alexander requested Xenocrates (his teacher?) to compose for him *Didactic Essays on Kingship*.[140] Conversely, the many sources attesting the alleged tutorship of Aristotle are without exception of a relatively late date, late enough to be classified as a part of that romantic Alexandrian tradition which, among other fanciful tales, would not hesitate to link together the great sage and the great conqueror.[141]

As a 'reward' for his instruction of Alexander, or for some other services he had rendered the king, or as an acknowledgement of the respect he enjoyed at the Macedonian court, Aristotle apparently secured Alexander's (or Philip's) promise to rebuild Stagira, which had been destroyed by Philip in 349–48 B.C. (DL V. 4).[142] Moreover, he is said to have drawn up a code of laws for the new Stagira (DL V. 4).[143] Since Aristotle was a native of Stagira and without doubt its greatest son, it is not surprising that tradition should maintain that throughout his whole life he remained attached to that city in one way or another, either as an *oicist* or as a *nomothetes*. Hermippus, we know, wrote a Περὶ νομοθέτων. In this work he probably also referred to, and elaborated on, Aristotle's legislative efforts on behalf of Stagira.[144] This composition might well be the ultimate source used here by Diogenes Laertius. DL V. 4, it will be noted, not only relates that Aristotle drew up a code of laws for Stagira, but also that, following the example set by Xenocrates in the Academy, he established certain rules and regulations for the management of his own school (the Lyceum?). Diogenes Laertius (or perhaps his source), by way of associating similar themes, apparently joins together two essentially unrelated topics or traditions concerning Aristotle's activities as an *oicist* and *nomothetes* (and as an *euergetes*): he was the 'rebuilder' as well as the lawgiver of his native city, Stagira, and also the founder as well as the 'organizer' of his own school (the Lyceum ?). This being so, the reference to Aristotle's efforts to promulgate rules and regulations for the conduct of his school is but a kind of *excursus* which in fact has nothing to do with his sojourn in Macedonia or with his activities at the Macedonian royal court. Dio Chrysostom also relates that in his old age Aristotle allegedly insisted that the only truly meritorious deeds he ever performed were his diplomatic activities which led to his becoming 'the [second] founder of his native city.'[145] In other words, the deep satisfaction or feeling of achievement he experienced over his success in having been instrumental in the restoration and reorganization of Stagira in itself was the greatest reward and the most honorable distinction that had ever been bestowed upon him.[146]

A tradition, represented by the *Vita Aristotelis Marciana*, the *Vita Aristotelis Vulgata* and by the *Vita Aristotelis Latina*,[147] as well as by the Syriac and Arabic *Vitae Aristotelis*,[148] but wholly ignored by Diogenes Laertius, records that after Aristotle's death the grateful inhabitants of Stagira brought back the body (or ashes) of their benefactor (*oicist* and *nomothetes*);[149] built an altar over his grave;[150] named the place of his burial *Aristoteleion* (which they subsequently used as a meeting place of the Council);[151] named one month of the year after Aristotle;[152] and celebrated an annual festival in his memory.[153] These are honors which in ancient Greece were occasionally bestowed upon some signally meritorious citizen, 'founder,' lawgiver or 'hero.' It might be surmised that all these accounts of the honors conferred upon Aristotle probably go back to Hermippus or, perhaps, to Demetrius of Phaleron (?). In all likelihood, they were part of a vitriolic attack upon the Athenians who in the year 323 B.C. treated Aristotle, the *euergetes* of Athens,[154] in a most shabby and ungrateful manner. While the little town of Stagira heaped the highest honors imaginable upon its greatest son, Athens disgraced herself, as she had done previously in the case of Socrates, by banishing one of her foremost residents.

The story (DL V. 5)—that before departing from Macedonia Aristotle left behind his nephew Callisthenes of Olynthus (perhaps to carry on or complete the education of Alexander, perhaps to maintain his influence at Pella);[155] that Callisthenes accompanied Alexander on his Persian campaign;[156] and that Callisthenes was foully murdered by Alexander[157]—on the whole is well attested by a number of ancient historians who wrote on the Persian expedition of Alexander.[158]

As regards the biographical tradition of Aristotle, the following major 'trends' may be observed: the *Vita Marciana* (as well as the *Vita Vulgata*, the *Vita Latina* and the *Vita Hesychii*) does not mention the Callisthenes episode, while the Arabic *Vitae*[159] merely record that Aristotle left Callisthenes with Alexander,[160] recommending him to the latter. It is quite possible that the tradition, which is one-sidedly favorable to Aristotle, omitted all incidents, such as the foul murder of Callisthenes which might make Aristotle appear in a bad light. Since Alexander allegedly was a pupil of Aristotle, some of his outrageous deeds might reflect on his teacher: 'Wherefore by their fruits ye shall know them.'[161]

The more important and in all likelihood more reliable 'Alexandrian tradition'—we shall mention here only Arrian[162] and Plutarch[163]—essentially recounts that after the senseless slaying of Clitus by Alexander, two philosophers, Callisthenes and Anaxarchus of Abdera (the Democritean),[164] tried to console the despondent king. Anaxarchus attempted to allay Alexander's grief by pointing out to him that a god-like king such as Alexander could do no wrong. Callisthenes, on the other hand, used 'moral language and gentle as well as soothing means' to bring the king to his senses,[165] refusing to admit, however, that whatever a king does is always well done. This refusal to cater to Alexander's whims and the king's steadily worsening temper probably brought about Callisthenes' gradually falling from Alexander's good graces.[166] The final catastrophe came, according to Plutarch,[167] when some sycophants among Alexander's associates accused Callisthenes of having been involved in Hermolaus' plot to assassinate the king. Although none of the conspirators, under torture, ever admitted that Callisthenes had any connection whatsoever with this plot,[168] he was cruelly put to death.

There are three different versions of the details of Callisthenes' punishment and death. Ptolemy maintains that by the express order of Alexander he was first tortured and then hanged;[169] Aristobulus relates that he was put in chains until he died from neglect and abuse;[170] and Chares of Mytilene insists that he was held in chains until he could be tried by Alexander himself, but that due to maltreatment and privation, he contracted a disease and died after seven months of inhuman sufferings.[171] In a remark which definitely seems to be out of place, Diogenes Laertius (DL V. 10) observes that according to some (antagonistic) source or sources Aristotle incurred Alexander's displeasure because he had introduced his nephew Callisthenes to, or had foisted him upon, the king. Moreover, this source also maintains that in order to annoy or offend Aristotle, Alexander deliberately honored Anaximenes[172] and sent presents to Xenocrates, the 'rival' of Aristotle.[173] There can be little doubt that this alienation between Aristotle and Alexander, which probably dates back to the time Alexander ascended to the throne of Macedonia in 336 B.C., was brought to a climax by Alexander's cruel treatment of Callisthenes. But while Diogenes Laertius (DL V. 10), or his source, makes it appear that it was Alexander who broke off his former friendship with Aristotle, it is quite likely that Aristotle, deeply offended by Alexander's general deportment and, in particular, by the murder of Callisthenes, turned against the king.[174] Plutarch also refers to a (spurious?) letter allegedly addressed by Alexander to Antipater (and others) in which Alexander threatened Aristotle by announcing rather bluntly that he 'would take care of, and punish, the people [*scil.*, Aristotle] who had sent Callisthenes to him, and who harbor those ... who conspire against my life.'[175] Perhaps it was only after Aristotle (and his friends and disciples) had broken with Alexander that the latter began to shower favors and presents upon Anaximenes of Lampsacus and Xenocrates.

Aside from stating briefly that 'when he thought he had stayed long enough with Alexander, he [*scil.*, Aristotle] departed for Athens' (DL V. 4), where 'he was head of the school for thirteen years' (DL V. 5),[176] Diogenes Laertius has nothing to say about what in the opinion of many scholars constituted the most important period in the scholarly life of Aristotle (335/34–323 B.C.). It was during these years that he is said to have produced some of his most significant philosophic works. This flagrant and almost shocking omission might possibly be due to the fact that neither Apollodorus nor Hermippus—the two main sources which Diogenes Laertius apparently consulted on this subject— have much to say about this particular period in the life of Aristotle. Perhaps it was, after all, scholarly not the most productive phase in his life.[177] This, then, might in turn also cast some doubt on the authenticity of some of the Aristotelian *pragmateia*, the vast majority of which is usually dated between 335–34 and 323 B.C.

According to Diogenes Laertius (DL V. 5–6), Aristotle 'withdrew to Chalcis [on the island of Euboea][178] because he had been indicted for impiety by the hierophant Eurymedon or, according to Favorinus in his *Miscellaneous History*, by Demophilus.'[179] The basis for the charges brought against Aristotle was probably the hymn he had composed in honor of Hermias of Atarneus.[180] The *Vita Aristotelis* of Al-Mubashir as well as that of Usaibia maintain, probably on the authority of

Ptolemy (-el-Garib), that Eurymedon deliberately gave a wholly distorted account of Aristotle's philosophy, claiming that the latter did not worship the gods and that he did not show them the proper respect.[181]

On the authority of Eumelus,[182] Diogenes Laertius (DL V. 6) reports that Aristotle died in Chalcis[183] at the age of seventy[184] by drinking aconite (hemlock). It goes without saying that the story told (or invented) by Eumelus parallels the life-span as well as the particular circumstances surrounding the death of Socrates, who seems to have been Eumelus' model.[185] As Diogenes Laertius (DL V. 6) himself concedes (by relying on Apollodorus' *Chronicle*, DL V. 10), this story is in conflict with the generally accepted facts.[186] Quoting Favorinus, Diogenes Laertius (DL V. 9) also relates that Aristotle was the first philosopher who under similar circumstances wrote a forensic speech in his own defense, denying the charge of impiety or blasphemy.[187] Probably in order to magnify or glorify his hero or heroes, Favorinus, the source used here by Diogenes Laertius, frequently claims that this or that philosopher was 'the first' to do or say something exceptional or original.[188] DL V. 9 also credits the departing Aristotle with having cited a hexameter from Homer, *Odyssey* VII. 120: 'Pear upon pear grows old, and fig upon fig.' This apophthegm, it may be assumed, alludes to the many professional informers or sycophants who made life in Athens almost unbearable. It is probably intended to provide an explanation and justification of the fact that Aristotle preferred to flee from Athens rather than face his accusers in court.[189] Socrates, who apparently had become the model of how the philosopher should act in such a situation, at least according to Plato's *Crito*, had refused to take to flight in order to escape death. But then again, Socrates was a native as well as a citizen of Athens, while Aristotle was a Macedonian alien temporarily residing in Athens.[190] Hence, DL V. 9 also contains something approaching an apology of Aristotle and his deportment in the face of his enemies or accusers.

Referring to Apollodorus' *Chronicle*, Diogenes Laertius (DL V. 10) states that Aristotle died a natural death[191] in Chalcis, in his sixty-third year (in 322 B.C.).[192] The stories recorded in DL V. 16, namely, that a large amount of dishes was found in the possession of Aristotle,[193] that he bathed in warm oil and that he placed a skin on his stomach, are probably connected with his failing health or old age. They might be indicative of his suffering from a serious stomach ailment. Some ancient authors, among them Lycon Pythagoraeus, gave these stories a nasty twist, claiming that Aristotle 'afterwards sold the oil' (DL V.

16).[194] This, then, would make him out to have been an avaricious 'skinflint.' The report that Aristotle's estate contained a great many dishes might also be a snide allusion to his alleged gluttony, a theme already touched upon by Theocritus of Chios (DL V. 11).[195] The somewhat sketchy account of Aristotle's flight from Athens and of his subsequent death in Chalcis can be supplemented by materials culled from ancient authors as well as from the other *Vitae Aristotelis*. The *Vita Marciana* (*VM* 41)[196] merely mentions that 'the Athenians turned against him,' while the Arabic *Vitae* (*II VA* 20 and *IV VA* 7) record that the hierophant Eurymedon had charged Aristotle with impiety. These accounts fail, however, to mention Aristotle's hymn to Hermias as the incriminating evidence substantiating the charge of impiety.[197] Moreover, some of these *Vitae* maintain that upon leaving Athens, Aristotle, plainly alluding to the fate that befell Socrates, remarked that he would not give the Athenians a second chance to sin against philosophy.[198] They also insist that he wrote to Antipater that 'it is dangerous to dwell among the Athenians (as a friend of Macedonia?),'[199] and that by citing the verse from Homer's *Odyssey* VII. 120,[200] he complained that Athens was crowded with 'troublemakers.'

Although the evidence relating to Aristotle's departure from Athens in 323 B.C. is rather confusing—and Diogenes Laertius contributes nothing in particular that might shed additional light on this incident—the following might be accepted as historical truth: Aristotle, besides being an alien, was always considered a philo-Macedonian. Consequently, he was forced to leave Athens due to political pressure.[201] The hymn or paean to Hermias,[202] if it was actually cited as evidence of Aristotle's alleged impiety, could have been a mere pretext,[203] especially since this hymn was not really a religious paean.[204] The real reason for the indictment of Aristotle would seem to have been his philo-Macedonian attitude. In the year 323 B.C., when Alexander had suddenly died and the imminent collapse of his empire was to be expected, the anti-Macedonian party in Athens for a short time gained the upper hand and immediately began to take action against all persons suspected of sympathizing with Macedonia, including Aristotle, the 'Macedonian.'[205]

Diogenes Laertius (DL V. 6) does not mention the particular circumstances of Aristotle's death in 322 B.C. It is fair to assume that Aristotle, after having drafted his last will and testament (DL V. 11–16), died a natural death and was in full possession of his mental powers at the time of his death.[206] It has already been stated that Eumelus, an utterly untrustworthy witness, maintains that like Socrates before him, he died by taking hemlock.[207] According to a third tradition which seems to have arisen somewhat later (and the beginnings of which can no longer be determined), Aristotle went to Chalcis allegedly for the purpose of studying at first-hand the ebb and flow of the Euripus,[208] the straits which separate the island of Euboea from the Greek mainland. It has also been maintained that he wrote or intended to write a learned treatise on the subject.[209] But when, according to this later tradition, he failed to solve the 'problem of the Euripus,' he either died from chagrin or, in a fit of despondency, took his own life.[210]

It is fair to surmise that in his *Vita Aristotelis* Diogenes Laertius largely follows the *Vita Aristotelis* of Hermippus, although he makes frequent use of other sources, some of which he actually cites by name. The *Vita* of Hermippus, the Peripatetic, undoubtedly was a sympathetic or favorable source and at times even an encomiastic report. It is safe to assume, however, that Hermippus also reported some derogatory stories about Aristotle. He probably did this in order to disprove certain unfavorable accounts or allegations which had been circulated and hence could not be completely ignored or simply suppressed. Diogenes Laertius, on the other hand, does not hesitate to intersperse rather liberally certain unfavorable (or fanciful) stories, some of which he might have found in Hermippus, while others he might have learned from a host of ancient authors and critics. But unlike Hermippus, as a rule Diogenes Laertius does not attempt to refute them.

The earliest biographers of Aristotle on which Diogenes relies for his information, probably made use of the scanty biographical data or 'facts' which could be culled from Aristotle's lost works,[211] from such personal documents as his last will and testament, from some letters of Aristotle, provided such letters existed,[212] from certain official decrees or 'records'[213] and from the accounts or opinions of some of Aristotle's contemporaries, students, members of the Peripatus, or authors and critics of the early third century B.C. It goes without saying that most of these accounts or opinions were often strongly influenced, if not decisively colored, by the bitter and protracted rivalries that existed between the many competing schools of philosophy throughout the early Hellenistic period, by violently championed political convictions or prejudices (anti-Macedonian or pro-Macedonian; anti-Alexandrian or pro-Alexandrian tendencies), and by the many literary, professional or personal feuds which enlivened this period, such as the rivalry between Aristotle and Isocrates and their respective schools, the bitter enmity between the Aristotelians and the Epicureans, and the prolonged antagonism between the Aristotelians and the Platonists. All these are probably the main elements from which the earliest biographers of Aristotle derived their materials as well as their information.

But there is a further historical factor whose decisive effects must be taken into consideration. The beginnings of the biographical treatment of Aristotle coincide with the essentially novel Hellenistic trend to pay increased attention to the individual in his historical uniqueness. In so doing, this trend displays a pronounced interest in the specific achievements of this individual, in his particular circumstances and in the more prosaic details of his life, including some of its most trivial incidents. At the same time it attempts to analyse his particular character, mentality, actions and motivations. This novel approach to biography in general, which is actually the beginning of all biographical literature in antiquity, was still in its infancy when the first authors began to concentrate on the life of Aristotle. In their inexperience as well as due to the frequent lack of adequate source materials or proper understanding as to how the few available sources should be handled, these first biographers often failed to distinguish between fact and fiction, thus perpetuating old fictions or creating new ones.

The first author, biographer or critic to make use of the so-called letters of Aristotle—the vast majority of them undoubtedly spurious—was probably Apellicon of Teos (*c.* 100–90 B.C.),[214] who thereby added some essentially new and so far mostly unused (and at the same time essentially unreliable) materials or sources to the biographical tradition concerning Aristotle. This, in turn, ushered in a somewhat altered approach to the whole history of Aristotelian biographies. After Apellicon (and Andronicus of Rhodes—*c.* the middle of the first century B.C.), it may be assumed that probably no strikingly novel additions to, or innovations of, the traditional biographical materials were made, although their particular exploitation and interpretation most certainly did undergo certain startling changes.

The *Vita Aristotelis* of Diogenes Laertius, then, is primarily a collection of excerpts from and references to a biographical tradition which in all its essential aspects and particular details had become crystallized during the third, second and first centuries B.C. We have noted, however, that Diogenes' particular collection of excerpts is often indiscriminately selected, arbitrarily assembled and ineptly interpreted. Presumably, Diogenes Laertius made a number of later insertions or additions to his original draft or text without properly integrating these insertions. This would also explain the obvious disjointedness of his frequently baffling reports. Hence, his *Vita* is not always a reliable or perhaps completely intelligible and consistent biography. Its many-faceted content and the large number of involved problems raised by this somewhat unusual biography make a proper and exhausting analysis well-nigh impossible, though always tempting.[215] To some extent and in a certain way this particular *Vita*, which also casts an ominous shadow on Diogenes Laertius' qualifications as a historian and biographer, probably will always remain something of a riddle. Any attempt to solve this complex riddle in all probability will have to rely on a certain amount of intelligent hypotheses and restrained as well as educated guesses. Together with the very brief and not too informative *Vita Aristotelis Hesychii* (*Vita Menagiana*), the *Vita Aristotelis* of Diogenes Laertius is the only surviving ancient biography which in a most haphazard fashion also relates stories pronouncedly unfavorable to Aristotle. In this it is radically different from the essentially encomiastic accounts or biographies of the Neo-Platonists.

Chapter IV

A Summary of the Syriac and Arabic
*Vitae Aristotelis**

It is commonly held that the two surviving Syriac and the four extant Arabic *Vitae Aristotelis* are ultimately based on the biographical tradition represented or inaugurated by Ptolemy (-el-Garib) and his (lost) *Vita Aristotelis*.[1] Probably in the course of the fifth or sixth century A.D., a Syriac translation was made of Ptolemy's *Vita* or, more likely, of an epitome of this *Vita*. Of this original translation, only two rather scanty abridgements by some Syriac biographers survive, namely, *I Vita Aristotelis Syriaca* and *II Vita Aristotelis Syriaca*, which might also be called short *résumés* of an older and more comprehensive Syriac translation of Ptolemy's original Greek *Vita Aristotelis* or of an epitome of this *Vita*.

The Syriac translation of either Ptolemy's *Vita* or that of an epitome of this *Vita*, together with some additional (probably Neo-Platonic) materials transmitted through several intermediary sources, ultimately became the foundation of the four Arabic *Vitae Aristotelis*. It has been surmised that towards the end of the ninth century A.D., Ishaq Ibn Hunayn translated into Arabic a Syriac rendition of Ptolemy's *Vita* or, rather, of a Syriac translation of an epitome of this *Vita*. In any event, the Arabic biographers, without exception, ultimately derived their information and materials, through the intermediary of Syriac translators, from Ptolemy, although they seem to have included in their *Vitae* not only some elements that were probably added (or invented) by the Syriac translators (or by the Arabic biographers themselves), but also bits of information gleaned from some other (Neo-Platonic?) reports or accounts. There exists no evidence, however, that the later Arabic biographers made direct use of Greek or Syriac sources. It might be correct to maintain, therefore, that the Syriac and Arabic biographers, like the Neo-Platonic School of Ammonius, derived most of their information concerning the life of Aristotle from Ptolemy (-el-Garib) and his *Vita Aristotelis*.[2]

The four major Arabic biographers of Aristotle are: Al-Mubassir (or Al-Mubashir, subsequently cited as *II VA*), who wrote during the latter part of the eleventh century;[3] Ibn Abi Usaibia (subsequently cited as *IV VA*), who wrote during the latter part of the thirteenth century;[4] Ibn an-Nadim (subsequently cited as *I VA*), who wrote near the end of the tenth century;[5] and Al-Qifti Gamaladdin (subsequently cited as *III VA*), who wrote during the first half of the thirteenth century.[6] A cursory examination of the Arabic (and Syriac) *Vitae Aristotelis* might indicate that especially *I VA*, *II VA* and *IV VA*, which are based on a single main source, are quite similar in content. Closer analysis reveals, however, that there exist quite a few significant differences in the facts selected and discussed by the different Arabic biographers. It is also obvious that some of the later Arabic biographers simply copied from some earlier Arabic author. Thus, Usaibia, for instance, occasionally seems to quote from Mubashir without, however, acknowledging his source.

In conformity with what appears to be a definite and probably widely used 'organizational arrangement,'[7] the Syriac and Arabic biographers begin with the name (and with an attempt at explaining the name) of the person whose life and accomplishments they recount. They all agree that the Stagirite's name was Aristotle. An-Nadim (*I VA* 1) adds the remark that this name signifies 'lover of wisdom' (confounding the name of Aristotle with the Greek term $\phi\iota\lambda\acuteo\sigma o\phi os$), 'the distinguished one,' 'the best one,' 'the perfect one,' or 'the excellent one.' Mubashir's (*II VA* 1) observation that this name means 'the perfect one' would indicate that neither he nor An-Nadim knew or understood Greek, something which may also be maintained about the intermediary source or sources which they consulted.[8] It is quite possible that the original source (Ptolemy's *Vita Aristotelis* or an epitome of this *Vita*) from which the Syriac (and Arabic) biographers ultimately derived their information, contained the following statement: 'Aristotle, the philosopher, was an excellent as well as distinguished man.' The Syriac translator, on whom the subsequent Syriac and Arabic biographers relied for their information, might have believed that this descriptive passage contained the etymology of Aristotle's name.

Next, there is a statement of the name of Aristotle's father, Nicomachus. On this, too, all of the *Vitae* agree,[9] except for Usaibia (*IV VA* 2) and Al-Qifti (*III VA*), who refer to Nicomachus-el-Gerasi, an obvious confusion with Nicomachus of Gerasa, the Neo-Pythagorean philosopher (*floruit c.* 140 A.D.). There is also mention of Aristotle's mother. *I VS* 3 calls her Parysatis, which is obviously an error;[10] An-Nadim

I VA 3) speaks of Phaestias, which is probably a mispelling of Phaestis; and both Mubashir (*II VA* 2) and Usaibia (*IV VA* 1–2) refer to her as Phaestis, which is the correct name.

When recounting the genealogy of Aristotle, *I VS* 3 merely relates that Nicomachus, the father of Aristotle, was a descendant of Asclepius; and Mubashir (*II VA* 2) as well as An-Nadim (*I VA* 2) record that Nicomachus was the son (descendant) of Machaon[11] and that through Machaon he traced his lineage back to Asclepius. Usaibia (*IV VA* 2), on the other hand, seems to confuse the whole of Aristotle's genealogy when he insists that Nicomachus traced his ancestry back to Asclepius, who fathered Machaon, who in turn fathered another Asclepius. The introduction of this second Asclepius into the genealogy of Aristotle is, most likely, a corruption.[12] According to *I VS* 3, Mubashir (*II VA* 2), Usaibia (*IV VA* 2) and An-Nadim (*I VA* 3),[13] Aristotle's mother, Phaestis, likewise descended from Asclepius. Hence, Mubashir (*II VA* 2) could rightfully maintain that Aristotle's family or ancestry 'was one of the most noble among the Greeks.'

I VS 1 and *II VS* 1 record that Nicomachus, the father of Aristotle, was a physician in Stagira, whereas Mubashir (*II VA* 2), Usaibia (*IV VA* 2) and An-Nadim (*I VA* 3) emphasize that he was not merely a physician, but the court physician of King Amyntas III of Macedonia and, hence, during his later years must have lived in Aegae (or Pella?) in Macedonia. They also seem to stress the fact that Amyntas III was the father of King Philip, who in turn was the father of Alexander the Great. In mentioning the position of Nicomachus at the royal court of Macedonia—obviously a position of confidence and intimacy in the eyes of the Arabs—the Arabic biographers wish not only to indicate Nicomachus' social position, professional standing and political connections, but also to point out the close personal ties which Aristotle's family had with some of the most powerful and most renowned dynasties of that time. Aside from indicating that Aristotle's father was an educated and cultured man—after all, he lived at the royal court of Macedonia—the Arabic biographers apparently also wish to stress the close personal ties that existed between the two 'Western heroes' of the Muslim world, Alexander the Great and Aristotle, the great philosopher.

All these *Vitae* agree that Aristotle was born in Stagira,[14] although they do not seem to know exactly where Stagira was located. *I VS* 2 maintains that Stagira was a town in Thrace, near Chalcidice and Olynthus; Mubashir (*II VA* 2), that it was located 'in the land of Chalcidice, belonging to the province of Thrace'; Usaibia (*IV VA* 1), that it was located near the towns of Olynthus and Methone, in 'a land called Chalcidice, which is a part of Thrace'; *II VS* 1, that it was located in Macedonia; and An-Nadim (*I VA* 3), that it was 'a Greek city.'[15] No *Vita*, however, mentions the date of Aristotle's birth. Moreover, neither the Syriac nor the Arabic *Vitae Aristotelis* refer either to Aristotle's brother, Arimnestus, or to his sister, Arimneste.[16] Although An-Nadim (*I VA* 16) states that Theophrastus was the son of Aristotle's sister, he does not mention her name.[17]

Mubashir (*II VA* 3) relates an unusual story about Aristotle's early training, a story not to be found in any other *Vitae Aristotelis*, be they Greek, Syriac or Arabic: when Aristotle was eight years old, his father, Nicomachus, brought him to Athens and placed him in the Lyceum, or to be more exact, handed him over to 'a school of poets, orators and schoolmasters.' Mubashir continues: 'This kind of learning [poetry and rhetoric], as well as this knowledge the Greeks called the "rounded or all-embracing education." They did so because every person needed this kind of knowledge which is an instrument as well as a guide to all sorts of wisdom and virtue—showing us, too, how each department of human knowledge had been developed.'[18] Aristotle stayed in this school nine years, until, according to the general tradition, he supposedly entered the school of Plato at the age of seventeen. If Mubashir's unusual account is correct, then Aristotle went to Athens for the first time in the year 376 B.C.[19] Thus, although we know that Aristotle's father died while Aristotle was rather young, that is, before he was sent to Athens in the year 367 B.C., Nicomachus must still have been alive in 376.

The story of Aristotle's stay at a 'school of poets, orators and schoolmasters'—repeated in substance by Usaibia (*IV VA* 28), although making no mention of Aristotle's exact age—might be explained as follows: There exists a tradition, not mentioned by the Syriac and Arabic biographers, according to which Aristotle went to Athens 'at the age of seventeen ... [where] he kept company with Socrates ... and stayed with him a short time until Socrates met his death. ... After that he joined Plato.'[20] In brief, some *Vitae Aristotelis* do not make it clear whether Aristotle originally went to Athens for the express purpose of joining Plato and the Academy, or whether he entered some other school first. Since Socrates died in 399 B.C., and Aristotle was born in 384 B.C., the story that Aristotle 'joined Socrates' contains a fatal anachronism.

A reasonable explanation of this account may lie in the biographers' or epitomizers' confusion of Socrates with Isocrates.[21] Assuming, then, that the name 'Socrates' is merely an erroneous substitution for the name 'Isocrates,' and in view of the tradition according to which Aristotle went to Athens in the year 367 B.C., we might also conjecture that perhaps in his first year or years in Athens, Aristotle actually became a member of Isocrates' school, at least for a while.[22] (It should also be borne in mind that early in 367 Plato went to Syracuse, not to return until 365–64.) In fact, the *Vita Marciana* 4, the *Vita Vulgata* 3 and the *Vita Latina* 4, as well as the biography of Mubashir (*II VA* 3) and that of Usaibia (*IV VA* 28)—Usaibia's report is an almost verbatim repetition of Mubashir's account—all stress that Aristotle's first thorough training was in rhetoric, a training which he might well have received in the school of Isocrates.[23] Tradition also has it that Aristotle's first didactic efforts at the Academy (between 360 and 355 B.C.) were connected with rhetoric,[24] and that his first literary effort—probably the *Gryllus*, which carries the significant subtitle of *On Rhetoric*—was likewise related to rhetoric.[25] And finally, the *Gryllus*, which was composed *c.* 360–59 B.C. or perhaps a little later, testifies to the bitterness of the rivalry between Aristotle and Isocrates (as does the Aristotelian *Protrepticus*, usually dated between 352 and 350 B.C., which is probably a rebuttal of Isocrates' *Antidosis*, published in 352 B.C.).[26] The *Gryllus* might be interpreted as an attempt on the part of Aristotle to justify his earlier 'secession' from Isocrates and his school.[27] Of course, all these explanations are conjectures, resting upon the assumptions that, in this instance, Socrates and Isocrates have been confused, and that at one time Aristotle had been associated with Isocrates and his school.[28]

There must also have existed a tradition, known to the Syriac and Arabic biographers, according to which Aristotle turned to philosophy only at the age of thirty, after having practiced medicine for some time. This information is to be found in *I VS* 6 and in An-Nadim (*I VA* 6), who relates that 'it is said that Aristotle started his study of philosophy only when he was thirty years old.' This tradition, which is rejected outright by all biographers, is not known to, or at least is not mentioned by, Mubashir. Usaibia (*IV VA* 12) tries apparently to 'set the record straight' by pointing out that those people are wrong 'who contend that he [*scil.*, Aristotle] did not devote himself to philosophy until he had reached the age of thirty, and that up to that time he had tried his hand at governing cities [*scil.*, was interested in politics], his aim being to improve the political conditions of these cities.'[29] The passage from Usaibia (*IV VA* 12) contends with certain derogatory stories about the young Aristotle, probably put into circulation by Epicurus and the Epicureans. According to these stories, in his youth Aristotle had been a medical quack, a peddler of drugs, a mercenary soldier and a squanderer who only after he had failed in everything else, turned to philosophy (at the age of thirty).[30]

I VS 4,[31] *II VS* 2, Mubashir (*II VA* 9),[32] Usaibia (*IV VA* 3) and An-Nadim (*I VA* 4) relate that at the age of seventeen Aristotle became the disciple of Plato, and that this arrangement was made on the advice of the Delphic oracle. Usaibia (*IV VA* 3) also records that after the death of his father, Nicomachus, the youthful Aristotle was 'handed over' to Plato by Proxenus, who apparently became Aristotle's guardian (?).[33] This Proxenus, Usaibia continues, acted in compliance with the dictate of the Delphic oracle or perhaps because he was a personal friend of Plato.[34] Mubashir (*II VA* 9–10), on the other hand, recounts that after having completed his 'preliminary' or 'pre-philosophic' studies at the age of seventeen, Aristotle attached himself to Plato at the Academy and became his disciple for twenty years.[35] According to Mubashir (*II VA* 9), Aristotle studied 'ethics, politics, mathematics, physics and theology [metaphysics]' under the personal guidance of Plato; and Usaibia (*IV VA* 28) says that he studied 'dialec-tics [logic], politics [which included ethics], mathematics, physics and theology' with Plato, and that at the beginning of these 'more advanced' studies he was seventeen years old.

All sources, except one (*II VS* 2), agree that Aristotle stayed with Plato twenty years. *II VS* 2 merely mentions that as long as Aristotle studied philosophy under Plato's supervision, he concentrated on Platonic philosophy until 'frightened by the execution of Socrates' he fled from Athens and stayed near the Hellespont (*II VS* 3).[36]

All sources also agree that Aristotle was taught by Plato personally. Mubashir (*II VA* 10) is more explicit in maintaining that, 'because of the extraordinary impression which Aristotle made upon him, Plato did not entrust him to be taught by Xenocrates, as he did with his other pupils.' *II VS* 2, as had already been shown, essentially relates the same story, insisting that during his stay at the Academy, Aristotle studied (exclusively?) under Plato's direction, concentrating on Platonic philosophy. The 'extraordinary impression' which Aristotle made upon Plato became manifest not only in the fact that Plato insisted upon instructing him personally, but also in the lavish praise which Plato apparently bestowed upon him. Thus, when it sometimes happened that Aristotle was not among Plato's audience, according to *I VS* 5, the latter would say, 'the "Mind" is absent,' or, 'the philosopher is far from the truth,' or, 'the audience is deaf.'[37] Mubashir (*II VA* 11–12) insists that Plato simply refused to hold scholarly discussions unless Aristotle was present, remarking that he did not care to discuss philosophy 'until the "Mind" is here.' And when Aristotle arrived, Mubashir continues, Plato would say: 'Begin to recite, the audience is complete,' or, 'read now, the "Mind" is present.'[38]

A further indication of the high esteem in which Aristotle was held by Plato, Mubashir (*II VA* 13) and Usaibia (*IV VA* 4) relate, was Aristotle's appointment as 'acting scholarch' of the Academy 'while Plato went to Sicily for a second time.' Mubashir and Usaibia, needless to say, are here in error. According to tradition, Aristotle entered the Platonic Academy in the late spring or early summer of 367 B.C. (unless he joined first Isocrates and his school),[39] while Plato departed on his second journey to Syracuse in the early spring of 367 B.C., not to return until 365–64 B.C. During Plato's absence, Eudoxus of Cnidus was the 'acting scholarch.'[40] In 361–60 B.C., Plato made his third and last visit to Sicily, and Heracleides of Pontus became the 'acting scholarch' during this period.[41] It is not entirely clear whether Mubashir and Usaibia refer to the second or third Sicilian journey of Plato.[42]

Usaibia (*IV VA* 4) relates that when Plato returned from Sicily (in 360 B.C. ?), 'Aristotle moved to the Lyceum and there founded a school of his own, which was named after the "walking philosophers".' Mubashir (*II VA* 14), on the other hand, reports that 'when Plato was dead, Aristotle went to a place in Athens called the Lyceum. There he founded a school of philosophy which was named after the "walking philosophers."'[43] And *II VS* 5 maintains that after having been the scholarch of the Academy for some time, Aristotle 'left it for the Lyceum. And when he had founded his own school there, his followers came to be known as the "Peripatetics" [the "walking philosophers"], because he used to lecture to them walking up and down in the Lyceum.'[44] An-Nadim (*I VA* 5) again claims that after Plato had gone to Sicily, Aristotle succeeded him in the scholarchate of the Academy.[45] The accounts of Usaibia (*IV VA* 4) and An-Nadim (*I VA* 5), it will be noted, might possibly reflect some of the unpleasant stories about Aristotle's alleged unconscionable conduct towards, or alleged 'rebellion' against, Plato and about his 'flagrant ingratitude' towards his teacher and benefactor.[46]

Mubashir (*II VA* 5) maintains that while Aristotle was 'engaged in the study [teaching?] of rhetoric,' this branch of learning came under severe attack by some 'outsiders.' It will be noted that Mubashir places this incident at a time when Aristotle allegedly was studying at the Lyceum with 'some poets, orators, grammarians and schoolmasters'

(Isocrates?), and prior to his joining Plato and the Academy.[47] Mubashir might possibly be here the victim of some confused sources, or he might confuse and misunderstand his sources. Insisting that 'to those slanderers belonged Epicurus and Pythagoras [Lycon Pythagoraeus],' Mubashir is guilty of a fatal anachronism. He probably had in mind the subsequent vicious attacks of Epicurus and the Epicureans on Aristotle and on the Peripatetics in general, as well as on their philosophic *paideia* in particular.[48] Mubashir (*II VA* 6–8)[49] continues by pointing out that Aristotle strongly defended the cause of rhetoric—the proper, that is, the Platonic notion of rhetoric—and that he insisted that rhetoric (dialectics and logic) is the true, stable and necessary foundation and pre-requisite of all scientific and philosophic knowledge: 'Man's superiority over animals,' Aristotle proclaims in the account of Mubashir, 'is founded on man's power of articulate speech. Only he is a man in the true sense of the term, who in his speech is capable of clarifying, by the use of clear concepts, an issue, and who is capable of expressing properly the thoughts of his mind—he who knows how to arrange words properly and effectively. . . . Since philosophic wisdom is the most exalted of all things, it must be expressed in the most lucid language . . . [and] be devoid of errors and mistakes. . . . Such defects obscure wisdom and truth, obstruct intercommunication, diminish perspicuity, befuddle the mind of the listener, defeat logic, and create ignorance.'[50]

As to Aristotle's intellectual and moral qualities, Mubashir (*II VA* 38) and Usaibia (*IV VA* 36) relate that he was an avid reader of books,[51] shunning empty talk. 'When a question was put to him,' Mubashir continues, 'he weighted every word and kept silent for a while before he gave his answer. He spent some time of the day in the fields or by the rivers. He liked music [the 'liberal arts'] as well as the company of mathematicians and logicians.'

'When Plato reproached him for his books and writings on philosophy,'[52] Mubashir (*II VA* 37) reports, 'Aristotle defended himself as follows: "As to the children and heirs of philosophy, I do not think it necessary to conceal anything from them. As to those who despise and hate philosophy, I do not deem it possible that these people could ever attain to philosophy, because of their ignorance of philosophic doctrines and because of their disdain and contempt for philosophy—a contempt which is really nothing other than their inability to gain access to so difficult a subject as philosophy. I have expounded the doctrines of philosophy as well as strengthened philosophy in such a manner as to make it impregnable. Hence, its detractors cannot climb

its gates, the ignorant cannot attain it, and the wicked cannot obtain it.
I have put philosophy into an orderly form, which causes no difficulty
whatever to the wise man, but is of no use to liars and impostors.'''
There exists a vague and probably unreliable tradition that Plato
reprimanded Aristotle for having written too many books on philosophy, thus making the latter accessible not only to the 'unworthy' or
'uninitiated,' but also to the 'detractors of philosophy,' exposing it to
the attacks of its enemies.[53]

An-Nadim (*I VA* 7) reports that Aristotle 'was the most eloquent
man among the Greeks and the most eminent Greek author of learned
books, after Plato the most distinguished scholar among all Greek
scholars, and the man who attained to the highest levels of philosophy.'
Usaibia (*IV VA* 16) informs us that Aristotle practiced goodness with
zest, and that he devoted himself to the promotion of happiness among
men (*IV VA* 24). According to Mubashir (*II VA* 25), he displayed a
great and abiding interest in public welfare and in the affairs of the
commonweal, supporting the feeble, getting maidens married, protecting orphans, assisting those who were eager to learn, and obtaining
alms for the poor (*II VA* 26).[54] These traits of character, which call to
mind the Muslim duties of charity, are also included in Al-Qifti's
(*III VA*) recital of the moral and intellectual qualities of Aristotle.
According to Usaibia (*II VA* 26), Aristotle was always very moderate,
modest and unassuming, considerate in his dealings with other people,
and always ready and willing to intercede on behalf of his friends,
using the bountiful influence he had among his fellow men (*IV VA*
15).

In what is probably a much idealized description of Aristotle's
personal appearance, Mubashir (*II VA* 38) narrates that he was fair, a
little bald-headed, of a good figure, and very bony; that he had small
(or close-set eyes) bluish eyes, an aquiline nose, a small mouth, and a
broad chest; and that he wore a thick beard. The report that Aristotle
had small or close-set eyes ($\mu\iota\kappa\rho\acute{o}\mu\mu\alpha\tau o\varsigma$) seems to be based on an old
tradition. Obviously, the Arabic biographers did not know that this
particular characterization had an unfavorable connotation with the
Greeks: $\mu\iota\kappa\rho\acute{o}\mu\mu\alpha\tau o\varsigma$ was said to be an indication of $\mu\iota\kappa\rho o\psi\upsilon\chi\acute{\iota}\alpha$
(pettiness, small-mindedness or meanness).[55] Usaibia (*IV VA* 36) fully
concurs with this description of Aristotle's physical appearance. He
claims, however, that he grew a sparse beard rather than a thick one.[56]
Mubashir (*II VA* 38) also states that when walking alone, Aristotle
would move hurriedly, but when in the company of friends, he would
move slowly. And finally, Mubashir (*II VA* 38) relates that Aristotle

was moderate in his clothing, eating and drinking habits, sexual relations and emotions.[57] Al-Quifti's (*III VA*) description of Aristotle's external appearance is essentially identical with that supplied by Mubashir and Usaibia.

The Syriac and Arabic biographers make only the briefest of reference to Aristotle's children. *I VS* 11, Mubashir (*II VA* 33) and Usaibia (*IV VA* 35) merely mention that on his death, Aristotle left one boy of tender age, called Nicomachus, and a young daughter, whose name is not mentioned. Aristotle's last will and testament, which is preserved by Usaibia, An-Nadim and Al-Qifti, however, has more to say about Aristotle's children.[58]

When Plato died, *II VS* 4 maintains, Speusippus took charge of Plato's school. Speusippus sent a message to Aristotle, who at the time was absent from Athens, requesting him to return and become the scholarch of the Academy.[59] This unknown Syriac biographer apparently also believed that Aristotle was scholarch of the Academy for a while, until he established his own independent school in the Lyceum (*II VS* 5).[60] Mubashir (*II VA* 14), on the other hand, insisted that when Plato died, 'Aristotle went to a place in Athens called the Lyceum, and there founded a separate school named after the "walking philosophers" [Peripatetics].'[61] Mubashir (*II VA* 17) seems to contradict himself, however, when he subsequently relates that after the death of Plato, 'Aristotle went to Hermias the slave, the ruler of Atarneus. And when the slave [Hermias] died, Aristotle returned to Athens.' Usaibia (*IV VA* 5), who apparently copies Mubashir, likewise records that after Plato's death Aristotle went to live with Hermias of Atarneus and that after Hermias' death he returned to Athens. Thus, the Hermias episode, which probably constitutes an important incident in the life of Aristotle, is mentioned only briefly in the Arabic *Vitae*,[62] its details being blatantly ignored.

Aristotle's connections with the Macedonian royal court likewise receive only a very scanty and rather uninformative treatment by the Syriac and Arabic biographers. *II VS* 6 merely observes that Alexander of Macedonia was the disciple of Aristotle; Al-Qifti (*III VA*) says that Aristotle was the preceptor of Alexander; and An-Nadim (*I VA* 8) remarks that he was held in high esteem by King Alexander, who conducted his affairs in accordance with Aristotle's philosophic principles and precepts. Mubashir (*II VA* 18) and Usaibia (*IV VA* 6)[63] relate that after the death of Hermias of Atarneus,[64] King Philip of Macedonia sent for Aristotle and that Aristotle went to Macedonia, teaching philosophy (to Alexander) until Alexander invaded Asia.

The Syriac and Arabic biographers say little about Aristotle's departure from Macedonia and his return to Athens (in 335-34 B.C.); they tell even less about the tragic fate of Callisthenes, the nephew or grand-nephew of Aristotle.[65] Mubashir (*II VA* 19) and Usaibia (*IV VA* 6) note briefly that when Alexander invaded Asia, Aristotle left Callisthenes as his 'successor' at the court in Macedonia and returned to Athens, where he stayed ten years teaching in the Lyceum. Mubashir (*II VA* 24-5) and Usaibia (*IV VA* 22-3) try once more to explain Aristotle's departure from Macedonia after the accession of Alexander, pointing out in a rather detached manner that when Philip had died and his son Alexander had succeeded to the throne and then left Macedonia in order to conquer the lands of Asia, 'Aristotle freed as well as disassociated himself from the affairs of the King.[66] He founded the afore-mentioned seat of learning,' the 'Peripatetic School.'[67] An-Nadim (*I VA* 10-11) says that when Alexander became king and marched off to war, Aristotle 'was free and without business and, hence, went to Athens. There he established a seat of learning, and this is the place which was named after the philosophers who taught while walking about.'[68]

As to Aristotle's intellectual activities and teaching in the Lyceum after his return from Macedonia, Mubashir (*II VA* 31) and Usaibia (*IV VA* 33) say only that 'he had many disciples ... among them Theophrastus, Eudemus, Arnimus [Hermias?, Hermippus?], Ashulus [this name cannot be identified] and many other famous men, distinguished for their learning, prominent in philosophy and renowned for the noble descent.' *II VS* 6 simply relates that 'among his famous pupils were Theophrastus, Eudemus, Alexander, king of Macedonia, and many others.' Mubashir (*II VA* 35) also seems to know that during his second and last stay in Athens Aristotle 'wrote many books, about one hundred and many more,' on a great variety of philosophic subjects.[69] Thus, what in the opinion of some Aristotelian scholars seems to have been the most important and, from the point of view of literary effort, most productive period in the life of the philosopher Aristotle—the period between the years 335-34 and 323 B.C., when Aristotle allegedly did his decisive work in the fields of systematic philosophy—is passed over rather lightly in the Syriac and Arabic *Vitae*, and for that matter, in all other ancient biographies.

Aside from having instructed (or advised) Alexander on the invitation of King Philip,[70] and in addition to his having exchanged many letters with kings and statesmen,[71] Aristotle, according to Usaibia (*IV VA* 15), had much influence among the great men of his time, 'as shown by the many honors bestowed upon him by kings.'[72] Moreover, Usaibia (*IV VA* 16) continues, 'he had many interviews [diplomatic dealings?] with contemporary kings. By these [diplomatic] negotiations he promoted their affairs and proved useful to them.'[73] Usaibia (*IV VA* 17) also speaks of the many beneficial deeds and outstanding services Aristotle performed for, or rendered, the city of Athens in particular, including his many intercessions with King Philip (and Alexander) on behalf of the Athenians. These intercessions procured the generosity of Philip and Alexander, and generally promoted the interest and welfare of the citizens of Athens.

Mubashir (*II VA* 27), Usaibia (*IV VA* 25) and An-Nadim (*I VA* 13) seem to refer to the rebuilding of Stagira when they insist that Aristotle 'erected the city of Stagira,' or that 'he erected the buildings of Stagira.' Stagira, as it is known, had been destroyed by King Philip in 349 B.C. At the instigation of Aristotle, the king had the town rebuilt.[74] But Aristotle apparently did not limit himself to the role of an *oicist* or 'builder of cities'; he also became the *nomothetes* or 'lawgiver' of Stagira. Thus, *I VS* 7 states that he was 'the lawgiver of Stagira,' and Usaibia (*IV VA* 14) maintains that he 'drew up a code of laws for the people of Stagira.' According to Mubashir (*II VA* 26-7), Aristotle must have been the *nomothetes* and *euergetes* (benefactor) not only of Stagira, but of other cities as well,[75] 'devoting himself to writing constitutions for these cities.' In fact, Usaibia (*IV VA* 12) claims that he 'tried his hand at governing cities, attempting to improve their conditions,' and that 'he did a great deal for the [Athenian] commonweal' (*IV VA* 24).

Upon the death of Aristotle, *I VS* 10 relates, the people of Stagira, wishing to honor their great benefactor and most eminent son, 'sent envoys to bring his ashes from Chalcis. And when they had brought the urn to Stagira, they deposited it in a place which they named *Aristoteleion*, where afterwards they made it a practice to hold their councils.' Mubashir (*II VA* 29-30), Usaibia (*IV VA* 30-1) and Al-Qifti (*III VA*) essentially repeat this story,[76] adding that the people of Stagira 'sought comfort at the place of his tomb, and peace of mind where his bones rested. When something of a philosophic or learned nature seemed to them to be too difficult for a simple solution, they went to this place and sat down for deliberations. There they talked with one another about these matters, until that which previously seemed obscure and difficult became clear, and until they were sure about the issue which had been under discussion. For they believed that by coming to the place where Aristotle's remains were buried, their minds would be purified, their judgment would improve and their understanding would become more subtle. They went there, too, in order to pay their respect to him after his death, and to show the misfortune they had suffered by the loss of the fountainhead of wisdom which he had been to them.'[77]

The following story, which is both an encomium of Aristotle and of the many public services he had rendered the Athenians and at the same time an indication of the troubles he was soon to experience in Athens, can be found in Usaibia (*IV VA* 17–21) but not in the other Syriac or Arabic *Vitae*: 'On account of Aristotle's many good deeds and the outstanding services he had rendered the city of Athens, the Athenians decreed to call an assembly and to vote on an inscription in his honor.[78] They had this inscription engraved on a stone column which they set up on the highest point of their citadel, called The Summit [the Acropolis].[79] In this inscription they related that Aristotle of Stagira, the son of Nicomachus, had served the city well by his many good deeds and by his numerous acts of assistance and kindness, as well as by all his services to the people of Athens and especially by his interventions with King Philip for the purpose of promoting their interests and for seeing to it that they were treated kindly [by Philip or Alexander].[80] Hence, the people of Athens wanted to make it quite clear that they were aware of, and grateful for, the good which resulted from all this; that they bestowed upon him distinction, honor and praise; and that they would keep him in faithful and honored remembrance. . . .[81] When the people of Athens had decided to set up this inscription, the decision was opposed by an Athenian named Aimaraus [Himeraeus].[82] He objected to this decision to honor Aristotle, and opposed it. He pounced upon the column, on which the Athenians had decreed to inscribe the words of praise and which they had set up on the place called The Summit of the City, and hurled it down. For doing this he was later seized by Antinoos [Antipater] and executed.[83] Afterwards, an Athenian by the name of Stephanus,[84] with the approval of many others, set up a stone column. On this column they recorded such praise of Aristotle as had been contained in the original inscription. Moreover, they also mentioned Aimaraus [Himeraeus], who had hurled down the [original] column, related what he had done, and recommended that he be exiled and that the city be purified.'[85] The Himeraeus incident, which reflects the internal turmoil at Athens during the years 323–22, casts an ominous shadow on the fate of Aristotle. When, after the death of Alexander in June of 323 B.C., the anti-Macedonian party at Athens assumed control for a short time, Aristotle, who was a 'resident alien' suspected of philo-Macedonian leanings as well as of aiding and abetting Macedonian control over Athens and Greece, found himself in serious trouble.

Aristotle's flight from Athens in the year 323 B.C. is reported in some detail by the Syriac and Arabic biographers. *II VS* 3 briefly remarks that 'being frightened by the execution of Socrates, Aristotle left Athens and retired near the Hellespont,'[86] and that Aristotle 'finally went to Chalcis in Euboea' (*II VS* 7). Mubashir (*II VA* 20-1) and Usaibia (*IV VA* 7-10), on the other hand, give a lengthy account of this event:[87] a hierophant named Eurymedon, prompted by jealousy and bearing an old grudge against Aristotle,[88] gave a distorted account of Aristotle's philosophy and subsequently charged him with having failed to worship the old gods properly, that is, indicted him for 'impiety.'[89] Usaibia (*IV VA* 7) adds to his story the remark that Aristotle reports all this in a letter addressed to Antipater. When Aristotle learned about Eurymedon's action (*II VA* 21; *IV VA* 8), or when the bill of indictment was served on him, he left Athens (*IV VA* 9) before any further official action was taken against him (*IV VA* 9). He did so because he feared that the Athenians would attempt to do to him what they had previously done to Socrates (*II VA* 21; *IV VA* 8).[90] No one interfered with Aristotle's withdrawal, or did him any harm before he departed (*IV VA* 9).[91] Usaibia (*IV VA* 10) denies the truth of a story according to which Aristotle wrote an apology or defense against the charges made by Eurymedon.[92]

The Syriac (*I VS* 8; *II VS* 7) and Arabic (*II VA* 21-2; *IV VA* 8) sources agree that Aristotle withdrew to Chalcis[93] on the island of Euboea. *II VS* 7 and Mubashir (*II VA* 22) also relate that while in Chalcis he watched (or studied) the flow of the Euripus (the narrows which separate the island from the mainland), and Mubashir adds that he also wrote a book on this subject.[94] Usaibia (*IV VA* 11), on the other hand, recounts only that Aristotle moved into his home in Chalcis and stayed there until he died, implying perhaps that he was already a sick man when he arrived in Chalcis. According to *I VS* 8, Aristotle died in Chalcis after having lived 67 years; according to *II VS* 8, Mubashir (*II VA* 23), Usaibia (*IV VA* 11) and Al-Qifti (*III VA*), 68 years; and according to An-Nadim (*I VA*), 66 years.[95] Mubashir (*II VA* 23) claims that he was buried in Chalcis,[96] but the same Mubashir (*II VA* 29) also relates that the grateful people of Stagira brought his body to Stagira, after it had moldered (had been cremated and temporarily buried in Chalcis). 'They collected the bones (ashes?), placed them into a bronze urn which they deposited [in Stagira] in a place called *Aristoteleion.*' Mubashir's account, in the main, is repeated by Usaibia (*IV VA* 30).

II VS 10 again states that 'the people of Stagira sent envoys to bring his ashes from Chalcis, and when they had brought the urn to Stagira, they deposited it in a place called *Aristoteleion*.'[97]

I VS 11–12, Mubashir (*II VA* 33–4) and Usaibia (*IV VA* 35) relate that on his death Aristotle left two children of tender age: a son, called Nicomachus,[98] and a daughter.[99] He also left a large estate, numerous male and female servants (slaves) and many other things.[100] He appointed Antipater executor of his last will and testament, along with many of his close friends.[101] Mubashir (*II VA* 34) presents the additional information that in his testament Aristotle proposed Theophrastus as one of his executors,[102] provided the latter should agree to assist Antipater in the administration of the estate.

The last will and testament of Aristotle, in an abridged form, is preserved by An-Nadim, Usaibia and Al-Qifti. These three Arabic versions are almost identical. They differ only slightly from the testament as it is quoted by Diogenes Laertius (DL V. 11–16). In all likelihood, these minor differences between the Arabic versions and the version preserved by Diogenes Laertius are the result of linguistic and technical (legal) misunderstandings.[103] Probably they are also due to the fact that the version found in Diogenes Laertius and the Arabic versions are different abridgments of the original document. The Arabic accounts of Aristotle's testament, which in some respects are probably more accurate than the account of Diogenes Laertius, among other matters call Herpyllis the 'handmaid' of Aristotle, thus dispelling the presumption that Herpyllis was Aristotle's lawful wedded wife. The Arabs, but not Diogenes Laertius, also refer to Nicomachus, the (illegitimate through probably adopted or legitimized) son of Aristotle and Herpyllis.

A long list of Aristotle's writings is preserved by Usaibia. This list or catalogue, which includes a number of *pseudepigrapha*, ultimately goes back to the list compiled by Ptolemy (-el-Garib).[104] A brief classification of Aristotle's works can also be found in An-Nadim (*I VA* 18). Mubashir (*II VA* 35), who maintains that Aristotle 'wrote many books, about one hundred, and that it is said that apart from these one hundred books he wrote others too,'[105] enumerates only twenty works which he claims to have seen, namely, 'eight books on logic; eight (actually seven) books on physics;[106] one book on ethics; one book on constitutions; one large book called *Metaphysics*, also known by the title of *Theology*, that is, *Divine Discourse*; one book on mathematics; and one book on mechanics.'[107]

A comparison of the Syriac and Arabic *Vitae Aristotelis* with other

Vitae—Diogenes Laertius V. 1–16,[108] *Vita Aristotelis Marciana, Vita Aristotelis Vulgata, Vita Aristotelis Latina* and *Vita Aristotelis Hesychii* (*Vita Menagiana* or *Vita Menagii*)—indicates that the Syriac and Arabic biographies supplement and implement, and must be implemented by, these other *Vitae*. Not to be found in the 'Western' biographies are the reports that at the age of eight Aristotle was sent to Athens to enter the Lyceum, 'a school of poets, grammarians, rhetoricians and school-masters' (Mubashir, *II VA* 3; Usaibia, *IV VA* 28); that there was a tradition according to which Aristotle was already thirty years old when he turned to philosophy (*I VS* 6; Usaibia, *IV VA* 12; An-Nadim, *I VA* 6; Al-Qifti, *III VA*),[109] and that until then he had practiced medicine (*I VS* 6); that at a very early stage of his career Aristotle defended rhetoric against its detractors and despoilers (Mubashir, *II VA* 5–8; Usaibia *IV VA* 27–8); that when Plato went to Sicily (in 361–60?) he made Aristotle the 'acting scholarch' (Mubashir, *II VA* 13; Usaibia, *IV VA* 4; An-Nadim, *I VA* 5); that Aristotle derived from Plato the maxim of 'training body and mind together'—an additional explanation of the origin of the term 'Peripatetic' (Mubashir, *II VA* 15);[110] that Plato reproached Aristotle for having written books on philosophy, and how Aristotle defended himself on that matter (Mubashir, *II VA* 37); that Aristotle went to Hermias of Atarneus in 348/47 because of an outbreak of anti-Macedonian feelings in Athens (*II VS* 3); that Aristotle addressed a letter to Antipater about his indictment in the year 323 B.C. (Usaibia, *IV VA* 7); that Aristotle did not write a defense against the charges made by Eurymedon (Usaibia, *IV VA* 10); that in Chalcis Aristotle studied the flow of the Euripus (*II VS* 7; Mubashir, *II VA* 22) and wrote a book about this phenomenon (Mubashir, *II VA* 22); that Aristotle engaged in philanthropic activities (Mubashir, *II VA* 26; Usaibia, *IV VA* 24; An-Nadim, *I VA* 12); that the Athenians erected a column in Aristotle's honor (Usaibia, *IV VA* 17–18);[111] that Himeraeus had this column overthrown and was executed for this by Antipater (Usaibia, *IV VA* 20); and that Stephanus had a second column erected honoring Aristotle (Usaibia, *IV VA* 21). Moreover, the Arabic *Vitae* (Mubashir, *II VA* 38; Usaibia, *IV VA* 36; Al-Qifti, *III VA*) quote some additional, and probably idealized, information about the physical appearance of Aristotle.

While the Syriac *Vitae Aristotelis*, in the main, are relatively insignificant, the Arabic biographies contain a large amount of fresh and extremely valuable information. The Arabs, especially Mubashir and Usaibia, refer to certain facts and data not contained in the other *Vitae*. At the same time they supplement, implement or elaborate certain cryptic or mystifying references found in the other biographies. Undoubtedly, the Arabic *Vitae* are replete with patent errors, blatant misunderstandings, naïve distortions, obvious mistranslations and well-intended embellishments, all of which can be explained as the mani-festations of an uncritical but excusable tendency to magnify and glorify Aristotle. This particular tendency, which permeates the whole of the 'Oriental' *Vitae*, can already be discerned in the Neo-Platonic *Vitae Aristotelis* from which the Arabs (and Syrians), through such intermediary sources as Ptolemy (-el-Garib),[112] borrowed extensively and at times uncritically. Behind the Syriac and Arabic texts, however, we can frequently detect characteristically Hellenistic idioms as well as a typically (late) Hellenistic mentality. Thus, despite occasional important and far-reaching differences between the 'Occidental' and the 'Oriental' *Vitae Aristotelis*, there exists an undeniably basic agree-ment between these two trends or tendencies: both trends are prone to eulogize Aristotle, although they differ somewhat as to the specific means or details of achieving this goal; and both trends have their common source in the Hellenistic or Neo-Platonic biographical tradition concerning Aristotle. One thing, in particular, seems to be emphasized by the Arabic *Vitae Aristotelis*, namely, the many and important political, diplomatic and statesman-like activities and achievements of Aristotle, as well as his many and perhaps decisive deeds which benefited kings, princes, ordinary people, nations and cities, including Athens.

A NOTE, LOOKING FORWARD TO CHAPTERS V–XV

In Chapters I–IV some of the extant biographical reports about Aristotle have been discussed and analyzed. These chapters, which are primarily a study and evaluation of some surviving biographical sources, should indicate the many and exasperating difficulties con-nected with this biographical tradition. Closer scrutiny of these sources divulges that aside from essentially chronological (and, on the whole, fairly reliable) accounts, such as, for instance, that of Dionysius of Halicarnassus (Chapter II), there exist, as Chapter I tries to show, two major biographical traditions: the tradition which, in all likelihood, was inaugurated by Hermippus of Smyrna, and that which was reflected in the biography of Ptolemy (-el-Garib). Unfortunately, in the course of time the original biographies of Hermippus and Ptolemy were lost in their entirety. They survive, however, in some of their

respective 'derivatives' which, on the whole, are but poorly epitomized and frequently badly mutilated accounts. The biography of
Diogenes Laertius (and perhaps that of Hesychius of Smyrna), as has
been shown (Chapters I and III), to some extent reflects the biographical
tradition inaugurated by Hermippus. The *Vita Aristotelis Marciana*, the
Vita Aristotelis Vulgata, the *Vita Aristotelis Latina*, the two anonymous
Syriac *Vitae Aristotelis* and the four extant Arabic *Vitae Aristotelis* (as
well as some other essentially unimportant *Vitae Aristotelis*), on the
other hand, in the main have been influenced by the biographical
tradition represented and perhaps inaugurated by Ptolemy. Hence,
Chapters III and IV contain presentations, discussions and analyses of
some of the surviving 'reflections' of either the Hermippian tradition
or of the Ptolemian tradition.

Beginning with Chapter V, some of the salient events in the life of
Aristotle, as well as some of the decisive dates and the circumstances of
their occurrence, are presented. These presentations, to a very large
extent, are based on or inferred from the information relayed by the
surviving ancient biographies of Aristotle. In other words, while in
Chapters I–IV some of these biographies are *analyzed* as to their origin,
method, reliability and particular prejudices, in Chapters V–XV (or
XVII) the facts and dates supplied by some of Aristotle's ancient
biographers (and by other ancient reporters or other ancient *testimonia*)
are *exploited* for the purpose of intelligently reconstructing certain
important and perhaps decisive historical events in the life of Aristotle.
Hence, a noticeable (and probably annoying) amount of repetition
becomes almost a necessity. Reports, that were originally analyzed
solely as reports, are now employed (and exploited) once more in order
to establish what appear to have been some of the most significant
events in the life of the Stagirite. Moreover, such historical facts or
incidents as the likely genealogy of Aristotle (Chapter V), his relation
with the historian Callisthenes of Olynthus (Chapter VI), his entry into
the Academy (Chapter VII), his first 'lectures' on rhetoric (Chapter
VIII), his first departure from Athens and from the Academy in
348 B.C. (Chapter IX), his tutoring of Alexander (Chapter X), his
return to Athens (Chapter XI), his second departure from Athens in
323 B.C. (Chapter XII), his likely involvements in the many political
schemes of King Philip of Macedonia (Chapter XIII), his alleged suicide
(Chapter XIV), and his last will and testament (Chapter XV)—all these
important historical facts or events, in the main, are treated as separate
and, in a way, 'isolated' and yet 'integrated' incidents whose decisive
significance makes them nonetheless integral to the life and work of

Aristotle. After all, this part of the book is not, and was never intended to be, a comprehensive or traditional biography of Aristotle. Conversely, the kind of presentation adopted in this book should enable a reader wishing to acquaint himself with a specific event in the life of the Stagirite, to find all relevant information, dates and sources related to that particular event, in the very place where this incident is being discussed. This will also relieve the reader from the often tedious and sometimes unrewarding labors of constantly leafing through the book for the confirmation and verification of any particular event. Needless to say, this kind of presentation, aside from resorting to much imaginative hypothesis and conjecture, apparently must rely on the frequent retracing of certain materials, as well as on the re-arguing of certain issues and the repetition of certain findings previously presented and discussed. This seems to be a necessary and even unavoidable aspect of a work which deals with so problematic, elusive and controversial a topic as a detailed account of the salient events in the life of Aristotle.

Chapter V

The Genealogy and Family of Aristotle*

Aristotle was born in the year 384 B.C. To be more exact, he was born during the archonship of Diotrephes (384–83), that is, in the first year of the 99th Olympiad.[1] Moreover, we are presently able to determine, with reasonable accuracy, the time of the year in which Aristotle was born. According to the majority of our sources, Aristotle died in the year 322 B.C. when he was sixty-two years old, or in his sixty-third year; he died during the archonship of Philocles (322–21), in the third year of the 114th Olympiad.[2] It is also held that his death occurred shortly before Demosthenes took his own life 14 October 322 B.C. Integrating these dates and bits of information, we arrive at the following conclusion: the archon, Philocles, assumed office during the month of July (*Hecatombaeon*) 322 B.C., and Demosthenes died 14 October 322. Hence, Aristotle's death occurred between July and October of 322. However, at the time of his death, he had passed his sixty-second birthday. This fact enables us to fix the date of his birth more precisely. As we have seen, Aristotle was born during the archonship of Diotrephes, that is, after (or during) July 384; he died during the archonship of Philocles, after having celebrated his sixty-second birthday, but before the death of Demosthenes. Thus, he must have been born between July and October of 384 B.C. For had he been born after October 384, he would have died at the age of sixty-one (or in his sixty-second year); or if he had been born prior to July 384 B.C., he could not have been born during the archonship of Diotrephes. It would be reasonable to maintain, therefore, that Aristotle was born in the summer of 384 B.C.

All sources agree on Aristotle's name. The Arabic biographers attempt to interpret his name to mean the 'lover of wisdom' (φιλόσοφος), 'the distinguished one,' 'the best one,' 'the perfect one or 'the excellent one.'[3] They also agree that he was born in Stagira or Stagirus (today Stavro), although some biographers apparently do not seem to know the exact location of Stagira. Thus *VH* 1 states that Stagira was a place in Thrace; *VM* 1 and *VL* 1 maintain that it was located in Thrace near Olynthus and Methone; and *VV* 1 insists that Aristotle was a Macedonian because he was born in Stagira. *I VS* 2 calls it a town in Thrace, near Chalcidice (this biography apparently holds that Chalcidice was a town) and Olynthus; *II VS* 1 considers it 'a city in the land of Macedonia'; *I VA* 3 refers to it as a 'Greek city'; *II VA* 2 calls it a town located in Chalcidice belonging to the 'province of Thrace'; *IV VA* 1 believes that it was a town situated in the neighborhood of Olynthus and Methone in 'a land called Chalcidice, which is part of Thrace, in the vicinity of Olynthus and Methone.'[4] According to Thucydides (IV. 88; V. 6. 1; V. 18), Stagira, which was located in the north-eastern corner of Chalcidice about three miles from the sea and facing the Strymonic Gulf, originally had been settled by the island of Andros (the island from which Aristotle's paternal ancestors originally came), which at the time of its settlement was dependent on Eretria located on the island of Euboea. According to Strabo (VII. frag. 35), it was a colony founded by Euboean Chalcis, the town from which, in the words of Dionysius of Halicarnassus (DH 5), Aristotle's maternal ancestors came. Hence, it is possible that, like so many Greek colonies during the seventh century B.C., Stagira was a joint enterprise of both Andros and Chalcis, or that colonists from Chalcis joined the original Andrian settlers at some later time.

The name of Aristotle's father is given as Nicomachus.[5] *II VA* 1 relates that this name signifies 'the warrior' or 'the conqueror.'[6] This Nicomachus (the father of Aristotle) was the descendant of another Nicomachus, who in turn descended from Machaon, the son of Asclepius, the renowned Homeric physician.[7] Nicomachus' (and Aristotle's) alleged descent from Asclepius and Machaon raises a number of interesting and involved issues. Asclepius and his son Machaon are mentioned in the *Iliad* (II. 729 ff.; IV. 193 ff.; XI. 501; and XI. 833). Greek epic tradition would indicate that Asclepius and Machaon originally came from Thessaly, while the Machaon cult seems to point to the Peloponnesus or, to be more exact, to Messenia. Pausanias relates that Glaucus, the king of Messenia, first instituted in Messenia the worship of Machaon; and that Glaucus' son Isthmius erected in Pharae in Messenia a sanctuary in honor of Gorgasus and Nicomachus, the two sons of Machaon by Anticlea, the daughter of Diocles. Both Gorgasus and Nicomachus became kings as well as famous physicians. Subsequently, they too were deified and honored by a special worship.[8] The source from which Pausanias derived this information is possibly Ephorus.[9] All this would indicate that the

Asclepius-Machaon-Nicomachus tradition, which is primarily a cult tradition, might ultimately be traced back to Messenia.

The report that Nicomachus, the father of Aristotle, was a descendant of Asclepius, Machaon and Nicomachus (and, perhaps, some other Nicomachi), suggests the following most confusing possibilities: (i) Aristotle was in fact a direct descendant of Asclepius-Machaon-Nicomachus. (ii) Nicomachus, the son of Machaon, and Nicomachus, the father of Aristotle, have in common only the name. For purely encomiastic reasons, Hermippus or his source erroneously connected Aristotle's immediate ancestors with Machaon's son Nicomachus. (iii) Nicomachus, the father or some other more remote ancestor of Aristotle, was intentionally named after Machaon's son Nicomachus, thus establishing the fraudulent claim of direct descent from one of the Homeric heroes—according to Theognis, a not uncommon practice throughout ancient Greece. (iv) The Asclepiad Nicomachus, who was a physician, at one time became the 'cult ancestor' of the Aristotelian Nicomachi, who likewise were physicians. This latter possibility creates further complexities: (a) Aristotle's more immediate ancestors apparently came from the island of Andros (his paternal ancestors) and from Chalcis (his maternal ancestors, who likewise claimed to have descended from Asclepius), but his more remote ancestors might originally have come from Messenia. They might have left Messenia during the first Messenian war (during the last quarter of the eighth century B.C.) or, more likely, during or after the second Messenian war (during the last quarter of the seventh century B.C.), when Messenia was conquered by the Lacedaemonians and its inhabitants reduced to helots. After leaving Messenia they might have settled on the island of Andros (or Euboea). (b) At some time there might have existed some family connections between Aristotle's ancestors and the city of Pharae in Messenia. (c) At some time the Messenian cult of Asclepius-Machaon-Nicomachus was transplanted to the island of Andros and to the island of Euboea (Chalcis). There it was adopted by Aristotle's ancestors, who subsequently claimed to be the direct descendants of Asclepius, Machaon and the Messenian Nicomachus, giving the name of Nicomachus to a son who, as a physician, was to follow the vocation of his 'cult-ancestors.'

Nicomachus, the father of Aristotle, likewise was born in Stagira. He was a physician and at one time became the court physician as well as the intimate friend and personal advisor of King Amyntas III of Macedonia.[10] We do not know much about the standing of court physicians in early Macedonia. Presumably, in order to enhance Nicomachus' status—perhaps the position of a court physician in early Macedonia was not much above that of an ordinary servant—Aristotle's biographers insist that he was also a personal friend and confidant of King Amyntas III. It is possible that (in one of his letters addressed to King Philip?) Aristotle reminded the Macedonian king that he, Aristotle, was the son of a close friend and advisor of Philip's father. From his position at the court of Macedonia and from Suda's remark that 'he wrote six books on medicine and one book on physics,'[11] provided this statement is correct, we might infer that Nicomachus was a learned and cultured man of considerable 'social standing.' It is also safe to assume that he was a fairly well-to-do person.

The family of Aristotle's father originally came from the island of Andros and settled at some time in Stagira.[12] When Nicomachus became the court physician of King Amyntas, he must have moved his family to Aegae, the old 'capital' of Macedonia. Since Aristotle was born in Stagira, this move must have taken place after 384 B.C. Hence, it may be assumed that Nicomachus became Amyntas' personal physician after 384 B.C. When Aristotle went to Athens in the spring of 367 B.C., he was brought there by Proxenus, his 'guardian.'[13] Thus, it may be surmised that Nicomachus died before 367 B.C. If the story is correct that Aristotle was eight years old (in the year 376/75 B.C.) when 'his father took him to Athens,'[14] then Nicomachus must have died some time between 376/75 and 367 B.C.

Aristotle's mother, Phaestis,[15] was likewise a descendant of Asclepius,[16] although the surviving sources do not reveal her exact lineage.[17] Her immediate ancestors apparently came from Chalcis on the island of Euboea.[18] Although she seems to have retained her 'ancestral home' in Chalcis,[19] it is safe to assume that she was born in Stagira. Phaestis probably was dead by the time Aristotle went to Athens in 367 B.C.[20] Thus, it may be assumed that she died while Aristotle was still rather young. In his last will and testament, the pious son stipulated that his 'mother's statue or likeness shall be dedicated to Demeter of Nemea or wherever the executors think best.'[21]

The background of both Aristotle's parents would seem to suggest one of culture, refinement and wealth. Both parents were of excellent Greek stock[22] and both were of 'aristocratic' descent. Through Nicomachus the family established close and, judging from subsequent events, lasting and profitable ties with one of the rising dynasties in the Hellenic world.

Aristotle had a sister, Arimneste, and a brother, Arimnestus.[23] This (younger?) brother, who apparently died rather young without leaving any issue, is mentioned again in Aristotle's last will and testament. Here the testator stipulates that the executors of the will 'shall set up the bust that had been executed of Arimnestus to be a memorial of him, inasmuch as he had died without issue.'[24] The sister, Arimneste, seems to have been married first to Demotimus (or Callisthenes) by whom she apparently had a daughter, Hero. After the death of Demotimus (or Callisthenes), Arimneste married Proxenus. When Nicomachus, the father of Arimneste and Aristotle, died, this Proxenus became the 'guardian' of young Aristotle[25]. In this manner Arimneste became also a kind of 'foster mother' to her younger brother, Aristotle.[26]

According to one tradition, Callisthenes of Olynthus (died in 327 B.C.), the historian of Alexander the Great, was a 'second cousin' (ἀνεψιαδοῦς) of Aristotle (Suda); according to another report, he was the son of Hero, the niece of Aristotle through Arimneste.[27] If this Hero, the alleged mother of Callisthenes—Suda calls Callisthenes the son of Demotimus or Callisthenes[28]—was indeed the niece of Aristotle, then Hero might have been a daughter of Arimneste by a previous marriage to Demotimus (or Callisthenes). All this would make Arimneste somewhat older than Aristotle (she would have been the grandmother of Callisthenes through Hero), for it appears that Callisthenes, the historian, was a contemporary of Ephorus and Theopompus,[29] and that he was born shortly after 370 B.C. Summarizing all these bits of information, we may assume that Arimneste was older than Aristotle, and that she was married, first to Demotimus (or Callisthenes) by whom she had a daughter, Hero, who became the mother of Callisthenes, the historian, and then to Proxenus, by whom she had a son, Nicanor. Since Arimnestus, the (younger?) brother of Aristotle, died without issue, Hero could not have been his daughter.

An-Nadim, the Arabic biographer of Aristotle, relates (*I VA* 16) that Theophrastus of Eresus was the son of Aristotle's sister, but he does not report her name. Al-Mubashir (*II VA* 32) and Usaibia (*IV VA* 34) call Theophrastus 'a second cousin' of Aristotle. There exists no additional evidence in support of these statements. It is possible, however, that these particular accounts reflect a 'transfer' of the relationship of Plato and Speusippus to that of Aristotle and Theophrastus. This transfer might also be connected in some way with the succession in the scholarchate of the Peripatus which is supposed to have followed the example established by the Academy, or which allegedly paralleled the events which took place in the Academy at the time of Plato's death: Speusippus, the nephew of Plato, succeeded his uncle in the scholarchate of the Academy, and Theophrastus, the alleged 'second cousin' or the nephew of Aristotle, succeeded the latter in the scholarchate of the Peripatus. The accounts of An-Nadim, Al-Mubashir and Usaibia might simply be a confusion of Theophrastus and Callisthenes, who was definitely a 'second cousin' of Aristotle. In his last will and testament (DL V. 52), Theophrastus refers to his property in Stagira; and in his last will (DL V. 11–16), Aristotle appoints Theophrastus a 'special trustee' or a 'special executor' of his estate, as well as a 'special guardian' of his daughter, Pythias, and of his (illegitimate) son, Nicomachus. Such provisions in a formal will, it will be noted, might indicate that Theophrastus and the testator were related, especially since, according to Athenian law of testamentary succession, as a rule a trustee or executor (or guardian) had to be a near relative. Conversely, in his last will and testament, Theophrastus refers to Nicomachus, the son of Aristotle.[30] This might be an indication that Theophrastus was related to Nicomachus and, accordingly, to Aristotle.

In his last will and testament, Aristotle also provides that the executors 'shall see to it that the image . . . of Nicanor's mother [Arimneste], executed by Gryllion, shall be set up.'[31] By this generous gesture the testator gratefully remembers not only his departed sister, but apparently also honors his former 'foster mother' to whom he must have been greatly attached. Moreover, in his last will Aristotle makes some very magnanimous provisions for Nicanor,[32] the son of Proxenus and Arimneste, thus commemorating also his 'foster parents.'

Since Aristotle's parents apparently both died while he was still rather young, Proxenus of Atarneus became his 'guardian' or the 'mandatory of his father.'[33] This Proxenus, who is said to have been a native of Atarneus (?)[34] and possibly a friend or an acquaintance of Plato,[35] might have been a remote relative of Aristotle. At one time he moved from Atarneus to Stagira,[36] where he married Arimneste after the latter had lost her first husband, Demotimus (or Callisthenes). He did so presumably after (?) Nicomachus, the father of Aristotle, had died, that is, some time before 367 B.C. If he was indeed a friend of Plato, he must have spent some time in Athens. Proxenus and Arimneste had a son, Nicanor, who is mentioned several times in Aristotle's last will (and who subsequently rendered some important services to Alexander the Great as well as to some of the Diadochi and to the city of Ephesus).

Judging from the detailed provisions contained in Aristotle's last will and testament,[37] by way of an analogy, Proxenus became the 'guardian' of Aristotle probably in the following manner. When Nicomachus was about to die, he made a will in which he stipulated that Proxenus should take care of Phaestis—provided she was still alive at the time—and of the children (Arimneste, Aristotle and Arimnestus), as well as of the whole estate. He also provided that Arimneste, who apparently had lost her first husband (Demotinus or Callisthenes), should be given in marriage to Proxenus. (It is presumed here that at the time of Nicomachus' death Arimneste was still fairly young.) Proxenus was to take care of the three children and of all matters that concerned them, including the estate (also an indication that he might have been a remote relative, for under Greek law only an agnatic relative was charged with such duties), as if he were their father and (older) brother. The corresponding passages in Aristotle's last will, where Nicanor, the son of Proxenus and Arimneste, assumes the role Proxenus probably held in the testament of Nicomachus, read as follows:[38] 'Until Nicanor shall arrive [presumably at the time Aristotle drafted his will, Nicanor was abroad, *note by the present author*], Aristomenes, Timarchus, Hipparchus, Dioteles and (if he should consent and if circumstances should permit) Theophrastus shall take charge of Herpyllis and the children [Pythias and Nicomachus] and of the property. When the girl [Pythias] shall be grown up, she shall be given in marriage to Nicanor. And if anything should happen to the girl before her marriage [to Nicanor] or before there are any [male] children, Nicanor shall have full powers, both with regard to the child [Nicomachus] and with regard to everything else . . . .'[39]

According to the ancient biographers of Aristotle, Proxenus brought Aristotle to Athens in the year 367 B.C. and handed him over to Plato, presumably because he and Plato were friends (or because of the advice of the Delphic oracle).[40] It is entirely possible, though not very likely, that Proxenus also adopted Aristotle.[41] Since Aristotle took young Nicanor into his home and brought him up,[42] it must be presumed that Proxenus (and Arimneste?) died while Nicanor was still rather young. According to some reports, Nicanor accompanied Aristotle to Macedonia in 343–42 B.C. Hence, it may be assumed that Proxenus (and Arimneste?) were dead by that year, although this is by no means certain. In his last will and testament, Aristotle gratefully remembers his 'foster father' when he provides that the image or bust of Proxenus, executed by Gryllion, 'should be set up.'[43]

Nicanor, the son of Proxenus and Arimneste, is mentioned several times in Aristotle's last will and testament, where the testator provides that when Pythias, the daughter of Aristotle, 'shall be grown up, she shall be given in marriage to Nicanor' (DL V. 12);[44] that 'if anything should happen to the girl [Pythias] . . . before her marriage [to Nicanor] or after she is married but before there are any [male] children, Nicanor shall have full powers both as regards the child [Nicomachus, the son of Aristotle and Herpyllis] and as regards everything else, to administer in a manner worthy of himself and of us' (DL V. 12); that 'Nicanor shall take charge of the girl [Pythias] and of the boy Nicomachus as he shall think proper in all that concerns them, just as if he were their father and [older?] brother' (DL V. 12); that 'if anything should happen to Nicanor [during his absence on some official mission?] . . . either before he marries the girl [Pythias] or when he has married her but before there are any [male] children, any arrangement he may have made shall be binding and valid' (DL V. 12); and that Nicanor 'shall take charge of the boy Myrmex' (DL V. 14).[45]

Thus, in keeping with a wide-spread Greek custom sanctioned by law, Nicanor, for the primary purpose of keeping Aristotle's estate within his immediate family, is to marry Pythias.[46] Since at the time of Aristotle's death both Pythias and Nicomachus still were minors, he was also to become their guardian as well as the trustee or administrator of Aristotle's estate. Moreover, together with the other executors, Nicanor is charged with taking care of Herpyllis (DL V. 13). At the time Aristotle drafted his will, Nicanor was abroad on a dangerous mission. This may be gathered from the provision in Aristotle's will that 'until Nicanor shall return (or can take over),' some other people 'shall take charge of Herpyllis and the children [Pythias and Nicomachus], as well as of the estate' (DL V. 12); and that in order 'to commemorate Nicanor's safe return [from this dangerous mission,]' the other executors 'shall set up in Stagira life-size stone statues of Zeus and Athena, the Saviours' (DL V. 16).[47]

VM 3, *VV* 2 and *VL* 3, as well as an Ephesian inscription in honor of Nicanor (of *c.* 318 B.C.?) which reads, Νικανόρι Ἀριστοτέλεος Σταγε[ιρίτηι],[48] call Nicanor the son of Aristotle by adoption. If such an adoption actually took place, it must have happened after the death of Proxenus (and Arimneste): Out of gratitude towards his former 'foster parents' Aristotle adopts their orphaned son. It is not certain and, as a matter of fact, quite doubtful, however, whether Aristotle ever adopted Nicanor, although the tenor of Aristotle's last will and testament seems to suggest such an adoption.[49] The important role assigned to Nicanor in Aristotle's will, and the fact that Aristotle took him into his home and educated him,[50] indicates that, especially after the death of Callisthenes in 327 B.C., Nicanor was very close to Aristotle and his family.

It might briefly be mentioned that Aristotle married Pythias, the daughter or niece or sister or the adopted daughter of Hermias of Atarneus.[51] The detractors of Aristotle call her a former concubine of Hermias,[52] although this story is probably based on some misunderstanding or on a deliberate attempt to slander Aristotle (and Hermias). It is reasonable to assume that Aristotle married Pythias during his sojourn in Assos or Ataerneus, that is, between 347 and 345–44 B.C. It has also been maintained that Aristotle married her out of pity—because after the violent death of Hermias she found herself without a protector.[53] If this be true, then Aristotle must have married her after 341–340 B.C., the year Hermias was captured and put to death by the Persians, and he must have married her in Stagira or, more likely, in Macedonia. Judging from a passage in Aristotle's last will and testament, namely, from the statement, 'wherever they bury me, there the bones of Pythias shall also be laid to rest, according to her own instructions' (DL V. 16), this marriage seems to have been a happy one. This is also borne out by the report that on her death 'Aristotle sacrificed to her [held memorial services in her honor] as the Athenians sacrifice to Demeter of Eleusis.'[54] One girl, named after her mother, Pythias, was the issue of this marriage.[55] At the time Aristotle drafted his last will (in 323–22 B.C.), young Pythias was about thirteen or fourteen years old, that is, not yet of marriageable age. Accordingly, she must have been born after 337 B.C. (in Macedonia?). Pythias, the mother, died some time before 322 B.C., although the exact date of her death cannot be ascertained. It is possible, however, that she died shortly after the birth of her daughter, that is, some time after 337 B.C. (?).

After the death of Pythias, Aristotle took up with Herpyllis, apparently a former handmaid of Pythias.[56] Tradition has it that Herpyllis originally came from Stagira,[57] although this is by no means certain. It is most unlikely that Aristotle ever married Herpyllis,[58] a fact which is also brought out by Aristotle's last will and testament, wherein the testator makes some very generous provisions for her.[59] Aristotle had an illegitimate son by Herpyllis. He was named after his paternal grandfather, Nicomachus.[60]

Aristotle's daughter and, presumably, his only legitimate child, Pythias, was still rather young—about thirteen or fourteen years old—at the time of her father's death in 322 B.C.[61] Some time after 322 B.C., she married Nicanor, her cousin and the son of Proxenus and Arimneste.[62] Nicanor was executed by Cassander in 317 B.C., apparently without leaving any children or male children of his marriage to Pythias. Subsequently, Pythias married Procles (or Procleus),[63] by whom she had two sons, Procles (or Procleus) and Demaratus. When her second husband died—the exact date of this event cannot be ascertained —Pythias married Medias[64] (later sources—Nemesius—call him Metrodorus), by whom she had a son, Aristotle, named after his maternal grandfather. This Aristotle, who probably was born during the last decade of the fourth century B.C., became a ('junior') member of the Peripatus. He is also mentioned in the last will and testament of Theophrastus.[65]

The last will and testament of Aristotle contains the following clause: 'As to my estate and my son [Nicomachus] there is no need for me to make a special will and testament.' This clause, which can be found in the Arabic versions of Aristotle's will, for some unknown reason is omitted in the version preserved by Diogenes Laertius. From this unusual clause it seems to follow that at one time Aristotle had adopted Nicomachus, or had formally declared him legitimate. Under Greek (Athenian) law of succession only legitimate or formally adopted sons could inherit intestate—and this seems to be the ultimate meaning of the clause recorded by the Arabic biographers—although a testator could make a limited bequest to his illegitimate son.[66] At the time of Aristotle's death in 322 B.C., Nicomachus apparently was still very young, presumably a 'little boy.'[67] At some later time he was personally instructed by Theophrastus,[68] but he must have been an indifferent student. This seems to follow from Theophrastus' remark reminding Nicomachus that he was not only the heir to Aristotle's estate, but also the heir to his father's intellectual achievements.[69] It is also related that Nicomachus died a young soldier in some war,[70] and that throughout his short life he was apparently a never-do-well.[71] On the strength of Theophrastus' last will and testament,[72] which was probably drafted shortly before 287–86 B.C., he must have been dead by that year.[73]

Chapter VI

Aristotle and Callisthenes of Olynthus*

Callisthenes, the close relative as well as disciple of Aristotle, the famed historiographer of Alexander the Great and the author of several important works on Greek history, was a native of Olynthus.[1] He must have been born prior to 348 B.C., the year the city of Olynthus was captured and destroyed by King Philip of Macedonia. It also seems that around the year 345 B.C., Callisthenes was already in his twenties. At about this time, or shortly thereafter, he apparently became more closely associated with Aristotle and his studies. Hence, it is reasonable to conjecture that he was born about the year 370 B.C., or a few years thereafter.[2]

Tradition has it that Callisthenes was a relative of Aristotle. Diogenes Laertius V. 4, calls him a 'kinsman' ($\sigma\upsilon\gamma\gamma\epsilon\nu\dot{\eta}\varsigma$); Plutarch, *Alexander* 52, a 'relative' ($o\grave{\iota}\kappa\epsilon\hat{\iota}o\varsigma$); Ammianus Marcellinus XVIII. 3. 7, a 'near relation' (*propinquus*); and Suda, a 'first cousin's son' (a 'second cousin,' $\grave{\alpha}\nu\epsilon\psi\iota\alpha\delta o\hat{\upsilon}\varsigma$) of Aristotle—the son of Hero to whom Plutarch, *Alexander* 55, refers to as 'a first cousin' or niece ($\grave{\alpha}\nu\epsilon\psi\iota\dot{\alpha}$) of Aristotle. If Hero, the alleged mother of Callisthenes, was indeed the niece of Aristotle rather than a remote cousin, then this Hero might have been a daughter of Arimneste, the sister of Aristotle. This would have made Callisthenes the grandson of Arimneste as well as the grandnephew of Aristotle.[3] Suda further relates that Callisthenes' father (grandfather?) was called Callisthenes (or Demotimus, a name which also appears in the testament of Theophrastus).[4] In Theophrastus' last will and testament, the name Callisthenes is also mentioned.[5] It is impossible, however, to ascertain whether the Callisthenes referred to in Theophrastus' last will and testament is a kinsman (son? or grandson?) of our Callisthenes and, hence, a remote relative of Aristotle.[6] If Arimneste was, in fact, the grandmother of our Callisthenes, then she must have been married at least twice.[7]

It appears that Callisthenes was educated by Aristotle, and that the latter took the young man into his home.[8] Hence, Aristotle raised not only Nicanor, the son of Arimneste,[9] but also Callisthenes, Arimneste's grandson (?). It is also claimed that Aristotle educated Callisthenes together with Alexander (in Macedonia—Mieza—after 343–42 B.C.);[10] that he educated Callisthenes and Theophrastus at the same time;[11] and that he applied to Theophrastus and Callisthenes what Plato had formerly said about Aristotle and Xenocrates,[12] namely, that Theophrastus needed a bridle and Callisthenes a spur.[13] This story might indicate that Callisthenes was not a brilliant student or, perhaps, that he was an indifferent or lazy person.[14]

Judging from Theophrastus' posthumous eulogy of Callisthenes,[15] a close tie of friendship must have existed between Callisthenes and Theophrastus who were of approximately the same age.[16] In all likelihood, these two men met first in Assos or Mytilene, where Aristotle and Callisthenes spent the years between 348/47 and 343/42 B.C. It is impossible, however, to ascertain the exact time Aristotle began to take over the education of Callisthenes. It appears that Callisthenes joined Aristotle after the latter had settled down in Assos or Atarneus in 348–47 B.C.,[17] that is, when, at the age of about twenty, Callisthenes was compelled to seek a new home after the destruction of Olynthus in 348 B.C. We also know that after 341–40 B.C. Callisthenes wrote a eulogy or encomium of Hermias of Atarneus,[18] the friend, protector and relative (by marriage) of Aristotle. This, in turn, might indicate that Callisthenes was personally acquainted with Hermias and, hence, might have lived for some time in Assos or Atarneus.

In the year 345–44 B.C., Aristotle left Assos in order to move to Mytilene on the island of Lesbos; and in 343–42 B.C. he proceeded to Macedonia (Pella or Mieza), apparently on the invitation of king Philip. Callisthenes accompanied him to both places. It is believed that in Macedonia, Callisthenes, with the approval or prompting of Aristotle, started his historical research. Possibly about this time, no doubt at the request of King Philip or that of Aristotle, he wrote, or started to write, the *History of the Sacred* (or *Phocian*) *War*.[19] At the same time he seems to have acted as Aristotle's amanuensis. It is safe to assume that he assisted Aristotle in compiling the *List of Victors at the Pythian Games*,[20] and also that he helped him in writing, or doing research for, a number of historical or antiquarian works. Undoubtedly, a list as long as that of the Pythian victors required extensive and thorough research in the Delphic archives. Since Callisthenes apparently collaborated in this scholarly enterprise, the *List of Pythian Victors* must have been compiled, and perhaps completed, several years before Callisthenes departed for Asia (in 334 B.C.), never to return. We may assume that while doing this research, Callisthenes did also prepare or edit his own *History of the Sacred War*. He had direct access to the Delphic archives and, hence, could study at first hand the particular circumstances, negotiations and detailed incidents surrounding this complex episode in the history of Greece. Thus, for several years Callisthenes was intimately connected with Aristotle's empirical or antiquarian investigations of historical or scientific detail. According to W. Jaeger, these investigations are not only typical of Aristotle's later intellectual activities and scholarly interests, but they also constitute novel and original contributions to historical research and to historical scholarship in general. In ancient days Callisthenes was called at times a 'philosopher,'[21] at times a 'sophist,'[22] and at times a 'historian.'[23]

When Aristotle returned to Athens in 335/34 B.C., he left Callisthenes with Alexander or, as some authors put it, recommended him as a possible member of Alexander's personal staff.[24] Ancient biographers of Aristotle relate that the Stagirite sent many letters to King Philip and Alexander recommending his friends and relatives.[25] It was perhaps thus that Aristotle recommended Callisthenes to Alexander. In his 'article,' *Mieza*, Stephanus of Byzantium reports that Callisthenes had the surname of Μιεζαῖος. This might indicate that at one time Callisthenes lived in Mieza where, according to tradition, Aristotle is said to have instructed Alexander.[26] If this is true, then Callisthenes might have been a 'classmate' of Alexander in Mieza and, hence, hardly needed a recommendation.[27] The probable reason or reasons why Aristotle recommended Callisthenes to Alexander are not fully apparent: he might have wished to maintain his close contacts with the Macedonian ruler through Callisthenes;[28] or Callisthenes, having become ambitious and wishing to do something on his own, might have intended to attach himself to Alexander and to accompany the latter to Persia as the official reporter and historian of Alexander's exploits and, hence, requested Aristotle to recommend him to Alexander. Callisthenes seems to have had a penchant as well as a distinct talent for historical reporting, something he might have learned from Aristotle. Perhaps he wished to 'get away' from, or 'get out' from being under the supervision of Aristotle. A further explanation for Callisthenes' resolve to stay with Alexander and serve him in the capacity of official historian, rather than to accompany Aristotle when the latter returned to Athens, may be found in the conjecture that, by his services to the king, he might persuade Alexander to rebuild the city of Olynthus which had been destroyed by King

Philip in 348 B.C.[29] Arrian, on the other hand, claims that Callisthenes attached himself to Alexander because he was of the opinion that the ultimate and abiding success of 'Alexander and his achievements were all dependent upon him and his history. He himself hoped for no glory in joining Alexander, but he rather expected to make Alexander famous in the eyes of mankind.'[30]

In any event, even after Aristotle and Callisthenes had become separated in 334 B.C., the latter apparently maintained some contacts with his former tutor and benefactor. It is also believed that Callisthenes sent Aristotle botanical and zoological specimens as well as other bits of information from Asia.[31]

Aristotle, it will be noted, seems to have had some reservations regarding Callisthenes' ability for 'getting along' with Alexander whose temperament and disposition he knew only too well. Diogenes Laertius[32] reports that when against the advice of Aristotle, Callisthenes talked too freely in the presence of Alexander, Aristotle rebuked him by citing in a prophetic mood the Homeric line, '[s]hortlived, I ween, wilt thou be, my child, by what thou sayest.'[33] Plutarch relates that Aristotle called Callisthenes a 'perfect speaker,' but also a man of poor judgment,[34] implying that the latter possessed unusual intellectual gifts but lacked plain commonsense.[35] And Arrian, who apparently had little use for Callisthenes, referred to the latter as 'something of a boor as regards his manners and character.'[36] Hence, Aristotle repeatedly warned Callisthenes 'to speak as seldom and as pleasantly as possible in the presence of a man [scil., Alexander] who had at the tip of his tongue the power over life and death.'[37]

When Alexander put Callisthenes to death in the spring of 327 B.C.,[38] the relationship between Aristotle and Alexander drastically deteriorated, although at one time they must have been on rather friendly terms.[39] It has already been mentioned that Aristotle apparently incurred Alexander's displeasure because he had introduced Callisthenes to the king. In any event, in a (spurious?) letter addressed to Antipater and others, Alexander threatened that 'he would take care of and punish the men [scil., Aristotle] who had sent Callisthenes to him, and who harbor those . . . who conspire against my life.' Plutarch adds that this letter was an unmistakable threat against Aristotle, 'in whose house Callisthenes . . . had been educated.'[40] There also exists a story that, in order to offend Aristotle,[41] Alexander honored Anaximenes of Lampsacus (Anaxarchus?)[42] and Xenocrates, the latter apparently a former 'rival' of Aristotle in the Academy.[43] In all likelihood, the alienation between Aristotle and Alexander, which might have been in the making for some time, was precipitated by Alexander's shameful and unfair treatment of Callisthenes, the pupil and close relative of Aristotle. Hence, by his barbaric treatment of Callisthenes, it was really Alexander who broke off his former friendship with Aristotle, and who thereby caused the latter to turn against him. Subsequently some friends and admirers of Alexander invented and circulated the story that after the year 327 B.C., Aristotle attempted to poison Alexander.[44] Arrian, a witness decidedly hostile towards both Aristotle and Callisthenes, maintains that 'Antipater sent him [*scil.*, Alexander] a poisonous drug . . . and Aristotle, already fearing Alexander on account of Callisthenes' death, concocted this drug for Antipater.'[45] This fear on the part of Aristotle might be alleged to have been caused by Alexander's threatening letter addressed to Antipater.[46] The story of Aristotle's attempt to poison Alexander is wholly unsupported and is probably a malicious fabrication of some pro-Alexandrian or anti-Aristotelian source or sources. In all likelihood, it was invented and circulated as a sort of 'propaganda material' during the prolonged and bitter struggles among Alexander's generals and among the Diadochi after the death of Alexander in 323 B.C.[47] Plutarch reports that 'at the time [of Alexander's death], no one had any suspicion of his being poisoned, but upon some information given six years later, they say that Olympias [the mother of Alexander] put many people to death, and scattered the ashes of Iolaus, then dead, as if he had given [the poison to Alexander]. But those who maintain that Aristotle counselled Antipater to do it, and that in this manner the poison was administered, cited a certain Hagnothemis as their authority, who, they insist, heard King Antigonus speak of the incident.'[48] It is quite possible that the story of Alexander's poisoning was originally propagated in a pamphlet, published six years after the death of Alexander, and perhaps composed by this Hagnothemis. It is not certain, however, whether Aristotle's name appeared in the original version of this story. In any event, neither Curtius Rufus nor Plutarch nor Diodorus Siculus accuses Aristotle of having been involved in the alleged poisoning of Alexander.[49]

The story that Aristotle poisoned Alexander, or that he assisted in the plot by preparing the fatal poison, not only had certain political and conspiratorial implications related to the bitter rivalry among Alexander's generals.[50] It might also have been a rather crude effort on the part of some pro-Alexandrian authors or romancers to blacken the character of Aristotle—a quaint though certainly effective manner of answering the charges of the pro-Aristotelian or pro-Callisthenian writers who had denounced and condemned Alexander for what he had done to Callisthenes and, through Callisthenes, to Aristotle. According to these pro-Alexandrian authors, the 'ungrateful' and 'treacherous' Aristotle, who was involved in the outrageous murder of Alexander, as well as his equally 'worthless' kinsman (Callisthenes), fully deserved Alexander's wrath as well as harsh treatment: Callisthenes, after all, was not only a fool and a despicable sycophant, but also a traitor;[51] and the same thing was probably maintained about Aristotle. The general effects of these conflicting and confusing stories can still be detected among the majority of Alexander's biographers and historians. It may be observed that some pro-Alexandrian authors claimed outright that Aristotle had planned to murder, and actually had participated in the murder of Alexander, while some anti-Alexandrian writers in fact maintained that Alexander had intended to kill Aristotle.[52]

A number of Greek authors, as a rule philosophers and opponents of Alexander, violently condemned, and even wholeheartedly scorned, the latter for his shameful treatment of Callisthenes. At the same time, they turned Callisthenes into a sort of martyr in the cause of Greek intellectual and moral life or aspirations, as well as in the cause of Greek political freedom.[53] Curtius Rufus seems to summarize this attitude when he maintains that 'there was no one whose death aroused greater hatred of the king among the Greeks, because the latter not only put to death a man endowed with a noble character and fine accomplishments, but one who had called him back to life when he, Alexander, had resolved to die after the murder of Clitus, but had also tortured him, and that without trial.'[54] They might indeed have praised Callisthenes' courage in objecting to Alexander's despotic ways, if it had not been for Callisthenes' prior subservience and indiscriminate flattery of the king (in his historical writings as well as in his personal dealings with Alexander). Hence, some ancient authors felt that Callisthenes fully deserved his fate for 'having compromised his philosophic principles in order to endear himself to the king.'[55]

Rightly, therefore, in my judgement, was Alexander angry with Callisthenes, both for his unseasonable freespokenness and for his foolish arrogance. I presume that this is why people easily believed those accusers of Callisthenes who insinuated that he had a part in the plot [of Hermolaus] against Alexander ... [and why] some people even maintained that Callisthenes instigated the plot.'[56]

Neither the *Vita Marciana* nor the *Vita Vulgata* nor the *Vita Latina* mentions Callisthenes or the Callisthenes incident. The *Vita Aristotelis*

Arabica of Al-Mubashir, as well as that of Usaibia, merely relates that, when Aristotle returned to Athens in 335–34 B.C., 'he left Callisthenes as his successor in Macedonia.'[57] This signal omission suggests that these particular *Vitae Aristotelis* were essentially encomia and, hence, suppressed all information which might possibly have cast an unfavorable light on Aristotle or Aristotle's kin. (And since the Arabs in particular were also great admirers of Alexander, they might have had an additional reason for ignoring the Callisthenes episode.) From all this, it might be inferred that the general literary tradition which sided with Callisthenes (and Aristotle) against Alexander apparently did not prevail, while those interpretations which insisted that Callisthenes had received his just deserts were widely accepted. Otherwise, the encomiastic biographers would not have felt compelled to suppress the Callisthenes incident.

Aristotle's personal reaction to the manner in which Callisthenes met his death is difficult to ascertain or assess. Plutarch relates that one of Callisthenes' servants or secretaries, a man called Stroebus, personally informed Aristotle of the whole incident,[58] and that the latter, who was fully aware of Callisthenes' lack of good sense and discretion, apparently was not altogether surprised at the tragic outcome. Aristotle probably blamed Callisthenes, at least in part, for what had happened, although he most certainly could not have condoned or approved of the manner in which Alexander had treated Callisthenes. It might be conjectured that in a way he had anticipated Callisthenes' ultimate tragic fate.[59] It has already been pointed out that on the occasion of Callisthenes' death, Theophrastus, who was an associate of Aristotle and apparently a close friend of Callisthenes, wrote an *in memoriam* in honor of the latter—the *Callisthenes or On Bereavement*.[60]—and that he did so probably at the suggestion of Aristotle. In this piece, Theophrastus also denounced Alexander as being a man who had attained supreme power and the height of good fortune, but who was utterly incapable of making proper and intelligent use of his attainments.[61]

It is quite possible that in his *Callisthenes*, Theophrastus also made use of *Nicomachean Ethics* 1123 b 1 ff., where Aristotle discusses magnanimity; and that he attempted to demonstrate that Aristotle's early efforts to mold the character of the young Alexander, and to instill in him a sense of restraint, were in no way responsible for Alexander's later excesses and uncontrolled emotional outbursts.[62] The *Callisthenes* of Theophrastus, and the manner in which it discusses the role that chance and fortune play in the lives of men, evoked much criticism as well as a great deal of opposition among ancient authors.[63] This work, aside from being a memorial in honor of Callisthenes, was as much an apology of Aristotle (and Callisthenes) as it was a moral indictment of Alexander. From the scanty surviving (indirect) evidence it might also be inferred that Theophrastus maintained that, thanks to Aristotle's didactic efforts, at one time Alexander emerged as a young man of great promise and high ideals. But the volatile gifts of chance and fortune, manifest in power and worldly success, subsequently corrupted Alexander and turned him into a vile monster. The Stoics, on the other hand, claimed that the evil traits of character subsequently displayed by Alexander were actually implanted in him by incompetent tutors who completely failed in their task. But they do not mention Aristotle among the teachers of Alexander.[64]

It is also quite likely that in his *Callisthenes*, Theophrastus expressed the general sentiments of the Peripatus (and of Greek intellectuals or philosophers in general), including the personal reaction of Aristotle who, however, seems to have preferred to remain silent. In their attacks on Alexander, the Peripatetics stooped low enough to charge Alexander with either sexual impotency or homosexuality. Theophrastus, for instance, suggests that Alexander was something less than a man. He does not claim, however, that Alexander was outright impotent—after all, he had a son by Roxane—but he calls him 'semi-impotent,'[65] and he ascribes this condition to excessive drinking.[66] The Peripatetics, who counted Callisthenes as one of their own, and Theophrastus in particular, claimed outright that, among other serious moral defects, Alexander was possessed of an evil character and an unpleasant disposition.[67] In this fashion, Theophrastus and the Peripatetics in general initiated a most unfavorable estimate of Alexander as the unrestrained tyrant and barbarous villain who was intoxicated with his power, dazzled by his military prowess, and corrupted by his fabulous success.[68]

This unfavorable estimate of Alexander, against which Plutarch, among others, vigorously protested in his *Alexander*, was further developed and exploited, frequently by way of outright exaggeration and baseless calumnies, by subsequent anti-Alexandrian philosophers, moralists and historians. Thus originated a thoroughly debased portrait of Alexander as a despicable despot, intemperate fool and uncouth barbarian, whose achievements were not due to virtue or personal merit, but solely to blind chance. He was presented as a contemptible person irredeemably ruined by the excesses of his own good fortune.[69] One might maintain, therefore, that Callisthenes succeeded in blackening Alexander's memory among ancient intellectuals and philosophers.

In a most unexpected manner did he achieve his avowed aim, namely, to make Alexander 'famous (actually infamous) in the eyes of mankind.'[70] It is also interesting to note that, on account of Alexander's brutal treatment of Callisthenes, the Peripatetics in particular transferred their original admiration for Alexander as the 'ideal ruler,' to Hermias of Atarneus.[71] This would also explain, at least in part, why Hermias came under violent and slanderous attacks by the enemies of Aristotle and by the detractors of the Peripatus in general.[72] It was also in the spirit of this contempt or hatred for Alexander that Demetrius of Phaleron, after 317 B.C., formally transferred the loyalty of the Peripatus to Cassander, the opponent of Alexander. Conversely, the admirers and eulogists of Alexander, as well as the detractors of Aristotle, insisted that the Macedonian king had acted properly and judiciously when he put away Callisthenes who, after all, had been involved in a plot to assassinate Alexander; that under the circumstances Callisthenes had received his just deserts; that Aristotle to a very large extent must be held responsible for the untimely death of Callisthenes; and that Aristotle himself had treacherously conspired against the life of Alexander.[73] It might be maintained, therefore, that Callisthenes, at least indirectly and in a manner he had never anticipated, not only influenced some of the events which shaped the last years of Aristotle's life, but also determined, to a large extent, the subsequent 'political outlook' of the Peripatus as well as some of the subsequent literary attitudes towards the Peripatus in general and towards Alexander and Hermias of Atarneus in particular.[74]

Chapter VII

Aristotle Enters the Academy*

According to a distinct biographical tradition, which in all likelihood goes back to Ptolemy (-el-Garib), Aristotle received what might be termed a 'well-rounded liberal education' while he was still a young boy.[1] But neither the *Vita Marciana*, nor the *Vita Vulgata*, nor the *Vita Latina*, nor, with one single exception, the Syriac and Arabic *Vitae Aristotelis* indicate whether he received this 'primary training' in Macedonia or somewhere else.[2] Al-Mubashir, on the other hand, insists that 'when he [*scil.*, Aristotle] was eight years old he was brought by his father [Nicomachus] to the country of Athens, known by the title of "the land of the wise men," and there the boy stayed at the Lyceum. His father handed him over to a school of poets, orators and schoolmasters, and he stayed there for nine years. This kind of instruction—the knowledge of language [*scil.*, rhetoric?]—was called by the Greeks the "all-embracing learning," because everyone stands in need of this knowledge which is an instrument as well as a guide to all sorts of wisdom and virtue, showing also how each branch of knowledge had been developed.'[3] Al-Mubashir's account that Aristotle was sent to Athens at the age of eight in order to receive there his basic education, and that he stayed there nine years, is not well substantiated. We may, however, accept the story that in his early youth he was given a 'well-rounded liberal education'[4] befitting the son of a well-to-do, cultured and educated Greek who not only was in the personal service of the Macedonian royal house, but who also descended from a noble family that had helped to found Stagira around the middle of the seventh century B.C., and which claimed Asclepius as one of its illustrious ancestors.

Some *Vitae Aristotelis* relate that after the death of Nicomachus (Aristotle's father), Proxenus of Atarneus[5] became the 'guardian' of Aristotle—the exact date of Nicomachus' death is unknown, but it must have occurred while Aristotle was still fairly young, that is, before he went to Athens in the year 367 B.C. at the age of seventeen or, better, when he was in his seventeenth year—and that Proxenus took over the 'primary education' of Aristotle.[6] Usaibia insists that 'when [Aristotle's] father died, Proxenus, the "mandatory of his father" [scil., the person whom Nicomachus had appointed his executor and Aristotle's guardian], handed over the young man to Plato. Some . . . say that he did this because he and Plato were friends.'[7] But the details of the role which Proxenus played in the education of the young Aristotle are not known.

Some biographies of Aristotle report that during his early years the Stagirite 'wrote' several 'books', including a work on *Homeric Questions*, an essay on rhetoric (the *Gryllus*?), a dialogue *On (the) Poets*, and that he made an edition of Homer's *Iliad*.[8] Obviously, these biographies confuse some of the works which Aristotle might have studied in his youth with works he wrote in later years. The reference to Aristotle's early literary activities is probably an effort on the part of Aristotle's admirers to counteract certain stories, invented by Aristotle's detractors, that in his youth he was an illiterate and dissipated never-do-well.[9] The encomiastic accounts which stress the excellence and thoroughness of Aristotle's education and which also report his early literary activities, can be traced back to certain Neo-Platonic authors (Ptolemy?), though the unfavorable reports about the young Aristotle, who is depicted as a boorish, dissipated and uneducated person, likewise were widely circulated and widely believed in antiquity. Epicurus, who was one of the earliest authors of these unpleasant stories, for instance, insisted that in his youth Aristotle recklessly squandered his patrimony (which must have been considerable) by riotous living; that at one time he became a mercenary soldier; that he was also a peddler of drugs (aphrodisiacs)[10]—the latter a vicious distortion of the fact that for a while he might have been interested in medicine; and that only after he had apparently failed in everything else did he enter the Academy in order to study (Platonic) philosophy,[11] a pursuit in which, at least according to Epicurus, he likewise failed. This whole account also implies that Aristotle turned to philosophy rather late in life, and certainly later than at the age of seventeen. It might be interesting to note here that Epicurus, the implacable enemy and vicious slanderer of Aristotle, boasted that he himself turned to philosophy at the age of fourteen.[12]

As mentioned above, there also exists a tradition, known to some biographers, which maintains that in his youth, Aristotle studied (or was interested in) medicine.[13] Since Aristotle's father, Nicomachus, himself was a physician, such preoccupation with or interest in medicine on the part of Aristotle would not be altogether unusual. Apparently the descendants of Asclepius and Machaon—and Aristotle was, or at least claimed to be, an Asclepiad on his father's as well as on his mother's side—passed down from generation to generation the 'art of healing' as a kind of family tradition. One Syriac *Vita Aristotelis* reports, on the other hand, that 'it is not in accordance with the true facts what is said about him [*scil.*, Aristotle], namely, that he did not turn to philosophy until he was thirty years old, and then only after he had [unsuccessfully?] practiced medicine [peddled drugs or aphrodisiacs, as Epicurus had insinuated?].'[14]

All extant *Vitae* concur that at one time Aristotle moved to Athens, but they do not always agree as to the exact date of this event nor as to the specific reason for this move. As a matter of fact, the several biographies seem to be in disagreement on these two points. Diogenes Laertius, on the authority of Apollodorus' *Chronicle*, in a rather cryptic manner states that Aristotle 'attached himself to Plato . . . having become his pupil at the age of seventeen.'[15] Dionysius of Halicarnassus, likewise on the authority of Apollodorus (?), maintains that 'after the death of his father, when he was in his eighteenth year, Aristotle went to Athens and joined Plato.'[16] Al-Mubashir, being somewhat more informative, relates that 'when he [*scil.*, Aristotle] had completed his studies of the poets, grammarians and rhetoricians, and when he was imbued with their knowledge,[17] he turned to ethics, politics, mathematics, physics and theology [metaphysics]. He attached himself to Plato and became his disciple and apprentice. He was now seventeen years old [or in his seventeenth year]. All this happened in a place called the Academy, situated in Athens in the country of the wise men.'[18] According to these reports, Aristotle apparently went to Athens at the age of seventeen (in his seventeenth year), and that he did so for the sole purpose of entering the Academy in order to study philosophy under the personal guidance of Plato.[19] But there exists still a further and somewhat puzzling tradition recorded by some biographers—a tradition which probably goes back to Ptolemy (?) and, perhaps, to some earlier sources—which maintains that 'at the age of seventeen . . . Aristotle kept company with Socrates and stayed with the latter a short time until Socrates met his death. . . . After that he did seek out Plato.'[20] Al-Mubashir, in turn, narrates that Aristotle went to Athens when he was eight years old,[21] and that he came in contact with Plato only when he was seventeen years old.[22]

In brief, the extant *Vitae Aristotelis* do not make it clear whether

Aristotle went to Athens for the express purpose of joining the Academy, and Plato in particular; nor do they agree as to the exact time Aristotle visited Athens (and joined the Academy). The *Vita Marciana*, which relies here on Philochorus, insists that all this happened during the archonship of Nausigenes (368–67 B.C.), when Aristotle was seventeen years old, that is, in his seventeenth year.[23] Dionysius of Halicarnassus, who estimates Aristotle to have been in his eighteenth year at the time, says that all this took place during the archonship of Polycelus (367–66 B.C.).[24] On the whole, the dating of the *Vita Marciana* (Philochorus) has been accepted. It has been suggested that Aristotle arrived in Athens either in May or June of 367 B.C., that is, during the latter part of Nausigenes' archonship, and that at the time he was in his seventeenth year without, however, having attained his seventeenth birthday.[25] This view is based on the fairly reasonable assumption that Aristotle was born between July and October of 384 B.C., that is, during the early part of Diotrephes' archonship (384–83 B.C.) or in the early months (July to October) of the first year of the 99th Olympiad.[26]

A number of reasons have been advanced by ancient biographers to explain why Aristotle went to Athens in the year 367 B.C. According to one tradition, which probably goes back to Ptolemy (-el-Garib), he did so because of the advice given by the Delphic oracle.[27] Usaibia, who likewise recites the injunction of the Delphic oracle, maintains on the other hand that 'this happened because Proxenus and Plato were personal friends.'[28] One might also conjecture here that Aristotle went to Athens for 'political reasons,' a possibility which, however, is not mentioned in the extant *Vitae Aristotelis*. King Amyntas III, the friend of Aristotle's father, died in 370–69 B.C. He was succeeded by his oldest son, Alexander II, who was murdered by his uncle Ptolemy of Alorus in 369 B.C. Ptolemy proclaimed himself regent, ruling Macedonia in the name of Perdiccas and Philip, the younger brothers of Alexander II. Ptolemy, in turn, was slain in 365 B.C. by Perdiccas who made himself king. Approximately five years before his death, King Amyntas III had concluded an alliance with Athens. Amyntas supported the Athenian policy in Thrace, while Athens abetted Macedonia's policy in Thessaly. Ptolemy, who had become regent of Macedonia thanks to the support of Athens (Iphicrates), initially leaned on Athens. But in 368 B.C., as a result of the second Theban invasion of Thessaly under Pelopidas, he switched his allegiance and declared himself for Thebes. In the year 365 B.C., thanks to the assistance by Athens, Perdiccas removed Ptolemy and declared himself for Athens. He maintained this allegiance with Athens until 362 B.C., when, after the battle of Mantinea, he shifted his allegiance and allied himself once more with Thebes against Athens. When Perdiccas was slain in battle fighting against the Illyrians in 359 B.C., his son Amyntas became the rightful heir to the throne. Since, at the time, Amyntas was a mere child, his uncle Philip assumed the regency. Philip, the astute diplomatist, soon came to terms with Athens.

It is not unreasonable to assume that Aristotle's family remained loyal to the legitimate heir or heirs of Amyntas III (Alexander II, Perdiccas, and Philip).[29] During the regency of Ptolemy and the fierce inter-dynastic struggles which convulsed Macedonia at the time, Aristotle might have taken political refuge in Athens (his immediate family probably belonged to the pro-Athenian faction in Macedonia) in order to escape persecution by the regent, who after 368 B.C. allied himself with Thebes, the enemy of Athens, and who probably tried to exterminate all persons whom he suspected to be friends and supporters of Amyntas III, Alexander II and Perdiccas. It is also possible that Aristotle's father, Nicomachus, was killed during these bloody inter-dynastic struggles. In any event, by the time Aristotle went to Athens in 367 B.C., Nicomachus, the personal physician, friend, adviser and, we must assume, the partisan of Amyntas III and his family, was dead (as was probably Aristotle's mother, Phaestis).[30]

It has already been noted that some *Vitae* maintain that when Aristotle came to Athens in the year 367 B.C., he first stayed with Socrates.[31] The *Vita Vulgata* and the *Vita Latina* actually speak of his three-year stay with Socrates.[32] As it stands, this story contains a fatal anachronism: Socrates died in 399 B.C., fifteen years before Aristotle was born. Aside from the problem inherent in the statement that Aristotle studied with Socrates, this account raises a number of involved issues difficult to resolve. If Aristotle actually stayed three years with Socrates, then he did become Plato's disciple only at the age of twenty (or in his twentieth year), provided he went to Athens at the age of seventeen. Conversely, according to universal and apparently reliable tradition, Aristotle stayed twenty years with Plato and the Academy, which would have been impossible if he came to Plato after a three-year stay with Socrates (367–64) and left Athens and the Academy in 348 B.C. Accordingly, the report contained in the *Vita Vulgata* and in the *Vita Latina* might be based on some misunderstanding. Perhaps an epitomizer (or his source) confused the period of Aristotle's association with Plato and the Platonic Academy (twenty years) and Aristotle's age at the time he entered the Academy. In order to account for the

missing three years—the three years between his arrival in Athens at
the age of seventeen and his joining Plato at the age of twenty—this
epitomizer or biographer simply invented the story that Aristotle
stayed three years with Socrates. Needless to say, this explanation is
pure conjecture. In any event, the report that Aristotle stayed three
full years with Socrates—but not necessarily the story that he stayed
for a while with Socrates, provided we are willing to assume that the
name 'Socrates' is but a mispelling (or confusion) of 'Isocrates'—
must be based on some misunderstanding. There might be another
possible explanation of the account that Aristotle stayed three years
with Socrates: at the time Aristotle arrived in Athens in 367 B.C.,
Plato was in Syracuse (or on his way to Syracuse), not to return until
365–64 B.C. Hence, not until about 364, that is, after he had been in
Athens for almost three years, did Aristotle come into personal contact with Plato. Perhaps some confused biographer or epitomizer,
being familiar with these facts, wished to account for the intervening
three years and, hence, simply invented the story that Aristotle stayed
three years with Socrates. A remote echo of this story might be detected in Al-Mubashir (*II VA* 9): 'When he [*scil.*, Aristotle] had completed
his study of the poets, grammarians and orators . . . he attached
himself to Plato and became his disciple and apprentice.'

It has already been pointed out that the report that Aristotle stayed
with Socrates and that he studied philosophy under his guidance,
contains a fatal anachronism. But there might be a reasonable and,
perhaps, persuasive explanation for this obvious mistake. Some
biographer or epitomizer might have confused Socrates with Isocrates;[33] or, the name of Socrates might be merely a scribal error for
Isocrates.[34] Assuming, then, that the name 'Socrates' is here merely an
erroneous substitution for Isocrates, we might further conjecture that
perhaps in the first year or years at Athens[35] Aristotle joined Isocrates'
school of rhetoric, which by that time eclipsed Plato and the Platonic
Academy both in fame and notoriety. During the early part of the
fourth century B.C., the renown of Isocrates as a literary man as well as
that of his school of rhetoric was widespread throughout the Hellenic
world and beyond, reaching into Macedonia and to the island of
Cyprus. It should also be borne in mind that during the last years of
the fifth century B.C., Isocrates had spent some time in Larissa in
Thessaly, where he was associated with the famous Gorgias of Leontini
and with Gorgias' influential school of rhetoric.[36] Thessaly, again,
had many close contacts with Macedonia. Hence, it may be assumed
that Isocrates and his work were known among the more cultured

Macedonians and, especially, among the Greeks or Greek settlers who lived in Macedonia and Chalcidice. All this would indicate that by the year 400 B.C. Greek intellectual culture had begun to penetrate the adjacent lands to the north. When Isocrates opened his own school in Athens (near the Lyceum) around the year 393 B.C., or perhaps, in 386–85 B.C.,[37] he attracted a great many distinguished 'students'— about one hundred[38]—from all parts of the eastern Mediterranean world.[39] Moreover, at the time Aristotle arrived in Athens (in 367 B.C.), Isocrates already had published some of his most renowned orations.[40] Under the circumstances it is only fair to surmise that the young Aristotle, if indeed during his early years he had received a 'liberal and well-rounded education' befitting a young man of noble Greek descent, read some of these orations which undoubtedly made a profound impression on him. This, in turn, probably induced Aristotle, the Macedonian, to seek out Isocrates and his school rather than Plato and the Platonic Academy, whose rapidly growing fame may as yet have escaped him.[41]

Additional support for the thesis that Aristotle might first have joined Isocrates and his school of rhetoric might be found in the fact that at the time Aristotle arrived in Athens in the year 367 B.C., Plato was away in Syracuse and did not return to Athens until 365–64 B.C. It may also be argued that while Aristotle was connected with the school of Isocrates, he became acquainted with some of Plato's writings. Impressed by what he had read, he decided to transfer to the Academy. This might possibly be inferred from one of Aristotle's earliest compositions, the *Nerinthus*,[42] which may have been a sort of 'autobiographical sketch.' In this *Nerinthus*, it has previously been shown, a Corinthian farmer (an illiterate or uncouth person, the young Aristotle?) reads Plato's *Gorgias* which denounces the rhetoric propagated by Gorgias (and, by implication, the rhetoric taught by Isocrates). As a result of this lecture he leaves his 'farm' (the school of Isocrates?) and joins the Platonic Academy.[43] If this story should actually contain a kind of autobiographical reference, then Plato's *Gorgias*, in a way, must have had the same effect on the intellectual development of the young Aristotle as Cicero's *Hortensius* (which ultimately may go back to Aristotle's *Protrepticus*) at one time had on the intellectual conversion of St Augustine.[44] Additional arguments could be advanced in support of the claim that Aristotle first attended Isocrates' school where he was subjected to a thorough training in rhetoric, and that only at some later time he transferred to the Platonic Academy: Several *Vitae* stress the fact that Aristotle first received a training in rhetoric—this could very well be the ultimate meaning of the 'liberal, all-embracing education' which he is said to have received while attending 'a school of . . . orators.'[45] It is not very likely that Aristotle was trained in rhetoric while he attended the Academy.

Al-Mubashir's account, although in a somewhat garbled and confusing manner, also might reflect the possibility that Aristotle first joined Isocrates and his school, and that he stayed with Isocrates for some time. This Arabic biographer, who ultimately derives his information from Ptolemy (-el-Garib), relates that, at least for a while, Aristotle attended 'a school of poets, orators and schoolmasters [at the Lyceum]. . . . This branch of learning, the knowledge of language, was called by the Greeks the 'all-encompassing,' because everyone needed this knowledge which is an instrument and at the same time a guide to all kinds of wisdom and virtue. . . . But there were among the wise men some who despised the knowledge of the orators, lexicographers and schoolmasters, and ridiculed those who devoted themselves to these pursuits. . . . They held that these activities were of no use in the acquisition of wisdom, since the grammarians were nothing but schoolmasters, the poets nothing but weathercocks and liars, and the orators nothing but slanderers, cajolers and fanatic revolutionaries. When this came to Aristotle's attention, he stepped forward to defend the schoolmasters, orators and poets, and pleaded their cause insisting that wisdom cannot do without their knowledge, since logic is instrumental of their knowledge. He also maintained that man's superiority over animals is based on man's power of speech. Only he is a man in the true sense of the term who in his speech is capable of being accurate and of deftly expressing the thoughts of his mind—who knows how to arrange the words properly and choose phrases which are as terse as they are graceful. Since wisdom is the most exalted of all things, it must be expressed in the most lucid language, by the most eloquent speech and in the most succinct form. It must be free from errors and fallacies, vulgarities and barbarisms, and verbal incompetence. For such defects obscure the light of wisdom, impede communication, diminish perspicuity, confuse the listener's mind, destroy logic, and perpetuate as well as spread ignorance. When he [scil., Aristotle] had completed his studies of the poets, grammarians and orators, and when he was imbued with their knowledge . . . he attached himself to Plato and became his disciple and apprentice . . . in the Academy.'[46] This 'school of poets, orators and schoolmasters (or lexicographers)' might well have been the school of Isocrates.

Al-Mubashir's somewhat puzzling account raises a number of

problems which might be explained as follows: the biographical tradition of Aristotle, at least that tradition which probably goes back to Ptolemy (-el-Garib), apparently maintained that on the insistence of his father, Aristotle received a thorough 'liberal' or 'primary' education while still a young boy. This is also brought out by some of the other *Vitae*.[47] Al-Mubashir, however, enlarges and embellishes the traditional story of Aristotle's early education by changing it into the story that Aristotle's father brought him to Athens—'to the country of the wise men'—when he was only eight years old, and that he placed him there in a school. Thus, unlike the other biographers, Al-Mubashir claims that Aristotle received his 'primary' intellectual training in Athens rather than in Macedonia or Stagira. This 'primary' training, which Aristotle received as a boy of eight, is immediately linked up with his 'pre-philosophic' education, which he began at the age of seventeen, presumably first under the guidance of Isocrates and later in the Platonic Academy. Describing further the education of the young Aristotle, Al-Mubashir combines (and perhaps confuses) Aristotle's 'pre-philosophic' education not only with the 'primary' training he received as a young boy of eight, but also with Aristotle's earliest literary, didactic and apologetic-critical efforts, as well as with his early intellectual feuds. But there is still more in Al-Mubashir's complex account: for some unexplainable reason, he includes in his report on Aristotle's education a lengthy reference to the many and at times bitter intellectual controversies and feuds over the nature of the true *paideia*, which during the fourth and third centuries raged between the several schools of philosophy. It is impossible, however, to ascertain from what source or sources Al-Mubashir derived his information about these controversies, or about Epicurus' and Lycon Pythagoraeus' denunciations of the traditional ἐγκύκλια παιδεία in particular.[48] And finally, Al-Mubashir's account implies that Aristotle received his 'pre-philosophic' education in a school other than the Platonic Academy. This other school is probably the school of Isocrates.

Hence, nothing prevents us from assuming that Aristotle first studied rhetoric in the school of Isocrates. As a matter of fact, Al-Mubashir insists that when Aristotle came to Athens, he first stayed at the Lyceum.[49] Only at a later date did he move to the Academy.[50] According to tradition, Isocrates' school, but not that of Plato, was located in the vicinity of the Lyceum. Tradition also has it that Aristotle's first didactic activities were connected with rhetoric,[51] and that his first major literary effort, probably the *Gryllus or On Rhetoric*, likewise was related to rhetoric.[52] And finally, the bitter and protracted rivalry between Aristotle and Isocrates, which apparently started with the *Gryllus* and probably culminated in Aristotle's *Protrepticus* (which has been called a rebuttal of Isocrates' *Antidosis*), might be interpreted as an attempt on the part of Aristotle to proclaim as well as justify his 'secession' from the school of Isocrates.[53] Naturally, all this is more or less conjecture based on the assumption that the story of Aristotle's stay with Socrates actually refers to his early association with Isocrates and his school. More than doubtful is the report that he stayed with Socrates (Isocrates) three years.[54] It must always be borne in mind that soon after Isocrates had opened his school of rhetoric in Athens he attracted a great many students from all parts of the Hellenic world, and even from beyond the Greek orbit. Among these students were men of wealth, influence and fame; and the 'alumni' of this renowned school certainly constituted a remarkable group of people.[55]

There also must have existed a tradition, obviously hostile to Aristotle, which advanced the story that the latter entered the Academy only at the age of thirty (or forty) years. This baffling tradition is reflected in Diogenes Laertius,[56] in the *Vita Marciana*,[57] in one of the Syriac *Vitae Aristotelis*[58] and in two of the Arabic *Vitae*.[59] These biographies, however, outright refute this account calling it totally erroneous and misleading, and denouncing it as sheer malicious gossip.[60] Nevertheless, together with the report that before entering the Academy, Aristotle had engaged 'in politics,'[61] that is, perhaps in 'political oratory' as it was taught by Isocrates, this account might possibly allude, though in a hopelessly confused form, to Aristotle's entrance into the Academy after he had spent some time in the school of Isocrates where he concentrated also on 'political oratory.'

If we were to assume that Aristotle actually entered the Academy late in the spring of 367 B.C. (during the archonship of Nausigenes), then we are faced with a further problem: Plato had departed for Syracuse in 367 B.C.[62] It has been surmised that Aristotle arrived in Athens in May or June of 367, and that Plato left for Sicily early in 367, most likely some time before the arrival of Aristotle. Tradition also has it that before embarking on his journey, Plato had put Eudoxus of Cnidus in charge of the Academy.[63] As a matter of fact, several of the *Vitae Aristotelis* clearly indicate that Aristotle joined the Academy at the time Eudoxus was the 'acting scholarch.'[64] If this is so, then Aristotle would not have met Plato until the latter returned from Syracuse in 365–64 B.C.,[65] that is, almost three years after his arrival in Athens.

These few observations should make it sufficiently clear that the old and somewhat shop-worn 'text-book story' of Aristotle's joining Plato and the Academy in the year 367 B.C. at the age of seventeen (or in his seventeenth year) is by no means as certain or as well established as some people would like us to believe. It is reasonable to assume that Aristotle arrived in Athens during the latter part of the first half of 367 B.C., but it is by no means fully established that this was perchance his first visit to Athens, or that immediately upon his arrival in Athens he joined the Platonic Academy. Neither is it certain that he went to Athens in the year 367 primarily for the purpose of acquiring a philosophic or 'well-rounded' education under the tutelage of Plato. For it is possible that in 367 B.C. he was brought to Athens in order to escape political persecution or worse by Ptolemy of Alorus and his partisans.[66] It is also possible, though by no means certain, that at some earlier time (in 376–75 B.C. ?) he attended an Athenian school for his 'primary' education—during this particular period the relations between Athens and Macedonia were friendly—and there exists the reasonable possibility that in the year 367 B.C. he frequented for a time Isocrates' famous school of rhetoric, only to transfer to the Academy at some later date.

In the light of the available evidence, which is both scanty and conflicting the exact details and the particular circumstances surrounding Aristotle's entrance into the Platonic Academy are not fully known and may never be fully known.[67] But it is a tantalizing thought that for a brief span of time Aristotle might have been the disciple of Isocrates—Socrates according to some sources. Perhaps it was due to the influence of Isocrates that Aristotle developed that refined and pleasant style of writing which is so characteristic of his earliest (lost) compositions, and for which he became famous throughout antiquity.[68] Perhaps it was due to his association with the school of Isocrates, no matter how brief it might have been, that he subsequently began to change the literary form as well as the method of argumentation in which philosophic issues could be presented more 'scientifically' and more effectively. In so doing, he started a major literary innovation or trend in the domain of philosophic discussion.[69] Perhaps the early training in rhetoric which he had received in the school of Isocrates accounts for the fact that his first literary effort was concerned with rhetoric, and that at a relatively early stage of his 'academic career,' he was considered fully qualified to take issue with Isocrates' particular brand of rhetoric[70] and, hence, was entrusted with offering in the Academy a full-fledged independent 'course of lectures' on rhetoric.[71]

And finally, it might be possible that on account of his former close association or contact with Isocrates and Isocrates' more realistic approach to matters of political and practical concern, as contrasted with the purely theoretic-idealistic treatment by Plato, Aristotle subsequently developed a more practical attitude towards certain problems of concrete life and political existence. This practical attitude comes to the fore in some of his early (lost) political writings, such as the *On Justice*, the *Politicus* and the *On Kingship*, as well as in his later political and ethical treatises. Together with the somewhat garbled report in *Vita Marciana* 5, *Vita Vulgata* 4 and *Vita Latina* 5 (and perhaps in *II VA* 3–8), all these arguments might be adduced in support of the assumption that in the year 367 B.C. Aristotle first joined the school of Isocrates, and that at some later date he transferred to the Platonic Academy.

It may also be observed that after his transfer to the Academy, Aristotle stayed there until the summer or early fall of 348 B.C.[72] Despite this rather long and certainly eventful association (which, especially after 365 B.C., that is, after the removal of Ptolemy of Alorus by Perdiccas, might have been interrupted by several visits to Macedonia), we possess little information concerning his personal relations with Plato or with the other members of the Academy. In view of the fact that for centuries afterwards philosophers and historians debated whether and to what extent the young Aristotle adhered to, modified or rejected some of Plato's basic teachings, this omission is somewhat puzzling not to say annoying. Aside from the report that during his stay at the Academy, Aristotle taught an independent course of lectures on rhetoric,[73] not to mention the wholly untrustworthy stories about some serious and ugly rifts between Aristotle and Plato,[74] there exist only three rather meager accounts which might shed some light on Aristotle's general activities during his early membership in the Academy: (i) the report that he was an assiduous worker as well as a great reader of books; (ii) the story that he was a prolific author; and (iii) the account that Plato, although he did not always agree with his philosophic views or with his conduct, had a high personal opinion of his intellectual abilities and mental endowments.

The *Vita Marciana* and the *Vita Latina* relate that Plato referred to Aristotle as the 'reader of books,'[75] that is, as a man so much engrossed in reading and studying that he apparently had little time to join in the philosophic discussions of the Academy—as a man who preferred to stay in his 'room' where Plato paid him an occasional visit. Aristotle's industry, polymathy and literary productivity has been extolled and commented on by many ancient reporters,[76] although polymathy allegedly had been denounced by Socrates[77] and, hence, might not have been encouraged by Plato and the Early Academy.[78]

Aristotle's biographers as well as a number of ancient authors also insist that the Stagirite wrote numerous books on a great many subjects.[79] Some of these books, we know, not only were composed while he was still a member of the Academy, but were also critical of certain aspects of Plato's philosophy. There exists a tradition according to which Plato reproached Aristotle for having written so much on philosophic topics.[80] Aristotle's reply to this reprimand was that his philosophic writings were such as to make philosophy more accessible to the initiated and to the friends of philosophy, but never to dilettantes, the ignorant, nor to the detractors of philosophy; and that he had reduced philosophy to a system which would be welcomed by the philosophers but wholly incomprehensible to the foes of philosophy.[81] Alexander, too, is said to have expressed his displeasure over the fact that Aristotle had published his philosophic views.[82]

Some biographers (Al-Mubashir) relate that Plato was so impressed by the intelligence of the young Aristotle that 'he did not entrust him to Xenocrates for instruction, as he did with the other disciples, but taught him himself.'[83] Moreover, Al-Mubashir also maintains that 'when Plato addressed his students [in a formal lecture or discussion] and was urged to open the discussion, [on noticing Aristotle's absence] would say: "Not until everyone is present." And when Aristotle arrived, he would remark: "Start reciting, the audience is complete [or perfect]." And he would often say: "Not until the Mind is here." And when Aristotle had arrived, he would observe: "Read now, the Mind is present."'[84] According to the *Vita Marciana* and *Vita Latina*, Plato would say whenever Aristotle was absent from a lecture or discussion: 'The Mind is absent,' or 'The audience is deaf.'[85] These remarks, provided they are historical,[86] seem to indicate that Plato considered Aristotle not only his most talented and most promising student—the only young man who possessed adequate intelligence to follow his involved philosophic arguments[87]—but apparently also his favorite pupil.

Chapter VIII

Aristotle's Earliest 'Course of Lectures on Rhetoric'*

Diogenes Laertius reports that 'in time the circle [of students] around him [*scil.*, Aristotle] grew larger. He then sat down to lecture [regularly?], observing that "it would be a base and shameful thing to remain silent and let Xenocrates [read: Isocrates] speak out." He also taught his pupils to discourse upon a set theme, besides training them in rhetoric.'[1]

Philodemus, the Epicurean, appears to be the only one among ancient authors who provides a detailed and articulate account of Aristotle's lecturing on rhetoric in the Academy during the fifties.[2] Philodemus, who among other matters berates Aristotle for having abandoned philosophy in favor of rhetoric (and politics—political rhetoric), also claims that Aristotle taught rhetoric primarily for the purpose of antagonizing and discrediting Isocrates, the bitter rival and opponent of Plato and the Academy. Philodemus' main arguments, which might ultimately date back to Epicurus (a rather persistent foe of Aristotle and Aristotelian philosophy) or to some other Epicurean source or sources equally hostile towards Aristotle, are the following: Aristotle taught rhetoric in the afternoon (in the Academy), maintaining that 'it would be a scandal to remain silent and let Isocrates speak out.'[3] He also composed treatises on rhetoric[4] and insisted that politics constitutes an essential branch of general philosophy.[5] Moreover, he spoke in a confused and obfuscating manner about the differences between rhetoric and politics. Aristotle, according to Philodemus, justified his preoccupation with politics by alleging that ignorance of politics keeps a man out of touch with existential reality;[6] that philosophy and philosophic culture can flourish only among politically enlightened citizens; and that the performance of contemporary politicians (and political orators) in general was outright disappointing.[7] But any person, Philodemus insists, who (like Aristotle?) runs a school of rhetoric primarily for the purpose of gaining notoriety and popularity among people who actually despise philosophy and who exalt rhetoric beyond all measure—especially if, because of his profligate youth, that person lacks the bare necessities of life[8]—such a person might obtain some pupils for a short while, until he should decide to return to philosophy.

Referring to what was undoubtedly Epicurean (anti-Aristotelian) polemics, Philodemus continues: Aristotle did not act the true philosopher when he said that it is a scandal to remain silent and let Isocrates speak out.[9] For if Isocrates' activities were of no consequence, he should have been simply ignored. If, on the other hand, the art of speaking is indeed important, Aristotle should have engaged in rhetoric and the teaching of rhetoric irrespective of what Isocrates did; and, if neither were the case, Aristotle should not have devoted himself to rhetoric, unless he feared that failure to do so would make him appear to be an incompetent, quarrelsome man, defeated by and envious of Isocrates. If in his conduct Aristotle was guided by the popular misconception that it was dishonorable to remain silent and let Isocrates speak out, he most certainly did not understand the proper purpose of rhetoric. But, if he had the proper purpose in mind, why did he not find it disgraceful to speak out in the law courts through his disciples, who deported themselves like hired forensic orators, rather than like divinely inspired philosophers? Why did Aristotle desert philosophy? Why did he urge young men to dedicate themselves to rhetoric rather than to philosophy?[10] In so doing, he incurred the hatred of Isocrates' disciples,[11] as well as the resentment of other teachers of rhetoric.

Assuredly, Philodemus observes, Aristotle implanted in his disciples an admiration for his genius. As soon as he deserted philosophy, he began to collect, with the assistance of his disciples, information about divers areas of human endeavors in order to impress people with his erudition.[12] He studied and taught rhetoric, politics, agriculture, cosmetics, mining and, worse, the several aphrodisiacs.[13] In so doing, he was even less respectable than the ordinary teachers of rhetoric who attempted merely to impart a certain familiarity with the principles and techniques of rhetoric. But if he was honestly searching for the truth, why did he not choose the rhetoric taught by Isocrates (which he ridiculed in many ways) rather than political rhetoric (which he considered different from that taught by Isocrates)? If, on the other hand, Aristotle was indeed practicing political rather than didactic rhetoric, it was rather imprudent for him to speak out against (Isocrates') rhetoric and teach political rhetoric at the same time. None of Aristotle's disciples ever achieved any success in either political or didactic rhetoric, and none of them ever taught in these areas. In due time, Isocrates progressed from rhetoric to philosophy.[14] By concentrating on rhetoric, Aristotle, on the other hand, neglected both natural philosophy and ethics.

The foregoing is an eclectic summary of Philodemus' lengthy and acerbic vituperations of Aristotle and his 'fling' at rhetoric. The remainder of his account, though perhaps an important and enlightening source of evidence attesting to the Epicurean hostility towards Aristotle and Aristotelian philosophy (as well as towards Plato), is of no particular interest to us.

Cicero insists that Aristotle's primary concern with the teaching of rhetoric was the successful amalgam of *elegantia* and *doctrina*. Aristotle realized, according to Cicero, that Isocrates had become a successful teacher as well as a successful man in general because of the excellence of his disciples and because of his abandonment of forensic oratory in favor of a popular and apparently shallow type of rhetoric. Accordingly, he changed the entire form and content of his instruction, combining the study of scientific or philosophic topics with the practice of rhetoric.[15] From these bits of information it would appear that while Cicero praises Aristotle for having combined (actually, re-united) philosophy and rhetoric, Philodemus rebukes Aristotle for having abandoned philosophy in favor of a shallow rhetoric. This, in turn, might suggest that Cicero made use of a source or sources sympathetic to Aristotle, while Philodemus used a source, namely Epicurus, ostensibly hostile to the Stagirite.[16] However, both Philodemus and Cicero seem to be guilty of an 'anachronism' when they imply that Aristotle had already taught philosophic subjects for some time before he decided to include rhetoric in his curriculum.

In *Tusculane Disputationes* I. 4. 7, on the other hand, Cicero insinuates that Aristotle started to teach rhetoric for the sole purpose of competing with Isocrates and his school. 'Stimulated by the professional success of Isocrates, the orator, he [*scil.*, Aristotle] began to teach young people how to speak [eloquently] and to combine philosophic wisdom with rhetorical elegance.'[17] Very similar is Quintilian's version which records that when Isocrates was already a very old man,[18] Aristotle started to teach the art of oratory in his afternoon classes, justifying this enterprise with the remark that 'it would be a base thing to remain silent and let Isocrates speak out.'[19] Syrianus relates that Aristotle offered 'afternoon classes' in which he discussed problems of rhetoric with his friends, insisting that there were two kinds of oral persuasion, namely, rhetoric and dialectic; and exhorting his students by saying that 'it would be a shameful thing to remain silent and let Isocrates speak out.'[20]

Between 360 and 350 B.C., and perhaps later, Cephisodorus, the pupil of Isocrates, wrote a work (in four books), entitled *Against Aristotle*. In this composition, among other matters, he criticized Aristotle for having come forward in order to denounce Isocrates. Moreover, Cephisodorus also decried Aristotle's didactic methods and general philosophic *paideia*. 'When he saw his teacher Isocrates attacked by Aristotle, Cephisodorus, though he was wholly ignorant of and unacquainted with Aristotle, yet perceiving that the works of Plato were highly esteemed, supposed that Aristotle's philosophy agreed with that of Plato. Trying to make war upon Aristotle, he struck at Plato. . . . Hence, instead of combatting the man with whom he was at war [*scil.*, Aristotle], Cephisodorus fought with the man against whom he did not wish to make war.'[21] It must be borne in mind that about 360 B.C., Aristotle wrote his *Gryllus or On Rhetoric*. In this work, which constitutes what appears to have been Aristotle's first major literary effort, Aristotle directly and rather vehemently attacked Isocrates[22] and the very principles on which the latter based his peculiar understanding of the nature and function of rhetoric.[23] It is also fairly safe to surmise that Aristotle expressed his criticism of Isocrates and Isocrates' kind of rhetoric not only in the *Gryllus*, but also in his 'lectures' on rhetoric which around the year 355 B.C. he offered in the Academy. Hence, it may be presumed that Cephisodorus' attacks upon Aristotle are also directed against the Aristotelian *Gryllus*.

A faint but somewhat confusing and confused echo of the story that Aristotle taught rhetoric at a fairly early stage of his 'Academic career' might also be detected in the *Vita Aristotelis* of Al-Mubashir (*II VA* 5–8): 'There were among the wise men [at Athens] some who depreciated the knowledge of the orators . . . and ridiculed those who devoted themselves to this art. To these deprecators belonged also Epicurus and Pythagoras [Lycon Pythagoraeus]. They held that this occupation was of no practical use in the acquisition of wisdom, since . . . the orators were mere calumniators, cajolers and fanatic revolutionaries. When this came to the attention of Aristotle, he stepped forward to defend the . . . orators. He pleaded their cause by saying: "[Philosophic] wisdom cannot succeed without their knowledge." He also maintained that "man's superiority over animals is founded on man's power of articulate speech. Only he is truly a man who in his speech is capable of being exact and of expressing coherently and concisely the thoughts of his soul—who knows how to arrange words properly, as well as to choose phrases which are both terse and graceful. Since [philosophic] wisdom is the most exalted of all things, it must be expressed in the most lucid language, by the most eloquent tongue and in the most succinct form, free from all mistakes and misconceptions, vulgarisms and barbarisms, and linguistic incompetence. For such defects obscure the light of wisdom, obstruct intercommunication, lessen perspicuity, confuse the listener's mind, destroy logic, and beget ignorance.'''[24] It is not impossible that some of the arguments or statements ascribed to Aristotle by Al-Mubashir (or Usaibia) or by the source used by Al-Mubashir, ultimately go back to Aristotle's Gryllus. Al-Mubashir (and Usaibia) also seems to include in his report some of the attacks subsequently made by Epicurus and the Epicureans upon Aristotle and upon his views on rhetoric and philosophy, and upon the nature of a liberal (intellectual) education in general. But as it stands, the account of Al-Mubashir (and Usaibia) contains a fatal anachronism: Epicurus and Lycon Pythagoraeus, an Epicurean, denounced Aristotle's theories of rhetoric some time after the death of Aristotle, that is, after the year 322 B.C. Epicurus and the Epicureans, we know, roundly condemned all forms of rhetoric, calling it a useless and even dangerous intellectual occupation. And finally, this whole account might reflect, though probably in a badly garbled fashion, the controversy between Aristotle and Isocrates, a controversy which also constitutes one of the major issues discussed in the Aristotelian Gryllus.

In recent times, the problem of the early Aristotelian 'lectures on rhetoric' was first tackled by A. Stahr who pointed out that in some way these lectures were related to the rivalry that existed between Aristotle (and the Academy) and Isocrates and his particular school.[25] Subsequently, H. Diels made the truly important and original suggestion that these lectures were at the basis of an early (and, perhaps, the earliest) 'draft' of certain parts of the extant Aristotelian Rhetoric.[26] Diels also insisted that during the lifetime of Plato, Aristotle taught a course in rhetoric in the Academy, and that the Τέχνης τῆς Θεοδέκτου Συναγωγῆς (in one book)[27] contains these lectures, which apparently were taken up and later published by Theodectes after Aristotle had left the Academy in 348–47 B.C.[28] In 1892, F. Blass advanced two major theses: First, that these lectures were delivered about 355 B.C., that is, shortly after the composition of the Aristotelian Gryllus (with which they may have been connected); and, second, that as to their doctrinal or philosophic content they were under the influence of the Platonic Phaedrus[29]—two far-reaching and yet seemingly correct assumptions.

Many scholarly investigations and conjectures have been made concerning the exact nature and date of the so-called Τεχνῶν Συναγωγὴ (in two books) attributed to Aristotle.[30] This 'florilegium' or 'hand-book' of the art of oratory, which was credited to Aristotle by Cicero,[31] Quintilian[32] and others,[33] appears to have been a sort of 'anthology' or 'manual' for the use in a course of lectures on rhetoric. To compile such a 'compendium' was fully in keeping with Aristotle's general didactic principle that in the several domains of human knowledge and human learning, it is always of great advantage to know something about the experiences, achievements and contributions (as well as the errors) of others. Hence, Aristotle makes it a practice to review the ideas of his predecessors on the subject he is about to discuss.[34] But it cannot be determined with any degree of certainty whether this particular 'florilegium' is related to the course of lectures which was delivered by the young Aristotle in the fifties while he was still a 'junior member' of the Academy, or whether it was connected with a course of lectures given by Aristotle in the Lyceum at a later date, some traces of which can be found in Aristotle's extant *Rhetoric*. Cicero, who highly praises the *suavitas et brevitas dicendi* of its author, observed that on account of these qualities, the Τεχνῶν Συναγωγή by far surpasses all other works of its kind.[35]

H. Diels related the Τέχνης τῆς Θεοδέκτου Συναγωγῆς (one book),[36] rather than the Τεχνῶν Συναγωγή, to Aristotle's early course of lectures on rhetoric.[37] The authorship of the Τέχνης τῆς Θεοδέκτου Συναγωγῆς, subsequently quoted as the Θεοδέκτου, is much debated, however. Several ancient authors, including Quintilian,[38] Dionysius of Halicarnassus[39] and others,[40] seem to credit this composition to Aristotle. Cicero, on the other hand, ascribes it to Theodectes.[41] Aristotle, *Rhetoric* 1410 b 2, is said to refer to the Θεοδέκτου, although it is impossible to determine whether he cites his own work or that of someone else.[42]

In the light of these conflicting ancient *testimonia*, more recent Aristotelian scholarship has developed a variety of rather startling theses. V. Rose first declared that, in *Rhetoric* 1410 b 2, Aristotle refers back to the Θεοδέκτου (which he considered the authentic work of Theodectes) rather than to the Τεχνῶν Συναγωγή.[43] However, Rose soon revised his opinion. Proceeding on the assumption that all of the so-called Aristotelian dialogues, including the Θεοδέκτου, were simply spurious and hence not properly assigned to Aristotle, he suggested that the reference found in *Rhetoric* 1410 b 2 is merely a scholion added to the Aristotelian text at a later date.[44] E. Heitz, who concurred with V. Rose on the fact that the reference in *Rhetoric* 1410 b 2 could very well be a later (and mistaken) scholion, was inclined to consider the Θεοδέκτου the work of Theodectes.[45] E. Zeller, who refused to commit himself on this involved issue, argued that, if the Θεοδέκτου were the authentic work of Aristotle (and there exists no evidence either to prove or disprove this), then the only way to explain this curious title is to assume that Aristotle had dedicated this work to his friend and pupil, Theodectes.[46]

Finally, H. Diels, who relied a great deal on the testimony of Valerius Maximus,[47] proposed that the Θεοδέκτου is an authentic Aristotelian composition, and that it constitutes the earliest and rather inadequate version or 'draft' of the extant Aristotelian *Rhetoric*.[48] In support of this thesis, Diels advanced the following argument: the Θεοδέκτου was written while Plato was still alive and while Aristotle offered a course of lectures in rhetoric at the Academy. Theodectes, formerly a disciple of Isocrates, came to be the pupil and close friend of Aristotle. When Aristotle left Athens in 348–47 B.C., Theodectes remained behind and took over the 'lectureship' in rhetoric which was vacated by Aristotle's departure. He made full use of the original materials or 'florilegium' which Aristotle had prepared and used when he himself taught this course (Τεχνῶν Συναγωγή ?). Theodectes later published these materials (or had them published by one of his disciples) under his own name. In 335–34 B.C., Aristotle returned to Athens only to discover that his old 'florilegium,' in all likelihood greatly enlarged and fully kept up to date by Theodectes, was a rather effective, if not an excellent, text. After the death of Theodectes, Aristotle resumed the teaching of rhetoric. He worked over and improved upon this 'florilegium' which, after many editorial revisions, ultimately came to be the extant Aristotelian *Rhetoric*.[49]

The hypotheses of H. Diels, as well as those advanced by other scholars, were successfully refuted by F. Solmsen. Solmsen maintained that since the ancient 'catalogues' of Aristotle's writings mention a Τέχνης τῆς Θεοδέκτου Συναγωγῆς, it follows that Aristotle simply made his own 'resumé' of the subject, using as his model the *Treatise on the Art of Rhetoric* originally composed by Theodectes.[50] Solmsen also pointed out that, judging from the few surviving fragments and doxographical references, Theodectes' theories of rhetoric were quite distinct from those advocated by Aristotle. Moreover, Solmsen insisted that in *Rhetoric*, Book III, chapters 13–19, Aristotle is largely inspired by, or at least makes constant references to, Theodectes' theories. Aristotle did so, in the opinion of Solmsen, in order to demonstrate the extent to which his own views differed from, or coincided with, those of Theodectes. Hence, *Rhetoric* III. 13–19, which undoubtedly constitutes a self-contained discussion, may also be called a confrontation between Aristotle and Theodectes (and Isocrates). This being so, it may be contended that in *Rhetoric* III. 13–19, Aristotle is somewhat influenced by Theodectes (or Isocrates); that for primarily didactic purposes, he outlines here Theodectes' views on rhetoric; and that he takes issue with these views. Already some of the ancient authors and literary critics took notice of this fact, but, due to a tragic misunderstanding, they labored under the erroneous notion that the Θεοδέκτου was originally composed by Aristotle.[51]

Some scholars have attempted to show that certain sections of the extant Aristotelian *Rhetoric* go back to Aristotle's earliest course of lectures on rhetoric. A. Kantelhardt, for instance, believed that he had discovered in the extant Aristotelian *Rhetoric* certain elements which belong to different periods in Aristotle's literary activities. Hence, he claimed that *Rhetoric* 1354 a 11 to 1355 b 23 is the oldest part of this work, dating back to the original Aristotelian course of lectures on rhetoric, or, to use W. Jaeger's terminology, to the ' *Urrhetorik*.'[52] Kantelhardt's genetic or evolutionary hypothesis, on the whole, was accepted and further expanded by F. Solmsen, the disciple of W. Jaeger, who added *Rhetoric* 1354 a 1–11 to the ' *Urrhetorik*.' This ' *Urrhetorik*,' Solmsen continued, in essence dates back to the time when Aristotle offered his first course of lectures on rhetoric in the Academy during the lifetime of Plato.[53]

The theses of Solmsen, in the main, were accepted by W. Jaeger,[54] but rejected by P. Gohlke,[55] the disciple of Jaeger's old antagonist, H. von Arnim. In a way, Gohlke revived the old hypothesis, already announced in the *Rhetorica ad Alexandrum*,[56] that Aristotle composed an early treatise on rhetoric which was subsequently published by Theodectes. This early treatise, Gohlke insisted, reflects Aristotle's teaching of rhetoric during his stay at the Academy.[57] I. Düring proposed that the greater part of the extant *Rhetoric*, namely, Books I and II, with the exception of chapters 23 and 24 of Book II, were composed between 360 and 355 B.C.[58]—a view which probably will not be widely accepted. In other words, Düring suggested nothing less than that the major parts, as well as the dominant doctrines of the extant *Rhetoric* in all their essential aspects, were shaped while Aristotle was still a disciple of Plato and a relatively young member of the Academy. Hence, only Book III and chapters 23 and 24 of Book II would be post-Academic.[59]

In view of the fact that scholars apparently have failed to reach what even remotely might be called a consensus concerning the chronology underlying the evolution of Aristotle's views concerning rhetoric, it is well-nigh impossible to establish with any degree of certainty either the doctrinal content, or the exact date, of Aristotle's earliest course of lectures on rhetoric or, perchance, that of the Τεχνῶν Συναγωγή.[60] Since with one possible exception (the *Gryllus*) none of Aristotle's earliest dialogues or exoteric compositions may be safely related to this 'course,' we will have to consider the somewhat unreliable *testimonia* of ancient biographers and 'literary critics,' as well as rely on some other 'circumstantial evidence,' in order to learn something more definite about this 'course.'

Judging from all the available *testimonia*, it might be maintained that Aristotle's earliest course of lectures on rhetoric owed its origin to the general and personal feeling of antagonism and resentment, a spirit of fierce rivalry, which existed between the Academy (or Aristotle) and Isocrates and his school of rhetoric.[61] Perhaps it stemmed from Aristotle's or the Academy's conviction that, both as an orator and a teacher of rhetoric, Isocrates was worse than disappointing[62] and that the particular brand of philosophy which he advocated in his rhetoric was pernicious to the basic philosophic outlook cultivated in the Academy. For Isocrates recommended a distinctly 'realistic,' practical and even pragmatic philosophy[63]—something which Plato and the Academy (and, judging from the *Protrepticus*, the young Aristotle), in their one-sidedly theoretic commitment, rejected outright. This course, then, might also have been instituted in order to combine and integrate rhetoric (Isocrates?) and dialectics (Plato?)[64] with the intention of making rhetoric more 'scientific,'[65] and dialectics more attractive and persuasive.[66] Perhaps Aristotle was also encouraged to offer this course and, incidentally, to attack Isocrates by elaborating on what Plato had said about rhetoric in his *Phaedrus* (268A ff.).[67]

Moreover, around 360 B.C., Aristotle had composed his *Gryllus*[68] which, apart from being influenced by the Platonic *Protagoras* and *Gorgias*, also betrays an acquaintance with Plato's *Phaedrus*, written shortly after 369–68 B.C.[69] The *Gryllus*, it has been suggested, already 'takes a slap' at Isocrates and the obsequious attitude the latter allegedly displayed towards Xenophon on the occasion of the death of Xenophon's son, Gryllus.[70] This seems to follow from Diogenes' statement that '[in the *Gryllus*] Aristotle mentions that there existed a great many authors ... of eulogies of Gryllus, who wrote, in part at least, in order to ingratiate themselves in a servile manner with Gryllus' father [Xenophon]. Hermippus ... asserts that even Isocrates composed an encomium of Gryllus.'[71] It should also be borne in mind that Isocrates was probably the most distinguished disciple of Gorgias of Leontini, whom Plato had viciously attacked in the *Gorgias*; and that in his *Gryllus*, Aristotle probably fashioned some of his invectives against Isocrates after Plato's *Gorgias*.[72] The thesis that in the *Gryllus* Aristotle denounces Isocrates (as well as some other rhetoricians) seems to find some additional support in Cephisodorus, a pupil of Isocrates. This Cephisodorus wrote an *Against Aristotle* (in four books), in which he denounced Aristotle for having maligned Isocrates[73] and for having criticized Isocrates' rhetorical methods, educational views and general philosophic outlook.[74]

Hence, the Platonic *Phaedrus* and the Aristotelian *Gryllus* might be considered the two 'pivotal points of reference' with the help of which we might attempt to determine the approximate date as well as the likely doctrinal content of Aristotle's course of lectures on rhetoric. The *Gryllus* probably became the occasion for Aristotle's offering (or being permitted to offer) this course in the Academy, especially since in this dialogue he seems to have demonstrated not only his qualifications as a teacher of rhetoric, but also his ability and determination to stand up to and denounce the mighty Isocrates, a man much disliked by Plato and the members of the Academy.[75] The Platonic *Phaedrus* and the notions about the true nature and proper use of rhetoric and dialectics cultivated in the Academy probably furnished the general program of how rhetoric should be taught.[76]

If this is so, then the technique of writing dialogues, of discussing an intricate topic or of arguing a complex philosophic issue also had to change. To some extent, philosophy had to abandon the 'old fashioned' rhetoric and dialectics, and develop in accordance with the new 'expository style' initiated by the Platonic *Phaedrus*. From now on the traditional dialogue came to depend more on its internal structure as a whole and on systematic argument, rather than on the specific character or ability of the discussants (as it did in the early dialogues of Plato). In this fashion, the dialogue as such gained not only in unity of scientific presentation and methodical progression, but also in real content and philosophic depth. Lengthy theoretical examinations of the subject matter under discussion as well as intricate scientific or logical demonstrations conducted in methodical progression take the place of scintillating verbal duels so characteristic of Plato's 'obstetric' dialogues. Already in his later dialogues, Plato had to come to realize the necessity of changing over from the 'obstetric question and answer game' to the tight logic of the 'dialogue of discussion.' This 'dialogue of discussion,' which Aristotle subsequently adopted in some of his early compositions, was simply a novel manifestation of the fact that the scientific or systematic element gradually and inexorably asserted itself also in the particular form in which philosophic discussions were carried on.[77] It is not impossible, rather indeed it is most likely, that in his course of lectures on rhetoric Aristotle also taught this 'new dialectics' or scientific form of philosophic argumentation and presentation.[78] Moreover, there can be little doubt that this new form of literary expression advocated as well as employed by Aristotle in his early writings owed a debt to Plato's oral teachings and, surprisingly enough, to Isocrates' prose style.

If we are correct in our assumption that the Platonic *Phaedrus* and the Aristotelian *Gryllus* constitute the 'two pivotal points of reference' in any determination of the approximate date as well as the probable doctrinal content of Aristotle's course of lectures on rhetoric and, incidentally, of the Τεχνῶν Συναγωγή, then it also would be fairly safe to surmise, as do F. Solmsen[79] and I. Düring,[80] that this course of lectures offered by Aristotle in the Academy was first delivered between 360 and 355 B.C. This thesis apparently receives additional support from the fact that the *Antidosis* of Isocrates, which among other matters, also contains some very sharp attacks upon Aristotle and the manner in which he taught rhetoric,[81] was published around 352 B.C.—an indication that Aristotle must have taught this subject for some time. More than that: the *Antidosis* might also reveal that in this course of lectures Aristotle attacked Isocrates and his views on rhetoric in a manner which warranted an equally stinging reply. This may be gathered from *Antidosis* 258 ff.: 'Even among the professors of disputations [Isocrates seems to refer here to the Platonic Academy and to Aristotle] there are some who talk . . . abusively of the art of speaking on general and useful topics . . . because they think that by denouncing this art they will enhance their own standing. I could probably say much nastier things of these people than they are saying of me, but I shall refrain from doing so. . . . I do not wish to descend to the level of men whom envy has made blind. . . . I shall show you clearly that we, who are occupied with political discourse and whom they call contentious, are more considerate than they are. Although they are always saying disparaging things about me, I shall not answer them in kind. . . . I do not, however, think it proper to apply the term "philosophy" to a training which is of no help to us in the present either in our speech or in our actions, but rather I would call it a sort of mental gymnastics. . . . I would advise young men to spend some time in these disciplines [*scil.*, in philosophy and logic], but not to allow their minds to be dried up by these essentially barren subtleties. . . . For I am of the opinion that such curiosities of thought are on a par with the juggler's tricks which, though they profit no one, still nonetheless attract great crowds of empty-headed people. . . .'[82]

It is not impossible, indeed it is quite probable, that the Τεχνῶν Συναγωγή, this 'florilegium' or 'manual' designed for the use in a course of lectures on rhetoric, was composed somewhere between 360 and 355 B.C. To date this work, as well as Aristotle's earliest course of lectures on rhetoric, later than the year 355, might run into serious problems: After 355, and possibly a little before that time, Aristotle began to concentrate on strictly philosophical topics, as evidenced, for instance, by the *On the Good* and the *On (the) Ideas*—two early dialogues which are commonly dated about, or shortly after, the year 357–56 B.C.[83] To date this course of lectures prior to the year 360–59 B.C., on the other hand, would be fatal to the reasonable assumption that the composition (and apparent success) of the *Gryllus*, which carried the significant 'subtitle' of *On Rhetoric*, and which is commonly dated around 360–59 B.C.[84] was instrumental in securing Aristotle the 'lectureship' in rhetoric at the Academy. Hence, the year 357 B.C., incidentally the probable year in which Aristotle completed his 'pre-philosophic studies' and commenced his philosophic studies as a member of the 'inner circle' of 'initiates'—when, in other words, he began actively to participate in the internal discussions of certain problems and issues of Platonic philosophy—appears to be the most likely date for his beginning to lecture on, or teach, the proper art of rhetoric. In the light of the available evidence, this assumption seems to be quite reasonable.

Chapter IX

Aristotle Leaves the Academy*

Plato died in 348–47 B.C., at the age of eighty or eighty-one, during the archonship of Theophilus or in the first year of the 108th Olympiad.[1] According to a widespread and almost universally accepted tradition, one which has found an honored and lasting place in our current books on the 'History of Ancient Greek Philosophy,' Aristotle left the Academy and departed from Athens soon after Plato's death, repairing to Atarneus or Assos in north-western Asia Minor, where he stayed with Hermias of Atarneus. It would appear, therefore, that the death of Plato was the prime, if not the sole reason for Aristotle's rather sudden departure in 348–47 B.C. Moreover, since he did not succeed Plato in the scholarchate of the Academy, he had no reason for staying any longer. It has been conjectured, however, that Plato died in the spring of 347 B.C., probably in May of that year,[2] although this is by no means certain. In any event, the particular circumstances surrounding the rather sudden withdrawal of Aristotle, not only from the Academy but also from Athens in the year 348–47 B.C., properly re-question the ultimate cause or causes of this significant as well as puzzling incident.

The widely accepted version or interpretation of the event, namely, that the death of Plato precipitated Aristotle's departure from the Academy (and from Athens), is most persuasive indeed. We know, for instance, that, although Plato apparently had a very high opinion of Aristotle and his intellectual ability and achievements,[3] and although Aristotle was rightly considered 'Plato's most genuine disciple,'[4] he was not chosen to succeed Plato in the scholarchate of the Academy. The post fell to Speusippus, presumably at the personal request of Plato who was Speusippus' uncle.[5] It seems more than likely, therefore, that Aristotle, disillusioned and frustrated and perhaps disappointed in the scholarly as well as human stature of Speusippus, should simply sever his connections with the Academy (and with Speusippus) and seek a more appreciative intellectual environment. But this still leaves unexplained the reason for Aristotle's rather sudden departure from Athens.

It has also been suggested that, since Aristotle was no longer in complete agreement with certain basic aspects of Plato's fundamental teachings, his departure was merely the final step in a gradual but apparently unavoidable process of intellectual alienation between teacher and disciple, which had been going on for some time. Out of personal respect for, or deference to, his aged and venerable preceptor and friend, Aristotle, who apparently was a sensitive and considerate person, simply had postponed taking this final and irrevocable step until after the death of Plato. There undoubtedly existed doctrinal, methodological and perhaps personal differences between the basic philosophic positions held by Plato and by the majority of Plato's associates in the Academy, and certain views which Aristotle had advanced in such early compositions as the *On the Good*, the *On (the) Ideas*, perhaps in the *Protrepticus*, and most certainly in the *On Philosophy*, provided the latter was written before the year 348–47 B.C.[6] Ancient literature is replete with stories about the many doctrinal or philosophic differences that existed between Plato and Aristotle while the latter was still a member of the Academy.[7] But not all these stories are reliable. Some were plainly invented by Aristotle's detractors who wished to make the latter appear to have been an ungrateful and conceited person. Others probably originated with certain pro-Aristotelian authors or biographers who wished to make it appear that Aristotle was an original thinker who owed little, if anything, to Plato's teachings. It should also be borne in mind that Plato himself was fully aware of the essentially mythical background of his ultimate philosophic position. Hence, he freely admitted that his position was but one among several possible premises.[8] In so doing, Plato, at least by implication, granted his disciples and associates in the Academy the right of going their own intellectual ways. This being so, it would be difficult to maintain that doctrinal differences with Plato prompted Aristotle to depart from the Academy and from Athens. After all, Xenocrates, Eudemus, Eudoxus and other members of the Academy likewise disagreed with some of Plato's views without finding it necessary to sever their connections with the Academy. Moreover, some *Vitae Aristotelis* emphasize that it was simply unthinkable that Aristotle, who as a Macedonian 'resident alien' in Athens had no influence or standing in that city, should quarrel with Plato, who counted among his friends and relatives some of the most powerful Athenian citizens.[9]

Tradition also has it that Aristotle was not on the best of personal terms with some of the more influential members of the Academy[10] and, we may surmise, with the vast majority of the Athenian populace.[11] In 367 B.C., he had come to Athens as a stranger from the 'barbaric' or 'semi-barbaric' north, and throughout the twenty years of his association with the Academy was probably looked upon by the decidedly bigoted, anti-intellectual and xenophobic majority of the Athenians as an unwelcome foreigner who lived in Athens by mere sufferance.[12] Accordingly, after Plato's death there there was apparently nothing to keep Aristotle in Athens and in the Academy. He pulled up stakes on his own initiative and left for Assos (or Atarneus or, perhaps, for Macedonia). The plausibility of these arguments is such that in the past no one dared to offer them serious challenge.

The reasons why in 348-47 B.C. Aristotle went to Hermias of Atarneus rather than, let us say, to Macedonia, Chalcis (on the island of Euboea) or, perhaps, to Stagira, are usually stated as follows: Proxenus, who had married Aristotle's sister, Arimneste, and who had been Aristotle's 'guardian,'[13] is said to have been a friend and countryman of Hermias.[14] Hence, there might have existed some personal ties or associations between Aristotle's family and Hermias.[15] It must also be borne in mind that Erastus and Coriscus, two former members of the Platonic Academy as well as natives of Scepsis (a town not too far from Assos), had moved to Atarneus or Assos prior to Plato's death, and had become closely associated with Hermias whom they counselled on matters of statecraft.[16] This being so, Aristotle might have expected to be welcomed in Atarneus or Assos, where he would find some old acquaintances or 'classmates' who would grant him a congenial refuge.[17] Here he might also find and enjoy that intellectual freedom which he apparently craved, and perhaps even a congenial atmosphere for renewed intellectual activities.

The following is probably a reasonable explanation of why in the year 348-47 B.C. Aristotle did not retreat to Chalcis where he had a house which originally belonged to his maternal ancestors:[18] on the instigation of King Philip of Macedonia, the island of Euboea had revolted against Athens (in 349-48 B.C.) and, hence, was in a state of turmoil. An attempt on the part of Athens to retake the island failed dismally. In view of these unsettled conditions, Aristotle might understandably have preferred not to go to Chalcis. Stagira, where Aristotle or his paternal ancestors had a house, had been destroyed by King Philip in 349 B.C. (thanks to Aristotle's intercession with Philip or Alexander, the town was apparently rebuilt at a later time). Hence, he could not return to his native city which in 348–47 B.C. was still in shambles.[19] This raises the further and certainly interesting question: why did Aristotle, the Macedonian, philo-Macedonian and the personal friend of King Philip as well as of the Macedonian royal house, not return to Macedonia? There are several plausible answers to this query. By the year 348–47 B.C., both of Aristotle's parents were dead, as were probably the majority of his Macedonian relatives. Unlike in the year 343–42 B.C., in 348 B.C. he had no formal invitation from King Philip to join the royal court in Pella (or Mieza). Perhaps he abhorred the idea of asking Philip for refuge. It is possible, however, that Aristotle first went to Macedonia for a short visit, as he had probably done in the more recent past. There he might have consulted with King Philip, an old friend of Aristotle's family. The present author has attempted to show that throughout his mature life Aristotle was frequently engaged in 'diplomatic activities' of one sort or another, something which also his ancient biographers seem to stress.[20] It is not impossible that King Philip, who planned the conquest of Thrace and, perhaps, an invasion of Persia or, at least, of Asia Minor, suggested to Aristotle to go to Hermias of Atarneus and act there as a sort of Macedonian 'political agent.' Hermias' domain was strategically located not too far from the Hellespont and, hence, could become an important basis for the encirclement of Thrace as well as a vital bridgehead for an invasion of Asia Minor and for an attack upon Persia which at that time was plagued by serious internal disorders. Subsequent events seem to indicate that Hermias had some political dealings with Macedonia. Naturally, this explanation of Aristotle's journey to Atarneus (or Assos) is conjecture. We do not know whether as early as 348–47 B.C. King Philip entertained plans for an invasion of Asia Minor. But by that time his plans to conquer Thrace had certainly matured. If our conjecture should prove to be correct, then it might also be assumed that Aristotle journeyed to Atarneus in the spring of 347 B.C., and that he went there from Macedonia where he had spent the winter of 348–47 B.C.[21]

Three passages found in the biographical tradition of Aristotle seem to substantiate a challenge to the hypothesis that Plato's death occasioned the departure of Aristotle from the Academy and from Athens. *II Vita Aristotelis Syriaca* 2–4, relates that 'at the age age of seventeen he [*scil.*, Aristotle] became a disciple of Plato, the philosopher. And as long as he studied philosophy under the guidance of Plato, he was constantly preoccupied with him [*scil.*, with Plato and Platonic philosophy]. But being frightened by the execution of Socrates, he [*scil.*, Aristotle] retired from Athens and stayed near the Hellespont. When Plato died, Speusippus ... took charge of Plato's school ... [and] sent a message [to Aristotle] asking him to come back and take charge of Plato's school.' [22] Eubulides maintains that Aristotle was not present (no longer in Athens or no longer an active member of the Academy?) at the time of Plato's death. [23] And Diogenes Laertius V. 2 laconically reports that 'Aristotle left the Academy while Plato was still alive.' [24] *II Vita Syriaca*, Eubulides and Diogenes Laertius, then, maintain (or imply) that Plato was still living at the time Aristotle left Athens and the Academy. But only *II Vita Syriaca* explicitly states a reason for the latter's departure: Aristotle was 'frightened by the execution of Socrates.' This curious remark calls for some explanation.

In the year 349 B.C., King Philip of Macedonia began to subdue the Greek cities in Chalcidice. In order to escape capture and possible destruction by the Macedonians, the city of Olynthus entered into a defensive alliance with Athens. When the city was threatened by the approaching Macedonian army, an Athenian relief force was promptly dispatched. But the aid arrived too late to prevent the storming and ravaging of Olynthus in the summer of 348 B.C. This incident, together with Demosthenes' fiery denunciations of King Philip (the *First Philippic* and the three *Olynthiac Orations*) aroused intense anti-Macedonian feelings among the majority of the Athenians. Aristotle, a 'resident Macedonian alien,' was probably suspected of sympathizing with the enemy. Moreover, he still had close ties with the Macedonian royal house and with King Philip in particular, [25] and it is not unlikely that in the recent past he had paid visits to Pella or Mieza, certainly a cause for suspicion and enmity among the patriotic (and xenophobic) Athenians. As so often in days of anxiety, stress and frustration, the city of Athens at that time was ripe with malicious gossip, general ill-feeling and an almost paranoid distrust of everyone, especially of persons who had more recently come from Macedonia to Athens. And finally, in his speech in support of Sophocles' abortive motion (of 306 B.C.) to have all alien philosophers expelled from Athens on account of their 'subversive' activities or attitudes, Demochares alleges that, among other treasonable acts, Aristotle had denounced the wealthiest citizens of Olynthus to Philip of Macedonia. [26] It may fairly be assumed that on account of their commercial interests or business connections, the rich Olynthiac merchants were politically affiliated with mercantile Athens and, hence, were 'pro-Athenian.' In the same speech Demochares also maintains that Aristotle had sent many 'letters' ('intelligence reports'?) to Macedonia, the enemy, and that these 'letters' had been intercepted by the Athenians. It is not impossible that these 'letters,' the content of which might have been detrimental to the political interests and aspirations of Athens during the crucial period of 349–348 B.C., supplied Philip with vital political information. Should the allegations of Demochares be correct, something which we cannot possibly ascertain, then during the last years of his association with Plato and the Platonic Academy, Aristotle would also have been guilty of anti-Athenian or, better, pro-Macedonian leanings and actions. Such an attitude would not be unusual for a Macedonian as well as a personal friend of King Philip such as Aristotle. Hence, after the fall of Olynthus in the summer of 348 B.C., Aristotle had every reason to fear the vindictiveness of the Athenians, who in their outrage over Philip's attack on Olynthus and its subsequent capture as well as destruction, were looking for a scapegoat on whom they could vent their anger.

In the heat of this widespread resentment, threats were probably flung at all Macedonian residents and sympathizers in the city and at Aristotle in particular. Fearing that under the circumstances he might suffer 'the fate of Socrates'[27]—that the Athenians might do to him some serious harm—Aristotle simply departed from Athens. He did so in the late summer or early fall of 348 B.C., that is, some time before the death of Plato, seeking refuge probably first in Macedonia and then with Hermias in Atarneus (or Assos),[28] which is, as reported in *II Vita Syriaca* 3, 'near the Hellespont.' Hence, his departure from Athens and from the Academy was not simply a change of locale or a leisurely withdrawal, but rather a hasty flight ultimately caused by the capture and sack of Olynthus by Macedonia.

Also of interest and possible importance is the statement found in *II Vita Syriaca* 4, that upon Plato's death, Speusippus 'sent a message to him [*scil.*, to Aristotle] asking him to come back and take charge of Plato's school.' There seem to be two possible interpretations of this report (unless the author of *II Vita Syriaca* confounds Aristotle with Xenocrates):[29] either at that time Aristotle was already in Assos (or Atarneus) or Macedonia, or he had seceded from the Academy at some earlier date and had already established his own independent school in Athens (a most unlikely development).[30] In view of Speusippus' failing health—at the time he assumed the scholarchate of the Academy he was already seriously ailing[31] and he was to die in 339–38 B.C.—it is not surprising that he should try to bring back a young man of the intellectual stature, energy and ability of Aristotle. Since Xenocrates likewise had left the Academy, there was still a greater need for Aristotle's talented assistance in running the Academy. In any event,

II Vita Syriaca 3–4 plainly states that at the time of Plato's death Aristotle was no longer with the Academy and, in all likelihood, had left Athens.

Should our interpretation of *II Vita Syriaca* 3–4 be correct, then this invaluable text would seem to furnish the sole surviving biographical evidence which satisfactorily accounts for Aristotle's sudden flight from Athens and from the Platonic Academy in 348 B.C., that is, before Plato's death.[32] It will be noticed, further, that the circumstances surrounding and producing this flight closely parallel those necessitating his hasty withdrawal in 323 B.C., about a year before he died.[33]

It may be observed that the view that doctrinal differences with Plato and with certain basic doctrines held by the Academy drove Aristotle from the Academy and from Athens in 348–47 B.C. makes little sense. Provided our information is reliable, these differences date back to at least the publication of Aristotle's *On the Good* and *On (the) Ideas*, which were composed around 357–55 B.C.[34] These two works were highly critical of certain basic doctrines propagated by Plato. Hence, if Aristotle really intended to spare Plato a sense of disappointment or embarrassment, he should have left in 355 B.C., or thereabouts, rather than wait until Plato's death, when there was little need for him to withdraw on grounds of philosophic dissent. A secession from the Academy and from its philosophic teachings, however, would not have entailed Aristotle's flight from Athens, unless we were to assume that in view of Plato's influence (and that of his friends and associates) among the politically and socially powerful men in Athens,[35] a withdrawal from the Academy was tantamount to an expulsion from Athens. It has already been pointed out that, according to *Laws* 898E, Plato himself did not regard his philosophic position as being absolutely binding on his associates and disciples who, thus, were granted, at least by implication, the right to disagree with their master and teacher and to enjoy a large measure of intellectual freedom.[36]

Against the thesis that the 'political climate' in Athens after the fall of Olynthus was the prime and, perhaps, the sole cause for Aristotle's rather sudden departure in 348 B.C., it has been argued that Aristotle left Athens and the Academy together with Xenocrates. Hence, it has been maintained that this dual departure was precipitated by Speusippus' election or appointment to the scholarchate of the Academy after the death of Plato: Aristotle and Xenocrates felt that they could not possibly remain associated with a school guided and controlled by a man whom they personally disliked and whose philosophic talents and interests they seem to have held in low esteem.[37] This argument, which attributes Aristotle's (and Xenocrates') departure from Athens and from the Academy in 348–47 B.C. not directly to the death of Plato, but rather to an incident connected with Plato's death, namely, to Speusippus' accession to the scholarchate of the Academy, seems to overlook the following: the existing Athenian laws of succession, it cannot be emphasized often enough, demanded that the estate of the deceased should be passed on to a near male relative and thus be kept within agnatic lines. Since Speusippus was the son of Plato's sister Potone (and since Plato himself had no direct descendants of his own), Speusippus' assumption of the scholarchate after the death of Plato, that is, the transfer of the title to the Academy to Speusippus *mortis causa* was, legally speaking, unavoidable, not to say, a foregone conclusion—a fact with which Aristotle (and Xenocrates) must have been acquainted for several years prior to the death of Plato. In any event, Speusippus' accession to the scholarchate was not the result of an arbitrary or capricious act, but rather the practical result of an established legal policy.[38]

In summary, it might be contended that Aristotle left Athens and the Academy *prior* to the death of Plato, which probably occurred early (May?) in 347 B.C. He left, or better, fled because of a rising tide of anti-Macedonian feelings which, especially after the capture and sack of Olynthus by King Philip in the summer of 348 B.C., became rampant in Athens. According to Demetrius, Aristotle wrote a letter to Antipater in which he stated that in the year 348 B.C. he 'journeyed to Pella because of the King [Philip] . . . .'[39] This bit of information, provided the letter is not a later forgery, seems to imply that because of Philip's conquest of Olynthus, Aristotle was forced to leave Athens and seek refuge in Macedonia. It is reasonable to assume, therefore, that he departed from Athens and from the Academy in the summer or early fall of 348 B.C. Thus, contrary to a widely held opinion which has become an almost sacred tradition, the death of Plato had nothing to do with Aristotle's departure. On this, as on other occasions, Aristotle's close personal and political ties with Philip of Macedonia and with the Macedonian royal house in general—ties which seem to date back almost to the time the Stagirite reached his boyhood— decisively determined some of the salient events in his life.[40]

Chapter X

Was Aristotle Actually the Chief Preceptor of Alexander the Great?*

According to general tradition, Aristotle went to Macedonia in 343–42 B.C., at the personal request of King Philip who invited him to take charge of the education of young Alexander.[1] Although this story seems to be firmly established and universally accepted, Edward Zeller[2] long ago pointed out that, barring the date, it lacks substantial confirmation or, to be more exact, finds little or no support in the surviving literature and historiography of the fourth century B.C. All we know, Zeller insisted, is that Onesicritus, a disciple of Diogenes of Sinope (the Cynic), gave an unreliable, encomiastic and frequently romantic as well as distorted account of Alexander's education.[3] Diogenes Laertius also relates that this account was primarily an encomium of Alexander, and that it was composed in imitation of Xenophon's *Cyropaedia*. If this is so, then Onesicritus' report would be part of that particular 'mirror-for-princes literature' which, it could be argued, probably begins with Antisthenes who composed a *Cyrus*,[4] a *Cyrus or On Sovereignty*,[5] a *Cyrus or the Beloved*[6] and a *Cyrus or The Scout*.[7] Xenophon's *Cyropaedia*, it has been argued, was strongly influenced by these Antisthenian works which, unfortunately, are completely lost. This, then, would relegate Onesicritus' *How Alexander was Educated* (the presumed title of his work) and Xenophon's *Cyropaedia* to the realm of fiction or semi-fiction.[8] Onesicritus' work, in particular, seems to have been a sort of 'didactic essay,' discussing in great detail, though not always reliably, the life and the training of Alexander. According to Zeller, Marsyas of Pella likewise refers to the early education of Alexander.[9] This Marsyas, who apparently was a Macedonian nobleman and perhaps a 'companion' of Alexander, claims in his report that he had been a 'fellow student' of Alexander. But he does not relate that he ever studied under the tutelage of Aristotle. Marsyas was the author of a *History of King Philip* which, in turn, might have been a part of a larger *History of Macedonia* (in ten books), as well as the possible author of an *Education of Alexander*. Unlike Onesicritus, Marsyas must be considered a serious and reliable historian. Neither Onesicritus nor Marsyas, however, mentions Aristotle as the preceptor of Alexander. It appears, therefore, that those reporters who are closest to the event either knew nothing about Aristotle's efforts to educate Alexander, or simply ignored the alleged role which Aristotle played in the upbringing and training of the young prince. This fact is in itself both puzzling and disturbing.

The account of Onesicritus, as a matter of fact, would indicate that Alexander might have studied Cynic philosophy (Antisthenes and Diogenes of Sinope),[10] rather than Platonic (or 'Aristotelian') philosophy under the tutelage of Aristotle. In any event, it has reasonably been claimed that Onesicritus was ultimately responsible for Alexander's alleged 'cosmopolitanism,' the more so, since cosmopolitanism is traditionally related to certain Cynic teachings. Aristotle's fundamental outlook, on the other hand, is said to have been distinctly 'chauvinistic.' The only early source corroborating the story that Aristotle was possibly the teacher of Alexander is the account of Alexinus of Elis, a notorious detractor and slanderer of Aristotle, who wrote about a generation after Aristotle. According to Aristocles, 'Alexinus ... makes Alexander, while he was still a boy, converse with his father Philip, and pour contempt on Aristotle's doctrines ....'[11] In other words, young Alexander vehemently and contemptuously objected to Philip's suggestion that Aristotle should undertake the education of the prince and heir apparent. And who would be able to determine whether the protests of Alexander, a strong-willed child to whom his father more often than not deferred, did not prevail in this argument? The unusual story related by Aristocles (or Alexinus) would also fit perfectly into the general tradition: according to ample and reliable information, after the year 343-42 B.C., Aristotle spent considerable time at the Macedonian court. We may assume that through his father Nicomachus, who had been the friend, intimate advisor and personal physician of King Amyntas III of Macedonia (the father of Philip), Aristotle had close and possibly intimate contacts with the Macedonian royal house. In view of the fact that Aristotle was staying in Pella and perhaps was a member of the royal household, it is possible that at one time Philip might have suggested to his son that he should study under the supervision of Aristotle, who seems to have enjoyed the respect as well as the confidence of both King Philip and his wife Olympias, the mother of Alexander.[12] This suggestion apparently met with ridicule and opposition on the part of Alexander and hence might have been withdrawn.

There also exists a tradition according to which Xenocrates, the Academician and, in a way, the 'rival' of Aristotle, rather than Aristotle himself, was the preceptor of Alexander. This might be inferred from Plutarch who quotes some older sources which insist that Alexander had requested Xenocrates (his preceptor?) to compose for him *Didactic Essays on Kingship* (Ὑποθῆκαι περὶ βασιλείας).[13] Indeed, Xenocrates is credited with having written an *Elementary Principles of Kingship, Dedicated* (or *Addressed*) *to Alexander* (Στοιχεῖα πρὸς Ἀλέξανδρον περὶ βασιλείας) in four books.[14] The claim that Xenocrates rather than Aristotle was Alexander's tutor might find additional support in the story that while on a (political?) mission to Philip from Athens (?), probably between 342 and 338 B.C., Xenocrates was the only member of his embassy who could not be bribed by Philip. Impressed by this strength of character,[15] Philip might well have asked Xenocrates to take over the education of his son.

Plutarch, probably relying on some earlier and apparently dependable sources, reports that Alexander's preceptors and teachers were Leonidas, a kinsman of Alexander's mother Olympias, and Lysimachus, the Acarnanian.[16] Leonidas apparently was a strict disciplinarian who taught Alexander how to endure physical hardships and privations. Lysimachus, on the other hand, seems to have been a more congenial person as well as a man of no particular intellectual refinement, who liked to compare himself to the Homeric Phoenix, King Philip to Peleus and Alexander to Achilles.[17] Only subsequently does Plutarch, who combines early and late traditions, mention Aristotle as the preceptor of Alexander, probably on the basis of a much later and possibly 'romantic' (Hellenistic) tradition.

It is also rather disturbing that the Syriac and, especially, the Arabic biographers of Aristotle have little, if anything, to say about Aristotle's alleged tutorship. This is even more surprising, and more disturbing, in view of the fact that the Arabs in particular had a very high regard for both Aristotle and Alexander. Hence, one may assume that they would have been inclined not only to link together their two 'heroes' in a relationship of teacher and pupil, but also to expand on this theme as well as embellish it with many anecdotes or moral comments. Mubsahir (*II VA*), although conceding that among the many illustrious disciples of Aristotle was 'King Alexander,'[18] rather briefly mentions that 'Philip sent for him [*scil.*, Aristotle] and he [*scil.*, Aristotle] went to him in Macedonia and stayed there teaching philosophy [to Alexander?] until Alexander marched off against the countries of Asia.'[19] And Usaibia (*IV VA*) simply records that 'Philip sent for him [*scil.*, Aristotle]. He went to Macedonia and taught there until Alexander moved across to the lands of Asia.'[20] But nowhere are we told in these reports, which probably go back to the *Vita Aristotelis* of Ptolemy(-el-Garib),[21] that Aristotle became the personal tutor or the chief preceptor of Alexander.

Equally disturbing and enlightening is the fact that the Stoics in their criticisms and disapproval of Alexander's 'moral deportment' do not expressly mention Aristotle as the tutor of the king. Quintilian,[22] who apparently relies on Diogenes the Babylonian (or Panaetius, a disciple of Diogenes),[23] reports that Leonidas—and not Aristotle—was the main preceptor of Alexander, and that Leonidas was an ineffective tutor who must be held largely responsible for Alexander's defects of character and disposition—for his emotional instability as well as inability to cope with chance and good fortune. Clement of Alexandria, likewise under the influence of Stoic pedagogical theories, also blames Leonidas for Alexander's excesses and intemperance, but does not mention Aristotle among the teachers of Alexander.[24] In short, according to the Stoic critics of Alexander, the vices of the latter were implanted by his (incompetent) tutors who apparently failed completely in their task of instilling in Alexander a sense of restraint. But the Stoics do not refer to Aristotle and his pedagogical influence when they point out Alexander's faulty intellectual, moral and emotional training.[25] This omission, which should not be taken lightly, in itself constitutes weighty evidence in support of the contention that Aristotle was probably not the preceptor of Alexander.

If we can give any credence to Plutarch, Alexander has been credited with having stated once that 'he received life from one [*scil.*, from his father Philip], while the other [*scil.*, Aristotle (?), Leonidas (?), Lysimachus (?), Onesicritus (?)] had taught him to live nobly.'[26] But this statement, which is probably apocryphal and which could very well be a later (Cynic?) invention, is really a Cynic apophthegm. If it does not refer to Aristotle but rather to Onesicritus, the Cynic, we would have another indication of the latter's intellectual influence on Alexander. Onesicritus, but not Aristotle, also accompanied Alexander on his expedition to Asia and so might have been one of the preceptors of Alexander. His influence can still be felt in this apophthegm, provided the latter is historical.[27] Assuming, however, that this apophthegm in fact refers to Aristotle as well as to Aristotle's effectiveness as the teacher of Alexander, then it might be considered part of that Hellenistic literary *genre* which for the pupose of creating a certain literary effect (and also for encomiastic reasons) invented the story that corporeally Alexander was the son of Philip of Macedonia, that is, of the most prominent political and military figure of his time, while intellectually or morally he was the product of the pedagogical genius of Aristotle, the most renowned philosopher of his age.[28] Plutarch, moreover, relates that Alexander was trained in—and capable of— submitting to a most austere life of abnegation, Spartan discipline and physical hardships.[29] These are, however, essential aspects of the Cynic 'ideal of life' which, in all likelihood, Onesicritus the Cynic and Leonidas, rather than Aristotle, had instilled in Alexander.

Finally, according to Gellius, Philip supposedly addressed a letter to Aristotle (in 356 B.C.) in which he announced the birth of Alexander. At the same time, Philip indicated that he had great hopes that one day Aristotle would take over the education of the boy.[30] This particular letter is probably a naïve (encomiastic) forgery dating back to the second century B.C. or, perhaps, to Andronicus of Rhodes. For in 356 B.C., the year Alexander was born, Aristotle was still an untried young man of twenty-eight years, a relatively unknown disciple of Plato who had just completed his 'pre-philosophic studies' at the Academy, a person of little experience, and certainly not one of any repute or fame. It is most unlikely, to say the least, that as early as 356 B.C., King Philip should express the desire to entrust the education of his only son and the heir apparent to the throne of Macedonia, to an unknown as well as inexperienced young man.[31] But if this particular letter is a late forgery, then there exists no particular reason why one should not also reject as spurious a letter by Aristotle supposedly addressed to Philip (about 343 B.C.?) in which the former advertises the fact that he had been Plato's disciple for twenty years and that this experience ought to be a weighty factor in securing for him the position of Alexander's tutor.[32] This letter, which reads like a 'letter of application,' is doubly suspect in view of the fact that at that time Aristotle had somewhat 'drifted away' from Plato and his teachings and, hence, might have been reluctant to mention his former association with Plato. Moreover, at that time Theopompus, the disciple of Isocrates and thus a persistent opponent of Plato (and Aristotle),[33] was a fairly influential man at the Macedonian court. Under the circumstances, a reference to Plato might actually prove to be a liability rather than an asset, a fact of which Aristotle must have been aware. Should this 'letter of application' actually be authentic, although the peculiar circumstances surrounding this incident seem to indicate that it is a belated forgery, then we might also assume that Theopompus, the 'court historian' at Pella and a disciple of Isocrates, probably used every bit of his influence to keep Aristotle from being called to Macedonia as Alexander's tutor. And who might tell whether or not Theopompus was successful?

These are some of the arguments that might be cited in support of the allegation that, after all, Aristotle possibly was *not* the tutor (or chief preceptor) of Alexander, as some later Hellenistic authors and biographers have alleged. Interestingly enough, the several sources attesting to the alleged tutorship of Aristotle are without exception of a relatively late date, late enough to be classified as a part of that romantic fiction which, perhaps for edifying, moralizing or entertainment purposes, at some time began to link together the great sage and the great conqueror, the great thinker and the great doer, the man of ideas and the man of action, in a relationship of teacher and pupil. Such stories, it will be noted, were not uncommon among Hellenistic writers,[34] who on occasion displayed a pronounced proclivity for moralizing and entertaining at the expense of historical truth.[35] But this is not the place to recite the many and wholly fantastic deeds and schemes ascribed recklessly and indiscriminately to Alexander by a host of authors and biographers, beginning about the third, second or first century B.C., for the purpose of glorifying him and entertaining a reading audience.[36] Neither would it be profitable to point out here the many and occasionally serious inconsistencies which frequently not only mar these late reports, but also make them appear mutually irreconcilable.

One plausible explanation for the fairly late tradition which makes Aristotle the tutor of Alexander is the following: After the death of Theophrastus in 287–86 B.C., so the hypothesis goes, the writings of Aristotle 'came to be lost,' only to be recovered (in a seriously damaged state) in the course of the first century B.C.[37] The retrieval of the *Corpus Aristotelicum* during the first century B.C. by Apellicon of Teos, Tyrannion of Amisus and by Andronicus of Rhodes, as might be expected, triggered off an intensive preoccupation with Aristotelian studies (which apparently had been neglected for a considerable length of time), including biographical studies of Aristotle. This preoccupation, which in some literary circles probably assumed the proportions and exaggerations of an intellectual fashion, could not fail to affect Hellenistic literature and Hellenistic biography in general. It is possible that in the course of time Aristotle became included among the great literary heroes and, as such, was linked with other literary heroes, such as Alexander. It might also be claimed that Andronicus of Rhodes, in the general 'Introduction' to his edition of the *Corpus Aristotelicum*—

an Introduction which probably also contained a 'Life of Aristotle'—invented, or at least propagated, the story of Aristotle's having been the preceptor of Alexander.

There is a further argument to bolster this hypothesis. As is commonly known, Alexander had Callisthenes of Olynthus, the nephew or close relative of Aristotle, executed in 327 B.C. The Peripatetics, as well as other philosophers, never forgave Alexander this foul deed. Soon after Alexander's death in 323 B.C., they began their literary attacks on the king, apparently with the full approval of Cassander, who for political reasons disliked Alexander and, hence, wished to discredit him.[38] Thus was started a literary tradition distinctly unfavorable to Alexander. It is very likely that at a later date there grew up a 'romantic tradition' about Alexander, intended primarily to counteract this hostile attitude. What could be more effective than to make Aristotle the preceptor of Alexander, thereby silencing the Aristotelians and countering the Peripatic charges with the allegation that if Alexander was indeed such a monster as the Peripatetics claimed, this was but the result of Aristotle's utter failure as an educator. Naturally, this particular explanation likewise is mere conjecture.[39]

A final, though by no means insignificant, argument in support of the thesis that, after all, Aristotle was not the teacher or chief preceptor of Alexander, is the following: the Peripatetics, and the Stoics in particular, loudly condemned Alexander for his many excesses of intemperance and bad judgment. In so doing, they put the ultimate blame on Alexander's tutors who, it is claimed, completely failed in their task of instilling in Alexander a modicum of reasonableness and moral restraint. But neither the Peripatetics nor the Stoics mention Aristotle among the teachers of Alexander.[40] While in the case of the Peripatetics such an omission might have been deliberate, the Stoics most certainly had no reason to 'protect' Aristotle. Moreover, as far as we know, Epicurus and the Epicureans, the persistent and frequently malicious slanderers of Aristotle, never mention the story that Aristotle had been the preceptor of Alexander. If this had actually been the case, they would most certainly have exploited this story by showing that Aristotle's pernicious influence on the young Alexander was the prime cause for the reprehensible moral and emotional conduct which the king subsequently displayed.

It should also be remembered that, according to what appears to be a well established tradition, in later years Aristotle and Alexander were not on the best of terms. It has already been shown that Alexander allegedly threatened Aristotle with dire reprisals, while Aristotle is said not only to have been mortally afraid of Alexander, but also to have played an active role in the alleged poisoning of Alexander. As a rule, however, the normal teacher–student relationship is one of lasting respect, gratitude and affection, feelings which often become more intense and more meaningful as time passes on. In the light of their mutual dislike, which actually bordered on hate, it might be argued that Aristotle could not have been the teacher of Alexander.[41]

In conclusion, it might be pointed out that the traditional and apparently widely accepted story which makes Aristotle the preceptor and, as a matter of fact, the chief tutor of Alexander, is by no means so firmly established as some people would like us to believe. It is quite possible, however, that between 434–42 and 340 (or 338) B.C. he gave some occasional instructions to Alexander in one form or another. The sources closest in time to this alleged incident in the life of Alexander, namely, Onesicritus and Marsyas, however, are conspicuously silent about Aristotle having been the (regular) preceptor or main tutor of Alexander. But the further in time we move away from this alleged event, the more definite and more detailed these reports become. Perhaps the whole account is just one of those stories which suddenly arise and for some reason become widespread, but whose origins are impossible to ascertain. Here, as elsewhere in the ancient biographical tradition of Aristotle and, for that matter, in the biographical tradition of any prominent personage in antiquity, it is well-nigh impossible to separate fact from fiction in a satisfactory manner.[42] The story that as a preceptor Aristotle had such a beneficial as well as dominant influence on Alexander and Alexander's conception of his regal duties that the latter supposedly exclaimed, 'because I did not benefit anyone, today I have not been a king,'[43] is probably a later invention. As such it should be relegated to the realm of late Hellenistic fabrications or *fabulae* which insisted that Aristotle's writings no less than his deeds, like the military and political accomplishments of Alexander, were deathless gifts to mankind.[44] Ptolemy (-el-Garib), who undoubtedly believed that Aristotle was the chief preceptor of Alexander, in his encomiastic biography of the Stagirite may also have stated or at least implied that by becoming the foremost tutor of Alexander, the conqueror and master of the whole world, Aristotle became the foremost tutor of the whole of mankind.[45]

Chapter XI

Aristotle's Return to Athens in the Year 335-34 B.C.[*]

Aristotle returned to Athens in 335-34 B.C.,[1] that is, during the archonship of Evaenetus (335-34 B.C.),[2] in the second year of the 111th Olympiad.[3] Dionysius of Halicarnassus claims that his return was in some way related to the sudden death of King Philip of Macedonia (in the summer of 336 B.C.).[4] Diogenes Laertius insinuates that the relations between Aristotle and Alexander had become somewhat strained during the preceding years and that Aristotle yearned to return to Athens. This biographer also maintains that when Aristotle thought he had stayed long enough with Alexander, he simply departed for Athens.[5] Al-Mubashir[6] and Usaibia,[7] on the other hand, relate that Aristotle left Alexander when the latter invaded Persia (in 334 B.C.). With Alexander gone off to Asia, Aristotle felt relieved of all duties and responsibilities: He simply disassociated himself from the affairs of the king, of whose plans he did not approve,[8] and thus was able to return to Athens.[9] It appears, therefore, that the ancient biographers of Aristotle had relatively little to say about his return to Athens in the year 335 B.C., and about the reasons why he did so.

In order to understand better the particular circumstances surrounding Aristotle's return to Athens in the year 335-34 B.C., it might be helpful to review briefly Greek and Macedonian history in the years 336 and 335 B.C. Philip of Macedonia was assassinated in the summer of 336 B.C. He was succeeded, though not without some serious difficulties, by his son, Alexander, who at once found himself threatened on all sides by foes and rivals. In Macedonia, Attalus and his followers claimed the throne for the infant son of Cleopatra, the niece (and ward) of Attalus and the second wife of Philip; others supported the bid of Amyntas, the son of Perdiccas and former 'ward' of Philip.[10] With a boldness and speed that bordered on madness, Alexander immediately brought Macedonia back in line. Attalus, Amyntas, and later Cleopatra and her infant, as well as some of the conspirators, were simply removed from the scene through execution or outright murder.[11] Greece, which on the news of Philip's sudden death had revolted against Macedonia, was frightened into quick submission by a speedy show of force. Philip, the founder of the League of Corinth (of 338 B.C.), did not live long enough to consolidate this League, which had been forced upon the Greek states after the battle of Chaeronea. When the news of Philip's assassination reached the Greeks, they regarded all previous agreements and alliances with Macedonia as terminated. The vast majority of the Greek states rejoiced over the death of Philip, believing that this event would once and for all spell the end of Macedonian rule. They discounted completely the ability and willingness of Alexander to restore the political and military supremacy of Macedonia. Demosthenes, who in all matters concerning Macedonia often allowed wishful thinking to control his judgment, actually reported to the general assembly in Athens that the city had nothing to fear from so young and inexperienced a boy as Alexander.[12] Ambracia, which had been smarting under a Macedonian garrison, simply expelled the latter; in a gesture of defiance Aetolia recalled all the anti-Macedonian exiles; and there was great rejoicing both in Athens and Thebes over the murder of Philip. In Thessaly the anti-Macedonian partisans seized political power, and in the east, north and west of Macedonia the Balkan peoples were rising in revolt.

Alexander first descended upon Greece. On the way south he put down the Thessalian uprising by having himself declared the leader (*tagus*) and supreme commander of the Thessalian League, thus securing the military support of the vital Thessalian light cavalry. He then convoked the Amphictionic League and had himself elected its protector. Greece proper, including Athens and Thebes, was simply stunned by this rapid advance. Completely unprepared to offer Alexander any effective resistance, all of Greece, except Sparta, submitted quickly and rather meekly. In a gesture of generosity, Alexander forgave Athens, Thebes and Ambracia for their display of hostility. Next, he re-established and convoked the League of Corinth and had himself elected its supreme commander for the impending war against Persia.[13] Subsequently, in the spring of 335 B.C., he turned upon the Illyrians, Epirotes and Thracians, all of whom he subdued after some spectacular and hard-fought campaigns.

While Alexander was fully preoccupied with these difficult and dangerous campaigns in the Balkans, the Greek cities and states, oblivious of their own impotence, continued agitating against the king. Darius Codomannus, the King of Persia, intended to provoke a protracted war between Greece and Macedonia and thus prevent, or at least postpone, Alexander's planned invasion of Asia. Hence, he sent money as well as agents for that purpose—money which was readily accepted by some of the Greek cities.[14] The threatening defection of Greece was both widespread and serious. Suddenly, the rumor was passed around that Alexander had been slain in battle somewhere in Illyria. Demosthenes, blinded by his furious hatred of Macedonia, actually produced a man who allegedly had witnessed the death of the king. Once more some of the Greek states raised the banner of revolt, calling for the abolition of Macedonian domination. At Thebes the anti-Macedonian democrats, exiled by Philip, immediately returned, seized power and resorted to open violence. They slew Timolaus and Anemoetas, two pro-Macedonian leaders, killed the commander of the Macedonian garrison in Thebes, and laid siege to the Cadmea which was held by Macedonian troops. The signal action of Thebes was followed by other uprisings and acts of violence. Athens sent weapons and supplies to Thebes, and promised to follow up with the dispatch of troops. Aetolia and Elis promptly denounced their allegiance, and the Arcadians marched to the Isthmus of Corinth, ready to join any military action against Macedonia. The hopes of the patriots ran high to the point of recklessness.[15]

Apparently out of nowhere Alexander suddenly appeared, descending upon Greece with lightning-like speed.[16] In a spirit of desperate heroism, Thebes hoped to defy the military might of the enraged king and was immediately put under siege. After a brief struggle, the city was stormed and razed. The fate of Thebes as well as the drastic action of Alexander dispelled all further thought of rebellion or resistance among the Greeks. The Arcadians, in a gesture of abject submission, condemned to death the men who had counselled them to march to the aid of Thebes; the people of Elis hastily recalled the pro-Macedonian exiles; and the Aetolians rushed to assure Alexander of their undying devotion and loyalty. The news of the Theban disaster reached Athens during the celebration of the Eleusian festival. An emergency meeting was called at once, and on the initiative of Demades a special resolution was made by the very men who, on the motion of Demosthenes, only a few days before had wildly clamored for the annihilation of Macedonia. They decided to send an embassy to Alexander congratulating him on his success at Thebes and praising him for his just punishment of the treacherous Thebans.[17] Alexander, who had his agents everywhere, knew only too well that the recent uprisings had actually been planned and supported by Athens, and that the Athenians had actively aided and abetted Thebes. Nevertheless, he accepted the submission of the Athenians. He demanded, however, that the leading anti-Macedonian patriots, among them Demosthenes, Lycurgus, Hyperides, Charidemus and Chares,[18] be handed over to him for punishment; and that the Theban refugees, who only a few days ago had been welcomed in the city, be immediately expelled. But for some reason Alexander suddenly relented—tradition has it that Phocion and Demades prevailed upon him—and withdrew his relatively modest demands. He insisted solely on the forthright banishment of Charidemus, a Thracian mercenary captain and adventurer. Alexander's demand for the expulsion of Charidemus was readily accepted, but the Athenians refused to deliver the Theban refugees to Alexander. Chares, on the other hand, left Athens on his own accord.[19]

The unusually generous treatment of Athens by Alexander—unusual under the circumstances—is generally explained, as was the case after the conclusion of the Peloponnesian War (in 404 B.C.) or after the battle of Chaeronea (in 338 B.C.), by calling attention to Athens's ancient glory and deathless renown, and especially, to its heroic stand against the Persians at Marathon and Salamis. It has also been pointed out that Alexander, by displaying clemency, hoped to establish lasting friendly relations with the most important and most famous city in the Hellenic world; and that he intended to secure the active support of the powerful Athenian fleet for his Persian venture by winning the good will of Athens through a signal display of magnanimity. It has also been claimed that soon after the destruction of Thebes, the ancient and renowned city founded by Cadmus and the birthplace of Dionysius and Heracles, Alexander had feelings of bitter remorse.[20] All this might be true, but we are still puzzled by Alexander's unusually lenient treatment of Athens known by the king as the main instigator of the recent Greek revolt. Moreover, aside from the fact that Alexander himself was not immune to impulsive outbursts of violence and vindictiveness, the Athenians had entered into treasonable negotiations with Persia, an unpardonable crime in the eyes of the man who was about to launch a panhellenic crusade against the Persian arch-foe. And finally, the destruction of Athens might well have served as an effective deterrent for the Greeks not to attempt any further uprisings while Alexander was preoccupied with the conquest of Asia.[21]

There might be, however, another and perhaps more satisfactory explanation for Alexander's unusually generous treatment of the Athenians in the fall of 335 B.C. It is commonly believed that Aristotle, himself a Macedonian, left Athens in the summer or early fall of 348 B.C., because of an outbreak of violent anti-Macedonian sentiment and agitation in the city. This agitation was provoked by Philip's capture and destruction of Olynthus, the ally of Athens.[22] Subsequently, Aristotle went to Atarneus or Assos, probably after having spent the winter of 348-47 B.C. in Macedonia, keeping in close contact with King Philip. In 343-42 B.C., he returned to Macedonia where, according to the biographical tradition, he 'tutored' Alexander.[23] What seems to be more likely, however, is that Aristotle took an active part in Macedonia's foreign policy, and that he performed many valuable services for King Philip, who was a great admirer of his talents.[24] It also appears that some of the services he rendered Philip were of a diplomatic and political nature.[25] It may be maintained, for instance, that Aristotle's visit to Hermias of Atarneus (347-345 B.C.) had political overtones: Philip attempted, through the intermediary of Aristotle, to win over Hermias to his political designs, thus gaining an effective bridgehead on the Asiatic side of the Hellespont for a planned invasion of Asia Minor as well as an important base for the strategic encirclement of Thrace. Subsequent events indicate, however, that this venture was not altogether successful.[26] In any event, Diogenes Laertius (DL V. 2) relates that at the time of Speusippus' death (in 339-38 B.C.) Aristotle was on a diplomatic mission (in Macedonia?). Other biographical sources maintain that Aristotle dealt often and successfully with foreign kings, potentates, governments and countries; and that because of his many acts of valuable assistance, he was highly esteemed and greatly honored by them as well as by Philip.[27]

It is quite possible and, as a matter of fact, quite reasonable, to assume that it was Aristotle who personally persuaded Alexander to deal mercifully and generously with the Athenians in 335 B.C. We know that in the summer or fall of 335 B.C. Aristotle was with the Macedonian king. During the past years, to be sure, the relations between these two men had somewhat deteriorated.[28] This deterioration apparently was caused by the fact that Aristotle was personally very close to King Philip. Alexander and Philip, on the other hand, were not on the best of terms. Philip had put away his wife Olympias, the mother of Alexander. Subsequently he had married Cleopatra, the niece of Attalus, promising that the first male issue of this marriage would succeed him to the throne of Macedonia. This seriously jeopardized Alexander's hopes of becoming one day king of Macedonia. Nevertheless, in 335 B.C. Aristotle still had considerable influence with Alexander. At the same time, Aristotle seems to have had a genuine liking for Athens,[29] where he had gone to school and where he had spent twenty apparently happy years (367–348 B.C.) in a congenial intellectual surrounding. The deep and lasting impression which Athens' intellectual culture must have made upon Aristotle during these twenty formative years, as well as his genuine affection for this renowned city and for his former teachers and associates in the Platonic Academy, probably explains his efforts to intercede with Alexander on behalf of Athens.

The likelihood that in the year 335 B.C. Aristotle personally—and successfully—interceded on behalf of Athens seems to receive vital support from the report of Usaibia: 'On account of the many useful deeds and good services [Aristotle had rendered the city of Athens], the Athenians went so far as to convoke an assembly and vote an honorific inscription [dedicated to Aristotle]. They had this inscription engraved on a stone column which they erected on the highest citadel of their city, called The Summit [scil., the Acropolis]. In this inscription they recorded that Aristotle of Stagira, the son of Nicomachus, had served the city well by performing many beneficial deeds, by the large number of his acts of assistance and beneficence, and by all his services to the people of Athens, especially, by his intervention with King Philip [and King Alexander] for the purpose of promoting their interests as well as their welfare, and for seeing to it that they were well treated—that the people of Athens therefore wanted it to be known that they appreciated and were grateful for the good that had come out of his efforts—that they conferred upon him distinction and praise—and that they would keep him in faithful and honored memory. Those among the Athenians holding high public offices, who are of the opinion that he is unworthy of such an honor, may themselves attempt after his death to accomplish what he succeeded in accomplishing, taking an active part in all those affairs of state in which they, in their own selfish interest, would like to intervene.'[30]

The honorific decree recited by Usaibia, which is actually a decree of *proxenia*, in the main reproduces the traditional form and style of such decrees.[31] It is not impossible, however, that the inscription or decree mentioned by Usaibia, which specifically refers to Aristotle's successful intercessions with King Philip, may be related to the events which transpired on the eve of the battle of Chaeronea (in 338 B.C.), when Athens negotiated with the Macedonian king. Aristotle, who at the time is said to have been visiting Macedonia, might have taken an active part in these negotiations, representing Athenian interests.[32]

Usaibia's account may also refer to the events after the battle of Chaeronea, when Athens, although utterly defeated in battle, was treated rather generously by Philip. This magnanimous treatment, which saved the city from suffering the dire consequences of its stubborn resistance to Philip, might have been the result of Aristotle's personal recommendation and intercession. And Aristotle, who apparently was highly respected by Philip, had much influence with the king. This account may, as it is contended here, relate to Aristotle's successful intercession with Alexander on behalf of the Athenians in the year 335 B.C. It may also refer to all three of these crucial occasions in which Aristotle apparently played so decisive a role. Hence it is possible that for some unknown reason, the name of Alexander may have been omitted in the version preserved by Usaibia. Thus, the honorific decree may originally have referred to Aristotle's 'many and successful interventions with both King Philip and King Alexander for the purpose of promoting the interest and welfare of the Athenians and for seeing to it that they were well treated by King Philip and King Alexander.' And finally, it may also refer to Aristotle's intercessions with Antipater after 334 B.C. For Aristotle and Antipater, Alexander's lieutenant in Europe, seem to have been close friends.

It might be in order to discuss some of the technical questions raised by the account of Usaibia. The reference to, and enumeration of, Aristotle's many services and benefactions to the city of Athens is rather typical of Athenian decrees of *proxenia*. The remark that the Athenians are grateful for his many good deeds, and that on account of these good deeds they would keep him in honored memory, however, is somewhat unusual. As a rule, such inscriptions or decrees also recorded that the grateful people of Athens bestowed upon their benefactor a golden wreath. This might possibly be the ultimate meaning of Usaibia's statement that the Athenians 'conferred distinction and praise upon him.'[33] Moreover, the traditional honorific inscriptions or decrees also mentioned that the person so honored was made a *proxenos* and was officially declared an *euergetes*, as well as awarded 'honorary citizenship.' It is possible, however, that the unsophisticated wording used by Usaibia (or by his source) implies the bestowal of *proxenia and euergesia*—two technical terms which Usaibia (or his source), who most certainly was not familiar with Athenian legalistic phraseology or technical nomenclature, probably did not fully understand and, hence, translated or reported inadequately and misleadingly.

Barring the last sentence of Usaibia's account, and making some concessions to the understandable unfamiliarity of the Syriac or Arabic translator with the lego-technical language and phraseology of Athenian official documents or decrees, the report of Usaibia fairly accurately recasts, though in its own peculiar words, the traditional terminology of the typical Athenian decree of *proxenia* of the fourth century B.C. This fact is in itself highly significant. For it is more than unlikely that Usaibia (or his source) should have outright invented this whole story as well as this unique and unmistakable phraseology merely for encomiastic reasons. Such a phenomenon unquestionably points to a model which, as is the case here, has been awkwardly reproduced as well as partly misunderstood. It will have to be conceded, however, that Usaibia (or his source) not only was unfamiliar with the bureaucratic language of Athenian officialdom, but also was probably baffled and perhaps repelled by its linguistic ungainliness and technical awkwardness. In any event, he never intended to reproduce *verbatim* the original decree, although echoes of this decree unmistakably still reverberate throughout his account. Be this as it may, the indisputable fact remains that the report of Usaibia without doubt retains some of the standardized or formulaic characteristics common to all Athenian decrees of *proxenia*. It is well-nigh unthinkable, therefore, that Usaibia (or his source) should outright have invented the story of Aristotle's being honored by the Athenians with a decree of *proxenia*, and even more incredible that Usaibia should have resorted to a fairly accurate stylistic imitation of its unusual wording. Since all decrees of *proxenia* always mentioned the name as well as the descent of the person so honored, the passage, 'Aristotle of Stagira, the son of Nicomachus'—a passage faithfully reproduced by Usaibia—should make it quite clear that this honorific award was conferred on Aristotle.

The last part of Usaibia's account, namely, the statement that '[t]hose among the Athenians holding high public office, who are of the opinion that he is unworthy of such honors, may themselves attempt after his death to accomplish what he had succeeded in accomplishing, taking an active part and sharing in all those affairs of state in which they, prompted by selfish motives, would like to interfere,' needless to say, was not part or the conclusion of the original decree of *proxenia* bestowed on Aristotle. It may fairly be surmised that Usaibia refers here to some comments made by certain biographers (Ptolemy?) who reported or discussed the meritorious deeds Aristotle had performed for Athens. These particular comments, among other matters, may also have lashed out against certain Athenian statesmen or politicians who in their blind anti-Macedonian prejudices probably caused Athens more harm than good. It is quite possible that Usaibia (or his source) felt that a comparison of Aristotle's meritorious and beneficial deeds with the destructive behavior of his opponents and detractors fitted only too well into his narrative and, hence, appended it to his account of the bestowal of a decree of *proxenia* on Aristotle. But in so doing, he no longer cites the decree.

Should our interpretation of Usaibia's account prove to be the correct one, then Aristotle, on the surrender of Athens in the fall of 335 B.C., directly and effectively interceded with Alexander on behalf of the Athenians. In so doing, he probably saved the city from destruction, and the Athenians had every reason to be eternally grateful to him and to commemorate his noble action. It must be borne in mind, however, that in 335–34 B.C. Aristotle for a second time made Athens his permanent abode. But in the eyes of the vast majority of the Athenians he returned, or was brought back, to Athens in the van of the conquering Macedonian phalanx, a most unfortunate coincidence. Hence, in the mind and memory of many people he re-entered the city not as a welcome guest, cherished friend or celebrated saviour, or perhaps, as the renowned philosopher, former pupil of Plato and respected teacher of Alexander, but rather as a conqueror and as the symbol of conquest—as the living reminder of an embarrassing incident in Athenian history. This impression, which obviously caused much annoyance and profound animosity in a city where fear, anger and frustration were rampant, could not but generate widespread resentment.[34] Undoubtedly, the eternally gossiping Athenians now saw in Aristotle a dangerous agent of Macedonian domination in their very midst—a political informer or 'spy' who regularly reported their moods, aspirations and moves to Antipater[35]—an assumption which, aside from its nasty implications, probably was not too far removed from the actual truth.[36]

A great many Athenians, among them rabid patriots as well as plain xenophobes, after 335–34 B.C. genuinely hated and feared Aristotle. The frequently unflattering and even slanderous remarks about Aristotle interspersed in ancient literature[37] in part reflect this general unpopularity with the majority of his Athenian contemporaries, who saw in him the pernicious instrument of Macedonian tyranny and oppression. As is so often the case in such tense situations, the average Athenian vented his futile anger by inventing all sorts of nasty stories about Aristotle's personal vices and depravities. In view of the particular circumstances which compelled Aristotle to withdraw rather hurriedly from Athens in the year 348 B.C., it is more than likely that he might never have returned to that city but for her military surrender to Alexander and her subsequent occupation by Alexander's troops. Hence, it is not surprising that he should be mistrusted and even disliked, nay feared, by the vast majority of the Athenians who only waited for the opportune moment to rid themselves of this unwelcome 'intruder.'[38] It might be maintained, therefore, that the years between 335–34 and 323 B.C., allegedly the years of Aristotle's greatest and most important philosophic productivity, probably were not the most pleasant years in the life of the Stagirite. This most unfortunate situation, in turn, may also have adversely, if not decisively, affected Aristotle and his whole philosophic work. An atmosphere of patent hostility is wholly destructive of that 'intellectual leisure' which constitutes the basic prerequisite of all philosophic creativity.[39]

Now we may also understand why in the year 323 B.C., when the news of Alexander's sudden death in Babylon (on 13 June 323 B.C.) reached Athens and when Antipater, who had been summoned to proceed to Asia, was unable to give Aristotle some military protection, Aristotle once more was forced to flee from Athens. He did so under circumstances almost identical with those which had caused him to depart from the city rather hurriedly in the summer or early fall of 348 B.C.[40] Tradition has it that in 323 B.C. Aristotle faced an official indictment for impiety and blasphemy.[41] Such an indictment, like the charges made against him, might have been a mere pretext—a screen issue intended to dispose of or drive out a much disliked and, at the moment, utterly defenseless Macedonian alien. The true reason for the final persecution of Aristotle and for his renewed flight from Athens was undoubtedly his political affiliations with Macedonia and, especially, with Antipater, the 'destroyer of Greek freedom.' This seems to be reflected in the account of Usaibia: 'After the Athenians had decreed to erect this inscription [honoring Aristotle],[42] the decision was opposed by an Athenian named Himeraeus. As regards Aristotle, this man voiced an entirely different opinion. [In stark opposition to the supporters and (philo-Macedonian) friends of Aristotle, this Himeraeus claimed that Aristotle in fact was the sworn enemy of all truly patriotic and freedom-loving Athenians, as well as a serious detriment to Athens and to its aspirations to political freedom and independence.] He pounced upon the *stele* on which the Athenians had decreed to engrave the laudatory inscription, and which they had erected in a place called The Summit of the city [*scil.*, the Acropolis], and hurled it down.'[43]

Usaibia's account probably refers to the following incident: in the year 323 B.C., the anti-Macedonian partisans in Athens, who most certainly hated Aristotle, the Macedonian, for a short period of time assumed political control over the city. Among these partisans were such men as Demosthenes, Lycurgus, Hyperides and Himeraeus. They probably vented their long pent-up resentment and dislike of Macedonia, and of Aristotle in particular, by removing the honorific *stele* commemorating the many outstanding services Aristotle had rendered the city of Athens. This incident, therefore, might be historical and as such might have taken place in the summer or early fall of 323 B.C., probably after Aristotle had left the city. If this be so, then this occurrence would lend weighty support to the thesis that at some earlier time the Athenians had actually erected a *stele* honoring Aristotle. In any event, the additional report of Usaibia is historical, namely, that Himeraeus was subsequently executed by Antipater[44] (though certainly not for the removal of the *stele*, but rather for his anti-Macedonian agitations and activities) after the latter had defeated the Greeks in the battle of Crannon (in 322 B.C.) and had re-occupied Athens. Usaibia also maintains that at some later time, this *stele*, which had been removed by Himeraeus, was restored thanks to the efforts of a man called Stephanus, who in this seems to have acted with the approval of many (philo-Macedonian?) Athenians:[45] 'On the [new] *stele* they engraved such praise of Aristotle as had been inscribed on the original *stele;* recorded what this Himeraeus had done; and recommended that he be exiled and the city purified.'[46] There is no way of verifying this latter account of Usaibia. We know, however, that in Athens damaged or wilfully destroyed honorific inscriptions and monuments were subsequently restored by a special decree of the popular assembly.

Seen in a larger context, it would appear that much of Aristotle's life was, in some ways, inextricably intertwined with Macedonia's political and military fortunes. In the year 348 B.C., Aristotle, the Macedonian, departed from Athens because of Philip's capture and destruction of Olynthus;[47] in 335–34 B.C. he returned to Athens after Macedonia's military might once more made the city accessible to him; and in 323 B.C., when the death of Alexander seemed to spell the end of Macedonian military and political power, he had to leave the city for a second time, never to return.[48] Although by his personal efforts, Aristotle probably had prevented the destruction of Athens in

335 B.C., the particular circumstances under which he returned to the city in that year made him highly suspect and decidedly unpopular with the majority of the Athenians. Never loath to deal harshly and unjustly with their benefactors, the Athenians repaid him with flagrant ingratitude. In this, Aristotle, the Macedonian, shared the fate of many of the greatest men in Greek antiquity.[49]

Chapter XII

Aristotle's Flight From Athens in the Year 323 B.C.*

Tradition has it that in 323 B.C., Aristotle withdrew from Athens to Chalcis where he died the following year.[1] The reason for his sudden departure is stated briefly by Diogenes Laertius: 'Aristotle . . . was indicted for impiety by the hierophant Eurymedon or, according to Favorinus in his *Miscellaneous History,* by Demophilus, the basis of the indictment being the hymn he had composed in honor of . . . Hermias, as well as the following inscription for Hermias' statue in Delphi: "This man in violation of the hallowed law of the gods was slain by the king of the bowbearing Persians, who overcame him, not openly with a spear in deadly combat, but by treachery with the aid of one in whom he had put his trust."'[2]

Athenaeus[3] vigorously denies that 'the poem addressed by the most learned Aristotle to Hermias of Atarneus' was a religious paean, 'as alleged by Demophilus. This Demophilus, suborned by Eurymedon, caused the indictment to be drawn against the philosopher for impiety, on the ground that he impiously sang a paean to Hermias every day in the common dining rooms.[4] But the song furnishes no evidence of being a paean, but rather a kind of *scolion.*[5] This I shall make plain from its own words: "Virtue, attained by mortals through much toil, is the fairest prize that life can win. It is an enviable lot in Hellas to die for thy virgin beauty, and to endure for thy sake violent and unwearied toils. Such is the fruit thou bestowest on the soul, a fruit like that the immortals enjoy, better than gold, better than noble ancestors, yea, better than soft-eyed sleep. For thy sake the sons of Zeus, Heracles, and those born of Leda, endured many toils in their quest of power from thee. In their yearning for thee, Achilles and Ajax went to the dwelling of Hades. For the sake of thy dear beauty, the nurseling of Atarneus hath, in his turn, made desolate the sun's light. Therefore the Muses, Memory's daughters, shall exalt him in story, immortal for his deeds, exalting the majesty of Zeus, the god of friendship, and this meed of friendship."[6] I know not whether anyone can discern in these verses anything especially characteristic of the paean. The author plainly admits that Hermias is dead when he says "for the sake of thy beauty, the nurseling of Atarneus hath made desolate the sun's light." Moreover, there is no refrain, characteristic of the paean, as there is in the true paean . . . .' According to Athenaeus, Aristotle 'himself says in his *Defense Against the Charge of Impiety* (if this speech is not a forgery): "If my purpose had been to sacrifice to Hermias as a god, I should never have built for him a monument as for a mortal, nor if I had wished to make him into the nature of a god, should I have honored his body with funeral rites."'[7] Thus, already in antiquity, weighty doubts were entertained as to whether Aristotle's memorial hymn to Hermias was of a religious nature and, hence, constituted an act of impiety or blasphemy. More than that: already in antiquity some doubts were apparently entertained, at least by implication, as to whether this allegedly blasphemous paean or hymn was indeed the true reason for Aristotle's indictment in the year 323 B.C.

Conversely, it will be noted that the memorial hymn to Hermias begins with a formal invocation of Arete and, hence, may definitely be classified as a ritualistic or religious hymn. This invocation as well as the passage, 'therefore the Muses, Memory's daughters, shall exalt him in story, immortal for his deeds,' might possibly be adduced as evidence in support of the charge of impiety or blasphemy. We may also assume that Aristotle, on receiving the news of Hermias' death and the circumstances surrounding this event, did institute solemn memorial (religious?) services in honor of his friend and kinsman. It will be observed that, according to the testimony of Areius Didymus,[8] Callisthenes apparently assisted Aristotle in these memorial services (and in the composition of the hymn?). A reference to this memorial hymn in honor of the departed Hermias can also be found in Himerius: 'Now Hermias became a close friend of the philosopher from Stagira and . . . by the practice of excellence, roused in his preceptor [*scil.*, Aristotle] a most fervent admiration. Many were the tokens of his love towards Hermias which Aristotle displayed, training him in philosophic discussion and exercising him in excellence of character. For Hermias alone among his friends did Aristotle compose an elegy to adorn his resting place.'[9] In this connection it should not be overlooked that the reference to the allegedly sacrilegious paean or memorial hymn or elegy in honor of Hermias may also have been a clever, as well as effective, way of reminding the anti-Macedonian Athenians of Aristotle's former connections with the philo-Macedonian Hermias. Accordingly, the reference to the allegedly blasphemous act on the part of Aristotle was primarily a devious means of proving that Aristotle was definitely an enemy of all patriotic Athenians (who were on principle anti-Macedonian), and of Athenian political interests as well as aspirations in general, in that he honored and extolled a renowned philo-Macedonian such as Hermias. For there can be no doubt that, from sheer necessity, during his last years Hermias was a friend, if not an ally, of Macedonia.

Probably on the authority of Ptolemy (-el-Garib),[10] both Al-Mubashir (*II VA* 20–1)[11] and Usaibia (*IV VA* 7–10)[12] maintain that a hierophant by the name of Eurymedon gave a seriously distorted account of Aristotle's philosophy;[13] that this Eurymedon did so primarily from jealousy and because of an old grudge he bore against Aristotle; and that Eurymedon had claimed that Aristotle neither worshipped the traditional gods of Athens nor otherwise showed them the proper respect.[14] According to Al-Mubashir, Eurymedon also denounced Aristotle as 'a man who should be shunned by everyone,' thereby inducing the Stagirite to depart from Athens.[15] *II VS* 3 relates that 'being frightened by the execution of Socrates, Aristotle left Athens,'[16] and *II VS* 7 records that Aristotle 'finally went to Chalcis on the island of Euboea.' This account is further elucidated by the story, found in Al-Mubashir (*II VA* 21), that when Aristotle learned about Eurymedon's plan to bring him to public trial he took flight 'because he feared that they [*scil.*, the Athenians] might do to him what they had done to Socrates . . . whom they executed by poison.' Usaibia (*IV VA* 8–9) records that when Aristotle 'heard about this [*scil.*, the indictment],' that is, when the bill of indictment had been served upon him, but before any further official action could be taken, 'he withdrew from Athens . . . because he did not want the Athenians to do unto him what they had done to Socrates . . . whom they had executed.'[17]

On leaving Athens, Aristotle, alluding to the fate that had befallen Socrates some seventy-six years previously, allegedly remarked that he would not give the Athenians 'a second opportunity to sin against philosophy'; that it was indeed 'perilous for a [Macedonian?] alien to live in Athens'; and that Athens was crowded with professional informers or sycophants (who apparently made life almost unbearable).[18] The additional story that (before departing from Athens?) Aristotle wrote a formal *Defense Against the Charges Made by Eurymedon*[19] is almost certainly a late and wholly unfounded biographical invention.[20] Usaibia, who in this probably relies on the testimony of Ptolemy (-el-Garib), flatly denies the authenticity of this account:

'It is not in accordance with the true facts that Aristotle ... wrote a *Defense* .... On no account should this story be regarded as being true. On the contrary, it has been palmed off on him.'[21]

The reports of Al-Mubashir and Usaibia, it will be noted, are strangely similar to the traditional story of the indictment and trial of Socrates in the year 399 B.C. It is possible, therefore, that some biographers of Aristotle simply interchanged and supplemented the account of Aristotle's prosecution with the reported incidents of 399 B.C. Anytus, one of the 'prosecutors' of Socrates, for instance, is also said to have been motivated by jealousy and an old grudge.[22] The charge of impiety brought against Aristotle in 323 B.C., like that brought against Socrates in 399 B.C., might have been a mere 'token charge,' a screen-issue for what was probably an essentially political conflict.[23] Curiously enough, the 'sacrilegious' hymn to Hermias of Atarneus and the honorific inscription for Hermias' statue in Delphi,[24] the two presumed foundations for the charge of impiety,[25] are not so much as mentioned in the *Vita Aristotelis Marciana*, the *Vita Aristotelis Vulgata*, the *Vita Aristotelis Latina* or in the Syriac or Arabic *Vitae Aristotelis*.[26] This blatant omission in itself is obviously significant.

To the vast majority of the Athenians, it must be borne in mind, Aristotle was always an unwanted and suspected 'resident alien' (*metic*) living in Athens, a city which had become increasingly intolerant and deplorably anti-intellectual—indeed, xenophobic, especially as regards Macedonians. *VM* 12 (and *VM* 42) as well as *VL* 12 go out of their way to stress the fact that he was a mere ξένος or *extraneus* (an 'alien'), and they emphatically contrast him, the powerless alien who had but a few friends and no influential connections in Athens, with Plato, the Athenian citizen, who had many powerful friends and relatives as well as many personal, social and political connections in Athens. In short, Aristotle lived in Athens more by sufferance than by right, always subject to arbitrary persecution, wanton prosecution and sudden expulsion.[27] The Lyceum was never his own personal 'school,' but rather a 'communal' building accessible to all sorts of people. The Academy or Museum, on the other hand, was the personal property of Plato who could leave, bequeath or transfer this personal property—the grounds, buildings, the library, the inventory etc., of the Academy—to any person of his choice, provided the latter was a male agnate. The notion that, between 335–34 and 323 B.C., Aristotle owned as well as taught in his 'own school' and that this school consisted of grounds and buildings (κῆπος) belonging to Aristotle where the latter also kept his library and other personal belongings, is wholly erroneous.[28] Thanks to the co-operation of Demetrius of Phaleron, the Peripatetics acquired a κῆπος only during the scholarchate of Theophrastus.[29] Hence, it is perhaps not entirely correct to call Aristotle the founder of the Peripatus or, perhaps, the first scholarch of the Peripatus, although he was unquestionably the founder of Peripatetic philosophy. Naturally, it could be argued that although there existed an Athenian law which prevented aliens or *metics* from acquiring or holding the title to land in Attica (ἔγκτησις), there were always instances where this law was blatantly ignored or circumvented, or where exceptions to this rule were granted. Thus, nothing prevents us from assuming that Aristotle did take advantage of these exceptions, that in his particular case this law was not enforced, or that he acquired the property by using an Athenian citizen as a 'front man.' These attractive and, perhaps, persuasive arguments, however, are seriously challenged, nay defeated, by the incontestable fact that, unlike the wills of later Peripatetic scholarchs, the preserved versions of Aristotle's last will and testament do not once refer to any real property, or to any school, in Athens. This signal omission, it goes without saying, cannot be ignored or, perhaps, simply played down.

Moreover, many of Aristotle's relatives, friends and family connections were in foreign lands and, as has already been shown, he probably had very few close personal friends and acquaintances among the Athenians. Apparently he had, however, a great many enemies, especially political enemies, not to mention people who simply disliked and distrusted his intellectual outlook and who disagreed with his philosophic views. This widespread and apparently deep-rooted attitude is clearly indicated, for instance, in Demochares' utterly prejudiced *Oration Against the Philosophers*, delivered in 306 B.C.[30] Among other matters, Demochares gave formal expression to these anti-intellectual and xenophobic views in general. At the same time, he seems to have singled out Aristotle as a particularly untrustworthy, treacherous and dangerous person. Excepting perhaps a small philo-Macedonian minority composed of some intellectuals and a few wealthy merchants,[31] the city of Athens, at least since the capture and destruction of Olynthus by King Philip in the summer of 348 B.C., and probably before that time, plainly loathed (and feared) Macedonia and Macedonians (who in the eyes of the proud Athenians were 'semi-barbarians'), including Aristotle, the Macedonian.[32]

Aristotle's close relationship or friendship with Hermias of Atarneus, especially after Theopompus and Theocritus of Chios had begun to launch their vitriolic attacks upon Hermias (and indirectly upon

Aristotle), was of course politically suspect, the more so since Hermias apparently had some political dealings with Macedonia. Theopompus and Theocritus had also insinuated that Aristotle's relations with Hermias were scandalous and morally reprehensible. All this most certainly became the source of much scandal-mongering among the eternally gossiping Athenians. Aristotle's situation in Athens was also made most difficult by his well-known contacts—official as well as personal—with the Macedonian royal house and with certain powerful Macedonians, especially with Antipater, the lieutenant of Alexander in Europe and the much hated 'oppressor' of Greece, as well as 'destroyer' of Hellenic political freedom. Matters were certainly not improved when Aristotle married Pythias, the niece or adopted daughter (or sister?) of Hermias, the 'Bithynian.' To the average Athenian, who gloried in his prejudices, Hermias was a 'lowly' native of Asia Minor, a former slave of the disreputable Eubulus, a despicable eunuch and an 'inferior barbarian' who had betrayed and murdered Eubulus, his former master and benefactor. It was also rumored that Pythias had been the concubine of Hermias, the petty tyrant and friend or ally of Macedonia, who had been credited by Theopompus and Theocritus with every vile deed imaginable. In view of his extremely precarious political situation vis-à-vis the Persians (whom he had defied for some time), Hermias, the father or uncle of Pythias, of necessity had been strongly pro-Macedonian—an unforgivable crime in the eyes of the essentially anti-Macedonian Athenians. Accordingly, the Athenians probably transferred their hatred and contempt to Aristotle's wife, provided Pythias was still alive when Aristotle returned to Athens in 335 B.C. Moreover, as an intellectual, Aristotle was immediately under suspicion as well as under the attack of the numerous philistines and 'know-nothings' who can always be found in any society—ancient, mediaeval and modern. How bad this situation actually was may be surmised from Demochares (a nephew of Demosthenes) and his vicious, but without doubt widely acclaimed and widely accepted, *Oration Against the Philosophers*, which was an eloquent but nasty speech in support of Sophocles' motion (in 306 B.C.) to have all foreign 'subversive' or pro-Macedonian philosophers expelled from Athens.[33] Demochares, who in his *Oration* probably also related some of the nasty gossip circulating in Athens during the lifetime of Aristotle, forthrightly claimed that Aristotle's letters and messages (intelligence reports?) to Antipater had been intercepted by the Athenians; that in these letters Aristotle had displayed a pronouncedly anti-Athenian attitude; that in 349 B.C.

Aristotle had personally betrayed Stagira, his native town, to Philip of Macedonia; and that in 348 B.C. Aristotle had denounced the wealthiest citizens of Olynthus, the ally of Athens, to Philip.[34] Hence, it is not surprising that shortly before his death Aristotle should write to Antipater that 'in Athens the same things are not permitted to an alien which are proper for an Athenian citizen'; and that 'it is dangerous [for a Macedonian alien] to live in Athens.'[35]

Already by the year 348 B.C. Aristotle had experienced the effects of a sudden wave of anti-Macedonian sentiment in Athens, occasioned by Philip's attack upon, and conquest of, Olynthus.[36] Then, too, he had withdrawn from Athens rather hurriedly. After the abortive anti-Macedonian revolt in the year 335 B.C. (that is, after the conquest and destruction of Thebes by Alexander), when the Athenians made their renewed submission to the Macedonian king, Aristotle dared to come back to Athens. Since at the time he apparently returned to the city in the van of the conquering Macedonian army, it is not surprising that he should be disliked more intensely than ever by the Athenian patriots. No doubt, by now the vast majority of the Athenians considered him a political agent or representative of their conqueror and oppressor—a fiendish traitor who brazenly lived in their very midst, enjoying the protection of the Macedonian army.[37] They apparently forgot that in 335 B.C. Aristotle might have interceded with Alexander on behalf of Athens and thus saved the city from possible destruction or, at least, from humiliating terms of surrender.[38] When, on the news of Alexander's sudden death in June of 323 B.C. in Babylon, Athens revolted once more against its Macedonian overlords, Aristotle was naturally a prime target. Aristotle's second sojourn in Athens, therefore, was closely bound to the Macedonian fortunes of war. A Macedonian military defeat or, perhaps, the sudden death of its great soldier-king (or the absence or impotence of Antipater, Alexander's lieutenant and 'watchdog' in Europe) automatically spelled disaster for the philosopher.

In support of the contention that Aristotle's flight from Athens in 323 B.C. was prompted primarily by political events, the following additional evidence may be introduced: a story, which is an eloquent description of the political troubles Aristotle was about to experience in Athens, can be found in the *Vita Aristotelis* of Usaibia.[39] Here we are told that some Athenians (some pro-Macedonian partisans?) decreed to dedicate a public inscription honoring and commemorating Aristotle for his many outstanding services to the city.[40] But this motion was violently opposed by an Athenian named Aimaraeus

(Himeraeus) who (in the somewhat garbled version recorded by Usaibia) hurled down the column erected to record Aristotle's meritorious deeds. Himeraeus, the son of Phenostratus and the brother of Demetrius of Phaleron, was a prominent as well as very active partisan of the anti-Macedonian faction in Athens during the twenties of the fourth century B.C.,[41] and probably a personal enemy of Aristotle, the 'Macedonian.' This Himeraeus most certainly considered Aristotle a philo-Macedonian, an enemy of those patriotic Athenians who were attempting to regain political independence for Athens by shaking off the Macedonian yoke and, hence, a person unworthy of such an honor.[42]

The Himeraeus incident, as recorded by Usaibia (and provided it is historically accurate), not only reflects the internal turmoil caused by the tensions between the philo-Macedonian and anti-Macedonian factions within the city of Athens, but it also shows what an ominous shadow overclouded the future fate of Aristotle. When the death of Alexander of Macedonia (and Antipater's absence from Europe) in the summer of 323 B.C. provided a brief opportunity for the anti-Macedonians in Athens to assume control of political affairs, Aristotle found himself in an acutely precarious position.

Aristotle's close personal and professional ties with King Philip,[43] Alexander and Antipater are too well known to warrant detailed discussion.[44] His father Nicomachus had been the personal physician and intimate friend or adviser of King Amyntas III, King Philip's father.[45] Aside from these personal contacts, Aristotle had official connections with several prominent Macedonians.[46] Hence, it is hardly surprising that he should be suspected of and charged with being an enemy of Athens and a major obstacle to throwing off the Macedonian yoke—a key foe of the anti-Macedonian or 'patriotic' party which included such prominent men as Demosthenes, Lycurgus, Hyperides and Himeraeus.

Al-Mubashir relates[47] that when charging Aristotle with impiety, Eurymedon gave a 'distorted account of his [scil., Aristotle's] philosophy.'[48] This bit of information, which cannot be found in any of the other Vitae Aristotelis, once more calls to mind the indictment and trial of Socrates[49] and hence might be based on confusion, or perhaps, should be considered a case of transfer. On the other hand, this particular statement may represent a somewhat garbled reflection of the many doctrinal controversies in which Aristotle and his particular teachings were embroiled, both during his lifetime and afterwards. In addition to his dissent from several of Plato's fundamental philosophic principles, Aristotle seems to have disagreed with such prominent members of the Platonic Academy as Speusippus, Xenocrates and Heracleides of Pontus. Isocrates and his distinguished school of rhetoric, which exerted much intellectual influence in Athens and throughout the Hellenic world, was decidedly hostile towards Aristotle and the philosophy he propagated. As early as *c.* 360 B.C., in his *Gryllus*, Aristotle had attacked Isocrates and the Isocratic ideals of rhetoric and cultural *paideia;*[50] and he had kept alive this antagonism in the *Protrepticus*, published *c.* 350 B.C.[51] About the same time, he clashed with Cephisodorus, a disciple of Isocrates, who wrote an *Against Aristotle* in four books.[52] Moreover, the Stagirite managed to arouse the lasting antipathy as well as enmity of the School of Megara (Eubulides) and subsequently that of the influential and vociferous Epicurus and the Epicureans.[53]

In summary, the extant *Vitae Aristotelis*, in the main, advance no less than three reasons for the official action taken against Aristotle in the year 323 B.C. by Eurymedon: (i) the allegedly blasphemous hymn in honor of Hermias of Atarneus and perhaps the 'sacrilegious' inscription for Hermias' memorial statue in Delphi; (ii) the close political and personal ties which Aristotle had with Macedonia and particularly with the Macedonian royal house and its lieutenant, Antipater; and (iii) the 'distorted interpretation' of Aristotle's teachings which apparently led many people to believe that he did not honor or worship the traditional gods of Athens and had failed to show the gods the respect due to them. Close scrutiny should reveal that the second reason was the primary and most urgent cause for Aristotle's indictment and flight in 323 B.C.[54]

Thus, it is persuasively clear that the peculiar political situation in Athens in the summer of 323 B.C. caused Aristotle to leave the city most precipitately. The news of Alexander's sudden death presented the Athenian patriots with the occasion to regain independence and power. They took full advantage of the chaotic conditions that followed in the wake of the king's death—a chaos that was heightened by the fact that at this very moment Antipater was on his way to meet Alexander in Persia[55]—to strike with a vengeance. Athens once again revolted, and did so more successfully than she had done in the year 335 B.C. on the false rumour that Alexander had been slain somewhere in Thrace. As other Greek cities joined the general uprising, Aristotle found himself surrounded by bitter hostility and mortal danger. Fearing the worst, he fled from Athens to Chalcis. It is possible that the Athenians were actually planning to bring formal charges against him, But these proceedings, if they were in fact initiated, were merely a technical pretext formally to channel the blind hatred of Athens for anything and anyone Macedonian. When, according to Usaibia, Aristotle voluntarily departed from Athens before formal legal proceedings were instituted against him, no one apparently interfered with him or tried to arrest him.[56] In any event, judging from his last will and testament[57] as well as from the remark of Lycon Pythagoraeus,[58] Aristotle was able to remove all of his personal property and servants from Athens. This seems to be a strong indication that no one tried to prevent him from leaving, and that the Athenians were satisfied with just ridding themselves of Aristotle, the unwanted and probably hated 'political enemy.' As it had happened before in the course of Athenian history, 'politics,' prejudice, false patriotic emotionalism and plain stupidity once again drove into exile a prominent man who, it appears, had been a great benefactor of the city. True to her fickle temperament, Athens once again managed to 'sin against philosophy,'[59] something which mankind has been doing since time immemorial.[60]

Chapter XIII

Aristotle, Athens and the Foreign Policy of Macedonia*

Several reasons have been advanced by Aristotle's biographers as to why in the year 367 B.C. the young Stagirite went to Athens, or was brought there by his 'guardian' Proxenus.[1] According to one tradition, he moved there because of the advice given by the Delphic oracle.[2] Usaibia also relates that, in keeping with some ancient reports, 'this happened because Proxenus and Plato were personal friends.'[3] But we do not know whether this particular explanation is based on historical fact, or whether it is just another instance of an essentially encomiastic and, hence, unreliable tradition about Aristotle. Nor are we able to ascertain where Ptolemy (-el-Garib), in all likelihood Usaibia's source, found this bit of information. Naturally, it could always be maintained that Aristotle went to Athens in 367 B.C. for the purpose of securing the best education available in the Hellenic world,[4] especially since by that year the fame of Isocrates and that of his school of rhetoric (and, judging from Pseudo-Plato, *Fifth Epistle*, perhaps that of the Platonic Academy) must have reached Macedonia.

There is, however, another and apparently more persuasive explanation for Aristotle's journey to Athens in the year 367 B.C.: Aristotle's father, Nicomachus,[5] was not only the court physician of King Amyntas III of Macedonia, but also an intimate friend and general adviser of the king. Hence, Aristotle's immediate family had rather close connections with the royal house of Macedonia; and his father must have been a man of some standing at the Macedonian court.[6] King Amyntas died in 370–69 B.C. He was succeeded by his oldest (minor) son, Alexander II. Alexander was soon murdered by Ptolemy of Alorus, who proclaimed himself regent as well as king, ruling Macedonia in the name of Perdiccas and Philip, the two younger brothers of the slain Alexander. In the ensuing inter-dynastic struggles, which ended only with the assassination of Ptolemy by Perdiccas in 365 B.C., Aristotle's father, who probably remained loyal to the sons of Amyntas III, might also have been killed.[7] This would explain why

Proxenus, the 'guardian' and brother-in-law of Aristotle, rather than Nicomachus himself, brought young Aristotle to Athens in 367 B.C.[8] In any event, the several *Vitae Aristotelis* insist that at the time Aristotle went to Athens in 367 B.C., Nicomachus was already dead.[9] It might be conjectured, therefore, that during the reign of Ptolemy, and after the death of Nicomachus, Aristotle was sent to Athens in order to get him 'out of harm's way.'[10]

Alexander II, and after him Perdiccas, pursued a philo-Athenian policy. Ptolemy of Alorus, on the other hand, was tied to Thebes, the political rival of Athens. When in the year 369–68 B.C. Ptolemy revolted against Alexander II, the Theban Pelopidas was called upon to settle this dispute. Pelopidas concluded an alliance between Macedonia and Thebes as well as confirmed the regency of Ptolemy. With the support of Eurydice, the widow of Amyntas III and the unnatural mother of Alexander II, Ptolemy subsequently murdered Alexander II. When another pretender to the Macedonian throne threatened Ptolemy, the latter turned to Athens for help. Thebes, however, was opposed to any Athenian interference in the internal affairs of Macedonia. Hence, in 368 B.C. Thebes compelled Ptolemy to abandon his alliance with Athens and to renew his alliance with Thebes. After the assassination of Ptolemy in 365 B.C. by Perdiccas, the younger brother of the slain Alexander II, Macedonia freed itself from Theban control and became allied with Athens. Accordingly, it would be reasonable to assume that, in the year 367 B.C., a partisan or the son of a partisan of the Amyntas-Alexander-Perdiccas faction in Macedonia, such as Aristotle and his immediate family, should seek political asylum in Athens, which was not likely to hand him over to the pro-Theban Ptolemy of Alorus.

This being so, Aristotle's arrival in Athens in the year 367 B.C., could very well have been an incident connected with the murderous inter-dynastic struggles and disorders which convulsed Macedonia between 370–69 and 365 B.C. Hence, already in his youth, Aristotle became familiar with and perhaps involved in, the dynastic intrigues and political schemes within Macedonia. The fact that he and his family apparently belonged to the political faction which remained loyal to the sons of Amyntas III (and to Philip in particular), undoubtedly had far-reaching and long-lasting repercussions regarding the whole future life of Aristotle: at the very outset, Aristotle's life came to be tied up with 'politics,' something which he apparently never forgot and which Philip probably never permitted him to forget. It also explains why throughout his life he remained closely attached to King Philip and, perhaps, why in later years he and Alexander who (after Philip's divorce from Olympias and subsequent marriage to Cleopatra) disliked and feared his father, became alienated. Although some of these facts have been previously discussed in some detail, it might be advisable as well as informative to briefly restate them in a detailed discussion of Aristotle's relations to Athens, and in an analysis of his personal involvements in and his many contributions to King Philip's political schemes and aspirations. In so doing, we might also gain novel insights into Aristotle's personal life—insights, that is, which so far seem to have escaped the attention of scholars.

According to an almost universally accepted tradition, Aristotle departed from Athens and from the Platonic Academy shortly after the death of Plato in 348-47 B.C., that is, during the archonship of Theophilus. This would make it appear that the death of Plato was the main, if not the sole, reason for Aristotle's withdrawal from Athens.[11] There exists, however, another and, perhaps, more persuasive explanation for Aristotle's departure from Athens in 348-47 B.C. *II VS* 3-4 relates that 'being frightened by the execution of Socrates, he [*scil.*, Aristotle] retired from Athens and stayed near the Hellespont. When Plato died, Speusippus . . . took charge of Plato's school . . . [and] sent a message [to Aristotle] asking him to come back. . . .' And Diogenes Laertius (V. 2) laconically reports that 'Aristotle left the Academy [and Athens] while Plato was still alive.'[12] Both *II VS* 3-4 and DL V. 2 maintain or imply that Plato was still alive at the time Aristotle departed from Athens, but only *II VS* 3 states a definite reason why he did so: he was frightened by 'the execution of Socrates.' This rather curious remark, which has been the subject of many misinterpretations and much misunderstanding,[13] certainly calls for additional as well as detailed explanation.

In the year 349-48 B.C., King Philip of Macedonia, in connection with his general 'eastward expansionist movement' against Thrace, undertook the gradual subjugation of the Greek colonies or settlements in Chalcidice. Thus, in 349 B.C. he took and destroyed Stagira. To escape possible capture and destruction by the Macedonians, Olynthus, the most important and wealthiest city on the Chalcidian peninsula, entered into a defensive alliance with Athens.[14] When Olynthus was actually attacked by King Philip in the summer of 348 B.C., an Athenian relief force was promptly dispatched to come to its assistance. This assistance, however, arrived too late to prevent the fall of Olynthus. This incident, together with Demosthenes' fiery and constant denunciations of Philip,[15] led to the outbreak of violent anti-Macedonian sentiments and actions among the outraged Athenians. Aristotle was a Macedonian alien residing in Athens and hence a man who was surely suspected of strong pro-Macedonian leanings or sympathies. It may also be surmised that he was not on the best of personal terms with the overwhelming majority of the Athenian populace.[16] In the year 367 B.C. he had come to Athens from the 'barbaric north' as a stranger and, perhaps, as a political refugee closely aligned with the partisans of Amyntas III's kinsmen and heirs—to a city which unashamedly discriminated against, and looked down upon, any non-Athenian. It is also quite likely that between 359 and 348 B.C. he had paid several visits to Macedonia and to King Philip in particular, thus arousing a strong feeling of suspicion, enmity and envy. Unfortunately, we have no detailed information about the specific purpose of these visits to Macedonia. Neither do we know whether these visits had political overtones. But if it is indeed true, as some sources claim, that in 349 B.C. he betrayed Stagira to Philip, and that in 348 B.C. he denounced to Philip the wealthiest citizens of Olynthus,[17] then we are justified in surmising that already during the last years of his association with the Platonic Academy Aristotle was politically active on behalf of Macedonia.

In any event, the average Athenian of that period, we know, could be as bigoted and anti-intellectual as he could be intolerant and xenophobic. In this general atmosphere of resentment, anger, fear and frustration (which thanks to Demosthenes' inflammatory perorations was vented on everyone and everything Macedonian), Aristotle feared that he might share 'the fate of Socrates.'[18] Accordingly, he decided to depart from Athens—probably in the summer of 348 B.C.—seeking refuge, it appears, first in Macedonia and then with Hermias of Atarneus. The reason why in 348 B.C. Aristotle decided not to retire to Chalcis on the island of Euboea (as he did in the year 323 B.C.), where he had a house he had inherited from his mother or from his mother's ancestors, is probably the following: on the instigation of King Philip, the island of Euboea had revolted against Athens in 349-48 B.C. An attempt on the part of the Athenians to retake the island by force miscarried. In view of this unsettled situation Aristotle preferred not to retire to Chalcis where he might be captured by the Athenians. Since Stagira had been destroyed by Philip in 349 B.C. (it was later rebuilt thanks to Aristotle's personal intercession with Philip or Alexander), he could not return to his native city which, after all, in 348 B.C. was part of Macedonia.

Assuming that this interpretation of the cryptic remark found in

II VS 3–4 is essentially correct, then this priceless text would constitute, though in a highly condensed and certainly somewhat garbled form, the sole surviving report which sensibly and satisfactorily accounts for Aristotle's precipitate flight from Athens in the year 348 B.C., that is, several months before Plato's death. In any event, Aristotle's departure from Athens (and from the Platonic Academy) in 348 B.C. seems to have been a hasty flight prompted by sudden political developments instigated by Macedonia, rather than a deliberate and leisurely secession from an intellectual community for intellectual reasons.[19] It appears, therefore, that the two major external events in Aristotle's early life, namely, his journey to Athens in 367 B.C., and his departure from Athens in 348 B.C., were decisively determined by certain events related to Macedonia's political history.

It is quite possible that after leaving Athens in the summer of 348 B.C., Aristotle went first to Macedonia where he might have preferred to stay indefinitely. It was perhaps during his brief sojourn in Macedonia— he probably stayed at the court of King Philip in Pella—that he was advised (or probably ordered) by Philip to proceed to Asia Minor and 'join' Hermias of Atarneus for 'political' or 'imperialistic' reasons.[20] King Philip, we know, envisioned the conquest of Thrace; and, as early as 342 B.C., and probably several years before that time, he was toying with the idea of a Pan-Hellenic war against Persia or, at least, with an invasion of Asia Minor or Western Persia. Hence, he might have suggested to Aristotle (or perhaps commanded him) to seek out Hermias of Atarneus, and by acting as the political emissary or diplomatic agent of Macedonia, win him over to the Macedonian cause by inducing him to support and collaborate with Philip's political designs. Hermias' domain, which was strategically located 'near the Hellespont,' could serve both as an ideal base for the encirclement of Thrace, and as an effective bridgehead for the invasion of Asia Minor, provided Hermias might be persuaded to collaborate with Philip's schemes. At the same time, Hermias himself was in a most precarious position as regards Persia. Due to grave and protracted internal disorders within Persia, he had managed to achieve and maintain for some time a measure of political independence. But now, with Persia attempting to reassert its former domination, he was confronted with the certainty of Persian conquest and retaliation. Hence, Hermias probably welcomed, and perhaps sought, a military or political alliance with Macedonia, the rising power in the Eastern Mediterranean. This being so, Hermias actually may have approached King Philip, asking him for protection; or Philip, being aware of

Hermias' precarious situation, might have contacted the latter through Aristotle, who had some connections with Atarneus through Erastus and Coriscus, two former members of the Platonic Academy, and perhaps through Proxenus, the husband of Aristotle's sister, Arimneste.[21] An alliance between Philip and Hermias would have been beneficial to both rulers: Philip's military power would safeguard Hermias' independence in north-western Asia Minor, and Hermias could supply Philip with a convenient military base in Asia Minor. This might well have been the ultimate reason why Aristotle went to Atarneus in 348–47 B.C. In 341–40, that is, a few years after Aristotle had left him, Hermias was captured and put to death for 'treason' by the Persians. This fact lends weighty support to the thesis that Aristotle's sojourn with Hermias (348/47–345/44 B.C.)—a sojourn which might actually have been suggested by King Philip—might possibly have been a 'political mission' rather than a 'philosophic excursion.' Hence, it is reasonable to assume that Aristotle proceeded to Atarneus in 348–47 B.C. or, more likely, in the spring of 347 B.C., that is, after having spent the winter of 348–47 B.C. in Macedonia.

The Persians apparently became aware of these schemes, and it might have been Demosthenes who gave them this information in the hope of winning over the Persians as possible allies against Macedonia.[22] Perhaps Aristotle's transfer to Mytilene on the island of Lesbos in 345–44 B.C. and his return (or recall) to Macedonia in 343–42 B.C. likewise were connected with the negotiations that were carried on between Philip and Hermias or with the fact that the Persians had some knowledge of these negotiations.[23] In any event, the evidence supplied by Demosthenes and Areius Didymus seems to indicate that some 'diplomatic' or political contacts existed between Macedonia and Hermias, and that Aristotle played an active and probably important role in these negotiations.[24] But there exists some further evidence which might lend support to the thesis that Aristotle's stay with Hermias was primarily a diplomatic or political mission. King Artaxerxes III Ochus, who ruled Persia from 358 to 338 B.C., displayed more energy and certainly more ability than his immediate predecessors who in their weakness had permitted the western lands to revolt against, or secede from, Persia. He undertook to bring back under his rule not only Phoenicia, Cyprus and Egypt, but also Asia Minor. To accomplish this, he commissioned Mentor, a distinguished Greek mercenary soldier in the service of Persia, to retake the coast of the Troad, including the domain of Hermias, forcing the latter to re-submit to Persian rule. Diogenes Laertius relates that among the writings of

Aristotle were 'Letters [of Aristotle] addressed to Mentor.'[25] It might be tempting to speculate that the addressee of these letters, none of which has survived, is this Greek mercenary soldier, and that in these letters, Aristotle tried to persuade Mentor to desert Artaxerxes and join the cause of Hermias and, incidentally, that of Macedonia. In other words, by acting as the 'political agent' of both King Philip and Hermias, Aristotle corresponded with Mentor not only in the hope of mediating between Hermias and Mentor, but perhaps also in the hope of winning over Mentor to Philip's political and military designs against Persia. After all, this Mentor was not only a Greek, but also, and this might have been even more important, a mercenary soldier, that is, an adventurer as well as a venal person who might be persuaded to 'change sides.' Judging from the scanty evidence, Mentor seems to have feigned some interest in the proposals made by Aristotle (or Hermias) and hence might have pretended collaboration with Philip and Hermias. In the end, however, he remained loyal to the Persian king. Through the use of a ruse, he trapped and captured Hermias. This might be gathered from the remark contained in the honorific inscription at Delphi which at some later time Aristotle dedicated to the memory of Hermias. Here we are told that Hermias was treacherously betrayed 'with the aid of a man [Mentor] in whom he had put his trust.'[26] Mentor, it appears, deliberately deceived Hermias by making him believe that he had accepted his (or Aristotle's) offer. After having captured Hermias (in 341–40 B.C.), Mentor sent Hermias in chains to Artaxerxes who, by the use of torture, tried in vain[27] to extract from Hermias information concerning Philip's ultimate designs.[28]

The view that Aristotle's stay in Assos or Atarneus was primarily a diplomatic or political mission seems to receive additional support from the following fact: according to Areius Didymus,[29] Hermias first kept Aristotle (and Erastus, Coriscus and Xenocrates) in Atarneus in order to enjoy and profit by this close association and by the counsels Aristotle gave him. But later, after Aristotle had advised him well on many political issues—thanks to these counsels Hermias succeeded in winning over to his side some of the cities of the Aeolid—allegedly out of gratitude, he 'assigned' the city of Assos to Aristotle as his permanent domicile, that is, a city which is more than one hundred miles from Atarneus by land and about sixty miles by sea. A number of reasons have been advanced for this unusual arrangement which impresses us as being something of an exile from Hermias' 'capital'. There exists, however, what appears to be a reasonable explanation for this rather unusual action on the part of Hermias. We know that after a while the Persians began to suspect Hermias of treasonable dealings with Philip of Macedonia; and that they probably suspected Aristotle of being the resident diplomatic agent or emissary of Philip. Accordingly, perhaps in order to dispel this suspicion and thus assuage the Persians, Hermias might have sent Aristotle to Assos, thus keeping him at a distance and yet within his domain. Moreover, if together with Erastus and Coriscus he should pursue philosophic or scientific studies in Assos, this might, indeed, convince the Persians that his stay there was a 'philosophic excursion' rather than a diplomatic or political mission on behalf of Philip. All this, however, is conjecture.

Although Aristotle's sojourn in Atarneus or Assos, in all likelihood, was a 'political mission' rather than a 'philosophic excursion,' the presence in Atarneus, Assos or Scepsis of some of his old friends and former associates or 'fellow students' in the Platonic Academy— Erastus and Coriscus—probably made this sojourn even more attractive and, perhaps, even more promising as regards the political implications of his stay there. This interpretation of Aristotle's protracted visit with Hermias of Atarneus as a primarily 'political mission,' needless to say, is highly speculative, although in the light of the surviving, though extremely scanty evidence, it is by no means utterly fantastic. Aristotle's political and diplomatic activities in Atarneus and Assos might well have been part of what his biographers have called Aristotle's 'many diplomatic and statesman-like negotiations with kings and rulers,' activities for which he was often honored and admired by the mighty of this earth.[30]

After his departure from Assos in 345–44 B.C., Aristotle went first to Mytilene and then, in 343–42 B.C., to Macedonia. The withdrawal to Mytilene likewise might have had 'political overtones.' Mytilene, a city at the eastern end of the island of Lesbos, was situated across from the domain of Hermias, from which it is separated by a relatively narrow channel. From there he still could exert some influence on Hermias, while at the same time he was safely beyond the reach of the Persians. This, in turn, might indicate that as early as 345–44 B.C., the Persians had become aware of Aristotle's political activities in Atarneus and hence perhaps attempted to get hold of him.

Although tradition has it that Aristotle returned to Macedonia in 343–42 B.C., primarily for the purpose of educating young Alexander, it is safe to assume that he continued there his political activities on behalf of King Philip. Diogenes Laertius (V. 2), for instance, reports that at the time of Speusippus' death (in 339–38 B.C.), Aristotle was on a diplomatic mission to King Philip of Macedonia (representing the political interests of Athens?).[31] Although it is difficult to visualize that a Macedonian 'alien,' such as Aristotle, should at this time represent Athens and Athenian political interests at the Macedonian court, we might accept the fact that in one way or another Aristotle took an active part in the decisive negotiations between Macedonia and the several Greek states, including Athens, which took place prior to the battle of Chaeronea in 338 B.C.

It appears, however, that after the year 344-43 or 343-42 B.C., Aristotle withdrew for a while from all political activities on behalf of King Philip. There existed, it seems, a good reason for his temporary political inactivity. After 344-43 or 343-42 B.C., Philip apparently 'sold out,' if not outright betrayed, Hermias of Atarneus, the friend and kinsman of Aristotle, to the Persians. We know that the Athenians, and Demosthenes in particular, attempted to persuade the Persians to join them in a political and military alliance against Macedonia. The Athenians apparently knew about Philip's intention to turn Hermias into an ally and to use Hermias' territory as a convenient bridgehead for a planned invasion of Asia Minor as well as for a direct attack upon Persia. Wishing to ingratiate themselves with the Persians, the Athenians informed the latter of Philip's designs.[32] In order to placate the Persians and thus prevent a possible alliance between Athens and Persia—an alliance which might have been fatal to Macedonia's political aspirations—Philip, who in such matters could be quite unscrupulous, simply abandoned Hermias to the Persians. As might be expected, the Persians promptly and mercilessly disposed of Hermias, but not before they had attempted, though apparently without success, to extract from him by way of torture some information concerning his dealings with Macedonia. This crude betrayal of Hermias, which might well have been part of Philip's *Realpolitik*, must have been profoundly resented by Aristotle. Finding himself in complete disagreement with the Macedonian king and his handling of the 'Hermias affair,' Aristotle probably fell out with King Philip and hence, for the time being, simply abstained from engaging in any political or diplomatic activities on behalf of Philip of Macedonia.[33]

Regarding Aristotle's return to Athens in the year 335-34 B.C. or in the second year of the 111th Olympiad, that is, during the archonship of Evaenetus,[34] the biographers have relatively little to say that might cast some light on this important event.[35] The majority of these biographers or authors seem to imply that when Alexander invaded Asia in 334 B.C., or was about to get ready for this invasion (of which

Aristotle apparently did not approve), Aristotle felt free to depart from Macedonia and to return to Athens. Relieved of all duties and obligations—Alexander apparently did not ask Aristotle to accompany him to Persia—he simply moved back to Athens, leaving his ill-fated nephew Callisthenes of Olynthus with Alexander. Some ancient authors claim, however, that Aristotle left Macedonia and Alexander primarily because of a steadily growing mutual estrangement. Plutarch, for instance, maintains that at one time Alexander 'admired Aristotle above all other men,' and that 'he loved him . . . more than his own father. Later, however, he held him more or less in suspicion, not to the extent of doing him any harm, but his attentions lacked their former warmth and affection towards him.'[36] Dionysius of Halicarnassus, in turn, connects Aristotle's return to Athens in 335–34 B.C. with the sudden death (assassination) of King Philip in 336 B.C.[37] According to this latter report, Aristotle might have felt that the death of Philip had relieved him of all obligations to serve the Macedonian royal house. Perhaps he did not wish to serve Alexander (whom he might have suspected of being implicated in the murder of Philip). Or possibly, in the light of Alexander's growing distrust of Aristotle, the young king felt that he could dispense with Aristotle's services.

Aristotle's return to Athens in the year 335–34 B.C., however, might have been connected with another incident in the expansionist foreign policy of Macedonia.[38] After the assassination of King Philip in the summer of 336 B.C., Alexander, by a speedy show of force, immediately restored the Synedrion or Confederacy of Corinth, originally established by his father in 338 B.C. He accepted the timely submission of the Greek states, including that of Athens. Subsequently, he turned upon the Illyrians, Epirotes and Thracians, who likewise had revolted. In the past, the Greek patriots at Athens and elsewhere had often prayed for the death of King Philip whom they hated with a passion. Now they hoped for the demise of Alexander. Suddenly, rumors began to spread throughout Greece that Alexander, whom many Greeks regarded a 'mere boy' not to be feared by anyone, had been slain in battle somewhere in Thrace.[39] The hopes of the patriots ran high, hopes which were at once translated into reckless action. Only too willing to believe what they wanted to believe, they acted immediately in a most foolish manner and without first ascertaining the truth of Alexander's alleged death. Thebes, Athens and other Greek cities or states once more rose in revolt against their Macedonian overlords. But Alexander was very much alive. With lightning-like speed he descended upon Greece for a second time. He took the city of Thebes by storm (early in September of 335 B.C.) and ruthlessly destroyed it. Then he moved on to Athens, which promptly submitted in abject surrender. All this happened in the fall of 335 B.C., that is, during the archonship of Evaenetus (2nd year of the 111th Olympiad), and it was about this time that, according to what seems to be reliable tradition, Aristotle returned to Athens. Thus it appears that Aristotle moved back to Athens almost in the van of the conquering Macedonia phalanx—that he came back, or was brought back, by the force of arms. In any event, it is a rather curious, if not suggestive, phenomenon that the enforced submission of Athens to the Macedonians in the fall of 335 B.C. and Aristotle's sudden re-appearance in Athens should so closely coincide.

But there is additional evidence in support of the assumption that Aristotle's return to Athens in the year 335–34 B.C. in some way was related to Alexander's retaking that city. Ancient tradition is replete with stories that Aristotle exchanged many letters with kings and statesmen;[40] that he had much influence among the great men of his time,[41] and that numerous honors were bestowed upon him by kings and cities.[42] Moreover, according to these reports, he had many interviews (diplomatic negotiations?) with kings.[43] By these negotiations and dealings he promoted the interests of these kings and proved very useful to them.[44] Aristotle's biographers also refer to the many beneficial deeds and outstanding services he had rendered the city of Athens in particular, as well as to his frequent intercessions with King Philip and Alexander on behalf of the Athenians in order to promote the interests of Athens and secure the generous treatment of that city by the Macedonians.[45] It is possible (and quite likely) that in the year 335 B.C., Aristotle personally and successfully interceded with Alexander on behalf of the Athenians. In any event, while Thebes was razed after the abortive uprising, Athens was not only spared by Alexander, but apparently most generously treated. This may have been the result of Aristotle's personal intercession. Now we might also understand the story, told in great detail by Usaibia,[46] that 'on account of . . . the outstanding services he [scil., Aristotle] had rendered them, the Athenians . . . had an inscription . . . set up . . . [in which] they related that Aristotle . . . had served the city well by his many . . . services to the people of Athens, and especially, by his interventions with King Philip [and Alexander] for the purpose of promoting their interests and for seeing to it that they were treated kindly [by Philip and Alexander]. Hence, the people of Athens wished to make it quite clear . . . that they bestowed upon him [scil., Aristotle] distinction, honor, and praise; and that they would forever keep him in faithful and honored memory.'[47] All these honors and expressions of praise or gratitude might have been bestowed upon Aristotle—if, indeed, they were bestowed—because in the year 335 B.C. he had personally interceded with Alexander urging him to spare Athens the fate of Thebes,[48] and most likely because on previous occasions he had probably intervened with King Philip on behalf of the Athenians.

Needless to say, the very circumstances under which Aristotle returned to Athens in 335-34 B.C. made him extremely suspect as well as very much disliked by the Athenian public in general. In 348 B.C., it will be remembered, the Athenians had suspected him of sympathizing with Macedonia and with Macedonia's imperialistic aims and aspirations which became manifest in the Chalcidian War and, especially, in the attack on Olynthus. Now, in the year 335-34 B.C., they were absolutely convinced that he was a Macedonian 'political agent' or representative in Athens, installed in their very midst by their Macedonian conquerors in order to keep a close watch over them and, if necessary, to report any anti-Macedonian stirrings in the city as well as in other parts of Greece.

According to the general biographical tradition, Aristotle finally withdrew from Athens probably in the summer or early fall of 323 B.C. or in the second year of the 114th Olympiad, that is, during the archonship of Cephisodorus, approximately one year before he died in Chalcis.[49] The reason or reasons for his second departure from Athens are stated by Diogenes Laertius as follows: 'Aristotle . . . was indicted for impiety by the hierophant Eurymedon or, according to Favorinus and his *Miscellaneous History*, by Demophilus, the basis of this indictment being the hymn he composed in honor . . . of Hermias, as well as the honorific inscription for Hermias' statue in Delphi. . . .'[50] Athenaeus, in turn, maintains that Eurymedon made the motion to have Aristotle indicted for impiety, while Demophilus actually pressed the official charges.[51] The same Athenaeus also vigorously and at great length denies that Aristotle's hymn dedicated to the memory of Hermias, was a religious paean or hymn (and, hence, an act of 'blasphemy'), as alleged by Eurymedon, but rather was a *scolion*.[52] Mubashir[53] and Usaibia[54] insist that a hierophant by the name of Eurymedon gave a 'wholly distorted account' of Aristotle's philosophy;[55] that this Eurymedon was prompted by personal jealousy and because he bore an old personal grudge against Aristotle; and that Eurymedon claimed that Aristotle neither worshipped the traditional gods of the city nor otherwise showed them the proper respect.[56]

According to Mubashir, Eurymedon also called Aristotle 'a man who should be shunned by everyone.'[57] 'When Aristotle learned about this,' Mubashir continues,[58] 'he withdrew from Athens . . . fearing that they [scil., the Athenians] might do to him what they had done to Socrates . . . whom they had executed.'[59]

The reports of Mubashir and Usaibia in substance seem to be in accord with the traditional stories connected with the indictment and trial of Socrates in the year 399 B.C. Like the accusations made against Socrates at that time,[60] the charge of impiety brought against Aristotle in 323 B.C. might very well have been a mere 'token charge'—a screen issue for what in reality was an essentially political incident motivated by political resentment and personal prejudice.[61] According to Usaibia, Aristotle departed from Athens voluntarily and before any further official proceedings were instituted against him. It also appears that no one interfered, or tried to interfere, with his departure or 'did him any harm before he departed.'[62] These facts seem to lend weighty support to the assumption that the charges made against Aristotle in 323 B.C. were in fact only 'token charges' or a mere pretext: the Athenian patriots just intended to rid themselves one way or another of an unwanted and highly suspect foreigner—of a man whom they suspected of being a political agent of their mortal foe.[63] This also seems to follow, (i) from the statement that Aristotle 'should be shunned by everyone,'[64] a remark which might imply that no self-respecting Athenian patriot would have anything to do with this avowed enemy of Athens; (ii) from the observation that Eurymedon turned against Aristotle 'from jealousy' and because of 'an old grudge,' an explanation or justification which might allude to the hatred which Eurymedon, an Athenian patriot, bore towards Aristotle, the Macedonian 'enemy'; and (iii) from the statement that this Eurymedon gave 'a wholly distorted account' of Aristotle's philosophy, a report which might signify that Eurymedon saw in Aristotle primarily the enemy rather than the benefactor of Athens and, hence, was not interested in Aristotle's philosophy or religious views, of which he probably knew little if anything.[65] Now we may also understand why the several *Vitae Aristotelis* emphasize again and again the many beneficial services Aristotle had rendered the city of Athens:[66] Under the pretext of moral scruples and religious orthodoxy, the shabby Athenians turned upon one of their greatest benefactors.

It has already been shown that, for the majority of the Athenians, Aristotle was always an unwanted, unpopular and highly suspect 'resident Macedonian alien.' He lived in the city more by sufferance than by right, always subject to arbitrary and capricious prosecution (and persecution) as well as to sudden expulsion.[67] After 335–34 B.C., in particular, the pro-Macedonian party in Athens, feeling secure under the military protection of Alexander and Antipater, brazenly stepped into the open. Hence, they were hated more than ever by the anti-Macedonian or patriotic faction in the city which could still vent its hatred and fears in oratorical contests (Demosthenes and Aeschines). Faced with the military might of Macedonia and the well-known efficiency of Antipater, however, the anti-Macedonian partisans found themselves utterly powerless to act at that time—something which drove them almost to a frenzy of frustration. Aristotle's close ties, personal as well as 'official,' with King Philip, Alexander and later with Antipater,[68] for some time had been a matter of common knowledge as well as the cause of much gossiping and profound resentment in essentially anti-Macedonian Athens.[69] Especially after his return to Athens in 335–34 B.C., Aristotle seems to have been under the special protection of Antipater, whom Alexander had left in Europe as his lieutenant, 'care-taker' or 'watchdog' and as the Macedonian military commander-in-chief in Macedonia and Greece. For some unknown reason, close ties of personal and lasting friendship developed between Aristotle and Antipater, between two men who otherwise had very little in common. It would not be too fanciful to assume that Aristotle, in the main, was in full accord with Antipater's political tasks and aims, although in keeping with his conciliatory disposition and friendly leanings towards Hellenic intellectual culture, he probably tempered some of Antipater's plans and methods. But outwardly he completely supported the policies and actions of the latter. No wonder, therefore, that the Athenian patriots, blinded by fierce hatred and short-sighted prejudice, should see in Aristotle primarily a mortal enemy as well as a dangerous Macedonian agent—a key foe of the anti-Macedonian or patriotic partisans (including Demosthenes, Lycurgus, Hyperides and Himeraeus), a vicious despoiler of Hellenic freedom, a relentless opponent of the 'good old political ways' and a most dangerous agent or instrument of Macedonian domination over the city— and that they should consider the men around him not perhaps as students or intellectual associates, but rather as members of a conspiracy bent upon keeping Athens in permanent submission to Macedonia.[70]

Already in the year 348 B.C., Aristotle had experienced the effects of a sudden outbreak of anti-Macedonian resentment among the Athenians. Then, too, he was compelled to flee Athens. Ten years later, the battle of Chaeronea tolled the end of Greek political independence. The unexpected assassination of King Philip in 336 B.C. for a brief moment revived the hopes of the patriots, as did the false rumor of Alexander's death in 335 B.C. After the abortive anti-Macedonian uprising in 335 B.C., when the Athenians made their timely submission to Alexander, Aristotle dared to come back to Athens and live openly among his former enemies, protected by the armed might of Macedonia. Then, in the year 323 B.C., the tidings reached Athens that Alexander had died in Babylon in the month of June. Although the patriots had been living on the slender hope that some disaster might befall Alexander, they fully realized that it would be plain madness to defy the king openly. Hence, almost to the man the Athenians, in the beginning, refused to believe the 'good tidings.' This time, however, the news proved to be correct: Alexander had died and Antipater, his lieutenant in Macedonia and Greece, at this very moment had been summoned to Asia and, hence, could no longer protect Aristotle or effectively enforce Macedonia's military control over Athens and Greece.[71] This situation, as is commonly known, led to the so-called Lamian War. Since in the year 335–34 B.C. Aristotle had returned to Athens in the van of the conquering Macedonian army, he was probably more intensely disliked than ever by the Athenians, who in all likelihood considered him the pernicious instrument of their conquerors and oppressors. This general and widespread opinion, after all, might not have been too far from the actual truth. Thus, twelve years later, in 323 B.C., when Athens once more revolted against its Macedonian overlords, Aristotle was naturally one of the prime targets of popular wrath and wanton persecution. In a way, it appears that Aristotle's sojourn in Athens, at least after 335 B.C., was irretrievably bound up with the Macedonian fortunes of war. A Macedonian defeat or the death of its great soldier-king (which would unavoidably have led to serious internal disorders in Macedonia as well as to fierce and prolonged struggles among his generals), or the absence or impotence of one of his lieutenants in Europe, automatically spelled disaster for Aristotle, cutting short his sojourn in Athens.[72]

In support of the contention that Aristotle's flight from Athens in the year 323 B.C. was prompted primarily by political factors and circumstances rather than by his allegedly 'blasphemous' deportment, the following additional piece of evidence may be adduced: a story can be found in Usaibia[73] which most eloquently presages the political troubles Aristotle was about to experience in Athens. (This story may even depict, though probably in a garbled fashion, what actually did happen.) Here we are told that some Athenians, presumably philo-Macedonian partisans, had moved, or perhaps decreed, that a public inscription should be erected on the Acropolis, honoring Aristotle and recording the many public services he had rendered the city.[74] This motion, Usaibia continues, was vehemently opposed by an Athenian named Aimaraeus (Himeraeus), who is also said to have subsequently removed or destroyed the honorific inscription or *stele*.[75] Himeraeus, we know, was a prominent as well as very active member of the anti-Macedonian faction in Athens, and probably a personal enemy of Aristotle.[76]

The extant *Vitae Aristotelis*, it cannot be emphasized often enough, advance no less than three major reasons for the official action taken against Aristotle in the year 323 B.C.: the 'blasphemous' paean or hymn in honor of Hermias of Atarneus as well as the honorific inscription dedicated to the memory of the unfortunate Hermias and erected at Delphi;[77] the close political and personal ties which existed between Aristotle and the Macedonian royal house;[78] and the 'distorted interpretation' of Aristotle's teachings, which had led people to believe that he did not worship properly.[79] But minute analysis of all these allegations should divulge that his political and personal connections with Philip, Alexander and Antipater in all likelihood constituted the primary and most urgent reason for the attacks upon Aristotle in the year 323 B.C., and concomitantly, became the prime cause for his hasty departure. Thus, it should be persuasively clear that the general political situation in Athens in the summer of 323 B.C. precipitated Aristotle's withdrawal to Chalcis. The confirmed news of Alexander's sudden death (and Antipater's absence) presented the Athenian patriots with an unexpected—and unprecedented—opportunity to regain political independence from Macedonian domination. Athens simply rose in revolt, as she had done previously in 335 B.C. on the false rumor of Alexander's unexpected death in Thrace. As other Greek cities joined the uprising (designated the Lamian War), Aristotle found himself surrounded on all sides by undisguised hostility. Fearing the worst, he simply left Athens, never to return. It is possible that the Athenians actually intended to bring formal charges and start legal proceedings against Aristotle.[80] But these proceedings, if they were in fact initiated, were really a mere pretext to vent formally the general hatred the average Athenian had for anything Macedonian and, in particular, for Aristotle, the suspect political agent of Macedonia. Of special interest to us is the report of Usaibia that no one apparently interfered with, or tried to prevent, his departure from Athens.[81] Judging from Aristotle's last will and testament as it is preserved by Diogenes Laertius[82] and also by some of the Arabic biographers,[83] Aristotle was permitted to take with him his many servants as well as all his movable property.[84] All this would indicate that the Athenians were primarily interested in ridding themselves of this unwanted and distrusted alien, whom they considered an enemy agent in their very midst, representing and promoting Macedonian political and imperialistic interest in Athens, the heartland of the Hellenic world.

The striking parallels between the political and military fortunes of Macedonia and the sojourns of Aristotle in Athens are highly suggestive, to say the least. They may possibly imply that Aristotle was something more than a withdrawn intellectual, something more than a mere 'ivory tower' philosopher who spent his time in the exclusive pursuit of philosophic truth and theoretic speculation. He was perhaps a kind of political agent working for Macedonia (and the Macedonian royal house in particular), doing yeoman's duties for Philip and later for Alexander and Antipater, Alexander's lieutenant in Europe. It is certainly not insignificant that, according to tradition, Aristotle exchanged a great many letters or communications with Antipater, and that in his last will and testament he appointed Antipater 'chief executor' of this will.[85] These letters, it must be repeated here, might have contained 'intelligence reports' on the political situation and events in Athens and, probably, in the rest of Greece.[86] Antipater, whose background and upbringing were radically different from those of Aristotle, certainly was neither a scholar nor a person interested in scholarship or philosophic discourse. Hence, it would be difficult to imagine that in these many letters Aristotle should have discussed philosophic subjects with Antipater. This leaves, and this cannot be stressed often enough, but one intelligent explanation for the ample correspondence which passed between these two men who otherwise had little in common: these letters were regular official accounts or intelligence reports. In his *Oration Against the Philosophers* of 306 B.C., it has already been pointed out several times, Demochares claims outright that many of Aristotle's letters addressed to Antipater had been intercepted by the Athenians, and that the content of these letters was found to be detrimental to Athens and to Athenian political interests.[87] Assuming that Demochares' allegations are true, then this charge would clearly indicate that Aristotle had supplied Antipater, and before that Philip and Alexander, with vital information concerning the political events in Athens and throughout Greece.

It would be unusual, indeed, if Aristotle, intellectually the most prominent Macedonian of his time, the best educated Macedonian conversant with Athenian and Greek conditions in general, and the close friend of King Philip and Antipater, should not have played an active and, perhaps, important role in the meteoric rise of Macedonia from a relatively insignificant and semi-barbaric mountain people to a cosmocracy within one generation—the generation of Aristotle. In keeping with his peculiar talents and interests, and by making use of his acquaintance with Athenian and Greek intellectuals, as well as consonant with his intellectual stature—qualifications which were extremely rare in Macedonia during the fourth century B.C.—it is only natural that Athens, the intellectual capital of the Hellenic world and one of the most important centers of Greek political activism, should become the place of Aristotle's political and diplomatic activities: he was dispatched to Athens in order to work for and, if possible, to facilitate the political aims and aspirations of Macedonia and, at the same time, to keep a watchful eye on any anti-Macedonian stirrings in Athens and throughout Greece.

By way of a summation of Aristotle's major political involvements, the following important facts must be emphasized even at the risk of becoming somewhat repetitious: in the year 348 B.C., when Aristotle was about thirty-six years old, he was compelled to flee from Athens because of King Philip's encroachment upon an Athenian sphere of political interest. He ultimately went to Hermias of Atarneus in order to escape a sudden outburst of intense anti-Macedonian sentiments in Athens over the capture of Olynthus by Philip. Tradition has it that he went to Assos or Atarneus in 348-47 B.C., because the Platonic Academy had established there a sort of 'foreign branch' in the persons of Erastus and Coriscus, two former members of the Academy.[88] It should not be overlooked, however, that Hermias' small but strategically located domain could possibly furnish an ideal base for military and political operations in the East,[89] provided Hermias could be won over to Philip's designs. It is possible, therefore, that Philip sent Aristotle to Hermias as his emissary or agent. Aristotle returned to Macedonia in 343-42 B.C. His departure from Assos or Atarneus, first for Mytilene and later for Macedonia, might have been occasioned or at least hastened by the fact that the Persians had become suspicious of Hermias' dealings with Macedonia through the intermediary of Aristotle and, hence, began to close in on Hermias.[90] He might have been recalled by Philip himself who apparently knew that the Athenians had approached the Persians informing them of Philip's plans and suggesting a possible political and military alliance against

Macedonia. In order to forestall such an alliance, he simply ordered Aristotle to leave Hermias.[91]

It may also be noted that upon leaving Assos or Atarneus, Aristotle did not immediately return to Macedonia, but rather went to Mytilene on the island of Lesbos, which is separated from the Asiatic mainland (and from the domain of Hermias) only by a relatively narrow channel. One might explain, therefore, Aristotle's temporary removal to Mytilene as follows: since the Persians could be expected sooner or later to move in on Hermias, it was no longer safe for Aristotle to stay on the mainland, where he might be abducted or murdered by the Persians. Hence he was sent to Mytilene, where he was relatively safe and yet close enough to Hermias to make his personal influence felt. Only when Philip realized the utter hopelessness of Hermias' situation in the face of Persia's determination to dispose of the latter, did he recall Aristotle to Macedonia, allegedly under the pretext that Aristotle should undertake the education of Alexander, leaving Hermias to his doom. Indeed, in 341-40 B.C., Hermias was captured and put to death by the Persians. It is also possible that Aristotle contacted, or wrote 'letters' to, Mentor from Mytilene, trying to win him over to the cause of Macedonia (?).

King Philip's deliberate and crude betrayal of Hermias might also shed some light on, and intelligently explain, the ultimate meaning of the following incident: when about to die under torture, after his treacherous capture by the Persians, Hermias is said to have sent a message to his friends (Aristotle?, Philip?) telling them that 'he had done nothing dishonorable or unworthy of philosophy.'[92] Perhaps this message implied that he had not betrayed to the Persians any political secrets or divulged the agreements he had reached with King Philip through the mediation of Aristotle.[93] Aside from the fact that he was the personal friend as well as the kinsman of Hermias (through his marriage to Pythias), Aristotle's lifelong admiration for Hermias, which was also shared by some of Aristotle's friends, might properly be explained by Hermias' staunch loyalty to Macedonia and by his refusal to betray, even under torture, his Macedonian friends and allies. Aristotle's eloquent reply to Hermias' courage and loyalty was the noble cenotaph he erected in Delphi in honor of Hermias, the moving hymn or elegy he composed in memory of Hermias and the elaborate funeral or memorial services he held for Hermias.[94] This seems to be the most persuasive as well as most logical explanation of these many posthumous memorials instituted by Aristotle in honor of Hermias— memorials which subsequently were resented and denounced by

Aristotle's detractors, and which were used by his enemies to indict him for 'blasphemy' or 'impiety' in 323 B.C. One might maintain that the death of Hermias spelled the end of certain political plans or aims for which Aristotle had been working for a long time. The cruel and treacherous treatment of Hermias by the Persians might also explain Aristotle's subsequent dislike and contempt for 'barbarians,' and for the 'barbaric' Persians in particular.[95]

The ancient biographies of Aristotle, it will be remembered, are replete with numerous accounts of the many noble and beneficial deeds the Stagirite had performed for Greek (and non-Greek) cities and peoples, and for Athens as well as for King Philip in particular. They likewise relate that he did all this by making use of his personal influence with King Philip, Olympias, Alexander, Antipater and other powerful people[96]—an influence which must have been considerable. We are also told of the many and important diplomatic missions he undertook on behalf of Macedonia, Athens and of other cities or peoples as well.[97] In the year 335–34 B.C., he returned to Athens, the key city of the whole Hellenic world and of the Corinthian Confederacy—the most renowned city in the Eastern Mediterranean. He returned there, we may surmise, in order to help establish, stabilize and enhance Macedonia's political influence and standing throughout Greece; and he probably also tried to make Macedonian domination more humane and more bearable to the Greeks.

One may ask here why Aristotle did not return to Athens immediately after the battle of Chaeronea in August of 338 B.C., especially since this battle, which amounted to a complete rout of the Greek forces, finally and irrevocably established Macedonian military and political control over the whole of Greece and hence made Athens once more accessible to him. Moreover, at about this time Aristotle's supposed 'education' of Alexander had come to an end.[98] Thanks to his close association with the Macedonian royal family and with King Philip in particular, Aristotle must have known that, in the words of Demaratus, Philip had 'filled his house with bitterness and division.'[99] When Philip put away his wife Olympias, the mother of Alexander, and married Cleopatra, the niece (and ward) of Attalus, Aristotle, who knew the temperament of Olympias as well as that of Alexander only too well, anticipated serious troubles, especially, since Philip's action also jeopardized Alexander's succession to the throne of Macedonia.[100] Perhaps King Philip, who would not brook objections, began to distrust Aristotle who, after all, probably expressed his strong disapproval of the manner in which Philip had betrayed Hermias of

Atarneus. It is also possible that Aristotle had counselled King Philip against divorcing Olympias and marrying Cleopatra, thus incurring the king's displeasure. Perhaps King Philip suspected Aristotle of sympathizing with Olympias and Alexander. Unfortunately, we do not know anything about the particular role, if any, Aristotle played in Philip's domestic troubles, although tradition has it that he was highly esteemed by Olympias.[101] We know, however, that after his divorce and remarriage, King Philip apparently began to suspect some of his former friends and confidants. In the light of all this, it might be presumed that for the time being Aristotle assumed an attitude of 'wait and see' before committing himself for either Philip or Alexander, two men who had become mutually estranged.

This impasse was resolved with the assassination of King Philip in the summer of 336 B.C. Philip was cut down by a certain Pausanias, an obscure man who claimed to have been wronged by Attalus. When Philip refused to redress this wrong, Pausanias simply slew him. The assassin was immediately cut down, but the true author or authors of this crime were never discovered. It was widely rumored, however, that Olympias had instigated the murder and that Alexander, who had most to gain by this foul deed, was privy to the plot. But there might have been further reasons or explanation for Aristotle's dilatory attitude or 'political inactivism' after c. 341-40 B.C. It has already been shown that about this time, King Philip, in order to forestall a possible political and military alliance between Athens and Persia, had simply abandoned Hermias of Atarneus to the Persians. Resenting this crude act of *Realpolitik*, Aristotle temporarily withdrew from all political activities on behalf of King Philip.[102]

When Alexander, the only man who could possibly hold together Macedonia and its many conquests (and its many ambitious generals), died unexpectedly 13 June 323 B.C., Aristotle's position in Athens, which had always been extremely precarious, became utterly untenable, the more so, since at this very moment Antipater was on his way to Persia, thus leaving him without adequate military protection. Antipater, to be sure, restored Macedonian control over Athens and Greece in the late summer or early fall of 322 B.C., by defeating the Greeks in the battle of Crannon. But by that time Aristotle was on his deathbed (in Chalcis), if not already dead. Otherwise, he might well have returned to Athens once more.[103]

The many and, at times, detailed biographical references to, or accounts of, Aristotle's numerous dealings and negotiations with kings and statesmen; to the apparently decisive influence he had with some of the leading political personalities of his time; to the many meritorious deeds he performed for cities and kings; and to the numerous honors which were bestowed upon him by grateful kings, princes, potentates, cities and communities [104]—all these reports are certainly significant. They cannot be ignored, nor can they simply be brushed aside as purely encomiastic inventions by some later authors who wished to exalt and magnify Aristotle and, accordingly, deliberately concocted these 'stories.' [105] This leaves us with but one intelligent explanation: Aristotle must have been actively and perhaps decisively (and successfully) involved in some of the many and far-reaching political activities and schemes of King Philip of Macedonia, [106] one of the shrewdest as well as most successful statesmen of Hellenic antiquity. It was this involvement which, among other experiences, forced him twice to leave Athens rather hurriedly and to 'run for his life.' It is intriguing to realize that one of the greatest intellects the ancient Mediterranean world has produced should play an important role in the crucial political events which not only re-shaped the whole of Greek history, but which also ushered in a wholly novel and crucially decisive epoch in Western history. In a manner and on a scale of which Plato could never have dreamed, this former member of the Platonic Academy carried out one of the basic aims as well as major tenets of the Academy: to re-shape and re-orientate the political and cultural affairs of the whole of Western mankind. [107]

Chapter XIV

The Myth of Aristotle's Suicide*

Diogenes Laertius V. 6 relates that 'according to Eumelus, in the fifth Book of his *Histories*, [Aristotle died] by drinking the hemlock, at the age of seventy.'[1] The *Vita Aristotelis Hesychii*, presumably on the authority of Eumelus (or a source used by Eumelus), likewise reports that Aristotle ended his life by drinking the hemlock at the age of seventy.[2] Whether this Eumelus is identical with the Peripatetic Eumelus who authored an *On the Old Comedy* (Περὶ ἀρχαίας κωμῳδίας), cannot be determined.[3] In any event, Eumelus, the source cited by Diogenes Laertius, apparently transfers to Aristotle the life span of Socrates as well as the manner in which the latter met his death. Accordingly, we may safely disregard the testimony of Eumelus and call it pure fiction.[4]

Being indicted for alleged 'impiety' and 'blasphemy,' or more likely, because of sudden and unfavorable political developments in the city, Aristotle fled from Athens in the later summer or early autumn of 323 B.C. He died in 322 B.C. in Chalcis on the island of Euboea, probably in the late summer or early fall of that year.[5] *II Vita Aristotelis Syriaca* maintains that 'Aristotle withdrew to Chalcis on Euboea and there ended his life watching (studying) the ebb and flow of the Euripus.'[6] Similarly, the *Vita Aristotelis Arabica* of Al-Mubashir narrates that Aristotle 'withdrew to Chalcidice [should read, Chalcis] . . . in order to study the ebb and flow of the gulf [should read, straits] of the Euripus close to Euboea, and in order to write a book about this phenomenon.'[7] It is possible, indeed, that during the last year of his life, that is, when he was sixty-one or sixty-two years old, Aristotle was still interested in, and preoccupied with, scientific studies and investigations. Phenomena of nature, according to a distinct tradition, apparently always had a special attraction for him. What is disturbing in this account, however, is the fact that this particular tradition, which credits Aristotle with having studied the tides of the Euripus shortly before his death, is apparently of a fairly late date, late enough to be possibly classified as a piece of Hellenistic fabrication. This particular account, which by no means is above suspicion, also records that Aristotle was unable to solve this problem and, in a fit of despondency over his failure, either took his own life or died of a 'broken heart.'[8]

It may be well to remember that Greek tradition abounds with stories of wise men and philosophers either deteriorating physically or ending their own lives after having experienced some unsupportable personal chagrin.[9] Diogenes Laertius reports, for instance, that when Diodorus Cronos, the pupil of Eubulides, stayed with Ptolemy Soter, Stilpo, the casuist, 'put certain dialectical questions to him. Being unable to solve them on the spot, he was reproached by the king [Ptolemy Soter] and, among other slights, the nickname Cronos [old fool] was attached to him by way of ridicule. He left the banquet and, after composing a pamphlet on the logical question, took his own life, being utterly despondent.'[10] Likewise, Homer is said to have died of shame because he failed to solve 'the riddle of the lice.'[11] There was Menedemus of Eretria who died of a broken heart after being suspected of the theft of some golden goblets from the temple of Amphiaraus in Oropus.[12] Again, Speusippus, the successor of Plato in the scholarchate of the Academy, in his old days became so melancholic over his poor health that he died by his own hand.[13] Finally, Menippus the Cynic hung himself when robbed of all his earthly goods by some fraudulent scheme.[14] Whether or not the above examples are true, we can readily understand the origin of this tale about Aristotle's chagrin and consequent death by suicide: as a philosopher who had failed to solve a scientific problem, he simply despaired and died either of a broken heart or by taking his own life.

The story of Aristotle's alleged suicide in certain respects resembles too closely the tale of Socrates' death, which for some Greek authors apparently had become the ideal *exodus* befitting the true philosopher who is faced with an insoluble problem. Probably some encomiastic biographer, who can no longer be identified, wished to exalt Aristotle and, accordingly, invented the myth of Aristotle's suicide. We may safely disregard this whole account as pure fiction.[15] It cannot be ascertained, however, whether the story of Aristotle's suicide goes back as far as Hermippus, who seems to have had a predilection for such morbid or sensational incidents in the life of philosophers.

Censorinus[16] and others credibly relate, on the other hand, that Aristotle died a natural death,[17] and that the cause of his death was a stomach ailment (ulcer or cancer of the stomach?).[18] Neither the *Vita Aristotelis Marciana*, nor the *Vita Aristotelis Vulgata*, nor the *Vita*

Aristotelis Latina makes any mention of Aristotle's alleged suicide. An-Nadim,[19] Al-Mubashir[20] and Usaibia,[21] as well as the *I Vita Aristotelis Syriaca*[22] and the *II Vita Aristotelis Syriaca*,[23] do not imply that Aristotle took his own life (or that he died of despair). Al-Mubashir, for instance, relates that 'death came to him [*scil.*, Aristotle] there [*scil.*, in Chalcis], and he died there'; and Usaibia remarks that 'when Aristotle had arrived at his home in Chalcis, he stayed there until he died.'[24] From all this we may infer that the biographical tradition of Aristotle as it had been established by Ptolemy (-el-Garib) was not familiar with any reports of a suicidal death of Aristotle, or that it outright rejected these reports. And it is on this tradition that the Syriac and Arabic biographers relied primarily, and on which the *Vita Aristotelis Marciana*, the *Vita Aristotelis Vulgata* and the *Vita Aristotelis Latina* rely to a large extent. Diogenes Laertius, who in the choice of his sources or authorities is oftentimes indiscriminately eclectic and, hence, is not always trustworthy, points out that Eumelus is in error when he maintains that Aristotle joined Plato only at the age of thirty and that he died at the age of seventy.[25] On the other hand, Diogenes seems to give credence to the story that Aristotle died by committing suicide when he writes in his epigram: 'One day Eurymedon, the priest of Demeter, resolved to indict Aristotle for impiety. But he [*scil.*, Aristotle], by a draught of poison, painlessly escaped prosecution, thus triumphing over groundless calumnies.'[26] Hence, one might argue that Diogenes Laertius, on the one hand, rejects Eumelus' statement that Aristotle joined Plato at the age of thirty and that he died at the age of seventy, while, on the other hand, he apparently accepts the story that he died by committing suicide. Moreover, Diogenes Laertius also seems to imply that Aristotle died in Athens.

From all this it appears that the most stable and most reliable traditions or accounts of Aristotle's death fail to mention so sensational an event as his suicide. These accounts, then, far outweigh those reports which originated with a much later (and perhaps romantic or encomiastic?) tradition. In any event, we may wholly ignore the unusual and unsupported story told by Eumelus which simply transfers to Aristotle not only some of the events which apparently transpired in the year 399 B.C. in connection with the death of Socrates, but also the age of Socrates at the time of his death as well as the manner in which he died. Eumelus also makes it appear that Aristotle may have committed suicide in Athens, although all extant ancient *Vitae Aristotelis* are quite emphatic about the fact that he fled to Chalcis where he met his death. Some *Vitae* go so far as to imply that Aristotle's withdrawal to Chalcis was a rather leisurely affair, permitting him to take along all of his personal property[27] as well as all his servants.

Aside from falsifying Aristotle's age at the time of his death, Eumelus also seems to overlook an important fact when he claims that Aristotle answered the indictment for impiety by committing suicide: Socrates stayed in Athens, his native city, and drank the hemlock after he had been condemned to death. Aristotle, the Macedonian alien, on the other hand, repaired to Chalcis before his trial was held. And in Chalcis there was certainly no need for him to take his own life because of the hostile attitude taken by his Athenian enemies. Since we know almost nothing about Eumelus, it is also impossible to ascertain whether his unusual story was perhaps influenced by the Stoic glorification of suicide.[28] But there might be a reasonable explanation for Eumelus' account: on leaving Athens in 323 B.C., according to some biographers, Aristotle is said to have justified his flight with the remark that 'he would not give Athens a second chance to sin against philosophy.'[29] This particular account might well be the biographer's rejoinder to the charge that Aristotle was really a coward and, hence, an 'unphilosophic man' who had run away rather than stay in Athens and, as Socrates had done, face his accusers or enemies in open court (and in the name of philosophy). Eumelus (or his source), it appears, goes one better. He rebuts the detractors of Aristotle, who had charged him with cowardice, by claiming outright that Aristotle died as Socrates had died: he did not leave Athens and he, too, drank the hemlock.

The epigram of Diogenes Laertius,[30] aside from the fact that it is probably one of the worst pieces of Greek 'poetry' ever published, cannot be taken seriously, not to mention the fact that its author contradicts himself,[31] in as much as he had previously rejected the story of Aristotle's alleged suicide. The account that Aristotle took his life in a fit of despondency because he had been indicted for impiety or because he had failed to solve the 'riddle of the Euripus,'[32] is wholly unsupported, not to say fantastic. In all likelihood, this account is a late (Hellenistic) fabrication, as is the equally fanciful report that he died of chagrin over his failure.[33] Eumelus' reference to Aristotle's age at the time of his death, insisting that he was seventy years old;[34] his account of the particular circumstances surrounding this event; and his statement of the specific manner in which he took his own life—all these stories clearly indicate that Eumelus' whole report is simply a naïve transfer of the 'death of Socrates' to that of Aristotle.

Viewed in a broader context, ancient tradition contains no less than five different (major) versions of Aristotle's death and the circumstances surrounding this event: (i) Aristotle withdrew (or fled) to Chalcis in 323 B.C., moved into the home of his maternal ancestors and died there a natural death (from a stomach ailment?) in 322 B.C. (ii) Shortly before his death Aristotle moved from Athens to Chalcis, presumably in order to study the mysterious ebb and flow of the Euripus and, perhaps, in order to write a scholarly treatise about this unusual phenomenon. However, he died of natural causes before he succeeded in resolving this problem. (iii) In his old age Aristotle went to Chalcis primarily in order to study the Euripus. But when he failed in this task, he died of a 'broken heart' over his failure. (iv) When Aristotle failed to solve the puzzle of the Euripus, he took his own life in a fit of despondency. And (v) Aristotle committed suicide (in Athens?) by taking the hemlock in order to escape persecution and possible condemnation by the Athenians (who utterly failed to understand him or to appreciate the many beneficial deeds he had performed for Athens). It is fairly safe to assume that versions ii–v are later Hellenistic inventions or perhaps later romantic fabrications which might have been put into circulation during the third, second and first centuries B.C. Version (v), in particular, aside from being an obvious transfer of the death of Socrates, definitely smacks of Hellenistic romanticism. It takes up an issue which, since the time of Plato's *Phaedo*, and probably before that time, had apparently preoccupied many philosophers and biographers: how does the true philosopher face death, and how does his philosophy stand up in the hour of death? The manner in which the philosopher meets death in a large manner decides not only what sort of a man he was and what kind of a life he had lived, but it also determines the ultimate significance as well as the final worth of the particular philosophy he professed. Unless in his tragic confrontation with mankind's universal wickedness and stupidity the gentle philosopher is willing to lay down his life for his philosophy and for philosophy in general, in truth he has no philosophy worthy of the name nor does he truly love philosophy— an interesting though by no means novel version of John 15:13: 'Greater love hath no man than this, that a man lay down his life for his friends.' Conversely, version (i) probably relates what seem to have been the true historical facts, provided we keep in mind that Aristotle's removal to Chalcis was really a flight occasioned by the hostility the Athenians openly displayed towards him.

One of the rather puzzling aspects of Western tradition in particular seems to be the almost impulsive insistence that a 'hero' or human benefactor is not supposed to die a natural or peaceful death. Otherwise he probably might not be accepted as a true 'hero' or human benefactor. We have but to remember the ultimate fate of Prometheus, Hercules, Palamedes or that of Socrates, to mention only a few outstanding examples in Hellenic antiquity. Moreover, this 'hero' frequently also had to be a martyr of his own noble convictions or of his humanitarian accomplishments, whose many beneficial deeds for mankind dramatically were repaid by flagrant ingratitude on the part of those who benefited most by his accomplishments or teachings. Perhaps some encomiastic biographers or plain romancers, wishing to turn Aristotle into a true 'hero' conforming to this particular 'hero-pattern,' simply invented the story of Aristotle's 'unnatural death' into which he was driven by the ingratitude and stupidity of the very people who owed him an everlasting debt, as well as by the general human wickedness or viciousness. In this manner Aristotle also was turned into a 'witness unto philosophic truth,' a martyr in the cause of philosophy.

Chapter XV

Aristotle's Last Will and Testament*

The text of Aristotle's last will and testament, or at least an abridged version of it, has been preserved by Diogenes Laertius (DL V. 11–16), Ibn An-Nadim, Al-Qifti Gamaladdin and Ibn Abi Usaibia.[1] Without question, this important legal instrument or document is wholly authentic, although in the course of its transmission it may have been somewhat mutilated or, perhaps, slightly abridged. At the same time, it is the most revealing as well as the most extensive and most important piece of primary evidence from among the few surviving documents relating to the life of Aristotle. Most scholars are of the opinion that the particular version preserved by Diogenes Laertius ultimately goes back to Hermippus, possibly through the intermediary of Favorinus, and that Hermippus himself probably derived his (abridged?) text of Aristotle's will from Ariston of Ceos.[2] The versions recorded by An-Nadim, Al-Qifti and Usaibia, on the other hand, go back to Ptolemy (-el-Garib) and, ultimately, to Andronicus of Rhodes,[3] who in turn might have consulted or used (at least indirectly and probably through several intermediaries or reporters) Hermippus or Ariston of Ceos, or both, unless he had direct access to the original document, an unlikely surmise.

It is widely believed that around the year A.D. 900, Ishaq Ibn Hunayn made an Arabic translation of Ptolemy (-el-Garib)'s *On the Life of Aristotle,* either directly from the Greek original, or more likely, from a Syriac translation (or epitome) of Ptolemy's work.[4] Ibn Hunayn was a very accurate and most conscientious translator, although he (or his Syriac source) might have had some difficulties with certain Greek legal or technical terms and phrases. In any event, the indisputable fact is that there exist certain compelling similarities common to all Arabic *Vitae Aristotelis.* This fact, in itself, forces us to concede that, in the final analysis, the Arabic biographers of Aristotle all used one and the same source: Ptolemy's *Vita Aristotelis.* They used it either directly or through some intermediary sources which could have been a Syriac source, or more likely, Hunayn's Arabic translation of this *Vita*. Ptolemy's original work, it will be noted, probably bore the title of *On the Life of Aristotle; His Last Will and Testament; And a List* (or *Classification) of His Writings.*[5]

The *Vita Aristotelis Marciana* 43 and the *Vita Aristotelis Latina* 46, both of which in this instance rely on Ptolemy-el-Garib (who in turn relies on Andronicus of Rhodes), mention the last will and testament of Aristotle without, however, reciting any of its detailed provisions or its rather intricate technical text. It is safe to assume that the ancient biographers of Aristotle derived or inferred much of their information and data from this will. Concomitantly, this important document supplies the modern historian with some interesting facts which in many instances have been obscured, altered or simply omitted in the traditional (and preserved) biographies of Aristotle.

It is known that the testament of the Early Peripatetic scholarchs, including that of Aristotle, were carefully preserved and finally collated by Ariston of Ceos in his *Collection [of the Wills of the Peripatetic Scholarchs]*.[6] Aside from a sense of piety and reverence for the founder as well as for the former heads of the school, the primary reason why these testaments were so carefully preserved is the following: under Athenian law, as well as according to the 'by-laws' of the Early Peripatus as they were established during the scholarchate of Theophrastus (died in *c.* 286 B.C.), the school, including the grounds, the buildings, the library, etc., was the personal property of the scholarch who frequently also supported the whole venture out of his own private estate. Hence, in his last will and testament the scholarch could, and as a rule did, bequeath the school property, including the all-important library,[7] to whomever he should choose, that is, to whomever he wished to succeed him in the scholarchate. Conversely, barring other evidence, the testament of the preceding scholarch also established the legitimacy of the succeeding scholarch and, hence, was of vital importance for the whole issue of succession as well as for the legitimate continuation of the school as such. This important fact, which among other matters becomes evident from the testaments of Theophrastus,[8] Straton of Lampsacus[9] and Lycon,[10] should also help to explain why these testaments have been carefully preserved as well as incorporated in what seems to have been an official *Collection* made by Ariston of Ceos.[11]

Although Aristotle had spent many years in Athens (367–348 and 335/34–323 B.C.), his last will does not once refer to that city. Accordingly, it must be surmised that he wrote his testament after his flight from Athens in the summer or early fall of 323 B.C.,[12] that is, between the fall of 323 B.C. and the late summer or early fall of 322 B.C., the likely time of his death; that he wrote this will in Chalcis on the island of Euboea; that as a *metic* or 'resident Macedonian alien' he did not, and under Athenian existing laws could not, hold any real property— any buildings or any grounds—in Athens; and that on his departure from Athens in the year 323 B.C., he took with him many of his servants as well as all his personal possessions[13] which, judging from his last will and other evidence, must have been considerable.

THE TEXT OF ARISTOTLE'S WILL

Diogenes Laertius V. 11–16:   *An-Nadim and Usaibia (Al-Qifti):*

I All will be well. But in the event anything should happen, Aristotle has made the following [testamentary] provisions: (DL V. 11)

II Antipater shall be the [chief] executor as regards all testamentary matters and in general. (DL V. 11)

By this will and testament I for - ever appoint Antipater [chief] executor of everything of which I shall die seized.

III But until Nicanor shall return (or, can take over), Aristomenes, Timarchus, Hipparchus, Dioteles and, provided he shall consent and circumstances shall permit him to do do, Theophrastus shall take charge both of Herpyllis and the children [Pythias and Nicomachus], and of the estate. (DL V. 12)

Until Nicanor shall arrive (or, can take over), Aristomenes, Timarchus, Hipparchus and Dioteles shall assume charge of all matters that require attention and take the necessary measures concerning my estate, my maid-servant Herpyllis, my other maid-servants and men-servants, and the estate I shall leave. And if Theophrastus shall consent and be in a position to assist them in this task, he shall take charge as well.

IV When the girl [Pythias] shall be grown up, she shall be given in marriage to Nicanor. (DL V. 12)

When my daughter [Pythias] shall be grown up, Nicanor shall administer her affairs.

V But if anything should happen to the girl [Pythias]—which heaven forbid and no such thing will happen—before her marriage [to Nicanor], or after she is married but before there are any [male] children, Nicanor shall have full powers, both as regards the child [Nicomachus, the son of Aristotle] and as regards everything else, to administer [the estate] in a manner worthy of himself and of us. (DL V. 12)

If she [Pythias] should die before she is married [to Nicanor], or after she is married but before she has a [male] child, Nicanor shall administer both her estate and that of my son Nicomachus.

VI Nicanor shall take charge of the girl [Pythias] and of the boy Nicomachus as he shall think proper in all that concerns them, just as if he were their father and [older?] brother. (DL V. 12)

It is my intention that he [Nicanor] shall take charge of all this as he thinks proper, in all that concerns them [scil., Pythias and Nicomachus], just as if he were their father and [older?] brother.

VII And if anything should happen to Nicanor—which heaven forbid—either before he marries the girl [Pythias] or when he has married her but before there are any [male] children, any arrangement he may have made shall be valid and binding. (DL V. 12)

And if Nicanor should die before my daughter [Pythias] is married to him, or after her marriage [to Nicanor] but before she has a [male] child [by Nicanor], and if Nicanor in his will should make any arrangements concerning the property which I now have, this shall be admissible and binding.

VIII And if Theophrastus should be willing to live with [marry?] her [Pythias], he shall have the same powers and rights as Nicanor. (DL V. 13)

If [after having married Pythias] Nicanor should die intestate, and if Theophrastus should consent and be willing to take his place, it shall be the same with him in all matters in which Nicanor was in charge of my son's [Nicomachus'] affairs, and also as regards my estate.

IX Otherwise the executors, in consultation with Antipater, shall administer [the estate and take care of] my daughter and

And if Theophrastus should be unwilling to take upon himself this trusteeship, then the executors appointed by me shall again turn to the boy as seems to them to be best. (DL V. 13)

X The executors and Nicanor, in memory of me and the constant affection which Herpyllis has borne towards me, shall take care of her in every other respect. (DL V. 13)

Antipater and in collaboration with him consider what they are to do with my estate and then make such arrangements as they see fit. The executors and Nicanor shall bear me in mind when they make arrangements for Herpyllis. For judging from what I saw of her earnestness in rendering service to me and her zeal for all that was becoming for me, she has deserved well of me. They shall give her all she needs.

XI And if she should desire to be married, they shall see to it that she is given [in marriage] to one not unworthy of us. (DL V. 13)

And if she should desire to be married, they shall see to it that she is given [in marriage] to a man of good repute.

XII And besides what she has already received they shall give her a talent of silver out of the estate and three hand-maids whomsoever she shall choose, besides the maid she has at present, and the man-servant Pyrrhaeus. (DL V. 13)

And besides what she already possesses, she shall be given one talent, equivalent of 125 Roman *librae*, and three hand-maids whomsoever she shall choose, besides the maid she has at present and her man-servant.

XIII And if she should choose to remain in Chalcis, [she shall have] the lodge by the garden; if in Stagira, my father's house. (DL V. 14)

And if she should choose to remain in Chalcis, she shall live in my house, in the guest-house by the garden [to be exact]. And if she should choose to live in Stagira, she shall live in my father's and grandfather's house.

XIV And whichever of these two houses she shall choose, the executors shall furnish with such furniture as they think proper and as Herpyllis herself may approve. (DL V. 14)

And whichever of these two houses she shall choose, the executors shall furnish with such household articles as they think proper and as she may need and also whatever she may claim as necessary for her wants.

XV

As to my estate and my son [Nicomachus], there is no need for me to make a [formal] last will and testament.

XVI Nicanor shall take charge of the boy Myrmex and see to it that he be taken to his own people in a manner worthy of me, together with the property of his which we received. (DL V. 14)

Nicanor shall take charge of the boy Myrmex and see to it that he is finally sent back to his home with all his property in any manner he desires.

XVII Ambracis shall be given her freedom and, on my daughter's marriage, shall receive five hundred drachmas and the maid-servant she now has. (DL V. 14)

My maid-servant Ambracis shall be given her freedom, and if, after she has been emancipated, she remains in my daughter's service until my daughter marries, she shall receive five hundred drachmas and the maid-servant she now has.

XVIII To Thales shall be given, in addition to the maid-servant he now has and who was bought for him, one thousand drachmas and a [another] maid-servant. (DL V. 14)

To Thales shall be given the young girl we recently bought, a boy from among our servants, and one thousand drachmas.

XIX Simon [or Simos], in addition to the money heretofore paid to him towards another servant, shall either have a servant purchased for him or receive an additional sum of money. (DL V. 15)

To Simon [or Simos], in addition to the boy he already has received, shall be given money for another boy whom he may buy for himself, and besides this he shall further receive what the executors may deem proper.

XX Tycho [Tachon], Philo, Olympius and his child [boy-servant?] shall have their freedom when my daughter [Pythias] shall be married. (DL V. 15)

As soon as my daughter [Pythias] shall be married, my boys Tachon, Philo and Olympius shall be given their freedom.

XXI None of my [young] servants who waited upon me shall be sold, but they shall continue to be employed, and when they reach the proper age they shall have their freedom if they deserve it. (DL V. 15)

Neither the son of Olympius, nor any of the other boy-servants who have waited upon me shall be sold, but shall continue their service as servants until they reach their manhood, and when they reach the proper age, they shall have their freedom. And what shall then be given to them shall be determined in accordance with what they have deserved [if God Almighty so decides].

XXII   When the images which
Gryllion has been commissioned
to execute are completed, my
executors shall see to it that
these images are set up; namely,
that of Nicanor; that of Proxenus,
which it was my intention to have
executed; and that of Nicanor's
mother [Arimneste]. (DL V. 15)

XXIII Moreover, they shall set up the
bust which has been executed
of Arimnestus to be a memorial
to him, seeing that he died
childless. (DL V. 15)

XXIV   They shall also dedicate my
mother's statue to Demeter of
Nemea or wherever they
think best. (DL V. 16)

XXV   And wherever they bury me, there
the bones of Pythias shall be
laid to rest, in accordance with
her own instructions.
(DL V. 16)

XXVI   And to commemorate Nicanor's
safe return, as I have vowed on
his behalf, they shall set up in
Stagira stone statues of life size
[four cubits high] in honor of
Zeus and Athena, the Saviours.
(DL V. 16)

Al-Mubashir, it will be noted, contains a brief but interesting as well
as accurate summary of some of the provisions contained in Aristotle's
last will and testament: 'At his death he [*scil.*, Aristotle] left one boy of
tender age, Nicomachus, and a young daughter [Pythias]. He also left
a large estate, many men-servants and maid-servants, and other things.
He appointed Antipater [chief] executor of his will, together with a
number of friends to assist Antipater. He gave Theophrastus a free
hand to join the executor [Antipater], if he should desire to do so, and
to assist Antipater in the administration of the estate.'[14]

Before discussing or analyzing the detailed provisions of Aristotle's
last will and testament, it might be appropriate to say a few words

about Greek (Athenian) law controlling intestate and testamentary succession as it is reflected in Aristotle's will. It must be borne in mind, however, that any attempt to sketch an intelligible outline of Greek (Athenian) law of succession encounters at the very outset a number of almost insurmountable difficulties. Apart from a few not always reliable references to, or citations from, Solon's legislation found in the speeches of certain Athenian forensic orators (logographers) or 'lawyers' (who probably selected from among existing legal materials or authorities whatever best suited their particular purpose), we have to rely primarily on the legal arguments made by paid and, hence, partisan advocates who addressed a court of law composed of laymen.

The legal arguments made, for instance, by Isaeus and Demosthenes do not always make it clear whether they actually recite existing Athenian law, whether they merely 'rationalize' existing social customs, or whether they are attempting to tell the court what the law 'ought to be' in a particular case. It is presumed, however, that they refer to a Solonian law which accounted for certain social patterns that existed during the early part of the sixth century B.C. and, hence, may only partially be related to the pattern of social (and legal) practices that were observed during the time Isaeus and Demosthenes made their arguments.

From the legal arguments made by certain lawyers or logographers during the fourth century B.C., three major propositions or legal principles (policies) seem to emerge: first, the introduction of a valid formal will was not in itself dispositive of the issue in dispute. An Athenian jury could always implement or override the interpretation suggested by the instrument or advocated by the lawyer by resorting to its own sense of what was fair and equitable under the circumstances, acting thereby in the light of its own knowledge and understanding of existing social patterns and generally accepted social customs. Second, it was extremely difficult for any testator, no matter how adroitly he had phrased his last will and testament, to escape the limitations, restrictions and prohibitions imposed by existing social patterns and social customs. Third, the apparent fluidity and frequent ambiguity of Athenian testamentary law were somewhat mitigated or overcome by the fact that legal decisions in such matters were made by people who were fully aware of the particular social context and the dominant social patterns in which testamentary transactions occurred. This, then, would also explain why Athenian courts, on the whole, seem to have been averse to recognize wills which, no matter how insignificantly, deviated from the standard social patterns.

The controlling legal policy in matters of intestate as well as testamentary succession seems to have been the principle that above all else the individual is merely a link in the chain of his race or clan. In greater detail: the general rule of intestate succession was that male descendants (or their male descendants) took precedence over female descendants. On the death of the father, the son or sons took the whole estate[15] (unless there was a valid will). If there were several sons, they took equal shares. Barring the dispositive right of adopted sons, no distinction was made between sons of different mothers or adopted or legitimized sons, provided the latter were adopted or legitimized during the lifetime of the father (and not merely in the father's last will and testament).[16] Limited legacies to other persons could be made by a formal will. They were restricted, however, to small bequests, manumissions and gifts of life tenancies. The existing laws or social customs made the alienation of the whole estate, especially that of landed property, simply impossible. Accordingly, the son or sons (or their male descendants) or, if there was only a daughter, her male descendants through an agnate male relative (next of kin through males) who was expected to marry her, were always the ultimate takers.

In principle, daughters, whether single or married, had no claim against their father's estate, except in the case of unmarried daughters who, either by practice or custom or perhaps by law, had a claim to maintenance until they were married, as well as a claim to a dowry to be paid to their future husband. But a testator, by a formal and valid will, could always leave part of his estate to his daughter or daughters. If the only surviving descendant of a father who died intestate was an unmarried daughter, the estate so to speak 'went with her' to the nearest male agnate who would claim her in marriage or, if no agnate husband was forthcoming, to the husband to whom the nearest male agnate gave her in marriage. In this case, the estate was temporarily transmitted to the prospective son-in-law to be kept for the anticipated grandson or grandsons by the daughter. Thus, where a father died leaving only one (legitimate) daughter but no sons, her nearest male agnate, if she had no surviving grandfather, could claim her in marriage and through her gain temporary control over the estate.[17] This right of the agnate rested upon his relationship, and the daughter's position was akin to that of a plot of land—she had nothing to say about this matter.[18] This mode of succession, which was called ἐπίκληρος, assured continuity in the passage of the family property along agnatic lines of descent.

The purpose of all this was to keep the estate in the father's family by using the daughter, so to speak, as a channel for transmitting the estate to any male heir born to her. Only in this sense could she and the agnate who claimed her in marriage be called 'heirs.' Because the estate did not really go to her husband—he was at best an 'interim heir' who had a 'temporary estate'—the latter had only the management of the estate for the family's benefit until the wife's sons came of age (at the age of eighteen).[19] Hence, these sons (the grandsons of the deceased), as the ultimate takers, actually became entitled to the estate at birth. This being so, the grandsons of the deceased, in the final analysis, were the true heirs to their grandfather's estate on the principle that their father, as the husband of the deceased's daughter (and 'heiress'), was taken into the family in order to insure their inheritance. If the daughter was not yet of marriageable age, her nearest kinsman on her father's side became her 'guardian' until she attained the proper age, unless the deceased had already appointed such a 'guardian' by betrothing her to some relative.

If the deceased father had failed to provide a dowry for his daughter or daughters, the latter had an actionable claim against the estate for a suitable dowry. Where the deceased had left only an adopted son, and where also a legitimate daughter survived, the adopted son had no right to alienate the estate left by the deceased. He had only what we would call a life estate, subject to his duty to provide a suitable dowry for the daughter (his sister by adoption), together with a fiduciary obligation to preserve the estate for the ultimate takers: the legitimate male children of the deceased's daughter.[20] In case a person died intestate, and no descendants of the deceased survived, the brother or brothers (by the same father) or the male descendants of the brother or brothers inherited. If there were no brothers or married sisters (with a male child) of the deceased, collaterals through the paternal grandfather inherited.

Since the days of Solon (early part of the sixth century B.C.), the testamentary power of a male freeman was legally recognized. Any free male of age, being without a male descendant, could make a formal will, provided he was a person of sound mind and body and not affected by drugs, coercion, constraint or undue female influence. However, his testamentary powers were subject to certain restrictions so as to keep the bulk of the estate within the family or 'clan.' A father could formally disinherit a son for cause. This had to be done by solemn proclamation in the presence of witnesses during the lifetime of the father. A will was put into writing or executed in the presence of several witnesses. As a rule, it was deposited with some 'person or persons of standing' and, if possible, with a magistrate. For additional safety, several copies of the will were made. However, as long as there were legitimate male descendants, the testator could make only limited bequests to persons other than his natural male descendants. It is interesting to note that the Athenian courts, as a rule, were highly suspicious of wills. They were inclined to ignore a formal will and, with it, the last intentions of the deceased, in favor of a near (male) relative.

The last will and testament of Aristotle, in particular, poses a number of involved technical problems, not the least of which is the question, almost impossible to answer, namely, what particular local laws or customs controlled this legal instrument. We know that Aristotle was born in Stagira, which at the time of Aristotle's death was part of Macedonia. This might explain why he appointed Antipater 'general executor (administrator or trustee, *tutor honoris causa datus*).' Stagira, however, was originally a colony of Andros[21] or Chalcis (on the island of Euboea).[22] It is reasonable to assume that it was a joint colonial venture of both Andros and Chalcis.[23] After spending his early youth in Stagira and Macedonia (at the court of King Amyntas), Aristotle lived in Athens (367–348 B.C. and 335–34 to 323 B.C.), in Macedonia (343–42 to 335 B.C.), in Assos or Atarneus (348–47 to 345–44 B.C.), in Mytilene (345–44 to 343/42 B.C.) and in Chalcis (323–322 B.C.). We also know that he owned real property in Stagira and Chalcis, and it must be presumed that throughout his life he remained a Macedonian citizen. Conversely, as a Macedonian alien residing in Athens he did not, and under the existing laws of Athens could not, legally own any real property in Athens or Attica. Since he never became an Athenian citizen, Athenian law and custom, the law of Solon, did not necessarily control his testament or his estate. However, Stagira was a colony of Chalcis (and Andros), and Chalcis is said to have been a colony of Athens. Hence, it is possible that Athenian law was observed, at least in part, in Stagira and especially in Chalcis, the place where he probably made his last will and testament. Moreover, both Chalcis and Stagira at one time had been members of the Delian League which, being dominated by Athens, imposed the jurisdiction of Athenian law courts over certain civil and criminal issues arising within the member-states of the League.[24] All this, however, is by no means certain. Of the particular laws or customs of either Stagira or Chalcis we have no information.[25]

SOME COMMENTS TO THE SPECIFIC PROVISIONS OF
ARISTOTLE'S LAST WILL AND TESTAMENT

No. I

For some unknown reason, this purely formal clause is not to be found in the Arabic versions of the will. The sentence, '[A]ll will be well,' or '[A]ll is well," is a rather common introductory phrase in a formal Athenian will,[26] as is the passage, '[But] in the event something should happen [to the testator],'[27] that is, in the event the testator should suddenly die or meet with some other misfortune. Such introductory remarks are, in the main, mere formalities meant to have a reassuring effect on the testator's immediate family, implying that there are no grounds for undue concern just because a will has been made. They are somewhat akin to our introductory clause, frequently found at the beginning of a testament: 'I, John Doe, being of sound and disposing mind and aware of the unpredictable incidents of human life, declare this to be my last will and testament.' Wills in ancient Greece also frequently have such general endorsements as, 'This is the last will of John Doe.' Moreover, this introductory clause may also have the legal effect of disclaiming any and all coercion or undue influence on the testator by interested persons.[28] Under Athenian law, such coercion or undue influence would invalidate the whole will and, hence, might constitute grounds for contesting this will. Since Herpyllis, a beneficiary under the terms of Aristotle's will, was Aristotle's mistress but never his lawful wife, and since Nicomachus, likewise a beneficiary, was Aristotle's illegitimate son by Herpyllis (though adopted by Aristotle during the lifetime of the latter), such a precautionary clause was doubly important.

It will also be observed that Aristotle (or Diogenes Laertius who probably epitomized the original document) uses here the past tense as well as the third person ('Aristotle has made these [testamentary] provisions'), while the wills of Theophrastus, Straton of Lampsacus and Lycon[29] use the present tense as well as the first person ('I make these [testamentary] provisions'). It is not impossible, therefore, that in the case of Aristotle's will, Diogenes Laertius relies on an epitomized version or paraphrase of the original will—an epitome which perhaps goes back to Favorinus (or to Hermippus or Ariston of Ceos)—or that Diogenes Laertius himself abridged and rephrased this will.

No. II

Antipater, the 'acting regent' of Macedonia and Alexander's lieutenant in Europe, is appointed what the Romans called *tutor honoris causa*, a kind of 'honorary' or general executor (administrator) of the estate or, perhaps, is made a 'general trustee.'[30] Although basically different in background, education, outlook and occupation, Antipater and Aristotle had been close friends for some time, as is evidenced by the ample correspondence which passed between these two men—a correspondence of which ancient literature contains many traces.[31] Antipater's authority and status is a guarantee that the provisions of Aristotle's will would be strictly observed and, if necessary, fully enforced.[32] Moreover, this appointment also puts the heirs, legatees and beneficiaries (as well as the other executors or trustees) and their claims against Aristotle's estate—part of this estate is in Macedonia (Stagira), part in Chalcis—under the personal protection of the powerful and apparently fair-minded Antipater who, if necessary, might invoke Macedonian jurisdiction over the will. And finally, it should be borne in mind that Aristotle himself was a Macedonian citizen who, it appears, on the whole had been treated well by the Macedonian royal house and its immediate ministers and lieutenants.

No. III

Nicanor was the son of Proxenus and Arimneste, the (older?) sister of Aristotle and, hence, was Aristotle's nephew and nearest male agnate as well as the 'husband designate' of Pythias, Aristotle's legitimate daughter by his wife Pythias.[33] As a matter of fact, under Athenian law Nicanor had the 'privilege' of marrying Aristotle's daughter. Nicomachus, Aristotle's illegitimate (though adopted) son by Herpyllis, actually is the 'universal heir' or, better, as an adopted illegitimate son has a life interest in the estate.[34] But at the time Aristotle made his will, Nicomachus was still very young, though probably no longer a 'baby.'[35] As the 'interim heir designate,' Nicanor was to take actual possession of the whole estate,[36] barring those specified chattels which expressly had been bequeathed to other legatees. If it is correct that at one time (prior to his death) Aristotle had formally adopted Nicomachus (see No. XV), then the male issue of a marriage of Pythias and Nicanor would still be the ultimate takers. For an adopted son, as we have seen, had no right to dispose of or devise his father's estate, but had merely what we would call a 'life estate.' From all this it would follow that Nicanor also had an interest and a duty in seeing to it that Aristotle's estate would not be depleted or alienated by Nicomachus and, thus, in fact denied to the ultimate takers, Nicanor's prospective male children by Pythias.

VM 3, *VV* 2 and *VL* 3 maintain that Aristotle had formally adopted Nicanor, a statement which is not supported by the surviving evidence.[37] The provision in No. VI, namely, that Nicanor should act 'as if he were the father and (older?) brother' of the two minor children, Pythias and Nicomachus, does not bear out this contention.

At the time of Aristotle's death in the late summer or early fall of 322 B.C., or at the time Aristotle wrote his will in Athens or, more likely, in Chalcis, that is between the summer of 323 B.C. and the time of his death, Nicanor apparently was abroad on what appears to have been a 'dangerous mission.'[38] Hence, he was unable to 'take over' the estate as stipulated in Aristotle's will. It has been surmised, though on rather tenuous grounds, that he had been sent by Alexander to the Olympic Games in the year 324 to announce there to the assembled Greek states that Alexander had pardoned all political exiles (about 20,000 of them), that he had ordered the allied Greek states to receive back their banished citizens,[39] and that he claimed divine honors.[40] We also know that the people of Ephesus conferred upon Nicanor the honorific privilege of *proxenia* as the reward for some meritorious deed or deeds he had performed on behalf of that city.[41] It is not impossible that there exists a connection between this work for Ephesus or his activities on behalf of Alexander (or Cassander or some of the other Diodochi), and the 'dangerous mission' alluded to in No. VII (and No. XXVI). Since it appears that Nicanor in some ways was connected with certain political activities of Alexander and later became associated with Cassander, it might be assumed that at one time he belonged to the king's 'inner circle'—something which in the light of Alexander's steadily worsening temper in itself constituted a constant 'danger.' Equally dangerous was Nicanor's subsequent association with Cassander who, as it turned out, had Nicanor executed in 317 B.C. Perhaps Aristotle also remembered the tragic fate of his nephew Callisthenes of Olynthus, who was arbitrarily and cruelly put to death by Alexander in the year 327 B.C.[42] In brief, association with Alexander or with any of his successors invariably spelled danger.

Aristomenes, Timarchus, Hipparchus and Dioteles were probably close friends,[43] or perhaps relatives, of Aristotle.[44] But we do not know from what city or part of Greece they hailed—whether they were Athenians, Macedonians, Chalcidians or Stagirites. There exists the remote possibility that these men were also the witnesses present at the time Aristotle made his will. In case the will should be contested, they would testify to the fact that the testator had executed this particular will and that at the time he did so he was not under undue influence.

They were not, as is the case with the testament of Theophrastus, members of the 'school' or κοινωνία for, in 323–22 B.C., Aristotle had no 'school' of his own. These four men are to act in consultation with Antipater[45] should any of the following situations arise: (i) in case Aristotle should die before Nicanor returns from his 'dangerous mission'; (ii) in case Nicanor should die on his 'dangerous mission' and, hence, be unable to 'take over'; (iii) in case Nicanor should return safely but die before he marries Pythias, the daughter of Aristotle; (iv) in case Nicanor should return safely, marry Pythias, but die before Pythias had a male child or heir by him; and (v) in case Nicanor should return safely, marry Pythias, have a male child or heir by Pythias, but die intestate—provided in all cases Theophrastus should be unwilling or unable to 'take charge of Herpyllis, the children and the estate.' Accordingly, these friends or relatives are also 'alternates' for Theophrastus. The latter, long a close friend of the family and perhaps a relative (?), is the chief trustee or executor after Nicanor, not counting Antipater, who is really an honorary trustee or executor. As it turned out later—Nicanor died rather early (in 317 B.C.), but not before he had married Pythias (though there were no male children from this union)[46]—Theophrastus did in fact take charge of Nicomachus[47] and Pythias, although he did not marry the latter. Finally, the will provides that if everyone and everything else should fail, Antipater, the honorary 'general executor' or honorary 'general administrator' or honorary 'general trustee,' should have the final authority in all matters pertaining to Herpyllis, the children and the estate,[48] and as such should make the final dispositions.

There exists a minor difference between the text of Diogenes Laertius and that of the Arabs—a variation that might support the inference that Diogenes' is an abridged version: the Arabs refer to Theophrastus' particular status in a separate sentence or clause which makes it quite clear that in case certain conditions should materialize, Theophrastus would take over the children as well as the whole estate. The passage in DL V. 39 (where we are told that Theophrastus was the teacher of Nicomachus) and the provision in Theophrastus' will (DL V. 53) seem to indicate that when Nicanor died (in 317 B.C.), Theophrastus in fact did assume Nicanor's place and did take care of Nicomachus as well as of Pythias, and at a later time, of Aristotle, a son of Pythias' third marriage.

The most telling difference between the version recorded by Diogenes Laertius and that preserved by the Arabs, however, is that the former simply alludes to Herpyllis, the mother of Nicomachus, while the latter speaks expressly of 'my maid-servant Herpyllis.'[49] This raises the involved problem of Herpyllis' true status in Aristotle's household. For apparently encomiastic and hence significant reasons, Herpyllis is not mentioned at all in the other *Vitae Aristotelis*, except in the *Vita Hesychii* 4 and in Diogenes Laertius V. 1. The author (Aristippus?) of *Aristippus or On the Luxury of the Ancients* (DL V. 3–4) relates that 'Aristotle fell in love with a concubine of Hermias [Pythias?, Herpyllis?] and married her with the consent of Hermias.'[50] This particular passage is, without doubt, badly garbled. Aristotle apparently never married Herpyllis, who might have been a former concubine of Hermias (?) or, more likely, the hand-maid of Pythias. Pythias, the lawful wife of Aristotle, on the other hand, was not Hermias' concubine, but rather his adopted daughter or niece. Diogenes Laertius, citing Timaeus, also reports that Aristotle had a son, Nicomachus, 'by Herpyllis, his concubine.'[51] Naturally, it is possible that Aristotle married Herpyllis after the death of his wife Pythias, the mother of Pythias. However, the specific terms of the Aristotelian will throw serious doubt on such a marriage.

According to Eusebius, Herpyllis originally came from Stagira,[52] although this is by no means certain and, as a matter of fact, is rather doubtful. If Herpyllis was indeed a native of Stagira, then Aristotle might have taken up with her after his return to Macedonia or Stagira in 343–42 B.C., and after the death of Pythias. But this assumption would vitiate the story that Herpyllis at one time had been the concubine of Hermias, though not the claim that she was a 'woman of ill repute.'[53] The problems of Aristotle's connections with Pythias, Herpyllis and, perhaps, an unnamed concubine of Hermias are most confusing, to say the least. The author (Aristippus?) of *Aristippus or On the Luxury of the Ancients*, a rabid detractor of Aristotle, claims that 'Aristotle became enamored with a concubine of Hermias and married her with the consent of the latter.'[54] This statement implies either that Pythias, the daughter, adopted daughter or niece (whom he adopted as his daughter) of Hermias, at one time was also Hermias' concubine; or that Aristotle married an unnamed concubine of Hermias whom he later abandoned in order to marry Pythias; or that Herpyllis was originally this concubine of Hermias, and that at one time, perhaps after the death of Pythias, Aristotle married her. Ignoring all slanderous exaggerations and fictions, it might be safe to assume the following: Aristotle married Pythias; he married her either in Assos or Atarneus between 347 and 345 B.C., allegedly in order to 'flatter' Hermias, or, at some later time, because 'he felt sorry for her.'[55] In the latter case

Aristotle's marriage to Pythias must have taken place in Macedonia (or Stagira), after the death of Hermias in 341–40 B.C., an event, which left Pythias without a protector and, hence, made her the object of Aristotle's compassion. But it is unlikely that Pythias ever was the concubine of Hermias. Herpyllis, on the other hand, originally might have been the handmaid or servant of Pythias. Tradition has it that she was born in Stagira.[56] This would indicate that she became Pythias' handmaid only after Aristotle's return to Macedonia or Stagira in 343–42 B.C. Naturally, it is entirely possible that Herpyllis had already joined Pythias in Assos or Atarneus, and that, as the handmaid of Pythias, she was also one of Hermias' concubines. In any event, thanks to the persistent efforts of certain detractors of Aristotle, the whole problem of Aristotle's 'domestic relations' has become hopelessly confused. However, judging from the last will and testament of Aristotle,[57] his (brief?) marriage to Pythias must have been a happy one.[58]

The remark found in No. XV (Arabic version, but omitted by Diogenes Laertius), namely, 'as to my estate and my son [Nicomachus] there is no need for me to make a [formal] last will and testament,' would indicate that Nicomachus was a legitimate (or adopted or legitimized) son. For only legitimate (or adopted or legitimized) sons could inherit intestate. This highly significant passage, then, might imply the following: (i) that at one time in his life Aristotle had adopted Nicomachus;[59] (ii) that during his life he had him declared legitimate; (iii) that he had subsequently married Herpyllis (very doubtful); (iv) that at the time of Nicomachus' birth, he was legally married to Herpyllis (very doubtful); or (v) that Nicomachus was actually the son of Aristotle and Pythias (very doubtful). Had Nicomachus, at the time of Aristotle's death, actually been an illegitimate non-adopted or non-legitimized son of the Stagirite, then Aristotle would probably have made some special testamentary provisions or legacies for him. Under Athenian law, an illegitimate son had a claim to a special bequest, not exceeding 1,000 drachmas. Moreover, the fact that in his will Aristotle made some very generous provisions for Herpyllis,[60] and, especially, the fact that in the Arabic versions of Aristotle's will the testator refers to his 'maid-servant Herpyllis,' should make it sufficiently clear that he never married her, but that he probably adopted or legitimized Nicomachus.

Although in his biography of Aristotle, Diogenes Laertius admits that Herpyllis was Aristotle's concubine[61] as well as the mother of his (illegitimate) son Nicomachus, it appears that for some (encomiastic or apologetic?) reason the same Diogenes Laertius (or his source) omits any reference to her true status in his particular version of Aristotle's will. In so doing he creates, and perhaps intends to create, the impression that, after all, she was Aristotle's legitimate wife. It is possible that Herpyllis, who originally might have been the handmaid of Pythias, after the death of the latter and perhaps in compliance with Pythias' last wish, became a freedwoman. In any event, the provisions in Aristotle's will, insofar as they relate to Herpyllis, seem to indicate that, by the time Aristotle drafted his will, she was a freedwoman. The passage in the will, 'if she [*scil.*, Herpyllis] should desire to be married, they [*scil.*, the executors or trustees] shall see to it that she is given [in marriage] to one not unworthy of us,'[62] seems to indicate that she was never married before (and, by implication, that Aristotle had a high opinion of her). In conclusion, it might be noted that with the exception of Diogenes Laertius, the *Vita Aristotelis Hesychii*,[63] and the versions of Aristotle's last will and testament as they were recorded by Diogenes Laertius and by some of the Arabic *Vitae Aristotelis*, not to mention the implacable detractors of Aristotle,[64] no other *Vita Aristotelis* refers to Herpyllis or to her status. This fact, in itself, may be highly significant. It may also be indicative of the general confusion and uncertainty among ancient authors or biographers (who apparently did not really know what to make of her) about the true status of Herpyllis. Moreover, since the majority of these biographies are predominantly encomiastic, they are only too willing to suppress the whole 'Herpyllis affair.' This, in turn, would indicate that she was generally considered a 'person of ill repute,' and that Aristotle's association with her probably was regarded a distinct liability.

No. IV

Unless their source or sources were at fault, the Arabic biographers obviously did not understand the technical meaning of the Greek term ἐκδόσθαι ('shall be given in marriage [to Nicanor]'). The Arabs probably were of the opinion that this expression meant 'to be entrusted to the care of,' or 'to be taken care of.' Hence, there exists a startling difference between the Arabic text and that preserved by Diogenes Laertius. This mistranslation, which completely corrupts the meaning of the Arabic version, is also carried over into the following provision (No. V). There can be no doubt that the text transmitted by Diogenes Laertius is the correct one.

It was a common practice in Athens (and under Athenian law) for a male agnatic relative to take temporary possession and control (custody) of the estate by marrying the daughter of the deceased or testator, or to gain this temporary control because he was eventually expected to marry her. Accordingly, he also became a sort of guardian of the decedent's (minor) daughter. As mentioned above, whenever the only descendant was a young and unmarried daughter, the estate of her father went not *to* her, but rather *with* her to the nearest agnate who would marry her (or to whom the nearest agnate would give her in marriage).[65] In this fashion, the estate of the deceased was actually transmitted to her anticipated son or sons who, upon attaining their majority, would become the ultimate takers.[66] In the meantime, the husband (Nicanor) would have a temporary estate or interest. This seems to be the meaning, or the intended legal effect, of No. IV—a meaning which is also indicative of the fact that at the time Aristotle drafted his last will, Pythias was still rather young, and that she had not previously been married. As a matter of fact, soon after Aristotle's death in the late summer or early fall of 322 B.C., Nicanor married Pythias. He died, however, soon afterwards without issue.

We know that Nicanor became Cassander's lieutenant as well as the commander of Munichia in 319–18 B.C. Late in 318 B.C., he won a naval battle over Polyperchon. Subsequently, he fell out with Cassander, was charged with treason and was executed, probably in the spring of 317 B.C.[67] According to Sextus Empiricus, after the death of Nicanor Pythias married Procles (or Procleus) by whom she had two sons, Procles and Demaratus.[68] In his will, usually dated about 286 B.C., Theophrastus mentions Demaratus as one of the full-fledged members of the philosophic community of the Peripatus.[69] By then, Demaratus must have been a grown man. This would imply that Pythias married Procles approximately one year after Nicanor's death, and Demaratus, presumably the younger of her two sons by Procles, was born *c.* 314–13 B.C. After the death of her second husband, Procles, Pythias married Medias (some sources call him Metrodorus), the physician, by whom she had a son, Aristotle, named after his maternal grandfather. At the time of Theophrastus' death (*c.* 286 B.C.), this Aristotle was still a youth.[70] This seems to follow from Theophrastus's last will and testament, namely, from the following provision: 'Let the community [of the Peripatus] consist of Hipparchus, Neleus, Straton, Callinus, Pancreon and Nicippus. Aristotle, the son of Metrodorus [should read: Medias] and Pythias, shall also have the right to study and associate with these men, if he desires to do so. And the oldest of them [*scil.*, of the community of the Peripatus] shall pay every attention to him, in order to ensure for him the utmost proficiency in philosophy.'[71] This passage should make it quite clear that at the time of Theophrastus' death Aristotle was too young to be included among the regular or full-fledged members of the Peripatetic community or κοινωνία.

No. V

This provision is abridged and somewhat mutilated by the Arabic biographers who consistently misunderstand or mistranslate the Greek term ἐκδόσθαι.[72] The version found in Diogenes Laertius, on the other hand, should make it amply clear that under the terms of Aristotle's will, Nicanor, the nearest agnate as well as the prospective husband of Pythias, for the time being is to take charge of the whole of Aristotle's estate, and that he is to acquire a temporary interest in the estate. Moreover, this particular provision also empowers him, under certain circumstances and within the terms of the will, to use and administer the estate as he sees fit, provided he keeps within the limitations imposed upon him by law, and provided he does not alienate or squander the estate to the detriment of the ultimate takers—his prospective sons by Pythias. All this is wholly in keeping with the general legal or social policy characteristic of the Greek or Athenian law of succession, namely, that in the case of an unmarried (minor) daughter, the estate went for the time being to the nearest agnate or 'temporary heir designate,' who would either marry the girl (and thus acquire a temporary estate or interest), or see to it that she would find a suitable husband. In this manner, the estate was actually transferred first to the prospective son-in-law of the deceased or testator and, ultimately, to the prospective grandson or grandsons. If the daughter should die either before marrying the heir designate or before she had a male child, the heir designate was authorized to do with the estate as he saw fit, provided there were no other male heirs in the agnate line, including an adopted heir. Since at the time of Aristotle's death (in 322 B.C.), his daughter Pythias was not yet old enough to be married, she must have been born c. 336 B.C., and probably a little later (in Macedonia?). This would imply that Aristotle had married Pythias, her mother, either shortly before or soon after the death of Hermias in 341-40 B.C. It is also reasonable to conjecture that Pythias, the mother, died fairly soon after the birth of her daughter. This might be inferred from the fact that by the year 322 B.C., Nicomachus, the son of Aristotle and Herpyllis was no longer a 'baby,' but a 'young boy.'[73] Judging from Diogenes Laertius V. 16, Aristotle's marriage to Pythias must have been a happy one. Hence, it is fair to surmise that he 'took up' with Herpyllis only after the death of Pythias. One might conjecture, therefore, that Nicomachus was probably born about 330 B.C., that is, some time after Aristotle's return to Athens.

No. VI

While Diogenes' version makes Nicanor appear to be a sort of guardian of the two children, Pythias and Nicomachus,[74] the Arabic versions in a more general manner merely refer to Nicanor's right or power to administer, in his discretion, all matters pertaining to the children and to the estate. Like Diogenes, the Arabs (An-Nadim excepted) also report Aristotle's express wish that Nicanor should act as if he were the 'father and [older] brother' of the two minor children. This latter statement has been interpreted, though probably erroneously, to mean that Aristotle had previously adopted Nicanor.[75] To adopt a prospective son-in-law and thus keep the estate in the father's family, however, was not an uncommon practice in ancient Athens or in ancient Greece.

No. VII

Sextus Empiricus, *Adversus Mathematicos* I. 258, relates that Nicanor returned from his 'dangerous mission' or 'journey' and subsequently married Pythias.[76] But he died soon thereafter (in the spring of 317 B.C.),[77] apparently without leaving any male issue. In any event, the provision No. VII seems to confirm the fact that Nicanor, as the nearest male agnatic relative, was the 'interim heir designate.' As such he could apparently make valid provisions for the administration of the whole estate (which he held temporarily), as well as for the care of the two minor children. The other heirs, the residuary heirs and remaindermen, as well as the trustees or executors, would be bound by these provisions.[78] But unless he had been adopted by Aristotle during the lifetime of the latter, something which is very doubtful, Nicanor would control the estate only until Nicomachus came of age, or until any male children born of Nicanor's marriage to Pythias reached their manhood at the age of eighteen.[79] Since, however, Nicomachus was only an adopted son of Aristotle (adopted during Aristotle's lifetime), according to Greek (Athenian) law, he could acquire only a life estate.[80] On his death, therefore, the estate would revert to the male children of Nicanor and Pythias or, if there were no male children and if Nicanor should outlive Nicomachus and Pythias, to Nicanor. Hence, under the terms of the will, in the latter case Nicanor would become the ultimate taker and, accordingly, have the right to pass on the estate *mortis causa* to whomever he should choose, provided he kept the estate within agnatic lines and provided Nicanor was not an adopted son of Aristotle. This, in turn, implies that he would probably leave the estate to the prospective husband of his widow Pythias, or to be more correct, to the anticipated male offsprings of Pythias' second marriage. If, however, Nicanor had been adopted by Aristotle during the life-time of the latter, he would hold the estate only until his death, but he would be debarred from devising it *mortis causa*, that is, he would have no interest to pass on this estate on his death.[81]

This whole provision, however, is still somewhat puzzling. Under Athenian law, a guardian (provided Nicanor was the guardian of Nicomachus and Pythias) could not, as a rule, make any arrangements as regards the estate (or future estate) of his ward or wards. If, on the other hand, Nicanor was the adopted son of Aristotle (which seems very doubtful),[82] then he could not make any testamentary provisions regarding the estate of Aristotle or the estate he had inherited from Aristotle, and in which he held only a life interest. Perhaps this whole passage refers to the fact that, in case of his premature death, Nicanor was empowered to make arrangements concerning the guardianship, rather than the estate, of Nicomachus and Pythias.

No. VIII

Diogenes' text, it will be noted, is somewhat abridged and hence, by itself, difficult to understand or interpret. The Arabic version, on the other hand, makes it quite clear why and under what circumstances Theophrastus might 'take the place' of Nicanor in case the latter should die prematurely without having made any provisions as regards the guardianship of Nicomachus and Pythias and as regards the estate. In such a case, Theophrastus would become 'interim heir designate' (on the same terms as Nicanor had been appointed 'interim heir designate') as well as the guardian of Nicomachus and Pythias, pro-vided Theophrastus should consent to this arrangement. Theophrastus would have the same rights, powers and duties as had previously been granted Nicanor. The version preserved by Diogenes Laertius also implies that, if he wishes to do so, Theophrastus could 'live with' (marry?) Pythias, of whose affairs he would be in charge. Judging from the scanty evidence, Nicanor died intestate soon after marrying Pythias and did so without leaving a male heir.[83] Theophrastus apparently 'took his place' but did not marry Pythias. This is evidenced by Diogenes Laertius V. 53, where we are told that in his last will and testament Theophrastus made certain provisions for Aristotle, the son of his 'ward,' Pythias, by Pythias' third husband, Medias (or Metrodorus). It must also be assumed that it was Theophrastus who, after the death of Nicanor, gave Pythias in marriage, first to Procles (or Procleus) and then, after the death of Procles (by whom she had two sons), to Medias (or Metrodorus).[84] It is possible that by the year 286, the year Theophrastus apparently died, Pythias had lost her third husband. Diogenes Laertius V. 53 seems to imply this.

The provision found in No. VIII is somewhat ambiguous and puzzling. It might signify that if Nicanor should die and Theophrastus should be willing to marry (or 'live with') Pythias, Theophrastus should also become the guardian of Nicomachus and Pythias. It has already been pointed out that under Athenian law a guardian could not make any binding arrangements regarding the property of his ward. Hence, the Arabic version is somewhat confusing.

An-Nadim[85] calls Theophrastus the son of Aristotle's sister (Arimneste?),[86] while Al-Mubashir[87] as well as Usaibia[88] refer to him as 'the son of his [scil., Aristotle's] mother's sister (second cousin).' This latter version might be the result of a confusion with, or transfer of, Plato's relationship to Speusippus who was the son of Plato's sister Potone. None of the other Vitae Aristotelis claim that Theophrastus was in any way related to Aristotle. A number of weighty factors, however, might possibly indicate that, after all, Theophrastus might have been a remote relative of Aristotle: (i) In Aristotle's will, Theophrastus holds a position of great prominence—a position usually reserved only for relatives; (ii) in his own will Theophrastus refers to Demaratus,[89] the grandson of Aristotle through Pythias (and Procles);[90] (iii) in his will, Theophrastus provides for a commemorative statue in honor of Nicomachus, the illegitimate, though adopted, son of Aristotle;[91] (iv) Theophrastus owned property (a house) in Stagira;[92] (v) Theophrastus educated and took care of Nicomachus;[93] and (vi) in his own will, Theophrastus appointed Callisthenes, a son or grandson of the historian Callisthenes (died in 327 B.C.)[94] and hence the grandnephew or great-grandnephew of Aristotle, and a member of the inner circle of the Peripatus, a trustee or executor of his estate as well as of the Peripatus.[95]

No. IX

Here, too, the Arabic version is more detailed, more definite and probably closer to the original text of the testament than is Diogenes' report, which is obviously an abridgement. In a way, No. IX repeats some of the provisions that had already been laid down in No. II, where Antipater was appointed 'general executor' or 'general trustee.'[96] No. IX reaffirms that if all other devices or provisions, listed in Nos III–VIII, should fail for some reason or other, the other trustees or executors (Aristomenes, Timarchus, Hipparchus, Dioteles and, perhaps, Theophrastus) should turn to Antipater and, in collaboration with Antipater, look after the children and the estate. Since, however, Theophrastus apparently took charge of all matters as stipulated in No. VIII,[97] there did not arise the need for putting this clause into effect.

A brief review of the provisions and stipulations found in Nos III–IX would seem to indicate that Athenian law, after all, was to govern not only Aristotle's last will and testament, but also the interpretation of this instrument. This, then, would suggest that Aristotle, or whoever assisted him when he drafted his will (Theophrastus? who seems to have been something of a legal expert), had some knowledge of the Athenian law of testamentary succession as well as a profound understanding of human nature. This is borne out, for instance, by No. III, which designates as executor or guardian an agnatic kinsman, Nicanor, who would marry Aristotle's legitimate daughter, Pythias. This executor, for the time being, is to take Aristotle's estate in default of a legitimate adult male heir (including an adopted son) in accord with the Athenian legal rule of agnatic descent in order to keep the whole estate within the family. No. IV provides that Pythias, the legitimate daughter of the testator, is to be given in marriage to Nicanor, the agnatic kinsman, who, in keeping with Athenian law, was privileged to marry the decedent's daughter in case the testator should die without leaving a legitimate son. No. V reaffirms Nicanor's legal position (or that of his male children by Pythias) as ultimate taker(s) in default. For, according to Athenian law, an adopted son such as Nicomachus could not devise or alienate his father's estate. Accordingly, the male offsprings of a legitimate daughter of the deceased—in our case the son or sons of Pythias and Nicanor—would, upon reaching the proper age, automatically take their grandfather's estate at the death of Nicomachus, the adopted son of the testator. In keeping with Athenian law, No. V also stipulates that if the marriage of Pythias and Nicanor should fail of male issue, Nicanor, as the nearest agnatic kinsman, is to take the whole estate upon the death of the adopted son, Nicomachus. In the meantime, Nicanor will also act as the administrator of Aristotle's estate,[98] which under certain circumstances he might ultimately inherit. No. VI reiterates that

Nicanor's appointment as executor and guardian was determined by sentiments of kinship rather than by strict fiduciary concepts, while No. VII reiterates and confirms the legality (under Athenian law) of Nicanor's actions as executor and guardian, stipulating that his arrangements are to be binding, at least pending the appointment of a new executor or guardian in case of his premature death. No. VIII designates Theophrastus as the new executor and guardian in case of Nicanor's untimely death and, by implication, confers upon Theophrastus the privilege of marrying Pythias in case Nicanor should die prematurely. No. IX, finally, contains provisions intended to meet the contingency of Theophrastus' refusal to assume this executorship or guardianship (and to marry Pythias). All these provisions and stipulations, in the main, seem to be in accord with Athenian law.

No. X

This part of the will, like Nos XI–XIV, contains a number of provisions or legacies for Herpyllis.[99] Like the Arabic versions of No. III,[100] No. X, especially the Arabic text, makes it quite clear that Herpyllis was the maid-servant or the 'mistress' of Aristotle rather than his lawful wife.[101] No. X also stresses the fact that Herpyllis was always a loyal and devoted servant, deserving, as the Arabic versions emphasize, to be provided for in a most generous manner: that is—and the Arabic versions stress this—in a manner not unworthy of the grateful testator: 'The executors shall bear me in mind when they make arrangements for Herpyllis.'

Since Aristotle apparently died of a stomach ailment[102] in the late summer or early fall of 322 B.C., Herpyllis probably nursed him during his last illness. This seems to be borne out by the remark of Athenaeus who maintains that Aristotle lived with Herpyllis 'until his death.'[103] But while Diogenes Laertius only refers in general to the 'constant affection (or goodness?)' which Herpyllis had displayed towards Aristotle, the Arabs are more specific, extolling her earnestness in serving him and her solicitude for his well-being. It might be conjectured that the Arabic version, which stresses Herpyllis' loyalty and devotion to Aristotle, is closer to the original Aristotelian text than is the version preserved by Diogenes Laertius. This would seem more in keeping with the generally magnanimous tenor of the whole will. That Herpyllis was never Aristotle's legitimate wife, and that she was of humble origin is also confirmed by the fact that in his will Aristotle makes no provisions for the repayment of a dowry[104] or for her return to her own kin. However, when the executors or trustees are charged with 'taking care of Herpyllis,' this seems to imply that she was a freedwoman.

No. XI

The main, though relatively insignificant difference between Diogenes' version of this clause and that of the Arabs is that Diogenes Laertius speaks here of a husband for Herpyllis 'not unworthy of us,' that is, of Aristotle and his kinsmen, while the Arabs refer more generally to 'a man of good repute.'[105] In brief, Aristotle apparently wishes to make it known that in case Herpyllis should consider marriage, she should choose (or be given in marriage by the executors or trustees to) a husband who would not bring disgrace upon her and, through her, upon the whole family as well as upon the friends and associates of Aristotle.[106] It will be noted that the phrase 'not unworthy of us' is also used in No. XVI. Aristotle apparently is rather concerned with maintaining the good reputation (and social standing) of his family, his friends and that of the members of his entire household.

No. XII

In this instance the two versions are essentially identical, except that Diogenes Laertius mentions the name of the man-servant (Pyrrhaeus) who is to be given to Herpyllis. But the Arabs make a most interesting addition to their version: they assess the talent of silver referred to by Diogenes at '125 Roman *librae*.'[107] This anachronistic comment, which alludes to the Roman monetary system, is probably based on a much later gloss that might go back to Andronicus of Rhodes, who wished to explain to his Roman reader the 'current value' of a talent of silver. In any case, this stipulation, like the following provisions, is indicative of the fact that Herpyllis was well treated by Aristotle and generously provided for in his will—a testimonial to the philosopher's generosity.

No. XIII

This particular stipulation provides for a permanent dwelling place for Herpyllis, but it does not imply the transfer of title to one of the two houses to Herpyllis, the legatee. Rather, the two houses will remain the property of the heir or heirs, and thus remain in the testator's family or male agnatic descendants. Herpyllis is merely given an option: she may live in Aristotle's house in Chalcis—or to be more exact, in the guest-house or lodge by the garden (near the house); or she may move to Stagira and reside in the house which Aristotle owns there.[108] We know that Aristotle had a house in Chalcis which he inherited from the ancestors of his mother, Phaestis, who was a descendant of some settlers who at one time had migrated from Chalcis to Stagira.[109] It was this house to which he retired, together with Herpyllis and the children, in the year 323 B.C. Here he probably made his last will and here he died in 322 B.C. But if she preferred to do so, Herpyllis, who according to some sources was a native of Stagira,[110] could go to Stagira and move into Aristotle's ancestral home (the Arabs refer to Aristotle's father's and grandfather's house).[111] He had inherited this particular house from his father, Nicomachus, who had died while Aristotle was still rather young. Stagira, including probably Aristotle's paternal home there, had been destroyed by King Philip of Macedonia in 349 B.C. Tradition has it that at the intercession of Aristotle, Philip (or Alexander) rebuilt the town at some later time.[112] Aristotle's will would confirm this.

No. XIV

In this instance, both texts are almost identical, with the following minor exception: Diogenes Laertius relates that Herpyllis may have the furniture or household articles of which she approves. The Arabs, on the other hand, refer to those household goods she may need or 'claim as necessary for her wants.' To bequeath household articles to loyal servants of long and devoted service seems to have been a fairly common practice in ancient Greece.[113]

No. XV

For some unknown reason, the version preserved by Diogenes Laertius does not contain the rather important stipulation, '[a]s to my estate and my son [Nicomachus] there is no need for me to make a [formal] last will and testament.' This most significant passage seems to attest to the fact that Nicomachus apparently was to have what we would call a comprehensive 'life estate' in Aristotle's property. Conversely, in the light of No. XV, Nicanor would be a sort of 'interim heir designate' or trustee, or administrator, or guardian and the male offspring of a marriage between Nicanor and Pythias would be the ultimate takers. Or to be more detailed: under Athenian law, Nicomachus, as the illegitimate son of Aristotle who apparently had been adopted (or legitimized) by his father during the latter's lifetime, would inherit the whole estate whenever he reached the age of eighteen.[114] But being only an adopted son, Nicomachus could not devise or alienate the estate of his father, which on Nicomachus' death would automatically revert to the male offspring of Nicanor and Pythias.[115] This being so, Nicomachus acquired only a 'limited life estate,' and the son or sons of Nicanor and Pythias, if there should be any sons, would be the ultimate takers. If, on the other hand, Nicanor should outlive Nicomachus, and if Nicanor (or Pythias) should have no legitimate male offsprings, then Nicanor, the nephew of Aristotle through Arimneste, would become the ultimate taker after the death of Nicomachus. As such he would have the right to pass on the estate *mortis causa* to whomever he should choose, provided the estate stayed within agnatic lines. This might also shed some additional light on the provision in No. VII, where Aristotle stipulates that 'any arrangement he [*scil.*, Nicanor] may have made shall be valid and binding.'

No. XV, however, raises some further problems. In Athens, during the fourth century B.C., the privileges of full citizenship, including the right to hold title to land or landed property, as a rule were restricted to persons who were born of parents who were validly married Athenian citizens. An illegitimate offspring of an unrecognized union between two aliens—and in Athens both Aristotle and Herpyllis were aliens living in concubinage—could not inherit or acquire a life estate through adoption during the lifetime of the testator or deceased. Moreover, as has already been shown, under Athenian law adoption could not be used to legitimize an illegitimate son, or to give citizen status to an alien.[116] All this would indicate that No. XV would have no legal effects in Athens, though it would probably be effective in other Greek jurisdictions.[117] It may be assumed, therefore, that Athenian law was not meant to control this particular provision in the will of Aristotle. Conversely, No. XV may also indirectly refer to a particular Athenian legal rule in that it possibly implies the following: since Nicomachus is the illegitimate offspring of an unrecognized union between two aliens, he cannot inherit under any circumstances, at least not under Athenian law, even though he had been formally adopted or legitimized during the lifetime of the testator. Hence, there is no need for the testator to mention him in his will, or 'to make a [formal] last will and testament' regarding Nicomachus. This, then, might suggest that Athenian law, after all, controlled the provisions found in Aristotle's will. But under Athenian law, Nicomachus may still have a claim to a special bequest (νοθεία),[118] not to exceed 1,000 drachmas. Since Aristotle's will does not contain such a special bequest, it might be argued that (i) Athenian law, after all, did not control Aristotle's will; or (ii) that the passage, 'as to my estate and my son there is no need for me to make a [formal] last will and testament,' is actually an indirect reference to this special bequest—a reference which might have been badly garbled by the Arabic biographers (or their Syriac sources) who were not conversant with Greek legal nomenclature or legalistic phraseology; or (iii) that Aristotle deliberately refused to make such a special bequest; or (iv) that Aristotle intended Nicanor (or Theophrastus) to take care of Nicomachus[119] and hence felt that there was no need for him to make special provisions for Nicomachus—provisions which, under existing Athenian law, anyway would be null and void.

Hence, we might have the following situation: (i) Nicanor, the nephew of Aristotle and presumptive husband of Pythias, is the guardian, trustee, administrator and 'interim heir designate' of Aristotle's estate. (ii) When Nicomachus comes of age he will be the heir. (iii) In case Nicomachus should die before he comes of age, the estate goes temporarily to Nicanor who holds it in trust for his anticipated son or sons by Pythias. (These sons would be the ultimate takers.) (iv) On the death of Nicomachus, assuming he did come of age, the estate goes to Nicanor or to his male children by Pythias. (v) If at the time of Nicomachus' death Nicanor should have died without any male issue, the estate will go to the male children of Pythias by a second (or third) husband. (vi) Pythias, as the daughter of Aristotle, always has a claim against the estate for a dowry and for maintenance (until her marriage). As can readily be seen, No. XV, which is not to be found in the version preserved by Diogenes Laertius, greatly complicates the interpretation of Aristotle's will, especially if this instrument is controlled by Athenian law.

The phrasing of No. XV induces us to assume that at one time Nicomachus had either been legitimized or adopted by Aristotle. However, it does not imply, as some scholars have conjectured, that at one time Aristotle had married Herpyllis, the mother of Nicomachus, or that Nicomachus was the legitimate son of Aristotle and Pythias.[120] Now we may also understand why Aristotle made such a detailed will concerning his personal estate: had he died intestate, Nicomachus upon reaching the age of eighteen, would have inherited, or better, would have acquired a life estate or life interest in the whole estate of Aristotle to the exclusion of Pythias (and her male children). Hence, it is most unlikely that this particular passage is merely a later interpolation or, perchance, a late encomiastic attempt to alter the original wording of the will in order to 'legitimize' Nicomachus.[121] But then it must always be borne in mind that the version recorded by Diogenes Laertius, which omits this clause, is only an abridgement, based on either Favorinus or Hermippus, both of whom probably made use of the text quoted in Ariston of Ceos, and either of whom might themselves have epitomized Ariston's original text. This being so, Diogenes Laertius, or one of his sources, could very well have omitted some rather 'obvious' stipulations which to him seemed 'self-evident.'[122]

The legal problems connected with No. XV are many and complex.[123] If Nicomachus was indeed the legitimate son of Aristotle—if Aristotle married Herpyllis (which is to be doubted) or had Nicomachus declared legitimate or had him adopted (which seems to be almost certain)—then under existing Athenian law (provided Athenian law was controlling) Nicomachus was the sole heir, subject to the restrictions imposed on the inheritance of an adopted son—adopted during the lifetime of the testator. In that case there would be no need for a formal will, something which the Arabic version points out, although Aristotle still could have made some limited bequests to other persons. For, according to the law of Solon, only a male of age and of sound mind without a male descendant or male agnatic kin had unrestricted testamentary freedom.[124] Thus, if Nicomachus was indeed the sole heir, then the whole testament of Aristotle, aside from appointing trustees for the estate and guardians for the two minor children, would be nothing more than a series of limited bequests to persons other than Nicomachus, such as a life interest in, or life use of, one of Aristotle's two houses (in Stagira or Chalcis) for Herpyllis,[125] a list of manumissions and emancipations,[126] and some provisions for memorials in honor of certain relatives of Aristotle. The stipulations relating to Nicanor would be tantamount to his appointment as the guardian of Nicomachus and Pythias, and nothing more[127]—a view held by some scholars. If, on the other hand, Nicomachus was indeed an illegitimate child, and if Aristotle had not adopted him prior to his death, then Nicomachus would not have had any legal claim to Aristotle's entire estate, but merely a possible claim to a special bequest (νοθεία) not exceeding 1,000 drachmas.[128] In such a case Pythias would be the sole heir.[129] Since, however, a daughter could not inherit, the nearest male agnate had the right (and actually a duty) to marry her and, through this marriage, become 'interim heir' for the purpose of transmitting the estate to his male children by the daughter of the deceased, that is, to the grandchildren of the deceased. Moreover, if Nicomachus was indeed an illegitimate child (and had not subsequently been adopted or legitimized by Aristotle), then Aristotle probably could not have appointed Nicanor guardian of Nicomachus. All this would again suggest that at one time Aristotle had adopted Nicomachus or had him declared legitimate, and that this adoption had taken place prior to Aristotle's death and not merely in his last will and testament.

No. XVI

It will be noted that Nos XVI–XXI contain a number of provisions concerning the servants or slaves, both male and female, who were part of Aristotle's household or estate at the time of his death. Under Athenian law, assuming Athenian law controlled Aristotle's testament, a testator could choose to emancipate his slaves in a number of different ways, including outright and unconditional manumission, manumission on the expiration of a specified period of time, manumission after the attainment of a designated age, manumission upon the occurrence of a special event, and manumission upon the fulfilment of a specified condition.[130] In his last will and testament, Aristotle makes use of all these possibilities. The large number of Aristotle's servants or slaves, not including Herpyllis (she was probably a freedwoman), indicates that Aristotle was well-to-do.[131] Those from among Aristotle's servants or slaves who had served him faithfully and efficiently over a long period of time are to be set free immediately. They are also to receive some fairly generous legacies.[132]

No. XVI, in particular, which provides for the emancipation (?) and return of young Myrmex to his kinsmen, manifests two slight differences between the text transmitted by Diogenes Laertius and that preserved by the Arabs: Diogenes refers here to 'a manner worthy of me,'[133] while the Arabs speak of 'a manner he [Myrmex] desires.' Moreover, Diogenes Laertius also mentions 'the property (presents?) which we received [together with the boy?]' while the Arabs only allude to Myrmex's property.[134] Myrmex, it must be surmised, had a special status in Aristotle's household. Perhaps he had been given or loaned (together with some presents) by relatives, friends or admirers of Aristotle to live in the latter's house in order to be trained or educated by Aristotle; perhaps he was a remote relative (of Aristotle? or of Herpyllis?) who had stayed with Aristotle for a while; perhaps he was a special gift which Aristotle wished to return. It has also been suggested that this Myrmex, who was not only to receive special attention but is also mentioned in the testament between Herpyllis and Ambracis (a slave woman who is to be emancipated immediately, see No. XVII), might have been an illegitimate son of Herpyllis, or perhaps an illegitimate child of Aristotle and Herpyllis[135] who, unlike Nicomachus, had not been adopted by Aristotle. If this were the case, then the instruction found in No. XVI (Arabic version) that Myrmex 'be sent back . . . with all his property,' might refer to the special request (νοθεία) to which an illegitimate son was entitled under Athenian law; and that he was to be turned over to his mother's (Herpyllis'?) people. It is impossible, however, to verify these last two conjectures.

No. XVII

This section stipulates that Ambracia, apparently an elderly and trusted maid-servant, be emancipated immediately. The Arabic version adds the significant clause that Ambracia shall receive an additional but conditional bequest if, and only if, she stays in the service of Aristotle's daughter Pythias until the latter has married Nicanor. Diogenes Laertius, on the other hand, implies that Ambracia would receive this additional bequest on Pythias' wedding day without having rendered further service to Aristotle's family. Although it is impossible to determine which of these two versions is the correct one, it is reasonable to assume that Diogenes Laertius, who probably epitomized this passage, intended to convey the same notions as the Arabs do. In any event, the Arabic version seems to make better sense: for additional services, Ambracia is to receive an additional bequest.

No. XVIII

Although not expressly mentioned in the will, Thales[136] too was presumably to be emancipated at once, unless he (or she?) had not already been set free at some earlier time. Moreover, he was to receive an additional servant or slave. Aside from the fact that Diogenes Laertius refers to an additional *maid*-servant, while the Arabs mention an additional *boy*-servant that shall be given to Thales, there exists only a slight difference in the specific wording of these two versions: according to Diogenes Laertius, it appears that Thales has already had his first servant for some time, while according to the Arabs he had only recently received his first servant and could now expect a second servant as well as the sum of one thousand drachmas.[137]

No. XIX

Diogenes Laertius, whose abridged text seems to be badly mutilated, implies that in addition to the amount of money he had previously received towards the purchase of another servant, Simon (or Simos) was to have either a further servant bought especially for him or was to receive, in cash, the equivalent of the purchase price.[138] Presumably, Simon is likewise to be set free without delay, unless he had already been emancipated. The Arabs, on the other hand, relate that in addition to the servant he had previously received, Simon should be given some money for the purchase of an additional boy-servant whom he may buy himself, as well as an additional sum of cash money, the exact amount to be determined by the executors. Unlike the Arabs, Diogenes Laertius does not mention that this additional amount of cash money is to be determined by the executors. Here, as elsewhere, the Arabic version seems to make better sense and is probably closer to the original document.[139]

No. XX

It is impossible to determine with any degree of certainty whether the name of the man-servant is Tachon or Tycho. Diogenes Laertius' reference to Olympius' child (son)—it is rather unlikely that a boy-servant of Olympius is meant here—can be found in the Arabic version of No. XXI, where, unlike Diogenes' text, the boy does not receive his freedom after Pythias is married, but only after he has attained a certain age and then only on the condition that he deserves this boon. Tachon, Philo and Olympius—three adult men-servants—are to have their freedom after Pythias' marriage to Nicanor.[140]

No. XXI

While Diogenes Laertius reports that none of the other servants may be auctioned off under any condition, the Arabs modify (correctly?) this passage by relating that only the young son (or boy-servant) of Olympius, as well as the other boy-servants of Aristotle, may not be sold. They must continue serving (Pythias?, Nicanor?, Herpyllis?, Nicomachus?) until they have reached the proper age (Diogenes Laertius) or their manhood (the Arabs). Then, and only then, shall they have their freedom.[141] Hence, the Arabic text implies that some of the older slaves may, after all, be sold, provided the trustees or executors see fit to do so.[142] The Arabs, but not Diogenes Laertius, also relate that when the above-mentioned boy-servants receive their freedom, the executors or trustees may decide what, in accordance with their merits, shall be given to them.

215

No. XXII

Nos XXII–XXVI are concerned with the erection of certain memorials in honor or memory of some of Aristotle's closest relatives, with Aristotle's final resting place, and with some votive statues to be set up in Stagira. Any testator, wishing to have the memory of his ancestors (or that of some near relative or that of himself) honored by appropriate measures, usually charged his heirs, executors or trustees to establish and maintain certain memorial cults or to erect statues of himself or of those persons (mostly ancestors, near relatives or, occasionally, dear friends) he had named in his will.[143] It may also be observed that a testator frequently intended to have his memory and that of his ancestors honored with appropriate feasts or sacrifices. Since he might entertain doubts about the piety of his own children, he often included in his will provisions setting up special 'trust funds' to be applied to this particular purpose; and he frequently appointed in his testament as trustee a kind of 'association' consisting of close relatives or trusted friends, which would see to it that these commemorative acts would be carried out. Perhaps from religious prejudice, the Arabic biographers omitted this part of Aristotle's last will and testament, which they probably considered to be declaratory of certain 'reprehensible' or pagan practices violative of the provisions of the Koran forbidding the use of graven images. Perhaps they simply regarded these provisions as unimportant.

In No. XXII, in particular, Aristotle stipulates that the 'images' (busts or statues) of Nicanor, Proxenus and that of Arimneste, the (older?) sister of Aristotle, should be set up. These 'images' are yet to be executed by Gryllion. With this generous gesture, Aristotle manifests his gratitude towards Proxenus, who as his 'guardian' (?) had taken care of the young Aristotle after the latter had lost his father (Nicomachus) and probably his mother (Phaestis); and towards Arimneste, his sister and the wife of Proxenus. Arimneste, we may presume, had been a 'second mother' to Aristotle after Phaestis had died and while Aristotle was still a boy. Dionysius of Halicarnassus,[144] as well as some of the other *Vitae Aristotelis*, imply that Aristotle's father (and perhaps his mother) died before Aristotle went to Athens and entered the Platonic Academy in 367 B.C.[145] The fact that Aristotle took over the education and care of Nicanor might indicate that Nicanor's parents, Proxenus and Arimneste, had both died while Nicanor was still rather young.[146] Proxenus and Arimneste certainly were dead in 323–22 B.C., the year in which Aristotle probably drew up his last will. In setting up the 'image' of Nicanor, who was still alive in 323–22 B.C., Aristotle also wishes to acknowledge his indebtedness to Nicanor's parents. The sculptor Gryllion (or Grylion), who had been commissioned to execute these 'images,' cannot be identified.

No. XXIII

Here Aristotle provides for a bust in memory of his (younger?) brother, Arimnestus. This Arimnestus apparently had died rather young without leaving any issue and hence had no one but his surviving brother, Aristotle, to remember and honor him as the duty of piety required.[147]

No. XXIV

The pious and apparently affectionate son stipulates that a statue (or 'likeness') of his mother Phaestis should be dedicated to, or erected in the temple of, Demeter at Nemea, or wherever the trustees or executors think best. Protogenes of Rhodes, a famous painter, is said to have painted the portrait of Aristotle's mother.[148] Whether or not the 'likeness' mentioned by Diogenes Laertius is this portrait cannot be determined. No temple of Demeter at Nemea (or of Nemea) has so far been identified, and we do not know the particular reason why Aristotle should insist that his mother's statue or 'likeness' be dedicated to Demeter.[149] For some inexplicable reason, Aristotle does not mention his father, Nicomachus. Perhaps he had died before the child Aristotle could have formed a lasting impression of him, perhaps there once had existed some serious tensions or disagreements between the young Aristotle and his father.

No. XXV

This passage implies that Aristotle had not designated his final resting place, but had left this decision to his executors or heirs.[150] Aristotle's specific wish that the bones of his long-departed wife, Pythias, should be buried together with his own remains, as Pythias herself apparently had wanted, indicates that Aristotle's (brief?) marriage to Pythias must have been a happy one.[151] It should also make it clear that he considered Pythias his only lawful wife, and that Herpyllis was not his second wife, as some people have suggested.

No. XXVI

The stipulation that, in compliance with Aristotle's vow, the executors or trustees should set up in Stagira life-size statues of Zeus and Athena (in order to ensure, or show thanks for, the safe return of Nicanor) bears out the fact, also alluded to in Nos III and VII, that at the time of Aristotle's death Nicanor was abroad on a 'dangerous mission.' To provide for such votive statues in a will was not an uncommon practice in ancient Athens and Greece. This gesture also attests that Aristotle was a pious and god-fearing man,[152] and that he must have been very fond of Nicanor, the intended husband of his only daughter.[153] The actual measurements of the votive statues are to be 'four cubits high,' which for some unknown reason were taken by certain scholars to mean 'four animal figures.'[154]

From a technical or legalistic point of view, the last will and testament of Aristotle poses a number of problems, most of which can be resolved, it is believed, in a reasonably satisfactory manner. Some scholars have denied outright, however, that this legal instrument is in fact a will; others are in disagreement as to its ultimate meaning; and still others believe that in the process of transmission it has been severely mutilated and badly distorted. There is no conclusive evidence, however, in support of any of these allegations.

Barring a few relatively minor details, there exists an undeniable agreement or accord between the general tenor of the Greek text of Aristotle's last will and testament preserved by Diogenes Laertius, and the Arabic version or translation. It is fairly safe to assume that, in some instances, Diogenes' version is slightly abridged or condensed, while the Arabic version is probably closer to the original document. To call the Arabic version an 'expanded interpolation' of the original text, however, is not warranted by the evidence. Only on two major and, perhaps, crucial points do these two versions disagree. The Arabs explicitly refer to Herpyllis as Aristotle's hand-maid.[155] This important statement should dispell any doubt as to Herpyllis' true status in Aristotle's household. Moreover, the Arabic version, but not that preserved by Diogenes Laertius, contains the provision that 'as to my estate and my son [Nicomachus] there is no need for me to make a [formal] last will and testament.'[156] This provision should make it clear that at one time Aristotle had adopted or legitimized Nicomachus, his son by Herpyllis. Aside from shedding some light on the status of either Herpyllis or Nicomachus, Aristotle's will also indicates that by

323–22 B.C., the likely year Aristotle drafted this instrument, Stagira must have been rebuilt, at least in part. For otherwise, the provision that if Herpyllis should elect to stay in Stagira, she could live in Aristotle's paternal home,[157] would be meaningless, as would the provision that stone statues in honor of Zeus and Athena should be erected in Stagira.[158]

The will of Aristotle also indicates that he must have been a well-to-do man;[159] that when he fled from Athens in the year 323 B.C. he managed to take with him most of his movable property as well as his fairly large staff of servants; and that he owned no house or other real property in Athens. Unlike the testaments of the Peripatetic scholarchs, namely, those of Theophrastus, Straton of Lampsacus and Lycon, the last will and testament of Aristotle does not contain any provisions or stipulations concering a 'school property of the Peripatus.' According to Strabo,[160] Aristotle donated his personal library to Theophrastus, probably at the time he had to leave Athens rather hurriedly in 323 B.C. (and, perhaps, in order to indicate that he wished Theophrastus to become his 'successor').[161] Since Aristotle was a *metic* or 'resident alien' in Athens, under the existing Athenian laws he could not have owned any real property there, including his own school buildings or 'garden.' The Lyceum was a 'municipal building' and hence not his to bequeath as, for instance, Theophrastus could bequeath the grounds and buildings of the Peripatus, which he had acquired thanks to Demetrius of Phaleron,[162] to whomever he chose. Aristotle merely taught or discussed philosophic issues at the Lyceum, as did other teachers. Moreover, it is highly improper to call Aristotle the first scholarch of the Peripatus, although he is certainly the founder of Peripatetic philosophy. Not being the scholarch of the Peripatus or, for that matter, of any distinct 'school' in terms of specific buildings or grounds, he could not dispose *mortis causa* of the school property.[163]

More broadly speaking, Aristotle's last will and testament is a truly noble document, attesting to the generosity, nobility and piety of the testator. To the point of being over-meticulous, Aristotle generously provides for all persons near and dear to him. Within the restrictions imposed upon him by law, he makes most magnanimous provisions for Herpyllis, who shared his life during the last years, had borne him his only son, and who had nursed him during his last illness. In a spirit of humanity and generosity, he not only frees his servants and slaves, but he also sees to it that they receive additional remunerations for their long and loyal services. In the waning days of his life, he recalls in a spirit of piety and reverence his far-away paternal home in Stagira, where he had spent what must have been a happy childhood. He remembers as well as honors his long-departed mother, to whom he must have been very much attached, but whom he could remember only as he had seen her while he was still a young boy; his (younger?) brother Arimnestus, who apparently had died at an early age; his foster-father (?) Proxenus, who had taken charge of the boy Aristotle after the death of his father, raising him and seeing to it not only that he would grow up safely, but also that he would receive the best liberal education available in the Hellenic world; his (older?) sister Arimneste, the wife of Proxenus, who had become his second mother; and his prospective son-in-law, Nicanor, the son of Proxenus and Arimneste, who had been like a son to Aristotle, and to whom he wishes to repay the everlasting debt he owed to Proxenus and Arimneste. To honor these beloved people, he decrees that their memory should be preserved in graven stone. He desires that his remains be buried together with those of his long-departed wife, Pythias, the beloved mother of his only daughter, as had been also Pythias' wish. The technical language of Aristotle's last will and testament cannot obscure its spirit of true humanity and genuine piety which forever attests to the fact that the testator was a great man. In more than one sense, this testament is the abiding memorial and the eloquent testimony of a noble human being.[164]

Chapter XVI

Aristotle's Religious Convictions*

The casual reader of Aristotle's doctrinal treatises may come away with the impression that 'science' and 'scientific research,' supported by methodological considerations and bolstered by some antiquarian investigations, dominated his whole active life and his entire intellectual concern. Accordingly, there remained little or no room for religious thought or theological speculation. However, this is not the place to discuss at length the religious and theological implications possibly contained in the traditional *Corpus Aristotelicum*. It is sufficient to point out that different scholars, often motivated by their own religious commitments, have come up with a great variety of widely conflicting suggestions and interpretations with regard to the religious content of the *Corpus Aristotelicum*. These suggestions range all the way from an allegedly complete 'religious indifferentism' on the part of Aristotle, to his fervent affirmation as well as deeply felt awareness of certain fundamental religious problems faced by all thoughtful people. This much, however, appears to be certain: the vital connection between science and *Weltanschauung* always remained the problematic issue as well as the focal point of Aristotle's philosophy and of his basic intellectual orientation. Especially in his earlier writings, which are gradually being brought to light, the Stagirite seems to have stressed the living and necessary interaction between an 'other-world-directedness'—a legacy which Plato and the Platonic Academy had bequeathed to him—and a distinct 'this-world-concern,' which constitutes an essential and original aspect of his basic philosophic endeavor. It was this living interaction which apparently gave him a deeper insight into the transcendental world and, at the same time, a more satisfactory and more secure footing in the existential-historical reality. Even if we were to assume that to Aristotle philosophy meant the total sphere of the sciences, and nothing more, we still would have to concede that the very concept of a 'total sphere,' which always calls for an integrated and compelling organization of science and reality, may never completely ignore the fact of religion. Religion, then, is a vital aspect of Aristotle's philosophic thought which has been almost completely overlooked or, still worse, simply ignored—ignored because the conventional views concerning Aristotle's basic philosophy and philosophic orientation would have to be abandoned if we were to realize that much of his philosophy was inspired and determined by his innermost religious convictions.

In what appears to be an intimate confession made probably during the last years of his life, and what might be called a 'baring of his soul,' Aristotle is said to have written to his friend Antipater: 'The lonelier and the more isolated I am, the more I have come to love myths.'[1] These moving words, which in their frankness should dispel all doubt as to their authenticity, clearly reveal that Aristotle knew as well as understood the two main avenues to personal religious experience: an adequate insight into the workings of the human spirit, and a true piety based on reverence and awe. In Aristotle's case, this piety assumes the form of symbols and 'myths.' The term 'myth' used here as a 'meta-rational' or 'meta-logical' meaning, but never signifies something 'irrational' or 'illogical.' It refers to something 'intuitively suggestive,' to an intuitive, immediate certainty or awareness which transcends science and method—to something deeply rooted in a 'world beyond' as well as in man himself. 'Myth,' then, is the ultimate, undefinable expression of an essentially undifferentiated ('pre-philosophic') thought which, in contrast to structured, articulated or conceptual thinking, intuitively formulates and comprehends something within and through itself. The truth of 'myth' lies at the level of the inner experience it expresses, while the 'myth' itself is the loving search of reason for something which really transcends reason—for something in which the ever questing intellect participates and to which this intellect seeks to attune itself in the perennially reciprocal and wholly intimate relationship of knower and known. The Platonic Academy, especially during the last years of Plato's philosophic endeavors, by its ability to construct, and by its determination to work with, symbols and 'myths,' created a new and positive piety among the members of the κοινωνία. This piety, through the intermediary of symbols and 'myths,' produced an innermost certainty and ultimate justification of religion and the true objects of religion. These symbols and 'myths,' also made it abundantly clear that a deeper and more satisfying form of religion is possible only as a personal experience— as a passionate commitment—based on faith and founded in wonder, awe and reverence transcending dispassionate rational or logical consideration.

The avowed commitment to 'myths,' in the final analysis, signifies to Aristotle a fuller and more satisfying understanding of the human spirit—of the real human condition—and a more profound appreciation of those facts or factors which are the main sources of religious inspiration and, at the same time, constitute the appropriate fountainhead of a more adequate effort to realize the ultimate meaning of life. More than that: the touching words uttered by Aristotle in his waning days should also reveal to the attentive reader that his life and work were deeply rooted in a second life which, barring a few fleeting moments, apparently remained wholly personal and hence completely hidden not only from the world at large, but seemingly also from his friends and more intimate associates. Most assuredly, this second life has also remained unknown to those scholars and commentators, both past and present, who in a spirit of unimaginative scholiasm have tried, and are still trying, to reduce Aristotle to a mere 'methodologist,' to a pioneering and successful architect of ancient formal logic, or perhaps to a sort of over-simplified 'text book.' Judging from the lost, but undoubtedly authentic, early works of the Stagirite, this hidden personal life and these personal experiences clearly indicate that Aristotle was both a profoundly religious man and a deeply sensitive person. Moreover, they also cast a novel light on a man who, to many people, was and still is little more than a scholarly philosopher, a masterly logician, a profoundly learned person and a wholly aloof intellectual.

It seems to be fully in keeping with Aristotle's ultimate attitude towards religion, piety and reverent awe when he is credited with having maintained that 'we should be nowhere more modest than in matters of religion. If we compose ourselves before we enter temples... how much more should we do this when we are discussing . . . the nature of the gods. In this latter case we must be on guard not to utter anything rashly and imprudently.'[2] Here Aristotle speaks unmistakably of a feeling of awe and reverence in the presence of the divine—in the presence of something which, in the final analysis, is infinitely above and infinitely superior to man. This awe and reverence, he insists, requires a certain 'inner composure' which, in his opinion, constitutes the fundamental attitude towards all religion, true religious feeling and genuine devotion. Just as we do not venture to enter the house of God until our feelings and thoughts are composed, so too, whenever we speak of the Most Sublime dwelling in the wondrous universe, we must enter the sacred temple of the cosmos in a thoroughly devotional spirit.[3] Accordingly, the pious contemplation of the universe in itself is akin to an initiation into religious faith. Probably under the influence of Aristotle (and under that of the Stoics), Plutarch could maintain, therefore, that 'the universe is the most sacred temple, worthy of God Himself. Man is introduced into this temple by being born into it . . . [and by becoming] a spectator of this ever-living reality . . . . Human life itself, therefore . . . is an initiation into this divine reality and, concomitantly, a most perfect ritual initiating us into the mysteries.'[4] In brief, 'by nature (actually, by his birth)' man is directed towards the eternal and divine[5]—towards God Who dwells within as well as above this awe-inspiring and miraculous universe.

Aristotle was apparently fully aware of the important and far-reaching distinction between reason and faith, rational understanding and sentiment, ratiocination and commitment, knowing and feeling: 'Those who are initiated into the mysteries,' he insisted, 'are not expected to grasp anything intellectually (discursively), but only to have a certain inner experience and thus can be put into a particular frame of mind, assuming they are capable of such an inner experience.'[6] A similar view is contained in a statement which is likewise traced back to Aristotle: 'I undertook to teach you what I myself have learned, not what I have personally experienced [within my innermost self] . . . . One is a matter for teaching, the other for mystical experience. The first one comes to men by listening; the second comes when the soul itself has experienced some "inner illumination," which Aristotle has described as mysterious and akin to the Eleusian initiation rites. For in these, he who was initiated into the mysteries was being molded, not taught. Whoever by virtue of rational operations reaches the conclusion that the soul is immortal, does so because he had been taught [how to use his powers of reasoning] and, hence, is a "taught person." However, he who through immediate spiritual vision or intuition sees the soul in its true essence, or he who without spiritual contemplation spontaneously and immediately apprehends its immortality, this man has an inspiration or "inner illumination" and hence is an "initiated person."'[7] A distant echo of this notion can still be detected in the *Eudemian Ethics*: 'Those are called fortunate who, whatever they start, succeed in it without being good at reasoning. Rational deliberation is of no advantage to them, for they have in them a principle which is better than intellect and rational deliberation . . . . They have inspiration, but they cannot deliberate . . . . Their insights (or inspirations) are speedy . . . [and these insights] in some instances are due to [mystical?] experience, in others to habituation in the use of reflection. And both [mystical] experience and habituation make use of God . . . . For the moving principle seems to become stronger when the reasoning power is relaxed.'[8]

Here Aristotle seems to speak of an 'inner illumination'—of an 'act of grace' that comes from the 'outside' and, hence, might be called the 'gift of faith.' Such an experience cannot adequately be reduced to mere logical or rational demonstration.[9] This 'inner illumination' is spontaneous contemplation of the divine and the divine infinite. It is a wholly personal, immediate and incommunicable state of mind through which the soul experiences the divine within itself. Inner illumination sheds light on the unintelligible and thus makes the latter intelligible on a higher plane. In this sense Aristotle could also maintain that mystical intuition—true faith—is illumination of the passive intellect and, hence, a kind of ecstasy.[10] He who has been initiated into the mysteries of the divine, like he who saw the light of faith or was illuminated by faith, has received a 'sign' rather than formal instruction: he has been given the 'gift of faith.' In this state of inner illumination, which is a special state of the soul, man realizes immediately and without intermediate proof the existence and reality of the divine as well as the immortality of his own soul, which is capable of receiving this illumination or grace.[11]

We might also conjecture that here Aristotle attacks certain aspects of traditional Greek religious cults which, through an essentially ritualistic formalism, had completely eliminated the element of personal and intimate relationship between the truly pious man and his God. At the same time Aristotle emphasizes the mysteries which stress the mystical (personal and intimate) union of, and communion between, man and God. Hence, the initiation into these mysteries, as well as the personal spiritual fervor with which man abandons himself to these mysteries, became for Aristotle the hallmark of true piety and meaningful religion. A commitment to God, an abandonment without questioning and an absolute will to believe must, Aristotle insists, replace calculating and reassuring ratiocination—sentiment must overcome reason to a point where the *credo quia absurdum* overrides all rational obstacles. This 'faith above reason,' this personal belief which borders on total abandonment to the sublime, was typical of the Greek mystery cults. This spiritual 'commitment no matter what' apparently attracted Aristotle, the rational philosopher who believed that, in the final analysis, religion and piety, unless they should degenerate into an essentially meaningless formalism—into a monumental irrelevance— are always an inner or spiritual experience of devotion and awe. The scanty evidence found in the lost works of Aristotle shows that the

Stagirite did seek this highly personal union and communion with God—a union and communion founded in wonder, awe and reverence.

In keeping with this basic religious attitude, Aristotle also insists that 'there is something above the "pure intellect" (νοῦς) as well as above being. This is shown by his [*scil.*, Aristotle's] general assertion, found at the end of his book *On Prayer*, that God is either "pure intellect" or something even beyond "pure intellect."'[12] From this statement we may infer that Aristotle believed in an incorporeal Supreme Being which he identified with 'pure intellect,' and that for him the Supreme God is 'pure mind' or *actus purus*—the 'Mind of minds' and perhaps something beyond mind (the human mind?) in that it transcends corporeal existence and sensibility.[13] Taken as a whole, Aristotle not only stresses the pure 'intellectuality' or pure 'spirituality' of God, but also emphasizes the fact that God transcends the 'pure intellect' or 'pure mind' and, concomitantly, is forever beyond the divine cosmos as well as beyond the human intellect.[14] It may also be conjectured, and it seems correctly, that in his *On Prayer*, Aristotle postulated that mortal man should approach God only 'in spirit' and pray to Him only in and through the intellect which, as Aristotle so emphatically stressed in the *Protrepticus*, is the 'only thing divine dwelling in us,' and which alone endows mortal life with 'a certain element or aspect of the divine.'[15] For, in keeping with the Greek notion that only like can communicate with like, the divine 'pure intellect' can be reached only through another intellect, that is, through 'spiritual' and intellectual truth—through the 'divine dwelling in us.'[16] Essentially the same notion is brought out once more in *Nicomachean Ethics* 1179 a 23 ff.: 'He who exercises and cultivates his intellect (νοῦς) seems to be both in the best state of mind and most dear to the gods. For if the gods have any care for human affairs, as they are thought to have, it will be reasonable to surmise that they should delight in that which is best and most akin to them (e.g., the intellect), and that they should reward those who love and honor this most, as caring for the things that are dear to them, and as acting both rightly and nobly. That all these attributes belong most of all to the philosopher is manifest. He, therefore, is dearest to the gods.'[17]

In the *De Virtutibus et Vitiis*, Aristotle insists that 'first among the acts of justice come the acts towards the gods. . . . Among these is piety, which is either a part of justice or an accompaniment of it.'[18] In brief, there cannot be true justice unless there is a reverence for the divine—unless people are committed to a firm belief in a Supreme Being. Hence, true justice and the belief in a single 'divine norm,' as well as the belief in the existence of a Supreme Being, always go hand in hand. This, then, would also indicate that Aristotle postulated, and probably held to, a theistic ethic. Justice without an ultimate, that is, divine and eternal 'point of reference' is impossible. Conversely, such a 'God-oriented' justice demands that we properly revere the ultimate and absolute norm of all that is right and just: God. Essentially the same idea is once more stated in the *Eudemian Ethics*: 'For God . . . is the end with a view to which prudence issues its commands. Whatever choice . . . will most readily produce the contemplation of God, that particular choice . . . is the best. This is the most exalted standard. But any choice that . . . prevents man from the contemplation of or services to God is bad. This ability to choose man possesses in his soul; and this is the best standard for the soul. . . .'[19]

Plato already insisted that 'there are two things which lead men to believe in the gods. . . . One is the argument about the soul . . . the other an argument from the order of the motion of the stars, and of all things under the dominion of the Mind which ordered the universe.'[20] Aristotle, who in this matter is probably under the influence of Plato's *Laws*, maintains that man can derive a knowledge of God's existence from two sources: from the inspired powers of the soul (revelation?), and from the starry heavens and the wonders of the visible world. According to Aristotle, 'also the heavenly bodies contributed to men's belief [in the existence of God]. Seeing by day the sun moving in its circular course, and by night the well-ordered movements of the other stars, men have come to think that there is a God Who is the cause of such movement and order.'[21] Pursuing the same argument further, Aristotle declares that 'some men, when they realize the unswerving and well-ordered movement of the heavenly bodies, say that in this realization the thought of gods had its origin. . . . Those who first looked up to the heavens and saw the sun running its race from its rising to its setting and the orderly dances of the stars looked for the [divine] Craftsman of this perfect design, and surmised that it came about not by chance, but through the agency of some mightier and imperishable nature, which was God.'[22]

In consequence, Philo of Alexandria could insist that 'Aristotle was surely speaking in a pious and devoted manner when he insisted that the universe is ungenerated and imperishable; and when he charged with serious godlessness those who proclaimed the opposite, that is, those who thought that the Visible God, Who contains in truth the sun and the moon and the remaining pantheon of planets and fixed stars, is no better than the work done by man's hands.'[23] It might be conjectured here that to Aristotle the starry (divine) universe was truly the 'Visible God' or, perhaps, the most perfect form in which God reveals Himself to man. It may even be conjectured that Aristotle might have believed that this divine universe in a certain way is 'God Incarnate.' In any event, such a highly conjectural assumption might be drawn from Philo of Alexandria, *De Aeternitate Mundi* III. 10. The sight of the starry heavens as well as his essentially religious feeling for the orderly cosmos, it will be noted, filled Aristotle with devotional wonder and awe. Thus, he gave expression to a timeless sentiment which defies precise definition or dogmatic analysis and hence becomes the ultimate and wholly irrefutable argument which since time immemorial man has made when standing face to face with the grandeur of the inexorable and ineffable. It was this sublime confrontation which not only led Aristotle to the belief in the existence of a Supreme Being,[24] but also determined his undeniable reverence and piety towards this Supreme Being as well as towards Its manifestations in the wondrous universe. This reverential awe and innermost piety is emphasized once more in *Metaphysics* 982 b 12 ff., where Aristotle confesses that 'it was owing to wonderment that men both now begin and at first began to philosophize. They wondered ... about the phenomena of the moon and those of the sun and of the stars, and about the genesis of the universe. And a man who is puzzled and wonders thinks himself ignorant. Whence even the lover of myths in a certain sense is a lover of wisdom or philosopher, for the myth is composed of wonders. ...' Only a wise man could have reached such a conclusion, and only a sincere person could have drawn the inescapable consequences from this conclusion. All this will also explain why, in contrast to Plato, Aristotle took a wholly affirmative attitude towards the visible world.

The thoughtful contemplation of, and the mystical insight into, the miraculous universe forced Aristotle to accept religion: it compelled him to realize that behind and beyond all this splendor there is, and must be, a divine artificer and director, a Supreme Being. In the spirit of this realization, he urges all men to think as well as reach beyond what is strictly human: 'The full possession of [true philosophy] might justly be regarded as being beyond human power. For in many ways human nature is in bondage ... and it is unfitting that man should not be content to seek the knowledge that is suited to him. ... The divine power, however, cannot be jealous, nor should any other science be considered more honorable than one of this sort. For the most divine science is also the most honorable. ...'[25] And again: 'We must not heed those who advise us, being human, to think only human things, and being mortal, only mortal things. But we must, so far as we can, make ourselves immortal, and strain our every nerve to live according to the best things in us.' [26] In short, we must reach (and can reach) beyond our human limitations and give more rein to the 'divine dwelling in us' if we intend to become 'god-like.' [27] When Aristotle attempts to prove the existence of God from the order and beauty of the visible universe, he does so not perhaps from the standpoint of dispassionate or disinterested intellectual curiosity, but rather in order to enable others to partake of what he himself has experienced in a sublime vision which almost amounts to ecstasy. Undoubtedly he was fully conscious of the fact that even the most refined and advanced logic 'can never attain to that irresistible force of inner conviction which arises out of the inspired . . . soul' [28] confronting the universe.

Aristotle's basic concern with the possibility of knowing God, or, at least of knowing God through contemplation, wonder and awe, is to some extent mysticism—an attitude which was prepared by Plato's *Laws* (books X and XII), by the *Epinomis* (provided the *Epinomis* is prior to the Aristotelian *On Philosophy*), and by the general philosophic and religious mood which permeated the Academy during the last years of Plato. But this contains the important implication, fully in accord with Aristotle's doctrine of causes, that we cannot know either the world or ourselves unless we have some knowledge of God— unless we know something about Him Who originated and still maintains both the world and us. Hence, with Aristotle, the famous Socratic 'know thyself' actually underwent a radical change. With him it came to mean that in order to know ourselves or, perhaps, in order to understand the world that surrounds us, we must know God or at least know of Him and of His existence. [29] Now we may also comprehend why Aristotle insists that 'all things have by nature something divine in them' [30]—why in the *Protrepticus* he maintains that 'reason is "the divine dwelling in us" ' . . . and because of reason, mortal life possesses a certain element or aspect of the divine.' [31] But this implies that a knowledge of God really comes to us 'from without.' Hence, if the true self of man is his intellect and if the intellect is really 'the divine dwelling in us,' then it is also through the intellect properly employed that we may gain a knowledge of God. This, then, would also explain why Aristotle should insist that God is 'pure intellect' or something above 'pure intellect,' and why mortal man may approach God and pray to Him only in and through the intellect. [32]

Aristotle's ultimate attitude towards and treatment of religion—we purposely refrain here from using the term 'theology'—is grounded, in the final analysis, upon three basic premises: First, 'all men have some conception of the nature of the gods, and all who believe in the existence of gods at all, whether barbarian or Greek, agree in allotting the highest place to the deity; [33] second, the mystic personal experience and the innermost religious life of individual man; and third, the more profound intuitive understanding of the awe-inspiring universe. Thus Aristotle attempted—and in our opinion successfully—to provide an empirical, a psychological and a rational explanation of and justification for the ultimate truth of religion, religious experience and the final reality of God. At the same time, the Stagirite was also aware of the fact that reason in and by itself can only in part satisfy the ultimate spiritual aspirations and needs of man. This being so, he was compelled to supply another vital element or factor which had already been advocated by Plato, though for a somewhat different purpose: a piety and reverential awe in the presence of the Most Sublime—in the face of something which by its very exaltedness must forever remain inexorable and ineffable. This piety and reverential awe find their metaphoric and, at the same time, most appropriate expression in symbols and myths. It is ultimately in the realm of mysticism that Aristotle, the great rational thinker and deathless logical architect of Western thought, discovered and formulated the personal relationship which exists between the God-seeking virtuous man and God Himself. Mysticism, which is man's spontaneous spiritual communion with God, always gives preference to personal spiritual experiences over dispassionate intellectual or impersonal logical considerations. For Aristotle, then, mysticism proclaims that true religion and true piety are possible only as personal commitment in the form of devotional awe—as a special kind of experience which, although it is the most profound of all experiences, does not require profound thought or a great store of learning. It might be contended, therefore, that Aristotle's whole philosophical outlook arose out of the apparently inescapable tension which so frequently exists between intellectual endeavor and religious longing. This, then, is also the ultimate meaning of Aristotle's last profession or confession: 'The lonelier and the more isolated I am, the more I have come to like myths.' [34] One may well transliterate these words as follows: The more I know about my soul and about the marvelous world in which I live, the more I realize in my reverent awe of the wondrous universe that all these wonders are ultimately the handiwork of a single Supreme Artificer. And the more I ponder over the fact that I am capable of knowing something about this world, the more I rise above this world of ours in my deeper under-standing of its ultimate origin and exalted meaning. And the more I rise above this world—above this divinely ordained handiwork of the Deity—although I shall always be, and shall always want to be, part of it, as I am part of the Divine, the more I understand this world in its magnificence and the more I shall find a secure refuge and a comforting haven in the world of faith which is, indeed, the world of God, wherein all true and worthwhile knowledge has its everlasting root as well as its ultimate significance and final justification.[35] In the light of this solemn profession, which amounts to an exalted prayer, Aristotle's well-known assertion that philosophy starts in wonder[36] acquires a novel and assuredly profounder meaning.[37]

Chapter XVII

Aristotle's 'Self-Portrayal'*

Some of the ancient *Vitae Aristotelis* attempt to portray Aristotle, touching upon his character, outlook on life, prominent virtues (and vices), scholarly attitude and the like. How reliable these reports are is difficult to assess, especially since most of the extant biographies are enthusiastically laudatory.[1] On the other hand, a number of more casual references to the Stagirite in Hellenistic and Patristic literature are often blatantly prejudiced and even deliberately hostile. Thus, the general impression we gain of Aristotle's character seems to depend to a large extent on the source or sources we consult. There is, however, a third ample and, it appears, reliable source which offers almost unlimited possibilities to 'reconstruct' Aristotle's main traits of character —a source which has hardly been tapped: His own writings as they have been preserved either in the extant *Corpus Aristotelicum*[2] or in some of the fragments from his 'lost' works. It is reasonable to assume that in his many writings Aristotle should divulge something about himself. Authors, especially prolific authors, frequently project their own personality into their compositions—a fact which is known to all who are familiar with literary criticism.

Judging from a variety of passages found in the *Corpus Aristotelicum*, as well as in the lost works, Aristotle must have had an abiding passion for truth and truthfulness: 'All men have an adequate natural instinct or desire for what is true and, as a rule, do arrive at the truth.'[3] Hence, 'we must honor truth above friends,'[4] because 'whatever is true . . . has a natural (inherent) tendency to prevail over its opposite.'[5] This passion for truth, empirical as well as philosophic, is probably best expressed in his statement that full credence must be given 'rather to empirical observation than to pure theories, and to theories only if what they allege agrees with the empirical facts.'[6] This being so, 'we may not reasonably attribute to anything any characteristics but those which observation detects in many or all instances.'[7] In other words, we should take for our working hypotheses only what we know

through experience and through observation to be generally or universally true. Theses and hypotheses, which fly in the face of scientifically observed facts, are 'next door to madness.'[8] Hence, 'we ought
never to shun philosophic truth'[9] and 'those who gainsay truth ought
to be punished.'[10] Aristotle's passion for truth also manifests itself in
his intellectual honesty. According to the testimony of Plutarch, the
Stagirite did not find it painful or distressing to have his own opinion
changed by others or to change his own mind on any subjects: 'He...
gave up some of the opinions which formerly satisfied [him]... without fuss or chagrin and even with pleasure.... Therefore, when truth
appears, reason gladly inclines to it and abandons falsehood.'[11]

It also appears that Aristotle was a kind and tolerant man, full of
understanding and compassion for the frailties of human nature and
the inadequacies of existential reality: 'We must as a second best...
take the least of evils,'[12] for true 'goodness is both rare and laudable,
as well as noble.'[13] One must always understand and forgive those
'who do something that ought not to be done, especially when they
act under duress which overstrains human nature and which no
average human being could withstand.'[14] Nowhere, perhaps, does
Aristotle's tolerance—wholly unknown to Plato—become more
apparent than in a remark found in the *Protrepticus*: 'Just as in the case
of material goods where the same kind of possession is, as regards
men, not conducive to both life and the good as well as happy life, so
it is with philosophic knowledge or wisdom. For in my opinion we
do not need the same kind of philosophic knowledge or wisdom as
regards plain ordinary life that we need for living the perfect (philosophic) life. The majority of men may wholly be excused and justified
for doing this—for being satisfied with that sort of knowledge which
is sufficient to lead a normal, average life. These people, to be sure,
wish for a higher form of happiness, but on the whole they are content
if they can simply stay alive.'[15] Aristotle's well-known tolerance
towards those who disagree with him and his philosophic views also
becomes manifest in *Politics* 1323 a 35, where he reminds us that we
must always take into account the fact that different people may
rightly disagree about the relative desirability or value of certain
goods.

The *De Virtutibus et Vitiis*, 1250 b 18 ff., testifies to Aristotle's piety
and reverence: 'First among the acts of justice come those towards
the gods... which are called piety.' But even more significant is his
statement that 'also the heavenly bodies contributed to man's belief
[in the existence of God]. Seeing by day the sun moving in its circular

course, and by night the well-ordered movements of the other stars, men have come to think that there is a God Who is the cause of such movement and order.'[16] And again: 'Some men, when they realize the unswerving and well-ordered movement of the heavenly bodies, say that in this realization the thought of gods had its origin. . . . Those who first looked up to the heavens and saw the sun running its race from its rising to its setting, and the orderly dances of the stars, looked for the Craftsman of this perfect design and surmised that it came about not by chance, but through the agency of some mightier and imperishable nature, which was God.'[17] Hence, Philo of Alexandria could maintain that 'Aristotle was surely speaking piously and devotedly when he insisted that the [divine] universe is ungenerated and imperishable; and charged with serious godlessness those who proclaimed the opposite—who thought that the visible God, Who contains in truth the sun and the moon and the remaining pantheon of planets and fixed stars, is no better than the work done by man's hands.'[18] Aristotle's attempts to prove the existence of God from the orderly beauty of the visible universe, it must be admitted, are above all passionate efforts on his part to enable others to experience what he himself had experienced when, in an inspired mood, he stood face to face with the wondrous universe. It is also in keeping with Aristotle's attitude towards religion and piety when he is credited with having said that 'we should nowhere be more modest than in matters of religion. If we compose ourselves before we enter temples . . . how much more should we do this when we are discussing the nature of the gods.'[19] In his early work *On Prayer*,[20] Aristotle declares that God is 'pure intellect' or 'something above the pure intellect.'[21] Hence, we must approach God and pray to Him only through the intellect, that is, on the highest possible level of communication befitting the sublimity of the Supreme Being. Essentially the same idea becomes manifest in the statement ascribed to Aristotle, that 'we must not offer anything defective to the gods, but things perfect and whole, and that which is complete is perfect, and garlanding oneself is a sort of completion.'[22]

Aristotle also seems to accept divine providence as well as divine concern for human affairs and for man in general: 'He who exercises his intellect and cultivates it seems to be both in the best state of mind and most dear to the gods. For if the gods have a care for human affairs, as they are thought to have, it would be reasonable to assume that they should delight in that which is best [in man] and most akin to them [*scil.*, the intellect], and that they should reward those who love and honor this most, as caring for the things that are dear to them, and as acting both in a right and noble manner. And it should be manifest that all these attributes belong most of all to the philosopher. He, therefore, is most dear to the gods.'[23] Hence, 'if there is any gift of the gods to man, it is reasonable to assume that happiness should be god-given, and certainly the most god-given gift of all human things inasmuch as it is best.'[24] In other words, true happiness is a divine gift bestowed upon those who, by their proper and intelligent conduct, have endeared themselves to the deity.

The prodigious scholarly output of Aristotle is in itself the most eloquent proof of the fact that he was an indefatigable as well as painstaking worker; and that he saw in intellectual work and scholarly effort the most profound meaning of life itself: the life of the 'doer' is the best life.[25] For 'happiness is activity.'[26] Hence, 'happiness, if not god-given, comes as a result of virtue, study and effort.'[27] 'We certainly should not spare any labor and expense in the pursuit of philosophic wisdom.'[28] Achievements for which we work hard and persistently are unquestionably the most pleasant and most rewarding of all experiences.[29] 'Learning things and wondering about them, as a rule, are also pleasant. But wondering implies the desire of learning [and working]. . . . In learning [and working] man is brought into his natural condition.'[30] 'The work connected with philosophic wisdom is admittedly the most delightful of all virtuous activities. In any event, the pursuit of philosophic wisdom is believed to offer pleasures outstanding for their purity and enduringness; and it is expected that those who know [and work for the acquisition of knowledge] will pass their time . . . most pleasantly. . . .'[31] 'To learn [and to work intellectually] is in itself superior to all physical pleasures and delights.'[32] For it is better for a man 'to exercise his soul (intellect) than merely to possess a soul (intellect).'[33]

Aristotle goes on, giving some excellent advice. 'The practice of anything, therefore, is the following: if something can be done only in one way, it is done when one does just that thing. If it can be done in more than one way, however, it is done when one does it the best possible way.'[34] 'Now, if living as such is for every animal its true being, then it should become evident that the thinking or rational animal has being in the highest degree and in the most compelling sense, and most of all if it uses this faculty or power in the intellectual contemplation of what is most knowable.'[35] 'It is for this reason that we declare the man who is awake [that is, who is doing something] . . . to be truly living and to be truly alive—the man who thinks, rather than the man who is without thought. And we also insist that the delight of [active] living is that kind of pleasure we derive from the activities of the soul (intellect). For this is, indeed, true life.'[36] 'A pleasant life and the capacity for true enjoyment, therefore, belong only, or most of all, to intellectual men who are thinking,'[37] that is, who work intellectually and dedicate their lives to intellectual pursuits. 'The doing of just acts is pleasant to the lover of justice, and acts that are in general virtuous are pleasant to the lover of virtue.... Their life, therefore, has no further need of pleasure as a sort of ornamental charm, but contains its own pleasures.'[38] Hence, Aristotle reaches the conclusion that true happiness and real contentment are the reward of unremitting intellectual work—of constant learning and tireless effort.[39] 'It is for the sake of practicing (of working) and learning (philosophic wisdom) that we have come into being ... and, hence, we also exist for that purpose.'[40] In brief, Aristotle, himself a prodigious intellectual worker as evidenced by his stupendous literary output, believes that sustained work endows life with a more profound meaning and, in all probability, with its ultimate meaning. The record seems to support the claim that he fully practiced what he preached.

Aristotle's approach to scholarship and scientific research is well illustrated in what appears to be an autobiographical sketch as well as a justification of his scholarly work: 'Of the things constituted by nature some are ungenerated, imperishable and eternal, while others are subject to generation and corruption. The former are most excellent ... but less accessible to knowledge. The evidence which might throw light upon them ... is furnished but sparingly by the senses, whereas in the case of perishable plants and animals we have abundant information, living as we do in their midst ... if only we are willing to take adequate pains. Both departments, however, have their unique charm. The scanty conceptions to which we can attain of celestial things give us ... more pleasure than all our knowledge of the world in which we live; just as half a glimpse of persons we love is more delightful than the leisurely view of other things, whatever their number or dimensions. On the other hand, in certitude and completeness our knowledge of terrestrial things has the advantage. Moreover, their greater nearness and affinity to us balance somewhat the loftier interest in the heavenly things which are the objects of the higher philosophy.'[41] And again: 'We should select also from the written text books on argumentation, and we should draw up outlines of them ... organizing them under separate headings, to wit, "On the Good," or "On Life." And the "On the Good" should deal with every form of good, beginning with the category of essence. On the margin, too, one should indicate also the respective opinions of individual thinkers. . . . For any one might assent to the saying of some widely accepted authority.'[42]

In the passage just quoted from the *De Partibus Animalium*, Aristotle proclaims that the human intellect has an innate desire to comprehend the world by knowing the first principles and causes:[43] *anima naturaliter philosophica*. He frequently recounts the joys and pleasures inherent in philosophic and scientific inquiry; and he insists that man is destined to philosophize and engage in scientific investigations from the moment 'he casts his eyes upon the discernible world.'[44] The passage from the *Topics*, on the other hand, is a reminder that in order to properly philosophize and pursue scientific studies we must work in an orderly and systematic fashion—that we must master the facts and be familiar with the findings and hypotheses of others. In short, science and philosophy presuppose a certain method, a definite approach and a consistent procedure, supported by a vast amount of historical knowledge. We must know and understand what preceding philosophers and scientists have held, in order to build upon their evidence and ideas, and also in order to refute them effectively wherever necessary.[45]

Aristotle's views on scientific method and scientific knowledge are also stated in the *Posterior Analytics*. When resorting to demonstration, scientific knowledge presupposes a knowledge of primary premises. This, in turn, raises a number of problems: whether the apprehension of these primary premises is the same as the apprehension of the conclusions; whether there is a scientific knowledge of primary premises and of the conclusions; whether there is a scientific knowledge of the conclusions, but a different kind of knowledge of primary premises; and whether the developed states of knowledge are acquired in some way or are perhaps innate but at first unnoticed. If they are innate, we would actually possess apprehensions which are more accurate than demonstrations, but we would be unaware of this. If we acquire primary premises, then the question arises as to how we may apprehend them without primary premises. From all this, it would follow that primary premises are neither innate nor are they simply acquired. Hence, we must possess a capacity of some kind, but not of the sort that ranks higher in accuracy than conclusions.[46]

Animals, according to the *Posterior Analytics*, possess a congenital discriminative capacity called sense perception. Out of repeated sense perceptions comes memory, and from frequently repeated recollection of the same things develops experience. From experience, again, originates the skill of the craftsman and the knowledge of the man of science. Thus, when a number of logically indiscriminable particulars 'have made a stand,' the earliest universal is present in the soul or mind as 'memory.' Although the act of sense perception is of the particular, its content is universal. A 'fresh stand' is made among these rudimentary universals, and this process is continued until the indivisible concepts, the true universals, are established. Accordingly, 'we must get to know the primary premises by induction. For the method by which sense perception implants the universal is inductive. Now of the thinking states by which we grasp truth, some are unfailingly true, while others admit of error. . . . But scientific knowledge and intuition are always true. . . . No other kind of thought, except intuition, is more accurate than scientific knowledge, but primary premises are more knowable than demonstrations, and all scientific knowledge is discursive. From all this, it follows that there cannot be a scientific knowledge of primary premises. This also follows from the fact that demonstration cannot be the originative source of demonstration nor, concomitantly, scientific knowledge the originative source of scientific knowledge. Hence . . . intuition is the originative source of scientific knowledge. This originative source of scientific knowledge grasps the original basic premise, while science as a whole is similarly related . . . to the whole body of facts.'[47] In other words, the beginning of all rational (analytical) knowledge as well as that of all rational (analytical) procedures, in a way, is really 'meta-rational' or 'meta-logical' in an analytical sense, but not 'irrational' or 'illogical.'

In the *Nicomachean Ethics*, Aristotle restates once more his basic views on scientific method or procedure: 'Scientific knowledge is judgment about things that are universal and necessary; and the conclusions of demonstration—and for that matter, all scientific knowledge —follow from first principles (for scientific knowledge involves apprehension of a rational ground). This being so, the first principle, which follows from what is scientifically known, cannot be an object of scientific knowledge. . . . For that which can scientifically be known can also be demonstrated. . . . Nor are these first principles the object of philosophic wisdom, for it is the mark of the philosopher to have demonstration about some things. If, therefore, the states of mind by which we possess truth and are never deceived about things invariable or even variable, are either scientific knowledge or practical wisdom or philosophic (theoretic) wisdom or intuitive reason—and it cannot possibly be any of the first three (to wit, scientific knowledge, practical wisdom or philosophic wisdom)—then the remaining alternative is that it must be intuitive reason which grasps the first principles.'[48]

The striking similarity between the passage from the *Posterior Analytics* and that taken from the *Nicomachean Ethics* should make it abundantly clear that throughout his creative life—Book II of the *Posterior Analytics* is said to have been composed prior to the year 350 B.C., while Book VI of the *Nicomachean Ethics* apparently was written during the last twelve years of Aristotle's literary activities, that is, between 335-34 and 323 B.C.—Aristotle consistently adhered to a single conception of the scientific method and scientific knowledge.

Though Aristotle sometimes evinces a strain of pessimism—a man who knew the world as Aristotle knew it and who had experienced, as he had, the general viciousness of man, had some cause to be at times pessimistic—he generally professed his abiding confidence in the ultimate ascendency of good over evil, of the beautiful over the ugly: 'Even if things are at times depressing, yet nobility and beauty always shine through, especially, when a man bears with resignation many great misfortunes, not through insensibility . . . to pain, but through nobility (beauty) and greatness of his soul'[49]—a statement which almost amounts to a self-revelatory confession. For 'even in inferior creatures there is some natural good.'[50] At the same time, he clings to an irrepressible faith in the irresistible progress of science: 'It would seem that anyone is capable of carrying on and articulating what has once been properly outlined; and that time is a good discoverer or partner in such an undertaking. To this fact, the advances in the arts and sciences are due. For any one can implement what is lacking.'[51] And again: 'The investigation of the truth is in one way hard and difficult, in another way easy. An indication of this is to be found in the fact that no single man is capable of attaining the whole truth adequately, while, on the other hand, we do not fail collectively. For everyone says something about the nature of things that is true. Thus, while individually we contribute little or nothing to truth, by the collaboration of all we are able to collect a considerable amount of factual truth.'[52]

In these last two passages, Aristotle re-affirms his fundamental belief that patient and systematic work, based on the achievements of past efforts and discoveries, will inevitably lead to improved results and thus promote human understanding and human progress. These remarks also affirm that scientific progress is a joint human endeavor. While an isolated individual effort might miss 'the target' either completely or in part, the combined efforts of the many, as a rule, may prove more successful. For 'the many, of whom each individual is but an ordinary person, when they join or work together, may very likely be better than the few good men by themselves, if regarded not individually but collectively. . . . Each individual among the many has a share of virtue and prudence; and when they meet together, they become in a manner of speaking one man. . . . The many are better judges than a single man. For some understand one part, and some another, but among them they understand the whole.'[53] Because 'when men meet together [and collaborate], their perceptions are quite good . . . but each individual left to himself forms a defective judgment.'[54] This is also an eloquent appeal to 'scientific teamwork,' a practice which Aristotle himself seems to have initiated and which in modern times has contributed so much to the advancement of science and human knowledge. More than that: Aristotle also attaches great significance to tradition which in his opinion embodies real experience. Hence, he insists that we must also consider every problem in the light of current opinion, inasmuch as all data are in accord with current opinions.[55] Current opinions, at least for Aristotle, always express some real fact: 'It is impossible that the views held by many people as well as by the men of old should be entirely mistaken.'[56] This is so, Aristotle argues, because 'men have a sufficient natural instinct for what is true and usually arrive at the truth.'[57] Essentially the same notion is expressed in the statement that 'every man has some contribution to make to truth.'[58] But the value of current opinions is greatly increased if they can look back on a long tradition (that is, if they go back to ancient times),[59] since that 'which has been established for a long period of time seems to be akin to what exists by nature.'[60] In short, the very antiquity of a tradition or view is some justification of its truth. For what exists for a long time, does not exist in vain.

Aristotle contends that the inexorable development of science promises a brighter future and nobler hope for mankind: 'In the case of all discoveries, the results of previous efforts, which have been handed down from others, have been advanced bit by bit by those who have taken them on. And whereas the original discoveries generally constitute an advance which is small at first, it is often much more useful and significant than the subsequent development which later follows these original discoveries. For it may be that in everything, as the saying goes, "the first start is the main part." And for this reason, the first beginning is also the most difficult.'[61] For 'just as in the legislative assemblies the general practice is to propose an amendment to the existing body of laws, and if the amendment constitutes an improvement the people repeal an existing law, so one ought to act in a like manner in the case of [scientific] definitions.'[62] But 'change or progress is only gradual and takes a long time.'[63]

Aristotle manifests his modesty and humility when he pays his respect to the achievements of his predecessors. He acknowledges that he is simply building upon the foundations laid by others: 'Let us always keep in mind that we should never discount the experience of the ages. In the course of many years these things . . . most certainly did not remain unknown. Almost everything has been found out, although in some instances these things were not put together. In other cases, men do not make use of the knowledge they have.'[64] For 'the same ideas, one must believe, occur and re-occur in the minds of men, not just once, but again and again.'[65] 'The same opinions appear in circles among men, not once nor twice, but infinitely many times.'[66] It was 'necessity which may be supposed to have taught men the inventions that were absolutely necessary [for survival]. When these had been taken care of, it was natural that other things, which would adorn and enrich life, should be devised by degrees.'[67] One must always bear in mind that 'probably every art and every science has often been developed as far as this is possible, and again has disappeared.'[68] But if there is an analogy between the recurrence of these necessary inventions and the recurrence of fundamental ideas, then there also must be a kind of necessity behind these fundamental ideas. The forces that cause the same ideas to appear again and again in a way are 'by nature': tradition starts with nature, or better, with a natural instinct for what is true, good and beautiful; its continuity throughout the ages indicates that it is 'by nature'; and its recurrence is a manifestation of the fact that it is determined 'by nature.' Hence, 'for our study . . .,' Aristotle avers, 'it is necessary, while formulating the problems, if we are to discover the solutions in our further investigations, that we consult the views of those of our predecessors who have uttered opinions on this particular subject, in order that we may profit by whatever is sound in their suggestions. . . .'[69] Accordingly, our main contributions to the views handed down to us by tradition is scientific systematization and co-ordination. Such systematization and co-ordination, in the opinion of Aristotle, is but the clarification of tradition as it has been handed down to us: 'By advancing from true but obscure statements [made in the past], man will arrive at clear statements, provided at every stage we assume a more scientific position or posture in exchange for the traditional confused statements.'[70] Such an 'exchange' does not involve, however, a drastic transformation of the traditional views, but merely implies a scientific or methodological improvement upon or modification of those traditional views (and former methods): 'We should therefore take over and make the best use of what has already been adequately discussed and expressed before us, and confine ourselves to the discovery of what heretofore has been omitted.'[71] This being so, 'it is only proper that we should be grateful, not only to those whose opinions we may share, but also to those who have expressed more superficial views. For the latter, too, contributed something. . . . From the better thinkers we have inherited certain opinions, while the others have been responsible for the appearance of better thinkers.'[72] For 'he who can observe things in their first growth and origin . . . will obtain the clearest and most perfect view of them.'[73]

In the field of rhetoric, Aristotle concedes that much good work had previously been done. But since 'the ordinary authors of text books [on rhetoric] treat non-essentials . . . and are more inclined towards forensic oratory,'[74] he proposes a novel approach which, however, still takes account of past achievements. Hence, 'let us start with a review of the theories of other thinkers. For the proofs of a theory are difficulties for the contrary theory. Besides, those who have first heard the pleas and arguments of our adversaries will be more likely to give credit to the assertions which we are going to make. We shall be less open to the charge of securing judgment by default. To make a satisfactory decision as to the truth, it will be necessary to be an arbitrator rather than a party to the dispute.'[75] In this latter passage, Aristotle suggests that truth ought always to be argued before the tribunal of reason where all parties to the discussion should be properly heard: *audiatur et altera pars.*

Realizing the importance of factual or historical knowledge, Aristotle became the great collector of information culled from history. The *Physics, Metaphysics, Politics, Rhetoric, Poetics* and the works on ethics, to mention only the most important Aristotelian writings, are treasure troves of historical materials, not to mention such compilations of facts and data as the *List of Olympian Victors*, the *List of Pythian Victors* or the *Constitutions of 158 Cities*. As a rule, Aristotle's systematic analyses are prefaced by historical observations or discussions. This is in itself indicative not only of his high regard for the intellectual accomplishments of his predecessors and for history in general—one might almost call him an 'antiquarian'—but also testifies to his firm belief that history is not only the repository of past achievements, but also an inspiration to further progress.[76] Apparently he believed that ignorance of history condemns man to repeat ancient mistakes as well as preventing him from making deliberate and significant progress. In keeping with his penchant for methodical work, however, he is never a mere compiler of facts. He is, rather, a systematizer of information.[77] He does not write as a historian or archivist, but he does try to relate the philosophers he quotes to philosophic, that is, to systematic truth. And his pursuit of truth is not motivated by utilitarian considerations.[78] Neither does he merely report on, or enumerate, the views held by the older philosophers. He invariably makes every effort to explain their teachings, and he attempts to give reasons why they did arrive at their particular conclusions. Frequently he organizes and arranges his historical materials in terms of scientific discovery and scientific progress rather than along purely chronological lines.[79]

In *Metaphysics* 984 a 11 ff., when discussing Empedocles' four basic elements, Aristotle points out that 'Anaxagoras of Clazomenae, though older than Empedocles, was later in his philosophical activities.' And in *Metaphysics* 984 b 15 ff., he maintains that 'when one man [namely, Anaxagoras] said that "reason" was present . . . as the cause of all order and arrangement, he seemed like a sober man in contrast to the wild talk of his predecessors. We know that Anaxagoras certainly adopted these views, but Hermotimus of Clazomenae is credited with expressing them earlier.' When discussing the problems of Being or of the One, Aristotle insists that the opinions of Xenophanes (*floruit* about 540–36 B.C.) were somewhat naïve and, hence, should be ignored, while Parmenides (*floruit* about 480–75) 'in places appears to speak with more insight.'[80] These few examples, which could be augmented *ad nauseam*, illustrate Aristotle's conviction that a mastery of historical fact as well as a thorough understanding of the history of philosophy is an indispensable prerequisite for all philosophic endeavor and all philosophic progress. Nowhere does he express this notion more succinctly than in *Nicomachean Ethics* 1181 b 16: 'First, then, if anything has been said well in detail by earlier thinkers, let us try to review it'; or in *Politics* 1260 b 27 ff.: 'It is our aim to consider what political community is the best for all those who are most able to realize their ideal life. We must therefore examine not only the [ideal] constitution, but also other constitutions, both those which actually exist . . . and any theoretic forms which are held in esteem. We shall do this in order that that which is good and useful may be brought to light. . . . We shall engage in this inquiry only because all the constitutions with which we are acquainted are faulty.' Hence, 'the reason why I speak of this [namely, of the opinions of the earlier philosophers] is that we want to learn from them the principles which they advocated. . . . Such a presentation is germane to our inquiry.'[81]

Constant reference to the views advanced by earlier philosophers not only assists us in understanding the difficulties inherent in all philosophic speculation, but is also constructive in giving us valuable hints as to what the real problems and issues are: 'Let us call on those for aid who have tackled the investigations about Being and have philosophized about reality long before us. . . . To go over their views, then, will be of advantage to our present inquiry, for we shall either find another kind of principle (cause), or be more convinced of the correctness of those principles (causes) which we are now about to propose.'[82]

Aristotle also had a genuine appreciation for and understanding of beauty or the beautiful, which to him was inseparably linked to every-thing rational and purposive. Together with intellectual knowledge, beauty was for Aristotle the ultimate end of man and of human acti-vity—the ultimate end of purposive nature: 'If some animals have no attractiveness to charm the senses, yet even these animals, viewed from the standpoint of science, disclose to intellectual perception the artistic-aesthetic spirit which designed them. In this they give abundant pleasure to all those who are able to trace links of causation and have a penchant for philosophic thought. Indeed, it would be strange if mimic representations of these animals were attractive (because they disclose the mimic skill of the painter or sculptor) and the original realities themselves were not more interesting, to all those at any rate who have eyes to discern the reason which presided over their original formation. We therefore must not recoil with childish aversion from the examination of the humbler animals. Every domain of nature is simply marvelous and beautiful. . . . Hence, we should venture into the study of every kind of animal without distaste. For each and every one will reveal to us something natural and, at the same time, something intrinsically beautiful. Absense of haphazardness and conduciveness of everything to an end are both to be found in the works of nature to the highest degree. The resultant end of nature's generations and combinations is indeed a form of the beautiful.'[83] In short, Aristotle was fully convinced that 'nature always follows the best course possible,'[84] and that the best course possible always produces what is most beautiful.[85] A cursory survey of Aristotle's writings readily discloses that he had a deep understanding of beauty and its infinite manifestations, either in the awe-inspiring starry sky, or in the stirring declamations of the poetic arts, or in the intricate wonders of nature.

Although Aristotle most certainly disagrees with some of the philosophic tenets of his friends, teachers, associates and benefactors— the statement, *amicus quidem Socrates, sed magis amica veritas*, has been ascribed to the Stagirite[86]—his admiration and reverence for Plato becomes manifest in his Elegy, dedicated to the honored memory of Plato (or Eudemus of Cyprus):

'Coming to the famed plain of Cecropia,
He [*scil.*, Aristotle] piously set up an altar of sacred friendship
For the man [*scil.*, Plato] whom to praise is not lawful for bad men,
Who alone or first of all mortals clearly revealed
By his own life and by the methods of his teachings
That a man becomes good and happy at the same time.
Now no one can ever attain to these things again.'[87]

For his disagreement with certain aspects of Plato's philosophy he almost apologizes: 'It would perhaps be thought to be better and indeed to be our duty, for the sake of upholding the truth, even to deny what touches us most closely, especially, since we are philosophers and lovers of wisdom (truth). For, while both (friends and truth) are dear to us, piety requires us to honor truth above our friends.'[88] Aristotle's deep attachment to his teachers and to the friends he made while studying at the Academy is expressed in his statement that 'one should return to those with whom one has studied philosophy. For their worth cannot be measured against money, and they can get no honour which will repay them for their services. But it might be enough, as is the case with the gods or with one's own parents, to give them whatever one can.'[89] For Eudoxus of Cnidus, whose views he could not possibly accept, Aristotle has some very kind words: 'His [*scil.*, Eudoxus'] arguments [namely, that pleasure was the ultimate good] gained eminence more on account of the excellence of his character than for their own sake.'[90] Objecting to Plato's suggestion (*Laws* 737E) that there should be 5,000 warriors in the ideal city, Aristotle remarks that Socrates' discourses in Plato's dialogues 'are never commonplace. For they always exhibit grace, originality and profound thought, but perfection in everything can hardly be expected.'[91] How strongly he remained attached to his friends and benefactors is also evident in the Hymn to Hermias,[92] as well as in the honorific inscription he dedicated to Hermias at Delphi.[93] In 348–47 B.C., Hermias had not only given Aristotle shelter, but also friendship. Thus, a great and humble man not only acknowledges his everlasing indebtedness to his friends, teachers and benefactors, but also eloquently praises friendship.[94]

From Aristotle's last will and testament[95] we also learn that he was a man of great humanity, generosity and piety. In this document, he provides that those of his servants or slaves who had served him loyally shall be set free. More than that: in order to prevent these servants from becoming destitute in their old age, he stipulates that they shall receive legacies to provide for their future needs.[96] To Herpyllis, the mother of his illegitimate son Nicomachus, who in Aristotle's own words had served him with devotion and had nursed him during his last illness, he made over a considerable part of his estate and provided her with a comfortable home.[97] He instructs his executors to set up a statue in the memory of his mother Phaestis and to dedicate this statue to Demeter of Nemea.[98] He also gratefully remembers his guardian and foster-father Proxenus, who had raised him after his father Nicomachus had died prematurely; Proxenus' wife Arimneste (the sister of Aristotle), who had become his foster-mother after the death of Phaestis; Arimnestus, his brother who had died without issue; and Nicanor, the son of Proxenus and Arimneste and Aristotle's intended son-in-law.[99] Statues in memory of all these people, whom he must have loved dearly, are to be erected so that their memory may be properly preserved forever in graven stone. And finally, he desires that his mortal remains be buried together with those of Pythias, his long-departed and beloved wife, the mother of his only daughter.[100]

Like all great men, Aristotle must have been a terrifyingly lonely man—a loneliness which he expressed in his moving confession, in all likelihood contained in a letter written by him during his last years: 'The more lonely and isolated I am, the more I have come to love myths.'[101] These are the words of a reserved, austere and solitary man, withdrawn into himself and hidden from the world by the unconquerable ramparts of his awesome learning. Somewhere behind these ramparts dwells the true Aristotle—the man who anchored his concept of the philosophic life in a second life, wholly personal, almost unknown and essentially 'other-world-directed.'[102] Only a superficial and ill-informed observer could maintain that Aristotle's whole life was uncompromisingly and exclusively committed to scholarly and scientific work.[103] In a way, it may be observed that Aristotle's dialectical, logical and metaphysical notions were inspired by his deeply rooted religious beliefs and commitments—that they were the tangible products of an 'inner compulsion' which urged him on to find some demonstrable expressions or proofs for what he himself had experienced, and thus to communicate to others what was the innermost conviction of his whole life. This basic aspect of Aristotle's intellectual activities has been either completely ignored or deliberately overlooked, perhaps because the conventional estimate of him and his life's work would have been upset if we should concede that his fundamental philosophic outlook or *Weltanschauung* was inspired from within by a fervent and innermost religious belief.

These fragmentary references, chosen at random, could be considerably augmented. They encompass the whole span of Aristotle's productive life, from the time he was still a member of the Platonic Academy to the last years of his literary activity. They bespeak an astonishing consistency which he maintained even in the face of changing philosophic and scientific interests or emphases, as well as in the face of changing fortune and circumstance. In short, while Aristotle's fundamental philosophic outlook underwent some notable changes in the evolution of his thought and in the general direction of his scholarly concerns, Aristotle the man remained essentially the same throughout his life. Judging from his writings, in which he reveals the dominant traits of his character, we may conclude the following: in all his intellectual endeavors and scholarly enterprises he was motivated by a passion for truth—truth in its moral as well as intellectual meaning. Concomitant with his passion for truth—his honest and almost humble effort to understand the actual conditions of the existential world—is his sense of toleration and tolerance which at times borders on gentle compassion proclaiming a spirit of humane 'good will' towards the world. His piety and deeply religious convictions, his reverence for the sublime and divine, always edify the reader who seeks in Aristotle's works more than mere attempts at systematizing human knowledge or categorizing empirical evidence.

Like so many believers, Aristotle sincerely tried, through incessant intellectual work, to reach beyond the world of the senses, sense perceptions and empirical reality. He was undoubtedly a deeply religious man, and in a very real sense he lived the motto, *laborare est orare*. His approach to the problem of knowledge and understanding is not primarily 'metaphoric' or 'mystical' or 'mythical,' as it is with Plato, but scholarly and scientific. At the same time he realized that reason by itself cannot completely satisfy the ultimate intellectual and spiritual longings of man, and that in a spirit of reverential awe man must acknowledge the existence as well as the efficacy of something which (although it may forever remain inexorable and ineffable) constitutes the ultimate reason of all knowability and of all true knowledge. In so doing, he also discovered that there exists and always must exist a personal spiritual experience as well as a personal moral and intellectual commitment, which is at the basis of man's ultimate communion with truth. He firmly believed that all men have an innate desire to know and to understand, and that it is man's duty to satisfy this lofty desire by promoting human knowledge and human understanding. But this craving for knowledge and understanding can only be achieved by disciplined scholarly effort and unremitting work. In a spirit of noble and humanistic optimism, he professed his deeply-rooted faith in the gradual scientific progress of mankind, a progress which would be paralleled by a similar moral evolution. Like all decent and learned men, he manifested a genuine reverence and a generous respect for the past as well as for past scientific and moral performances. He was fully aware that the past constitutes the firm footing of the present and the bright hope for the future. In this, he displayed a serene attitude towards life in general—an attitude which is both realistic and contemplative without being tragic.[104] He had a profound understanding and appreciation of beauty which to him is consonant with truth. When he insists that 'philosophy begins in wonder and wonderment,'[105] he frankly concedes that all worthwhile knowledge and worthwhile truth originates with contemplative awe and reverent contemplation of the ultimate truth and ultimate beauty. He was always the loyal friend who professed an abiding and genuine affection for and an undying gratitude towards his teachers, benefactors and associates. And finally, to the very end he was generously mindful of those persons who were particularly near and dear to him. In commemorating them, he unknowingly erected to himself the greatest human monument.[106]

Conclusion

Whether the extant ancient *Vitae Aristotelis* contain consistently reliable information about the life and the deeds of Aristotle is extremely difficult to ascertain. With the possible exception of the *Vita Aristotelis* of Diogenes Laertius (DL V. 1–16) and the *Vita Aristotelis Hesychii*, these ancient *Vitae* are pronouncedly and even one-sidedly encomiastic. Hence, it is safe to assume that they relate a *mélange* of fact and fiction— a conglomerate of true or almost true stories, often slanted in favor of Aristotle. This also seems to have been the case with the *Vita Aristotelis* of Hermippus and most certainly with the *Vita Aristotelis* of Ptolemy (-el-Garib). Both these *Vitae*, which appropriately may be termed the traditional *Vitae Aristotelis*, are lost, although some epitomes or abridgments of these traditional *Vitae* have survived in one form or another.[1] Of these surviving epitomes, the *Vita Aristotelis* of Diogenes Laertius[2] and the *Vita Aristotelis Hesychii*, in the main, apparently rely on the *Vita* of Hermippus, although both Diogenes Laertius and Hesychius make use of other sources as well.[3] This might also explain why these two *Vitae* relate and discuss side by side both favorable and unfavorable reports about Aristotle. Conversely, the *Vita Aristotelis Marciana*, the *Vita Aristotelis Vulgata* (*Vita Pseudo-Ammoniana* or *Vita Pseudo-Elias*), the *Vita Aristotelis Latina*, the two anonymous *Vitae Aristotelis Syriacae* and the four *Vitae Aristotelis Arabicae*, namely, those of Ibn An-Nadim, Al-Mubashir, Al-Qifti Gamaladdin and Ibn Abi Usaibia, in the main go back to, or are more or less successful abbreviations of, the *Vita Aristotelis* of Ptolemy (-el-Garib).[4] This is further confirmed by the fact that these nine particular *Vitae*, on the whole, are fairly uniform in their general tenor as well as basic content, although on occasion they manifest some interesting differences of detail or emphasis. Hence, all the extant ancient and mediaeval *Vitae Aristotelis*, in one form or another, are ultimately based on either the *Vita* of Hermippus or the *Vita* of Ptolemy.

Judging from its two surviving derivates, namely, the *Vita Aristotelis* of Diogenes and the *Vita Aristotelis Hesychii*, the dominant characteristic of Hermippus' original *Vita Aristotelis* seems to have been at times a bewildering fusion of history and anecdote, praise and slander, truth and fiction. Perhaps the most telling aspect of Hermippus' work is his practice of citing side by side both favorable and unfavorable reports about Aristotle. There can be no doubt, however, that on the whole he intends to extoll Aristotle, and to present him as a first-rate thinker and splendid person who intellectually and morally owed little or nothing to Plato. Whenever Hermippus relates some unfavorable and unpleasant story or account of Aristotle, he tries, we must assume, to minimize or controvert it by pointing out that this particular report is based on false information, deplorable misunderstanding or deliberate malice.[5] Ptolemy, on the other hand, appears to have been a one-sidedly encomiastic reporter who undertook to suppress, gloss over or refute any and all unfavorable accounts about Aristotle. It cannot be determined, however, to what extent, if at all, Ptolemy made use of Hermippus' *Vita*, or of some intermediary sources (Andronicus of Rhodes) which ultimately go back to Hermippus. One thing, however, is rather striking about the *Vita Aristotelis* of Ptolemy: it appears to have stressed, and discussed at great length, the many diplomatic, political and statesman-like activities, preoccupations and successes of Aristotle, something which the nine extant derivatives of this particular *Vita* likewise emphasize.[6] This, in turn, might compel us to revise some of the traditional views about Aristotle as the withdrawn and unworldly theoretic man who spent his whole life in philosophic contemplation and in producing a host of scholarly publications. These seem to have been the main features of the *Vita Aristotelis* of Hermippus and of the *Vita Aristotelis* of Ptolemy, provided the proposed, though certainly conjectural, 'reconstruction' of their main contents has been successful.

The *Vita Aristotelis* of Dionysius of Halicarnassus is essentially a fairly accurate chronology of the main events in the life of Aristotle,[7] while the *Vita Aristotelis* of Diogenes Laertius (V. 1–16) is most certainly a very complex and frequently puzzling biography. Aside from relying heavily on the *Vita Aristotelis* of Hermippus, the biography of Diogenes Laertius also draws information from a number of other historians, authors and philosophers, including writers who are decidedly hostile towards Aristotle. In this, the *Vita Aristotelis* of Diogenes Laertius is also something of a spectrum as well as a kind of survey of the many conflicting stories circulated about Aristotle in antiquity by both his admirers and detractors. Because of its inherent complexity and the fact that it is not intended to be a deliberate and one-sided exaltation of Aristotle, the *Vita* of Diogenes Laertius poses many problems, some of which are almost impossible to resolve.[8] In its tendency to relate both favorable and unfavorable (including outright slanderous) reports about Aristotle, it differs considerably from the two Syriac and four Arabic *Vitae Aristotelis* (as well as from the *Vita Aristotelis Marciana*, the *Vita Aristotelis Vulgata* and the *Vita Aristotelis Latina*), which through certain intermediary sources, including an earlier and apparently complete Syriac translation of the whole of the *Vita Aristotelis* of Ptolemy (-el-Garib), are more or less accurate and detailed epitomes of Ptolemy's *Vita*. Like their ultimate source or model, the essentially encomiastic Syriac and Arabic *Vitae Aristotelis* also stress and extoll, as we have seen, the many political and social activities of Aristotle, thus making it appear that he played an important and, perhaps, decisive role in the meteoric rise of Macedonia to a cosmocracy during the reign of King Philip.[9]

The several ancient biographies of Aristotle, as well as the writings of a number of ancient historians and authors, enable us not only to reconstruct the genealogy of Aristotle and some vital data of his life,[10] but also to gain an insight into the history of his more immediate family.[11] The story that he was a direct descendant of Asclepius and especially of Machaon—a story which may safely be discarded—might possibly indicate that his more remote paternal ancestors originally came from Messene. In any event, this genealogy makes it quite clear that his paternal and maternal ancestors were Greek. The most prominent among his closer relatives—Theophrastus excluded, provided the latter was indeed a relative—was undoubtedly Callisthenes of Olynthus, the historian. Callisthenes apparently entered the household of Aristotle and was educated by the latter. He also seems to have collaborated with Aristotle in compiling the *List of Victors at the Pythian Games* as well as in collecting materials for some other works authored by the Stagirite. In 327 B.C. Callisthenes was put to death by Alexander, whom he had accompanied on his Persian venture as the official reporter or historian. This sordid incident resulted not only in a further alienation between Aristotle and Alexander, but also in the subsequent moral condemnation of Alexander by the Peripatetics (and Stoics). This condemnation had far-reaching effects on certain aspects of the literary tradition concerning Alexander's moral or emotional weaknesses and main traits of character.[12]

In the late spring of 367 B.C., at the age of approximately seventeen years, Aristotle went to Athens. It is possible that he sought there political refuge from the murderous inter-dynastic struggles between the followers of Amyntas III and Alexander II, and those of Ptolemy of Alorus—struggles which convulsed Macedonia between c. 369 and 365 B.C. At the time of his arrival in Athens, Aristotle was orphaned (his father Nicomachus probably was a follower of Amyntas III and Alexander II and might have been killed by the partisans of Ptolemy), and Plato had journeyed to Syracuse, whence he did not return until late in 365 or early in 364 B.C. During Plato's absence, Eudoxus of Cnidus had been installed as the 'acting scholarch' of the Academy. Several *Vitae Aristotelis* insist that upon his arrival in Athens in 367 B.C., Aristotle studied or kept company with Socrates for some time. In view of the fatal anachronism contained in this bit of information, we are entitled to presume that he studied for a while with Isocrates. This assumption seems to find additional support in the *Vita Aristotelis* of Al-Mubashir as well as in a fragment ascribed to the lost Aristotelian composition, entitled *Nerinthus*. After a presumably short stay with Isocrates and his school, Aristotle 'transferred' to the Academy where he came under the personal tutelage of Plato. It might be surmised that he joined the Academy after Plato's return from Syracuse, although it is quite possible that he did so at an earlier time, that is, during the scholarchate of Eudoxus.[13]

After the completion of his preliminary or pre-philosophic studies at the Academy, Aristotle was apparently put in charge of an independent course of lectures on rhetoric, a signal honor for so young a member of the Academy. This fact seems to be borne out by the statements of certain ancient authors, as well as by some of the earlier writings of Aristotle, including the so-called *Urrhetorik* (Jaeger). Moreover, this significant incident may also be construed as an indication that during his association with the Academy, Aristotle must have subscribed to the basic tenets of Plato's philosophy; that at one time he must have received a thorough training in rhetoric (by Isocrates?); that he must have advocated Plato's teachings concerning rhetoric (as the latter had promulgated them in the *Gorgias* and the *Phaedrus*) rather than those of Isocrates; that at one time he must have criticized and rejected the teachings of Isocrates; and that from the very beginning, he must have been an outstanding 'student' who enjoyed Plato's confidence and admiration.[14]

Aristotle left Athens and the Academy in the summer or early fall of 348 B.C., several months before the death of Plato. Being a Macedonian 'resident alien,' he departed (or better, fled) because of the sudden outbreak of serious anti-Macedonian agitations in Athens which had been provoked by King Philip's seizure and destruction of Olynthus in the summer of 348. Hence, contrary to a widely held belief, the death of Plato (which probably occurred early in 347 B.C.) had nothing to do with Aristotle's hasty departure.[15] Presumably, after having fled from Athens, Aristotle returned to Macedonia and, perhaps in the spring of 347 B.C., went, or was sent by Philip, to Hermias of Atarneus. It is quite plausible that Aristotle's visit with Hermias was, in truth, a political or diplomatic mission intended to win over the ruler of Atarneus to Philip's future political designs and plans of conquest. Hermias' domain was strategically located and could effectively be used as a bridgehead for an invasion of Asia Minor or as a basis for the encirclement of Thrace—two aims in the political schemes of Philip. Moreover, Hermias, who thanks to some serious political upheavals within the Persian empire, had gained a certain measure of independence, knew only too well that without outside assistance he would sooner or later be crushed by the Persians. While in Assos or Atarneus, Aristotle became the close personal friend of Hermias, whose daughter (adoptive daughter) Pythias he subsequently married. In the year 345–44 B.C. Aristotle departed from Hermias and went to Mytilene. It is possible that his transfer from Assos (or Atarneus) to Mytilene was primarily a 'safety measure,' and that he was finally recalled to Macedonia by King Philip himself who, for the time being (and in order to prevent an Athenian-Persian alliance against Macedonia), apparently abandoned his political designs as regards Hermias. Presumably over the protests of Aristotle, Hermias was crudely betrayed by his Macedonian ally and soon overpowered (and put to death) by the Persians who seem to have been aware of his political negotiations with Macedonia.[16]

In the year 343–42 B.C., Aristotle returned to Macedonia, presumably in order to undertake the education of Alexander. The story that Aristotle was the preceptor or chief tutor of the young prince is by no means above suspicion.[17] It might well be a later literary invention devised to magnify two outstanding men—to bring together the great thinker and the great doer, the man of ideas and the man of action, in a relationship of teacher and pupil. There also exists the possibility that Philip's rather crude betrayal of Hermias, the friend and kinsman of Aristotle, for a while was strongly resented by the Stagirite. Although this incident might have caused a brief personal alienation between Aristotle and King Philip—an alienation which probably induced Aristotle temporarily to withdraw from all public or political activities on behalf of King Philip—we may conjecture that soon afterwards Aristotle once more began to play an important role in the diplomatic schemes of the Macedonian king. Presumably, he assumed an active, if not decisive, part in a number of political negotiations which took place between Macedonia and some of the Greek states, including Athens, both before and after the battle of Chaeronea (in 338 B.C.). In any event, throughout his mature life, Aristotle seems to have been actively associated with many of Macedonia's diplomatic and political moves or manoeuvres.[18]

In the year 335–34 B.C., after the abortive revolt of the Greek states against their Macedonian overlords had been put down by the force of arms, Aristotle returned to Athens. It appears that after the meek surrender of Athens he, the Macedonian, moved back to that city in the van of the conquering Macedonian army. It is possible, however, that he personally interceded with King Alexander on behalf of the Athenians, thus saving Athens from possible destruction or humiliating terms of submission imposed by the outraged Alexander. There exists some evidence that at one time the Athenians erected or planned to erect, a honorific *stele* commemorating Aristotle's many beneficial services to Athens, including perhaps his successful intercession with Alexander to spare the city.[19] It is also possible that between 335–34 and 323 B.C., he was something of a 'political agent' for Macedonia in Athens. Presumably, the Athenians knew about or suspected him of being an agent of their enemy. In any event, the many 'letters' ('intelligence reports'?) he apparently sent to Antipater during this period lend some weighty support to this assumption. Some of these 'letters,' which allegedly contained information detrimental to Athens and to the Athenian aspirations to regain political freedom, are said to have been intercepted by the Athenians. Aristotle's 'official position' in Athens during his second stay in that city—a period which traditionally has been called the philosophically most productive years in his life or his philosophic *Meisterjahre*—must have made his second sojourn in Athens a rather unpleasant and trying experience.[20] This might also question the general assumption that between 335–34 and 323 B.C. Aristotle composed his most important doctrinal treatises.

After the sudden death of Alexander on 13 June 323 B.C., which subsequently brought on a widespread anti-Macedonian uprising in Athens and other parts of Greece (Lamian War), Aristotle once more found himself in serious jeopardy. He fled again from Athens, where formal proceedings for alleged *asebeia* were instituted against him. He withdrew to Chalcis where he died the following year.[21] Judging from the terms of his last will and testament as well as in the light of the existing Athenian laws pertaining to resident aliens, Aristotle apparently never acquired or possessed a school of his own, or to be more exact, a distinct school *building* of his own. Hence, it is doubtful whether he ever had his own independent school in Athens which was on an equal footing with the Academy. This, in turn, raises the far-reaching question of whether Aristotle was indeed the founder of the Peripatetic School or Peripatus, although with some modifications he may fairly be called the originator of Peripatetic philosophy.

The last will and testament of Aristotle,[22] his lost early works, his many letters and his later doctrinal treatises, provided the latter *in toto* are fully authentic, divulge that he was a deeply religious person[23] as well as a man possessed of a very attractive personality.[24] Moreover, assuming that the extant ancient *Vitae Aristotelis* in the main contain reliable information, Aristotle must have been a very active and a very successful statesman-diplomat, a dedicated benefactor of many people and many nations or states, a person deeply concerned with the general well-being of his fellow man, and a profoundly learned scholar.

Some of the extant *Vitae Aristotelis*, it has been shown, seem to indicate that after the year 348 B.C. Aristotle apparently spent much of his time and energies in diplomatic and statesman-like activities, working for the political aspirations of both King Philip and King Alexander (and Antipater).[25] Particularly during the years between 335–34 and 323 B.C., which are traditionally considered the period when he allegedly authored his most important philosophic treatises—when, in other words, he is said to have laid the foundations of what subsequently has been called his basic philosophy—Aristotle seems to have been heavily engaged in the promotion of the political aim of Macedonia to keep Athens and the whole of Greece in total submission. Presumably as kind of 'political agent' or 'observer' stationed in Athens, he probably did not have the necessary leisure or perhaps find the mental tranquillity and happy surroundings required by all major and sustained intellectual enterprises. This in turn might cast an ominous shadow on the authenticity of those philosophic writings which he allegedly wrote between 335–34 and 323 B.C., unless it is admitted that these writings were composed prior to the year 335–34 B.C. It might also defeat the widely held assumption that during these uneasy and trying years he founded his own school of philosophy in Athens and that he concentrated on teaching philosophy at the Lyceum. Under existing Athenian law, Aristotle, the Macedonian resident alien, was prevented from acquiring any real property or 'school buildings' (κῆπος) in Athens which he might have called his own, and in which he could gather his associates and students, do his teaching and keep a 'school library.'[26] The fact that Aristotle never owned a distinct school (or school building) in Athens is also clearly brought out by the following rather persuasive evidence: while in their respective testaments Theophrastus, Straton of Lampsacus and Lycon make rather detailed provisions as regards the school (Peripatus) and the school property, Aristotle's last will and testament does not contain any reference whatever to such a school or school property in Athens or elsewhere. Moreover, the term or designation 'Peripatus' came into general use only after the death of Aristotle, that is, during the scholarchate of Theophrastus. Concomitantly, many ancient reporters call Theophrastus rather than Aristotle the first scholarch of the Peripatus.

Discussions and analyses of Aristotle's many political or diplomatic activities in particular, no less than detailed presentations of certain decisive incidents in his life, in the past have been either neglected or simply ignored, and this apparently for a number of reasons: such discussions, it must be admitted, would not only disturb the traditionalist view we have entertained for a long time about Aristotle as an unworldly 'ivory tower philosopher' who spent his whole time in intellectual contemplation, teaching and in the production of learned works. They might, by implication, also cast an ominous shadow on the authenticity of some of the compositions traditionally credited to Aristotle. Perhaps the most intriguing aspect of a realistic investigation into the biographical treatment of Aristotle, both as a philosopher and as a historical man who lived in a historically crucial and even decisive period of antiquity, is the realization that he was one of the greatest intellectuals in Hellenic antiquity and, at the same time, frequently played an important role in the many and perhaps decisive political events which changed the whole of Greek history, as well as ushered in a novel and extremely fruitful epoch in Western history: the Hellenistic age. In a manner and on a scale Plato would never have imagined, this former member of the Platonic Academy did carry out and in part realized one of the basic aims as well as major tenets of Plato and the Academy: to re-shape and re-orientate the political, intellectual and cultural affairs of the whole of Western mankind.[27] In this particular sense, it might be contended, Aristotle apparently remained always an orthodox Platonist.

Notes

PREFACE

1 For essentially unfavorable discussions or reviews of Zürcher's work, see
A. Mansion, 'Travaux d'ensemble sur Aristote, son oeuvre et sa philosophie', *Revue Philosophique de Louvain*, vol. 57 (1959), pp. 67 ff.; A. Mansion,
in *Mededelingen van de Koninklijke Vlamse Academie voor Wetenschappen,
Letteren en Schone Kunsten van Belgie, Klasse der Letteren*, Jaargang XVI
(1954), no. 3, pp. 18 ff.; G. Reale, 'Josef Zürcher e un tentativo di rivoluz-
zione nel campo degli studi aristotelici,' *Aristotele nella Critica e negli Studi
Contemporanei, Scritti di Emanuele Severino . . . Giovanni Reale, etc.* (Milan,
1956), pp. 115 ff.; E. J. Schächer, *Ist das Corpus Aristotelicum Nach-
Aristotelisch?* (Munich, 1963), *passim*; E. Barbotin, in *Revue Thomiste*,
vol. 54 (1954), pp. 676 ff.; J. De Munter, in *Tijdschrift voor Filosofie en
Theologie*, vol. 15 (1953), pp. 156 ff.; K. Ennen, in *Scholastik*, vol. 28 (1953),
pp. 411 ff.; O. Gigon, in *Deutsche Literaturzeitung*, vol. 76 (1955), pp. 263 ff.;
S. Heller, in *Centaurus*, vol. 5, no. 4 (1955), pp. 34 ff.; J. E. Hofmann, in
Centaurus, vol. 3 (1954), pp. 247 ff.; G. B. Kerferd, in *Classical Review*,
vol. 29 (new series, vol. 5, no. 1, 1955), pp. 263 ff.; E. Lampe, in *Philo-
sophischer Literaturanzeiger*, vol. 9 (1955), p. 93; G. Rudberg, in *Lychnos*
(1953), pp. 356 ff.; A. S. Tarouca, in *Anzeiger für die Altertumswissenschaft*,
vol. 10 (1957), cols. 36 ff.; L. Torraca, in *Sophia*, vol. 26 (1958), pp. 35 ff.;
É. Weil, in *Revue de Métaphysique et de Morale*, vol. 57 (1952), pp. 446 ff.;
R. Weil, in *Revue des Études Grecques*, vol. 67 (1954), pp. 550 ff. For partly
unfavorable, partly favorable reviews, see R. Brumbaugh, in *Review of
Metaphysics*, vol. 7 (1953–4), pp. 609 ff.; P. Kucharski, in *Revue Philosophique de la France et de l'Étranger*, no. 143 (1953), pp. 466 ff.; E. Lahay, in
Nouvelle Revue Théologique, vol. 75 (1953), pp. 550 ff.; P. Louis, in *Revue
de Philologie, de Littérature et Histoire Ancienne*, vol. 28 (1954), pp. 279 ff.;
A. Naber, in *Gregorianum*, vol. 34 (1953), pp. 288 ff.; D. Saffrey, in *Revue
des Sciences Philosophiques et Théologiques*, vol. 37 (1953), pp. 333 ff.;
A. Smeets, in *Ephemerides Theologicae Lovanienses*, vol. 5, no. 29 (1953),
pp. 118 ff.; J. Rohner, in *Revue des Sciences Religieuses*, vol. 28 (1954),
pp. 177 ff. For favorable or generally favorable discussions or reviews, see
M. Adriani, in *Giornale di Metafisica*, vol. 8 (1953), pp. 610 ff.; I. Brady, in

New Scholasticism, vol. 27 (1955), pp. 305 ff.; R. B. Drudis, *Revista di Filosofia* (Madrid), vol. 14 (1955), pp. 420 ff.; E. Elorduy, in *Pensiamiento*, vol. 8 (1952), pp. 325 ff.; M. C. Hernandez, in *Annuario di Filosofia del Derecho*, vol. 1 (1953), pp. 397 ff.; C. Lacorte, in *Rassegna di Filosofia*, vol. 1 (1952), pp. 355 ff.; C. Lacorte, in *Giornale Critico della Filosofia Italiana*, vol. 31 (1952), pp. 422 ff.; J. M. Le Blond, in *Critique*, vol. 8 (1952), pp. 858 ff.; N. Picard, in *Teoresi: Rivista di Cultura Filosofica*, vol. 5, no. 8 (1953), pp. 166 ff.; N. Picard, in *Studi Francescani*, vol. 25 (1953), pp. 290 ff.; M. Gigante, in *Giornale Italiano di Filologia*, vol. 5, no. 6 (1953), pp. 267 ff.; E. Platzek, in *Antonianum*, vol. 27 (1952), pp. 595 ff.; I. Quiles, in *Cienca y Fee*, vol. 9, nos 35–6 (1953), pp. 73 ff.; A. B. Wolter, in *Modern Schoolman*, vol. 31 (1953–54), pp. 137 ff. E. J. Schächer, this note, himself a severe critic of Zürcher and his work, has discussed in detail some of these reviews or review articles, especially those which are critical of and unfavorable to Zürcher's main theses.

2 For detail, see A.-H. Chroust, 'The miraculous disappearance and recovery of the *Corpus Aristotelicum*,' *Classica et Mediaevalia*, vol. 23, vasc. 1–2 (1962), pp. 51–67.

3 Since the days of J. Bernay's, *Die Dialoge des Aristoteles* (Berlin, 1863), it has been held with varying success that the expression, λόγοι ἐξωτερικοί, refers to the dialogues which Aristotle wrote while he was still a member of the Platonic Academy. With a few exceptions, ancient authors and critics insist that the 'exoteric works' of Aristotle are less 'scientific' than his 'esoteric' or 'intra-mural' writings. Cicero (*De Finibus* V. 5. 12), Strabo (XIII. 1. 54), and Plutarch (*Adversus Coloten* 14), for instance, call the *exoterica* 'popular writings' composed for a general reading public, and Gellius (*Attic Nights* XX. 5), calls them compositions which discuss rhetoric, politics and 'topics.' For a different view, see W. Wieland, 'Aristoteles als Rhetoriker und die Exoterischen Schriften,' *Hermes*, vol. 86 (1958), pp. 323–46.

4 It is interesting to note that Epicurus and the Epicureans, the seemingly implacable opponents of Aristotle and his philosophic teachings, in their relentless attacks upon the latter apparently did not take issue with the 'Aristotelianism' manifest in the traditional *Corpus Aristotelicum*, but rather with what Aristotle had said in his early or lost works. This has been noticed and discussed, for instance, by E. Bignone, *L'Aristotele Perduto e la Formazione Filosofica di Epicuro*, 2 vols (Florence, 1936), *passim* (and his many learned articles dealing with the Epicurus' attitude towards the early lost works of Aristotle). Hence, it may be surmised that the 'doctrinal treatises' credited to Aristotle were not accessible to Epicurus and the Epicureans. Bignone has also pointed out that the Epicurean writings might contain valuable guides for the possible recovery and interpretation of the lost early works of the Stagirite.

5 The surviving ancient 'catalogues' of Aristotle's writings (see P. Moraux, *Les Listes Anciennes des Ouvrages d'Aristote*, Louvain, 1951) are of a relatively

late date and as such do not always contain reliable information. They were compiled after the 'recovery' of what was then considered the authentic *Corpus Aristotelicum*.

6 See H. D. P. Lee, 'Place-names and the date of Aristotle's biological works,' *Classical Quarterly*, vol. 42 (1948), pp. 61–7; P. Louis, 'Sur la chronologie des oeuvres d'Aristote,' *Bulletin de l'Association G. Budé*, n.s., no. 5 (1948), pp. 91–5; P. Louis, *Aristote: Les Parties des Animaux* (Paris, 1955), Introd., pp. xix–xxxi; P. Louis, *Aristote: Histoire des Animaux*, Books I–IV (Paris, 1964), Introd., pp. xiv–xviii; D. W. Thompson, *The Works of Aristotle*, vol. IV (Oxford, 1910), Introductory Note, p. vii; Fr Nuyens, *L'Évolution de la Psychologie d'Aristote* (Louvain, 1948), pp. 147–9; L. Torraca, *Ricerche sull' Aristotele Minore* (Padua, 1959), pp. 53–72. See also Pliny, *Hist. Nat.* VIII. 16. 44. These scholars have pointed out that a great many place-names as well as a large part of the examples or illustrations used in Aristotle's writings on animals (and plants) are to be found in northwestern Asia Minor or on the island of Lesbos. This being so, it has been surmised that these particular works were composed during Aristotle's sojourn in Assos (348–47 to 345–44 B.C.) or in Mytilene (345–44 to 343–42 B.C.). I have attempted to show (see Vol. I, Chapter XIII) that Aristotle's sojourn in Assos or Atarneus, and probably also his stay in Mytilene, had strong 'political' overtones and, hence, were replete with exciting as well as time-consuming incidents resulting from the particular nature and purpose of his mission to Atarneus. Accordingly, the 'Assian period' in the life of Aristotle probably was not conducive to extensive scientific research or perhaps to the production (or preparation) of involved scientific works. This, in turn, might suggest that the several works on animals or plants, traditionally credited to Aristotle, were in fact not authored by the latter (whose particular philosophic training in the Platonic Academy was not exactly the ideal preparation for this kind of scientific undertaking), but were possibly written by Theophrastus who, aside from his pronounced penchant for the natural sciences and for systematic investigations of natural phenomena, lived for many years in these parts of the Eastern Mediterranean.

7 Since the manuscript of this book was completed in 1972, I have published the following additional papers which are related to the topics discussed here: 'Philosophy Starts in Wonder (Aristotle, *Metaphysics* 982 b 12 ff.),' *Divus Thomas*, vol. 75 (1972), pp. 56–66; 'Speusippus Succeeds Plato in the Scholarchate of the Academy,' *Revue des Études Grecques*, vol. 84 (1971), pp. 338–41; 'Aristotle and the Foreign Policy of Macedonia,' *Review of Politics*, vol. 34 (1972), pp. 367–94; 'Aristotle's Sojourn in Assos,' *Historia: Zeitschrift für Alte Geschichte*, vol. 21 (1972), pp. 170–6; 'Comments on Aristotle's *On Prayer*,' *New Scholasticism*, vol. 46 (1972), pp. 308–30; 'A Comment on Aristotle's *On Noble Birth*,' *Wiener Studien*, vol. 6 (Neue Folge, 1972), pp. 19–32; 'Mystical Revelation and Rational Theology in Aristotle's *On Philosophy*,' *Tijdschrift voor Filosofie*, vol. 34 (1972), pp.

500–12; 'A Fragment of Aristotle's Lost *On Philosophy*?: Aristotle, *Metaphysics* 982 b 12–983 b 11,' *Rivista Critica di Storia della Filosofia*, vol. 27 (1972), pp. 287–92; 'Aristotle's Alleged "Revolt" against Plato,' *Journal of the History of Philosophy*, vol. 12 (1973), pp. 91–4.

INTRODUCTION

1 For some brief comments on the several *Vitae Aristotelis*, see Chapter I, notes 8–19. The following Neo-Platonic commentaries to the works of Aristotle contain brief but, on the whole, significant biographical references to the Stagirite: Olympiodorus, *Prolegomena et in Aristotelis Categorias Commentarium, Commentaria in Aristotelem Graeca (CIAG)*, vol. XII, part I (ed. A. Busse, Berlin, 1902), p. 13, lines 7 ff.; Elias (*olim* David), *Commentaria in Porphyrii Isagogen et in Aristotelis Categorias, CIAG*, vol. XVIII, part I (ed. A. Busse, Berlin, 1900), p. 107, lines 8 ff.; p. 112, lines 17 ff.; p. 113, lines 17 ff.; p. 114; lines 1 ff.; p. 15, lines 14 ff.; p. 116, lines 15 ff.; p. 117, lines 15 ff.; Philoponus (*olim* Ammonius), *In Aristotelis Categorias Commentarium, CIAG*, vol. XIII, part I (ed. A. Busse, Berlin, 1898), p. 7, lines 16 ff. General 'introductions' to Aristotle and Aristotle's philosophy can also be found in Ammonius, *Commentaria in Aristotelis Categorias, CIAG*, vol. IV, part 4 (ed. A. Busse, Berlin, 1895), pp. 1 ff.; Simplicius, *In Aristotelis Categorias Commentarius, CIAG*, vol. VIII (ed. C. Kalbfleisch, Berlin, 1907), pp. 10 ff.

2 See, for instance, Ammonius, *Commentaria in Aristotelis Categorias, CIAG*, vol. IV, part 4, p. 6, lines 25–7; Elias (*olim* David), *Commentaria in Porphyrii Isagogen et in Aristotelis Categorias, CIAG*, vol. XVIII, part I, 1900, p. 114, lines 15 ff.

3 See *Metaphysics* 1028 b 21; 1069 a 36; 1072 b 30; 1075 a 34; 1075 b 37; 1076 a 21; 1076 b 12; 1080 b 14; 1080 b 26; 1084 a 13; 1085 a 32; 1086 a 2; 1086 a 29; 1087 b 6; 1087 b 26; 1090 a 7; 1090 a 25; 1090 b 17; 1091 a 34; 1091 b 23; 1091 b 32; 1092 a 11–1092 b 7; *Nicomachean Ethics* 1096 b 7; 1104 b 24; 1153 b 4; 1172 a 28.

4 *Metaphysics* 1028 b 25; 1069 a 35; 1076 a 20; 1076 b 12; 1080 b 22; 1080 b 29; 1083 b 1; 1085 b 7; 1086 a 6; 1088 b 28; 1090 b 30; 1091 b 35.

5 See Chapter XVII.

6 See Aristotle, *Eudemus or On the Soul*, discussed in vol. II, Chapters V and VI.

7 In Aristotle, *Protrepticus*. See vol. II, Chapter IX.

8 In Aristotle, *On Kingship*. See vol. II, Chapter XVII. See also Aristotle, *Alexander or A Plea for Colonies* (or *Colonization*), discussed in vol. II, Chapter II; vol. I, Chapters VI and X.

9 In Aristotle, *On Philosophy*, and in Aristotle, *On Prayer*. See Chapter XVI, and vol. II, Chapters II and Chapters XIII–XVI.

10 In Aristotle, *On Noble Birth*. See vol. II, Chapter II.

11 In Aristotle, *On Education*. See vol. II, Chapter II.

12 In Aristotle, *On Pleasure*. See vol. II, Chapter II.

13 In Aristotle, *On Wealth*. See vol. II, Chapter II.

14 See, for instance, Cicero, *Ad Quintum Fratrem* III. 5. 1; Cicero, *Ad Atticum* XIII. 19. 4; Elias (*olim* David), *Comment. in Porphyrii Isagogen et in Aristotelis Categorias, CIAG*, vol. XVIII. part 1, 1900, p. 115, lines 3–5, and *ibid.*, p. 124, lines 3–6; Cicero, *De Oratore* III. 21. 80; Cicero, *Ad Familiares* I. 9. 23; Dio Chrysostom, *Oratio* LIII. 1; Plutarch, *De Virtute Morali* 7 (*Moralia* 447F ff.);Simplicius, *Comment. in Aristotelis De Caelo, CIAG*, vol. VII (ed. J. L. Heiberg, Berlin, 1894), p. 288, lines 31 ff.

15 See Chapter XV.

16 See W. Dittenberger, *Syll. Inscript. Graec.*[3] 275, and the literature thereto cited in I. Düring, *Aristotle in the Ancient Biographical Tradition*, Acta Universitatis Gothoburgensis, vol. 63, no. 2 (Göteborg, 1957), pp. 339–40.

17 See R. Heberdey, in *Festschrift für Theodor Gomperz* (Vienna, 1902), pp. 412–16.

18 See here also *II VA* 29–30; *IV VA* 13; *I VS* 10.

19 See Chapter XI.

20 In Olympiodorus, *In Platonis Gorgiam Comment.* (ed. W. Norvin), p. 197. See also *VM* 26; *VV* 11; *VL* 30; frag. 673, Rose.

21 DL V. 27 (no. 145).

22 DL V. 27 (no. 146).

23 DL V. 6; Himerius, *Oratio* VI. 6; Areius Didymus, *In Demosthenis Orationes Commenta* (ed. H. Diels and W. Schubart, Berlin, 1904), col. 6, 36 ff. See also frag. 674, Rose.

24 DL V. 7–8; Athenaeus, *Deipnosophistae* XV. 696A ff.; Areius Didymus (see note 23), col. 6, 18 ff.; Himerius, *Oratio* VI 6. See also frag. 675, Rose.

25 See DL V. 27 (no. 144); *VH* 10 (no. 137); *IV VA* (nos 93 and 96). According to Usaibia (*IV VA*), the edition of Aristotle's works by Andronicus of Rhodes contained a collection of twenty books of letters written by Aristotle (no. 96). Usaibia also mentions a collection of letters by Aristotle in eight books (no. 93). See also *VM* 5; 16; 27; 42; *VV* 16; 20; *VL* 5; 16; 44; frags 651–70, Rose; and the many ancient authors who refer to, or cite, letters written by Aristotle.

26 See also M. Plezia, *Aristotelis Epistolarum Fragmenta cum Testamento* (*Auctorum Graecorum et Latinorum Opuscula Selecta*, fasc. III, ed. C. Kumaniecki and V. Steffen, Warsaw, 1961), pp. 43–7.

27 DL V. 50.

28 See Eudemus, frag. 6, Wehrli.

29 It would certainly not be true to maintain that conservative scholars are unimaginative, but it might be nearer to the truth to say that unimaginative scholars are conservative.

CHAPTER I   A BRIEF ACCOUNT OF THE (LOST) *Vita Aristotelis* OF
HERMIPPUS AND OF THE (LOST) *Vita Aristotelis* OF PTOLEMY
(EL-GARIB)

* In a different and much less detailed form, and under a different title, this
  chapter was first published in *Revue des Études Grecques*, vol. 77, nos 364-5
  (1964), pp. 50-69.
1 W. Jaeger, *Studien zur Entwicklungsgeschichte der Metaphysik des Aristoteles*
  (Berlin, 1912). It should be noted, however, that T. Case, in his article
  'Aristotle,' *Encyclopaedia Britannica* (11th ed., 1910), vol. II, pp. 501-22,
  already anticipated some of Jaeger's evolutionary theses.
2 W. Jaeger, *Aristoteles: Grundlegung einer Geschichte seiner Entwicklung*
  (Berlin, 1923).
3 See, for instance, A.-H. Chroust, 'The first thirty years of modern
  Aristotelian scholarship (1912-42),' *Classica et Mediaevalia*, vol. 23, fasc. 1-2
  (1963), pp. 25-57. A German translation (and expansion) of this paper,
  under the title of 'Die ersten dreissig Jahre moderner Aristoteles-
  Forschung,' can be found in *Wege der Forschung*, vol. LXI: *Aristoteles in
  der Neueren Forschung*, ed. P. Moraux (Darmstadt, 1968), pp. 95-143.
4 See I. Düring, *Aristotle's Protrepticus: An Attempt at Reconstruction*, Studia
  Graeca et Latina Gothoburgensia, vol. XII (Göteborg, 1961); A.-H.
  Chroust, *Aristotle: Protrepticus—A Reconstruction* (Notre Dame, 1964);
  P. Moraux, *A la Recherche de l'Aristote Perdu: Le Dialogue 'Sur la Justice,'*
  Aristote, Traductions et Études, Collection Publiée par l'Institut Supérieur
  de Philosophie de l'Université de Louvain (Louvain, 1957); M. Unter-
  steiner, *Aristotele: Della Filosofia* (Rome, 1963); P.-M. Schuhl (ed.),
  *Aristote: Cinq Oeuvres Perdues: De la Richesse—De la Prière—De la
  Noblesse—Du Plaisir—De l'Éducation*, par J. Aubonnet, J. Bertier, J.
  Brunschwig, P. Hadot, J. Pépin, P. Thillet: Fragments et Témoignages
  (Publications de la Faculté des Letters et Sciences Humaines de Paris-
  Sorbonne, Séries 'Textes et Documents', vol. XVII, Paris, 1968). Several
  scholars at present are attempting to reconstruct some of the more
  important lost works of Aristotle: O. Gigon, *Aristoteles Dialog 'Eudemos':
  Ein Versuch der Wiederherstellung*; P. Wilpert, *Aristoteles Dialog 'Über die
  Philosophie': Ein Versuch der Wiederherstellung*; S. Mansion and É. de
  Strycker, *Aristote 'Du Bien': Éssai de Reconstruction*; and G. E. L. Owen,
  Aristotle's Essay 'On Ideas': An Attempt at Reconstruction. All these attempted
  reconstructions await publication in the near future. See also, in general,
  E. Berti, *La Filosofia del Primo Aristotele*, Università di Padova, Pub-
  blicazioni della Facoltà di Lettere e Filosofia (Padua, 1962). (After having
  completed his manuscript, the author received the sad news that Professor
  P. Wilpert had died early in 1967.)
5 See, in general, I. Düring, *Aristotle in the Ancient Biographical Tradition*,
  Acta Universitatis Gothoburgensis, vol. 63, no. 2 (Göteborg, 1957).
6 Except for the purpose of shedding some additional light on the several

Vitae Aristotelis, no attention will be paid here to occasional biographical references to Aristotle by a host of ancient authors, historians, grammarians, critics and commentators. For an exhaustive treatment of our subject, see also I. Düring (see note 5), *passim*; O. Gigon, 'Interpretationen zu den Antiken Aristotelesviten,' *Museum Helveticum,* vol. 15 (1958), pp. 147–93. Also, no mention is made here of the 'abridgment' or 'chronology' found in Dionysius of Halicarnassus, *I Epistola ad Ammaeum* 3–5. This epitome, it will be noted, is based on several *Vitae Aristotelis* that were in circulation during the latter part of the first century B.C. See A.-H. Chroust, 'The *Vita Aristotelis* of Dionysius of Halicarnassus (*I Epistola ad Ammaeum* 5),' *Acta Antiqua Academiae Scientiarum Hungaricae,* vol. 13 (1965), pp. 369–77, and Chapter II.

7 See O. Gigon (see note 6); I. Düring (see note 5), pp. 29–56; P. Moraux, 'La composition de la "Vie d'Aristote" chez Diogène Laërce,' *Revue des Études Grecques,* vol. 68 (1955), pp. 124–63; A.-H. Chroust, 'A Brief Analysis of the *Vita Aristotelis* of Diogenes Laertius (DL V. 1–16),' *Antiquité Classique,* vol. 34, fasc. 1 (1965), pp. 97–129, and Chapter III.

8 This *Vita,* which contains an important 'list of Aristotle's writings,' is also known as the *Vita Menagiana* or *Vita Menagii.* It is reprinted in V. Rose, *Aristotelis Qui Ferebantur Librorum Fragmenta* (Leipzig, 1886), pp. 9–18; I. Düring (see note 5), pp. 82–9.

9 This relatively unimportant *Vita* is a brief compilation from Diogenes Laertius and from the *Vita Hesychii.* See I Düring (see note 5), pp. 92–3.

10 This important *Vita* was first edited by L. Robbe, *Vita Aristotelis ex Codice Marciano Graece* (Leiden, 1861); V. Rose (see note 8), pp. 426–36. See also A. Busse, 'Neuplatonische Lebensbeschreibung des Aristoteles,' *Hermes,* vol. 28 (1893), pp. 252–73; I. Düring (see note 5), pp. 96–106; O. Gigon, *Vita Aristotelis Marciana: Kleine Texte für Vorlesungen und Übungen,* Heft no. 81 (Berlin, 1962). The *Vita Marciana,* in the main, is dependent on an abridgment of Ptolemy's lost *Vita Aristotelis.*

11 This *Vita,* which is also called *Vita Pseudo-Ammoniana* or *Pseudo-Elias,* is probably an abridgment of Ptolemy's *Vita Aristotelis* or is based on such an abridgment. It contains some additions which can also be found in an anonymous commentary to Porphyry's *Isagoge.* See A. Busse, *Die Neuplatonischen Ausleger der Isagoge des Porphyrios* (Berlin, 1892), *passim*; V. Rose (see note 8), pp. 437–41; I. Düring (see note 5), pp. 131–6.

12 This *Vita* is an unimportant abridgment of the *Vita Marciana.* See I. Düring (see note 5), pp. 140–1; A. Továr, 'Para la formación de la *Vita Marciana* de Aristoteles,' *Emerita,* vol. II (1943), pp. 180–200; V. Labate, 'Per la biografia di C. Lascaris,' *Archivo Storico Siciliano* (1901), pp. 222–40; L. Alfonsi, 'Su una Vita di Aristotele scritta da C. Lascaris,' *Giornale di Metafisica,* vol. 4 (1949), pp. 381 ff.

13 This *Vita,* which can be found in V. Rose (see note 8), pp. 442–50, is a rather 'liberal' thirteenth-century Latin translation of a Greek epitome of Ptolemy's *Vita* or of the *Vita Marciana* (which likewise is based on such an

epitome), with some minor additions from the *Vita Vulgata* (?). See I. Düring (see note 5), pp. 142–63.

14 This brief *Vita*, which might be called a Syriac version of the Greek *Vita Vulgata* (see note 11), ultimately goes back to Ptolemy's *Vita* (or to an abridgment of this *Vita*), which probably was brought to Nisibis when Emperor Zeno closed down the Neo-Platonic school in Edessa. It was edited and translated by A. Baumstark, *Syrisch-Arabische Biographien des Aristoteles* (Leipzig, 1900), appendix to p. 130, and *ibid.*, p. 38. See I. Düring (see note 5), pp. 185–6.

15 This very short and relatively unimportant *Vita*, which is likewise based on Ptolemy's *Vita*, was translated by A. Baumstark (see note 14), p. 116. See I. Düring (see note 5), pp. 187–8.

16 This *Vita*, which follows the *Vita* of Ptolemy, was translated by A. Baumstark (see note 14), pp. 39 ff. See I. Düring (see note 5), pp. 193–5.

17 This *Vita*, which shows the influence of Ptolemy's *Vita*, the *Vita Syriaca I* and *II*, and of the *Vita Arabica I*, was translated by A. Baumstark (see note 14), pp. 39–51 and 120–4; and by J. Lippert, *Studien auf dem Gebiete der Griechisch-Arabischen Übersetzungsliteratur* (Braunschweig, 1894), pp. 4–19. See I. Düring (see note 5), pp. 197–201.

18 This *Vita*, which is a sort of 'article' on Aristotle, to a large extent is based on the *Vita* of Ptolemy as excerpted by several Arabic authors. See J. Lippert, *Ibn al-Qifti's Tarih-al-Hukama* (Leipzig, 1903); M. Steinschneider, *Al-Farabi: Des Arabischen Philosophen Leben und Schriften* (St Petersburg, 1869), pp. 187–91; I. Düring (see note 5), pp. 211–12.

19 This *Vita*, which likewise follows Ptolemy's *Vita*, contains a 'catalogue' of Aristotle's writings which ultimately goes back to Ptolemy-el-Garib. See P. Moraux, *Les Listes Anciennes des Ouvrages d'Aristote* (Louvain, 1951), *passim*; I. Düring (see note 5), pp. 211–31. The important and influential Greek *Vita Aristotelis* of Ptolemy, which underlies the Syriac and Arabic *Vitae Aristotelis* (and the *Vita Marciana*, the *Vita Vulgata* and the *Vita Latina*), has come down to us only in the garbled, mutilated and abridged form of these *Vitae*. See below. A discussion of the *Vitae* mentioned in notes 9–19 can also be found in I. Düring (see note 5), *passim*; the *Vitae* mentioned in notes 14–19 are analysed in A.-H. Chroust, 'A brief summary of the Syriac and Arabic *Vitae Aristotelis*,' *Acta Orientalia*, vol. 29, nos 1–2 (1965), pp. 23–47, and Chapter IV.

20 These scholars were opposed by V. Rose, J. Bernays, H. Diels, A. Gercke and others, who insisted that the primary source of information used by Diogenes Laertius was Adronicus of Rhodes, the alleged 'restorer' of the *Corpus Aristotelicum* around the middle of the first century B.C. This thesis, which sees in Andronicus the original source of Diogenes Laertius, by now has been mostly abandoned.

21 See Demochares' *Oration Against the Philosophers* in support of Sophocles' motion to have all 'subversive' philosophers expelled from Athens (in 306 B.C.). DL V. 38; Athenaeus, *Deipnosophistae* XIII. 610EF, and XI. 509B;

Pseudo-Plutarch, *Vita Decem Oratorum* (*Moralia* 850B ff.); Eusebius, *Praeparatio Evangelica* XV. 2. 6; Pollux IX. 42. Demochares denounced Aristotle in particular (whom he charged with having committed many acts detrimental to Athenian political interests) as well as the philosophers in general.

22 Straton of Lampsacus probably went to Egypt because he was an 'undesirable alien' in Athens as well as a Peripatetic. Demetrius of Phaleron left because, aside from his association with the Peripatus, he was in political difficulties. See note 21.

23 DL V. 52. See also A.-H. Chroust, 'The miraculous disappearance and recovery of the *Corpus Aristotelicum*,' *Classica et Mediaevalia*, vol. 23, fasc. 1–2 (1962), pp. 50–67.

24 Athenaeus, *Deipnosophistae* I. 3AB. See also I. Düring, *Notes on the History of the Transmission of Aristotle's Writings* (Acta Universitatis Gothoburgensis, vol. 56, Göteborg, 1950), pp. 59–60.

25 I. Düring (see note 5), pp. 464–7. See also M. Plezia, 'De Hermippi Vita Aristotelis,' *Charisteria Th. Sinko Quinquaginta abhinc Annos Amplissimis in Philosoph. Honor. Ornato ab Amicis Collegis Discipulis Oblata* (Warsaw, 1951), pp. 271–67; P. Moraux (see note 19), pp. 243–5.

26 DL V. 2. See also Eusebius, *op. cit.*, XV. 2. 3; and XV. 2. 13. The story of Aristotle having 'ousted' or 'replaced' Plato in the Academy apparently was also accepted by Aelian, *Varia Historia* IV. 9; by Theodoretus, *Graecorum Affectionum Curatio* IV. 46; and by St Augustine, *De Civitate Dei* VIII. 12. When Speusippus died in 339–38 B.C., Aristotle, the 'most genuine disciple of Plato,' rather than Xenocrates, should have been made the new scholarch of the Academy. But at the time Aristotle was at the court of King Philip of Macedonia, presumably on a diplomatic mission on behalf of Athens. When Aristotle returned to Athens in 335–34 B.C., he finally managed to establish his own independent school which came to be a competitor of the Platonic Academy. Together with the account of Aristotle's early secession from the Academy (and his philosophic disagreements or confrontations with Plato) while Plato was still alive, these two stories are, in brief, probably Hermippus' main contributions to the biographical tradition concerning Aristotle. See also DL V. 2–3; P. Moraux (see note 19), *passim*. It is highly doubtful, however, whether after 335–34 B.C. Aristotle in fact founded and owned an organized and independent school of his own comparable to the Platonic Academy. See below.

27 See also Aelius Aristides, *Oratio* XLVI. 249. 10.

28 I. Düring (see note 5), pp. 465–7.

29 See also *VM* 1–2; *VV* 1–2; *VL* 1–2; *VH* 1–2; *VS* 1–3; *I VA* 1–3; *II VS* 1; *I VA* 2–3; 16; *II VA* 1–2; *III VA*; *IV VA* 1–2.

30 See note 29.

31 *VH* 1; *VM* 5–7; *VV* 4–5; 12; *VL* 5–7; *I VS* 4–5; *II VS* 2; *I VA* 3; *II VA* 9–13; *III VA*; *IV VA* 3; 28–9. *VM* 4, *VV* 3 and *VL* 4 also mention that

Aristotle received a 'good liberal education' while he was still 'very young.'

32 See note 31. See also Dionysius of Halicarnassus, *I Epistola ad Ammaeum* 1.

33 See also *VH* 1; *II VA* 38; *IV VA* 36; Aelian, *Varia Historia* III. 19; Plutarch, *De Adulatore et Amico* 9 (*Moralia* 53C); Plutarch, *De Audiendis Poetis* 8 (*Moralia* 26B).

34 See also *VM* 9; 25–9; *VV* 6–11; *VL* 9; 25–9; Aelian, *op. cit.*, IV. 9; Helladius, in Photius, *Bibliotheca* (p. 533 b 13, ed. I. Bekker). See note 26.

35 See also Aelian (see note 34); Helladius (see note 34); Aelius Aristides, *Oratio* XLVI. 249. 10.

36 See also *VM* 9–12; *VV* 6–7; *VL* 9–12; Aelian (see note 34); Eusebius, *op. cit.*, XV. 2. 13 (Aristoxenus, Aristocles); Aelius Aristides (see note 35); Origen, *Contra Celsum* II. 397.

37 See also *VM* 13–15; *VV* 13–15; 21; *VL* 13–15; *I VS* 4; *II VA* 24; 27; *IV VA* 6; Philodemus, *Academicorum Philosophorum Index Herculanensis*, col. 6, 28 (p. 37, ed. S. Mekler, 1902).

38 See also Cicero, *De Oratore* III. 35. 141; Cicero, *Tusculanae Disputationes* I. 4. 7; Quintilian, *Institutio Oratoria* III. 1. 14; Gellius, *Attic Nights* XX. 5; Syrianus, *Scholia in Hermogenem* IV. 297 (ed. G. Walz). See also A.-H. Chroust, 'Aristotle's Earliest Course of Lectures on Rhetoric,' *Antiquité Classique*, vol. 33, fasc. 1 (1964), pp. 58–71, and Chapter VIII.

39 See also *VH* 2; 4; *II VA* 17; *IV VA* 5; *II VS* 3; Areius Didymus, *In Demosthenis Orationes Commenta* (Berliner Klassikertexte, vol. I, Berlin, 1904, ed. H. Diels and W. Schubart) col. 5, 21 ff.; col. 5, 51 ff.; Philodemus (see note 37), p. 22, col. 6; Eusebius *op. cit.*, XV. 2. 13–15.

40 See also *VH* 2; 4; *VM* 2; *VL* 2; Athenaeus, *Deipnosophistae* XIII. 589C; Eusebius (see note 39).

41 See also Areius Didymus (see note 39), col. 5, 64 ff.; vol. I, col. 6, 50 ff.

42 Areius Didymus (see note 39), col. 6, 18.

43 See also Areius Didymus (see note 39), col. 6, 36.

44 See also *VM* 14; *VV* 14; *VL* 14; *II VA* 18; 31; *IV VA* 6.

45 See *VM* 17–18; *VV* 17; *VL* 17; 19–20; *I VS* 7; *I VA* 13; *II VA* 27; 29–30; *IV VA* 13–14; Diodorus Siculus XVI. 52. 9; Valerius Maximus V. 6. 5; Pliny, *Hist. Nat.* VII, 109; Plutarch, *Alexander* 7; Dio Chrysostom, *Oratio* II 79, and *Oratio* XLVII. 8 (frag. 657, Rose); Aelian, *Varia Historia* XII. 54; III. 17; Plutarch, *Adversus Coloten* 33 (*Moralia* 1126F).

46 See also *VM* 17; *I VS* 7; *II VA* 27; *IV VA* 14; Plutarch, *Adversus Coloten* 32 (*Moralia* 1126C).

47 See also *VM* 17–18; 20; *VV* 17; 19–20; *I VS* 10; *II VA* 29–30; *IV VA* 13; 30–1.

48 This might contain Hermippus' (a Peripatetic) slap at the Academy: Aristotle, the 'most genuine' disciple of Plato as well as the great benefactor of Athens and of the Academy who, by his intercessions with King Philip and Alexander, had rendered the Athenians and the Academy many valuable services, is repaid with ingratitude. It might also imply

that by making Xenocrates rather than Aristotle the new scholarch of the Academy, the Platonists displayed their utter lack of good sense.

49 See here also DL V. 10; Plutarch, *Alexander* 53 ff.; 55; Arrian, *Anabasis* IV. 9. 10; Valerius Maximus VII. 2. 11; Themistius, *Oratio* X 130 A (p. 155, 6, Dindorf); *Oratio* VII 94 A (p. 122, 12); Suda, article 'Callisthenes'.

50 *VM* 24; *VV* 18; *VL* 24; *II VS* 5; Gellius, *Attic Nights* XX. 5. See also *I VA* 11; *II VA* 14; 25; *IV VA* 4; 6; 23.

51 See also DL V. 10; *VH* 5; *VM* 23; *VV* 18; *VL* 23–4; *II VS* 4–5; *I VA* 10–11; *II VA* 14–16; 24–6; 31; *IV VA* 4; 6; 22–4; 33.

52 See also *VH* 6; *VM* 41; *VV* 19; *VL* 43; *I VS* 8; *II VS* 7; *II VA* 21–2; *IV VA* 8.

53 See *VM* 41–2; *VV* 19–20; *VL* 43–4; *II VA* 21; *IV VA* 7–8; Philochorus, in: *VM* 9–12 (Jacoby, *Frag. Hist. Graec.* 328, F. 233); Aelian, *op. cit.*, III. 36; Origen, *Contra Celsum* I. 380 (Migne II, p. 781B); Elias (*olim* David), *Commentaria in Porphyrii Isagogen et in Aristotelis Categorias, CIAG*, vol. XVIII, part 1, p. 123, lines 15 ff.; Eustathius, *In Odyss. H* 120–1; Seneca, *Dialogus* VIII. 8. 1. See also A.-H. Chroust, 'Aristotle's Flight from Athens in the Year 323 B.C.,' *Historia*, vol. 15, no. 2 (1966), pp. 185–92, and Chapter XII.

54 *VH* 6–7; *VM* 43; *VV* 19–20; *VL* 45–6; *I VS* 8; *II VS* 7–8; *I VA* 15; *II VA* 20–3; *IV VA* 7–11. See also Strabo X. 1. 10; Aelian, *op. cit.* IX. 23; Gellius, *Attic Nights* XVII. 21. 25; XVII. 21. 34; XIII. 5; Justin Martyr, *Cohortatio ad Graecos* 34B; Gregory of Nazianzus, *Oratio* IV. 72; Procopius VIII. 6. 20; Censorinus, *De Die Natali* XIV. 16; Suda, 'article' Aristotle. According to one tradition (Eumelus), which might have been cited by Hermippus, Aristotle died by committing suicide; according to others, he died while watching the flow of the Euripus or, probably, of a stomach ailment. See A.-H. Chroust, 'The Myth of Aristotle's Suicide,' *Modern Schoolman*, vol. 44, no. 2 (1967), pp. 177–8, and Chapter XIV.

55 See *VH* 6–7; *VM* 9–12; 43; *VV* 30; *VL* 45–6; *I VS* 8; *II VS* 7–8; 23; *I VA* 15; *II VA* 20–3; *IV VA* 7–11. See also Philochorus, in *VM* 9–12 and *VL* 9–12, and some of the references cited in note 54.

56 See Gellius, *Attic Nights* XIII. 5. Gellius probably derived this story from Favorinus, who in turn probably found it in Hermippus. Since Aristotle was never the scholarch or owner of a distinct 'school,' this story is apocryphal. But in a garbled form it may convey the story that on the eve of his flight from Athens in 323 B.C., Aristotle might have donated (or sold) his private library to Theophrastus. The sale of scholarly libraries is mentioned in Athenaeus, *Deipnosophistae* I. 3A; DL IV. 5; Gellius, *op. cit.*, III. 17; Strabo XIII. 1. 54.

57 See also Areius Didymus (see note 39), col. 6, 43 ff.; E. Diehl, *Anthologia Lyrica Graeca*, vol. I (2nd ed.), p. 127 (Theocritus of Chios); Plutarch, *De Exilio* 10 (*Moralia* 603C); Eusebius, *op. cit.*, XV. 2. 12.

58 See also Athenaeus, *op. cit.*, XIII. 589C. The Arabic *Vitae Aristotelis* contain a version of Aristotle's will which differs somewhat from that cited in

DL V. 11-16. See A.-H. Chroust, 'Aristotle's Last Will and Testament,' *Wiener Studien*, vol. 80 (1967), pp. 90-114, and Chapter XV.

59 See also Eusebius, *op. cit.*, XV. 2, 8-9; Pliny, *Hist. Nat.* XXXV. 162; Theodoretus, *Graecorum Affectionum Curatio* VIII. 34; XII. 50-1.

60 See also *VH* 8; 10; *VM* 45-50; *VL* 48; 50-2; *II VS* 6; *I VA* 16; *II VA* 31-6. The catalogue of Aristotle's writings in the *Vita Hesychii* 10, at least titles 1-139, in the main coincides with that found in Diogenes Laertius V. 22-7. Hence, it is assumed that the catalogue contained in the *Vita Hesychii* is based on Hermippus, at least in part. The catalogue found in the Arabic *Vitae*, which goes back to Ptolemy (-el-Garib) and ultimately to Andronicus of Rhodes, on the other hand, is very incomplete and differs considerably from that of Diogenes Laertius.

61 See I. Düring (see note 5), p. 466. The remainder of Diogenes Laertius' *Vita Aristotelis*, that is, V. 28-35, which contains a brief and rather superficial account of Aristotle's philosophy, in all likelihood is not based on Hermippus. O. Gigon (see note 6) has subjected the *Vita Aristotelis* of Diogenes Laertius and its reliance on Hermippus to a searching and most learned analysis. See also A.-H. Chroust, 'A Brief Analysis of the *Vita Aristotelis* of Diogenes Laertius (DL 1-16),' *Antiquité Classique*, vol. 34, fasc. 1 (1965), pp. 97-129, and Chapter III. O. Gigon, it will be noted, occasionally disagrees with some of the findings of I. Düring and, in all probability, will also disagree with some of the statements made by the present author. See also P. Moraux (see note 7).

62 See note 61.

63 See below.

64 See also note 46.

65 See note 103.

66 P. Moraux (see note 19), pp. 243-7 *et passim*. See also the criticism of Moraux's theses by G. Verbeke, 'Les listes anciennes des ouvrages d'Aristote,' *Revue Philosophique de Louvain*, vol. 50 (1952), pp. 90-112. For a summary (and criticism) of Moraux's views, see also I. Düring, 'Ariston or Hermippus?,' *Classica et Mediaevalia*, vol. 17 (1956), pp. 11-21.

67 DL V. 64.

68 P. Moraux (see note 19), p. 244.

69 We possess five minor fragments of Ariston's biography discussing his predecessors in the scholarchate of the Peripatus. See F. Wehrli, *Die Schule des Aristoteles: Text und Kommentar*, Heft VI: *Lykon und Ariston von Keos* (Basle, 1952), frags 28-32.

70 See DL V. 11-16; V. 51-7; V. 61-4; V. 69-74; V. 64. Diogenes Laertius actually speaks of a *Collection* (συνήγαγε) made by Ariston of Ceos. The reason why the testaments of the Peripatetic scholarchs were so carefully preserved is the following: Under the existing Athenian law, the legal title to the whole 'school property,' including the buildings, the grounds, the library, the inventory, etc., was vested in the scholarch. Hence, at the time of his death, he had to pass on this property, or the title to this property, to whomever he wished to succeed him in the scholarchate.

Conversely, on the strength of this testament the successor or heir could legally claim not only the whole of the school property, but also his right to, and legitimacy of, his succession. Since Aristotle's last will and testament (DL V. 11–16) does not contain any provisions regarding either the library or the school property, some scholars have denied that this document is actually a testament (see Chapter XV), claiming that it is concerned only with the appointment of a guardian (Nicanor) and of some trustees for the children of Aristotle. This argument overlooks the facts (i) that Aristotle never had or owned an 'organized school' in Athens similar to the Academy; (ii) that as a foreigner or *metic* he could not own any real property in Athens; (iii) that Aristotle, therefore, was not the scholarch of a school in the legal sense of the term and, hence, had no 'school property' to pass on to a successor; and (iv) that Nicomachus, Aristotle's son by Herpyllis, was his real heir. See the provision in the Arabic version of Aristotle's will (not to be found in the version preserved by Diogenes Laertius): 'As to my estate and my son [Nicomachus], there is no need for me to be concerned about any testamentary provisions.'

71 See also K. Praechter, *Die Philosophie der Griechen*, in Ueberweg-Heinze, *Grundriss der Geschichte der Philosophie*, vol. I (12th ed., Berlin, 1926), p. 485.

72 Ariston of Ceos is also credited with having composed a general history of the several philosophical schools in antiquity.

73 I. Düring (see note 66).

74 See, for instance, Athenaeus, *op. cit.*, XIII. 589C; XV. 696F; DL V. 1.

75 See here H. Usener, *Analecta Theophrastea*, in *Kleine Schriften*, vol. I. (Leipzig, 1910), pp. 50 ff. That Hermippus was interested in compiling lists of the works of famous authors, in the opinion of I. Düring (see note 66), p. 18, is confirmed by DL VIII. 85; 88.

76 See H. Usener (see note 75), vol. I, p. 69. See also Plutarch, *Sulla* 26.

77 See, for instance, DL V. 27 (Aristotle); V. 50 (Theophrastus). See also *ibid.*, IV. 5 (Speusippus); IV. 14 (Xenocrates).

78 P. Moraux (see note 19), pp. 242–3, insisted, however, that the 'stichometric method' antedates the Alexandrian library. I. Düring (see note 66), p. 19 with equal determination maintained that this method was first used in the Alexandrian library and, perhaps, even invented there.

79 I. Düring (see note 66), pp. 19 ff.

80 See here also I. Düring (see note 5), pp. 464 ff.

81 Düring doubted, however, whether Ariston's biographies included detailed catalogues. These catalogues, Düring surmised, probably were compiled by Hermippus. See I. Düring, 'Ariston or Hermippus?,' *Classica et Mediaevalia*, vol. 17 (1956), p. 20.

82 *Ibid.*, p. 20.

83 See note 8.

84 *VH* 1, for instance, sounds very much like DL V. 1. Diogenes' biography of Aristotle, as has been shown, to a large extent relies on Hermippus.

85 Or, perhaps, on some of the sources used by Ptolemy.

86 *VH* 2 and DL 3 indicate that both make use of a source unfavorable to Aristotle. This particular source might have been Theocritus of Chios or, perhaps, Demetrius of Magnesia. See DL V. 3.

87 Compare *VH* 4 and DL V. 1, where Timaeus is cited. See also Eusebius, *op. cit.*, XV. 2. 3; Suda, 'article' Aristotle; Athenaeus, *op. cit.*, VIII. 342C; Polybius XII. 8. Timaeus, the historian, who lived a generation after Aristotle, was a staunch 'conservative,' a sort of 'anti-intellectual,' a violent anti-Macedonian and a follower of the school of Isocrates (which was hostile to Aristotle because the latter had attacked Isocrates). He loathed Carthage (see Diodorus Siculus XIII. 43. 5; XIII. 59. 6; XIII. 90. 2; XIII. 111. 5; XIV. 46. 3; XIV, 52. 2; XIV. 59. 1) and, hence, resented the fact that Aristotle in a way had praised the constitution of Carthage. See Aristotle, *Politics* 1272 b 24 ff. See, in general, R. Laqueur, article 'Timaeus,' in Pauly-Wissowa, *Realencyclopädie der classischen Altertumswissenschaft* (second series, R–Z, 11th half-volume, Stuttgart, 1936), pp. 1075–1203, especially, pp. 1194–6.

88 Compare *VH* 6 and DL V. 6, where Eumelus is cited.

89 P. Moraux (see note 19), pp. 195–288, especially, pp. 195–209.

90 Since the days of W. Christ (see Christ-Schmid, *Geschichte der Griechischen Literatur*, vol. I, 6th ed., 1912, p. 723, note 4), this Ptolemy has been identified with Ptolemy Chennos, who lived and wrote during the latter part of the first and early part of the second century A.D. The surname 'Chennos,' it was surmised by some scholars, probably came to be identified with the Greek word *xenos* (ξένος)—'the Stranger.' Hence the Arabic word 'el-Garib,' which signifies 'the Stranger.' See A. Chatzis, 'Der Philosoph und Grammatiker Ptolemaios Chennos,' part I, *Studien zur Geschichte und Kultur des Altertums*, vol. VII, Heft 2 (1914), pp. IX ff.; E. Zeller, *Die Philosophie der Griechen*, vol. II, part 2 (3rd ed., Leipzig, 1879), p. 54, note 2. For additional literature, see P. Moraux (see note 19), pp. 292–3, notes 15–22; for additional information about Ptolemy Chennos, see Suda, 'article' *Ptolemy*, and 'article' *Epaphroditus*. According to some scholars, our Ptolemy was born in Alexandria after 160 A.D., where he also received his education. He spent some time in Rome and authored a mystery play entitled *The Sphinx*, an *Epope* consisting of twenty-four rhapsodies, an *Anti-Homer*, a *History of Unusual Events* and a *Strange* (καινή) *History*, which was much used by Eustathius and Tzetzes. Other scholars (see below), again, hold that our Ptolemy was an Alexandrian Neo-Platonist who probably was a member of, or influenced by, the Neo-Platonic school of Iamblichus (fourth century A.D.). In any event, since the name of Ptolemy was rather common, the exact identification of the author of the *Vita Aristotelis* is almost impossible, although the view which identifies him with a member of the Neo-Platonic school of Iamblichus is most likely the correct one.

91 See K. Praechter (see note 71), p. 561.

92 P. Moraux (see note 19), pp. 292–4.

93 I. Düring (see note 5), pp. 210; 469 ff.; 475.

94 V. Rose, *De Aristotelis Librorum Ordine et Auctoritate Commentatio* (Berlin, 1854), p. 45, already had identified our Ptolemy with a Neo-Platonist of the same name mentioned by Iamblichus, Proclus and Priscinus.

95 See also I. Düring (see note 5), p. 475; M. Plezia, *De Andronici Rhodii Studiis Aristotelis* (Polske Akademia Umiejetnosci, Archivum Filologiczne, no. 20, Cracow, 1946), pp. 18–35; M. Plezia, 'Supplementary remarks on Aristotle in the ancient biographical tradition,' *Eos*, vol. 51, pp. 247 ff. The surname 'el-Garib,' according to I. Düring, was given to our Ptolemy in order to distinguish him from Ptolemy, the author of the *Almagest*. *Ibid.*, pp. 208 ff., and p. 475. See also note 90.

96 P. Moraux (see note 19), pp. 289 ff.

97 I. Düring (see note 5), pp. 469 ff.

98 See notes 10, 11 and 13 and the corresponding texts.

99 See notes 14 and 15 and the corresponding texts.

100 See notes 16, 17, 18 and 19 and the corresponding texts.

101 This Arabic translation, which dates back to the ninth or early tenth century A.D., was probably the work of Ishaq Ibn Hunayn (died in 910 or 911). See Chapter IV, notes 1–6, and the corresponding texts.

102 Ptolemy probably relied on, or made use of, the 'Collection of Letters (of Aristotle),' by Artemon (?) as well as on a later 'Collection' by Andronicus of Rhodes. Only after about the middle of the first century B.C. were the so-called letters of Aristotle used by his biographers to a larger extent.

103 From Hermippus, for instance, Ptolemy might have derived the story that, because Aristotle was on a 'diplomatic mission' to (or for) King Philip of Macedonia (or for Athens) and, hence, absent from Athens, he was not elected scholarch of the Academy after the death of Speusippus in 339–38 B.C. See DL V. 2; *VM* 20; *VL* 20; Philodemus, *Academicorum Philosophorum Index Herculanensis*, col. 6, 28 (p. 37, ed. S. Mekler). *IV VA* 17–21, which relates the many public services Aristotle had rendered the city of Athens, might reflect Hermippus' story that because of his absence on account of a diplomatic mission on behalf of Athens, Aristotle failed to be elected scholarch of the Academy in 339–38 B.C. See also note 140, and notes 37 and 48; Chapter III, notes 49–52. M. Plezia (see note 95), pp. 246 ff., maintains that Andronicus of Rhodes wrote a *Vita Aristotelis* which subsequently was much used by Ptolemy. See also M. Plezia, *De Andronici Rhodii Studiis Aristotelicis* (Polska Academia Umiejętnosci, Archivum Filologiczne, no. 20, Cracow, 1946), pp. 18–35.

104 I. Düring (see note 5), pp. 472–4.

105 According to Elias, Ptolemy wrote about Aristotle's 'list of writings, about his life and about his last will and testament.' Elias (*olim* David), *Commentaria in Porphyrii Isagogen et in Aristotelis Categorias*, *CIAG*, vol. XVIII, part 1, p. 107, line 11. See also *I VA* 19: 'Ptolemy-el-Garib . . . is the author of a book "On the Life of Aristotle, His Death and the Classification of His Writings."' Similarly *III VA*, and *IV VA*. Combining all

available information, we might conjecture that the original title of Ptolemy's works was something like 'On the Life of Aristotle, His Last Will and Testament and a List of His Writings.'

106 The etymology of Aristotle's name (*I VA* 1; *II VA* 1; *III VA*) and the epigram on his descent (*VM* 1; *VV* 1; *VL* 1) cannot be found in Diogenes Laertius and, hence, in all probability were not part of Hermippus' *Vita Aristotelis*. When *I VA* 1 and *II VA* 1 state that Aristotle's name signifies 'the distinguished one,' 'the perfect one' or 'the excellent one,' they merely indicate that they, or their immediate source, did not know Greek; and that they probably found this bit of information in a Syriac source. This 'explanation' or 'translation' of Aristotle's name most certainly could not have been contained in Ptolemy's *Vita*, although the latter might have written something like, 'Aristotle, this most excellent man.' When *I VA* 1 adds that the name Aristotle means 'lover of wisdom,' we may surmise that Ptolemy wrote something like, 'Aristotle, the philosopher . . . this most excellent man. . . .' See Chapter IV, note 8, and the corresponding text.

107 *I VS* 3 calls her Parysatis, an obvious error most likely not to be found in Ptolemy, and *I VA* 3 refers to her as Phaestias, probably a misspelling of Phaestis. *VH* 2, *VM* 2, *VV* 2 and *VL* 2, but not the Syriac and Arabic biographers, also mention Aristotle's sister (Arimneste) and his brother (Arimnestus). Hence, it may be presumed that Ptolemy did record them. *I VA* 16 states that Theophrastus was the son of Aristotle's sister. This might have been recorded in Ptolemy's *Vita*, although it is by no means certain that Theophrastus was a son of Aristotle's sister or that he was related to Aristotle. See Chapter XV, notes 85-95.

108 Judging from *VM* 1, *VV* 1, *VL* 1, *I VS* 3, *I VA* 2-3, *II VA* 2 and *IV VA* 2, Ptolemy must have maintained that both Nicomachus and Phaestis ultimately descended from Asclepius. This would be in keeping with the encomiastic tendency of Ptolemy's account. See note 29.

109 With some minor exceptions all the *Vitae* based on Ptolemy agree on this, although not all of them seem to be certain exactly where the city of Stagira was located.

110 *I VA* 3; *II VA* 2; *IV VA* 2. *I VS* 1 and *II VS* 1 simply record that Nicomachus was a physician. Obviously, Ptolemy would not have failed to point out that Aristotle and his family had close contacts with, and were intimately befriended by, one of the great dynasties of his time. See also notes 29-30.

111 *VM* 4; *VV* 3; *VL* 4. *II VA* 3-4 contains an elaborate but probably badly garbled account of Aristotle's early education: 'When he [*scil.*, Aristotle] was eight years old, he was sent or brought by his father to the country of Athens . . . and there the boy stayed at the Lyceum. His father handed him over to a school of poets, orators and school-masters, where he stayed for nine years. This branch of learning, namely, the knowledge of language, was called the "all-embracing [education]" by the Greeks. . . .' This

elaboration on Aristotle's earliest education in all likelihood goes back to Ptolemy and his somewhat exaggerated efforts to counteract certain stories, unfavorable to Aristotle, which contended that before he met up with Plato he was a boorish and uneducated barbarian. See, for instance, Eusebius (see note 21), XV. 2. 1; Epicurus, frag. 171, Usener. The remark found in *VM* 2, namely, that 'from his father [who was a descendant of Asclepius], and in keeping with family tradition, he [*scil.*, Aristotle] inherited an inclination towards the natural sciences and towards medicine,' might imply that, in keeping with old family tradition (and family worship—Aristotle's mother is said likewise to have been a descendant of Asclepius), the young Aristotle was initiated into the science of medicine. E. Barker, *The Politics of Aristotle* (Oxford, 1946), p. xi, for instance, suggests that the young Aristotle studied anatomy; and J. Aubonnet, *Introduction à Aristote*, vol. I (Paris, 1960), p. ix, believes that in his early youth Aristotle studied the works of Hippocrates. See also H. D. Hantz, *The Biological Motivation in Aristotle* (New York, 1939), *passim*; see note 31.

112 *VM* 5, *VV* 4 and *VL* 5 maintain that Aristotle stayed with Socrates (Isocrates?) three years. For a more detailed discussion of this puzzling problem, see A.-H. Chroust, 'Aristotle Enters the Academy,' *Classical Folia*, vol. 19, no. 1 (1965), pp. 21–9, especially, pp. 25–9, and see Chapter VII. *II VA* 3 relates that Aristotle first entered 'a school . . . of orators' in the Lyceum before joining Plato in the Academy. This 'school of orators' in the Lyceum might well be the school of Isocrates who taught in or near the Lyceum.

113 *VM* 3; *VV* 2; *VL* 3; *IV VA* 3. Usaibia (*IV VA* 3) reports that 'some [authors] maintain that he [*scil.*, Aristotle] was entrusted to Plato [by Proxenus] . . . because Proxenus and Plato were personal friends.' This explanation might possibly go back to Ptolemy who could use the friendship of Proxenus of Atarneus and Plato to justify Aristotle's subsequent sojourn with Hermias of Atarneus—an episode in his life which became the source of many slanderous attacks upon him.

114 *VM* 5; *VV* 4; *VL* 5; *I VS* 4; *I VA* 4; *IV AV* 3. *II VA* 3 states that Aristotle was brought to Athens by his father at the age of eight. See notes 111 and 113. *I VA* 4 expressly mentions that Ptolemy says that Aristotle was handed over to Plato on the advice of the Delphic oracle. Such a story may well have been invented by a Neo-Platonist. *II VA* 9 emphasizes that Aristotle joined Plato only at the age of eighteen, and that he was brought to Athens by Proxenus.

115 *VM* 5; *VV* 4; *VL* 5; *II VS* 2; *II VA* 9 (at the age of eighteen). The statement in *VM* 11 that Aristotle was approaching forty when he entered the Academy is probably based on a scribal error. Diogenes Laertius (V. 6), who attributes this story to Eumelus (a detractor of Aristotle), reports that at the time he entered the Academy, Aristotle was thirty years old. *VL* 11, which completely garbles its source or sources, states that Aristotle

stayed with Plato forty years. *I VS* 6 points out that 'it is not true what has been said about [Aristotle], namely, that he did not turn to philosophy until he was thirty years old, and after having practiced medicine.' See also *I VA* 6: 'He [*scil.*, Aristotle] began the study of philosophy at the age of forty.' *IV VA* 12: 'Those who maintain that he [*scil.*, Aristotle] did not devote himself to the study of philosophy until he had reached the age of thirty, and that up to that time he had tried his hand at governing cities, are wrong.' These stories, which are unfavorable to Aristotle, probably had already been refuted by Ptolemy, as might be gathered from *VM* 9–12 and *VL* 8; 9–12.

116 *VM* 11 (ἐπὶ Εὐδόξου); *VL* 11 (*tempore Eudoxi*). This bit of information, not to be found in the other *Vitae*, might go back to Philochorus from whom Ptolemy could have taken it. Plato was in Syracuse from 367 to 365–64 B.C. This might also explain why DL VIII. 90 (on the authority of Apollonius) relates that Eudoxus flourished between 368 and 364. Some people have interpreted this ἐπὶ Εὐδόξου (*VM* 11) to mean that Aristotle entered the Academy during the 'archonship of Eudoxus.' There was no archon called Eudoxus during this period.

117 *VM* 11; *I VS* 6; *I VA* 12. *I VS* 6 mentions that Aristotle practiced medicine, *IV VA* 12, that he practiced politics until he was thirty (forty) years old. Perhaps in the course of time ἰατρική and πολιτική came to be confused by some biographer; perhaps both versions, though with different connotations, were contained in Ptolemy's *Vita*. See also note 115.

118 *VM* 4; *VV* 3; *VL* 4; *II VA* 3; *IV VA* 28.

119 Found in all *Vitae*, except *VL* 11 which relates that he stayed in the Academy for forty years. See note 115. Al-Mubashir's (*II VA* 9–10) phrasing seems to lend support to the statement that Aristotle studied first rhetoric with Isocrates, but at some later date transferred to the Academy. It also conveys the message that Aristotle's earliest intellectual concern was with rhetoric. Undoubtedly, Al-Mubashir's account is both confused and confusing, but he may ultimately have derived his information, through several confused intermediaries, from Ptolemy who probably was himself not clear on this issue. See note 112.

120 *I VA* 9; *II VA* 28.

121 *VM* 6–7; *VV* 5; *VL* 7; *I VS* 5; *II VA* 11–12; *III VA*; *IV VA* 29. These sources also relate that Aristotle was 'a great worker' (and a busy author?). In *II VA* 38 we are told that Aristotle 'was a persistent reader of books.' See also *IV VA* 36. Some of the stories which make Aristotle's attitude towards Plato appear in an unfavorable light are expressly (or by implication) refuted by the encomiastic Ptolemy. See, for instance, *VM* 25; *VV* 6; *VL* 25; *I VA* 5; *II VA* 10; 13; *IV VA* 4. See also *II VS* 2. Some doctrinal disagreements between Plato and Aristotle are likewise explained in a manner essentially favorable to Aristotle, See *VM* 28–30; *VV* 7–10; *VL* 26–9; *II VA* 37. Here we may discern the hand of Ptolemy, the

syncretist Neo-Platonist, who would play down doctrinal differences between Plato and Aristotle. For additional unfavorable stories, see, among others, Aelian, *Varia Historia* III. 19; IV. 9; Eusebius, *op. cit.*, XV. 2, *passim*; as well as the many derogatory reports which go back to Theopompus, Theocritus, Alexinus, Lycon Pythagoraeus, Epicurus (and the Epicureans), Timaeus, Demochares, Cephisodorus (and the disciples of Isocrates in general), Eubulides, Aristides, Eumelus and many others.

122 *I VA* 4; *II VA* 10. *II VS* 2 relates that Aristotle studied under Plato's (personal?) guidance. See also notes 30–2.

123 *I VA* 5; *II VA* 13; *IV VA* 4. *II VS* 5 seems to have garbled this story. It will be noted that *II VA* 13 and *IV VA* 4 (or Ptolemy) apparently confuse the second (367–365/64) and third (360–61) Sicilian journey of Plato. While on his second journey, Plato appointed Eudoxus of Cnidus acting scholarch (see note 115), and while on his third (the second during Aristotle's stay at the Academy) journey, he made Heracleides of Pontus acting scholarch. See Heracleides (Suda), frag. 2, Wehrli.

124 *II VA* 5–8; *IV VA* 7. Ptolemy might possibly allude here to Aristotle's controversy with Isocrates as it becomes manifest, for instance, in Aristotle's *Gryllus* and *Protrepticus*, and in Isocrates' *Antidosis* or in the *Ad Demonicum*. See note 38. He might also allude to Cephisodorus' *Against Aristotle*. See Eusebius, *op. cit.*, XIV. 6. 9; XV. 2. 7; Athenaeus, *Deipnosophistae* II. 60DE; VIII. 354B ff.; Dionysius of Halicarnassus, *I Epistola ad Ammaeum* 1; Dionysius of Halicarnassus, *Isocrates* 18; Themistius, *Oratio* XXIII. 285A.

125 *II VA* 37. See also Plutarch, *Alexander* 7. Gellius, *Attic Nights* XX. 5, mentions that Plato reproached Aristotle for publishing too much, and that Aristotle countered with the remark that his works were understandable only to the 'initiated.' This story might go back to Ptolemy.

126 *I VA* 7; *II VA* 38; 25–6; *III VA*; *IV VA* 36; 16; 24; 26.

127 *II VA* 38; *III VA*; *IV VA* 36. See also note 33.

128 *II VA* 38; *IV VA* 36.

129 *II VA* 38; *IV VA* 36. See also *VM* 31; *VV* 24, *VL* 33.

130 *II VA* 38; *IV VA* 36.

131 *I VA* 7. See also *IV VA* 15, where we are told that Aristotle 'had great influence among his contemporaries.'

132 *II VA* 25–6; *III VA*; *IV VA* 15–16; 24; 26. See also *VM* 16–17; *VV* 16–17; *VL* 16–17.

133 *IV VA* 26; 16.

134 *VM* 31; *VV* 24; *VL* 33; *II VA* 38; *III VA*.

135 *II VA* 38; *III VA*; *IV VA* 36. Al-Mubashir (*II VA* 38) claims that Aristotle had a thick beard, Usaibia (*IV VA* 36) that he had a sparse beard. *VM* 31 and *VV* 24 relate that Aristotle had a 'well-proportioned figure.'

136 *I VS* 11; *II VA* 33; *IV VA* 35. See also *VM* 44; *VL* 47. The children are also mentioned in Aristotle's last will.

137 *VM* 25; *VL* 25. The ultimate sources of these unfavorable stories are probably Aristoxenus, Lycon, Aristides, Theocritus, Eumelus, Timaeus, Alexinus and others. See notes 26, 34–36, and 121.

138 *VM* 26; *VV* 11; *VL* 30. See here also Olympiodorus, *Scholia in Platonis Gorgiam* (ed. W. Norvin, 1913), pp. 192–7, especially, p. 197. Olympiodorus reproduces here Aristotle's 'Elegy on Plato' (some scholars maintain that it was dedicated to the memory of Eudemus of Cyprus), which contains the famous line calling Plato the man 'who alone or first among mortal men revealed it clearly for everyone to see that man becomes happy because he is good.' An echo of this Elegy can still be detected in *VM* 26, *VL* 30 and perhaps in *VL* 11. Hence, it is likely that Ptolemy quoted this Elegy, although *VM*, *VL* and *VV* probably garbled it.

139 *VM* 27. See also M. Plezia, *Aristotelis Epistolarum Fragmenta* (Warsaw, 1961), pp. 100 ff.

140 *VM* 13–14; *VV* 13–14; *VL* 13–14. This statement, which is an exact replica of DL V. 2, might indicate that Ptolemy made use of Hermippus. See note 103. *II VS* 4 reports that 'when Plato died, Speusippus, since he was his nephew, became scholarch. He [Speusippus] sent a message [to Aristotle] requesting him to return and take charge of Plato's school.' See also notes 37 and 48.

141 *II VS* 4. See note 140.

142 *II VA* 17; *IV VA* 5. See also *II VS* 3, which might refer to Aristotle's stay with Hermias. These statements might indicate that Ptolemy mentions (briefly?) Aristotle's sojourn with Hermias. Although the Hermias episode, on the whole, casts an unfavorable light on Aristotle, and despite his studied efforts to turn his *Vita Aristotelis* into an encomium of Aristotle, Ptolemy could not suppress entirely this whole incident. The Hermias episode cannot be found in *VM*, *VV* or *VL*, an indication that Ptolemy dealt with it briefly. See, however, *VH* 2; 4; DL V. 3–4. Thanks to the biased efforts of Theopompus and Theocritus of Chios, Hermias has been much maligned, as have been some of his friends and associates, such as Aristotle. The unfavorable and even slanderous stories about Hermias (and Aristotle), which are largely untrue, were widely circulated. They seem to have haunted Aristotle all his life. Subsequently they came to be part of the anti-Aristotelian (and anti-Peripatetic) literature, and they were incorporated into the later biographies of Aristotle.

143 This statement is incorrect. Hermias was captured and executed in 341–40 B.C.; Aristotle went to Macedonia in 343–42. See also notes 41–2.

144 *VM* 14; *VV* 14; *VL* 14; *II VA* 18; *III VA*; *IV VA* 6. See also *II VS* 6, and note 44.

145 *VM* 15; *VL* 15. See also *VV* 15; *I VA* 8; *II VA* 28; *IV VA* 15.

146 *II VA* 24–5; *IV VA* 22–3. See also *VM* 23; *VV* 23; *VL* 23.

147 *I VA* 10; *II VA* 19; 24; *IV VA* 6; 22–3. *I VA* 10 indirectly refers to Ptolemy as its source. See also note 146.

148 *II VA* 19; *IV VA* 6. This bit of information might go back to Hermippus.

See DL V. 4. We know that Callisthenes, the nephew of Aristotle, accompanied Alexander on his Persian expedition. He was unjustly accused of having been involved in a conspiracy against Alexander and was cruelly put to death in 327 B.C. See note 49.

149 *VM* 23; *VV* 23; *VL* 23. The abridgment used by these *Vitae* might have confused Aristotle and Callisthenes. This bit of information might not have been contained in Ptolemy's *Vita*.

150 *VM* 23. This story might have been an invention of Ptolemy, who as a Neo-Platonist probably had a predilection for the 'supernatural.'

151 *VM* 23; *VV* 23; *VL* 23. This statement is based on a misunderstanding: Aristotle returned to Athens after Alexander had retaken the city in 335 B.C.

152 *VM* 23; *VL* 23. This information is based on a misunderstanding: Philip died in 336 B.C., Alexander in 323 B.C. and Aristotle in 322 B.C. Perhaps the abridgment used by these *Vitae* confuses the death of Alexander with that of Philip.

153 *VM* 24; *VV* 18; *VL* 24. These sources relate that on his return to Athens, Aristotle, along with Xenocrates, jointly succeeded Speusippus in the scholarchate of the Academy and the Lyceum. As it stands, this story implies that at one time the Academy and the Lyceum were joined under one scholarch (Speusippus) and that, after the death of Speusippus, they became separated into two distinct schools, Xenocrates taking over the Academy and Aristotle the Lyceum. It is difficult to make much sense out of this account. See here also Philochorus, frag. 224, F. Jacoby, *Frag. Graec. Histor.*, part III, vol. 2 (1954), p. 484.

154 *II VS* 5; *I VA* 11; *II VA* 14; 25; 31; *IV VA* 4, 6; 23; 33. The same sources contain an explanation of the origin of the term 'Peripatetics.' See also Clement of Alexandria, *Stromateis* I. 14; DL V. 2 (Hermippus?). Originally, it seems, Aristotle was referred to only as 'the founder of the Peripatetic school.' Only after the death of Theophrastus were the members of this school called 'Peripatetics.' It is not impossible that the story of Aristotle's founding of the Lyceum ultimately goes back to Hermippus. It would be fully in accord with Hermippus' encomiastic effort to maintain that Aristotle, who in the opinion of Hermippus was an absolutely original genius who owed nothing to Plato, seceded from the Academy while Plato was still alive; that he established his own independent school at the Lyceum already during the lifetime of Plato; and that this new school was on an equal footing with, if not superior to, the Platonic Academy. See note 50.

155 See preceding note. See also notes 50–2.

156 *II VS* 6; *II VA* 31; *IV VA* 33. See also *VM* 44; *VL* 47.

157 *II VA* 31; *IV VA* 33. See also *VM* 44; 46; *VL* 49. Eusebius, *Praeparatio Evangelica* XV. 2. 11 (Aristocles), refers to Aristotle's 'friendship with kings.'

158 *II VA* 35. See also *VM* 45; *VL* 48.

159 *II VA* 25; *IV VA* 17–18. See also *I VA* 11.

160 *I VA* 12; *II VA* 25–6; *III VA*; *IV VA* 16; 24.

161 *I VA* 9; *II VA* 36; *IV VA* 16; 25. See also *VM* 16; 27; *VV* 16; *VL* 16.

162 *I VA* 7–8; *II VA* 28; *IV VA* 15. See also *VM* 15; 23; 46; *VV* 21; *VL* 15; 23; 49; Eusebius (see note 157), XV. 2. 11.

163 *VM* 16; *VL* 16; *II VA* 25. See also *VV* 15; *VL* 15 ('he did much work for the King').

164 *IV VA* 17–18. See also *VM* 20; *VL* 20.

165 *VM* 17; 18; *VV* 17; *VL* 17; 18; *I VA* 13; *II VA* 27; *IV VA* 25.

166 *I VS* 7; *IV VA* 14. See also *II VA* 26–7.

167 *VM* 17–18; *VL* 19; *I VS* 10; *II VA* 29; *IV VA* 13; 30.

168 *VM* 18; *VV* 17; *VL* 19; *I VS* 10; *II VA* 29–30; *III VA*; *IV VA* 13; 30–1. Al-Mubashir (*II VA* 30), who is also quoted by Usaibia (*IV VA* 31), relates: 'They [the citizens of Stagira] sought comfort at the place of his tomb, and peace and tranquillity where his bones rested. When something in the domain of philosophy or learning seemed to them too difficult, they went to that place and sat down to deliberate. They talked there with one another about the matter, until that which previously had been obscure became clear, and until they were certain about that which had been the object of dispute. For they believed that their coming to the place where Aristotle's remains were buried would purify their minds, improve their judgment, and increase their understanding of things. They went there, too, in order to pay their respect to him after his death, to show their mourning for his departure, and to manifest their grief over the misfortune they had sustained by the loss of the source of wisdom that he had been to them.' These stories indicate not only that Aristotle's last resting place became a *bouleuterion* or council house (named *Aristoteleion*), but also that a visit to his burial place, aside from being an act of homage to the memory of Stagira's benefactor and greatest son, gave wisdom to the visitor as well as purified the mind—definitely a Neo-Platonic twist. Hence, we may safely assign this story to Ptolemy who in his encomiastic tendency turns Aristotle's tomb into a sacred shrine as well as a council house. See also *II VA* 32, and note 200.

169 *IV VA* 17–21. Subsequently, the Athenians are said to have set up a new *stele* to atone (?) for the removal of the first inscription. This story, which cannot be verified, might have been told by Ptolemy. See also *VM* 20; *VL* 20, and Chapter XI.

170 *II VA* 20–1; *IV VA* 7–10. See also note 52.

171 *Ibid.*

172 *II VA* 21; *IV VA* 6.

173 *IV VA* 9.

174 *VV* 19; *II VS* 3; *II VA* 21; *IV VA* 8.

175 *VM* 41; *VV* 19; *VL* 43; *II VA* 21; *IV VA* 8.

176 *VM* 42. See also *VM* 41; *VV* 18–20; *VL* 44; *IV VA* 8.

177 *VM* 41–2; *VV* 19–20; *VL* 43–4.

178 *IV VA* 9.

179 *IV VA* 10. Athenaeus, *Deipnosophistae* XV. 697AB, refers to this 'Defense,' but adds the remark, 'provided this "Defense" is not a forgery.' *VH* 10 (catalogue, no. 189), cites an *Apology against the Charge of Impiety Addressed to Eurymedon* among the spurious works of Aristotle.

180 *VM* 41; *VV* 19; *VL* 43; *I VS* 8; *II VS* 7; *II VA* 21–2; *IV VA* 8. See also *VH* 6. Al-Mubashir (*II VA* 21–2) and Usaibia (*IV VA* 8) apparently confused Chalcis with Chalcidice. See also note 54.

181 *IV VA* 11.

182 *II VS* 7; *II VA* 22–3; *IV VA* 11. See also *VH* 6.

183 *II VA* 22. This might be a reference to the (spurious?) Περὶ τῆς Ἀίδου (DL V. 26, no. 125; *VH* 10, no. 117), or to the (spurious?) Περὶ τῆς τοῦ Νίλου ἀναβάσεως (*VH* 10, no. 159; Ptolemy, no. 25).

184 *VM* 43; *VL* 46; 19; *I VS* 8; *II VA* 22–3; *IV VA* 11.

185 For some unknown reason (scribal error?), *I VS* 8 makes Aristotle 67 years at the time of his death; *II VS* 7, 68 years; *I VA* 15, 66 years; and *II VA* 23, *III VA* and *IV VA* 11, 68 years. *II VS* 7 and *II VA* 22–3 state that he died 'watching the ebb and flow of the Euripus.' See also note 55.

186 *I VS* 9.

187 See Porphyry, *De Antro Nympharum* 19. Since Ptolemy, like Porphyry, was a Neo-Platonist, it is probable that he mentioned this in his *Vita*.

188 *VM* 43; *VL* 46; *I VA* 17; *II VA* 33–4; *III VA*; *IV VA* 34. *VM* 43 and *VL* 46 indicate that Aristotle's last will and testament was recorded by Andronicus of Rhodes as well as by Ptolemy. See also DL V. 11–16; A.-H. Chroust, 'Aristotle's Last Will and Testament,' *Wiener Studien*, vol. 80 (vol. I, new series, 1967), pp. 90–114, and Chapter XV.

189 *VM* 44; *VL* 47; *I VS* 11; *II VA* 33; *IV VA* 36.

190 *VM* 44; *VL* 47; *I VS* 11–12; *II VA* 33–4; *IV VA* 35–6. This also follows from Aristotle's testament.

191 *I VA* 16; *II VA* 32; *IV VA* 34. See also note 56. It might be more correct to call Theophrastus rather than Aristotle the founder and first scholarch of the Peripatus. See note 154.

192 This is stipulated in Aristotle's testament. See note 188.

193 *VM* 44; *VL* 47; *II VS* 6; *II VA* 31; *III VA*; *IV VA* 33. It is quite possible that Ptolemy listed some additional disciples of Aristotle.

194 *VM* 15–16; 46; *VV* 15–16; *VL* 15–16; *I VA* 12; *II VA* 26: '[Aristotle began to devote himself] to supporting the feeble; to getting maidens married; to protecting orphans; to assisting those who were anxious to learn and acquire an education, whoever they might be and whatever schooling they might desire, and to obtaining "scholarships" for that purpose; to collecting alms for the poor....' *IV VA* 24 repeats *II VA* 26 almost *verbatim*. See *III VA*.

195 At Aristotle's request, King Philip (or Alexander) rebuilt Stagira. *VM* 17; *VV* 17; *VL* 17; *I VA* 13; *II VA* 27; *IV VA* 25. Aristotle devised a code of laws for Stagira. *I VS* 7; *II VA* 27; *IV VA* 14. Because of Aristotle's

intercession, Philip spared Eressus (or Eresus). *VM* 19; *VV* 17; *VL* 18. Some of these stories can also be found in DL V. 4, and, hence, might go back to Hermippus. Plutarch, *Adversus Coloten* 33 (*Moralia* 1126F), and Plutarch, *Ne Suaviter Quidem Vivi Posse Secundum Epicurum* 15 (*Moralia* 1097B) claims, however, that Eresus was 'saved' (actually rescued from tyranny) thanks to the intercession of Theophrastus and Phaenias (or Phanias) rather than on account of Aristotle's efforts.

196 *VM* 20; *VL* 20; *IV VA* 17; 18. Usaibia (*IV VA* 18) mentions that Aristotle 'had intervened [on behalf of the Athenians] with King Philip, and had succeeded in persuading the King that they should be treated generously. . . .' This passage might be a summary (and Usaibia's version) of the content of an inscription honoring Aristotle. See *IV VA* 17–18. It might also refer to the possibility that Aristotle interceded with Alexander on behalf of the Athenians after the abortive revolt of 335 B.C. This might explain also why in 335 B.C. Athens was treated generously by Alexander, while Thebes was razed. See also note 164 and Chapter XI.

197 *VM* 21 (see also 22); *VV* 22; *VL* 21; *I VA* 12; *II VA* 25–6; *IV VA* 16; 24. *VM* 21 and *VL* 22 specifically cite Aristotle's *On Kingship* as one of the significant contributions to the welfare of mankind. *VV* 22 merely mentions this work. Throughout these sources, the impression is created that Aristotle's writings were deathless gifts to mankind. Al-Mubashir (*II VA* 25) relates that Aristotle 'devoted himself to working for the commonweal.' Similarly *VM* 15. Usaibia (*IV VA* 16) maintains that 'he strove to serve well his fellow men,' and that 'by [diplomatic?] negotiations he promoted their affairs and proved to be of great service to them.'

198 *VM* 15; 46; *VV* 15; *VL* 15; 49. *VM* 15 and *VL* 15 also contain the information that King Philip erected a statue in honor of Aristotle. A statue erected in honor of Aristotle by Philip (or Alexander?) in Stagira is mentioned by Pausanias VI. 4. 8.

199 *VM* 23; 49; *VV* 21; *VL* 49; *I VA* 8; *II VA* 28; *IV VA* 15.

200 *VM* 17–18; 20; *VV* 17; *VL* 17; 19–20; *I VS* 10; *II VA* 29–30; *III VA*; *IV VA* 13; 17–18; 21; 30–1. For his meritorious deeds the people of Stagira celebrated an annual festival in his honor, called *Aristoteleia*, and they named a month of the year *Stageirites*. *VM* 17; *VV* 17; *VL* 17. They also erected an altar and a monument in his honor (*VL* 19), and named a place (council house) *Aristoteleion* in his honored memory. *IV VA* 13. See also note 168. The story that the Athenians erected (or attempted to erect) a *stele* with a laudatory inscription in Aristotle's honor(*IV VA* 17–18), is discussed in Chapter XI. (The Athenians also erected a *stele* in honor of King Philip and later voted a decree of *proxenia* honoring Alexander and Antipater.) There also exists an inscription dedicated to Aristotle and expressing the gratitude of the Amphyctionic League at Delphi for his meritorious services to the League (for compiling the 'List of Pythian Victors'). See W. Dittenberger, *Syll. Inscript. Graec.*[3], no. 275; D. M. Lewis, 'An Aristotle Publication Date,' *Classical Review*, vol. 72 (1958), p. 108.

201 *VV* 25; *VL* 41; *I VA* 6. An-Nadim (*I VA* 7) states: 'He [*scil.*, Aristotle] was the most eloquent among the Greeks as well as their most eminent author of learned books, the most distinguished of the philosophers, after Plato, and the one person who attained the highest reaches of philosophy.' See also *III VA*; Plutarch, *Alexander* 9: 'He sent after Aristotle, the most learned and most celebrated philosopher of his time.'

202 *VM* 45; *VL* 48; *II VA* 35; and the *Index Librorum* in *I VA* 18, *II VA* 35, *III VA* and *IV VA*. *II VA* 36 mentions the 'public' and 'private' letters of Aristotle. See also *VH* 10, and the 'catalogue' in Diogenes Laertius. For additional detail, see P. Moraux (see note 19), *passim*, and note 60.

203 *VM* 29-40; 47-9; *VV* 24-9; *VL* 35-42; *II VA* 6-9; 37; *III VA*; *IV VA* 27.

204 See note 103 and the corresponding text.

CHAPTER II THE *Vita Aristotelis* OF DIONYSIUS OF HALICAR-
NASSUS

* In a somewhat different and abridged form, this chapter was first published in *Acta Antiqua Academiae Scientiarum Hungaricae*, vol. 13 (1965), pp. 369-77.

1 Dionysius of Halicarnassus, *I Epistola ad Ammaeum* 5. See also F. Jacoby, *Frag. Hist. Graec.* 244, F. 38.

2 Dionysius of Halicarnassus, *op. cit.*, 1.

3 *Ibid.*

4 *Ibid.*, 2.

5 *Ibid.*, 3. For a list of Demosthenes' early orations, see *ibid.*, 4.

6 See F. Olivier, *De Critolao Peripatetico* (Doctoral thesis, Berlin, 1895), pp. 33 ff. See also Philodemus, *De Rhetorica: Volumina Rhetorica* (ed. S. Sudhaus, Leipzig, 1896), vol. II, p. 102, and *Supplementum*, pp. XXXVII ff., which appears to be a direct citation from Critolaus. Critolaus, it will be noted, was in Rome in 156-55 B.C., when he was already a very old man. For a Peripatetic such as Critolaus it would not be unusual to claim, in an encomiastic effort, that Aristotle was the teacher of Demosthenes, the most renowned Greek orator.

7 The passages from the Aristotelian *Rhetoric*, cited by Dionysius in his *Epistle* in support of his argument that Demosthenes was wholly independent of Aristotle's theory of rhetoric, can be found in Book II, chapters 23-4, and Book III of the Aristotelian *Rhetoric*. It has been held, however, that Book I and Book II (with the exception of chaps. 23-4) of Aristotle's *Rhetoric* are part of the so-called '*Urrhetorik*' (Jaeger), or are based on this '*Urrhetorik*,' which is believed to have been written before 354 B.C. Book II, chapters 23-4, and Book III, on the other hand, are said to be of a fairly late date.

8 In his argument, Dionysius seems to overlook a few relevant facts. Undoubtedly, the first orations of Demosthenes antedate Book II, chapters 23-4, and Book III of the extant Aristotelian *Rhetoric*, although it is by no means certain that they antedate the so-called '*Urrhetorik*.' It is fairly certain that Aristotle taught a course of lectures on rhetoric in the Academy

as early as 355 B.C., and perhaps earlier. See A.-H. Chroust, 'Aristotle's earliest course of lectures on rhetoric,' *Antiquité Classique*, vol. 33, fasc. 1 (1964), pp. 58–72, and Chapter VIII. It is also fairly safe to assume that Aristotle wrote the Τεχνῶν Συναγωγὴ (DL V. 24, no. 77; *VH* 10, no. 71; Ptolemy-el-Garib, no. 24) and, perhaps, the Τεχνῆς τῆς Θεοδέκτου Συναγωγῆς (DL V. 24, no. 82; *VH* 10, no. 74), and that he wrote these two works before 354 B.C. It is not impossible that Demosthenes attended the lectures offered by Aristotle in the Academy, and that he became acquainted with the above-mentioned writings of Aristotle, including the 'Urrhetorik.' Dionysius of Halicarnassus, *I Epistola ad Ammaeum* 4, maintains that Demosthenes was born in the 'year preceding the 100th Olympiad' (381–80 B.C.), but from Demosthenes, *Oratio XXX.* 15, we may infer that he was born during the archonship of Diotrephes (384–83 B.C.). Accordingly, he was of about the same age as Aristotle. Tradition also has it that he was a disciple of Plato. It is not clear whether this account refers to the 'school of Plato' where he might have come in contact with Aristotle. See Plutarch, *Demosthenes* 5; DL III. 47; Plutarch, *Vita Decem Oratorum (Moralia* 844D); Anonymous, *Scholia in Platonem* 318; Suda, 'article' Demosthenes.

9 Dionysius of Halicarnassus, *op. cit.*, ch. 3.

10 *Ibid.*

11 *Ibid.*, ch. 6.

12 DL V. 9–10.

13 A study of DL V. 9–10, which contains Apollodorus' 'chronology' of Aristotle's life, seems to suggest this. Diogenes' text, however, is slightly confused: he carelessly recites Aristotle's sojourn in Mytilene before mentioning the death of Plato; and again, due to carelessness, he dates the flight of Aristotle from Athens in the third year of the 114th Olympiad (322–21 B.C.). See note 16.

14 *VM* 9–12 (and *VL* 9–10), which has been identified as a fragment of Philochorus' *Atthis*. See F. Jacoby, *Frag. Histor. Graec.* 328, F. 223. See also I. Düring, *Aristotle in the Ancient Biographical Tradition* (Göteborg, 1957), pp. 249–50; O. Gigon, *Vita Aristotelis Marciana* (Kleine Texte für Vorlesungen und Übungen, Berlin, 1962), pp. 46–51.

15 Dionysius, *op. cit.*, chap. 6.

16 DL V. 9–10; F. Jacoby, *Frag. Histor. Graec.* 244, F. 38. The reference to the third year of the 114th Olympiad (322–321 B.C.) indicates the year of Aristotle's death, not the year of his flight from Athens (in 323 B.C.). Dionysius, *op. cit.*, on the other hand, makes it appear that Aristotle died during the archonship of Cephisodorus (323–22 B.C.), that is, during the second year of the 114th Olympiad. Aristotle left Athens during the archonship of Cephisodorus (323–22 B.C.), that is, in the second year of the 114th Olympiad. He died in Chalcis during the archonship of Philocles (322–21 B.C.), that is, in the third year of the 114th Olympiad (between July and early October of 322 B.C.). See note 20 and the corresponding text.

17 *VM* 10 (*VL* 10), which is based on Philochorus. See F. Jacoby, *Frag. Hist. Graec.* 328, F. 223. Most scholars now accept the dating proposed by Philochorus.

18 Alexander was born in the summer of 356 B.C. If the information is correct that Alexander was in his fifteenth year at the time of Aristotle's return to Macedonia, then the latter must have arrived in Pella (or Mieza) during the latter half of the year 342 B.C. But Diogenes Laertius is again a bit careless: in 343 B.C., Alexander was only thirteen years old, that is, in his fourteenth year.

19 See A.-H. Chroust, 'Was Aristotle Actually the Preceptor of Alexander the Great?,' *Classical Folia*, vol. 18, no. 1 (1964), pp. 26–33, and Chapter X.

20 During the early part of Cephisodorus' archonship, that is, in the second year of the 114th Olympiad, presumably in the late summer or, more likely, in the early fall of 323 B.C. See note 16.

21 Philochorus (*VM* 10; *VL* 10; F. Jacoby, *Frag. Hist. Graec.* 328, F. 223) also maintains that Aristotle died during the archonship of Philocles (322–21 B.C.).

22 *VM* 1–2; *VV* 1–2; *VL* 1; *VH* 1; DL V. 1; *I VS* 1; 3; *II VS* 1; *I VA* 2; 3; *II VA* 1; 2; *III VA*; *IV VA* 1; 2. See also A.-H. Chroust, 'A Brief Analysis of the *Vita Aristotelis* of Diogenes Laertius (DL V. 1–16),' *Antiquité Classique*, vol. 34, fasc. 1 (1965), pp. 97–129, and Chapter III; A.-H. Chroust, 'A brief survey of the Syriac and Arabic *Vitae Aristotelis*,' *Acta Orientalia*, vol. 29, fasc. 1–2 (1965), pp. 23–47, and Chapter IV.

23 Parysatis, it will be remembered, was the wife of King Darius II of Persia, and the mother of Cyrus the Younger. The third (or fourth) wife of Alexander likewise was called Parysatis.

24 *VM* 1; *VV* 1; *VH* 1; *VL* 1; DL V. 1; *I VS* 2; *II VS* 1; *I VA* 3; *II VA* 2; *III VA*; *IV VA* 1. Some of the Syriac and Arabic biographers do not seem to know exactly where Stagira was located.

25 DL V. 1; *VH* 1; *VM* 1; *VV* 1; *VL* 1; *I VS* 3; *I VA* 2; *II VA* 2; *IV VA* 2. For the many and involved problems connected with Aristotle's alleged descent from Asclepius and Machaon, see A.-H. Chroust, 'The genealogy of Aristotle,' *Classical Folia*, vol. 19, no. 1 (1965), p. 141, note 7, and Chapter V.

26 This would explain why in 323 B.C. Aristotle retired to Chalcis: He did so because his mother or his mother's ancestors had a house there which he probably inherited. See DL V. 14.

27 *VM* 1; *VV* 1; *VL* 1; *I VS* 3; *II VA* 3; *IV VA* 2.

28 *VM* 2; *VV* 1; *VL* 2; DL V. 1; *II VA* 2; *IV VA* 2.

29 *VM* 5; *VV* 4; *VL* 5; DL V. 9; *II VS* 2; *II VA* 9; *IV VA* 28. See also note 17 and the corresponding text.

30 *VM* 5; *VV* 4; *VL* 5; *I VS* 4; *I VA* 4; *IV VA* 3. See, however, *IV VA* 9–10.

31 *II VA* 3. *VM* 4, *VL* 5 and, in an abridged form, *VV* 3, contain the information that while still a very young man, that is, before he joined Plato and the Platonic Academy in 367 B.C., Aristotle received a broad 'liberal

education.' We are not told, however, in what particular 'school' he received this 'liberal education.' *VM* 5, *VV* 4 and *VL* 5 also maintain that Aristotle stayed for a while with Socrates (Isocrates?) before joining Plato. *VV* 4 and *VL* 5 claim that he stayed three years with Socrates. For an interpretation of this unusual story, see A.-H. Chroust, 'Aristotle Enters the Academy,' *Classical Folia*, vol. 19, no. 1 (1965), pp. 21-9, and Chapter VII; O. Gigon (see note 14), p. 42.

32 That is, from 367 to 348-47 B.C.

33 The Hermias episode, which has been exploited for the purpose of maligning and discrediting Aristotle, is mentioned (and expanded) by a number of ancient authors and biographers. See A.-H. Chroust, 'Aristotle leaves the Academy,' *Greece and Rome*, vol. 14, no. 1 (1967), pp. 39-43, and Chapter IX; Chapter III, *passim*; and Chapter XIII, *passim*.

34 DL V. 9.

35 None of the other biographers report that Aristotle was Alexander's tutor for a period of eight years.

36 *II VA* 17 claims, however, that after the death of Hermias (Hermias was treacherously captured by Menon and put to death by the Persians in 341-40 B.C.), Aristotle returned to Athens. *II VA* 18, on the other hand, seems to contradict this statement when it insists that after Hermias' death Aristotle went to Macedonia. See also *VM* 14; *VV* 14; *VL* 14; DL V. 2; 4; 9; *I VS* 8; *IV VA* 6. As a matter of fact, Aristotle returned to Macedonia in 343-42 B.C., that is, before Hermias died, and he returned to Athens in 335-34 B.C., that is, about six years after Hermias' death.

37 See A.-H. Chroust (see note 19).

38 *VM* 24; *VV* 18; *VL* 24. *VM* 23, *VV* 23 and *VL* 23, probably confounding Aristotle and Callisthenes, erroneously claim that Aristotle accompanied Alexander to Persia.

39 The Arabic biographers, who had a very high esteem for both Aristotle and Alexander, do not mention any 'alienation' between these two men. Accordingly, they completely ignore the cruel treatment of Callisthenes by Alexander. See DL V. 5; Chapter III, notes 155-75, and the corresponding texts; Chapter VI.

40 *I VA* 10; *II VA* 24-5; *IV VA* 22-3. See also *VM* 23; *VL* 23.

41 See also DL V. 10, where Aristotle's last stay in Athens is also reckoned at thirteen years. This information might go back to Apollodorus. It has already been shown that Diogenes Laertius included in his reckoning the year 323 B.C., the year in which Aristotle fled to Chalcis. See text. See also Chapter XI.

42 See here also *VM* 23-4; 44-6; *VV* 18; *VL* 23-4; 48-9; *I VA* 11; *II VA* 14; 25; 31; *IV VA* 4; 6; 23; 31; 33.

43 See note 33.

44 *VM* 41, *VV* 19 and *VL* 43 simply record that 'the Athenians turned against him.' *IV VA* 17-20, which discusses this incident in great detail, records that a decision to erect a monument in his honor 'was opposed by

Himeraeus,' a leader of the anti-Macedonian party. *II VS* merely remarks that he went to Chalcis. See also *VM* 41–2; *VV* 19–20; *VL* 43–4; A.-H. Chroust, 'Aristotle's flight from Athens in the year 323 B.C.,' *Historia*, vol. 15, no. 2 (1966), pp. 185–92, and Chapter XII.

45 DL V. 5, on the authority of Favorinus' *Miscellaneous History*, also mentions Demophilus as one of Aristotle's accusers.

46 *II VS* 3; *II VA* 21; *IV VA* 8. See also *VM* 18; 41; *VV* 19; *VL* 18; 46.

47 See also Aelian, *Varia Historia* IX. 23. Eumelus, according to DL V. 6, claims that he committed suicide. Justin Martyr, *Cohortatio ad Graecos* 34B; Gregory of Nazianzus, *Oratio* IV. 72; and Procopius VIII. 6. 20, maintain that he took his own life in a fit of despondency because he had failed to explain the flow of the Euripus. See A.-H. Chroust, 'The Myth of Aristotle's Suicide,' *Modern Schoolman*, vol. 44, no. 2 (1967), pp. 177–8, and Chapter XIV.

48 Eumelus, according to DL V. 6, claims that Aristotle died at the age of seventy (by committing suicide). This is an obvious transfer from Socrates and the manner in which the latter met his death at the age of seventy. See A.-H. Chroust (see note 47).

49 See note 8.

50 See note 17.

51 The date of Aristotle's death can be ascertained fairly accurately, provided we accept the suggestion that he died during the archonship of Philocles: Philocles entered upon his office early in July of 322 B.C.; Demosthenes died on the island of Calauria 14 October 322 B.C.; and Aristotle died shortly before Demosthenes.

CHAPTER III   AN ANALYSIS OF THE *Vita Aristotelis* OF DIOGENES LAERTIUS (DL V. I–16)

* In a substantially different, less detailed, and less searching form, this chapter was first published in *Antiquité Classique*, vol. 34, fasc. 1 (1965), pp. 97–129.

1 Diogenes Laertius, in the main, has remained an obscure author. There exists no certainty even about his correct name. Eustathius (*Comment. in Iliadem M 153*, vol. III, p. 103, ed. G. Stallbaum) calls him Laertes, while some authors (Stephanus of Byzantium and Photius, for instance) refer to him as Laertius Diogenes. The approximate date of his *Vitae* has been fixed provisionally in the first decade or decades of the third century A.D., that is, shortly after the year A.D. 200, although some scholars would prefer to place the *Vitae* closer to the year A.D. 300. The latest philosopher whom Diogenes cites in his work is Saturninus (DL IX. 116), an otherwise unknown disciple of Sextus Empiricus (*floruit* towards the end of the second century A.D.). If our assumption should be correct, namely, that Diogenes Laertius wrote shortly after 200 A.D., then he was the younger contemporary of Clement of Alexandria, Galen and Philostratus. See, in

general, E. Schwartz, 'Diogenes Laertius,' in Pauly-Wissowa, *Real-encyclopädie der classischen Altertumswissenschaft*, vol. V (Stuttgart, 1905), pp. 738-63.

2 See P. Moraux, 'La Composition de la Vie d'Aristote chez Diogène Laërce,' *Revue des Études Grecques*, vol. 68 (1955), pp. 124-63; I. Düring, *Aristotle in the Ancient Biographical Tradition* (Acta Universitatis Gothoburgensis, vol. 63, no. 2, Göteborg, 1957, pp. 29-79, *et passim*; O. Gigon, 'Interpretationen zu den Antiken Aristoteles-Viten,' *Museum Helveticum*, vol. 15 (1958), pp. 147-93. I. Düring, *op. cit.*, pp. 25-6, aptly calls the *Vita Aristotelis* of Diogenes Laertius 'a compilation of literary sources ranging over a period of about 500 years. It lacks stylistic unity. It is probable that the author went on making insertions and adding marginal notes until he partly spoiled his original arrangement. It is probable, too, that some of these additions were rather carelessly inserted in the text. . . . This makes Diogenes' work appear more disorderly, not to say sloppier, than it really is. It is habitual to sneer at Diogenes as an insipid and stupid author. . . . The texts which he excerpted were of course not without textual errors, and we must expect that he inherited many of these ancient errors. . . . The assumption that he was stupid is mainly based on the epigrams with which he adorned his work: they beat the record in bathos and bad taste. But this manifestation of insipidity does not give us the right to dismiss him once and for all as an ignorant ass. . . . [H]e has undoubtedly collected for us a material without which our knowledge of the history of ancient philosophy would be much poorer; he has traced and used some excellent sources; and he has put his material in a tolerably good order.'

3 Whenever and wherever the situation demands it, some of the sympathetic sources or biographies turn at times into outright, though fanciful, apologies, while some of the unsympathetic or hostile sources or biographies, though by no means all of them, lapse into invective and slander. Naturally, there are also those sources which, on the whole, seem to be fairly 'neutral' and objective.

4 In opposition to the majority of scholars, P. Moraux insists that Ariston of Ceos, rather than Hermippus, is the main source consulted by Diogenes Laertius—a thesis which will not readily be accepted. See P. Moraux, *Les Listes Anciennes des Ouvrages d'Aristote* (Louvain, 1951), pp. 243-7. See, in general, A.-H. Chroust, 'A brief account of the traditional *Vitae Aristotelis*,' *Revue des Études Grecques*, vol. 77, nos. 364-5 (1964), pp. 50-69, especially, pp. 54 ff., and Chapter I, notes 66-79, and the corresponding text.

5 Unless Hermippus already confounded Isocrates and Xenocrates, assuming that there actually is a confusion here between these two men. See note 73 and the corresponding text.

6 It might be noted that, in quoting Apollodorus' *Chronicle*, Diogenes Laertius is guilty of a minor inaccuracy. See Chapter II, notes 16, 20 and 21.

7 This is probably Anaximenes of Lampsacus (or Anaxarchus?), according

to DL II. 3, 'the rhetorician, who wrote on the accomplishments of Alexander,' and who is considered the author of the *Rhetorica ad Alexandrum*, a work which has been credited also to Aristotle.

8 It is quite possible that in reproducing the last will and testament of Aristotle, Diogenes Laertius makes use of Ariston of Ceos. In any event, DL V. 64 contains the information that the last will and testament of Straton of Lampsacus, as quoted by Diogenes Laertius (DL V. 61–4), is ultimately derived from Ariston's *Collection [of the Wills of the Peripatetic Scholarchs?]*. It is believed that Ariston collected and published the will of Aristotle as well as the wills of the first three scholarchs of the Peripatus (Theophrastus, Straton of Lampsacus and Lycon—see DL V. 11–16; DL V. 51–7; DL V. 61–4; DL V. 69–74). Diogenes Laertius might also have found Aristotle's will in Favorinus. See Chapter XV and Chapter I.

9 See also Chapter I, text after note 28, and Chapter IV, note 7. It might be interesting to remember here the two *Vitae Platonis*, namely, that of Olympiodorus and an anonymous *Vita* (ed. C. F. Hermann). The *Vita* of Olympiodorus shows the following pattern: (a) A general introduction or foreword; (b) a special introduction; (c) Plato's immediate family or genealogy, including his birth; (d) his primary or 'pre-philosophic' training; (e) his meeting with Socrates; (f) some of his other (and later) teachers; (g) his travels; (h) his school (the Academy) and the manner in which he taught; and (i) his death and his funeral. The anonymous *Vita* (or *Prolegomena*) contains (a) a general introduction; (b) Plato's genealogy and name; (c) his general character and temperament; (d) the time, place and circumstances of his birth; (e) his 'pre-philosophic' training; (f) his relations with Socrates; (g) his other (and later) teachers; (h) his travels; (i) the founding of the Academy; (j) his disciples; (k) his philosophic attainments; and (l) his death and posthumous fame.

10 *VM* 1; *VV* 1; *VL* 1; *II VA* 1–2; *IV VA* 1–2. *I VS* 3 states that the name of Aristotle's mother was Parysatis, thus confusing her with the mother of Cyrus the Younger or with the third (or fourth) wife of Alexander of Macedonia; *I VA* 3 maintains that her name was Phaestias. The fact that the name of Aristotle's mother is mentioned here is somewhat unusual as is the reference to her genealogy: The mother, too, traces her ancestry back to Asclepius. See *VM* 1; *VV* 1; *VL* 1; *I VS* 3; *II VA* 3; *III VA*; *IV VA* 2. Dionysius of Halicarnassus, *I Epistola ad Ammaeum* 5, records that Phaestis' ancestors originally came from Chalcis on the island of Euboea (where Aristotle died in 322 B.C.). Diogenes Laertius (V. 14) relates that Aristotle had a house in Chalcis which he probably inherited from his maternal ancestors. Presumably, Aristotle withdrew to Chalcis in the year 323 B.C. because he had this house there. It was in this house that he died in 322 B.C.

11 All the extant *Vitae Aristotelis* agree on this, although some of them disagree on the exact location of Stagira (today Stavro). See Strabo VII, frags. 33 and 35. In the course of history, the border separating Macedonia

and Thrace was progressively moved eastward. Hence different authors who wrote at different times, assign Stagira either to Macedonia or Thrace. Stagira (also Stageiros or Stagiros) was founded during the 31st Olympiad or 656–52 B.C. (Eusebius, *Chronica*, p. 87, ed. A. Schöne). It was a joint colony of Andros (Thucydides IV. 88. 1, and V. 6. 1) and Chalcis. The island of Andros is the place from which Aristotle's paternal ancestors hailed, and Chalcis is the town from which Aristotle's maternal ancestors came (Dionysius of Halicarnassus (see note 10)). During the fifth century Stagira was a member of the Delian League, paying an annual tribute of a mere 1,000 drachmae. This might be an indication that Stagira was a relatively poor and unimportant town. Stagira was destroyed during the Chalcidian War (349–48 B.C.). Thanks to the personal intercession of Aristotle with either Philip or Alexander, it was rebuilt, but we do not know when. See note 89. Strabo (see earlier in this note) maintains, however, that after 349–48 B.C. Stagira remained 'unpopulated,' implying that it was rebuilt only in part, if at all. Dio Chrysostom, *Oratio* XLVII 9–10, refers to a letter written by Aristotle in which the latter expressed his disappointment over the many difficulties he was encountering in his efforts to have Stagira rebuilt. Aristotle also complained that attempts had been made to keep Stagira a κώμη and prevent it from becoming a πόλις. Dio Chrysostom maintains further than in his own time (second half of the first century A.D.) Stagira was uninhabited. But this might have been due to a later process of depopulation.

12 This 'genealogy' (see note 17) is plainly nonsensical. Asclepius and Machaon (father and son) are mentioned in *Iliad* II. 729 ff.; IV. 193 ff.; XI. 501 ff.; XI. 833. Hence, they cannot possibly have been the grandfather or great-grandfather of Nicomachus, the father of Aristotle, but they might have been his remote ancestors. See A.-H. Chroust, 'The Genealogy of Aristotle,' *Classical Folia*, vol. 19, no. 2 (1965), p. 141, note 7, and Chapter V. But we know that Machaon had a son called Nicomachus. See Chapter V, notes 8–9. The etymology of the name Nicomachus, however, might possibly point in the direction of Machaon, provided Machaon is derived from μαχάω. Such a warlike name seems to be appropriate to someone who battles and vanquishes the demons that cause sickness. It is also doubtful whether Aristotle's paternal grandfather was called Nicomachus, although there were probably some Nicomachi among his paternal ancestors.

13 *VM* 2; *VV* 1; *VL* 2; *VH* 1; *I VS* 3; *II VA* 2; *IV VA* 2.

14 It is quite possible that during the early part of the fourth century B.C. the position of a court physician at the royal court of Macedonia was not much above that of an ordinary servant. Hence, for encomiastic reasons the biographers of Aristotle may have added the remark that Nicomachus was also a personal friend and intimate advisor of King Amyntas. Suda, 'article' Nicomachus, also relates that Nicomachus 'wrote six books on medicine and one book on physics.' This, too, is probably part of an

encomiastic tradition, although we do not know the source from which Suda derived his information.

15 Pliny, *Hist. Nat.* XXXV. 106, reports that Protogenes of Rhodes, a famous painter, had painted a portrait of Aristotle's mother. It cannot be determined, however, whether this portrait is identical with the 'likeness' of Phaestis referred to in Aristotle's will. See DL V. 16, and Chapter XV, notes 148–9, and the corresponding texts.

16 *VM* 3, *VV* 2, *VL* 3, *IV VA* 3, and Dionysius of Halicarnassus, *I Epistola ad Ammaeum* 5, contain the information that Nicomachus (and Phaestis?) died while Aristotle was still rather young, and that Proxenus of Atarneus became the guardian (?) of the orphaned Aristotle, taking over his upbringing and education. (The connection of this Proxenus with Atarneus might also explain Aristotle's later sojourn in Atarneus, and his friendship with Hermias of Atarneus.) *IV VA* 3 reports that Proxenus brought Aristotle to Athens to study under the guidance of Plato, and that Plato was allegedly Proxenus' personal friend. In his testament (DL V. 15), Aristotle stipulated, perhaps out of gratitude towards Proxenus, that a bust of Proxenus should be set up. He also made some generous provisions for Nicanor, the son of Proxenus (DL V. 12) and Arimneste, a sister of Aristotle. Moreover, he expressed the wish that Nicanor, his nephew, marry his daughter Pythias (by his wife Pythias). On the strength of Aristotle's testament, it has been surmised that Proxenus married Aristotle's sister Arimneste, and that Nicanor was the issue of this marriage.

17 Arimnestus and Arimneste are mentioned in *VM* 2, *VL* 2 and *VH* 2. This, according to Diogenes Laertius, would be Aristotle's 'genealogy' (see also note 12):

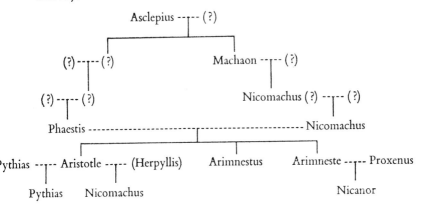

18 Dionysius of Halicarnassus, *Epistola ad Cn. Pompeium* 1. This is not the place to discuss the involved and still hotly debated problem of whether Aristotle was at any time a 'Platonist.' Some ancient authors (Aelius Aristides, Philochorus, Aristocles, Aristoxenus, Aelian and many others) claim that

from the beginning Aristotle disagreed with Plato on almost every major 'doctrinal issue.' See notes 38 and 52.

19 See *infra*. Some of the other *Vitae Aristotelis*, too, emphasize that Plato had a very high opinion of Aristotle and his philosophic attainments. See *VM* 6-7; *VV* 5; *VL* 6-7; *II VA* 11-12; *IV VA* 29; etc.

20 See also *VH* 1; Plutarch, *De Adulatore et Amico* 9 (*Moralia* 53C); Plutarch, *De Audiendis Poetis* 8 (*Moralia* 26B). This story might possibly be a transfer from Herodotus IV. 155, where we are told that Battus of Cyrene, aside from having closely set eyes, stammered and spoke with a lisp. The same Timotheus, it will be noted, also reports that Plato had 'a weak voice' (DL III. 51), that Speusippus' 'body was wasting away' (DL IV. 4), and that Zeno the Stoic had a 'wry neck,' 'thick legs,' and that he was 'flabby and delicate' (DL VII. 1). Plutarch, *De Adulatore et Amico*, *loc. cit.*, and Plutarch, *De Audiendis Poetis*, *loc. cit.*, also relates that Plato was a hunchback. All these stories and descriptions call to mind the many and frequently unflattering caricatures of philosophers found in Greek comedy.

21 It has been suggested that these particular accounts might go back to Ariston of Ceos and his *Collection* (DL V. 64), although it would seem that Epicurus (see Eusebius, *Praeparatio Evangelica* XV. 2. 1), Cephisodorus (*ibid.*, XV. 2. 7) or some other detractors of Aristotle (see, in general, I. Düring (see note 2), pp. 373-95) originated these derogatory stories. See also Aelian, *Varia Historia* III. 19, and notes 24-9.

22 *II VA* 38 relates that Aristotle was fair, a little bald-headed, of a good figure and very bony. He had small (or close-set) eyes and grew a thick beard; his eyes were blue, his nose aquiline, his mouth small and his chest broad. *IV VA* 36 concurs with this description but claims that Aristotle had a sparse beard.

23 See Pseudo-Aristotle, *Physiognomica* 808 a 29-31.

24 This might be gathered, among others, from Aelian, *Varia Historia* III. 19, where Aristotle's external appearance is described in the same 'derogatory' manner, with the additional information that he tied his shoes in an extravagant fashion.

25 Aelian, *loc. cit.*

26 In Eusebius, *op. cit.*, XV. 2. 1. Aristocles cites here some of the invectives which, in all likelihood, originated with Epicurus and the Epicureans.

27 This might be a partial transfer from Aristotle, the son of Pythias (the daughter of Aristotle of Stagira) and Metrodorus (or Medias) and, hence, the grandson of our Aristotle; or from Nicomachus, the (illegitimate) son of our Aristotle and Herpyllis. Nicomachus and Aristotle, the grandson of our Aristotle, seem to have been never-do-wells. See Chapter V at the end.

28 See *I VS* 6, where we are told that it is not true that Aristotle 'did not turn to philosophy until he was thirty years old and then only after he had practiced medicine.' See also *I VA* 6; *III VA*; *IV VA* 12: '... after he had tried his hand at politics.' See note 78.

29 This, then, would make out the Platonic Academy to have been a sort of

refugium peccatorum. See also Athenaeus, *Deipnosophistae* VIII. 354BC. In Eusebius (see note 26) we are told that, according to Epicurus, 'the Academy was thrown open to all sorts of people' in that it admitted and sheltered any and every person however intellectually incompetent or morally defective. Many of the slanderous accounts about the young Aristotle can ultimately be traced to Epicurus, the implacable and prejudiced enemy of the Stagirite, who 'called Aristotle a profligate, who after having squandered his patrimony took up soldiering and peddling drugs.' See DL X. 8. Derogatory stories about Aristotle also were told by Timaeus, likewise a prejudiced and tireless detractor of Aristotle. See Jacoby, *Frag. Histor. Graec.* 566, F. 156; Polybius XII. 8; Athenaeus, *op. cit.*, VIII. 352D; VIII. 354B.

30 See *VM* 4; *VV* 3; *VL* 4.

31 See also *VH* 4. The other *Vitae Aristotelis* do not mention Herpyllis or, for that matter, Aristotle's sojourn with Hermias of Atarneus, *II VA* 17, *IV VA* 5 and perhaps *II VS* 5 (as well as the versions of Aristotle's last will and testament, DL V. 11–16; *I VA*; *II VA*; *IV VA*) excepted. Nicomachus, the (illegitimate) son of Herpyllis and Aristotle, aside from being mentioned in Aristotle's last will and testament (DL V. 12), is also referred to in DL V. 39, DL V. 52 and DL VIII. 88. In *VM* 2, *VV* 2 and *VL* 2 we are told that Aristotle had named his (illegitimate) son Nicomachus in order to honor and commemorate his father, Nicomachus. See also Eusebius, *op. cit.*, XV. 2. 15. *VM* 2 and *VL* 2 recount that Aristotle addressed the *Nicomachean Ethics* to his son Nicomachus. This remark touches on the old and still unresolved problem as to the ultimate meaning of this title. See, for instance, R. E. Gauthier, *Aristote: L'Éthique à Nicomaque*, vol. I (Louvain-Paris, 1970), pp. 83 ff. DL V. 52 contains some stipulations in Theophrastus' last will and testament which imply that by the year 287–86 B.C. Nicomachus was dead. See also Suda, 'article' Nicomachus. The Arabic version of Aristotle's last will and testament, as it can be found for instance in *IV VA*, contains an interesting provision which has been omitted in the Greek version (DL V. 11–16) of this will: 'As to my estate and my son [Nicomachus] there is no need for me to make a formal last will (or special provisions in my will).' Should this passage from the Arabic version of the testament be authentic, then it would imply, at least according to Athenian law of succession, that Nicomachus was the legitimate son of Aristotle: Aristotle might either have adopted him or declared him legitimate (prior to making his will); or he might have married Nicomachus' mother Herpyllis after the death of his first wife Pythias (doubtful) and subsequently adopted him or declared him legitimate; or, perhaps, Nicomachus was the legitimate son of Aristotle and Pythias, a most unlikely possibility. Under Athenian law controlling succession, only a legitimate (or adopted son, adopted during the lifetime of the deceased) male child could inherit intestate—and this seems to be the legal meaning of the Arabic version cited above. For an illegitimate

non-adopted male child special testamentary provisions would have to be made. For additional legal details see, for instance, J. W. Jones, *The Law and Legal Theory of the Greeks* (Oxford, 1956), pp. 189-97, *et passim*. See also Chapter XV, *passim*. In *Gnomologium Vaticanum* (Cod. Vat. Graec. 743), no. 330, p. 130 (ed. L. Sternbach, Berlin, 1963), we find the following interesting story: 'Whenever Nicomachus [the son of Aristotle and Herpyllis] displayed a lack of interest in his philosophic studies, Theophrastus would remind him that he was not only the heir to his father's estate, but also the heir to his father's philosophic achievements.' This story would support the thesis that Nicomachus inherited Aristotle's estate.

32 This also seems to follow from Athenaeus, *op. cit.*, XIII. 589C. According to Eusebius, *op. cit.*, XV. 2. 15 (Aristocles), Herpyllis originally came from Stagira, a not altogether unlikely possibility.

33 The fact that in his last will and testament Aristotle made some rather generous provisions for Herpyllis (DL V. 13-14), might indicate that he never married her. See also the preceding notes. Aristocles (Eusebius, *op. cit.*, XV. 2. 15) relates, however, that Aristotle married Herpyllis. We may safely disregard this account as unfounded. See Chapters V and XV.

34 Pythias, the daughter or adopted daughter or niece (adopted) or sister (adopted) of Hermias of Atarneus as well as the legitimate wife of Aristotle (and the mother of Aristotle's legitimate daughter, Pythias), is mentioned in *VH* 2; *VM* 3; *VV* 2; *VL* 3; DL V. 16; as well as by a number of ancient authors. At the time Aristotle made his last will (probably in 323-22 B.C.), Pythias was dead, although we do not know exactly when or where she died. This follows from the statement, found in Aristotle's will, 'wherever they bury me, there the bones of Pythias shall also be buried.' DL V. 16. See also Eusebius, *op. cit.*, XV. 2. 12; XV. 2. 14.

35 DL V. 12-13; 15. See also *VH* 2; *VM* 3; *VV* 2; *VL* 3.

36 DL V. 16. See note 34.

37 See Chapter XV, especially notes 65-97, 150, and the corresponding texts.

38 See also *VM* 9; *VV* 6; *VL* 9.

39 See Eusebius, *op. cit.*, XV. 2. 3; XV. 2. 5; XV. 2. 13.

40 See Eusebius (see note 39); Aelian, *Varia Historia* III. 19; IV. 9; Aelius Aristides, *Oratio* XLVI. 249. 10; St Augustine, *De Civitate Dei* VIII. 12; Theodoretus, *Graecorum Affectionum Curatio* IV. 46; Philoponus, *Comment. in Arist. Analytica Posteriora*, *CIAG*, vol. XIII, part 3 (ed. M. Wallies, Berlin, 1909), p. 133, line 30.

41 Aelian, *Varia Historia* III. 19.

42 As frag. 6 (Wehrli) indicates, Heracleides apparently reported some of the more interesting incidents which transpired at the Academy during the scholarchate of Plato.

43 See DL IV. 3; *Epistolographi Graeci: Epist. Socrat.*, nos. 32-4 (ed. R. Hercher, Paris, 1873). See also note 63 and the corresponding text.

44 Dionysius of Halicarnassus, *I Epistola ad Ammaeum* 7, on the other hand, flatly denies that Aristotle ever founded or conducted his own independent

school or that he had his own disciples while Plato was still alive. See also *VM* 9 (Philochorus); *VL* 9; Chapter I, note 26. Conversely, Aristotle himself seems to have professed his enduring loyalty towards, and abiding admiration for, Plato. This follows not only from some of his later writings (see, for instance, *Nicomachean Ethics* 1096 a 12–17), but also from his Elegy which he presumably dedicated to the hallowed memory of Plato (or Eudemus?). See Olympiodorus, *Comment. in Platonis Gorgiam* (ed. W. Norvin), p. 197. That Plato himself had a high regard for Aristotle and his philosophic attainment might be inferred from the story that he referred to the Stagirite as 'the νοῦς,' provided this story is authentic. See *VM* 7; *VL* 7; *I VS* 5; *II VA* 12; *IV VA* 29; A.-H. Chroust, 'Brevia Aristotelica,' *Modern Schoolman*, vol. 39 (1965), pp. 165–7. See also *VM* 12 (Philochorus) and *VL* 12, where we are told that Aristotle could not possibly have turned against Plato, simply because it would have been utterly foolhardy for a Macedonian 'alien' such as Aristotle to tangle in Athens with an Athenian citizen, especially with so renowned and powerful a citizen as Plato, who had many politically and socially influential relatives and friends in Athens. Obviously, *VM* 12 and *VL* 12 (Philochorus) are efforts on the part of the 'pro-Aristotelian' biographers to disprove or discredit the reports of alleged clashes between the ungrateful Aristotle and the generous Plato. See also *VM* 29; *VV* 8; *VL* 27.

45 See also notes 50, 54–63. There can be little doubt that this whole account goes back to a friend or admirer of Xenocrates. Heracleides of Pontus might well have been this friend.

46 Origen, *Contra Celsum* II. 397, as a matter of fact, compares the alleged defection of Aristotle from the Academy with the defection of Chrysippus from Cleanthes' school.

47 This apophthegm can also be found in Aelian, *Varia Historia* IV. 9. See also Aelius Aristides, *Oratio* XLVI. 249. 10.

48 The plaintive tenor of this apophthegm, it seems, would speak against its authenticity.

49 The story of Aristotle's 'diplomatic mission' to Macedonia around the year 339–38 B.C., might be reflected in *IV VA* 17–21, where we are informed of the many generous and useful services Aristotle had rendered the city of Athens. See also *VM* 20 and *VL* 20, and Chapters XI and XIII. The extant *Vitae Aristotelis* are replete with stories and accounts of Aristotle's numerous diplomatic and statesmanlike dealings with kings and potentates, his great influence and popularity with princes and rulers, frequent correspondence with great and important people (DL V. 27 mentions letters of Aristotle addressed to Alexander, Philip, Olympias, Mentor and Antipater), and of the many public services he rendered cities and communities, including Athens. See also Philodemus, *Academicorum Philosophorum Index Herculanensis*, col. 6, 28 (p. 37, ed. S. Mekler).

50 See Chapter IX.

51 See note 66. DL IV. 8–9 relates that Xenocrates was a member of an

Athenian embassy to King Philip of Macedonia (between 340 and 338 B.C.?), which Aristotle might have joined (or with which he might have negotiated as a representative of Macedonia).

52 See DL V. 2. The stories about Aristotle's alleged ingratitude or outright irreverence towards Plato are legion. See note 38. In all likelihood these unpleasant stories owe their origin to (deliberate?) misunderstandings, exaggerations or plainly slanderous or malicious fabrications. Now we may also understand DL V. 1, where we are informed that Aristotle 'was the most genuine disciple of Plato.' Presumably, in Hermippus' *Vita* this statement was connected with the 'succession problem' in either 348–47 or 339–38 B.C., but in Diogenes Laertius, for some unknown reason, it became 'misplaced.' Hermippus apparently tried to make it absolutely clear that Aristotle was a better, worthier and more qualified man than either Speusippus or Xenocrates, both of whom succeeded in becoming scholarchs of the Academy, while Aristotle was by-passed at least twice.

53 For additional detail regarding the Athenian law of succession, see Chapter XV, and the literature cited there.

54 See, for instance, E. Bignone, *L'Aristotele Perduto e la Formazione Filosofica di Epicuro*, vol. I (Florence, 1936), pp. 223–5; Ph. Merlan, 'Zur Biographie des Speusippos,' *Philologus*, vol. 103 (1959), p. 206; 209–10; W. Jaeger, *Scripta Minora*, vol. 1 (Rome, 1960), pp. 341–3; A.-H. Chroust, 'Speusippus Succeeds Plato in the Scholarchate of the Academy,' *Revue des Études Grecques*, vol. 84 (1971), pp. 338–41.

55 Athenaeus, *op. cit.*, XII. 530D.

56 DL IV. 7–8 relates several stories about Xenocrates and his integrity as well as incorruptibility. These stories might also contain an indirect attack upon Aristotle who apparently accepted gifts and favors from King Philip, Alexander and Antipater.

57 See, for instance, Strabo XIII. 1. 57; *VM* 24; *VV* 18; *VL* 24. See also note 71.

58 See note 54.

59 See Chapter 1, notes 26–7, and the corresponding text.

60 See, for instance, *VM* 24; *VV* 18; *VL* 24.

61 Philodemus (see note 49), col. 6, 28 ff. (pp. 37 ff., ed. S. Mekler).

62 See DL V. 2, a passage which goes back to Hermippus and his anti-Xenocratic attitude.

63 See DL V. 3; Themistius, *Oratio* XXI. 245D (p. 310, ed. L. Dindorf); *Epistolographi Graeci* (ed. R. Hercher, Paris, 1873), nos 32–4.

64 *II VS* 4. See also Aelian, *Varia Historia* III. 19. The tradition relied upon by Aelian seems to have been hostile towards Aristotle. It wishes to emphasize that it was Xenocrates rather than Aristotle who preserved the Academy and its intellectual tradition. See, in general, O. Gigon, *Vita Aristotelis Marciana* (Kleine Texte für Vorlesungen und Übungen, Berlin, 1962), p. 64. See also notes 38–45 and the corresponding text; Chapter IX.

65 Practically all Hellenistic biographies of famous men seem to dwell upon

the connections which their subject had with some ruling dynasty. See note 9. Eusebius, *Praeparatio Evangelica* XV. 2. 11, for instance, remarks on 'the friendship Aristotle had with kings.'

66 It is not impossible that in one way or another Aristotle took part in the diplomatic negotiations between Athens and King Philip which were carried on shortly before the battle of Chaeronea (in 338 B.C.), or that at the time these negotiations took place he happened to be in Pella or Mieza. See note 49. During the greater part of his adult life, Aristotle had some official (political) contacts with Macedonia and the Macedonian kings, especially, with King Philip (and later also with Antipater, Alexander's lieutenant in Europe between 334 and 323 B.C.). See Chapter XIII.

67 See Eusebius, *op. cit.*, XV. 2. 6; Plutarch, *Vita Decem Oratorum* (*Moralia* 850B ff.); Pollux IX. 42. See also DL V. 38.

68 The other *Vitae Aristotelis* likewise mention the many and valuable services Aristotle had rendered Athens. See note 49; A.-H. Chroust, 'Aristotle and Athens: Some Observations on Aristotle's Sojourns in Athens,' *Laval Théologique et Philosophique*, vol. 22, fasc. 2 (1966), pp. 190-1, and Chapter XIII; A.-H. Chroust, 'Aristotle returns to Athens in the year 335 B.C.,' *ibid.*, vol. 23, fasc. 2 (1967), pp. 248 ff., and Chapter XI. But more than that: according to ancient tradition, Aristotle was not only the benefactor of Athens and the Athenians, but also that of many individuals, whole cities (Stagira and Eresus?) and of the whole of mankind. See, for instance, *VM* 15-22; *VV* 15-21; *VL* 15-22; *I VS* 7-10; *I VA* 12-13; *II VA* 25-30; *IV VA* 13-21; 24-5; 30; not to mention a host of other ancient authors, biographers, historians and reporters.

69 In a most penetrating and persuasive analysis of this passage, P. Moraux suggests that Diogenes Laertius combined here two distinct traditions. The first tradition, which is concerned with the development and organization of Aristotle's own school, contained the following bits of information: (a) in the beginning (b) Aristotle had practically no pupils (c) and, hence, taught 'walking up and down'; (d) but later, (e) when he had many students, (f) he taught sitting down. The second tradition, which touches upon the program of instruction at his school, reported the following facts: (g) in the morning, (h) but only to a small group of (advanced) students, (i) Aristotle taught philosophy, (j) while in the afternoon, (k) to a larger and more general audience, (l) he taught rhetoric. According to Moraux, Diogenes Laertius (DL V. 2) culled from these two different traditions (which Diogenes Laertius naïvely combined into one report) the following items: (c), (d), (e), (i), and (l). See P. Moraux (see note 2), p. 155.

70 See also *VM* 24; *VV* 18; *VL* 24; Clement of Alexandria, *Stromateis* I. 14; Philodemus (see note 49); Cicero, *Academica Post.* I. 4. 17.

71 Strabo XIII. 1. 57. See also note 57.

72 Frag. 785, Dindorf; frag. 796, Nauck².

73 See here also Quintilian, *Institutio Oratoria* III. 1. 14; Cicero, *De Oratore*

III. 35. 141; Syrianus, *Scholia in Hermogenem* II. 59. 21 ff. (ed. H. Rabe); Philodemus, *De Rhetorica: Volumina Rhetorica* (ed. S. Sudhaus), vol. II, p. 50, col. 48, 36. See also below. Conversely, Aristotle's many disagreements with Isocrates are also a matter of record. See, for instance, Cicero, *Orator* XVIII. 62; LI. 172; Cicero, *Tusculanae Disputationes* I. 4. 7; Athenaeus, *Deipnosophistae* II. 60DE; III. 122 B; VIII. 354C; Eusebius, *op. cit.*, XIV. 6. 9; Dionysius of Halicarnassus, *De Isocrate* 18; Dionysius of Halicarnassus, *I Epistola ad Ammaeum* 5; Themistius, *Oratio* XXIII. 285AB; DL II. 55; Quintilian, *Institutio Oratoria* II. 17. 14. See also Aristotle, *Rhetoric* 1354 a 11 ff.

74 Concerning the different meanings of the terms περίπατος and περιπατεῖν, see, in general, Philodemus (see note 49) (ed. S. Mekler), p. 22; Aristoxenus, frag. 64 (Wehrli); Quintilian, *Institutio Oratoria* III. 1. 14; DL V. 52 (the last will and testament of Theophrastus); Cicero, *De Oratore* III. 28. 109; Cicero, *Academica Post.* I. 4. 17; Plutarch, *De Alexandri Fortuna aut Virtute* I. 4 (*Moralia* 328A); Plutarch, *Moralia* 796D (Dicaearchus, frag. 29, Wehrli); Plutarch, *Adversus Coloten* 14 (*Moralia* 1115A); Gellius, *Attic Nights* XX. 5; Athenaeus, *op. cit.*, V. 214D; XII. 547D ff.; Ammonius, *In Aristotelis Categorias Commentarius*, CIAG, vol. IV. part 4 (ed. A. Busse, Berlin, 1895), p. 3, lines 8 ff.; Olympiodorus, *Prolegomena et in Categorias Comment.*, CIAG, vol. XII, part 1 (ed. A. Busse, Berlin, 1902), p. 5, lines 18 ff.; David, *Prolegomena et in Porphyrii Isagogen Comment.*, CIAG, vol. XVIII, part 2 (ed. A. Busse, Berlin, 1904), p. 121, lines 8 ff.

75 Hence, Hermippus might be guilty of an anachronism which Diogenes Laertius naïvely copies (?). The earliest use of the term περίπατος seems to have been by Colotes (see Plutarch, *Adversus Coloten* 14, *Moralia* 1115AB), and by Antigonus of Carystus (see Athenaeus, *op. cit.*, XII. 547D).

76 See, for instance, Aristotle, *Eudemian Ethics* 1214 b 22–4.

77 Apparently the original source from which this story is derived attempted to combine Aristotle's knowledge of medicine (which he might have received from his father and which has been attested by a number of sources) with his speculative or philosophic expertise. It will also be noted that in the Neo-Platonic tradition (Ammonius, Olympiodorus, Elias, Philoponus and David) Plato is depicted as having taught while walking around and as having done so for therapeutic reasons: *mens sana in corpore sano*. Plato, in *Phaedo* 66BC maintains that the body 'is liable also to diseases which overtake and impede us in the pusuit of true being.'

78 *VM* 2. See also *VL* 2. This story is not to be found in the other *Vitae*, but *I VS* 6 mentions that Aristotle had practiced medicine before he turned to philosophy (at the age of thirty). See also the preceding note. That Aristotle was thirty years old when he turned to philosophy is also mentioned in *I VA* 6, *III VA* and *IV VA* 12. When *IV VA* 12 relates that he was preoccupied with 'governing cities' until he was thirty years old, then this seems to be a confusion of ἰατρική and πολιτική. See note 28.

79 Since the days of Antisthenes (and probably before him) the philosopher

has been identified with the 'physician of the morally sick soul', and philosophy with the ἰατρικὴ τέχνη. See, for instance, DL VI. 4 (Antisthenes); VI. 6; VI. 30; VI. 36; Plutarch, *De Cohibenda Ira* 2 (*Moralia* 453D ff.); Plutarch, *An Viciositas ad Infelicitatem Sufficiat* 3 (*Moralia* 498E ff.); Seneca, *Epistola* 118. 4 ff.; *Epistola* 28. 9; *Epistola* 50. 4; Lucian, *Vitarum Auctio*. 8; Lucian, *Demonax* 6; Epictetus, *Discourses* III. 23. 30; III. 21. 8 ff.; I. 9. 10 ff.; Dio Chrysostom, *Oratio* XIII (p. 431, ed. L. Dindorf); *Oratio* XII (pp. 374 ff. ed. L. Dindorf); Stobaeus, *Florilegium* XIII. 25; III. 62; Stobaeus, *Eclogues* II. 40 (Philo of Larissa); Gellius, *Attic Nights* V. 1 ff.; Porphyry, *De Abstinentia* I. 31; etc. Already Plato (*Republic*, 489B; *Theaetetus* 167B) had compared the philosopher to the physician.

80 See note 69. In Plato's *Protagoras*, it will be remembered, Protagoras walks around (314E), while Hippias sits down (315BC). DL IV. 19 reports that Polemon 'would not even sit down to deal with the themes of his students, but would argue walking up and down.' No mention is made here of the story, found in Gellius, *Attic Nights* XX. 5, that Aristotle gave his 'exoteric lectures' in the afternoon or evening (sitting down?), while the 'esoteric lectures (or discussions)' were delivered in the morning (walking up and down?). See also Quintilian, *Institutio Oratoria* III. 1; Strabo XIV. 1. 48; Syrianus, *Scholia in Hermogenem* IV. 297 (ed. C. Walz), II. 59. 21 (ed. H. Rabe); Philodemus, *De Rhetorica: Volumina Rhetorica* (ed. S. Sudhaus), vol. II, pp. 50 ff.; Cicero, *Tusculanae Disputationes* II. 3. 9 (who insists that the morning was spent studying rhetoric, the afternoon studying philosophy). The story that Aristotle first taught walking up and down, but later, when the number of his students increased, he sat down to lecture, might also imply that in the beginning he had only a few students, but that when his reputation grew, that is, when he became known as a successful teacher, he attracted a great many students. Hence, he sat down and began to speak 'with authority' (*ex cathedra*) on a definite topic. It may be surmised, therefore, that this whole account is an attempt to extol Aristotle's excellence as a teacher.

81 See here also Cicero, *Orator* XIV. 46.

82 That this thorny problem had already been discussed in early times may be gathered, for instance, from Cicero, *Ad Atticum* IV. 16. 2; Cicero, *De Finibus* V. 5. 12 (Cicero relies here on Antiochus of Ascalon), as well as from some of the commentators of Aristotle, such as Ammonius, Simplicius and Elias.

83 See A.-H. Chroust, 'Aristotle's Earliest Course of Lectures on Rhetoric,' *Antiquité Classique*, vol. 33 (1964), pp. 58–72, especially, pp. 70 ff., and Chapter VIII.

84 Frag. 140, Rose. See also DL V. 24 (no. 77); *VH* 10 (no. 71); Ptolemy-el-Garib (no. 24).

85 In his *Gryllus or On Rhetoric*, probably composed around 360 B.C., Aristotle likewise seems to have taken issue with Isocrates. He not only chastizes Isocrates for having tried to ingratiate himself with Xenophon,

the father of Gryllus (or Grylus), by composing an obsequious and senti-
mental memorial in honor of Gryllus, but also objects to Isocrates' general
contention that his particular brand of rhetoric is τέχνη in the Platonic
sense. See DL II. 55; Quintilian, *Institutio Oratoria* II. 17. 14. See also A.-H.
Chroust, 'Aristotle's First Literary Effort: The *Gryllus*—A Lost Dialogue
on the Nature of Rhetoric,' *Revue des Études Grecques*, vol. 78, nos. 371–3
(1966), pp. 576–91, and vol. II, Chapter III. According to Athenaeus,
Deipnosophistae XIII. 592D, Hermippus wrote a work entitled Περὶ
'Ισοκράτους. In this work he probably also touched upon the relations
between Aristotle and Isocrates.

86 See note 73.

87 An exception might be DL V. 3 which contains the information that
Hermias gave Aristotle his daughter (adopted daughter, niece, or sister)
Pythias in marriage—a story which Diogenes Laertius credits to Demetrius
of Magnesia. See also Eusebius, *op. cit.*, XV. 2. 12; XV. 2. 14.

88 See, in general, Areius Didymus, *In Demosthenis Orationes Commenta*
(Berliner Klassikertexte, vol. I, ed. H. Diels and W. Schubart, Berlin,
1904), col. 5, 21 ff. (pp. 17 ff.); Demetrius of Magnesia, *De Elocutione* 293;
Philodemus, *Academicorum Philosophorum Index Herculanensis* (ed. S.
Mekler, 1902), p. 22; Himerius, *Oratio* VI. 6; Strabo XIII. 1. 57; Suda,
'article' Hermias; etc.

89 With the exception of *VH* 2 (and 4), *II VA* 17 and *IV VA* 5, the majority
of the extant *Vitae Aristotelis*, which on the whole are one-sidedly favorable
to Aristotle, simply ignore, suppress or play down the Hermias episode.
Some of the Syriac and Arabic *Vitae* (*II VS* 3; *II VA* 17; *IV VA* 5) touch
briefly upon this incident. Thus, *II VS* 3 states rather cryptically that
Aristotle 'stayed near the Hellespont.' Hermippus, on whom Diogenes
Laertius relies when reporting about the relationship of Aristotle and
Hermias, undoubtedly tried to make the whole Hermias incident appear
in the most favorable light. Hermippus is one of the main authors of the
tradition favorable to Hermias.

90 Areius Didymus (see note 88), col. 5,21 ff. See also Jacoby, *Frag. Hist.
Graec.*, 115, F. 250.

91 Some scholars are of the opinion that Aristippus was the author of the
Περὶ παλαιᾶς τρυφῆς. From this unknown author (and, perhaps, from
Theopompus and Theocritus of Chios), Diogenes Laertius ultimately
derives the story that Aristotle 'was on very affectionate terms with
Hermias.' See DL V. 3; Eusebius, *op. cit.* XV. 2. 5; Himerius, *Oratio* VI. 6.

92 Eusebius (see note 91); Himerius (see note 91).

93 See also Strabo XIII. 1. 57. Strabo makes it appear that Aristotle married
Pythias after the capture of Hermias, and that after having married Pythias,
he fled from Atarneus in the face of the advancing Persians.

94 Demetrius of Magnesia probably derived his information from Theopompus or Theocritus of Chios. Some of the unpleasant stories told about
Hermias and his wickedness might be transfers from Eubulus, the former
master of Hermias. See below.

95 Eusebius, *op. cit.*, XV. 2. 14. See also note 93.

96 Eusebius, *op. cit.*, XV. 2. 8.

97 Eusebius, *op. cit.*, XV. 2. 10.

98 Eusebius, *op. cit.*, XV. 2. 5 (Eubulides).

99 Compare Theocritus' epigram and Aristophanes, *Frogs* 83–5: 'Agathon, a convivial man . . . has gone [to the court of King Archelaus of Macedonia] . . . to join the blessed at their banquets.'

100 See DL V. 5; V. 6–8.

101 For this hymn (or paean) see also Areius Didymus (see note 88), col. 6, 22 ff.; Athenaeus, *op. cit.*, XV. 696A ff.; *VH* 6.

102 Areius Didymus, *op. cit.*, col. 5. 21 ff.

103 See, for instance, Dionysius of Halicarnassus, *Epistola ad Cn. Pompeium* VI. 6; Cornelius Nepos, *Vita Alcibiadis* 11. See also Athenaeus, *op. cit.*, IV. 166F ff.; VI. 260D ff.; Polybius, VIII. 9 (11). 5 ff.; VIII. 10 (12), 1 ff.

104 These prejudices become manifest in Areius Didymus, *op. cit.*, col. 5. 21 ff. Here Areius Didymus cites from Theopompus' *Epistle to Philip*, and from his *Philippica*.

105 Aristotle, on the other hand, calls Hermias a 'noble Greek.'

106 This, then, might lend some support to the thesis that Hermias, perhaps through the mediation of Aristotle, had allied himself with King Philip of Macedonia against Persia. See, for instance, Chapter XIII.

107 See Chapter XII.

108 See Herodotus VIII. 104–6. It should also be noted that the episode reported by Herodotus took place in Atarneus. Hermias may actually be an abridgment of Hermotimus (?), and Panionius, one of the chief actors in this sordid incident, was a Chian. Demetrius, *De Elocutione* 293, records that because Hermias was a eunuch, he always shuddered at the mere mention of amputations, excisions or scalpels. Some of the unattractive traits of character ascribed to Hermias by his detractors might in fact be partial transfers from Eubulus, the Bithynian and former 'master' of Hermias, who had been a money-changer and apparently a despicable rascal.

109 See Chapter VI.

110 See here also Himerius, *Oratio* VI. 6–7.

111 Areius Didymus (see note 85), col. 5, 64 ff.

112 That Hermias was not a barbarian as, for instance, Theopompus (Areius Didymus, see note 88, col. 5, 24) and Theocritus of Chios allege, may be inferred from the fact that he succeeded in persuading the Eleans to observe the Olympic truce (*ibid.*, col. 5, 29), something no 'barbarian' would have done. In his 'article' Hermias, Suda, who apparently tries to make out Hermias as a civilized and cultured person, claims that the latter was the author of a book entitled *On the Immortality of the Soul*. Needless to say, this is most certainly a naïve transfer from Hermeias of Alexandria, who authored such a work. See, in general, C. M. Mulvany, 'Notes on the legend of Aristotle,' *Classical Quarterly*, vol. 20 (1926), pp. 155–67; D. E. W. Wormell, 'The literary tradition concerning Hermias of Atarneus,' *Yale Classical Studies*, vol. 5 (1935), pp. 57–92; J. Bidez,

'Hermias d'Atarnée,' *Bulletin de la Classe des Lettres de l'Académie Royale de Belgique*, vol. 29 (1943), pp. 133–46.

113 See DL VIII. 60 (Empedocles); DL II. 23 (Socrates); DL II 48–9 (Xenophon); DL III. 29 (Plato); DL V. 39 (Theophrastus). It will be noted that not a few ancient authors took moral issue with the Platonic *Symposium*, claiming that it propagated homosexual eroticism. See U. von Wilamowitz-Moellendorff, *Antigonos von Karystos* (Philologische Untersuchungen, Heft 4, Berlin, 1881), pp. 48–53.

114 See above.

115 See Eusebius, *op. cit.*, XV. 2.5, where Eubulides refers to Aristotle's 'intimacy with Hermias.'

116 Himerius, *Oratio* VI. 6.

117 See the following note.

118 This hymn or paean is recorded in DL V. 6–8, Areius Didymus, *op. cit.*, col. 6, 18 ff., and Athenaeus, *op. cit.*, XV. 696A–696E.

119 In Eusebius, *op. cit.*, XV. 2. 5.

120 In Eusebius, *op. cit.*, XV. 2. 8.

121 See text, above. Aristocles and Apellicon of Teos (Eusebius, *op. cit.*, XV. 2. 14), relying on what appears to be a spurious letter addressed by Aristotle to Antipater, insinuate that Aristotle married Pythias (whom they call Hermias' sister) after the death of Hermias in 341–40 B.C. because he felt sorry for Pythias' plight. This unlikely story is perhaps fashioned after Aristotle, *On Noble Birth* (Plutarch, *Aristides* 27. 2; DL II. 26; Athenaeus, *op. cit.*, XIII. 555D ff.; frag. 93, Rose; frag. 3, Ross), where we are informed that Socrates married Myrto, the impoverished daughter (?) or, more likely, granddaughter or great-granddaughter of Aristides the Just, and that he married her because he felt compassion for her. See also Vol. II, Chapter II.

122 See Eusebius, *op. cit.*, XV. 2. 8 (Lycon Pythagoraeus).

123 See Areius Didymus, *op. cit.*, col. 5, 64 ff.; Athenaeus, *op. cit.*, XV 696 Aff.; DL V. 4; 6–8. See also note 118. The hymn or paean in honor of Hermias and the religious ceremonies held by Aristotle (and Callisthenes) in memory of Hermias in all likelihood were recorded by Hermippus (from whom Diogenes Laertius derived some of his information). We may assume that, in relating all this, Hermippus wished to demonstrate that Aristotle was a decent man who gratefully remembered and honored his friends and benefactors. In all likelihood, Hermippus also described Hermias as a noble and generous person. The above mentioned hymn or paean probably was sung or recited during the memorial services for Hermias. Together with these religious services, it was subsequently used by Aristotle's political enemies to indict him for impiety and blasphemy, and by his philosophic detractors to charge him with 'moral depravity.' In any event, this hymn as well as these religious memorial services apparently played an important role in Aristotle's official indictment in the year 323 B.C. See below, and, especially, Chapter XII.

124 Lucian, *Eunuchus* 9. See also Himerius, *Oratio* VI. 6–7.

125 See also U. von Wilamowitz-Moellendorff (see note 113), pp. 52 ff.

126 See Diodorus Siculus XVII. 108; Pausanias I. 37; Athenaeus, *op. cit.*, XIII. 595A ff.

127 DL V. 16.

128 See Philodemus, *Philosophorum Academicorum Index Herculanensis* (ed. S. Mekler, 1902), col. 5, 22.

129 Athenaeus, *op. cit.*, VII. 279F; Strabo XIII. I. 57; *Epistolographi Graeci* (ed. R. Hercher, Paris, 1873), *Epistolae Socraticorum* 36. 3 (p. 635b). See also R. Stark, *Aristotelesstudien: Philologische Untersuchungen zur Entwicklung der Aristotelischen Ethik* (Zetemata: Monographien zur Klassischen Altertumswissenschaft, Heft VIII, Munich, 1954), p. 22; I. Düring (see note 2), p. 279; E. R. Hill, *Journal of Hellenic Studies*, vol. 77, no. 1 (1957), p. 171. By implication, this story is apparently refuted by Plato (?), *Sixth Epistle* 322E, where Plato (?) implies that he had never met Hermias. As to the authenticity of the *Sixth Epistle*, see, for instance, E. Howald, *Die Briefe Platons* (Zürich, 1923), *passim;* F. Novotny, *Platonis Epistolae Commentariis Illustratae* (Brno, 1930); L. Edelstein, *Plato's Seventh Letter* (Leyden, 1966), pp. 122–3.

130 Areius Didymus, *op. cit.*, col. 5, 50–63.

131 See Plato (?), *Sixth Epistle, passim.* The many problems connected with Aristotle's stay in Assos or Atarneus (348/47–345/44 B.C.) have not yet been fully resolved. For some detailed discussions of these problems, see, for instance, P. Foucart, 'Étude sur Didymos d'après un Papyrus de Berlin,' *Mémoires de l'Académie des Inscriptions et Belles Lettres*, vol. 38, no. 1 (Paris, 1906); C. M. Mulvany, 'Notes on the legend of Aristotle,' *Classical Quarterly*, vol. 20 (1926), pp. 155 ff.; D. E. Wormell, 'The literary tradition concerning Hermias of Atarneus,' *Yale Classical Studies*, vol. V (1935), pp. 55 ff.; J. Bidez, 'Hermias d'Atarnée,' *Académie Royale de Belgique: Bulletin de la Classe des Lettres*, series V, vol. 29 (1943), pp. 133 ff.; C. Pavese, 'Aristotele e i filosofi ad Asso.' *La Parola del Passato*, vol. 16, fasc. 77 (1961), pp. 113 ff.; R. E. Gauthier, *Aristote: L'Éthique à Nicomaque* (Louvain-Paris, 1970), pp. 30 ff.; Chapter XIII.

132 Areius Didymus (see note 130).

133 See, for instance, Chapter XIII.

134 See, among others, *VM* 14; *VV* 14; *VL* 14; *II VS* 6; *II VA* 18; 31; *IV VA* 6; 33; DL V. 4; Plutarch, *De Alexandri Fortuna aut Virtute* I. 4 (*Moralia* 327E ff.); Quintilian, *Institutio Oratoria* I. 1. 23; Dio Chrysostom, *Oratio* XLIX. 4; Dionysius of Halicarnassus, *I Epistola ad Ammaeum* 5; Plutarch, *Alexander* 7–8; Plutarch, *De Exilio* 12 (*Moralia* 604D); Strabo I. 66 (Eratosthenes); etc. See also frag. 658, Rose.

135 See also A.-H. Chroust, 'Was Aristotle actually the preceptor of Alexander the Great?,' *Classical Folia*, vol. 18, no. 1 (1964), pp. 26–33, and Chapter X. It is interesting to note that with the exception of DL V. 9 (where he quotes Apollodorus' *Chronicle* for the fact that Aristotle 'went

to Mytilene during the archonship of Eubulus in the fourth year of the 108th Olympiad [345–44 B.C.]'), Diogenes Laertius does not mention Aristotle's sojourn in Mytilene (345/44–344/43 B.C.) or association with Theophrastus in Mytilene, implying thereby that he went directly from Assos or Atarneus to Macedonia. See DL V. 3–4: '[Aristotle] left [Athens] in order to stay with Hermias .... Next he stayed in Macedonia at the court of Philip ....' See also *II VA* 18. It will be observed, however, that in DL V. 9, Diogenes Laertius first refers to Aristotle's journey to Mytilene (345–44 B.C.) and only afterwards to the death of Plato (348–47 B.C.), an obvious chronological inversion.

136 DL VI. 84. Onesicritus gives a somewhat romantic account of Alexander's education, presumably fashioned after Xenophon's *Cyropaedia*. See Strabo XV. 1. 28; II. 1. 9. See also A.-H. Chroust (see note 135), and Chapter X.

137 See, in general, Suda, 'article' Marsyas.

138 Plutarch, *Alexander* 7; 22; 25. Relying on what appear to be fairly early sources, Plutarch relates that Leonidas, a kinsman of Alexander's mother Olympias, and Lysimachus, the Acarnanian, were the teachers of young Alexander. Plutarch may have made use of Onesicritus' *Report on the Education of Alexander*, a work which is mentioned in DL VI. 84. Quintilian, *Institutio Oratoria* I. 1. 9, and Clement of Alexandria, *Paedagogus* I. 7, likewise call Leonidas the preceptor of Alexander. It will be noted that the Stoic critics of Alexander, who denounce him for his emotional intemperance, do not mention Aristotle as the tutor of Alexander. This fact, in itself, is highly significant. See J. Stroux, 'Die Stoische Beurteilung Alexanders des Grossen,' *Philologus*, vol. 88 (1933), pp. 222–40.

139 Eusebius, *op. cit.*, XV. 2. 4, and Chapter X. In DL II. 109, Alexinus, who lived about a generation after Aristotle, is given the nickname of Elenxinus.

140 Plutarch, *Adversus Coloten* 32 (*Moralia* 1126 CD). As a matter of fact, Xenocrates is credited with having composed *Elementary Principles of Kingship Addressed to Alexander*. See DL IV. 14.

141 There can be little doubt, however, that Aristotle spent considerable time at the Macedonian royal court (between 343–42 B.C. and 335 B.C.), and that he was highly regarded by King Philip and his wife Olympias. See, for instance, *VM* 15; 46; *VV* 15; *VL* 15; 49; *I VA* 8; *II VA* 28; *IV VA* 15; Plutarch, *De Alexandri Fortuna aut Virtute* I. 4 (*Moralia* 327E). The surviving *Vitae Aristotelis* as well as some ancient authors refer to the many honors bestowed upon Aristotle by kings and princes and especially by Philip, Olympias and Alexander.

142 *VM* 17; *VV* 17; *VL* 17; *I VA* 13; *II VA* 27; *IV VA* 25. See also Pliny, *Hist Nat.* VII. 109; Plutarch, *Ne Suaviter Quidem Vivi Posse Secundum Epicurum* 15 (*Moralia* 1097B); Plutarch, *Alexander* 7; Dio Chrysostom, *Oratio* II. 79; Dio Chrysostom, *Oratio* XLVII. 8 (frag. 657, Rose); Aelian, *Varia Historia* III. 17; XII. 54; Diodorus Siculus XVI. 52. 9; Valerius Maximus V. 6. 5; Plutarch, *Adversus Coloten* 33 (*Moralia* 1126E). See also note 11. Dio Chrysostom, *Oratio* XLVII. 10–11, concludes his account

by reporting that in his own time (second half of the first century A.D.) Stagira was still 'unpopulated,' insinuating that it was never rebuilt. Naturally, it is quite possible that during the third or second century B.C. Stagira gradually declined and, hence, came to be abandoned. See also Strabo, VII, frag. 35.

143 *I VS* 7; *II VA* 27; *IV VA* 14. See also Plutarch, *Adversus Coloten* 33 (*Moralia* 1126C).

144 Aelian, *Varia Historia* III. 46, mentions a 'law of the Stagirites.' This law might well be the 'code' drawn up by Aristotle for Stagira.

145 Dio Chrysostom, *Oratio* XLVII. 9-10. This 'theme' reminds us of Goethe's *Faust*, part II, at the end, where Faust confesses that the only true happiness he had ever experienced in his life was the realization that he had become the benefactor of his people.

146 DL V. 14 mentions that in his last will and testament, drawn up presumably in 323-22 B.C., Aristotle provided that if Herpyllis wished to live in Stagira, she could use the house of Aristotle's father in Stagira. In his will (DL V. 16) Aristotle also stipulates that life-size stone statues of Zeus and Athena shall be erected in Stagira. DL V. 52 reports that in his will Theophrastus bequeathed his estate in Stagira to Callinus. All this implies that Stagira must have been rebuilt, at least in part, by 323-22 B.C., and certainly not later than 287-86 B.C. See also Theophrastus, *Historia Plantarum* IV. 16. 3.

147 *VM* 17-18; 20; *VL* 17; 19-20; *VV* 17.

148 *I VS* 10; *II VA* 29-30; *IV VA* 13; 30-1.

149 *VM* 18; *VL* 19; *IV VA* 13.

150 *VL* 19; *VM* 18. See also *VV* 17.

151 *IV VA* 13; *VL* 19; *VM* 18. See also the detailed account in *II VA* 29-30.

152 *VM* 17; *VV* 17; *VL* 17.

153 *VM* 17; *VV* 17; *VL* 17.

154 See also above and Chapter XI.

155 *II VA* 19; *IV VA* 6.

156 There exists a tradition, recorded by Plutarch, *Alexander* 53, that Callisthenes accompanied Alexander on his Persian venture in the hope that by his services to the king (see Arrian IV. 10. 2) he might be able to persuade the latter to rebuild Olynthus, the birthplace of Callisthenes, which had been destroyed by King Philip in 348 B.C. This, then, would be a 'duplication' of the story that, in return for the many services he had rendered Philip (or Alexander), Aristotle persuaded him to restore Stagira. See also the report that Aristotle persuaded Philip to spare Eresus. *VM* 19; *VV* 17; *VL* 18. Plutarch, *Ne Suaviter Quidem Vivi Posse Secundum Epicurum* 15 (*Moralia* 1097B), maintains, however, that Eresus was 'saved' (actually rescued from tyranny) due to the efforts of Theophrastus and Phanias. See also Plutarch, *Adversus Coloten* 33 (*Moralia* 1126F).

157 Theophrastus' *Callisthenes or On Bereavement* (DL V. 44) seems to have dealt with the philosophic implications of Callisthenes' cruel fate.

158 See, in general, Arrian, *Anabasis* IV. 10-14; Plutarch, *Alexander* 53 ff.; 55;

Valerius Maximus VII. 2. 11; Curtius VIII. 8. 22; Themistius, *Oratio* X.
130A(p. 155,Dindorf); *Oratio* VII. 94A(p. 122); Suda, article 'Callisthenes'.
See also A.-H. Chroust, 'Aristotle and Callisthenes of Olynthus,' *Classical
Folia*, vol. 20, no. 1 (1966), pp. 32–41, and Chapter VI.

159 *II VA* 19; *IV VA* 6.

160 *VM* 23, *VV* 23 and *VL* 23 evade the unpleasant Callisthenes incident by
erroneously implying that Aristotle, rather than his nephew Callisthenes,
accompanied Alexander to Asia. Naturally, the source or sources used by
these *Vitae* (*VM* 8; *VL* 8) might have confused Callisthenes and Aristotle,
or they might have referred to Aristotle's stay with Hermias of Atarneus.
There exists another possibility of explaining the story that Aristotle went
with Alexander to Asia. This story might have been a rather poor attempt
to justify and explain the meeting between Aristotle and Hermias, which
some of the encomiastic *Vitae* try to suppress or, at least, to 'play down.'
For if Aristotle accompanied Alexander, he might not have been able to
avoid meeting Hermias. This explanation, needless to say, is highly
conjectural and contains a fatal anachronism. After all, Hermias died in
341–40 B.C., and Alexander invaded Asia in 334 B.C.

161 Matthew 7:20. See also Luke 6:43–4. This explanation of the fact that some
Vitae Aristotelis hardly touch upon the Callisthenes episode is highly
conjectural.

162 Arrian, *Anabasis* IV. 10–14.

163 Plutarch, *Alexander* 52–5. *See also* Themistius, *Oratio* VII. 94A (p. 112,
Dindorf); *Oratio* X. 130A (p. 155); Tatian, *Oratio Adversus Graecos* 2
(Migne, vol. VI. p. 808).

164 DL IX. 58–60.

165 Plutarch, *Alexander* 52, contains a witty exchange between Callisthenes and
Anaxarchus which would suggest that the two men were rivals and not
altogether on friendly terms. See also Arrian, *Anabasis* IV. 11.

166 There exist two stories relating the particular reasons why Callisthenes fell
out with Alexander. According to one story, Callisthenes' 'outspokenness'
became his undoing. See DL V. 5, where Aristotle points out to Callisthenes
the dangers of being too outspoken. According to Plutarch, *Alexander* 54,
Aristotle is said to have told Callisthenes that he lacked good sense. The
other story, told in Plutarch, *op. cit.*, 54–5, reports that Callisthenes'
refusal to prostrate himself before the king (*proskynesis*) caused this fatal
rift. See also Arrian, *Anabasis* IV. 12. 3–7. For additional explanations, see
Chapter VI *passim*, especially note 45.

167 Plutarch, *Alexander* 55.

168 In letters addressed to Cratinus, Attalus and Alcetas, Alexander conceded
that even under torture the conspirators admitted that no other person or
persons, including Callisthenes, were privy to the plot. It cannot be
determined whether these letters are authentic. They might be later
forgeries to vindicate Callisthenes, or attempts to blacken the character of
Alexander. After the death of Callisthenes, the Peripatetics in particular

were willing to do anything to discredit Alexander. Conversely, Ptolemy and Aristobulus asserted independently that the conspirators confessed under torture that Callisthenes had 'inspired' them. It has also been claimed that Alexander suspected Callisthenes of having been an agent of the anti-Macedonian party in Greece. See J. B. Bury and R. Meiggs, *A History of Greece* (3rd ed., London, 1951), p. 797.

169 Jacoby, *Frag. Graec. Hist.* 138, F. 17; Plutarch, *Alexander* 55.

170 Jacoby, *Frag. Graec. Hist.* 139, F. 33; Plutarch, *loc. cit.*

171 Jacoby, *Frag. Graec. Hist.* 125, F. 15; Plutarch, *loc. cit.* Jacoby remarks that the reports of Aristobulus and Chares (that Callisthenes died a natural death) are attempts to absolve Alexander of all responsibility for this crude murder. It seems, however, that some authors (among them, perhaps, Hermippus) considered the treatment of Callisthenes to have been even more outrageous than would have been the case if he had been forthrightly executed. DL V. 5, following what seems to have been a later tradition, states that Callisthenes 'was confined to an iron cage and carried about until he became infested with vermin through the lack of proper attention. Finally, he was thrown to a lion and thus met his death.' Justin Martyr XV. 3. 3-7, maintains that Alexander had him multilated, cutting off his hands, feet, ears and nose, and had him locked in a small iron cage together with a dog. Moved by this pitiful sight, Lysimachus tried to put him out of his misery by passing some poison into the cage. This act of mercy was foiled, however, and, on orders by Alexander, Lysimachus was thrown to a lion.

172 This is obviously Anaximenes of Lampsacus, the rhetorician (DL II. 3) who has been credited with the authorship of the *Rhetorica ad Alexandrum*.

173 See notes 7, 55-64, and the corresponding texts.

174 There exists a wholly unsupported story that Aristotle attempted to poison Alexander. See Plutarch, *Alexander* 77; Arrian, *Anabasis* VII. 27. 1; Curtius Rufus X. 10; Dio Cassius LXXVII. 7. 3; Zonaras, *Annales* IV. 14 (Migne 134, 356); Pliny, *Hist. Nat.* XXX. 16. This story is probably an effort on the part of some pro-Alexandrian authors to blacken Aristotle's character—a quaint way of answering the pro-Aristotelian authors who denounced Alexander for what he had done to Callisthenes, and through Callisthenes, to Aristotle: this 'vile', 'ungrateful' Aristotle and his clansman fully deserved Alexander's harsh treatment. See also M. Plezia, 'Arystoteles Trucicielem Aleksandra Wielkiego (Aristotle as the poisoner of Alexander the Great),' *Meander*, vol. III (1948), pp. 492-501; R. Merkelbach, *Die Quellen des Griechischen Alexanderromans* (Zetemata, Heft IX, Munich, 1954), pp. 126 ff.

175 Plutarch, *Alexander* 55. See also Dio Chrysostom, *Oratio* LXIV. 20: Alexander 'planned to murder Aristotle.' See, in general, A.-H. Chroust (see note 158), and Chapter VI.

176 See Chapter XI.

177 See also Chapters XI and XIII.

178 See also *VH* 6; *VM* 41; *VV* 19; *VL* 43; *I VS* 8; *II VS* 7; *II VA* 22; *IV VA* 8.

179 According to Athenaeus, *Deipnosophistae* XV. 696A, Eurymedon merely made the motion to have Aristotle indicted for impiety, while Demophilus actually pressed the official charges. The parallel with Anytus and Meletus in the handling of Socrates' trial in 399 B.C. is rather obvious. See also A.-H. Chroust, 'Aristotle's flight from Athens in the year 323 B.C.,' *Historia*, vol. 15, no. 2 (1966), pp. 185-92, and Chapter XII.

180 DL V. 6 also mentions an inscription which Aristotle composed for a (projected) honorific statue or *stele* of Hermias at Delphi. Contrary to DL V. 6 (Favorinus), this particular inscription, it appears, had nothing to do with the official indictment of Aristotle in the year 323 B.C. It is possible, however, that Aristotle composed this honorific inscription after his withdrawal from Athens in 323. In Athenaeus, *op. cit.*, XV. 696A ff., we are told that Aristotle had been charged with impiety by Eurymedon and Demophilus, because he had daily recited a (religious?) hymn (or paean?) in honor of Hermias. Hermippus, the source of Athenaeus, apparently denied that this was a religious hymn or paean, as does Athenaeus. See here also Areius Didymus, *In Demosthenis Orationes Commenta* (ed. H. Diels and W. Schubart, Berlin, 1904), col. 6, 22 ff., and Chapter XII, especially notes 3-7, and the corresponding text. In this connection, Hermippus also refers to an *Apology of Aristotle* composed by the Stagirite, the authenticity of which is questioned, however, by Athenaeus, *loc. cit.* See also *IV VA* 10. In his 'catalogue' of Aristotelian works, Hesychius lists among the spurious works of Aristotle a *Defense (Apology) Against the Charge of Impiety Addressed to Eurymedon*. *VH* 10 (no. 189).

181 *II VA* 20; *IV VA* 7. This story recasts almost exactly the accounts of Socrates' indictment and trial in 399 B.C. Mubashir (*II VA* 20) and Usaibia (*IV VA* 7) add the information that Eurymedon's action was motivated by personal jealousy as well as by an old grudge which he bore Aristotle. Usaibia (*IV VA* 7) remarks that Aristotle speaks of this in a letter addressed to Antipater. In brief, Anytus becomes Eurymedon. *II VA* 20 also relates that Eurymedon denounced Aristotle as a person 'that should be shunned by everyone.' Moreover, *IV VA* 8-9 reports that when Aristotle was informed of his indictment, 'he departed [from Athens] before any further official steps were taken against him. No one did him any harm [or interfered with his departure] . . . .' This seems to be borne out by the fact that he was able to remove all of his considerable property, something which may be inferred from his last will and testament as well as from such authors as Diogenes Laertius (V. 16) and Lycon Pythagoraeus (Eusebius, *op. cit.*, XV. 2. 8).

182 Eumelus is difficult to identify. He might—and again might not—be the Peripatetic who composed a Περὶ ἀρχαίας κωμῳδίας.

183 See also *VH* 7; *VM* 43; *VL* 46; *II VS* 7; *II VA* 23; *IV VA* 11. *VH* 7 states

that Aristotle died of an illness, as does DL V. 10 (Apollodorus). See also Censorinus, *De Die Natali* XIV. 16; Gellius, *Attic Nights* XIII. 5. See note 191.

184 *VH* 7, *VV* 30 and *VL* 45 state that he was sixty-three years old (or in his sixty-third year) when he died; *II VS* 8, *II VA* 23, and *IV VA* 11, that he was sixty-eight; *I VA* 15, that he was sixty-five; and *I VS* 8, that he was sixty-seven.

185 See Chapter XIV.

186 Diogenes Laertius (DL V. 8), however, seems to accept the story of Eumelus when he composes the following lines in commemoration of Aristotle: 'One day Eurymedon, the priest of Demeter, resolved to indict Aristotle for impiety. But he [*scil*. Aristotle], by a draught of poison, painlessly escaped prosecution, thus triumphing over groundless calumnies.' Diogenes Laertius' versifications or epigrams have been called probably the worst verses ever published. Diogenes' epigram also implies that Aristotle committed suicide in Athens, something which might be inferred from the unusual account of Eumelus.

187 In contrast to the story told by Eumelus (who apparently attempts to bring out the alleged parallelisms between the trial and death of Socrates and the indictment and death of Aristotle), Favorinus, in his *Miscellaneous History*, seems to have stressed the differences between these two men and their ultimate fate: Socrates, according to the testimony of Plato, Xenophon and others, flatly refused to compose (or accept) a forensic speech in his own defense. Athenaeus, *Deipnosophistae* XV. 697B, Origen, *Contra Celsum* I. 380, and Mubashir (*IV VA* 10) emphatically deny that Aristotle ever wrote (or delivered) a speech in his own defense against the charges made by Eurymedon and Demophilus. See also notes 180, 200.

188 See, for instance, DL II. 20 (Socrates and his pupil Aeschines were the first to teach rhetoric); DL III. 24–5 (Plato was the first to introduce arguments by using the question and answer method or 'obstetric method'); DL VIII. 12 (Pythagoras was the first to introduce a special diet for athletes); DL VIII. 47–8 (Pythagoras was the first to call the heavens the universe and the earth a sphere); DL VIII. 83 (Alcmaeon was the first to compose a treatise on physics); and DL IX. 24 (Parmenides was the first to detect the identity of the evening star and the morning star). Hence, it is not surprising that Favorinus should claim that 'Aristotle was the first philosopher to compose a forensic speech in his own defense written for this law suit.' DL V. 9.

189 See also Aelian, *Varia Historia* III. 36.

190 *VM* 12, *VV* 6 and *VL* 12, for instance, emphasize that as a ξένος (*extraneus*) Aristotle had no standing in Athens (or in an Athenian court). See also Chapter XIV, text after note 29.

191 From the last part of DL V. 16, which seems to record some of the 'cures' or anodynes used by Aristotle during the last months of his life, it may be

inferred that he died a 'natural death,' that is, from the effects of some disease (stomach ailment?). For some unknown reason this bit of information came to be separated from DL V. 6. See here also Aelian, *Varia Historia* IX, 23; Censorinus, *De Die Natali* XIV. 16; Gellius, *Attic Nights* XIII. 5; Eusebius, *op. cit.*, XV. 2. 8 (Lycon Pythagoraeus); Valerius Maximus V. 6, ext. 5; Dionysius of Halicarnassus, *I Epistola ad Ammaeum* 5.

192 DL V. 10 claims that Aristotle died in the same year as Demosthenes. This information might in some way be related to the story that it was Aristotle's instruction which contributed much to Demosthenes' ultimate success as an orator. See Dionysius of Halicarnassus, *I Epistola ad Ammaeum* 2. The point here is apparently that the greatest teacher of rhetoric and his greatest disciple died the same year. It has been calculated (see Chapter V) that Aristotle died between early July and early October of 322 B.C. Demosthenes took his own life October 14, 322, and Aristotle, whose death occurred during the archonship of Philocles (early July 322 to early July 321 B.C.), died shortly before Demosthenes committed suicide. At the time of his death, Aristotle was sixty-two years old, that is, in his sixty-third year.

193 See also Eusebius, *op. cit.*, XV. 2. 8-9.

194 See Eusebius, *op. cit.*, XV. 2. 8.

195 See also Eusebius, *op. cit.*, XV. 2. 12 (Aristocles); XV. 2. 7 (Cephisodorus); Plutarch, *De Exilio* 10 (*Moralia* 603C); Polybius XII. 8.

196 See also *VV* 19; *VL* 43.

197 In all likelihood, the source (Ptolemy-el-Garib) or sources used by the Arabs were predominantly friendly towards Aristotle and, hence, omitted all references to Hermias. See above and Chapter XII.

198 *VM* 41; *VV* 19; *VL* 43; *IV VA* 7. *II VA* 21 merely mentions that Aristotle left Athens 'fearing that the Athenians might attempt to do to him what they had done to Socrates, the temperate, whom they executed by giving him poison.' See also Athenaeus, *op. cit.*, XV. 696A ff.; Aelian, *Varia Historia* III. 36; and the problematic passage in *II VS* 3.

199 *VM* 42; *VV* 20; *VL* 44; *IV VA* 7.

200 DL V. 9; *VM* 42; *VV* 20; *VL* 44. The reference to Socrates as well as the hexameter from Homer's *Odyssey*, VII. 120, can also be found in Aelian, *Varia Historia* III. 36. See note 189. According to Elias (*olim* David), *Comment. in Porphyrii Isagogen et in Aristotelis Categorias, CIAG*, vol. XVIII, part 1 (ed. A. Busse, Berlin, 1900), p. 123, lines 15 ff., this reference and the hexameter were contained in a letter which Aristotle addressed to the Athenians.

201 This might be gathered, for instance, from *IV VA* 20, where we are informed that the decision (by the philo-Macedonian party in Athens?) to set up on the Acropolis an inscription recording and honoring the many meritorious deeds of Aristotle on behalf of Athens, 'was opposed by an Athenian by the name of Himeraeus [a member of the anti-Macedonian party]. Himeraeus, we know, was afterwards seized and executed by

Antipater (*ibid.*, 21), after the latter had restored Macedonia's supremacy over Athens as the result of the battle of Crannon in 322 B.C. See also Chapter XII.

202 Hermias died in 341–40 B.C., and the hymn or paean was composed shortly after his death.

203 The same might be said about the trial of Socrates. The official charges against him, which also were charges of impiety, might have been mere 'token charges.' The real reason for his being tried might have been his previous association with oligarchs and, especially, with some of the Thirty Tyrants. See A.-H. Chroust, *Socrates: Man and Myth—The Two Socratic Apologies of Xenophon* (London, 1957), pp. 170 ff.

204 Since Eurymedon, the accuser of Aristotle, was a hierophant connected with the Eleusian mysteries, it could be argued that Aristotle's conduct was considered a violation or blasphemy of the Eleusian rites or cult. This, then, would call to mind what DL V. 3–4, on the authority of the author of *Aristippus or On the Luxury of the Ancients* (Aristippus?), had said about Aristotle, namely, that he brought sacrifices to his living wife, Pythias, 'as the Athenians did to Demeter of Eleusis.' See Eusebius, *op. cit.*, XV. 2. 8 (Lycon Pythagoreaus); Athenaeus, *op. cit.*, XV. 696A ff. Athenaeus *loc. cit.*, emphatically denies that Aristotle's hymn honoring the memory of Hermias was a religious paean and, hence, blasphemy. See also note 121. It might be maintained, however, that Aristotle's indictment for impiety (γραφὴ ἀσεβείας) in 323 B.C. was perhaps related to the sacrifices he brought to Pythias after her death (Lycon Pythagoraeus), or while she was still alive (author of *Aristippus or On the Luxury of the Ancients*), rather than to Aristotle's hymn or paean in memory of Hermias.

205 See, in general, A.-H. Chroust (see note 179).

206 This is also borne out be Aelian, *Varia Historia* IX. 23; *II VA* 23; *VH* 7. See also DL V. 10, and note 191. For Aristotle's last will and testament, see DL V. 11–16, *I VA*, *III VA*, and *IV VA*, which contain four almost identical versions of this will. See Chapter XV.

207 DL V. 6. See also notes 182–4 and the corresponding text; A.-H. Chroust, 'The Myth of Aristotle's Suicide,' *Modern Schoolman*, vol. 44, no. 2 (1967), pp. 177–8, and Chapter XIV. Eumelus also maintains that like Socrates, Aristotle died at the age of seventy.

208 *II VS* 7; *II VA* 22.

209 *II VA* 22. Mubashir (or his source) might have had in mind the (spurious?) Περὶ τῆς τοῦ Νἱλου ἀναβάσεως (*VH* 10, no. 159; frags. 246–8, Rose), or the Περὶ τῆς λἱθου (DL V. 26, no. 125; *VH* 10, no. 117).

210 Justin Martyr, *Cohortatio ad Graecos* 34B; Gregory of Nazianzus, *Oratio* IV. 72; Procopius VIII. 6. 20. An interesting parallel can be found in DL II. 11–12, where we are told that Diodorus Cronos committed suicide because he had failed to solve a logical problem put to him by Stilpo. Death or suicide because of despondency over some failure or misfortune are fairly common in Diogenes Laertius. See, for instance, DL I. 95

(Periander); DL II. 142 (Menedemus of Eretria); DL IV. 3 (Speusippus); DL V. 78 (Demetrius of Phaleron); and DL VI. 100 (Menippus). DL II. 142, DL V. 78 and DL VI. 100 are based on Hermippus. See also A.-H. Chroust (see note 207), *passim*, and Chapter XIV, notes 9–14.

211 The later doctrinal treatises, provided they are in their entirety by Aristotle, supply almost no biographical data. The early (lost) works or dialogues of Aristotle, on the other hand, must have contained some valuable bits of personal information, especially since Aristotle is one of the interlocutors, and in some instances, the main interlocutor in these dialogues.

212 Many of the letters subsequently credited to Aristotle are forgeries of a later date.

213 There still survive (i) an honorific decree issued by the Amphictionic League in 329–28 B.C., commemorating Aristotle's (and Callisthenes') services to the League (see W. Dittenberger, *Syll. Inscript. Graec.*³ 275); (ii) an honorific inscription by the city of Ephesus (of 318–17 B.C.) referring to 'Nicanor, the son of Aristotle of Stagira' (see R. Heberdey, in *Festschrift für Theodor Gomperz*, Vienna, 1902, pp. 412–16); and (iii) what appears to be a reference to an honorific inscription dedicated (after 335 B.C.?) by the Athenians to Aristotle in commemoration of his many services to Athens (see *IV VA* 17–21). It is not impossible that the reports about the honors bestowed upon Aristotle by Stagira (see *VM* 17–18; *VV* 17; *VL* 17; 19; *II VA* 29–30; *IV VA* 13; 30) ultimately go back to some authentic honorific inscription or decree.

214 See here also Eusebius, *op. cit.*, XV. 2. 14. This Apellicon of Teos is said to have acquired the remnants of the 'papers' as well as the library of Aristotle (and that of the Early Peripatus) from the heirs of Neleus of Scepsis (who had inherited them from Theophrastus, see DL V. 52) early in the first century B.C. See Strabo XIII. 1. 54; Plutarch, *Sulla* 26; Athenaeus, *op. cit.*, V. 214D; A.-H. Chroust, 'The miraculous disappearance and recovery of the *Corpus Aristotelicum*,' *Classica et Mediaevalia*, vol. 23 (1962), pp. 50–67.

215 The *Vita Aristotelis* of Diogenes Laertius might also furnish a promising starting point for a systematic investigation and evaluation of those ancient biographical accounts which are decidedly hostile towards Aristotle.

CHAPTER IV   A SUMMARY OF THE SYRIAC AND ARABIC *Vitae Aristotelis*

* In a different form, this chapter was first published in *Acta Orientalia* (Denmark), vol. 29, nos 1–2 (1965), pp. 23–47.

1 See A.-H. Chroust, 'A brief account of the traditional *Vitae Aristotelis*,' *Revue des Études Grecques*, vol. 77, nos 364–5 (1964), pp. 50–69, especially, pp. 60–9, and Chapter I. The title of Ptolemy's *Vita Aristotelis* probably was something like '*On the Life of Aristotle, His Last Will and Testament, and*

a List of His Writings.' See Elias (*olim* David), *Commentaria in Porphyrii Isagogen et in Aristotelis Categorias, CIAG,* vol. XVIII, part 1 (ed. A. Busse, Berlin, 1900), p. 107, line 7, where we are told that Ptolemy wrote about Aristotle's 'list of writings, about his life, and about his last will and testament.' *I VA* 19 (An-Nadim) reports that 'Ptolemy-el-Garib . . . is the author of a book "On the Life of Aristotle, His Death, and the Classification of his Writings."' See also *IV VA* (Usaibia), at the beginning.

2 For the Syriac and Arabic *Vitae Aristotelis,* see, in general, F. A. Müller, 'Die griechischen Philosophen in der arabischen Überlieferung,' *Festschrift der Frankischen Stiftungen für Professor Bernhardy* (Halle, 1873); F. A. Müller, 'Das Arabische Verzeichnis der Aristotelischen Schriften,' *Morgenländische Forschungen: Festschrift für H. L. Fischer* (Leipzig, 1875); M. Steinschneider, 'Die arabischen Übersetzungen aus dem Griechischen,' *Centralblatt für Bibl.-Wesen,* Beiheft no. II, part 5 (Leipzig, 1890–1), and Beiheft no. IV, part 12 (Leipzig, 1893); J. Lippert, *Studien auf dem Gebiete der Griechisch-Arabischen Übersetzungsliteratur* (Braunschweig, 1894); A. Baumstark, 'Lucubrationes Syrio-Graecae,' *Jahrbuch für Klassische Philologie,* Supplement, vol. 21 (Leipzig, 1894), pp. 333–524; A. Baumstark, *Syrisch-Arabische Biographien des Aristoteles* (Leipzig, 1900); J. Lippert, *Ibn al-Qiftis Tarih al-Hukama* (Leipzig, 1903). For additional and detailed information about the literature on our subject, see M. Guidi and R. Walzer, 'Studi su al-Kindi I: un scritto introduttivo allo studio di Aristotele,' *Memor. della Reale Academia Nazionale dei Licei.* Classe di Scienze Morali, series VI, vol. VI, fasc. 5 (Rome, 1940), pp. 375–419; R. Walzer, 'New light on the Arabic translations of Aristotle,' *Oriens,* vol. VI (1953), pp. 91–142; I. Düring, *Aristotle in the Ancient Biographical Tradition,* Acta Universitatis Gothoburgensis, vol. LXIII, no. 2 (Göteborg, 1957), pp. 183–92, 193–246.

3 His full name is Abu-(e)l-Wafa al-Mubashir (or Mubassir) Ibn Fatik. He authored the *Kitab Mukhtar al-Hikam wa-Mahasin al-Kilam (The Book of Selections of Wisdom and Wonderful Sayings).* For simplicity's sake the accents on the Arabic words have been omitted. See also Chapter I, note 17.

4 He authored the *Kitab uyun al-Anba fi Tabaqat al-Atibba (The Book of Sources for Information Concerning the School of Physicians).* Usaibia, who died in 1270, was a physician. See also Chapter I, note 19.

5 His full name is Ibn Abi Yaqub an-Nadim. He authored the *Kitab al-Fihrist,* which was written before the year 987. This work, like that of Al-Qifti (see note 6), is more in the nature of a 'biographical encyclopedia.' See also Chapter I, note 16.

6 His full name is Al-Qifti Gamaladdin al-Qadi al-Akram. He authored the *Tabaqat al-Hukama (The School of Wise Men).* He died in 1248. See note 5 and Chapter I, note 18. Neither the work of An-Nadim nor that of Al-Qifti will be used extensively.

7 See Chapter I, p. 4.

8 Al-Qifti (*III VA*) likewise begins his biographical sketch with an etymology of the name 'Aristotle.' See Chapter I, note 106.

9 *II VA* 1 maintains that the name 'Nicomachus' means the 'fighter,' the 'conqueror' or the 'victorious warrior.' This etymology might indicate that Nicomachus is derived from μᾶχος or μαχεῖν, as is perhaps the name Machaon, the supposed ancestor of Nicomachus. According to *VM* 3 and *VL* 3, Nicomachus died before 367 B.C. See below.

10 Parysatis is the name of the wife of King Darius II of Persia, the mother of Cyrus the Younger, as well as the name of one of Alexander's wives.

11 Machaon, the son of Asclepius, is said to have been the ancestor of Nicomachus, the father of Aristotle. Machaon had two sons by Anticleia (the daughter of Diocles), Gorgasus and Nicomachus, who became famous physicians. See Pausanias, IV. 3. 1–2; IV. 3. 9–10; IV. 30. 3. Undoubtedly, some of the more remote descendants of Asclepius-Machaon likewise were named Nicomachus. For an analysis and interpretation of Aristotle's highly problematic genealogy, see A.-H. Chroust, 'The genealogy of Aristotle,' *Classical Folia*, no. 19, no. 2 (1965), pp. 139–46, especially p. 141, note 6; and Chapter V.

12 'Asclepius,' which could be a scribal error, should read 'Nicomachus' (?), namely, Nicomachus the Elder, a more immediate ancestor of our Nicomachus (the father of Aristotle) or, perhaps, Nicomachus, the son of Machaon and, hence, the grandson of Asclepius. See note 11. Patronymics were frequently used by persons engaged in hereditary occupations. See Aristophanes, *Acharnians* 595–7.

13 An-Nadim (*I VA* 3) states that Aristotle's mother (Phaestis) descended from 'Asclepiades.' This is either a scribal error or an error due to faulty translation. 'Asclepiades' is a clan or gens designation. Any descendant of Asclepius is an Asclepiad.

14 *I VA* 2; Mubashir (*II VA* 2); Usaibia (*IV VA* 1); An-Nadim (*I VA* 3).

15 The obvious uncertainty about the exact location of Stagira resulted from the fact that during the fourth century B.C. the borders between Macedonia, Chacidice and Thrace were in constant flux. The towns of Olynthus, Methone and Stagira were probably known to the Syriac and Arabic biographers through Thucydides V. 6; IV. 88; V. 18. *I VS* 2, as a matter of fact, insists that Stagira was a town 'in Thrace, near Chacidice and also near Olynthus, a locality mentioned by Thucydides in the fifth book, where he enumerates the allied cities.' It is quite possible that Usaibia (*IV VA* 1) derived his information from *I VS* 2, or from a source used by *I VS* 2.

16 *VH* 2; *VM* 2; *VL* 2; DL V. 15–16 (only Arimnestus).

17 This seems to be a confusion with Speusippus who was the son of Plato's sister, Potone. Theophrastus might have been Aristotle's maternal cousin (?). See Mubashir (*II VA* 32) and Usaibia (*IV VA* 34).

18 Obviously, the expression 'rounded or all-embracing education' is the Arabic rendition of the Greek ἐγκύκλια παιδεία.

19 *VM* 4, *VV* 3 and *VL* 4 state that Aristotle received a 'liberal education' while he was 'still very young.' But at the age of seventeen (or sixteen) he was likewise a νέος.

20 *VM* 5, *VV* 4 and *VL* 5, but none of the other *Vitae*, report this tradition. *VL* 5 also relates that Aristotle stayed with Socrates three years, and that this bit of information was originally contained in a letter of Aristotle addressed to King Philip of Macedonia. We know that Plato stayed away from Athens for almost three years (367–365/64) during his second journey to Sicily.

21 See A.-H. Chroust, 'Aristotle Enters the Academy,' *Classical Folia*, vol. 19, no. 1 (1965), pp. 21–9, especially, pp. 25–7, and Chapter VII.

22 By the year 367 B.C., Isocrates and his school had gained a great reputation not only in Greece proper, but also in Macedonia and Thessaly. Hence, it would not be surprising that Aristotle should have joined this school, especially, since by 367 the renown of the Platonic Academy had not yet been firmly established beyond Greece proper.

23 Mubashir (*II VA* 3) reports that Aristotle went first to the Lyceum. According to tradition, Isocrates taught for a while in or near the Lyceum.

24 See. A.-H. Chroust, 'Aristotle's earliest course of lectures on rhetoric,' *Antiquité Classique*, vol. 33, fasc. 1 (1964), pp. 58–72, and Chapter VIII.

25 See also A.-H. Chroust, 'Aristotle's First Literary Effort: The *Gryllus*, A Lost Dialogue on the Nature of Rhetoric,' *Revue des Études Grecques* vol. 78, nos 371–3 (1965), pp. 576–91, and Vol. II, Chapter III.

26 Isocrates' *Antidosis*, in part, might also be an effort to discredit the 'apostate' Aristotle. Aristotle's *Protrepticus* is believed to be a 'rebuttal' of the *Antidosis*, at least in part. The *Ad Demonicum*, authored by a pupil of Isocrates, is possibly a reply to the Aristotelian *Protrepticus*.

27 Aristotle's lost dialogue *Nerinthus* (DL V. 22, no. 6; *VH* 10, no. 6), according to Themistius (*Oratio* XXIII, p. 356, Dindorf—Themistius mistakenly calls the *Nerinthus*, '*Corinthius*'), contains the story of a 'farmer' (an illiterate: the young Aristotle?) who joins Plato and his school after having read the Platonic *Gorgias*. He leaves his farm (the school of Isocrates?) and enters the Academy. This account, then, might possibly be an autobiographical sketch.

28 For details, see A.-H. Chroust (see note 21), pp. 21–9, and Chapter VII.

29 *I VS* 6 and *IV VA* 12, however, can be reconciled. The original source used by the author of *I VS* was probably based on a Greek text which used the term ἰατρική, while the source used by Usaibia (*IV VA* 12) was based on a Greek text which contained the term πολιτική. Some of Aristotle's detractors insist that Aristotle was a 'late learner' (ὀψιμαθής) and, hence, started the study of philosophy only at the age of thirty. See also *VM* 11; *VL* 11 (at the age of forty); DL V. 6 (Eumelus). This story goes back to Timaeus (frag. 156, Jacoby; Polybius XII. 8) or to Epicurus (Eusebius, *Praeparatio Evangelica* XV. 2. 1; Athenaeus, *Deipnosophistae* VIII. 354B).

30 See Eusebius, *op. cit.*, XV. 2. 1; DL X. 8; Timaeus, in Jacoby, *Frag*.

Histor. Graec. 566 F. 156; Athenaeus, *op. cit.*, VIII. 352D; VIII. 354B; Polybius XII. 8. Since Aristotle's father was a physician, it is probable that Aristotle had some knowledge of medicine. In ancient times certain skills were handed down from father to son as a matter of course. See note 29.

31 *I VS* 4 reports that Aristotle 'joined the students assembled around Plato,' but does not mention Aristotle's age at the time he did so. See also *VM* 5; *VV* 4; *VL* 5.

32 *II VA* 9 does not relate that Aristotle joined Plato 'on the advice of the Delphic Oracle.'

33 This bit of information would indicate that by the year 367 B.C., Nicomachus was dead. Tradition has it that Aristotle lost his father (and mother) fairly early. See *VM* 3; *VV* 2; *VL* 3. Here we are told that Aristotle was orphaned at the time he went to Athens in 367 B.C.

34 This bit of information is quite interesting. It might explain Aristotle's connections with Hermias of Atarneus. Proxenus, who supposedly hailed from Atarneus, is said to have been a friend of Plato and Hermias. See also *VM* 5; *VV* 4; *VL* 5.

35 The phrasing of the passage might support the conjecture that at one time Aristotle 'transferred' from the school of Isocrates to the Platonic Academy. See above.

36 This badly corrupted account seems to connect two wholly unrelated incidents in the life of Aristotle, namely, his flight from Athens to Chalcis in the years 323 B.C. (see note 86) and his visit with Hermias of Atarneus (which is in fact near the Hellespont) in 348-47 B.C. Should our assumption be correct, then according to *II VA* 3, Aristotle stayed with Plato (or the Academy) from 367 to 348 B.C., that is, about twenty years. See, however, note 62 and Chapter IX. *VL* 11 erroneously insists that Aristotle stayed with Plato forty years.

37 The Syriac translator obviously did not understand the meaning of the Greek νοῦς ἄπεστι. Hence, he offered two alternatives, both of which are wrong. This story can also be found in *VM* 6-7, *VV* 5 and *VL* 7. According to DL II. 6, Anaxagoras was called 'νοῦς.'

38 Usaibia (*IV VA* 29) in essence repeats this story which he probably borrowed from Mubashir. See also *VM* 7; *VV* 5; *VL* 7.

39 See notes 22 and 27.

40 This follows from *VM* 11 and *VL* 11 (Philochorus).

41 See Suda, 'article' Heracleides; frag. 2, Wehrli.

42 Plato's first Sicilian journey must be dated *c.* 387 B.C. or slightly before that time. See Plato, *Seventh Epistle* 324A.

43 When copying Mubashir, Usaibia (*IV VA* 4) apparently combined *II VA* 13 and *II VA* 14, thus making it appear that when Plato returned from Sicily, Aristotle moved to the Lyceum and founded there the 'Peripatetic school.'

44 See also DL V. 2. The story that Aristotle founded his own independent school while Plato was still alive (or was absent in Sicily in 361-60 B.C.),

may be based on some tradition hostile to Aristotle. See Eusebius, *op. cit.*, XV. 2. 3. It may also have originated with Hermippus who, in an ecomiastic effort, wished to demonstrate here that Aristotle was an absolutely original thinker who owed nothing to Plato. See Chapter I, notes 22–7, and note 34, and the corresponding text; Chapter III, notes 38–48, and the corresponding text. This story is refuted by Philochorus, whose refutation is to be found in *VM* 9–12 (*Frag. Histor. Graec.* 328, F. 223, Jacoby). See also *VM* 25–9; *VV* 5–11; *VL* 9; 25–9; Aelian, *Varia Historia* IV. 9.

45 As a matter of fact, Aristotle never became the scholarch or 'acting scholarch' of the Academy.

46 According to one of these stories, invented and circulated by Aristotle's detractors, Aristotle attempted to force Plato from the Academy and, presumably, tried to take over the school. See, for instance, Aelian, *op. cit.*, III. 19; IV. 9; Eusebius, *op. cit.*, XV. 2. 3; XV. 2. 13; Aelius Aristides, *Oratio* XLVI. 249. 10. See also Chapter III, notes 41–5, and the corresponding text.

47 See Mubashir (*II VA* 3), and note 18.

48 See, for instance, Aelian, *op. cit.*, IV. 9; Cicero, *De Natura Deorum* I. 33. 93; DL X. 8; Athenaeus, *op. cit.*, VIII. 352D–354E; Sextus Empiricus, *Adversus Mathematicos* I. 1. But Mubashir might also refer to Cephisodorus, the disciple of Isocrates, who in his *Against Aristotle* (written *c.* 355 B.C.) denounced Aristotle and the kind of rhetoric he advocated. See Dionysius of Halicarnassus, *De Isocrate* 18; Dionysius of Halicarnassus, *Epistola ad Cn. Pompeium* 1; Athenaeus, *op. cit.*, II. 60DE; III. 122B; VIII. 354B; Eusebius, *op. cit.*, XIV. 6. 9.

49 Usaibia's report (*IV VA* 27) differs only slightly from that of Mubashir.

50 This story might contain an allusion to Aristotle's *Gryllus or On Rhetoric*, composed about 360–59 B.C., where the young Stagirite defends true (Platonic) rhetoric against Isocrates and his school. See A.-H. Chroust, (see note 25), and Vol. II, Chapter III. Aristotle probably wrote the *Gryllus* while he was still preoccupied with his 'pre-philosophic studies.' Moreover, between *c.* 360 and 355 B.C., Aristotle offered a course of lectures on rhetoric in the Academy. See A.-H. Chroust, 'Aristotle's Earliest Course of Lectures on Rhetoric,' *Antiquité Classique*, vol. 33, fasc. 1 (1964), pp. 58–72, and Chapter VIII. Mubashir (*II VA* 6–8) and Usaibia (*IV VA* 27) might refer to this course of lectures in which Aristotle probably defended rhetoric against its detractors and despoilers. See DL II. 55. The phrase, 'since philosophic wisdom [φρόνησις?] is the most exalted of all things,' might also be a reference to Aristotle's *Protrepticus* which extolls the unsurpassed excellence of philosophic wisdom.

51 *VM* 6, *VV* 5 and *VL* 6 insinuate that Aristotle was a 'great reader of books'; and DL I. 16 and DL X. 27, as well as *VM* 11 and *VL* 11, relate that he wrote a great many books.

52 According to Plutarch, *Alexander* 7, Alexander wrote Aristotle a letter in which he stated: 'You have not done well to publish your books of oral

doctrine. For what is there left now that we excel others in, if those things in which we have been particularly instructed should be laid open to all?' Aristotle defended his many publications against the charges levelled by Alexander by stating that 'his books on metaphysics are composed in a style which makes them useless for ordinary teaching, and instructive only, in the way of memoranda, for those who are already conversant with this kind of learning.'

53 The Arabic biographers of Aristotle probably found in Al-Farabi the story that Plato had reprimanded Aristotle for writing too many books. See F. Dieterici, *Alfarabis Philosophische Abhandlungen* (Leiden, 1890), p. 11. In all likelihood, this story was also contained in the *Vita Aristotelis* of Ptolemy (-el-Garib). It might have been based on two letters, quoted in Gellius, *Attic Nights* XX. 5, and mentioned by Andronicus of Rhodes.

54 See also Usaibia (*IV VA* 24) who relies either on Mubashir (*II VA* 26) or on a source used by Mubashir.

55 See, for instance, Pseudo-Aristotle, *Physiognomica* 808 a 29-31. See also DL V. 2, and Chapter III, note 23.

56 Usaibia prefaces his description of Aristotle's physical appearance with the remark: 'I saw a description of Aristotle's appearance in some books.' Among the books Usaibia consulted was probably the *Vita Aristotelis* of Mubashir.

57 Mubashir (*II VA* 38) also maintains that Aristotle held in his hand an astrolobe. This account might indicate that Mubashir's description of Aristotle's external is taken from some 'idealized picture' of Aristotle. It might also be based on a misunderstanding of the story, told by Diogenes Laertius (DL V. 16), that when Aristotle 'went to sleep, a bronze ball was placed in his hand with a vessel under it, in order that, when the ball dropped from his hand into the vessel, he might be awakened by the sound.' That Aristotle was moderate in everything he did is confirmed by *VM* 31, *VV* 24 and *VL* 33.

58 See below and Chapter XV, *passim*. Aristotle's two children are also mentioned in *VH* 2; 4; *VM* 44; *VV* 47.

59 Aristotle's absence from Athens at the time of Plato's death might have been connected with his visit to Hermias of Atarneus, although *II VS* 4 does not specifically mention Hermias or the 'Hermias episode.' In any event, *II VS* 4 lends some support to the thesis that Aristotle left Athens and the Academy prior to the death of Plato. See A.-H. Chroust, 'Aristotle leaves the Academy,' *Greece and Rome*, vol. 14, no. 1 (1967), pp. 39-43, and Chapter IX.

60 See note 44.

61 See notes 43-4 and the corresponding text.

62 *II VS* 3 mentions that Aristotle withdrew from Athens to a place 'near the Hellespont.' This might be an allusion to Aristotle's sojourn with Hermias. See notes 36, 86. Neither *VM* nor *VV* nor *VL* mentions Hermias or Aristotle's stay with Hermias. See, however, *VH* 2; 4; DL V. 3-4.

63 Usaibia (*IV VA* 5) actually states that after the death of Hermias, Aristotle returned to Athens, and that it was in Athens that he received King Philip's invitation to come to Macedonia.

64 This statement is incorrect. Hermias was captured by Mentor and subsequently put to a cruel death in 341-40 B.C. Aristotle went to Macedonia before that time. See also *VM* 14; *VV* 14; *VL* 14.

65 The Arabs, in particular, had a very high opinion of Alexander the Great. Al-Qifti (*III VA*) claims that it was Aristotle and Alexander who brought philosophy to the Muslim world. Accordingly, they probably suppressed the sordid Callisthenes incident (see Arrian, *Anabasis* IV. 10-14; Plutarch, *Alexander* 53 ff.; Valerius Maximus VII. 2. 11; Curtius Rufus VIII. 8. 22; Themistius, *Oratio* X, p. 155, ed. Dindorf; Suda, 'article' Callisthenes) which casts an unfavorable light on Alexander. See also Chapter VI.

66 This particular passage might contain an allusion to the fact that after Alexander's accession to the throne of Macedonia, and especially after the foul murder of Callisthenes, the relationship between Aristotle and Alexander deteriorated. See also *VM* 23; *VL* 23; Plutarch, *Alexander* 55; Dio Chrysostom, *Oratio* LXIV. 20; Arrian, *Anabasis* VII. 27. 1.

67 Mubashir (*II VA* 25) adds to the last sentence the remark that after his return to Athens Aristotle also 'began to devote himself to the promotion of the commonweal.' It will be noted that Mubashir (*II VA* 23) and Usaibia (*IV VA* 6) relate that Aristotle's second sojourn in Athens lasted ten years (rather than twelve or thirteen years, that is, from 335-34 to 323 B.C.).

68 An-Nadim (*I VA* 12) relates that during this period Aristotle 'devoted himself to the promotion of happiness among men.' See also *VM* 16-17; 20; VL 16-17; 20.

69 See notes 52-3 and the corresponding text.

70 Mubashir (*II VA* 31) reports that, in addition to Alexander, Aristotle had many kings and princes for his disciples. There exists some doubt, however, as to whether Aristotle was in fact the teacher of Alexander. See A.-H. Chroust, 'Was Aristotle actually the preceptor of Alexander the Great?', *Classical Folia*, vol. 18, no. 1 (1964), pp. 26-33, and Chapter X. See also *VM* 14 and *VL* 14, which enumerate some of Aristotle's distinguished pupils.

71 See, for instance, Usaibia (*IV VA* 16) and An-Nadim (*I VA* 9). Similarly, Mubashir (*II VA* 36) and Usaibia (*IV VA* 25). DL V. 27 lists letters of Aristotle to Philip, Alexander, Antipater (nine books), Mentor and Olympias. See also *VM* 16; 27; *VV* 16; *VL* 16.

72 See also Mubashir (*II VA* 26); An-Nadim (*I VA* 6-7); *VM* 15; 23; 46; *VV* 31; *VL* 15; 23; 49. Eusebius, *op. cit.*, XV. 2. 11, refers to Aristotle's friendship 'with many kings.' See also Chapter XIII.

73 See Mubashir (*II VA* 25), where Aristotle's concern for the commonweal is extolled. *VM* 16 and *VL* 16, which in all likelihood rely on the *Vita Aristotelis* of Ptolemy (-el-Garib), record that these facts came to light in

letters which Aristotle addressed to kings and princes. See also *VV* 15 and *VL* 15, which relate that he did much work for King Philip.

74 The rebuilding of Stagira by Philip or Alexander at the request or due to the intercession of Aristotle is also attested to by *VM* 17; *VV* 17; *VL* 17; DL V. 4; Dio Chrysostom, *Oratio* II. 79; Pliny, *Hist Nat.* VII. 109; Plutarch, *Alexander* 7; Aelian, *Varia Historia* III. 17; XII. 54; Diodorus Siculus XVI. 52. 9; Valerius Maximus V. 6. 5; Plutarch, *Ne Suaviter Quidem Vivi Posse Secundum Epicurum* 15 (*Moralia* 1097B); Plutarch, *Adversus Coloten* 32 (*Moralia* 1126C); Strabo VII, frag. 35; Dio Chrysostom, *Oratio* XLVII. 8–11. See also note 61.

75 *VM* 19, *VV* 17 and *VL* 18 also report that Aristotle was instrumental in preventing the 'destruction' of Eresus. On the other hand, Plutarch, *Ne Suaviter Quidem Vivi Posse Secundum Epicurum* 15 (*Moralia* 1097B), and Plutarch, *Adversus Coloten* 33 (*Moralia* 1126F), maintains that Eresus was 'saved' (actually rescued from tyranny) thanks to the intercession of Theophrastus and Phanias, rather than through the efforts of Aristotle.

76 Mubashir (*II VA* 29) relates that they collected Aristotle's remains and placed them into a bronze urn. See also *VM* 17–18; *VV* 17; *VL* 19.

77 This is Mubashir's account, which in essence is repeated by Usaibia (*IV VA* 30–1). An echo of this attractive story might be detected in Usaibia (*IV VA* 32), who quotes here Al-Masudi. Usaibia reports that in a mosque (church) in Messina, Sicily, the likeness of 'a Greek wise man, namely, that of Aristotle, was hanging on a wooden block [a crucifix?] from the ceiling.... The Christians extol the miraculous or miracle-working powers of this idol.... They also say that the reason for hanging him between heaven and earth was that people come here and pray for rain or for some other important matter which make them seek comfort in God Almighty as, for instance, in times of misfortune or disaster or when they try to settle disputes.' See also W. Hertz, *Gesammelte Abhandlungen* (Stuttgart-Berlin, 1905), pp. 398–412.

78 According to DL VII. 10–12, the Athenians voted a decree honoring Zeno, the Stoic. See also DL IV. 9. We know that a statue of Aristotle was erected in Stagira by King Philip and Olympias. See *VM* 15; *VL* 15; Pausanias VI. 4. 8.

79 We do not know for certain whether the Athenians ever passed such a decree, or whether they ever erected such a *stele* in honor of Aristotle. It is not impossible that, in the biographical tradition of Aristotle, the statue erected in honor of King Philip in 338 B.C. or the later decrees of *proxenia* honoring Alexander and Antipater were subsequently transferred to Aristotle. Usaibia might also refer here to the following facts: at one time the Amphyctionic League dedicated to Aristotle an honorific inscription in Delphi. See W. Dittenberger, *Syll. Inscript. Graec.*3, no. 275; Aelian, *Varia Historia* XIV. 1. See also D. M. Lewis, 'An Aristotle publication date,' *Classical Review*, vol. 72 (1958), p. 108. Late in 323 B.C., when the Am-

phyctionic League joined the anti-Macedonian uprising (Lamian War), this inscription was removed and apparently thrown into a well (where it was found in modern times).

80 This may also refer to Alexander's unusually lenient treatment of Athens in the year 335 B.C., after the abortive Athenian uprising against Macedonia—a leniency which Aristotle might have suggested to Alexander who otherwise might have razed the city. See Chapters XI and XIII. See also *VM* 20; *VL* 20.

81 In a summary manner, Usaibia (*IV VA* 18) relates what might well have been the content of an honorific decree. This seems to follow from the text of Usaibia, who reproduces the wording of an Athenian decree of *proxenia*. See E. Drerup, 'Ein athenisches Proxeniendekret für Aristoteles,' *Mittheilungen des Kaiserlichen Deutschen Archeologischen Instituts* (Athenische Abteilung), vol. 23 (1898), pp. 369–81. The date of this decree or *stele*, provided such a decree was ever proposed and passed and that such a *stele* was ever erected, might have been either the year 340–39 B.C., when Athens was negotiating with King Philip, using Aristotle as an intermediary (?)—see DL V. 2; or the year 338 B.C., when after the battle of Chaeronea, perhaps on the intercession of Aristotle, Philip treated Athens rather generously; or the year 335 B.C. (or shortly thereafter), when, thanks to Aristotle's intercession with Alexander, the latter spared Athens the fate of Thebes.

82 Himeraeus, the son of Phenostratus of Phaleron and the brother of Demetrius of Phaleron, was a very prominent partisan of the anti-Macedonian faction in Athens during the thirties and twenties of the fourth century B.C. Hence, it is not altogether surprising that he should be a staunch opponent of Aristotle, the Macedonian, the pro-Macedonian and perhaps the 'agent' of King Philip or Antipater.

83 Together with other prominent anti-Macedonian leaders, Himeraeus was executed by Antipater on 5 October 322 B.C. This execution, which had nothing to do with the above-mentioned incident, took place in connection with the Lamian War and Antipater's recapture of Athens after the battle of Crannon in 322. When the news of Alexander's sudden death in Babylon (13 June 323 B.C.) reached Athens, the Athenians threw out the Macedonian garrison and the philo-Macedonian partisans (or indicted some of the latter for 'treason'), including Aristotle. See below; A.-H. Chroust, 'Aristotle's Flight from Athens in the Year 323 B.C.,' *Historia*, vol. 15, no. 2 (1966), pp. 185–92, and Chapter XII. When Antipater re-took Athens, Himeraeus and Hyperides fled to Aegina. There they were captured by Archias of Thurii, who sent them to Antipater. See Plutarch, *Demosthenes* 28. Demosthenes, the most prominent leader from among the anti-Macedonian partisans, committed suicide, 14 October 322 B.C., on the island of Calauria in order to escape execution.

84 The Stephanus mentioned by Usaibia (*IV VA* 21) is difficult to identify.

He might be Stephanus, the son of Menecles (Demosthenes, *Oratio* XLV. 8), or Stephanus, the son of Antidoridas (Athenaeus, *op. cit.*, XIII. 593F ff.; Demosthenes, *Oratio* LIX, 43), or some other Stephanus.

85 If this story about Stephanus is true, then this incident must have taken place after the battle of Crannon, that is, in the year 322 B.C., or shortly thereafter. There survive a number of Athenian decrees ordering the restoration or repair of damaged or destroyed honorific inscriptions or *stelai*. See, in general, Chapter XI.

86 This curious passage, it appears, combines and probably confuses two different incidents in the life of Aristotle. Being indicted for 'impiety' in 323 B.C., Aristotle feared that he might have to suffer the fate that befell Socrates in 399 B.C. and, hence, retired or fled to Chalcis. See *II VS* 7. The reference to the Hellespont, unless it is a confusion with the Euripus, on the other hand, might be an allusion to Aristotle's departure from Athens in the year 348 B.C., as well as to his sojourn with Hermias of Atarneus (348-47 to 345 B.C.), whose domain was located 'near' the Hellespont (actually near the island of Lesbos). Thus, our biographer seems to confuse (and combine) Aristotle's withdrawal to Atarneus (or Assos) in 348-47 B.C. with his flight from Athens to Chalcis in 323 B.C. See notes 26 and 62. *II VS* 3, again, might also refer to the following incident: in the summer of 348 B.C., King Philip took the city of Olynthus, which was allied with Athens. After this incident, which sparked a wave of anti-Macedonian resentment among the Athenians, Aristotle, the 'resident Macedonian alien,' no longer felt safe in Athens. In the heat of this widespread resentment, threats were probably uttered against Aristotle, the Macedonian. Fearing serious trouble—the 'fate of Socrates'—Aristotle departed from Athens taking refuge with Hermias in Atarneus 'near the Hellespont.' Should our interpretation of *II VS* 3 prove to be correct, then this unusual text would constitute the only known biographical reference stating what seems to be the true reason for Aristotle's rather sudden departure from Athens and precipitate journey to Atarneus (or Assos) in the year 348 B.C. In the year 323, it will be noted, this situation repeated itself. This time Aristotle fled to Chalcis, presumably because he had a house there, and because Euboea (as well as Chalcis) was philo-Macedonian. See A.-H. Chroust, 'Aristotle Leaves the Academy,' (see note 59) and Chapter IX; A.-H. Chroust, 'Aristotle's Flight from Athens in the Year 323 B.C.' (see note 83) and Chapter XII; A.-H. Chroust, 'Aristotle and Athens: some observations on Aristotle's sojourns in Athens,' *Laval Théologique et Philosophique*, vol. 22, no. 2 (1966), pp. 186-96, and Chapter XIII.

87 The following reports are almost an exact replica of the indictment and trial of Socrates in the year 399 B.C. It is not unlikely that some biographers transferred incidents which transpired in 399 to the 'indictment' of Aristotle in 323 B.C. This was done, for instance, by Eumelus. See DL V. 6.

88 Anytus, one of the prosecutors of Socrates, is also said to have been prompted by jealousy and an old grudge. This is the version found in

Plato's and Xenophon's *Apologies* of Socrates. Eusebius, *op. cit.*, XV. 2. 11, reports that Aristotle was envied by many, 'both for his friendship with kings and for his superiority in argument.'

89 Mubashir (*II VA* 20) also relates that Eurymedon denounced Aristotle as a person that 'should be shunned by everyone.'

90 See also *VM* 42; *VV* 20; *VL* 44.

91 This may be gathered from the fact that, according to Aristotle's last will and testament, he apparently was able (or permitted?) to remove all his considerable personal possessions from Athens to Chalcis. See also Eusebius, *op. cit.*, XV. 2. 8, quoting Lycon Pythagoraeus.

92 *VH* 10 (no. 189) cites among the spurious works of Aristotle an Ἀπολογία ἀσεβείας πρὸς Εὐρυμέδοντα. Athenaeus, *op. cit.*, XV. 697AB, remarks that Aristotle's *Defense Against the Charge of Impiety* might very well be a forgery. The charge of impiety brought against Aristotle in the year 323 B.C. might have been a mere 'token charge' in what was in fact a 'political trial.' This might also be derived from Usaibia (*IV VA* 20). See notes 82-3. Hence, it may be maintained that in 323 B.C. Aristotle was indicted because he was suspected of philo-Macedonian or anti-Athenian leanings. The suspicion that he was philo-Macedonian was certainly not without foundation in fact. Aristotle, it must be borne in mind, was a Macedonian 'resident alien' (*metic*) in Athens (see also *VM* 12; 42; *VL* 12)— he originally came from Macedonia—and apparently had retained his close connections with Macedonia and the Macedonian royal house as well as with Antipater. Presumably, the Syriac and Arabic biographers (and probably also Ptolemy) did not fully understand or appreciate the particular political situation which prevailed in Athens in the years 323-22 B.C.

93 Mubashir (*II VA* 21) and Usaibia (*IV VA* 8) refer here to Chalcidice, which is but a mispelling of, or confusion with, Chalcis. It might also indicate that Mubashir and Usaibia used the same (corrupted) source or, more likely, that Usaibia copied from Mubashir. See also *VM* 41; *VV* 19; *VL* 43.

94 Mubashir (or his source) might have had in mind the Περὶ τῆς τοῦ Νείλου ἀναβάσεως, a (spurious?) work which has been ascribed to Aristotle. See frags. 246-8, Rose; *VH* 10 (no. 159); Ptolemy, no. 25. Mubashir might also refer to Aristotle's (?) Περὶ τῆς Λίθου. See DL V. 26 (no. 125); *VH* 10 (no. 117).

95 An-Nadim also maintains that Aristotle died during the last days of Alexander. *I VA* 15. Alexander, however, died 13 June 323 B.C., while Aristotle died during the archonship of Philocles, that is after the early part of July, 322 B.C., and prior to the death of Demosthenes which occurred 14 October 322 B.C.

96 *I VS* 9 reports: 'It is said that a swarm of bees was found around the urn containing his [*scil.*, Aristotle's] ashes.' The bee was a symbol of the soul of a righteous and virtuous man. See Pophyry, *De Antro Nympharum* 19.

97 See also *VM* 17-18; *VV* 17; *VL* 17; 19.

98 Nicomachus was the illegitimate son of Aristotle and Herpyllis. It is

believed that he had been adopted or legitimized by Aristotle during the latter's lifetime. Herpyllis, who never became Aristotle's legitimate wife (see, however, Eusebius, *op. cit.*, XV. 2. 15), is not mentioned by the Syriac or Arabic biographers, except in Aristotle's last will and testament as it has been preserved by these biographers.

99 This daughter, whose name—Pythias—is not mentioned by the Syriac or Arabic biographers, is also referred to in Aristotle's last will and testament. She was the legitimate child of Aristotle and Pythias. Pythias, the mother, was the daughter (?), sister (?), or adopted niece of Hermias of Atarneus. She is not mentioned by the Syriac and Arabic biographers either. See also *VM* 44; *VL* 47.

100 This is borne out by Aristotle's last will and testament. See also *VM* 44; *VL* 47; Eusebius, *op. cit.*, XV. 2. 8–9.

101 This, too, is borne out by Aristotle's last will and testament.

102 This, too, is borne out by Aristotle's last will and testament.

103 For a comparison (and discussion) of the Arabic versions of Aristotle's last will and testament, and the version preserved by Diogenes Laertius V. 11–16 (Hermippus; Ariston of Ceos; Favorinus; Andronicus of Rhodes?), see A.-H. Chroust, 'A brief analysis of the *Vita Aristotelis* of Diogenes Laertius (DL V. 11–16),' *Antiquité Classique*, vol. 34, fasc. 1 (1965), pp. 126–9; A.-H. Chroust, 'Aristotle's last will and testament,' *Wiener Studien*, vol. 1, Neue Folge (1967), pp. 90–114, and Chapter XV.

104 Usaibia also contains a short survey of Aristotle's writings. This survey is based upon, or taken from, Ibn Said Al-Qordubi.

105 The number 'one hundred' is probably a mistranslation or misreading of the Greek χίλιοι (one thousand), which can be found in *VM* 45 and *VL* 48.

106 Like An-Nadim (*I VA* 18), Mubashir (*II VA* 35) actually recites only seven titles on 'physics.'

107 Mubashir (*II VA* 36) also mentions the 'public' and private letters of Aristotle. These 'public' letters might well contain the 'official reports' which Aristotle sent to Macedonia and to Antipater in particular. In his *Oration Against the Philosophers* of 306 B.C., Demochares implies that Aristotle 'conspired' with Macedonia against Athens. See DL V. 38; Athenaeus, *op. cit.*, XIII. 610EF; XI. 509B; Pollux IX. 42; Pseudo-Plutarch, *Vita Decem Oratorum (Moralia* 850B ff.); Eusebius, *op. cit.*, XV. 2. 6; XV. 2. 11. See also Chapter XIII.

108 A.-H. Chroust, 'A Brief Analysis of the *Vita Aristotelis* of Diogenes Laertius (DL V. 11–16),' pp. 97–129, and Chapter III.

109 See, however, Eumelus, in DL V. 6, and note 29.

110 This 'additional explanation' might have been derived from some Neo-Platonic commentator. See, for instance, Olympiodorus, *Prolegomena et in Categorias Comment.*, *CIAG*, vol. XII, part 1 (ed. A. Busse, Berlin, 1902), p. 5, lines 18 ff.

111 See, however, *VM* 20; *VL* 20.

112 In keeping with the general Neo-Platonic tradition, Ptolemy (-el-Garib)'s

Vita Aristotelis is essentially an encomium of Aristotle: under his pen the Stagirite becomes the 'divine Aristotle' who excels all other men, Plato excepted. In his determination to extol Aristotle and his many virtues, outstanding qualities and unrivalled excellence (Plato always excepted), Ptolemy somewhat one-sidedly seeks out materials which glorify and almost deify Aristotle, attributing to him nearly super-human faculties. Conversely, he deliberately suppresses, or tries to refute, all those stories and traditions which might possibly detract from the perfect image of his hero. Without the slightest hesitation or scruple, Ptolemy credits Aristotle with achievements, honors and distinctions which may actually belong to other historical personalities. In this fashion, Aristotle is turned into an inimitable idol worthy of being venerated by the whole of civilized mankind. See A.-H. Chroust (see note 1), and Chapter I, notes 102-3, and the corresponding text, and the last paragraph of Chapter I. This, then, is the primary model from which the Syriac and Arabic biographers derive most of their materials.

CHAPTER V   THE GENEALOGY AND FAMILY OF ARISTOTLE

* In a different and much shorter form, and under a different title, this chapter was first published in *Classical Folia*, vol. 19, no. 2 (1965), pp. 139-46.

1 Dionysius of Halicarnassus, *I Epistola ad Ammaeum* 5; DL V. 9; *VM* 10; *VL* 10. The *Chronicle* of Apollodorus, cited in Dionysius of Halicarnassus, *loc. cit.*, DL V. 9, *VM* 10 and *VL* 10, might ultimately go back to Philochorus, *Atthis*. See *Frag. Histor. Graec.* (Jacoby) 328, F. 233. See also Gellius, *Attic Nights* XVIII. 21. 25.

2 DH 5; DL V. 6; V. 10 (Apollodorus); *VM* 10; *VV* 30; *VL* 10; 45. According to *I VS* 8, Aristotle died at the age of 67; according to *II VS* 8, Mubashir (*II VA* 23), Al-Qifti (*III VA*), and Usaibia (*IV VA* 11), at the age of 68; according to An-Nadim (*I VA* 15), at the age of 66; and according to Eumelus (DL V. 6), who apparently confuses Aristotle with Socrates, at the age of 70. All these reports are in error. An-Nadim (*I VA* 15) also maintains that he died during the last days of Alexander, who died in 323 B.C. See also Chapter IV, note 95, and the corresponding text.

3 *I VA* 1; *II VA* 1; *III VA*; *IV VA* (introductory note, taken from Al-Masudi). All these 'translations' or interpretations of Aristotle's name indicate that the Arabic biographers or their more immediate sources did not know the Greek language, or that they took an adjective attached to Aristotle or a reference to his 'status' and standing for a translation of his name. See Chapter IV, note 8.

4 The geographic knowledge of the Syriac and Arabic biographers as to the exact location of Stagira is clearly erroneous. See also Chapter IV, note 15, and the corresponding text. Some of these biographers probably knew of Olynthus, Methone and Stagira through Thucydides V. 6 and V. 18. See

also Thucydides IV. 88. *I VS* 2, in fact, says: 'Olynthus is a locality mentioned by Thucydides in the fifth book, where he enumerates the allied cities.' *IV VA* 1 might have derived its information from *I VS* 2. Herodotus VII. 115 and Thucydides IV. 88; V. 6; V. 18, call the town Στάγιρος or Στάγειρος. We do not know when and why it was renamed Στάγιρα. DL V. 14 (the last will and testament of Aristotle), and V. 52 (the last will and testament of Theophrastus), refer to Στάγειρα. Eusebius, *Chronica* (p. 87, ed. A. Schöne), reports that Stagira was founded during the 31st Olympiad (656-52 B.C.). Thucydides IV. 88 calls it a colony of Andros, and DH 5 relates that colonists from Chalcis (on the island of Euboea) helped found Stagira. The border between Macedonia and Thrace, it has been pointed out previously, was gradually moved eastwards and hence was somewhat in flux. According to Hecataeus (*Frag. Histor. Graec.*, Jacoby I, F. 146), the river Axius seems to have been this border, according to Thucydides I. 61, the river Strymon, and according to Strabo, VII, frags. 33-5, the river Nestus. Only according to Hecataeus, would Stagira have been a Thracian town.

5 DL V. 1; *VH* 1; *VM* 1; *VV* 1; *VL* 1; *I VS* 1; 3; *II VS* 1; *I VA* 2; *II VA* 1; *III VA*; *IV VA* 2.

6 *IV VA* 1 (and *III VA*) refer to Nicomachus-el-Gerasi, an obvious confusion with Nicomachus of Gerasa, the Neo-Pythagorean philosopher (*floruit c.* 140 A.D.). See Chapter IV. The name Nicomachus might possibly have been derived from μάχομαι (to fight or combat—see Chapter IV, note 9) and νίκη (victory), and hence may mean 'conquering warrior.' Such a name would, for the early Greeks, befit a man who, as a physician, 'battles' and 'conquers' the evil forces which cause illness.

7 DL V. 1; *VH* 1; *VM* 1; *VV* 1; *VL* 1; *I VS* 3; *I VA* 1; *II VA* 2; *III VA*; *IV VA* 2. *IV VA* 2 also relates that 'Asclepius was the father of Machaon, and Machaon the father of another Asclepius [Nicomachus?].' This second Asclepius (Nicomachus?) was the father of Nicomachus, the remote ancestor of Aristotle. Needless to say, this particular 'genealogy' is quite confusing, not to say nonsensical. See Chapter III, note 12; Chapter IV, notes 11-12, and the corresponding observations in the text following Chapter III, note 9. The epitomizers of Ptolemy's *Vita* (or the Syriac or Arabic translators of an epitome of Ptolemy's *Vita*) simply botched the genealogy of Aristotle, as did Diogenes Laertius (DL V. 1). We may assume that the earliest biographers of Aristotle (Hermippus and Ariston of Ceos) related that Nicomachus, the father of Aristotle, ultimately descended from Machaon, the son of Asclepius, and from Nicomachus, the son of Machaon (through some other Nicomachi).

8 Pausanias IV. 3. 1-2; IV. 3. 9-10; IV. 30. 3.

9 *Frag. Histor. Graec.* (Jacoby) 265, F. 38-46, and Jacoby's remarks found on p. 121.

10 DL V. 1; *VH* 1; *VM* 2; *VV* 1; *VL* 2; *I VS* 1; *II VS* 1; *I VA* 3; *II VA* 2; *III VA*; *IV VA* 2. The report found in *I VA* 3 that Nicomachus was the

personal physician of King Philip of Macedonia might be a mistake in name. Nicomachus was dead at the time Philip became king. It might be possible, however, that at one time Nicomachus attended Philip while the latter was still a child or young man. With some interruptions, Amyntas III reigned from *c.* 392 or 390 to 370–69 B.C. See Diodorus Siculus XIV. 92; XV. 19; XV. 60; XX. 78; Xenophon, *Hellenica* V. 2–3; Aelian, *Varia Historia* IV. 8; XII. 43; Isocrates, *Panegyricus* 126. Amyntas had three sons, Alexander II (who was murdered by Ptolemy of Alorus in 369–68 B.C.), Perdiccas III (the addressee of Pseudo-Plato, *Fifth Epistle*—see also Athenaeus, *Deipnosophistae* XI. 508DE), who ruled from 365 to 359 B.C., and Philip (359 or 356 to 336 B.C.).

11 Suda, 'article' Nicomachus. We have no means, however, of checking the report of Suda. More likely than not this information is incorrect.

12 Thucydides IV. 88. See also Strabo VIII frag. 35; and note 4.

13 *VM* 3; *VV* 2; *VL* 3; *IV VA* 3. *VM* 3 *VV* 2 and *VL* 3 also mention that by the year 367 B.C. Aristotle was 'orphaned.'

14 *II VA* 3.

15 DH 5; DL V. 1; *VM* 1; *VV* 1; *VL* 1; *II VA* 2; *IV VA* 1. *VH* 1 and *I VA* 3 call her Phaestias and *I VS* 3 calls her Parysatis. Phaestis is again mentioned in Aristotle's last will and testament (though not by name). DL V. 16.

16 *I VA* 3 relates that Phaestis (at times spelled Thestis) descended from Asclepiades—a scribal error or more likely a *gens* designation. Any descendant of Asclepius was an Asclepiade.

17 *VM* 1; *VV* 1; *VL* 1; *I VS* 3; *I VA* 3; *II VA* 2; *IV VA* 2. See also note 7. O. Gigon, *Vita Aristotelis Marciana: Kleine Texte für Vorlesungen und Übungen* (Berlin, 1962), p. 25, denies that the epigram in *VM* 1 (also in *VV* 1 and *VL* 1) establishes that both parents of Aristotle descended from Asclepius. The attribute δῖος in the epigram might possibly suggest that this epigram is of fairly late (Neo-Platonic?) origin.

18 DH 5: '[Aristotle's] mother, Phaestis, descended from one of the colonists who led the [Greek] settlers from Chalcis to Stagira.' *Frag. Hist. Graec.* (Jacoby), F. 423, mentions an historian, Aristotle of Chalcis, who might have been a remote relative of our Aristotle. Diogenes Laertius (V. 36) mentions seven additional men who were named Aristotle.

19 In his last will and testament, Aristotle provided that Herpyllis, 'if she should choose to remain in Chalcis, shall have the lodge by the house' (DL V. 14), a provision which can also be found in the Arabic versions of Aristotle's will. See A.-H. Chroust, 'Aristotle's last will and testament, *Wiener Studien*, vol. 80 (vol. I, Neue Folge, 1967), pp. 90–114; A.-H. Chroust, 'Estate planning in Hellenic antiquity: Aristotle's last will and testament,' *Notre Dame Lawyer*, vol. 45, no. 4 (1970), pp. 629–62; Chapter XV, notes 108–12. It will remembered that Aristotle died in 322 B.C. in his mother's house in Chalcis, and that he had retired to Chalcis in 323 B.C., probably because he had this house (and because Euboea and Chalcis at the time were philo-Macedonian).

20 *VM* 3; *VV* 2; *VL* 3; see also note 13.

21 DL V. 16. Pliny, *Hist. Nat.* XXXV. 10. 106, mentions a 'likeness' of Phaestis made by Protogenes. It is impossible to determine whether this 'likeness' is identical with the 'statue' mentioned in Aristotle's last will and testament.

22 This should dispel the widespread but wholly erroneous notion that Aristotle was of 'barbarian' descent. See, for instance, Epiphanius, *De Graec. Sectis Exc.* 31, in H. Diels, *Doxographi Graeci* (Berlin, 1879), p. 592. Equally erroneous is the notion that he was 'half-Greek.' Aristotle's lost (early) composition, *On Noble Birth* (see Vol. II, Chapter II), perhaps contained a 'biographical' or 'genealogical' sketch of his family and descent.

23 *VH* 2; *VM* 2; *VL* 2. See also DL V. 15.

24 DL V. 15–16.

25 See note 33.

26 Judging from Aristotle's last will and testament, Arimneste died before 323–32 n.c. See DL V. 15.

27 See Plutarch, *Alexander* 55. *Ibid.*, 52, Plutarch calls Callisthenes a 'relative' of Aristotle, as does Ammianus Marcellinus XVIII. 3. 7, and DL V. 4.

28 See here also DL V. 53; V. 55; V. 56; A.-H. Chroust, 'Aristotle and Callisthenes of Olynthus,' *Classical Folia*, vol. 20, no. 1 (1966), pp. 32–44; and Chapter VI, at the beginning.

29 See Diodorus Siculus IV. 1. 2 ff.

30 See DL V. 53; Chapter XV, notes 47, 91 and 93, and the corresponding text.

31 DL V. 15.

32 DL V. 11–16, and the corresponding provisions in the Arabic versions of Aristotle's last will and testament. See note 37.

33 *VM* 3; *VV* 2; *VL* 3; *IV VA* 3. This incident might have taken place *c.* 370–369 B.C., or shortly thereafter.

34 *VM* 3; *VV* 2; *VL* 3. This might also explain Aristotle's later connections with Hermias of Atarneus. It cannot be proven, however, that Proxenus actually came from Atarneus.

35 *IV VA* 3 relates that 'Proxenus and Plato were friends,' and that on account of this friendship, Proxenus 'handed over the young Aristotle to Plato' (in 367 B.C.). See also *VM* 5; *VV* 4; *VL* 5. Proxenus might have visited Athens before 370 B.C. He also might have been a friend of Hermias of Atarneus. This, then, would explain Aristotle's subsequent friendship with Hermias of Atarneus. We are unable to verify whether Proxenus was indeed a friend of Plato (or Hermias).

36 Sextus Empiricus, *Adversus Mathematicos* I. 258, calls Proxenus (and his son by Arimneste, Nicanor) 'a Stagirite,' and 'a relative (by blood?) of Aristotle.'

37 DL V. 11–16. A translation of the Arabic version of Aristotle's last will, which is incomplete and which differs somewhat from the version pre-

served by Diogenes Laertius, can be found in I. Düring, *Aristotle in the Ancient Biographical Tradition* (Göteborg, 1957), pp. 219–20, 238–40. See also A.-H. Chroust (see note 19), and Chapter XV; A.-H. Chroust, 'A brief analysis of the *Vita Aristotelis* of Diogenes Laertius (DL V. 1–16),' *Antiquité Classique*, vol. 34, fasc. 1 (1965), pp. 126–9.

38 DL V. 11–12.

39 The Arabic biographers (An-Nadim, Al-Qifti and Usaibia, or their source) apparently did not understand this particular passage. Hence they rendered it as follows: 'When my daughter [Pythias] shall be grown up, Nicanor shall administer her affairs.'

40 *VM* 5; *VV* 4; *VL* 5; *IV VA* 3. See also note 35.

41 This might be inferred from Aristotle's last will and testament, especially, from the provision that the 'image' or bust of Proxenus by Grylion (or Gryllion), which Aristotle had ordered to be executed, should be set up in the honored memory of Proxenus. It is very doubtful, however, that Proxenus ever adopted Aristotle.

42 *VM* 3; *VV* 2; *VL* 3.

43 DL V. 15. See also note 31.

44 For the Arabic version of this provision, see note 39.

45 This boy Myrmex cannot be identified. In his last will and testament Aristotle stipulates that Myrmex shall 'be taken back to his own people . . . together with the property of his which we have received.' DL V. 14. See Chapter XV, notes 133–5, and the corresponding text.

46 See Chapter XV, notes 19–20, *et passim*, and the corresponding text.

47 For this whole paragraph, see the corresponding passages in Chapter XV, *passim*.

48 W. Dittenberger, *Syll. Inscript. Graec.*[3], p. 275; *Frag. Histor. Graec.* (Jacoby) 124, T. 23.

49 See Chapter XV, note 37, and the corresponding text.

50 See *VM* 3; *VV* 2; *VL* 3.

51 DL V. 3; *VH* 2; *VM* 3; *VV* 2; *VL* 3. Pythias, the wife of Aristotle and the mother of his daughter (Pythias) and only legitimate child, is difficult to identify. According to DL V. 3, Pythias was the daughter of Hermias' brother, and had been adopted by Hermias who is said to have been a eunuch; according to *VH* 2, she was Hermias' natural (illegitimate) child, although Hermias was a eunuch; according to the author (Aristippus?) of the *Aristippus or On the Luxury of the Ancients* (DL V. 3), she was Hermias' concubine; according to Demetrius of Magnesia (DL V. 3) and Strabo XIII. 1. 57, she was the daughter of Hermias' brother; according to Aristocles or Apellicon (Eusebius, *Praeparatio Evangelica* XV. 2. 14), she was the sister of Hermias; and according to Aristocles (Eusebius, *op. cit.*, XV. 2. 12), she was a sister of Hermias who subsequently adopted her as his daughter. See also Chapter III, notes 93–7, 122 and 126, and the corresponding text.

52 DL V. 3–4.

53 Eusebius, *op. cit.*, XV. 2. 14.

54 *Ibid.*, XV. 2. 8; DL V. 4. Lycon Pythagoraeus (Eusebius, *loc. cit.*) claims that he did this after the death of Pythias. The author (Aristippus?) of *Aristippus or On the Luxury of the Ancients* (see note 51) insists that he did so while Pythias was still alive.

55 DL V. 12–13; V. 15, and the corresponding passages in the Arabic version of Aristotle's last will and testament. See also *VM* 3; *VV* 2; *VL* 3; Pliny, *Hist. Nat.* XXIX. 1; Sextus Empiricus, *Adversus Mathematicos* I. 258.

56 Athenaeus, *op. cit.*, XIII. 589C. See also DL V. 1; Timaeus, *Frag. Histor. Graec.* (Jacoby) 566, F. 157. It may be presumed that Herpyllis was considerably younger than Aristotle. This might be inferred from a passage in Aristotle's last will and testament (DL V. 13), where the testator stipulates that 'if she [Herpyllis] desires to be married, they [*scil.*, the trustees] shall see to it that she is given in marriage to a man not unworthy of us.' The corresponding Arabic version states that in this case 'she should be given in marriage to a man of good repute.' This provision is also an indication of the high esteem in which Herpyllis was held by Aristotle.

57 Eusebius, *op .cit.*, XV. 2. 15.

58 The Arabic version of Aristotle's last will and testament (see Chapter XV, note 49) expressly refers to Herpyllis as Aristotle's 'handmaid' or 'maid-servant.' This remark is not to be found in the version preserved by Diogenes Laertius. Eusebius, *op. cit.*, XV. 2. 15, claims, however, that Aristotle 'married Herpyllis of Stagira.'

59 DL V. 13–14. See also the corresponding passages in the Arabic version of Aristotle's will. See note 58.

60 DL V. 1; V. 12; V. 39; V. 52; VIII. 88; Eusebius, *op. cit.*, XV. 2. 15; *VH* 4; *VM* 2; 44; *VV* 2; *VL* 2; 47.

61 DL V. 12–13; V. 15, and the corresponding passages in the Arabic version of Aristotle's last will and testament. See also *VH* 2; *VM* 3; *VV* 2; *VL* 3.

62 Sextus Empiricus, *Adversus Mathematicos* I. 258. Nicanor, who is also mentioned by Dinarchus, Diodorus Siculus, Hypereides and others, was honored by Ephesus for certain meritorious services he had rendered that city. See note 48. In 324 B.C. he was charged by Alexander with announcing in Olympia to the assembled Greeks that the king had pardoned all the political exiles (and that Alexander demanded divine honors). In 319–18 B.C., as one of Cassander's lieutenants, he became the military commander of Munichia, and late in 318 B.C. he defeated Polyperchon in a naval battle. For further detail, see H. Berve, 'Nicanor,' Pauly-Wissowa, *Realencyclopädie der classischen Altertumswissenschaft*, Halbband 33 (Stuttgart, 1936), pp. 267–9.

63 Procles (or Procleus) was a descendant of the ill-famed Spartan king, Demaratus. See Xenophon, *Hellenica* III. 1. 6; Xenophon, *Anabasis* II. 1. 3; VIII. 8. 17. Demaratus, the son of Procles and Pythias, is also mentioned in the will of Theophrastus where he is refered to as one of the members of the Peripatetic community. See DL V. 53.

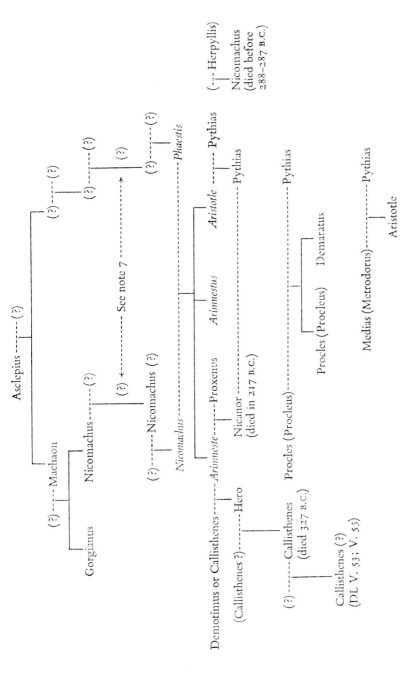

64 See DL VII. 186.

65 See DL V. 53.

66 See Chapter XV, notes 114–29, and the corresponding text.

67 *II VA* 33; *IV VA* 35.

68 DL V. 38–9.

69 See *Gnomologium Vaticanum* (Cod. Vat. Graec. 743), no. 330, p. 130 (ed. L. Sternbach, Berlin, 1963).

70 Eusebius, *op. cit.*, XV. 2. 15.

71 Some scholars are of the opinion that this Nicomachus was a never-do-well. See *Gnomologium Vaticanum* (see note 69). They base their view on the following facts: when Epicurus, the bitter and relentless antagonist of Aristotle, and the Epicureans in general, attacked and denounced Aristotle, claiming that in his youth the latter had lived a profligate life, squandering his patrimony, practicing medical quackery and trying his hand at soldiering (see Eusebius, *op. cit.*, XV. 2.1.; Athenaeus *Deipnosophistae* VIII. 354C; Philodemus, *De Rhetorica: Volumina Rhetorica*, vol. II, ed. S. Sudhaus, Leipzig, 1896, col. 49, 37, p. 52), they actually had in mind Nicomachus (or perhaps Aristotle, the grandson of the Stagirite and the son of Pythias and Medias, the third husband of Pythias). See also S. Sudhaus, 'Aristoteles in der Beurteilung des Epikur und Philodemos,' *Rheinisches Museum*, vol. 48 (1893), pp. 552 ff.; S. Sudhaus, 'Noch Einmal Nausiphanes und Aristoteles bei Philodemos,' *Philologus*, vol. 54 (1895), pp. 80 ff.; E. Bignone, *L'Aristotele Perduto a la Formazione Filosofica di Epicuro*, vol. II (Florence, 1936), pp. 89 ff.

72 DL V. 52.

73 The geneaology (and the immediate family) of Aristotle is probably as shown on page 329.

CHAPTER VI   ARISTOTLE AND CALLISTHENES OF OLYNTHUS

* In a different form, this chapter was first published in *Classical Folia*, vol. 20, no. 1 (1966), pp. 32–41.

1 See, in general, DL V. 4; Suda, 'article' *Callisthenes*; Plutarch, *Alexander* 52 ff.; Arrian, IV. 10. 1 ff.; Philostratus, *Vita Apollonii* VII. 2; Plutarch, *Sulla* 26; Plutarch, *De Repugnantiis Stoicis* 20 (*Moralia* 1043D), and the several references to Callisthenes in the notes to this Chapter, as well as in some ancient historians of Alexander the Great.

2 Diodorus Siculus IV. 3. 1., calls Callisthenes a contemporary of Theopompus and Ephorus. Since the exact dates of these two men are unknown, this reference does not assist us in establishing the exact date of Callisthenes' birth.

3 Hero could not have been the daughter of Arimnestus, Aristotle's (younger?) brother, who died without issue. See DL V. 15: 'They [*scil.*, the executors] shall set up the bust which had been executed of Arimnestus, to be a memorial to him, seeing that he died childless.' See also A.-H.

Chroust, 'The genealogy of Aristotle,' *Classical Folia*, vol. 19, no. 2 (1966), pp. 139-46, and Chapter V, note 24. Arimneste apparently married first Demotimus or, more likely, Callisthenes, by whom she had a daughter, Hero. Hero, in turn, became the mother of Callisthenes, the historian.

4 DL V. 53; V. 55; V. 56. It might also be possible that Callisthenes was the grandfather and Demotimus the father of our Callisthenes (the historian).

5 DL V. 53; V. 55; V. 56.

6 Our Callisthenes died in the spring of 327 B.C. (see this Chapter), while Theophrastus died in *c.* 287-86 B.C. Callisthenes and Theophrastus, who might have been remote (?) relatives (*I VA* 16 calls Theophrastus the son of Aristotle's sister (Arimneste?), and *II VA* 32 as well as *IV VA* 34 refer to him as a 'second cousin' of Aristotle), were born about the same time, that is, *c.* 370 B.C., or shortly thereafter, although Theophrastus outlived Callisthenes by approximately forty years. See Chapter V.

7 See Chapter V, notes 25-9, and this chapter, note 3. After the death of Demotimus (or Callisthenes), Arimneste married Proxenus, by whom she had a son, Nicanor, who became the first husband of Aristotle's daughter, Pythias. See Chapter XV, *passim*.

8 See *VM* 3; *VV* 2; *VL* 3; Plutarch, *Alexander* 55; Suda, 'article' *Callisthenes*; Valerius Maximus VII. 2. ext. 11; Ammianus Marcellinus XVIII. 3. 7; Arrian IV. 10. 1.

9 See Chapter V, note 42.

10 See Justinus, *Epitome Trogi* XII. 6. 17. See also note 24.

11 DL V. 39; Cicero, *Tuscul. Disput.* III. 9. 21.

12 DL IV. 6.

13 See note 11.

14 The influence of Aristotle's teachings and writings on Callisthenes might be detected in the following: Anonymous, *Comment. in Arist. Ethica Nicom.*, *CIAG*, vol. XX (ed. G. Heylbut, Berlin, 1892), p. 189, lines 13 ff., reports that, according to Callisthenes, the Spartans were seeking the friendship of the Athenians. In order to accomplish this, they emphasized Athens' many past services to Sparta. This passage might well be a reference to what Callisthenes had said in his *Hellenica*, where he probably quoted Thucydides II. 40. 2: '[The Athenians] make friends by giving favors, not by receiving them.' Aristotle, who elaborates on this passage (*Nicomachean Ethics* 1124 b 9 ff.), might have been Callisthenes' more immediate source. Another fragment of Callisthenes (frag. 44, Jacoby) likewise seems to indicate that the latter shared Aristotle's opinion concerning the moral, political and literary significance of Thucydides' speeches. See, for instance, Aristotle, *Poetics* 1450 b 5-12.

15 DL V. 44: *Callisthenes or On Bereavement*. This work was composed to commemorate and deplore the cruel fate of Callisthenes. See also Cicero, *Tuscul. Disput.* III. 9. 21; V. 9. 25; and note 60.

16 See note 6.

17 For the date of Aristotle's departure from Athens in 348 B.C., see A.-H.

Chroust, 'Aristotle leaves the Academy,' *Greece and Rome*, vol. 14, no. 1 (1967), pp. 39-43, and Chapter IX.

18 Areius Didymus, *In Demosthenis Orationes Commenta*, col. 5, 64 ff., *Berliner Klassikertexte*, vol. I (ed. H. Diels and W. Schubart, Berlin, 1904), pp. 23 ff.; W. Crönert, 'Neue Lesungen des Didymuspapyrus,' *Rheinisches Museum*, vol. 62 (1907), pp. 380-9; P. Foucart, 'Étude sur Didymos d'après un Papyrus de Berlin,' *Mémoires de l'Académie des Inscriptions et Belles Lettres*, vol. 58, no. 1 (Paris, 1906); J. Bidez, 'Hermias d'Atarnée,' *Académie Royale Belgique: Bulletin de la Classe des Lettres*, series 5, vol. 29 (1943), pp. 33-146; D. E. W. Wormell, 'The literary tradition concerning Hermias of Atarneus,' *Yale Classical Studies*, vol. V (1935), pp. 57-62. This encomium must have been composed after Hermias' death in 341-40 B.C., and after Aristotle and Callisthenes had moved to Macedonia. It suggests that Callisthenes had befriended Hermias, probably through Aristotle (or perhaps through Proxenus?). We cannot ascertain, however, whether this encomium was also intended to be a rebuttal of Theopompus, who in Book 46 of his *Philippica* violently attacked and maligned Hermias. See also Areius Didymus, *op. cit.*, col. 5, 21 ff. Like Theocritus of Chios, Theopompus, the Chian, loathed Hermias because the latter had interfered in the political affairs of Chios; and he disliked Aristotle because he was a close friend of Hermias. See Chapter III, notes 102-5, and the corresponding text.

19 Athenaeus, *Deipnosophistae* XIII. 560BC; Cicero, *Ad Familiares* V. 12. 2.

20 DL V. 26 (no. 131); *VH* 10 (no. 123). Hesychius also relates that the *List* compiled by Aristotle and Callisthenes surpassed (or superseded) the list made up by Menaechmus. The fact that Callisthenes assisted Aristotle in compiling this *List* is borne out by an honorific inscription at Delphi. See W. Dittenberger, *Syll. Inscript. Graec.*[3] 275. The stone mason's bill for cutting a tablet of the *List of Victors at the Pythian Games* has been preserved. It has been estimated that this tablet contained about 60,000 words, and that its completion must have taken several years. The bill bears the date of Caphis, the Delphic archon of the year 327-26 B.C. See D. M. Lewis, 'An Aristotle publication-date,' *Classical Review*, vol. 72 (1958), p. 108. It is also possible that Callisthenes assisted Aristotle in compiling the *List of Olympic Victors* (see DL V. 26, no. 130; *VH* 10, no. 122; *Papyr. Oxyrh.* 222, col. I, 41) and perhaps *The Constitutions of 158 Cities* (see DL V. 27, no. 143; *VH* 10, no. 135; Ptolemy, no. 86).

21 Plutarch, *Alexander* 52; Justinus, *Epitome Trogi* XII. 6. 17; XV. 3. 3.

22 Plutarch, *Alexander* 55; Athenaeus, *op. cit.*, X. 434D (Lynceus).

23 Diodorus Siculus IV. 1. 3; XIV. 117. 8; Pliny, *Hist. Nat.* XXXVI. 36. See also some of the historians of Alexander the Great.

24 DL V. 4; Suda, 'article' Callisthenes; Justinus, *Epitome Trogi* XII. 6. 17; Ammianus Marcellinus XVIII. 3. 7; Arrian IV. 10. 1; Valerius Maximus VII. 2, ext. 11; Curtius Rufus VIII. 8. 22; Themistius, *Oratio* VII. 94A (p. 112, Dindorf) X. 130A (p. 155); *II VA* 19; *IV VA* 6: Plutarch, *Alexander* 55.

25 *VM* 16; *VV* 16; *VL* 16.

26 See note 8.

27 See, in general, T. S. Brown, 'Callisthenes and Alexander,' *American Journal of Philology*, vol. 70 (1949), pp. 225–48.

28 *II VA* 19; *IV VA* 6. DL V. 10 relates that Aristotle incurred Alexander's displeasure 'because he had introduced Callisthenes to him.' See also Plutarch, *Alexander* 55.

29 Plutarch, *Alexander* 53; Plutarch, *De Repugnantiis Stoicis* 20 (*Moralia* 1043D). This might be a 'duplication' (or transfer) of the story that Aristotle had persuaded King Philip (or Alexander) to rebuild Stagira. See DL V. 4; *VM* 17; *VV* 17; *VL* 17; *II VA* 27; *IV VA* 25; Pliny, *Hist. Nat.* VII. 109; Plutarch, *Ne Suaviter Quidem Vivi Posse Secundum Epicurum* 15 (*Moralia* 1097B); Dio Chrysostom, *Oratio* II. 79; Dio Chrysostom, *Oratio* XLVII. 8 (frag. 657, Rose); Aelian, *Varia Historia* III. 17; XII. 54; Diodorus Siculus XVI. 52. 9; Valerius Maximus V. 6. 5; Plutarch, *Adversus Coloten* 33 (*Moralia* 1126E).

30 Arrian IV. 10. 2.

31 See Simplicius, *Comment. in Arist. De Caelo*, *CIAG*, vol. VII (ed. J. Heiberg, Berlin, 1894), p. 506, line 11. Pliny, *Nat. Hist.*, books XII and XIII, which are said to be based on Callisthenes' 'scientific reports,' and Epiphanius, *Adversus Haereses* I. 1. 3 (Migne, *Patrol. Graec.*, vol. CXL, p. 177), seem to imply that Callisthenes was a 'botanist.'

32 DL V. 5.

33 Homer, *Iliad* XVIII. 95. See also Valerius Maximus VII. 2. 11.

34 Plutarch, *Alexander* 54.

35 See also Ioannes Lydus, *Liber de Mensibus* (ed. R. Wuensch, 1898) IV. 77.

36 Arrian IV. 10. 1.

37 Ammianus Marcellinus XVIII. 3. 7.

38 About the manner in which Callisthenes was put to death by Alexander and the circumstances which led to this incident, see Chapter III, notes 162–75, and the corresponding text.

39 Plutarch, *Alexander* 55. See also the many accounts of the relationship of Aristotle to Alexander contained in the extant *Vitae Aristotelis*, or reported by a host of ancient authors and historians.

40 Plutarch, *Alexander* 55. Seneca, *Suas.* I. 5, maintains, though probably erroneously, that at one time Callisthenes was the teacher of Alexander. According to Arrian VII. 27. 7, after the foul murder of Callisthenes, Aristotle was afraid of Alexander.

41 DL V. 10.

42 This man is also credited with having authored the *Rhetorica ad Alexandrum* which subsequently was attributed to Aristotle. See Plutarch, *Alexander* 8.

43 It has already been shown that although Aristotle was 'the most genuine disciple of Plato' (DL V. 1), he was passed over at the election (or appointment) of the new scholarch of the Academy after the death of Speusippus in 339–38 B.C. See DL V. 2. See also DL V. 3, where we are told that, in a

'spirit of rivalry' and defiance, Aristotle remarked that 'it would be a shameful thing to keep silent and let Xenocrates speak out.' See Quintilian, *Institutio Oratoria* III. 1. 14; Cicero, *De Oratore* III. 35. 141; Philodemus, *De Rhetorica*, vol. II, p. 50 (ed. S. Sudhaus), col. 48, 36; Syrianus, *Scholia in Hermogenem*, vol. II, col. 59, 21 ff. (ed. H. Rabe). See also Chapter III, notes 72–3, and the corresponding text.

44 Plutarch, *Alexander* 77; Dio Cassius LXXVII. 7. 3; Pliny, *Hist. Nat.* XXX. 53. 149; Zonaras, *Annales* IV. 14 (Migne, vol. CXXXIV, p. 356); Diodorus Siculus XVII. 118; Curtius Rufus X. 10; Arrian VII. 27. 7.

45 Arrian VII. 27. 7.

46 See note 40. Dio Chrysostom, *Oratio* LXIV. 20, claims that Alexander 'planned to murder Aristotle.' See also Arrian VII. 27.7.

47 See R. Merkelbach, *Die Quellen des Griechischen Alexander-Romans* (Zetemata, vol. IX, Munich, 1954), pp. 126 ff.; W. Tarn, *Alexander the Great*, vol. II (Cambridge, 1948), pp. 301 ff.

48 Plutarch, *Alexander* 77.

49 See also M. Plezia, 'Arystoteles trucicielem Aleksandra Wielkiego (Aristotle as the poisoner of Alexander the Great),' *Meander*, vol. III (1948), pp. 492–501.

50 See R. Merkelbach (see note 47).

51 See, for instance, Timaeus, a dedicated detractor of Aristotle. Polybius XII. 12B, relates that Timaeus 'calls Callisthenes a flatterer ... very far from being a philosopher ... adding that Alexander was quite right in punishing him, as he had corrupted his [*scil.*, Alexander's] mind as far as he could.'

52 See, for instance, Dio Chrysostom (see note 46). We do not know from what particular source or sources Dio Chrysostom derived this information.

53 See, for instance, Plutarch, *De Cohibenda Ira* 9 (*Moralia* 458B); Seneca, *Natur. Quaestiones* VI. 23. 2; Themistius, *Oratio* VII (p. 112, ed. L. Dindorf), and *Oratio* XIII (p. 215, ed. L. Dindorf); Curtius Rufus VIII. 8. 22; Valerius Maximus IX. 3, ext. 1. But there are also those who insist that Callisthenes received his well-earned deserts. See note 51.

54 Curtius Rufus VIII. 8. 22. See also Seneca, *Natur. Quaest.* VI. 23.2: 'The immortal crime of Alexander can never be expiated by either virtue or military achievements.' Cicero, *De Officiis* I. 26, contains what appears to be a reference to Alexander's turpitude.

55 See Philodemus, *Papyr. Hercul.* 1674 (*Vol. Hercul. Coll. Alt.* I. 1–15); Timaeus, cited in note 51. Both Philodemus and Timaeus were outspokenly hostile to Aristotle.

56 Arrian IV. 12. 7. See also *ibid.*, IV. 14. 1: 'Aristobulus indeed declares that they [*scil.*, the conspirators] said that it was Callisthenes who had urged them to the plot; and Ptolemy agrees. But most authorities do not say so, but only that by reason of Alexander's dislike for Callisthenes ... [the king] easily believed the worst story about Callisthenes.' Curtius Rufus VIII. 6. 1: 'Against Callisthenes, who had previously been suspected of

insubordination, his [*scil.*, Alexander's] wrath was more persistent.'
Plutarch, *Alexander* 55, for instance, denies that Callisthenes was involved
in Hermolaus' conspiracy to murder Alexander.

57 *II VA* 19; *IV VA* 6. DL V. 5, on the other hand, makes a short reference to
the murder of Callisthenes. See Chapter III, notes 155 ff., and the corresponding text.

58 Plutarch, *Alexander* 54.

59 See notes 32–5 and the corresponding text.

60 DL V. 44.

61 Cicero, *Tuscul. Disput.* III. 21; V. 25. See also note 60. Of Theophrastus'
Callisthenes or On Bereavement only a few fragments survive. See Cicero,
loc. cit.; Cicero, *Ad Atticum* XIII. 28.

62 See here also Tatian, *Oratio adversus Graecos* 2 (Migne, vol. VI. p. 808).
Tatian refers to the fact that, although Aristotle had taught Alexander
moderation and magnanimity, the latter ignored these teachings when
dealing with Callisthenes.

63 See, for instance, Cicero, *Tuscul. Disput.* V. 25. It is also held that Plutarch,
De Fortuna (*Moralia* 97C–100), was directed against Theophrastus' *Callis-
thenes*. See F. Dümmler, *Akademika* (Giessen, 1889), p. 206. Other ancient
authors who discussed the problem of chance and fortune in connection
with Theophrastus' *Callisthenes* were Demetrius of Phaleron (see Polybius
XXIX. 21), Ariston of Chios (see Cicero, *Tuscul. Disput.* V. 27), the
Stoics and Epicurus. See E. Bignone, *L'Aristotele Perduto e la Formazione
Filosofica di Epicuro*, vol. II (Florence, 1936), pp. 441 ff.

64 See J. Stroux, 'Die stoische Beurteilung Alexander des Grossen,' *Philologus*, vol. 88 (1933), pp. 222–40. See also Chapter X; Ph. Merlan, 'Isocrates, Aristotle and Alexander the Great,' *Historia*, vol. III (1954), pp. 60–1.

65 See Athenaeus, *op. cit.*, X. 435A.

66 *Ibid.*, X. 443F.

67 *Ibid.*, XIII. 603AB.

68 C. A. Robinson, 'The extraordinary ideas of Alexander the Great,'
American Historical Review, vol. 62 (1956–7), pp. 340–1, attempts to explain
Alexander's barbaric treatment of Callisthenes in the following manner:
For some time there had developed among the generals of Alexander a
growing opposition to the king. By resorting to drastic actions—to a sort
of *Politik der Schrecklichkeit*—and by abandoning the comradely deportment which he had previously displayed towards his generals and personal
advisers, Alexander hoped to put an end to all plots or dissents which might
threaten not only his plans, but also his life.

69 See, in general, T. S. Brown (see note 27), *passim.*

70 Arrian IV. 10. 2. See note 30.

71 See, for instance, Himerius, *Oratio* VI. 6. See also Chapter III, note 88.

72 Subsequently, the Stoics roundly condemned and denounced Alexander
for his 'glaring defects of character.' Undoubtedly, Alexander's cruel
treatment of Callisthenes contributed heavily to the Stoic dislike of

Alexander. See J. Stroux (see note 64), *passim*. In view of the 'cosmopolitan achievements' of Alexander, who attempted to bring together East and West, one might have expected that the Stoics, who in their philosophy entertained 'cosmopolitan' and 'pan-humanitarian' notions, would have considered Alexander their 'hero.'

73 See notes 44–6. The fact that after 327 B.C. Aristotle escaped the vindictiveness of Alexander (see note 40) may be explained as follows: due to the intrigues of Olympias, the mother of Alexander, Antipater, Alexander's lieutenant in Europe, came to be suspected of treason and conspiracy against the Macedonian king. (In 323 B.C. Antipater was summoned to Persia by Alexander who no longer trusted him.) Under the circumstances it is quite reasonable to assume that Antipater should refuse to take any drastic action against Aristotle. After all, Aristotle supposedly concocted for Antipater the poison with which the latter is said to have killed Alexander. See Arrian VII. 27. 7; and see note 45.

74. For some interesting observations on our subject, see also Ph. Merlan (see note 64), pp. 60–81.

CHAPTER VII   ARISTOTLE ENTERS THE ACADEMY

* In a different form, this chapter was first published in *Classical Folia*, vol. 19, no. 1 (1965), pp. 21–9.

1 *VM* 4; *VV* 3; *VL* 4. Diogenes Laertius, who derived his information mainly from Hermippus, does not refer to Aristotle's early education. Neither does the *Vita Aristotelis Hesychii*. Conversely, some of Aristotle's detractors claim that in his youth Aristotle was an uncouth and dissipated person. See notes 8, 10, and 11.

2 Some ancient authors or biographers display a marked interest in the early education of certain famous men. See, for instance, Plutarch, *Pericles* 2–4; Aristoxenus, frag. 66, Wehrli; Xenophon, *Cyropaedia, passim*.

3 *II VA* 3–4.

4 DL V. 31 refers to ἐγκύκλια μαθήματα. In *Politics* 1338 b 2 ff., Aristotle stresses the need for a 'well-rounded liberal education' which he calls an indispensable prerequisite for all 'higher studies' (philosophy). Al-Mubashir or his source apparently knew of Epicurus' efforts to ridicule this 'well-rounded liberal education.' See, for instance, Epicurus, frag. 117, Usener. Al-Mubashir insisted that Aristotle energetically and, it seems, successfully defended the need for such an education. See *II VA* 5–6. What escaped Al-Mubashir, however, was that Aristotle's defense was probably directed against Isocrates (and certainly not against Epicurus) or, perhaps, against Cephisodorus. See Eusebius, *op. cit.* XIV. 6. 9; Athenaeus, *Deipnosophistae* II. 60DE; VIII. 354BC; Themistius, *Oratio* XXIII. 285A.

5 On the strength of Aristotle's last will and testament (DL V. 11–16 as well as some of the Arabic biographers) and other sources, it has been conjec-

tured that Proxenus married Aristotle's (older) sister Arimneste (probably after the death of Nicomachus), and that he was the father of Nicanor.

6 *VM* 3; *VV* 2; *VL* 3. It is quite possible that Nicomachus was killed during the fierce dynastic struggles which convulsed Macedonia after the death of King Amyntas III in 370–69 B.C. See note 30, and the corresponding text.

7 *IV VA* 3. *I VS* 4, *II VS* 2, *I VA* 4 and *IV VA* 3 also relate that Proxenus did this on the advice of the Delphic oracle. See *VM* 5; *VV* 4; *VL* 5.

8 *VM* 4; *VV* 3; *VL* 4. Some of these writings are listed in the 'catalogues' of Aristotle's works compiled by Diogenes Laertius, by the author of the *Vita Aristotelis Hesychii* and by Ptolemy (-el-Garib) as the latter has been excerpted by some of the Arabic *Vitae Aristotelis* (Usaibia).

9 See notes 10–11. For a detailed discussion of *VM* 4, see also O. Gigon, *Vita Aristotelis Marciana*, Kleine Texte für Vorlesungen und Übungen (Berlin, 1962), pp. 36–40.

10 DL X. 8; Philodemus, *De Rhetorica: Volumina Rhetorica*, vol. II (ed. S. Sudhaus, Leipzig, 1896), pp. 50 ff., col. 48, 37–8; Athenaeus, *op. cit.*, VIII. 354B; Aelian, *Varia Historia* V. 9; Eusebius, *op. cit.*, XV. 2. 1 (Aristocles). See also E. Bignone, *L'Aristotele Perduto e la Formazione Filosofica di Epicuro*, vol. II (Florence, 1936), pp. 89–91; S. Sudhaus, 'Aristoteles in der Beurteilung des Epikur und Philodemos,' *Rheinisches Museum*, vol. 48 (1893), p. 562; S. Sudhaus, 'Noch Einmal Nausiphanes und Aristoteles bei Philodemos,' *Philologus*, vol. 54 (1895), pp. 80 ff. We know that Aristotle had an illegitimate (though adopted) son by Herpyllis, named Nicomachus. This Nicomachus, it appears, never amounted to much. See *Gnomologium Vaticanum* no. 330 (p. 130, ed. L. Sternbach); Chapter V, notes 69–71. He became a mercenary soldier, probably squandered his patrimony (the estate which Aristotle bequeathed to him; see Chapter XV, notes 114–29, and the corresponding text), and died rather young. See Eusebius, *op. cit.*, XV. 2.15. Epicurus probably had in mind this Nicomachus (or, possibly, Aristotle, the son of Pythias—Aristotle's daughter—and Medias, who likewise never amounted to much) when he slandered Aristotle of Stagira. Epicurus might have attempted to show by the example of Nicomachus (or by that of Aristotle, the grandson of our Aristotle) that the father (or grandfather), Aristotle, in his youth likewise must have been a complete failure and a rogue: 'For the tree is known by his fruit.' Matthew 12:33; Luke 6:44.

11 This story, which probably goes back to Epicurus (or Cephisodorus), also contains a vicious attack upon Plato and the Platonic Academy which is made out to have been a sort of disreputable *refugium peccatorum*. See Eusebius, *op. cit.*, XV. 2. 1 (Epicurus); XV. 2. 7 (Cephisodorus); Athenaeus, *op. cit.*, VIII. 354B (Epicurus); VIII. 354C (Cephisodorus).

12 DL X. 2 (frag. 179, Usener).

13 *VM* 2; *VL* 2. Here we are informed that Aristotle inherited from his father or paternal ancestors an interest in medicine. *VM* 4 relates that in his youth Aristotle dealt with, or wrote about, 'problems of medicine.' See also

Aelian, *Varia Historia* IX. 22, who states that like the Pythagoreans or Plato, Aristotle was profoundly interested in medicine. Plutarch, *Alexander* 8, reports that it was Aristotle who awakened in Alexander an abiding interest in medicine.

14 *I VS* 6. See also *I VA* 6; *IV VA* 12; and notes 56–60; Usaibia (*IV VA* 12), confusing πολιτική and ἰατρική, relates that according to one tradition Aristotle was engaged in politics until he was thirty years old. See also *VM* 11 and *VL* 11. It might be noted that *I VS* 6, *I VA* 6 and *IV VA* 12 could be attempts on the part of some biographers to refute the many nasty stories which Epicurus, Cephisodorus and other detractors of Aristotle had told about the manner in which the Stagirite allegedly spent his youth. See notes 10–11.

15 DL V. 9. See also *II VS* 2: 'At the age of seventeen he [*scil.*, Aristotle] became a disciple of Plato.' *VM* 5; *VV* 4; *VL* 5; *II VA* 9.

16 Dionysius of Halicarnassus, *I Epistola ad Ammaeum* 5. Dionysius is probably in error when he claims that Aristotle joined Plato at the age of eighteen. Aside from the fact that all other *Vitae Aristotelis* insist that this happened when Aristotle was seventeen years old (in his seventeenth year), at the age of eighteen he would no longer be a 'ward' of Proxenus. Aristotle, it is safe to assume, was born in the late summer of 384 B.C., and he went to Athens probably in the spring or early summer of 367 B.C., before he had celebrated his seventeenth birthday. See Chapter V, at the beginning.

17 See note 3.

18 *II VA* 9. See also *IV VA* 28.

19 According to Philochorus (*VM* 10; *VL* 10), Aristotle arrived in Athens during the latter part of Nausigenes' archonship (368–67 B.C.), that is, probably in the spring of 367 B.C. According to Dionysius of Halicarnassus, *I Epistola ad Ammaeum* 5, he did so during the early part of Polycelus' archonship (367–66 B.C.), that is, in the summer or fall of 367 B.C. See the text, below, and notes 15–16, 23.

20 *VM* 5; *VV* 4; *VL* 5; 11.

21 *II VA* 3. See also note 3 and the corresponding text.

22 *II VA* 9. *IV VA* 28, which quotes Al-Mubashir (*II VA* 9) *verbatim*, likewise insists that Aristotle joined Plato at the age of seventeen.

23 *VM* 10. See also *VL* 10, and notes 16 and 19. If Aristotle arrived in Athens during the archonship of Nausigenes, he must have done so during the last months of Nausigenes' term of office (May or June).

24 Dionysius of Halicarnassus (see note 16). Dionysius seems to rely on the *Chronicle* of Apollodorus (?), or on a source used by Apollodorus. See also note 15. If Aristotle arrived in Athens during the archonship of Polycelus, he must have done so during the first months of Polycelus' term of office (July or August).

25 Diogenes Laertius, who relies here on Apollodorus' *Chronicle*, insists that Aristotle 'became Plato's disciple at the age of seventeen.' DL V. 9. See also notes 16, 19 and 23.

26 See A.-H. Chroust, 'The geneaology of Aristotle,' *Classical Folia*, vol. 19, no. 2 (1965), pp. 139-40; and Chapter V. See also note 19.

27 *VM* 5; *VV* 4; *VL* 5; *I VS* 4; *I VA* 4; *IV VA* 3.

28 *IV VA* 3. We have no additional evidence in support of this story. It has been suggested, however, that Proxenus did spend some time in Athens.

29 This might also explain the close personal ties of friendship which existed between Philip of Macedonia and Aristotle. See Chapter XIII. It might be worthwhile to keep in mind that Aristotle was born in 384 and Philip in 383 B.C. and hence that the two were approximately of the same age; that Aristotle spent much of his early youth at the Macedonian court (where his father was the personal physician of Amyntas III, the father of Philip); and that under the circumstances Aristotle and Philip probably were playmates and close friends.

30 *VM* 3; *VV* 2; *VL* 3. These sources also imply that by the year 367 B.C., Aristotle's mother, Phaestis, was dead.

31 See note 20. Neither the Syriac nor the Arabic *Vitae* mention Aristotle's alleged stay with Socrates. This is surprising in view of the fact that these *Vitae*, like the *Vita Marciana*, the *Vita Vulgata* and the *Vita Latina*, ultimately go back to Ptolemy's *Vita Aristotelis*.

32 *VV* 4; *VL* 5; 11 (but not *VM*). See also notes 20 and 35. According to *VL* 5 (see also *VM* 5), this information was contained in a letter which Aristotle addressed to King Philip.

33 A similar 'confusion' might be detected in DL V. 3, where Aristotle is credited with having stated: 'It would be a base and shameful thing to keep silent and let Xenocrates speak out.' Every classical scholar will recognize in this statement a paraphrase of Euripides, *Philoctetes*, frag. 785, Dindorf; frag. 796, Nauck[2]. Some scholars have put the name of Isocrates in place of that of Xenocrates, thus making it read: 'It would be a base and shameful thing to keep silent and let Isocrates speak out.' But the problem is not that simple. See Chapter III, notes 72-3, and the corresponding text.

34 A not altogether successful attempt has been made to identify this Socrates with one of the less known members of the Academy, that is, with Socrates the Younger (see Aristotle, *Metaphysics* 1036 b 24-32), or with the Socrates mentioned in Plato's *Theaetetus* (147D), *Sophist* (218B) and *Statesman* (257C ff.). See E. Kapp, in Paul-Wissowa, *Realencyclopädie der classischen Altertumswissenschaft* (Zweite Reihe, R-Z), Fünfter Halbband (Stuttgart, 1927), pp. 890-1; D. H. Vollenhoven, *Geschiedenis der Wijsbegeerte*, vol. I (Wever, 1950), pp. 482-5. Vollenhoven suggests that this reference is to Socrates the Younger, a man who advanced some unusual theories concerning the soul-body relation, and who attempted to integrate the philosophy of Anaxagoras and that of the Pythagoreans. When Socrates the Younger died in 366 B.C. Vollenhoven maintains, Aristotle entered the Academy. Another explanation of the story that initially Aristotle studied with Socrates might be the following: Plato had left for Syracuse before Aristotle arrived in Athens in 367 B.C. Hence, he joined the

'Socratics,' that is, the other members of the Academy who frequently and collectively were referred to as 'Socratics' by contemporary and subsequent authors. See DL II. 47. Due to a scribal error or to some confusion these 'Socratics' were identified with Socrates himself. It is also possible that upon his admission to the Academy (and during Plato's absence) Aristotle was instructed by Xenocrates, whose name subsequently was mutilated to read Socrates. It is known that in the Academy 'novices' usually were instructed by some of the lesser members of the community. See, for instance, II VA 10, where we are told that Aristotle 'was taught by Plato himself. Plato did not entrust him to be instructed by Xenocrates [or by any other member of the Academy], as he did with the other disciples.'

35 VV 4 and VL 5 (and ibid., 11) actually refer to three years. See notes 20 and 32. Provided Aristotle in fact stayed with Isocrates and his school, it would be safe to assume that he did so only for a relatively short period of time. The period of three years during which Aristotle is said to have studied with Isocrates may actually refer to the three years during which Plato was absent from Athens (367-65/64 B.C.).

36 See Isocrates, Antidosis 46-7; 155; Cicero, Orator LI. 176; Plato, Meno 70B; F. Blass, Attische Beredsamkeit, vol. II (2nd ed., Leipzig, 1892), p. 14.

37 It has been suggested that the passage in Pseudo-Plutarch, Isocrates 837B, where we are told that the statement that 'according to some he [scil., Isocrates] first established his own school ἐπὶ Χίου,' signifies that he did so during the archonship of [Μουστί]χιδος (386-85 B.C.).

38 See Pseudo-Plutarch, Isocrates 837C.

39 See, for instance, Isocrates, Antidosis 224-6, where Isocrates boasts of the fact that many of his illustrious students had come from Sicily as well as from the Black Sea regions or from other remote parts of the world, shunning neither the expense nor the dangers or exertions of long journeys to attend his school. See also ibid., 40; 107 ff.; Cicero, De Oratore II. 94; W. Jaeger, Paideia, vol. III (New York, 1944), pp. 138 ff. Dionysius of Halicarnassus, Isocrates 1, relates that Isocrates was the most illustrious teacher of his time and that he made his school the intellectual center as well as the image of Athens and of Hellenic intellectual culture in general.

40 Isocrates' The Team of Horses was published in c. 397-95 B.C.; the Trapeziticus in c. 394; the Against the Sophists in c. 390; the Busiris in c. 390-85; the Panegyricus in c. 380; the To Neocles and the Neocles or to the Cypriots in c. 374-72; the Plataeicus in c. 373-71; and the Helen in c. 370.

41 It may also be presumed that by the year 367 B.C., the writings of Plato, which have a certain 'esoteric' or 'intra-mural' flair, were not yet widely known outside either the Academy or Athens. If it is true that Aristotle read the Platonic Gorgias in his youth (and that this experience induced him to join the Academy, see note 43) then this probably happened after his arrival in Athens in the year 367 B.C.

42 DL 22 (no. 6); VH 10 (no. 6). But for a single fragment, preserved by

Themistius, *Oratio* XXIII, p. 256, ed. Dindorf (295CD), the *Nerinthus* (Themistius calls it *Corinthius*) is completely lost. See frag. 64, Rose; frag. 1, Ross.

43 When Themistius refers to the *Nerinthus* as *Corinthius*, then this might be a scribal error. See preceding note. Themistius mentions a Corinthian farmer who was converted to philosophy through the lecture of Plato's *Gorgias*. Hence probably the confusion of *Nerinthus* and *Corinthius*.

44 St Augustine, *Confessiones* III. 4. It may be noted that, according to DL VII. 2, Zeno, the Stoic, turned to philosophy after having read Book II of Xenophon's *Memorabilia* or, according to Themistius, *Oratio* XXIII, p. 356, Dindorf (296D), after having read Plato's *Apology*.

45 *II VA* 3-4; *VM* 4; *VV* 3; *VL* 4. See also *II VA* 6-8, where Aristotle is said to have defended this kind of rhetoric. In *II VA* 9 we are told that 'when he [*scil.*, Aristotle] had completed his studies of the poets, grammarians and orators . . . he turned to ethics, politics, mathematics, physics and theology [*scil.*, metaphysics]. He attached himself to Plato.' Al-Mubashir emphasizes that at the time 'he attached himself to Plato' he was seventeen years old. See also *IV VA* 28, notes 22 and 46.

46 *II VA* 3-9. See also *II VA* 28.

47 See, for instance, *VM* 4; *VV* 3; *VL* 4.

48 See frag. 117, Usener. For the many Epicurean (and other) attacks upon Aristotle, see I. Düring, *Aristotle in the Ancient Biographical Tradition*, Acta Universitatis Gothoburgensis, vol. 63, no. 2 (Göteborg, 1957), pp. 373–95, and notes 10–11.

49 *II VA* 3. Al-Mubashir insists, however, that this happened when he was eight years old. *Ibid.*

50 *II VA* 9.

51 See A.-H. Chroust, 'Aristotle's First Course of Lectures on Rhetoric,' *Antiquité Classique*, vol. 33 (1964), fasc. 1, pp. 58–72, and Chapter VIII.

52 See A.-H. Chroust, 'Aristotle's first literary effort: the *Gryllus*, a lost dialogue on the nature of rhetoric,' *Revue des Études Grecques*, vol. 78, nos 371-3, (1965), pp. 576–91; Vol. II, Chapter III.

53 Isocrates' *Antidosis* might also be an effort on the part of its author to discredit the 'apostate' Aristotle. The same might be said of the *Ad Demonicum*, composed probably by a disciple of Isocrates.

54 *VV* 4; *VL* 5; 11. See also notes 20 and 35.

55 See, for instance, Pseudo-Plutarch, *Isocrates* 837C; Isocrates, *Antidosis* 224 ff. See also notes 36–41.

56 DL V. 6 (thirty years), citing Eumelus as its source. The same Eumelus, in his *Histories*, also relates (DL V. 6) that Aristotle committed suicide by drinking the hemlock at the age of seventy—a flagrant 'transfer' of the age of Socrates and the circumstances of Socrates' death. This might be an indication of Eumelus' accuracy as a historical reporter. See A.-H. Chroust, 'The Myth of Aristotle's Suicide,' *The Modern Schoolman*, vol. 44, no. 2 (1967), pp. 177–8, and Chapter XIV.

57 *VM* 11, where we are told that Aristotle was forty years old when he joined Plato—obviously a mistake for thirty years. See note 56, *VL* 11, which completely confuses the story, relates that Aristotle stayed forty years with Plato. By making Aristotle thirty years old at the time he began the study of philosophy, his detractors wished to make him appear 'stupid' or 'retarded.' See also note 10.

58 *I VS* 6. See note 14. *I VA* 6 expressly denies that 'Aristotle . . . did not turn to philosophy until he was thirty years of age. . . .' See also *IV VA* 12: 'Those who allege that he [Aristotle] did not devote himself to philosophy until he had reached the age of thirty years are plainly in error. . . .'

59 *I VA* 6; *IV VA* 12. While *I VS* 6 relates that according to some reports Aristotle had 'practiced medicine' before he began the study of philosophy (at the age of thirty), *IV VA* 12 maintains that it is said that Aristotle had first been engaged in 'political activities' before he started the study of philosophy (at the age of thirty). See note 14. Perhaps *I VS* 6 and Usaibia (or their source) defend Aristotle against the calumnies of the Epicureans and those of other detractors. *II VA* 5 expressly mentions Epicurus as one of the calumniators of Aristotle. See notes 10–11.

60 It had been suggested that this hostile tradition insinuated either that in his youth Aristotle was a 'ne'er-do-well,' or that he was 'slow in grasping things.' See, for instance, Suda, 'article' *Aristotle*; Eusebius, *op. cit.*, XV. 2. 1; Timaeus, in Polybius XII. 8; Athenaeus, *Deipnosophistae* VIII. 354B. See also notes 10–11, and the corresponding texts; DL V. 1, which relates that according to some Aristotle had 'close-set eyes,' an indication of his narrow-mindedness.

61 *IV VA* 12. See also notes 14 and 58.

62 Dionysius the Elder died early in 367 B.C. It is reasonable to assume that upon receipt of the news Plato immediately made preparations to go to Sicily. See also Plato, *Seventh Epistle, passim*. Some scholars hold, however, that Plato went to Sicily in 366 B.C.

63 This would coincide with the remark found in DL VIII. 90 (based on Apollodorus' *Chronicle*), that the *acme* of Eudoxus of Cnidus fell in the 103rd Olympiad, that is, between 368 and 364 B.C.

64 *VM* 11; *VL* 11; *I VA* 5; *II VA* 13; *IV VA* 4. Some scholars have erroneously interpreted this statement to mean that Aristotle arrived in Athens 'during the archonship of Eudoxus.' During this period, it will be noted, there was no archon called Eudoxus. Philochorus (*VM* 9–12; *VL* 9–12) attempts to straighten out some of the erroneous notions about the chronology of Aristotle's stay at the Academy. If Eudoxus of Cnidus was 'acting scholarch' during the whole of Plato's absence in Syracuse (367 to 365–364 B.C.), then Aristotle could have entered, or transferred into, the Academy in 367, 366, 365 or early in 364 B.C. This might be derived from *VM* 11 and *VL* 11, where we are told that Aristotle entered the Academy ἐπὶ Εὐδόξου or *tempore Eudoxi*, that is, while Eudoxus was 'acting scholarch.'

65 The fact that Plato stayed in Syracuse for almost three years might have prompted *VV* 4 and *VL* 5 (and *ibid.*, 11) or their source to insist that Aristotle remained with Socrates (Isocrates ?) three years. See note 35.

66 If this is true, then there exists a certain parallel between the life of Zeno the Stoic and that of Aristotle. Around 320 B.C., Zeno is said to have originally come to Athens because of a shipwreck. See DL VII. 2.; VII. 4–5; Seneca, *Ad Serenum de Tranquillitate Animi* XIV. 3; Plutarch, *De Tranquillitate Animi* 6; Plutarch, *De Inimicorum Utilitate* 2. In a certain way Aristotle's arrival in Athens in the year 367 B.C. likewise was due to a calamity: the political or dynastic upheavals in Macedonia after 369 B.C. which forced him to seek shelter in Athens.

67 Naturally, in 365 B.C., that is, after the assassination of Ptolemy of Alorus by Perdiccas, Aristotle could have safely returned to Macedonia. But by that time he was probably so engrossed in his studies that he preferred to remain with the Platonic Academy in Athens.

68 See, for instance, Cicero, *De Inventione* II. 2. 6; Cicero, *Acad. Prior.* II.38. 119; Cicero, *De Oratore* I. 11. 49; Cicero, *De Finibus* I. 5. 14; Dionysius of Halicarnassus, *De Cens. Vet. Script.* 4; Dionysius of Halicarnassus, *De Verborum Compositione* 24; Quintilian, *Institutio Oratoria* X. 1. 83; XII. 11. 22.

69 This becomes manifest, for instance, in the Aristotelian *Protrepticus*, which effectively combines Platonic doctrine and the hortatory-literary form of argumentation characteristic of certain orations and addresses of Isocrates, such as the *Cypriot Orations*.

70 In the *Gryllus or On Rhetoric*, for instance.

71 See A.-H. Chroust (see note 51).

72 See Chapter IX.

73 See Chapter VIII.

74 The untrustworthiness of these stories is emphasized by *VM* 12, *VV* 4 and *VL* 12, where we are informed that in Athens a powerless 'resident Macedonian alien' such as Aristotle could not possibly have antagonized so influential an Athenian citizen as Plato, who counted among his friends and relatives some of the most prominent Athenian citizens.

75 *VM* 6; *VL* 6. See also Aristotle, *Topics* 105 b 12 ff.

76 See, for instance, DL V. 34, and *ibid.*, I. 16.

77 Xenophon, *Memorabilia* IV. 2. 1 ff.

78 See Chapter IV, notes 52–3, and the corresponding text.

79 See, for instance, *VM* 11; 45; *VL* 11; 48; *II VA* 35; and others, including the 'catalogues' of Aristotle's writings in DL V. 22–7; *VH* 10; *IV VA*. See also note 76.

80 *II VA* 37. See also Gellius, *Attic Nights* XX. 5.

81 *Ibid.*

82 Plutarch, *Alexander* 7. See also Gellius (see note 80); frag. 662, Rose.

83 *II VA* 10; *II VS* 2.

84 *II VA* 11–12. See also *I VS* 5; *IV VA* 29.

85 *VM* 7; *VL* 7.

86 It is quite possible that this story is a later encomiastic invention intended to counteract some of the unpleasant (and probably untrue) stories about certain serious rifts between Plato and the young Aristotle. See note 74.

87 See here Diogenes DL IV. 6, where Plato contrasts Aristotle's and Xenocrates' philosophic abilities, comparing the former to a spirited steed which needs a bridle and the latter to a slow jackass that needs a spur. This might also explain why Diogenes Laertius (DL V. 1) calls Aristotle 'Plato's most genuine disciple.' See also Dionysius of Halicarnassus, *Epistola ad Cn. Pompeium* 1.

CHAPTER VIII ARISTOTLE'S EARLIEST 'COURSE OF LECTURES ON RHETORIC'

★ In a slightly different form, this chapter was first published in *Antiquité Classique*, vol. 33, fasc. 1 (1964), pp. 58–72.

1 DL V. 3. See also Cicero, *Orator* XIV. 46.

2 Philodemus, *De Rhetorica: Volumina Rhetorica*, vol. II, pp. 50 ff. (ed. S. Sudhaus), col. 48,36–57,45. Here Philodemus might be following Epicurus (see E. Bignone, *L'Aristotele Perduto e la Formazione Filosofica di Epicuro*, vol. II (Florence, 1936) p. 97) or some other Epicurean or Epicureans. According to frags. 171, 235 and 237 (Usener), and DL X. 25, Epicurus, Metrodorus and Hermarchus viciously attacked Aristotle and his philosophy. In fact, Hermarchus wrote an *Against Aristotle*. See also H. M. Hubbell, 'The *Rhetorica* of Philodemus,' *Transactions of the Connecticut Academy of Arts and Sciences*, vol. 23 (1920), pp. 243–382; H. M. Hubbell, 'Isocrates and the Epicureans,' *Classical Philology*, vol. 11 (1916), pp. 405–18; I. Düring, *Aristotle in the Ancient Biographical Tradition* (Göteborg, 1957), pp. 299–314; E. Berti, *La Filosofia del Primo Aristotele* (Padua, 1961), pp. 175–85; W. Wieland, 'Aristoteles als Rhetoriker und die exoterischen Schriften,' *Hermes*, vol. 86 (1958), pp. 323–46.

3 See also Cicero, *De Oratore* III. 35. 141; Quintilian, *Institutio Oratoria* III. 1. 14; VL V. 3 (should read Isocrates rather than Xenocrates); Syrianus, *Scholia in Hermogenem* IV. 297 (ed. Ch. Walz); II. 59. 21 (ed. H. Rabe). See also Euripides, *Philoctetes*, frag. 796 (ed. A. Nauck), frag. 785 (ed. L. Dindorf). It is not impossible that this statement, like other statements made here by Philodemus, originally was contained in Aristotle's lost work, entitled *Gryllus or On Rhetoric* (DL V. 22, no. 5, in one book; *VH* 10, no. 5, where it is referred to as *On Politics or Gryllus*, in three books; *Vita Aristotelis* of Ptolemy—*IV VA*, no 3, in three books). Accordingly, it might also be claimed that this whole passage from Philodemus' *De Rhetorica* contains some fragments or allusion to the lost Aristotelian *Gryllus*. See Vol. II, Chapter III. According to Gellius, *Attic Nights* XX. 5, Aristotle gave his 'exoteric lectures' in the afternoon or evening, while the 'esoteric lectures' were delivered in the morning. This raises an interesting problem: did the Platonic Academy (and later the Peripatus) teach its 'esoteric' or intramural doctrines in the morning to a restricted circle of 'initiates' or

'advanced students,' and offer its 'exoteric,' 'popular' or 'introductory' lectures in the afternoon or evening to a general public, 'non-initiated persons' or 'undergraduate students,' as the Pythagoreans are believed to have done. See here also notes 19 and 20.

4 Philodemus seems to refer here to Aristotle's *Gryllus*, composed about 360–59 B.C. See also note 3.

5 That politics is a branch of general philosophy is restated in Aristotle, *Metaphysics* 1025 b 22–3; Aristotle, *Nicomachean Ethics* 1181 b 15.

6 E. Bignone (see note 2), vol. II, pp. 97–101, maintains that this remark refers to something Aristotle had said in his *Politicus* (a lost work).

7 E. Bignone, *op. cit.*, vol. II, p. 249, believes that this particular passage refers to something Aristotle had maintained in his *Eudemus or On the Soul*; I. Düring (see note 2), p. 303, suggests that it might refer to the Aristotelian *Politicus*. It is more likely, however, that it refers to the *Gryllus*. See DL II. 55, and notes 3–4.

8 This might be a reference or allusion to the wholly unsupported stories that in his youth Aristotle lived a profligate life. See DL X. 8 (frag. 171, Usener) and Aristocles (Eusebius, *Praeparatio Evangelica* XV. 2. 1). See also E. Bignone, *op. cit.*, vol. II, pp. 89–91; S. Sudhaus, 'Aristoteles in der Beurteilung des Epikur und Philodemos,' *Rheinisches Museum*, vol. 48 (1893), p. 562; S. Sudhaus, 'Noch einmal Nausiphanes und Aristoteles bei Philodemos,' *Philologus*, vol. 54 (1895), pp. 80 ff. See also note 13.

9 See note 3.

10 Philodemus might refer here to the *Protrepticus* or, more likely, to the *Gryllus*. See also E. Bignone, *op. cit.*, pp. 125–7. The *Protrepticus* was written probably after 352 B.C., and the *Gryllus* probably between 360–59 and 358–7 B.C. See A.-H. Chroust, 'The probable dates of some of Aristotle's lost works,' *Rivista Critica di Storia della Filosofia*, vol. 22, fasc. 1 (1967), pp. 3–5; 13–17; Vol. II, Chapter I.

11 That Aristotle (and Plato) was profoundly resented by Isocrates and his disciples is a matter of record.

12 This passage might be a reference to Isocrates, *Antidosis* 243 ff.; 258 ff. See also Philodemus, *op. cit.*, col. 52, 41–2, where Philodemus maintains that, together with his disciples (Theophrastus?, Callisthenes?), 'he [*scil.*, Aristotle] collected the laws, the arguments of the cities concerning their territorial boundaries, the main constitutions and the laws enacted at times of crises. . . .' Philodemus probably refers here to Aristotle's *Constitutions of One Hundred and Fifty-Eight Cities and Tribes*, of which only the *Constitution of Athens* has survived in its totality, although some two hundred fragments of the other parts of this work can be found in ancient grammarians, doxographers, lexicographers and scholiasts who, however, seem to have been interested primarily in fanciful stories or entertaining details. See K. von Fritz and E. Kapp, *Aristotle's Constitution of Athens and Related Texts* (New York, 1950), pp. VII ff. It is reasonable to surmise that the Aristotelian *Constitutions* was composed after 343–2 B.C.

13 Aphrodisiacs are mentioned in Aristotle, *Eudemian Ethics* 1225 b 4, and

(Aristotle?), *Magna Moralia* 1188 b 32–8. Philodemus' remark might be a snide allusion to the wholly unsupported story that in his youth Aristotle was a medical quack who tried his hand at selling aphrodisiacs. Eusebius, *op. cit.*, XV. 2. 1; XV. 2. 7; Athenaeus, *Deipnosophistae* VIII. 354B. See also note 8. The derogatory accounts about Aristotle recorded by Athenaeus, Eusebius and others, might be a transfer from Nicomachus, the (illegitimate) son of Aristotle by Herpyllis, or from Aristotle, the grandson of the Stagirite through his daughter Pythias, both of whom apparently were 'never-do-wells.' See Chapter V, last paragraph; Chapter VII, note 10.

14 See Isocrates, *Antidosis, passim*. This passage, it will be noted, amounts to a deliberate misrepresentation intended to belittle Aristotle: Aristotle perverted or debased philosophy to rhetoric—and rhetoric was something of an abomination in the eyes of the Epicureans (see note 24)—while Isocrates elevated rhetoric to philosophy. See S. Sudhaus (see note 8), *Rheinisches Museum* vol. 48 (1893), p. 561.

15 Cicero, *De Oratore* III. 35. 141. See also Cicero, *Orator* XIV. 46; XXXVI. 127; LI. 172.

16 I. Düring (see note 2), pp. 311; 313, suggests that Hermippus' *Vita Aristotelis* is Cicero's main and, perhaps sole source. Philodemus, on the other hand, makes use of the traditionally anti-Aristotelian writings of Epicurus and the Epicureans in general.

17 Cicero seems to avoid here the anachronism found in the *De Oratore* III. 35. 141. See also Cicero's many remarks about Aristotle's excellence as a rhetorician as well as a teacher of rhetoric in *Orator, passim*.

18 Isocrates was born in 436 B.C. Hence, in 355 B.C., the approximate year Aristotle started teaching rhetoric in the Academy, he was 81 years old.

19 Quintilian, *Institutio Oratoria* III. 1. 14. See also Strabo XIV. 1. 48, and note 3. Cicero, *Orator* LI. 172, points out that Aristotle was 'the most violent opponent of Isocrates.'

20 Syrianus, *Scholia in Hermogenem* IV. 297 (ed. Ch. Walz), II. 59, 21 ff. (ed. H. Rabe). See also Philodemus (see note 2), col. 48,36. See note 3.

21 Eusebius, *op. cit.*, XIV. 6. 9; Athenaeus, *op. cit.*, II. 60 DE; VIII. 354C; Dionysius of Halicarnassus, *Epistola ad Cn. Pompeium* 1; Dionysius of Halicarnassus, *Isocrates* 18; Themistius, *Oratio* XXIII. 285AB (p. 345, ed. L. Dindorf). See also note 73 and the corresponding text.

22 See DL II. 55. See also Cicero, *Orator* XVIII. 62: 'Aristotle challenged Isocrates.' *Ibid.*, LI. 172.

23 For additional detail, see A.-H. Chroust, 'Aristotle's first literary effort: the *Gryllus*—a lost dialogue on the nature of rhetoric,' *Revue des Études Grecques*, vol. 78, nos. 371–3 (1965), pp. 576–91, and Vol. II, Chapter III. See also note 3.

24 See also *IV VA* 27 (Usaibia). Pythagoras is undoubtedly Lycon Pythagoraeus, who lived about a generation after Aristotle. This Lycon was one of the most persistent slanderers of Aristotle whom he called a gourmand as well as a 'skin-flint.' See DL V. 16; Eusebius, *op. cit.*, XV. 2. 8–9;

Pliny, *Hist. Nat.* XXXV. 162. See note 23 and Aristotle, *Metaphysics* 980 b 23 ff.

25 A. Stahr, *Aristoteles: Leben, Schriften und Schüler des Aristoteles*, vol. I (Halle, 1830), pp. 63–70. Stahr did not realize as yet that the Aristotelian *Protrepticus* was the literary result (or one of the literary results) of this protracted rivalry, and that Aristotle's *Gryllus* likewise had been occasioned by Aristotle's animosity towards Isocrates, something which might also be inferred from Cephisodorus' attacks upon Aristotle. Cephisodorus, it will be remembered, was a disciple of Isocrates. See A.-H. Chroust (see note 23), especially, pp. 587 ff., and Vol. II, Chapter III.

26 H. Diels, 'Über das dritte Buch der aristotelischen Rhetorik,' *Abhandlungen der Königlichen Akademie der Wissenschaften zu Berlin*, Philologisch-Historische Klasse, vol. IV (Berlin, 1886) pp. 11–16.

27 DL V. 24 (no. 82): *VH* 10 (no. 74). The *Vita Hesychii*, which states that this work contained three books, gives it a slightly different title. Ptolemy (-el-Garib), on the other hand, does not mention this work in his 'catalogue.' See also L. Radermacher (ed.), *Artium Scriptores* (Sitzungsberichte der Österreichischen Akademie der Wissenschaften, Philologisch-Historische Klasse), no. 227, Abhandlung 3 (Vienna, 1961), pp. 202, 203.

28 H. Diels (see note 26).

29 F. Blass, *Die Attische Beredsamkeit*, vol. II (Leipzig, 1892), pp. 64–5. Blass also refuted G. Teichmüller's thesis that between 344 and 342 B.C. Aristotle re-entered the Academy for a brief spell, and that it was during this period that he delivered lectures on rhetoric. See G. Teichmüller, *Literarische Fehden im Vierten Jahrhundert vor Chr.* (Berlin, 1881), pp. 228–32.

30 DL V. 24 (no. 77); *VH* 10 (no. 71); Ptolemy (-el-Garib), no. 24. Hesychius and Ptolemy maintain that this work consisted of one book. See Diogenes Laertius, *loc. cit.*, who also lists a *Treatise (Handbook) on the Art of Rhetoric in Two Books* (no. 78); a *Treatise (Handbook) [on the Art of Rhetoric] in One Book* (no. 79); and an *Another Treatise (Handbook, Collection) on the Art of Rhetoric in Two Books* (no. 80), which might possibly be a revised version of no. 77. The corresponding numbers in the *Vita Hesychii* are nos 72 (three books) and 73. No. 80 of Diogenes Laertius is not listed by Hesychius. When compiling their respective 'catalogues,' both Diogenes Laertius and Hesychius seem to have used the same source. Scholars disagree, however, as to which of the two 'catalogues' is more reliable. With the exception of the hypercritical V. Rose, no scholar has seriously challenged the authenticity of the Τεχνῶν Συναγωγή. Τέχνη, as H. Bonitz, *Index Aristotelicus* 759 a 50 ff., has pointed out, signifies here the *ratio et doctrina artis (Kunstlehre)*, or the *praecipue institutio oratoria*. See also Aristotle, *Nicomachean Ethics* 1140 a 10–14; Aristotle, *Metaphysics* 981 a 5 ff.

31 Cicero, *De Inventione* II. 2. 6; Cicero, *De Oratore* II. 38. 160; Cicero, *Brutus* 12 (Quintilian, *Institutio Oratoria* III. 1. 8–13).

32 Quintilian, *Institutio Oratoria* III. 1. 13.

33 Dionysius of Halicarnassus, *De Isocrate* 18; Anonym., *Prolegomena in*

Isocratem, Scholia in Aeschinem et Isocratem (ed. L. Dindorf, 1852), p. 105. See also V. Rose, *Aristotelis qui Ferebantur Librorum Fragmenta* (Leipzig, 1886), pp. 118–20, frags 136–41.

34 See, for instance, Aristotle, *Nicomachean Ethics* 1181 b 6–12; Aristotle, *Metaphysics* 993 a 30 ff.; 993 b 11 ff.; 1074 b 10; Aristotle, *Topics* 105 b 12 ff.; Aristotle, *Politics* 1264 a 1 ff.; 1329 a 25 ff.; Aristotle, *De Anima* 403 b 20 ff.; Aristotle, *De Caelo* 270 b 5 ff.; Aristotle, *Meteorologica* 351 b 25 ff.; 339 b 28; Aristotle, *De Sophisticis Elenchis* 183 b 17 ff.; etc.

35 Cicero, *De Inventione* II. 2. 6. See also the remarks of P. Moraux, *Les Listes Anciennes des Ouvrages d'Aristote* (Louvain, 1951), pp. 96–7.

36 DL V. 24 (no. 82); *VH* 10 (no. 74). Hesychius entitles it Τέχνης τῆς Θεοδέκτου Συναγωγὴν (in three books).

37 H. Diels (see note 26), pp. 11–16.

38 Quintilian, *Institutio Oratoria* II. 15. 10 (frag. 125, Rose); IV. 2. 31 (frag. 126, Rose); I. 4. 18 (frag. 127, Rose). Quintilian is not certain whether he should credit this work to Aristotle or to Theodectes.

39 Dionysius of Halicarnassus, *De Verborum Compositione* 2 (frag. 127, Rose); *De Vi Demosthenis* 48 (frag. 127, Rose). Dionysius is not at all certain whether he should ascribe this work to Aristotle or to Theodectes.

40 Pseudo-Aristotle, *Rhetorica ad Alexandrum* 1421 a 38 (see V. Rose (see note 33), p. 114), where it is not made clear whether this work of Aristotle was edited by, or addressed to, Theodectes. Valerius Maximus VIII. 14. 3, who apparently relied on the *Rhetorica ad Alexandrum* as well as on Aristotle, *Rhetoric* 1410 b 2, reports that Aristotle had entrusted his disciple Theodectes with the editing of this work, but afterwards discovered to his regret that it was credited to Theodectes and circulated under his name. See also E. Heitz, *Fragmenta Aristotelis* (Paris, 1868), p. 124; V. Rose, *op. cit.*, p. 114; Anonymus Seguerianus, *De Orat. Polit.*, in L. Spengel, *Rhetorici Graeci*, vol. I, p. 454 (frag. 134, Rose), who considers it an authentic Aristotelian composition; *Scholia in Aristotelis Rhetoricam* 1410 b 2 (frag. 132, Rose), where it is called an authentic work of Aristotle dedicated to Theodectes. For additional sources see V. Rose, *op. cit.*, pp. 116–18.

41 Cicero, *Orator* LI. 172 (frag. 128, Rose); LVII. 194 (Quintilian, *Institutio Oratoria* IX. 4. 88; Rufinus, *De Metris* II. 2; XLIV. 218 frag. 129, Rose).

42 See here also H. Bonitz, *Index Aristotelicus* 104 a 33 ff.; '*suum se citare librum non distincte scribit Aristoteles, tamen ex formula citandi vero est simillimum.*'

43 V. Rose, *De Aristotelis Librorum Ordine et Auctoritate* (Berlin, 1854), p. 89.

44 V. Rose, *Aristoteles Pseudepigraphus* (Leipzig, 1863), p. 137. Rose went so far as to doubt the authenticity of the Aristotelian *Rhetoric* or, at least, of Book III. He based this somewhat extravagant thesis on the assumption that Aristotle could not possibly have claimed as his own a work (the Θεοδέκτου) which was authored by someone else.

45 E. Heitz, *Die Verlorenen Schriften des Aristoteles* (Leipzig, 1865), pp. 85–7. See also E. Heitz, *Fragmenta Aristotelis* (Paris, 1868), p. 124.

46 E. Zeller, *Die Philosophie der Griechen*, vol. II, part 2 (3rd ed., Leipzig, 1879), p. 76, note 2.

47 See note 40.

48 H. Diels (see note 26), pp. 11–16.

49 H. Diels, *loc. cit.* Diels also pointed out that in his *Rhetoric* (1410 b 2), Aristotle did not hesitate to refer back to Theodectes' version, thus avoiding the necessity of having to enlarge upon a point already made by Theodectes. This might be an indication of the high esteem in which Theodectes' work was held.

50 F. Solmsen, 'Drei Rekonstruktionen zur Antiken Rhetorik und Poetik, II: Theodektes,' *Hermes*, vol. 67 (1932), pp. 144–54. Solmsen's considered views seem to be beyond challenge.

51 F. Solmsen, *loc. cit.* See also P. Moraux (see note 35), p. 100. Of Theodectes' life we know only that he was from Phaselis in Lycia; that he taught rhetoric and 'tragediography'; and that he died in Athens at the age of 41, not long after the year 340. See F. Blass, *Attische Beredsamkeit*, vol. II (Leipzig, 1892), pp. 441–6; F. Solmsen, article 'Theodectes,' Pauly-Wissowa, *Realencyclopädie der classischen Alterumswissenschaft*, 2. Reihe, vol. V (1934), cols 1722–34. According to some sources, he was first a disciple of Isocrates, then of Plato, and finally of Aristotle. Suda, article 'Theodectes'; Dionysius of Halicarnassus, *De Isocrate* 19; *I Epistola ad Ammaeum* 2; Athenaeus, *Deipnosophistae* XIII. 566E; Cicero, *Orator* LI. 172. F. Blass, *loc. cit.*, surmises that he joined the Academy during the time Aristotle lectured on rhetoric. Together with the most prominent orators of his day (Naucrates, Isocrates and Theopompus), he was invited to Halicarnassus in 353 B.C. on the occasion of King Mausolus' death, in order to compose a eulogy of the deceased king. Pliny, *Hist. Nat.* XXXVI. 30; Gellius, *Attic Nights* X. 8. ff; Pseudo-Plutarch, *Vita Isocratis* 838B; Eusebius (see note 8), X. 3. 464C (Porphyry); Suda, *loc. cit.* All this would indicate that by 353 B.C. his reputation must have been considerable and hence that by this time, he probably was no longer a disciple of Aristotle. This would also lend support to our contention that Aristotle taught rhetoric in the Academy prior to 353 B.C. Suda, *loc. cit.*, mentions a Τέχνη ῥητορικὴ ἐν μέτρῳ. For additional detail see P. Moraux, *op. cit.*, p. 101.

52 A. Kantelhardt, 'De Aristotelis Rhetoricis' (Doctoral thesis of the University of Göttingen, 1911), *passim*.

53 F. Solmsen, *Die Entwicklung der Aristotelischen Logik und Rhetorik* (Berlin, 1929), pp. 208–29. Solmsen, *op. cit.*, pp. 208; 213; 215 ff.; 227, believed that in his earliest lectures on rhetoric Aristotle attacked Isocrates.

54 W. Jaeger, *Paideia*, vol. III (1944), pp. 251–2.

55 P. Gohlke, 'Die Entstehung der Aristotelischen Ethik, Politik, Rhetorik,' *Sitzungsberichte der Akademie der Wissenschaften in Wien*, Philologisch-Historische Klasse, vol. 223 (1944), fasc. 2, pp. 111–41.

56 See note 40.

57 P. Gohlke, *op. cit.* Gohlke also added to the earliest Aristotelian writings

on rhetoric the *Rhetorica ad Alexandrum*, considered spurious by the majority of scholars, as well as another early *Rhetoric*, now lost. This whole 'group of *Rhetorica*' Gohlke assigned to Aristotle's Academic period. It was composed prior to the *Topics*. After the *Topics*, but prior to the first revision of the *Analytics*, Aristotle made the first revision of what ultimately became the preserved *Rhetoric*. After the first revision of the *Analytics*, he made a second and final revision of the *Rhetoric*, which antedates the final revision of the *Analytics*.

58 I. Düring (see note 2), pp. 258-9. Düring justified his thesis by showing that Aristotle did not refer to, or comment upon, any passages from Demosthenes' famous speeches. Demosthenes, it will be remembered, made his first appearance in the law courts of Athens (on behalf of Leptines) in 354 B.C. See also I. Düring, *op. cit.*, p. 314.

59 Some scholars, relying on Dionysius of Halicarnassus, *I Epistola ad Ammaeum* 7, insist that in Book I of his *Rhetoric* (1355 a 21-9; 1356 a 35-1356 b 21) Aristotle quotes the *Topics* (1355 a 28-9), the *Analytics* (1356 b 9-10) and the (lost) *Methodics* (1356 b 18-19). From this it was inferred that Aristotle composed all these works, or at least their earliest versions (or 'parts'), before he wrote (or revised) his *Rhetoric*. I. Düring maintains (*op. cit.*, pp. 258-9) that Aristotle wrote the *Topics* and probably had completed parts of the *Analytics* before he composed the *Rhetoric*. Originally, Book III of the *Rhetoric*, also known as the *On Diction* (Περὶ λέξεως, DL V. 24, no. 87; *VH* 10, no. 79), did not form part of the *Urrhetorik* (Jaeger) which, according to the testimony of Cicero, consisted of two books. Accordingly, it might be maintained that Book III was 'added' by Andronicus of Rhodes (?). Book II, Chapters 23-4, likewise might be a later 'addition.' Originally, it might have been a separate composition (perhaps the ἐνθυμημάτων διαιρέσεις, in one book, DL V. 24, no. 86; *VH* 10, no. 76; or the ἐνθυμήματα ῥητορικά, in one book, DL V. 24, no. 84; *VH* 10, no. 78). Book III (1411 a 1-8), which refers to the Olynthian War (349-48 B.C.), as well as chapters 23 and 24 of Book II of the *Rhetoric* (which might be later 'insertions'), in all likelihood were composed after the death of Plato in 348-47 B.C.

60 See note 30.

61 See, for instance, Cicero, *Tuscul. Disput.* I. 4. 7; Cicero, *Orator* XVIII. 62; LI. 172.

62 See, for instance, Philodemus (see note 2); Cicero, *De Oratore* III. 35. 141 (see note 15). Aristotle's extant *Rhetoric* indicates, however, that in his later years he must have had a fairly high opinion of Isocrates and his rhetorical talents. See, for instance, *Rhetoric* 1368 a 5 ff., which contains a reference to Isocrates' *Evagoras* 45, *Panathenaicus* 32, and, perhaps, to the *Ad Nicoclem* 29; *ibid.*, 1399 a 3 ff. (*Helen* 18-48); 1399 a 5-6 (*Evagoras* 51 ff.); 1401 a 9-10 (*Evagoras* 65-9); 1414 b 26 ff. (*Helen* 1 ff.); 1414 b 33 ff. (*Panegyricus* 1-2); 1418 a 33 ff. (*Panegyricus* 110-14, *On the Peace* 27, *Helen* 23-38 and *Helen* 41-8, *Busiris* 21-9 and 38-40, *Panathenaicus* 72-84); 1418

b 27 ff. (*Philippus* 4–7, *Antidosis* 132–9 and 141–9); 1418 b 35 (*Archidamus* 50); etc. As a matter of fact, Aristotle's style in the extant *Rhetoric* manifests the influence of Isocrates. This would suggest that in the course of time, Aristotle, like his teacher Plato, changed some of his views about Isocrates and his rhetoric.

63 See, for instance, Isocrates, *Antidosis* 258 ff.

64 See, for instance, Syrianus (see note 20).

65 See, for instance, Quintilian, *Institutio Oratoria* II. 17. 1; II. 17. 4.

66 See Cicero, *Orator* XXXVI. 127: 'The graceful method of philosophic discussion goes back to Aristotle.' Cicero, it will be noted, included Aristotle among the authors whose style and presentation was 'eloquent, charming and polished.' Cicero, *De Oratore* I. 11. 49. Cicero also states that Aristotle 'poured forth a golden stream of eloquence' (*Acad. Prior.* II. 38. 119), and that he was the foremost fount for the art of rhetoric (*De Inventione* II. 2. 6). Quintilian, *op. cit.*, X. 1. 83, likewise extolls 'the charm' of Aristotle's language. See also E. Berti (see note 2), p. 182.

67 This has also been observed by F. Solmsen. See note 53.

68 See, in general, A.-H. Chroust (see note 23), and vol. II, Chapter III.

69 In the past, it has been held, though apparently without foundation in fact, that the *Gryllus* was an eulogy or a *consolatio mortis* composed in memory of Xenophon's son Gryllus (or Grylus), who had died in the battle of Mantinea in 362 B.C. Hence, the *Gryllus* would be akin to the Aristotelian *Eudemus or On the Soul*. See A.-H. Chroust, '*Eudemus or On the Soul*: A Lost Aristotelian Dialogue on the Immortality of the Soul,' *Mnemosyne*, vol. 19 (4th series), fasc. 1 (1966), pp. 17–30; and Vol. II, Chapter V.

70 See also F. Solmsen (see note 53), pp. 196–8. P. Thillet, 'Note sur le *Gryllos*, ouvrage de jeunesse d'Aristote,' *Revue Philosophique de la France et de l'Étranger*, vol. 82 (1957), p. 353, suggests that in the *Gryllus* Aristotle refers to Isocrates (in an uncomplimentary manner). See also note 69.

71 DL II. 55.

72 It has already been stated (note 69) that in his *Gryllus* Aristotle did not eulogize Gryllus (or Gryllus' father, Xenophon), but rather criticized and denounced those obsequious memorials (and their authors) for having debased rhetoric in order to appeal to emotions (and in order to ingratiate themselves with Xenophon). Accordingly, the connection between Gryllus' death in 362 B.C., and Aristotle's *Gryllus* is, indeed, artificial. See P. Thillet (see note 70), pp. 353 ff.; Vol. II, Chapter III. Hence, the Aristotelian *Gryllus* is not, perchance, a 'memorial' or a *consolatio mortis*. See note 69.

73 See, for instance, Cicero, *Orator* XVIII. 62; Dionysius of Halicarnassus, *Isocrates* 18; Dionysius of Halicarnassus, *I Epistola ad Ammaeum* 2; Athenaeus, *op. cit.*, II. 60DE; III. 122B: Themistius, *Oratio* XXIII 285AB (p. 345, ed. L. Dindorf); Eusebius, *op. cit.*, XIV. 6. 9; XV. 2. 7. See also note 21.

74 See note 21 and the corresponding text. F. Blass (see note 29), vol. II, pp. 451–3, is of the opinion that the *Against Aristotle* of Cephisodorus was

composed after the death of Isocrates (in 336 B.C.). E. Bignone (see note 2),
pp. 58–61, suggests that the *Against Aristotle* was a rebuttal of Aristotle's
Protrepticus (composed between 352 and 350 B.C.), and that it was composed
after Aristotle's return to Athens in the year 335–34 B.C. I. Düring (see
note 2), pp. 389–91, on the strength of the evidence found in Dionysius of
Halicarnassus, *Epistola ad Cn. Pompeium* 1, rightly assumed that the *Against
Aristotle* was primarily meant to 'set the record straight.' Düring also held
that it was written around 360 B.C. or shortly thereafter. Should Düring's
date prove to be correct, then the *Against Aristotle* might have been provoked by Aristotle's *Gryllus*. This would lend support to the theory that
in his *Gryllus* Aristotle criticized Isocrates and his methods. But, again, if
the year 360 B.C. should be accepted as the date for the composition of
Cephisodorus' *Against Aristotle*, then this work probably could not have
taken issue with Aristotle's course of lectures on rhetoric or with his
Protrepticus. Accordingly, we would have to concede either that Aristotle
began to teach rhetoric in the Academy some time before 360 B.C.—a most
unlikely assumption—or that the *Against Aristotle*, after all, was composed
not much earlier than 355 B.C., and probably somewhat later. See also P.
Moraux (see note 35), pp. 334–7.

75 See A.-H. Chroust (see note 23), p. 591. See also note 70.
76 See E. Berti (see note 66).
77 See here W. Jaeger, *Aristoteles: Grundlegung einer Geschichte seiner Entwicklung* (Berlin, 1923), English translation of 1948 (Oxford paperbacks,
1962), pp. 28–9.
78 F. Solmsen (see note 53), has pointed out that the development of Aristotelian rhetoric and Aristotelian logic go hand in hand. See also Cicero,
Orator XXXVI. 127; LI. 172.
79 F. Solmsen (see note 53), p. 218.
80 I. Düring (see note 2), pp. 258–9; 314. F. Blass (note 29), vol. II, p. 64,
already suggested this date in 1892.
81 See, especially, Isocrates, *Antidosis* 258 ff., quoted in part in the text, pp.
115–16. Aristotle's *Protrepticus*, which is believed to be a 'rebuttal' of the
Antidosis, in all likelihood was written after 353–52 B.C. See E. Einarson,
'Aristotle's *Protrepticus* and the structure of the *Epinomis*,' *Transactions and
Proceedings of the American Philological Association*, vol. 67 (Ithaca, 1936),
pp. 261–85, who maintains that the *Antidosis* definitely preceded the
Aristotelian *Protrepticus*, a view with which I. Düring and others concur.
P. von der Mühll, 'Isokrates und der *Protreptikos* des Aristoteles,' *Philologus*,
vol. 54 (1939–40), pp. 259–65; A. Lesky, *Geschichte der Griechischen
Literatur* (2nd ed., Berne-Munich, 1963), p. 600; A. Stark, in: *Göttinger
Gelehrter Anzeiger*, no. 217 (1965), p. 57, and others, however, insist
that the *Protrepticus* preceded the *Antidosis* and that the *Antidosis* was a
'rebuttal' of the *Protrepticus*.
82 See also, among others, Isocrates, *Helen* 3; 6; 7; 8–13; Isocrates, *Against
the Sophists* 1–3; 9; 11; 17 ff.; 19–20; Isocrates, *Panathenaicus* 1; 26–28;
Isocrates, *Fifth Epistle* (*Ad Alexandrum*) 3.

83 See A.-H. Chroust, 'The probable dates of some of Aristotle's lost works,' *Rivista Critica di Storia della Filosofia*, vol. 22, fasc. 1 (1967), pp. 3–23, especially, pp. 5 ff., and Vol. II, Chapter I.

84 See A.-H. Chroust (see note 83), pp. 3 ff.

CHAPTER IX   ARISTOTLE LEAVES THE ACADEMY

★ In a different form, this chapter was first published in *Greece and Rome*, vol. XIV, no. 1 (1967), pp. 39–43.

1 See DL III. 2; Apollodorus, *Chronicle*, in DL V. 9; Dionysius of Halicarnassus, *I Epistola ad Ammaeum* 5; Suda, 'article' Plato; Cicero, *Cato V.* 13; St Augustine, *De Civitate Dei* VII. 2; Athenaeus, *Deipnosophistae* V. 217B. See also *VM* 10 and *VL* 10, which relate that Plato died during the archonship of Theophilus (348–47 B.C.).

2 See, for instance, E. Zeller, *Philosophie der Griechen*, vol. II, part 1 (4th ed., Leipzig, 1889), p. 391, note; W. Jaeger, *Aristotle: Fundamentals of the History of His Development* (Oxford, 1948), pp. 105 ff.

3 This might be inferred from Plato's laudatory remarks about Aristotle's intellectual abilities. See, for instance, *VM* 7; *VL* 7; *I VS* 5; *II VA* 10–11; *IV VA* 29; etc. *II VA* 10 also speaks of 'the extraordinarily favorable impression which Aristotle made on Plato.' However, some ancient biographical reports, which are distinctly and one-sidedly hostile to Aristotle, maintain that serious rifts developed between Plato and Aristotle. For details, see Chapters I–IV. As a matter of fact, there exists an ample tradition (Eubulides, Epicurus, Theocritus, Theopompus, Lycon Pythagoraeus, Timaeus, Alexinus, Demochares and others), antagonistic to Aristotle, which, among other matters, charges the latter with flagrant ingratitude and undisguised hostility towards Plato. These reports, it is safe to assume, are blatantly prejudiced and hence wholly unreliable.

4 DL V. 1. It is reasonable to assume that Diogenes Laertius derived this information from Hermippus, a source decidedly sympathetic towards Aristotle.

5 It has already been pointed out that under the existing Athenian law of succession, Plato had little choice but appoint Speusippus, the son of his sister Potone and hence his nearest male agnatic relative, his successor to the scholarchate of the Academy as well as the heir to his estate which also included the Academy. See Chapter III, note 53, and the corresponding text; Chapter XV; note 38, and the corresponding text. Speusippus' appointment apparently did not meet with universal approval. According to *Philosophorum Academicorum Index Herculanensis* (ed. S. Mekler), pp. 37 ff., and DL IV. 1, Speusippus, aside from being a sick man, seems to have been a rather unattractive person of mediocre intellectual endowments. See, however, Athenaeus, *op. cit.*, XIII. 547F ff. Ancient tradition, which on the whole has only rather unpleasant things to say about Speusippus, seems to insinuate that only because of his close relationship with Speusippus, did

Plato appoint him his successor to the scholarchate. It has also been suggested that Aristotle (and Xenocrates) left the Academy in 348–47 B.C. primarily because he could not brook the thought of serving under a scholarch—Speusippus—of whose philosophic qualifications he had a rather low opinion. See note 37; Chapter III, note 54.

6 See A.-H. Chroust, 'The probable date of Aristotle's lost dialogue *On Philosophy*,' *Journal of the History of Philosophy*, vol. IV, no. 4 (1966), pp. 283–91; and Vol. II, Chapter XII.

7 See, for instance, Aelian, *Varia Historia* III. 19; IV. 9; Plutarch, *Adversus Coloten* 14 (*Moralia* 1115BC); Aelius Aristides, *Oratio* XLVI. 249; Dionysius of Halicarnassus, *Epistola ad Cn. Pompeium* 1; Eusebius, *Praeparatio Evangelica* XV. 2. 3 (Aristoxenus); Origen, *Contra Celsum* II. 397; Cicero, *Acad. Post.* I. 9. 33.

8 Plato, *Laws* 898E.

9 *VM* 12; 42; *VV* 6; *VL* 12; 44.

10 The laudatory remarks allegedly made by Plato about Aristotle (*VM* 7; *I VS* 5; *II VA* 10–11; *IV VA* 29), and Plato's resolve not to entrust Aristotle's preliminary education to Xenocrates (*II VA* 10), probably made Aristotle rather unpopular with some of the members of the Academy (and with Xenocrates). That Aristotle was not on the best of terms with Xenocrates may also be inferred from DL IV. 6, where Plato is quoted as, having said: 'The one [*scil.*, Xenocrates] needed a spur, the other [*scil.*, Aristotle] a bridle,' or from the statement, also credited to Plato: 'See what an ass [*scil.*, Xenocrates] I am training, and what a spirited steed [*scil.*, Aristotle] he has to run against' *ibid.* Such invidious comparisons must have aroused Xenocrates' resentment as well as that of some other members of the Academy. DL V. 3, and Quintilian, *Institutio Oratoria* III. 1. 14 (and others), record that Aristotle, paraphrasing Euripides' *Philectetes*, remarked that 'it would be a base and shameful thing to keep silent and let Xenocrates speak out.' According to Athenaeus, *Deipnosophistae* XII. 530D, Aristotle mocked Xenocrates for his prudery. See also DL IV. 7–9. There also exists a tradition according to which Xenocrates, rather than Aristotle, was the preceptor of Alexander the Great, a tale which must have irked Aristotle, the Macedonian and close friend of King Philip. See Chapter X. Plutarch, *Adversus Coloten* 32 (*Moralia* 1126C), quoting some earlier sources, relates the Alexander the Great requested Xenocrates to write for him *Didactic Essays on Kingship*. As a matter of fact, Xenocrates did compose an *Elementary Principles of Kingship, Dedicated to Alexander*. See DL IV. 14. Plutarch, *Alexander* 8, and DL V. 8, report that Alexander sent Xenocrates a large sum of money (in order to annoy Aristotle?). All this might indicate that Aristotle and Xenocrates were committed rivals. See Chapter III, notes 55–60, 70–3.

11 This is emphasized by *VM* 12; 42; *VL* 12; 44; *VV* 6.

12 Shortly before his death (and after he had fled from Athens in 323 B.C.), Aristotle is said to have written a letter to Antipater in which he pointed

out that 'in Athens things which are considered proper for a citizen are not permitted to an alien,' and that 'it is dangerous [for a Macedonian alien] to live in Athens.' See note 11.

13 *II VA* 3; *VM* 3; *VV* 2; *VL* 3.

14 *VM* 3, *VV* 2 and *VL* 3 narrate that Proxenus was a native of Atarneus. It is impossible to ascertain the correctness of this statement.

15 According to Athenaeus, *op. cit.*, VII. 279F, Strabo XIII. 1. 57, and *Epistolographi Graeci* (ed. R. Hercher, Paris, 1873): *Epistolae Socraticorum* 36. 3 (p. 635b), at one time Hermias visited Athens where he might have come into personal contact with Aristotle (and Plato?). This account, which has been challenged by some scholars, seems to be refuted, however, by Plato (?), *Sixth Epistle* 322E, where the author denies ever having met Hermias. It also appears that Hermias sent several invitations to Aristotle before and after the death of Plato, urging him to come to Atarneus. See *Philosophorum Academicorum Index Herculanensis* (ed. S. Mekler, 1902) col. 5, 22.

16 Plato (?), *Sixth Epistle* 322E, *et passim*. See also Areius Didymus, *In Demosthenis Orationes Commenta* (Berliner Klassiker Texte, vol. I, ed. H. Diels and W. Schubart, Berlin, 1904), col. 5, 21 ff.; W. Crönert, 'Neue Lesungen des Didymuspapyrus,' *Rheinisches Museum*, vol. 62 (1907), pp. 380–9; D. E. W. Wormell, 'The literary tradition concerning Hermias of Atarneus,' *Yale Classical Studies*, vol. 5 (1935), pp. 57 ff.; J. Bidez, 'Hermias d'Atarnée,' *Académie Royale de Belgique*, Bulletin de la Classe des Lettres, 5th series, vol. 29 (1943), pp. 133–46; P. Foucart, 'Étude sur Didymos d'après un papyrus de Berlin,' *Mémoires de l'Académie des Inscriptions et Belles Letters*, vol. 38 (Paris, 1906), *passim*; C. Pavese, 'Aristotele e i filosofi ad Asso,' *La Parola del Passato*, vol. 16, fasc. 77 (1961), pp. 113–19; C. M. Mulvany, 'Notes on the legend of Aristotle,' *Classical Quarterly*, vol. 20 (1926), p. 165, *et passim*. According to Areius Didymus, *op. cit.*, col. 5, 51–63, Erastus and Coriscus, and later Aristotle (and for awhile perhaps Xenocrates), frequently consulted with Hermias in Atarneus. It may be presumed, therefore, that Hermias made these men his personal councillors.

17 It has been suggested that since Aristotle frequently consulted with Hermias, he must have lived in Atarneus rather than in Assos. Assos might have been 'assigned' to Aristotle, not in the sense that the philosopher lived there permanently, but in the sense that the revenues of that city were given to Aristotle as a kind of compensation for his services to Hermias, a not uncommon practice in antiquity. Assos, it will be remembered, was acquired by Hermias through his moderate government, suggested probably by Erastus and Coriscus. See Areius Didymus (see note 16). Strabo XIII. 1. 57, however, maintains that Eubulus, the 'predecessor' of Hermias, had previously gained possession of Assos. See also Chapter XIII.

18 The ancestors of Aristotle's mother, Phaestis, originally came from Chalcis. See Dionysius of Halicarnassus, *I Epistola ad Ammaeum* 5. Apparently Phaestis, or her heirs (Aristotle), retained this ancestral home in

Chalcis. When in 323 B.C. Aristotle left Athens for the second time, he settled in Chalcis, presumably because he had inherited his mother's ancestral home. It was in this house that he died in 322 B.C. See Chapter XII.

19 See Diodorus Siculus XVI. 52. 9; Valerius Maximus V. 6. 5; Pliny, *Hist. Nat.* VII. 109; Plutarch, *Ne Suaviter Quidem Vivi Posse Secundum Epicurum* 15 (*Moralia* 1097B); Dio Chrysostom, *Oratio* II. 79; Dio Chrysostom, *Oratio* XLVII. 8; Aelian, *Varia Historia* XII. 54.

20 See A.-H. Chroust, 'Aristotle and Athens: some comments on Aristotle's sojourns in Athens,' *Laval Théologique et Philosophique*, vol. 22, no. 2 (1966), pp. 186–96, and Chapter XIII.

21 See note 39; Chapter XIII, note 20, and the corresponding text.

22 Naturally, it could be argued that *II VS* 3 is but a badly garbled account, a confusing combination of two wholly unrelated incidents—namely, Aristotle's departure from Athens and sojourn with Hermias of Atarneus in 348/47–345 B.C., and his official indictment for alleged impiety in 323 B.C., an indictment which prompted him to flee to Chalcis in order to escape condemnation and possible execution in Athens. The story, found in *II VS* 4, that Speusippus wrote a letter to Aristotle asking him to return to the Academy, however, might be the result of a confusion of Aristotle with Xenocrates. According to DL IV. 3, shortly before his death in 339–38 B.C., Speusippus 'sent a message to Xenocrates, requesting him to come back and take charge of the school [*scil.*, the Academy].' See also *Epistolographi Graeci*, nos 32–4; *Academicorum Index Herculanensis* (ed. S. Mekler, 1902), pp. 37 ff.; Themistius, *Oratio* XXI. 255B. All this would suggest (a) that Speusippus approached Xenocrates (after he had failed to persuade Aristotle to return to the Academy?); or (b) that some ancient author, biographer or epitomizer simply transferred to Aristotle the correspondence between Speusippus and Xenocrates. When *II VS* 3 relates that Aristotle went 'to a place near the Hellespont,' this remark might be an allusion to Atarneus or Assos which is indeed 'near the Hellespont' or, to be more exact, on the Asiatic mainland across from the island of Lesbos.

23 Eusebius, *op. cit.*, XV. 2. 5 (Eubulides) reports that Aristotle 'did not come to visit Plato when the latter was dying.' It is possible that Aristotle could not visit the dying Plato because he had already left Athens. Eubulides, a persistent detractor of Aristotle, probably attempted to interpret Aristotle's absence as a deliberate act on the part of Aristotle: this ungrateful and crude man does not pay his teacher and benefactor the proper respect. Eubulides, it seems, must have ignored or rejected the story (DL III. 2; Suda, 'article' Plato) that Plato died suddenly (of a heart attack?) while attending a banquet (given on the occasion of the marriage of Plato's niece?). Perhaps he accepted the fanciful report (DL III. 40) that Plato died of phtheiriasis.

24 The account in DL V. 2, which might possibly refer to the story that Aristotle allegedly seceded from Plato and from the Academy while Plato was still alive, is discussed at some length in Chapter III, notes 38 ff.,

and the corresponding texts. But DL V. 2 might also imply that Aristotle left the Academy (and Athens) before Plato died, that is, before the spring of 347 B.C., and that his departure was necessitated by certain political developments rather than by doctrinal or personal disagreements with Plato. In any event, there exists no persuasive evidence that Aristotle seceded from the Academy for doctrinal reasons, or that he 'founded his own school' while Plato was still alive. See also notes 30 and 32. I. Düring, *Aristotle in the Ancient Biographical Tradition* (Acta Universitatis Gothoburgensis, vol. 63, no. 2, Göteborg, 1957), p. 459, states that Aristotle 'withdrew to Atarneus shortly before the death of Plato.' Düring, however, does not adduce any evidence in support of his statement. Neither does he mention any reason for Aristotle's withdrawal.

25 Several *Vitae Aristotelis* refer to Aristotle's friendship with kings, including King Philip of Macedonia. See, for instance, *VM* 15–16; 44–6; *VV* 15; *VL* 15–18; 49; *II VS* 6; *I VA* 8; *IV VA* 33–4. Eusebius, *op. cit.* XV. 2. 11, maintains that people envied and hated him for his 'friendship with kings.'

26 Eusebius, *op. cit.* XV. 2. 6; Plutarch, *Vita Decem Oratorum* (*Moralia* 850B ff.); DL V. 38; Pollux IX. 42. See also I. Düring, *Herodicus the Cratetean* (Stockholm, 1941), pp. 149–51. Demochares' speech became an important source for subsequent defamations of Aristotle. It should be noted that in the opinion of many Greek (or Athenian) patriots, Greek cities joined Macedonia only because they had been 'betrayed' from within.

27 Socrates, too, might have been the victim of 'political entanglements' and animosities. It is not unreasonable to surmise that Socrates' trial in 399 B.C. was basically a political incident in the history of Athens. See A.-H. Chroust, *Socrates: Man and Myth—The Two Socratic Apologies of Xenophon* (London, 1957), pp. 164 ff.: Socrates had, or at least was suspected of having, close ties with some of the much despised Thirty Tyrants, especially, with Critias and Charmides.

28 See note 11.

29 See note 22.

30 Dionysius of Halicarnassus, *I Epistola ad Ammaeum* 7, flatly denies that Aristotle ever established his own independent school while Plato was still alive. Aristoxenus, a most unreliable witness, insinuates the opposite. See Eusebius, *op. cit.*, XV. 2. 3 (frag. 64, Wehrli); Aelius Aristides, *Oratio* XLVI. 249. 10 (who apparently relies on Aristoxenus). The influence of Aristoxenus is also felt in DL V. 2, *VM* 12; 35, and in Aelian, *Varia Historia* III. 19; IV. 9. For a refutation of Aristoxenus and his allegations, see *VM* 9–12 (taken from Philochorus) and *VL* 9–12. See also note 24.

31 See DL IV. 3–4.

32 See note 23; I. Düring (see note 21), pp. 276; 388; Ph. Merlan, 'Zur Biographie des Speusippos,' *Philologus*, vol. 103 (1959), p. 206, note 2.

33 See *I VA* 20–1; *II VA* 7–10; DL V. 5–6; *I VS* 8; *II VS* 7–8; *VM* 41–2; *VV* 19–20; *VL* 43–4. After the death of Alexander on 13 June 323 B.C., several Greek cities or states, including Athens, revolted against their

Macedonian overlords, an incident which led to the Lamian War. It was during this anti-Macedonian uprising that Aristotle was indicted for alleged impiety. See DL V. 5; *II VA* 7; Athenaeus, *op. cit.*, XV. 696A ff. See also A.-H. Chroust (see note 3), pp. 120 ff.; Chapter III, notes 178 ff., and the corresponding text; Chapter XII and Chapter XIII, notes 49 ff., and the corresponding text.

34 See A.-H. Chroust, 'The Probable Dates of Some of Aristotle's "Lost Works,"' *Rivista Critica di Storia della Filosofia*, vol. 23, fasc. 1 (1967), pp. 5–11, and Vol. II, Chapter I, *passim*.

35 See note 9 and the corresponding text.

36 See note 8 and the corresponding text.

37 Aristotle's philosophical disagreements with, and perhaps contempt for, Speusippus might be inferred from Aristotle, *Metaphysics* 1028 b 21; 1072 a 30–5; 1075 a 34; 1075 b 37; 1080 b 14; 1080 b 26; 1084 a 13; 1085 a 32; 1086 a 2; 1086 a 29; 1087 b 8; 1087 b 27; 1087 b 32; 1090 a 7; 1090 a 25; 1090 b 17; 1091 a 34; 1091 b 23; 1091 b 32; 1092 a 11–1092 b 8; Aristotle, *Nicomachean Ethics* 1153 b 4–7; 1172 a 27–1172 b 3. It has also been claimed that Aristotle's *Elegy* in the honored memory of Plato, especially the statement that 'it is not lawful for bad men' to praise Plato (Olympiodorus, *Comment. in Platonis Gorgiam*, ed. W. Norvin, p. 197; *VM* 26; *VV* 11; *LV* 30), contains an attack upon Speusippus and his friends or followers who are unworthy of their teacher, Plato. See E. Bignone, *L'Aristotele Perduto e la Formazione Filosofica di Epicuro*, vol. I (Florence, 1936), pp. 223–5; Ph. Merlan (see note 32); W. Jaeger, 'Aristotle's Verses in Praise of Plato,' *Scripta Minora*, vol. I (Rome, 1960), pp. 341–2. See also note 5.

38 See note 5.

39 Demetrius, *De Elocutione* 29; 154 (frag. 619, Rose).

40 For additional detail, see Chapter XIII, *passim*. Among other issues and events, Chapter XIII also discusses in some detail Aristotle's sojourn in Assos, Atarneus and Mytilene (348/47–343/42 B.C.) as well as the likely background and significance of this incident in the life of the Stagirite—an incident which, in the opinion of the present author, constitutes a vital part of Aristotle's personal involvements in the political schemes and aspirations of King Philip and Macedonia in general. Hence, there exists no need for subjecting the so-called 'Assian period of Aristotle' to a separate investigation in the form of a distinct chapter.

CHAPTER X   WAS ARISTOTLE ACTUALLY THE CHIEF PRECEP-
TOR OF ALEXANDER THE GREAT?

* In a different form, this chapter was first published in *Classical Folia*, vol. 18, no. 1 (1966), pp. 26–33.

1 DL V. 10. Diogenes Laertius, who relies here on Apollodorus' *Chronicle*, states that at the time Alexander was in his fifteenth year (fourteen years

old), while Apollodorus claims that this happened in the second year of the 109th Olympiad (343–42 B.C.), that is, during the archonship of Pythodotus (343–42 B.C.). Justinus, *Epitome Trogi* XII. 16, when relating to this incident, refers to Alexander's age as *exacta pueritia*. Alexander was born in the summer of 356 B.C. Accordingly, if Aristotle returned to Macedonia either during the last half of the year 343 or during the first half of 342 B.C., Alexander was thirteen years old (or, in his fourteenth year). Hence, the report of Diogenes Laertius that Alexander was in his fifteenth year implies that Aristotle returned to Macedonia (or became Alexander's preceptor) in the year of the 109th Olympiad (342–41 B.C.). Other authors or biographers (all fairly late) who make Aristotle the preceptor of Alexander are Quintilian, *Institutio Oratoria* I. 1. 23; Dionysius of Halicarnassus, *I Epistola ad Ammaeum* 5; Plutarch, *Alexander* 7–8; Plutarch, *De Exilio* 12 (*Moralia* 604D); Plutarch, *De Alexandri Fortuna aut Virtute* I. 4 (*Moralia* 327F—frag. 658, Rose); Dio Chrysostom, *Oratio* XLIX. 4; Eratosthenes (in Strabo I. 66); and others, including Hellenistic or Alexandrian biographers and historians of Alexander and his exploits. See also *VM* 21–2; *VV* 21–2; *VL* 21–2; *II VS* 6; *I VA* 6; *II VA* 18; 31; *III VA*; *IV VA* 6; 33.

2 E. Zeller, *Die Philosophie der Griechen*, vol. II, part 2 (3rd ed., Leipzig, 1879), and note 4. See also O. Gigon, 'Interpretationen zu den Antiken Aristoteles-Viten,' *Museum Helveticum*, vol. 15 (1958), pp. 184 ff.

3 DL VI. 84.

4 DL VI. 16.

5 *Ibid.*

6 DL VI. 18.

7 *Ibid.*

8 Strabo, we know, is rather contemptuous of Onesicritus as a reporter and historian, considering him an unreliable 'romancer.' See Strabo I. 28; II. 1. 9. See, in general, *Frag. Hist. Graec.* (Jacoby) II. no. 134.

9 See Suda, article 'Marsyas'; *Frag. Hist. Graec.* (Jacoby) II. no. 135; E. Zeller (see note 2).

10 In this connection one may recall the many anecdotes about the encounters between Diogenes of Sinope (the Cynic) and Alexander. Alexander apparently had a high opinion of Diogenes of Sinope. It is entirely possible that this favorable opinion is due to Alexander's acquaintance (through Onesicritus) with Cynic teachings which he seems to have held in high respect. Plutarch, *Alexander* 8, implies that Onesicritus was one of Alexander's favorites. See also *ibid.*, 65.

11 Eusebius, *Praeparatio Evangelica* XV. 2. 4. Alexinus, whose nickname was Elenxinus (because of his fondness for controversy), is mentioned in DL II. 109, where we are informed that he was a pupil of Eubulides (a persistent detractor of Aristotle). Eubulides, in turn, was a member of the School of Megara which had been founded by Euclides.

12 See, for instance, *VM* 15; 46; *VL* 15; 49. *VM* 15 and *VL* 15 also contain the information that Philip and Olympias erected a statue in honor of Aristotle,

an incident which is also mentioned by Pausanias VI. 4. 8. That Aristotle spent some time at the royal court of Macedonia is attested by all extant *Vitae Aristotelis* as well as by a number of ancient authors and historians, including Eusebius (*op. cit.*, XV. 2. 4) who cites Demochares, Theocritus, Eubulides and others as his sources. See also Plutarch, *Alexander* 7–8. Tradition also has it that Aristotle visited Macedonia several times as an emissary of Athens (?). See, for instance, DL V. 2; *VM* 13–14; 46; *VV* 13–14; *VL* 13–14; 49. *I VA* 8 relates that Aristotle was held 'in high esteem by kings' (and by King Philip); and *II VA* 28 maintains that 'great honors and high positions were conferred upon Aristotle by kings' (including by Philip), and that Aristotle 'had many disciples, among them kings and princes . . .', *ibid.*, 31. Al-Mubashir's (*II VA*) reports are reiterated by Usaibia (*IV VA* 15; 33).

13 Plutarch, *Adversus Coloten* 32 (*Moralia* 1126D). DL IV. 8 relates that Alexander gave Xenocrates a large sum of money. See also Plutarch, *Alexander* 8. *Ibid.*, we are also told that Aristotle and Alexander gradually became estranged, and that after a while Alexander began to honor Xenocrates and Anaxarchus. See also Dio Chrysostom, *Oratio* LXIV. 20.

14 DL IV. 14.

15 *Ibid.*, IV. 8–9.

16 Plutarch, *Alexander* 5. See also *ibid.*, 22; 24; 25; 55. It is not impossible that Plutarch makes use of Onesicritus' *The Education of Alexander* (see DL VI. 84). In his account, Plutarch seems to combine early and late versions of Alexander's education. He mentions Leonidas and Lysimachus together with Aristotle as the tutors of Alexander. Other authors who mention Leonidas (and others) as the tutor of Alexander are Quintilian, *Institutio Oratoria* I. 1. 9; Clement of Alexandria, *Paedagogus* I. 7; Hieronymous, *Epistola ad Laetam* (Epist. 107), *Corpus Script. Eccles. Lat.*, vol. 88 (1933), pp. 224 ff.; Pseudo-Callisthenes, *Alexandri Vita* I. 13 (ed. W. Kroll); Julius Valerius, *Res Gestae Alexandri* I. 7 (ed. B. Kübler).

17 Plutarch, *op. cit.*, 5. See also *Frag. Histor. Graec.* (Jacoby) 125, F. 7 (Chares). Suda, 'article' Philiscus, mentions an additional tutor of Alexander, namely, Philiscus. See also Pseudo-Callisthenes, *op. cit.*, I. 13. Eusebius, *op. cit.*, XV. 2. 4., reports that young Alexander 'approved of Nicagoras' (as his tutor?), but rejected Aristotle. See note 11. This Nicagoras, who was the tyrant of Zaleia (near Cyzicus), had the surname of Hermes. See Aristos of Salamis (*Frag. Histor. Graec.* 143, F. 4); Bato of Sinope (*ibid.*, 268, F. 2). Nicagoras, who seems to have been mentally deranged, not only claimed to be Hermes, but also walked about dressed like Hermes. Ephippus (*ibid.*, 126, F. 5) relates that Alexander likewise donned the dress of Hermes.

18 *II VA* 31, restated in *IV VA* 33. See also *II VS* 6: 'Among his [*scil.*, Aristotle's] famous disciples [was] . . . Alexander, the king of Macedonia.'

19 *II VA* 18.

20 *IV VA* 6.

21 See A.-H. Chroust, 'A Brief Account of the Traditional *Vitae Aristotelis*,'

Revue des Études Grecques, vol. 77, nos 364–5 (1964), pp. 60 ff.; and Chapter I.

22 Quintilian (see note 16), I. 1. 9.

23 It has been suggested that Quintilian, perhaps through some intermediary source, made use of Chrysippus' *On the Education of Children*. An *On the Education of Children* has erroneously been credited to Plutarch.

24 Clement of Alexandria, *Paedagogus* I. 7.

25 See J. Stroux, 'Die stoische Beurteilung Alexanders des Grossen,' *Philologus*, vol. 88 (1933), pp. 222–40.

26 Plutarch, *Alexander* 8. DL V. 19 relates: 'Teachers who educated children, he [*scil.*, Aristotle] stated, deserved more honor than parents who merely gave them birth. For bare life is furnished by the one, while the other ensures the good life.' See also Dio Chrysostom, *Oratio* II. 79, where King Philip expresses his satisfaction with Aristotle's performance as the teacher of Alexander.

27 DL VI. 84. The pronounced cosmopolitanism of the Cynics, which contrasts with the 'chauvinism,' 'parochialism,' 'particularism' or 'nationalism' of Aristotle, seems to fit Alexander's 'cosmopolitan designs' which he attempted to carry out in his conquest of Persia and western India. It should also be noted that Isocrates, certainly no friend of Aristotle, was in favor of a Panhellenic war against Persia (in his *Epistle to Philip*), while Aristotle, on the whole, seems to have been opposed to such a venture. (It might be conjectured that Aristotle, who himself was not a Greek in the strict sense of the term, had a low opinion of the Persians. In his opinion they were people destined 'by nature' to be slaves (see Aristotle, *Politics* 1255a 3 ff.), presumably on account of what they had done to his friend and kinsman Hermias of Atarneus.) Some recent authors have attributed to Alexander 'pan-humanitarian' ideals which antedate the idea of the Stoics on the same subject. See O. W. Reinmuth, 'Alexander and the World-State,' *The Greek Political Experience* (Oxford, 1941), pp. 109–24; W. W. Tarn, 'Alexander, Cynics and Stoics,' *American Journal of Classical Philology*, vol. IX (1939), p. 41; W. Kolbe, 'Die Weltreichsidee Alexanders des Grossen,' *Sitzungsberichte der Berliner Akademie*, vol. 24 (1937), pp. 199 ff.; H. Berve, 'Die Verschmelzungspolitik Alexanders des Grossen,' *Klio*, vol. 31 (1938), p. 135. W. W. Tarn, *Alexander the Great*, 2 vol. (Cambridge, 1948), *passim*; R. Andreotti, 'Die Weltreichsidee Alexanders des Grossen in Überlieferung und geschichtlicher Wirklichkeit,' *Saeculum*, vol. VII (1957), pp. 120–66; E. Badian, 'Alexander the Great and the unity of mankind,' *Historia*, vol. VII (1958), pp. 425–44. It would not be inappropriate to surmise that this 'pan-humanitarianism' of Alexander goes back to Cynic influences. It is also well known that some of the Stoic teachings were influenced by the Cynics. See, for instance, DL VII. 2–3, where we are told that Zeno was a pupil of Crates, the Cynic. DL VII. 4 relates that Zeno wrote his *Polity* 'on the tail of a dog,' implying that this work was strongly influenced by Cynic views.

28 See note 34 and the corresponding text.

29 Plutarch, *Alexander* 5; 22.

30 Gellius, *Attic Nights* IX. 3. This letter reads as follows: 'Philip to Aristotle, Greetings. Know that a son has been born to me . . . I hope that as a result of your training and instructing him he will prove to be worthy of us and of succeeding to our kingdom.'

31 Dio Chrysostom, *Oratio* XLIX. 4–5, attempts to explain why Philip entrusted the training of Alexander to Aristotle rather than undertake this task himself: 'Philip, who is reputed to have been the cleverest of kings, engaged Aristotle as teacher and preceptor of his son Alexander . . . The reason why he did this was that he did not feel it would be too great a risk if he should make a mistake where it concerned any one else as it would be if he should commit some error as regards [the education of] his son. . . . Although he [*scil.*, Philip] himself had had the good fortune of obtaining a good education, he did not dare to instruct Alexander himself.'

32 See, for instance, *VM* 5; *VL* 5; M. Plezia, *Aristotelis Epistolarum Fragmenta cum Testamento* (Warsaw, 1951), pp. 100 ff. We must also bear in mind that there existed some contacts between the Macedonian royal house and the Platonic Academy. This is brought out, for instance, by Pseudo-Plato, *Fifth Epistle*, which is addressed to King Perdiccas III of Macedonia, the brother of King Philip. See also Athenaeus, *Deipnosophistae* XI. 508DE; *Epist. Socrat.* 30–1. Moreover, several members of the Academy, such as Delius (Plutarch, *Adversus Coloten* 32—*Moralia* 1126D; Philostratus, *Vit. Soph.* I. 3) and Python (Plutarch, *op. cit.*, 32—*Moralia* 1126CD; Aeschines. *Oratio* II. 125) spent some time at the court of Macedonia. Plutarch, *Phocion* 14, relates, however, that there existed some 'frictions' between the Academy and Macedonia.

33 Theopompus not only composed a *Diatribe Against Plato*, but he also denounced Plato to King Philip of Macedonia. See *Frag. Hist. Graec.* T. 48; T. 7; F. 299; Athenaeus, *op. cit.*, XI. 506E. Several of Aristotle's early works, such as the *Gryllus or On Rhetoric* and the *Protrepticus* (and possibly the *Politicus*), as well as his first attempts at teaching rhetoric in the Platonic Academy during the fifties, were definitely critical of Isocrates, Isocrates' school of rhetoric (of which Theopompus had been a member), and of Isocrates' conception of the nature and function of rhetoric in general. See, for instance, A.-H. Chroust, 'Aristotle's First Literary Effort: The *Gryllus*—A Lost Work on the Nature of Rhetoric,' *Revue des Études Grecques*, vol. 78, nos 371–3 (1965), pp. 576–91, and Vol. II, Chapter III; A.-H. Chroust, 'Aristotle's Earliest Course of Lectures on Rhetoric,' *Antiquité Classique*, vol. 33, fasc. 1 (1965), pp. 58–72, and Chapter VIII.

34 This relation of Aristotle and Alexander supposedly paralleled that of Phoenix and Achilles. Alexander, who did cast himself in the role of Achilles, needed a Phoenix: Aristotle. Lysimachus, the Acarnanian and the tutor of Alexander (see note 16), had called himself the Phoenix of Alexander. But for later authors, this Lysimachus was too insignificant a person to be honored with such an important title or role.

35 See, in general, W. W. Tarn, *Alexander the Great*, vol. II (Cambridge, 1948), *passim*, especially, pp. 297, 376 and 396 ff. It should also be noted that part of the later 'Alexandrian legend,' especially the story of Alexander's alleged plans for the systematic conquest of the whole world (the facts, as far as they can still be ascertained, do not seem to bear out that Alexander ever planned such a systematic conquest of the world, see W. W. Tarn, *op. cit.*, vol. II, pp. 378 ff.), to some extent seems to coincide with the later Roman notion of the *Imperium Romanum*. See also R. Merkelbach, *Die Quellen des Grossen Alexander-Romans* (Zetemata, vol. IX, Munich, 1954), *passim*.

36 For examples, see W. W. Tarn, *op. cit.*, *passim*; R. Merkelbach, *op. cit.*, *passim*. Plutarch's account of Alexander's education by Aristotle, which was written during the second half of the first century or the early part of the second century A.D., in the main is part of this 'romantic' tradition.

37 See A.-H. Chroust, 'The miraculous disappearance and recovery of the *Corpus Aristotelicum*,' *Classica et Mediaevalia*, vol. 23 (1962–63), pp. 50–67.

38 See, for instance, W. W. Tarn, 'Alexander the Great and the unity of mankind,' *Proceedings of the British Academy* (1933), pp. 140–5; 166, *et passim*; W. W. Tarn (see note 35), pp. 378 ff.

39 See A.-H. Chroust, 'Aristotle and Callisthenes of Olynthus,' *Classical Folia*, vol. 20, no. 1 (1966), pp. 32–41, and Chapter VI. See also M. Brocker, *Aristoteles als Alexanders Lehrer in der Legende* (Doctorial Dissertation, Bonn, 1966); P. Merlan, 'Isocrates, Aristotle and Alexander the Great,' *Historia*, vol. III (1954), pp. 60–81.

40 See J. Stroux (see note 25), *passim*.

41 This mutual 'dislike' might also be explained as follows: when King Philip divorced Olympias, the mother of Alexander, and married Cleopatra, the niece of Attalus, Alexander's succession to the throne of Macedonia was in jeopardy. During the wedding feast, Attalus, perhaps at the prompting of King Philip, urged the guests to implore the gods to give Philip a *legitimate* heir through Cleopatra. (Gossip had it that Philip was not the father of Alexander.) It is only natural that after this incident Alexander should hate Philip as well as Philip's friends and associates, including Aristotle, a close friend of Philip. Conversely, rumor had it that Alexander was privy to the murder of Philip in the summer of 336 B.C. After all, Alexander had much to gain by this sordid deed, including the throne of Macedonia. Hence, Aristotle hated Alexander for killing his friend and protector, Philip.

42 For a thorough presentation and analysis of the ancient biographical tradition concerning Aristotle, see, in general, I. Düring, *Aristotle in the Ancient Biographical Tradition* (Acta Universitatis Gothoburgensis, vol. 63, no. 2, Göteborg, 1957); O. Gigon (see note 2), pp. 147–93; O. Gigon, *Vita Aristotelis Marciana* (Kleine Texte für Vorlesungen und Übungen, Berlin, 1962); and Chapters I–IV.

43 *VM* 21; *VL* 21. See also Elias (*olim* David), *Comment. in Porphyrii Isagogen*

et in Aristotelis Categorias, CIAG, vol. XVIII, part 1 (ed. A. Busse, Berlin, 1900), p. 112, lines 24–7; Suetonius, *The Lives of the Caesars* VIII (Titus) 1: 'On another occasion, remembering . . . that [as the emperor] he [*scil.*, Titus] had done nothing for anyone all that day, uttered that memorial and praiseworthy statement: "Friends, I have lost a day."' See also Xenophon, *Memorabilia* III. 9. 10–13.

44 *VM* 21 and *VL* 21 also refer to a work of Aristotle, entitled *On Kingship* (see DL V. 22, no. 18; *VH* 10, no. 16; *IV VA*, no. 8), which he supposedly wrote for Alexander (in the year 340 B.C.?), and which might have contained the maxim that to labor constantly for the promotion of the common weal is the ultimate function and the most noble justification of kingship in general. This, then, would make the *On Kingship* part of the general protreptic literature or, perhaps, a sort of 'mirror for princes.' See also Vol. II, Chapter XVII. DL V. 22 (no. 17) and *VH* 10 (no. 22) also mention a *To Alexander or On Colonization*, in one book.

45 This is also implied in *VM* 21 and *VL* 21. Plutarch, *Maxime Cum Principibus Philosophandum Esse* 1 (*Moralia* 776D), suggests that the philosopher who educates a king also educates the peoples over whom the latter rules. In this sense the philosopher becomes the benefactor of the whole people and, in some instances, of the whole of mankind.

CHAPTER XI   ARISTOTLE'S RETURN TO ATHENS IN 335/34 B.C.

★ With some changes, this chapter was first published in *Laval Théologique et Philosophique*, vol. 23, no. 2 (1967), pp. 244–54.

1 DL V. 4–5; *VM* 23; *VV* 21; *VL* 23.

2 Dionysius of Halicarnassus, *I Epistola ad Ammaeum* 5.

3 DL V. 10 (Apollodorus).

4 Dionysius of Halicarnassus (see note 2).

5 DL V. 4–5.

6 *II VA* 19, and *ibid.*, 24.

7 *IV VA* 6, and *ibid.*, 22.

8 *VM* 23, where we are told that since the omens were unfavorable, Aristotle tried to dissuade Alexander from invading Persia.

9 *I VA* 10–11. See also *II VA* 24–5; *IV VA* 22–3; *VM* 23; *VL* 23.

10 In 370–69 B.C., on the death of King Amyntas III (the father of Alexander II, Perdiccas and Philip), Alexander II succeeded to the throne of Macedonia. Since at the time Alexander II was a mere child, his uncle Ptolemy of Alorus became his 'guardian' as well as the regent of Macedonia. In 369–68 B.C., Ptolemy, with the connivance of Eurydice (the mother of Alexander II), murdered Alexander II and had himself proclaimed king (and also married Eurydice). Perdiccas, in turn, assassinated Ptolemy in 365 B.C., thus becoming king of Macedonia. Perdiccas, who had a son and heir to the throne, namely, Amyntas IV, died in battle in 360–59 B.C. After Perdiccas' death, Philip, the next of kin, became the 'guardian' of

Amyntas IV (who at the time was still a small boy) as well as the regent of Macedonia. Without resorting to the murder of Amyntas IV, Philip had himself declared king in 356 B.C. Hence Amyntas IV, who was still alive at the time of Philip's assassination in 336 B.C., had a legitimate claim to the throne of Macedonia.

11 See Diodorus Siculus XVII. 2. 4 ff.; XVII. 5. 1 ff.; Curtius Rufus VI. 9. 17; VII. 1. 13; Justin XI. 5. 1 ff.; XI. 7. 12; XII. 6. 14; Plutarch, *Alexander* 10; Pausanias VIII. 7. 5.

12 See Aeschines, *Contra Ctesiphontem* 160; Diodorus Siculus XVII. 3; Plutarch, *Alexander* 11; Plutarch, *Phocion* 16; Plutarch, *Demosthenes* 23.

13 See Diodorus Siculus XVII. 4; Arrian I. 7. 1-3; Justin XI. 3. 1-3.

14 Arrian II. 14. 6; Plutarch, *De Alexandri Fortuna et Virtute* (*Moralia* 327C); Plutarch, *Demosthenes* 20; Aeschines, *Contra Ctesiphontem* 156; 239 ff.; Dinarchus, *Contra Demosthenem* 10; 18.

15 Arrian I. 7. 1-3; Diodorus Siculus XVII. 8; Plutarch, *Demosthenes* 23.

16 The Theban leaders first tried to reassure the alarmed people by claiming that since Alexander was dead it must be Antipater who was approaching the city. Later they announced that it was not Alexander of Macedonia but Alexander of Lyncestis who had been seen in the vicinity of Thebes. See Arrian I. 7. 4-11; Diodorus Siculus XVII. 9. 10.

17 At the same time the Athenians welcomed the few Theban refugees who had managed to escape the holocaust, ordered the rural population of Attica to seek shelter behind the walls of Athens and prepared the city for a siege. See Arrian I. 10. 1-4; Plutarch, *Alexander* 13.

18 The complete list of these men is preserved in Suda, *Antipater*. Suda mentions also Polyeuctas, Ephialtes, Diotimus, Patroclus (should read Moerocles) and Thrasybulus. See also Arrian I. 10. 4, who omits Thrasybulus; Plutarch, *Demosthenes* 23, who omits Hyperides, Chares and Thrasybulus, but adds Demon and Callisthenes.

19 See Arrian I. 10. 6; Diodorus Siculus XVII. 15; Plutarch, *Demosthenes* 23; Plutarch, *Phocion* 17.

20 A contemporary orator compared the destruction of Thebes by Alexander with the tearing of the moon from the heavens. See Hegesias, frag. 2; Dinarchus, *Contra Demosthenem* 24; Arrian I. 9. 1-10; Plutarch, *Alexander* 13.

21 From his father, Philip, one of the shrewdest statesmen and most successful politicians in antiquity, Alexander might have learned that, according to the tenets of crude *Realpolitik*, such a wanton act might frighten the Greeks into total and lasting submission.

22 *II VS* 3: 'But frightened by the execution of Socrates, he [*scil.*, Aristotle] left Athens and stayed near the Hellespont.' See also A.-H. Chroust, 'Aristotle leaves the Academy,' *Greece and Rome*, vol. 14, no. 1 (1967), pp. 39-43, and Chapter IX; A.-H. Chroust, 'Aristotle and Athens: some comments on Aristotle's sojourns in Athens,' *Laval Théologique et Philosophique*, vol. 22, no. 2 (1966), pp. 188-9, and Chapter XIII.

23 There exists some doubt, however, as to whether Aristotle was indeed the tutor, or the chief preceptor, of Alexander. See, for instance, A.-H. Chroust, 'Was Aristotle actually the preceptor of Alexander the Great?,' *Classical Folia*, vol. 18, no. 1 (1964), pp. 26–33, and Chapter X.

24 See, for instance, *VM* 15–16; *VV* 15–16; *VL* 15–16; *I VA* 8; *II VA* 28; *IV VA* 15; Eusebius, *Praeparatio Evangelica* XV. 2. 6; XV. 2. 10.

25 See, for instance, *VM* 17; *VV* 17; *VL* 17; *IV VA* 16.

26 See Chapter XIII, notes 22–8.

27 See, for instance, *VM* 15–16; 17–18; 20; 23; 46; 49; *VV* 15–16; 17; 21; *VL* 15–16; 17; 19–20; 49; *I VS* 10; *II VA* 28; 29–30; *III VA*; *IV VA* 13; 15–16; 17–18; 21. DL V. 26 lists letters of Aristotle to Philip, Alexander, Antipater (in nine books), Mentor, Olympias, Hephaestion and to other prominent personalities. See also *VH* 10 (no. 137).

28 See, for instance, Dio Chrysostom, *Oratio* XLIV. 20; Plutarch, *Alexander* 8.

29 Later, in the year 323 B.C., when the Athenians drove Aristotle out of the city for a second time, he seems to have lost some of his love for Athens. It was in 323 B.C. that he supposedly wrote to Antipater that the city of Athens was crowded with professional informers (sycophants), that it was dangerous for a Macedonian alien to live in Athens, and that in Athens things which were permitted to an Athenian citizen were not permitted to a Macedonian alien. See *VM* 41–2; *VV* 19–20; *VL* 43–4; Elias (*olim* David), *Comment. in Prophyrii Isagogen et in Aristotelis Categorias*, CIAG, vol. XVIII, part 1 (ed. A. Busse, Berlin, 1900), p. 123, lines 15 ff.; DL V. 5 (Favorinus); Aelian, *Varia Historia* III. 36; Origen, *Contra Celsum* I. 380; Eustathius, *Comment. in Odyss.* VII. 120–1.

30 *IV VA* 17–19. This incident is briefly referred to in *VM* 20 and *VL* 20. A remote echo of this story might be detected in DL V. 2. Aristotle, it appears, was publicly honored at least four times: (1) by a statue erected in Stagira by King Philip (*VM* 15; *VL* 15; Pausanias VI. 4. 8); (2) by an honorific inscription at Delphi, dedicated by the Amphictionic League (W. Dittenberger, *Syll. Inscript. Graec.*3 275; Aelian, *Varia Historia* XIV. 1); (3) by Athens (*IV VA* 17–19; *VM* 20; *VL* 20); and (4) posthumously by Stagira (*VM* 17–18; *VV* 17; *VL* 17; 19; *I VS* 10; *II VA* 29–30; *IV VA* 30–1). See, however, Chapter XII, note 40.

31 See E. Drerup, 'Ein Attisches Proxeniendekret für Aristoteles,' *Mittheilungen des Kaiserlichen Deutschen Archaeologischen Instituts*, vol. XXIII (Athens, 1898), pp. 369–81. See also C. I. A. II. 68; II. 124; II. 161; II. 193; II. 194; II. 234; II. 249; II. 263; II. 264; II. 300; IV. 2. 107b; IV. 2. 264c; IV. 2. 264d—all cited in Drerup, *op. cit.*, p. 373. It goes without saying that the last part of Usaibia's report, beginning with, 'Those of the Athenians ...,' was not a part of the original decree of *proxenia*. See text, p. 138. DL VII. 10–12 reproduces the honorific inscription dedicated to Zeno, the Stoic, by the Athenians, although Zeno, like Aristotle, was an alien.

32 This might be gathered, for instance, from DL V. 2; *VM* 20; *VL* 20.

33 *IV VA* 18.

34 Usaibia's account (*IV VA* 17–18) makes it quite obvious that the decree of *proxenia* conferred upon Aristotle was moved by a spokesman of the pro-Macedonian factions in Athens and subsequently carried by the pro-Macedonian partisans who after 335 B.C. had the upper hand in the city. This might also lend some support to the contention that this decree was formally bestowed upon Aristotle because in the year 335 B.C. he had successfully interceded with Alexander on behalf of Athens. Conversely, the action of Himeraeus (*IV VA* 20), the well-known anti-Macedonian, probably took place in the summer of 323 B.C., when the news of Alexander's death reached Athens. It was then that the *stele* honoring Aristotle was removed. (At approximately the same time the Amphictionic League at Delphi, which joined the anti-Macedonian revolt in 323 B.C., destroyed the inscription at Delphi commemorating Aristotle's services to the League.) The restoration of the *stele* or honorific inscription removed by Himeraeus probably was undertaken some time after the battle of Crannon (in 322 B.C.), and after the re-occupation of Athens by Antipater. See also note 42.

35 See, for instance, Eusebius, *op. cit.*, XV. 2. 6, where Demochares is quoted as having maintained (in 306 B.C.) that many of the letters addressed by Aristotle to Antipater had been intercepted and that the contents of these letters (official reports?, 'intelligence reports'?) were found to be detrimental to the political interests of Athens. DL V. 26 relates that Aristotle wrote 'nine books of letters to Antipater.' Since, intellectually, Aristotle and Antipater had absolutely nothing in common, one may wonder about the content of these many 'letters' or 'reports.' In any event, according to Eusebius, *loc. cit.*, Demochares continues his condemnation of Aristotle as the sworn enemy of Athens by pointing out that the Stagirite had also betrayed Stagira, his native city, to the Macedonians; and that he had denounced the wealthiest citizens of Olynthus to King Philip. Accordingly, it may also be assumed that in his speech against 'subversive' or alien philosophers, Demochares accused Aristotle of having been an informer or 'political agent' working for Macedonia against Athens. See also Pseudo-Plutarch, *Vita Decem Oratorum* (*Moralia* 850B ff.); Pollux IX. 42; Athenaeus, *Deipnosophistae* XIII. 610EF; XI. 509B; DL V. 38.

36 See A.-H. Chroust, 'Aristotle and Athens: Some Comments on Aristotle's Sojourns in Athens' (see note 22), and Chapter XIII.

37 To mention only a few of these slanderers of Aristotle: Theopompus, Theocritus of Chios, Timaeus, Lycon Pythagoraeus, Alexinus, Eubulides, Demochares, Epicurus (and the Epicureans in general) and many others. Some of these slanderous stories were recorded by Diogenes Laertius and by the *Vita Aristotelis Hesychii*. See also Eusebius, *op. cit.*, XV. chap. 2.

38 The traditional accounts have it that the years between 335–34 and 323 B.C. were philosophically the most productive years—the philosophic *Meister-jahre*—in the life of Aristotle. In the light of the unpleasant as well as trying circumstances surrounding Aristotle's life in Athens during these years, this

view might have to be revised somewhat, as would the opinion that the whole of the extant *Corpus Aristotelicum* should without exception be credited to Aristotle. Tradition also has it that between 335-34 and 323 B.C., Aristotle founded his own distinct and independent school—a school which was on a par with the Academy—and that he was the first scholarch of the Peripatus (or Lyceum). These views, too, will have to be jettisoned. See note 49, and Chapter XV, note 117.

39 In his learned and informative book, *Aristotle in the Ancient Biographical Tradition* (*Acta Universitatis Gothoburgensis*, vol. 63, no. 2, Göteborg, 1957), p. 460, I. Düring explains Aristotle's return to Athens in 335-34 B.C. in rather idyllic terms: 'When in 334, after the destruction of Thebes, he [*scil.*, Aristotle] returned to Athens in order to stay there, he did not come as the celebrated philosopher known to everybody as Alexander's tutor. . . . He was merely one of the old dons of the Academy who returned, a professor among other foreign professors in Athens.'

40 See A.-H. Chroust, 'Aristotle's Flight from Athens in the Year 323 B.C.,' *Historia*, vol. 15, no. 2 (1966), pp. 185-92, and Chapter XII. See also Chapter IX.

41 DL 5-6; Athenaeus, *op. cit.*, XV. 696A ff.; VH 6; *II VA* 20-21; *IV VA* 7-10; *II VS* 3. *VM* 41, *VV* 19 and *VL* 43 only relate that the Athenians 'turned against Aristotle.'

42 *IV VA* 17-18.

43 *IV VA* 20-1.

44 *IV VA* 20.

45 *IV VA* 21.

46 *Ibid.*

47 See A.-H. Chroust, 'Aristotle Leaves the Academy,' *Greece and Rome*, vol. 14, no. 1 (1967), pp. 39-43, and Chapter IX. It may also be contended that originally, in the year 367 B.C., Aristotle went to Athens for 'political reasons,' that is, in order to escape the ruthless inter-dynastic struggles which convulsed Macedonia between 369-68 and 365 B.C. An echo of these events may still be detected in *VM* 3; *VV* 2; *VL* 3. See Chapter XIII, notes 5-10, and the corresponding text.

48 After the battle of Crannon in 322 B.C., Antipater once more restored Macedonian rule over Greece and Athens. However, by that time Aristotle was on his death bed, if not already dead. Otherwise he might very well have returned to Athens once more. See Chapter XIII, note 102.

49 This might also explain why, in his last will and testament, Aristotle never so much as mentions Athens. See Chapter XV, *passim*. But, then, it must always be kept in mind (i) that under existing Athenian laws, Aristotle, the 'resident Macedonian alien,' could not own any real property in Athens or Attica, that is, any real property which he might have bequeathed to his heirs; (ii) that upon his flight from Athens in 323 B.C., he took with him all of his movable property (it is said that he gave his private library to Theophrastus); and (iii) that he never owned a distinct school of

his own in Athens, that is, school grounds, school buildings, a school library etc. in Athens, comparable to the Platonic Academy, which he could leave and bequeath to the person he intended to make his successor as the 'head of the school.' See also note 38, and Chapter XV, note 117.

CHAPTER XII   ARISTOTLE'S FLIGHT FROM ATHENS IN THE YEAR 323 B.C.

* In a different form, this chapter was first published in *Historia*, vol. 15, no. 2 (1966), pp. 185–191.

1 Dionysius of Halicarnassus, *I Epistola ad Ammaeum* 5; DL V. 5–7; V. 10. Dionysius of Halicarnassus claims that Aristotle fled from Athens 'in the thirteenth year [of his second sojourn in Athens], after the death of Alexander [13 June, 323 B.C.] during the archonship of Cephisodorus [323–22 B.C.]. . . .' Diogenes Laertius, quoting Apollodorus, relates that 'in the third year of the 114th Olympiad [322–21 B.C.], Aristotle retired to Chalcis . . . during the archonship of Philocles [322–21 B.C.].' This latter reference dates Aristotle's death rather than his flight from Athens. See A.-H. Chroust, 'The *Vita Aristotelis* of Dionysius of Halicarnassus (*I Epistola ad Ammaeum* 5),' *Acta Antiqua Academiae Scientiarum Hungaricae*, vol. 13, nos 3–4 (1965), pp. 369–77, and Chapter II; A.-H. Chroust, 'A brief analysis of the *Vita Aristotelis* of Diogenes Laertius (DL V. 1–16),' *Antiquité Classique*, vol. 34, fasc. 1 (1965), pp. 97–129, and Chapter III, *passim*, especially, notes 180–1, and the corresponding text, and notes 201–5, and the corresponding text.

2 DL V. 5–7. For the hymn or paean, see DL V. 7–8. Athenaeus, *Deipnosophistae* XV. 696A, who also cites the hymn, maintains that Eurymedon merely initiated the legal motion to have Aristotle indicted for impiety, while Demophilus actually pressed the official charges. The parallel with the technical manoeuvres of Anytus and Meletus during the trial of Socrates in 399 B.C. is rather obvious. Neither *VM* nor *VV* nor *VL* mentions the indictment of Aristotle, though they relate that 'the Athenians turned against him.' *VM* 41; *VV* 19; *VL* 43. *II VA* 20 and *IV VA* 7 relate that Eurymedon had charged Aristotle with impiety (and blasphemy), but make no allusion to the hymn or paean in honor of Hermias as the incriminating evidence. *VH* 6, on the other hand, explicitly cites the 'sacrilegious' memorial hymn or paean. For this hymn, see also Areius Didymus, *In Demosthenis Orationes Commenta* (ed. H. Diels and W. Schubart, Berlin, 1904), col. 6, 22 ff.; for the epigram, see *ibid.*, col. 6, 36 ff.; for Callisthenes' encomium of Hermias, see *ibid.*, col. 5, 64 ff. As to the story that Aristotle sacrificed in a sacrilegious manner to Pythias as to a goddess, see note 14.

3 Athenaeus, *op. cit.*, XV. 696A–696E. See also frag. 675, Rose; Lucian, *Eunuchus* 9 (frag. 645, Rose); Himerius, *Oratio* VI. 6–7. Athenaeus' ultimate source is probably Hermippus. See Athenaeus, *op. cit.*, XV. 696EF.

4 The paean was originally associated with the worship of Apollo. To address a living human being in a paean was considered an act of sacrilege. The distinction between a paean and a hymn, however, is not always clear. It will be noted that Diogenes Laertius calls the 'memorial' in honor of Hermias a 'paean' (DL V. 4) as well as a 'hymn' (DL V. 6), while Areius Didymus, *op. cit.*, col. 6, 19, refers to this 'memorial' as 'paean' without further discussion.

5 A *scolion* was originally a song with a refrain which was 'passed around' at banquets, being sung in turn by each of the guests, to the accompaniment of a lute. It is said that the *scolion* was introduced by Terpander. See also Plato, *Gorgias* 451E ff.

6 See DL V. 7-8; Areius Didymus, *op. cit.*, col. 6, 18 ff.; C. M. Bowra, 'Aristotle's Hymn to Virtue,' *Classical Quarterly*, vol. 12 (1938), pp. 182-9; D. E. W. Wormell, 'The literary tradition concerning Hermias of Atarneus,' *Yale Classical Studies*, vol. 5 (1935), pp. 63-5.

7 Athenaeus, *op. cit.*, XV. 697AB. Concerning the *Defense Against the Charge of Impiety*, see pp. 147-8. See also Aristotle, *Rhetoric* 1400 b 5 ff.: 'When the people of Elea asked Xenophanes whether they should or should not sacrifice to Leocothea and mourn for her, he advised them not to mourn for her if they thought her a goddess, and not to sacrifice to her if they thought her a mortal woman.'

8 Areius Didymus, *op. cit.*, col. 5, 64.

9 Himerius, *Oratio* VI. 6.

10 For an attempt to reconstruct the essential content of Ptolemy (-el-Garib)'s *Vita Aristotelis*, see I. Düring, *Aristotle in the Ancient Biographical Tradition* (Acta Universitatis Gothoburgensis, vol. 63, no 2. Göteborg, 1957), pp. 472-3; A.-H. Chroust, 'A brief account of the traditional *Vitae Aristotelis*,' *Revue des Études Grecques*, vol. 77, nos 364-5 (1964), pp. 50-69, especially, pp. 62-9, and Chapter I, notes 106-204, and the corresponding text.

11 For a discussion and analysis of the Syriac and Arabic *Vitae Aristotelis*, see A.-H. Chroust, 'A brief survey of the Syriac and Arabic *Vitae Aristotelis*,' *Acta Orientalia* (Denmark), vol. 29, fasc. 1-2 (1965), pp. 23-47, and Chapter IV.

12 *IV VA* 7 adds that Aristotle reports all this in a letter addressed to Antipater.

13 See here also Origen, *Contra Celsum* I. 380.

14 *II VA* 20; *IV VA* 7. This account recasts some of the events which probably transpired in connection with the indictment and trial of Socrates in the year 399 B.C. DL V. 4 (Aristippus) and Eusebius, *Praeparatio Evangelica* XV. 2. 8 (Lycon Pythagoraeus), also relate that Aristotle allegedly sacrificed to his wife Pythias as the Athenians sacrifice to Demeter of Eleusis. This, too, might have been part of Aristotle's indictment for alleged 'impiety.' Aristippus claims that Aristotle did so while Pythias was still alive, Lycon insists that this happened only after her death.

15 *II VA* 20.

16 This remark may actually refer to Aristotle's departure from Athens in the year 348 B.C., a departure, which apparently was likewise occasioned by 'political pressures.' See A.-H. Chroust, 'Aristotle leaves the Academy,' *Greece and Rome*, vol. 14, no. 1 (1967), pp. 39–43, and Chapter IX, note 22.

17 *IV VA* 9 adds that apparently no one interfered with Aristotle's voluntary departure.

18 *VM* 41–2; *VV* 19–20; *VL* 43–4. See also Elias (*olim* David), *Comment. in Porphyrii Isagogen et in Aristotelis Categorias*, CIAG, vol. XVIII, part 1 (ed. A. Busse, Berlin, 1900), p. 123, lines 15 ff.; DL V. 9 (Favorinus); Aelian, *Varia Historia* III. 36; Origen, *Contra Celsum* I. 380; Eustathius, *Comment. in Odyss.* VII 120–1; Athenaeus, *op. cit.*, XV. 696A ff. While *VV* 19, *VL* 43, *II VS* 3, *II VA* 21 and *IV VA* 8 mention Socrates in this connection, *VM* 41 omits any such reference. The quotation from Homer, *Odyssey* VIII. 120, 'Pear grows upon pear, and fig upon fig,' is an oblique reference to the many professional informers (sycophants) who made life in Athens almost unbearable. It is possible that some of the dicta credited to the departing Aristotle were contained in a letter which he addressed to Antipater (see *IV VA* 7), provided such a letter (or letters) was actually written by Aristotle. DL V. 27 (no. 144) mentions *Letters to Antipater* in nine books.

19 DL V. 9 (Favorinus); Athenaeus, *op. cit.*, 697AB; Origen, *Contra Celsum* I. 380; *IV VA* 10.

20 See note 17, *supra*. Some Hellenistic authors (e.g. Artemon) probably transferred Theophrastus' *Defense Against Hagnonides* of 319 B.C. to Aristotle. See Aelian, *Varia Historia* VIII. 12. Favorinus, according to the testimony of DL V. 9, called this *Defense* a 'forensic speech.'

21 *IV VA* 10. This would indicate that in his *Vita Aristotelis* Ptolemy (-el-Garib) had denied the authenticity of this *Defense*. It will be noted that also Athenaeus, *op. cit.*, XV. 697B, doubts its authenticity. See note 7, and the corresponding text. *VH* 10 (no. 189) lists this *Defense* among the spurious works of Aristotle.

22 See Plato, *Apology* 17E ff.; Plato, *Meno* 94E ff.; Xenophon, *Defense of Socrates* 29.

23 See A.-H. Chroust, *Socrates: Man and Myth—The Two Socratic Apologies of Xenophon* (London, 1957), pp. 164 ff.; pp. 189 ff.

24 See DL V. 6; Athenaeus, *op. cit.*, XV. 696A. See also notes 3–7, and the corresponding text.

25 The *graphe asebeias*, it may be presumed, was no longer officially enforced in 323 B.C.

26 *VH* 6 mentions the 'hymn,' but not the Delphic inscription. See note 2.

27 It has been argued that since Aristotle had his 'own school' in Athens after 335–34 B.C., he must have had a respectable standing in the Athenian community. This reasoning, however, overlooks two salient factors: first, it is by no means certain that in 335–34 or any time thereafter Aristotle founded and owned such a separate school (in a legal or physical sense)

which was on an equal footing with the Platonic Academy (see Chapter XI, notes 38 and 49; Chapter XV, note 117); and, second, when Aristotle returned to Athens in 335-34 B.C., he did so with the help of Alexander and the conquering Macedonian army (to which the Athenians surrendered rather meekly), a fact which assuredly did nothing to enhance Aristotle's popularity with the majority of the Athenians. See, in general, this Chapter; Chapter XI, *passim*; Chapter XIII, *passim*.

28 Unlike the wills of Theophrastus (DL V. 51-7), Straton of Lampsacus (DL V. 61-4), and Lycon (DL V. 69-74), the last will and testament of Aristotle contains no stipulations whatever regarding a 'school property' or, for that matter, as regards any real property in Athens or Attica. See Chapter XI, notes 38 and 49; Chapter XV, note 117.

29 DL V. 39.

30 See notes 33-4.

31 This may be gathered, for instance, from Demosthenes' *Philippica*, *Olynthiacs* and *De Corona*.

32 The inflammatory speeches of Demosthenes and other anti-Macedonians (Lycurgus and Himeraeus) certainly contributed to Aristotle's general unpopularity.

33 DL V. 38; Athenaeus, *op. cit.*, XIII. 610EF; XI. 509BC; Pseudo-Plutarch, *Vita Decem Oratorum* (*Moralia* 850B ff.); Pollux IX. 42; DL V. 38.

34 Eusebius, *op. cit.*, XV. 2. 6.

35 *VM* 42. See also *VL* 44; Elias (*olim* David) (see note 18); Origen, *Contra Celsum* I. 380; Aelian, *Varia Historia* III. 36.

36 See note 16.

37 It is possible that, in his *Oration Against the Philosophers* of 306 B.C., Demochares revived some of the charges made by the anti-Macedonian partisans in Athens against Aristotle in the year 323 B.C. See Eusebius, *op. cit.*, XV. 2. 6, and notes 33-4. Perhaps he also made use of some of the slanderous stories about Aristotle that had been invented and circulated by Theopompus, Theocritus of Chios and by other detractors of Aristotle.

38 See A.-H. Chroust, 'Aristotle returns to Athens in the year 335 B.C.,' *Laval Théologique et Philosophique*, vol. 23, no. 2 (1967), pp. 244-54, and Chapter XI.

39 *IV VA* 17-21.

40 See also *VM* 20; *VL* 20; DL V. 2. At one time (probably after 329-28 B.C.; see D. M. Lewis, 'An Aristotle Publication-Date,' *Classical Review*, vol. 72, 1958, p. 108), the Amphictionic League dedicated an honorific inscription to Aristotle in Delphi for services he had rendered the League. See W. Dittenberger, *Syll. Inscript. Graec.*³, no. 275; Aelian, *Varia Historia* XIV. 1; Chapter VI, note 20. In 323 B.C., when the Amphictionic League joined the general Greek uprising against Macedonia (Lamian War), this inscription was removed. When Aristotle heard about this incident, according to Aelian, *loc. cit.*, he allegedly wrote a letter to Antipater in which he stated: 'About the decision of the Amphictionic League and their resolve to

deprive me of my honors, my feeling is that I am sorry, but not very sorry.' O. Gigon, *Vita Aristotelis Marciana* (Kleine Texte für Vorlesungen und Übungen, Berlin, 1962), p. 59, maintains that it is quite likely that the Athenians at one time erected a *stele* honoring or commemorating Aristotle; that this *stele* was removed in the year 323 B.C.; and that it was restored after the battle of Crannon (in 322 B.C.). Hence, according to Gigon, the report found in *IV VA* 17–21, after all, might be historical. I. Düring (see note 10), pp. 233–6, on the other hand, holds the opposite view. See also Chapter XI.

41 Together with other prominent anti-Macedonian political leaders, Himeraeus was executed by Antipater on 5 October 322 B.C., that is, after the battle of Crannon which led to the reoccupation of Athens by the Macedonians. This execution had nothing to do with the destruction of the Aristotle-*stele* in 323 B.C. Demosthenes committed suicide in order to escape execution. See Plutarch, *Demosthenes* 29.

42 For additional detail, see A.-H. Chroust (see note 38), and Chapter XI.

43 According to Eusebius, *op. cit.*, XV. 2. 5 (Aristocles), 'Eubulides in his book *Against Aristotle* . . . asserted that he [*scil.*, Aristotle] offended Philip. . . .' This remark might possibly be a transfer from the story, related in Athenaeus, *op. cit.*, XI. 506DE, that Plato slandered Archelaus, the king of Macedonia. See Plato, *Gorgias* 471A; Plato (?), *II Alcibiades* 141D. Athenaeus, *loc. cit.*, also relates that Speusippus wrote a letter to King Philip reminding him that he owed the throne of Macedonia to Plato's advice and, hence, should cease denouncing and slandering Plato.

44 Aside from the traditional *Vitae Aristotelis*, this fact is also stressed by Plutarch, Curtius Rufus, Arrian, Quintilian, Dio Chrysostom, Pliny, Aelian, Athenaeus and by many others. On the authority of Aristocles (Eusebius, *op. cit.*, XV. 2. 11), we know that Aristotle was envied as well as hated (by the Athenians?) 'for his friendship with kings.'

45 DL V. 1; *VM* 2; *VV* 1; *VL* 2; *II VA* 2; *IV VA* 2; Suda, 'article' Nicomachus.

46 See DL V. 2; *VM* 20; *VL* 20; *IV VA* 17–21; etc. All this seems to imply that Aristotle must have been very active in the political arena, something which is also borne out by the many letters (or reports?) which he sent to Philip, Alexander and Antipater. See DL V. 27, which refers to Aristotle's *Letters to Philip, Letters to Alexander* (in four books) and to *Letters to Antipater* (in nine books). See also *VM* 23, *VV* 23 and *VL* 23, where we are told that Aristotle was held in high esteem, and was much honored, by Antipater; and that thanks to his intercession with Philip or Alexander, he became instrumental in the rebuilding of Stagira. See *VM* 17; *VV* 17; *VL* 17; Diodorus Siculus XVI. 52. 9; Pliny, *Hist. Nat.* VII. 109; Plutarch, *Ne Suaviter Quidem Vivi Posse Secundum Epicurum* 15 (*Moralia* 1097B); Dio Chrysostom, *Oratio* II. 79; Aelian, *Varia Historia* III. 17; etc. See also Chapters XI and XIII.

47 See also Origen, *Contra Celsum* I. 380.

48 *II VA* 20.

49 See, for instance, Plato, *Apology* 18A ff.; 19A ff.; 21B ff.; 23A ff.; 23C ff.; 24B ff.; 26D ff.; 29C ff.; 33A ff.; 34B ff.; 37A ff.; 39C ff.; *et passim*; Xenophon, *Defense of Socrates* 10 ff.; *et passim*; Xenophon, *Memorabilia* I. 1. 1 ff.; *et passim*; DL II. 40; Plato, *Euthyphro* 3A; Plato, *Gorgias* 521E ff.; etc.

50 See A.-H. Chroust, 'Aristotle's first literary effort: the *Gryllus*—a lost dialogue on the nature of rhetoric,' *Revue des Études Grecques*, vol. 78, nos 371–3 (1965), pp. 576–91, and Vol. II, Chapter III.

51 See A.-H. Chroust, 'What prompted Aristotle to address the *Protrepticus* to Themison?', *Hermes*, vol. 94, no. 2 (1966), pp. 202–7, and Vol. II, Chapter IX.

52 See Eusebius, *op. cit.* XIV. 6. 9 (Numenius); Athenaeus, *op. cit.*, VIII. 352D–354E; II. 60DE; Dionysius of Halicarnassus, *Epistola ad Cn. Pompeium* 1; Themistius, *Oratio* XXIII. 285A.

53 The vitriolic and persistent (and prejudiced) attacks of Epicurus and the Epicureans on Aristotle almost amount to a special feature of Epicurean philosophy in general.

54 O. Gigon, 'Interpretationen zu den Aristoteles-Viten,' *Museum Helveticum*, vol. 15 (1958), p. 178, concedes, though somewhat reluctantly, that the charges against Aristotle might have been a mere pretext for dealing effectively with a much hated Macedonian alien. The same Gigon (see note 40) pp. 75–6, however disagrees with the view that these charges had political overtones. He admits, nevertheless that the accounts of Aristotle's flight from Athens in the year 323 B.C. 'present many difficulties.' Gigon continues: 'Undoubtedly one may always resort to the solution so popular with modern historians that the indictment [of Aristotle] for impiety was merely a cheap pretext to get at the friend of Antipater. Against this explanation it might be argued (a) that ancient tradition never once refers to such an interpretation of the whole incident; and (b) that even a mere hypothesis in order to be acceptable, must have a modicum of credibility.'

55 Antipater had been denounced to Alexander by someone (Olympias?). He was suspected by Alexander of disloyalty and of harboring conspiratorial designs against the king. Hence he was about to be removed from his position in Macedonia and Greece and summoned to Babylon. This being so, Antipater was unable to come to the assistance or rescue of Aristotle.

56 *IV VA* 9.

57 See DL V. 14–15, and the corresponding provisions in the Arabic versions of Aristotle's last will and testament.

58 Eusebius, *op. cit.*, XV. 2. 8–9. See also DL V. 16.

59 See *VM* 41; *VV* 19; *VL* 43; *II VS* 3; *II VA* 21; *IV VA* 8; Aelian, *Varia Historia* III. 36. See also note 18.

60 One reasonable and persuasive explanation for Aristotle's retreat to Chalcis

in 323 B.C. is the fact that he had a house there which he had inherited from his maternal ancestors. It is possible, however, that he went to Chalcis for the following reason: Chalcis, on the island of Euboea, is separated from the Greek mainland by a narrow channel, the Euripus, and about forty miles from Athens. Hence, he might have toyed with the idea of returning to Athens at some future time. When Antipater re-took Athens in 322 B.C., Aristotle was on his death-bed, however, if not already dead. Otherwise he might well have returned to Athens once more, this time with the military assistance of Antipater.

CHAPTER XIII   ARISTOTLE, ATHENS AND THE FOREIGN POLICY OF MACEDONIA

★ In a different form and under the title of 'Aristotle and Athens: some comments on Aristotle's sojourns in Athens,' this chapter was first published in *Laval Théologique et Philosophique*, vol. 22, no. 2 (1966), pp. 186–96. Admittedly, Chapter XIII covers as well as repeats some of the topics which have already been discussed in Chapters VII, IX, XI and XII. However, while these previous chapters attempt to establish the historicity or biographical significance of certain salient events in the life of Aristotle, Chapter XIII essays to demonstrate that many of these events had decidedly political overtones—that in some way they were closely connected with, and in some instances apparently caused by, certain political occurrences which took place in the Eastern Mediterranean world between *c.* 370–69 B.C. and 323 B.C., such as the death of King Amyntas III of Macedonia in 370–69 B.C.; the dynastic struggles which convulsed Macedonia between 369 and 365 B.C.; the ascendancy of King Philip after 359 B.C.; the early expansionist policies of King Philip in 349–48 B.C.; the further expansionist designs of King Philip as regards Thrace and the Thracian Chersonesus as well as his early plans to invade Asia Minor; the political confrontation between Greece and Macedonia prior to the battle of Chaeronea in 338 B.C.; the general political situation after the battle of Chaeronea; the death of King Philip and the ascendancy of King Alexander to the throne of Macedonia in 336 B.C.; the revolt of the Greek states against Macedonia and the submission of Athens to King Alexander in 335 B.C.; the 'occupation' of Athens by Macedonia between 335 and 323 B.C.; and the sudden death of King Alexander in June of 323 B.C. as well as the ensuing anti-Macedonian revolt in Athens and in Greece during the latter half of 323 B.C. All these events, some of which shaped the whole history of Western mankind in a most decisive manner, to a very large extent determined, or caused, some of the most important incidents in the life of Aristotle, the Macedonian. More than that: Aristotle's whole life not only seems to have been inextricably tied up with these world-shaking events, but it also appears that he himself played an important role in the shaping of some of these events. Hence, it is most appropriate to analyze and discuss anew the several topics which had already been treated separately in Chapters VII, IX, X and XII; and to integrate them into one single coherent narrative stressing their political significance or implications. Such an undertaking, which could also be presented under the subtitle of 'Aristotle, the Statesman,' should also make it sufficiently clear that the historical Aristotle was certainly more than a contemplative philosopher or a prolific author of philosophic works. This far-reaching and perhaps decisive insight which apparently has escaped the attention of most scholars, certainly deserves a separate and detailed discussion, even at the risk of seeming repetitious.

1 See A.-H. Chroust, 'Aristotle enters the Academy,' *Classical Folia*, vol. 19, no. 1 (1965), pp. 21-9, and Chapter VII.

2 *VM* 5; *VV* 4; *VL* 5; *I VS* 4; *I VA* 4; *IV VA* 3.

3 *IV VA* 3.

4 This is brought out, for instance, in *VM* 4; *VV* 3; *VL* 4; *II VA* 3-4. *II VA* 3 also maintains that Nicomachus, the father of Aristotle, personally turned over the latter to a 'school of poets, orators and schoolmasters' in Athens, and that he did so when Aristotle was a mere eight years old. This story, at least as it is presented by Al-Mubashir, is probably a later invention or, perhaps, the result of some confusion caused by the source used by Al-Mubashir. In any event, it is not well substantiated. See A.-H. Chroust (see note 1), pp. 21-2, and Chapter VII.

5 DL V. 1; *VM* 1-2; *VV* 1-2; *VL* 1-2; *I VA* 1; *II VS* 1; *II VA* 2; *III VA* 3; *IV VA* 2; *VH* 1; Suda, 'article' Nicomachus.

6 See A.-H. Chroust, 'The genealogy of Aristotle,' *Classical Folia*, vol. 19, no. 2 (1965), pp. 139-46, and Chapter V. Epiphanius, *De Graecis Sectis Exc.* 31, in H. Diels, *Doxographi Graeci* (Berlin, 1879), p. 592, relates that, according to some authors, Aristotle was a Macedonian, and according to others a Thracian, that is, a 'barbarian' or 'semi-barbarian.'

7 See *VM* 3; *VV* 2; *VL* 3; *IV VA* 3. See note 9.

8 See A.-H. Chroust (see note 6), pp. 144-5, and Chapter V. See also notes 1-3. According to Philochorus (*VM* 10; *VL* 10), Aristotle went to Athens during the latter part of Nausigenes' archonship (368-67 B.C.), that is, during the first year of the 103rd Olympiad, or to be more exact, during the spring or late spring of the year 367. According to Dionysius of Halicarnassus (Apollodorus?), *I Epistola ad Ammaeum* 5, he arrived in Athens during the early part of Polycelus' archonship (367-66 B.C.), that is, in the second year of the 103rd Olympiad, or to be more exact, in the late summer or fall of 367 B.C. On the whole, the dating of Philochorus has been accepted. Since, according to Philochorus, Aristotle was born in 384 B.C. (in the first year of the 99th Olympiad, during the early part of Diotrephes' archonship, 384-83), that is, probably in the summer of 384 B.C., he arrived in Athens before he had turned seventeen.

9 *VM* 3; *VV* 2; *VL* 3; *IV VA* 3. These *Vitae* insist that at the time Aristotle went to Athens (in 367 B.C.) he was 'orphaned.' See note 7.

10 This might very well have been the 'advice' given by the Delphic oracle. See note 2.

11 See A.-H. Chroust, 'Aristotle leaves the Academy,' *Greece and Rome*, vol. 14, no. 1 (1967), pp. 39-43, and Chapter IX. Aristotle withdrew from Athens (and from the Academy) in the first year of the 108th Olympiad, during the early part of the archonship of Theophilus, that is, probably in the summer or early fall of 348 B.C.

12 Eusebius, *Praeparatio Evangelica* XV. 2. 5 (Eubulides), also reports that at the time of Plato's death, Aristotle was no longer in Athens.

13 It might be argued here that *II VS* 3-4 is only a badly garbled account, or confused combination, of two wholly unrelated incidents in the life of Aristotle: Aristotle's sojourn with Hermias of Atarneus (348-47 to 345-44 B.C.), and the indictment of Aristotle in 323 B.C. for alleged impiety. See this Chapter and Chapter XII. It was this indictment in 323 B.C. which prompted Aristotle to flee to Chalcis in order to escape condemnation and possible execution. See Athenaeus, *Deipnosophistae* XV. 696A ff.; DL V. 5-6; *II VA* 20-1; *IV VA* 7; *VM* 41; *VV* 19; *VL* 43. When the author of *II VS* 3 insists that Aristotle went to a place 'near the Hellespont,' he might well be alluding to Assos (or Atarneus), which is 'near the Hellespont.' See A.-H. Chroust, 'Aristotle's Flight from Athens in the Year 323 B.C.,' *Historia*, vol. 15, no. 2 (1966), pp. 185-92, and Chapter XII. DL V. 2, on the other hand, might refer to the story, circulated by some detractors of Aristotle, that in order to annoy Plato, Aristotle left the Academy while Plato was still alive, and founded his own independent school in the Lyceum. See *VM* 9; 25-9; *VV* 6-11; *VL* 9; 25-9; Eusebius, *op. cit.*, XV. 2. 3; Aelian, *Varia Historia* IV. 9; Helladius, in Photius, *Bibliotheca* (533 b 13, ed. I. Bekker). See also Chapter III, notes 38-45, and the corresponding text.

14 On the occasion of the heated debates over the question of whether Athens should enter into a political and military alliance with threatened Olynthus, Demosthenes delivered his *Olynthiac Orations* which were animated by the same violent anti-Macedonian spirit as his *Philippics*.

15 In his *Philippics* and, especially, in his *Olynthiacs*.

16 Shortly before his death, Aristotle is said to have written a letter to Antipater in which he pointed out that 'in Athens things which are proper for a citizen are not proper for an alien'; and that 'it is dangerous [for an alien] to live in Athens.' *VM* 42; *VV* 20; *VL* 44. See also Elias (*olim* David), *Comment. in Porphyrii Isagogen et in Aristotelis Categorias* (proem.), *CIAG*, vol. XVIII, part 1 (ed. A. Busse, Berlin, 1900), p. 123, lines 15 ff. In his *Oration Against the Philosophers*, Demochares accused Aristotle of having betrayed Stagira to the Macedonians (in 349 B.C.), and with having denounced to King Philip the wealthiest citizens of Olynthus (in 348 B.C.), who on account of their commercial relations with Athens were probably pro-Athenian and, hence, in favor of a defensive alliance with that city. See DL V. 38; Athenaeus, *op. cit.*, XIII. 610EF; XI. 509B; Pseudo-Plutarch,

Vita Decem Oratorum (Moralia 850B ff.); Eusebius, *op. cit.,* XV. 2. 6; Pollux IX. 42; DL V. 38. See also Eusebius, *op. cit.,* XV. 2. 11, and notes 70, 72 and 87; U. von Wilamowitz-Moellendorff, *Antigonos von Karystos* (Berlin, 1881), p. 192; p. 270; I. Düring, *Herodicus the Cratetean* (Stockholm, 1941), pp. 149-51.

17 See note 16.

18 Socrates, too, might have been the victim of political entanglements and animosities. It is not unreasonable to conjecture that Socrates' trial and condemnation in 399 B.C. was basically a political incident in the bitter and protracted struggle between the 'democratic' and the oligarchic-aristocratic factions in Athens. See A.-H. Chroust, *Socrates: Man and Myth—The Two Socratic Apologies of Xenophon* (London, 1957), pp. 164 ff.; pp. 189 ff. Socrates had, or was suspected of having, close ties with some of the much despised Thirty Tyrants, especially with Critias and Charmides.

19 See also A.-H. Chroust (see note 11), and Chapter IX.

20 See Chapter IX, notes 20-1, and the corresponding text. This might also be the ultimate meaning of *VM* 15, *VV* 15 and *VL* 15, where we are told that Aristotle 'did much work for King Philip.'

21 Proxenus is said to have been a native of Atarneus. See *VM* 3; *VV* 2; *VL* 3. See also Chapter V, note 34.

22 See Demosthenes, *Fourth Philippic (Oratio* X) 32.

23 See text, this Chapter.

24 This might be inferred from Demosthenes, *Fourth Philippic (Oratio* X) 32, where we are informed that 'the agent [Hermias], who was privy to all of Philip's schemes against the King of Persia, has been captured, and the King will hear of all these plots . . . from the lips of the very man who planned and carried them out. . . .' Demosthenes refers here to the capture of Hermias by Mentor in 341-40 B.C., and to the possibility that under torture Hermias would divulge the secret negotiations which had been carried on between him and Philip of Macedonia through the mediation of Aristotle. See also Areius Didymus, *In Demosthenis Orationes Commenta* (ed. H. Diels and W. Schubart, Berlin, 1904), col. 5, 64 ff.; Diodorus Siculus XVI. 52. 5; Polyaenus VI. 48; Pseudo-Aristotle, *Oeconomicus* II. 11. 38; D. E. W. Wormell, 'The literary tradition concerning Hermias of Atarneus,' *Yale Classical Studies,* vol. V (1935), pp. 57-92; W. Jaeger, *Aristotle: Fundamentals of the History of His Development* (Oxford, 1948), pp. 117-20.

25 DL V. 27 (no. 144): 'Letters to Mentor, in one book.'

26 See DL V. 6: 'This man [*scil.,* Hermias], in violation of the hallowed laws of the Immortals, was unrighteously slain . . . by treachery with the aid of one [*scil.,* Mentor] in whom he had put his trust.' See also Areius Didymus (see note 24), col. 6, 36. It will be noted that in order to capture Hermias, Mentor used the same means Tissaphernes, according to Xenophon, had employed in capturing Clearchus, Agias, Menon and Socrates after the battle of Cunaxa in 401 B.C.

27 This might be the ultimate meaning of Hermias' last message to his friends in which he insists that he had done nothing 'unworthy of philosophy [that he had not betrayed his friends to the Persians].' Areius Didymus, *op. cit.*, col. 6, 13 ff.

28 See note 24.

29 See Areius Didymus, *op. cit.*, col. 5, 51 ff.

30 See, for instance, *VM* 16; 27; *VV* 16; *VL* 16; *I VA* 8; *II VA* 25; 36; *IV VA* 25. All the biographers of Aristotle are quite emphatic in the praise of his many 'public services.' See also Eusebius, *op. cit.*, XV. 2. 11.

31 With the exception of DL V. 2 (which in all likelihood is derived from Hermippus who wishes to stress the stupid ingratitude of Athens and of the Platonic Academy), no other biographer mentions this diplomatic mission of Aristotle (on behalf of Athens?), although several *Vitae Aristotelis* refer to the many valuable services he had rendered the city of Athens (and other cities as well). See, for instance, *IV VA* 17 ff.; Diodorus Siculus XVI. 77; XVI. 84; etc. See pp. 175-6.

32 See Demosthenes, *Oratio* X. 32, cited note 24.

33 This might be the ultimate meaning of Eubulides' statement that at one time Aristotle 'offended Philip.' See Eusebius, *op. cit.*, XV. 2. 3; XV. 2. 5, where we are told that Aristotle 'fell out with Philip.' Although betrayed by Philip, Hermias, even when subjected to torture, apparently did not betray Philip (or Aristotle) to the Persians. See note 26 and notes 89 and 92. This loyalty on the part of Hermias, it might be contended, prompted Aristotle to bestow many posthumous honors upon Hermias.

34 *VM* 24; *VV* 23; *VL* 24; *I VA* 10-11; *II VA* 19; 24-5; *IV VA* 6; 22-3; Dionysius of Halicarnassus, *I Epistola ad Ammaeum* 5; Apollodorus, *Chronicle*, in DL V. 10. See also Chapter XI. Dionysius of Halicarnassus, *loc. cit.*, states that this happened during the archonship of Evaenetus (335-34 B.C.), and Apollodorus, *loc. cit.*, maintains that it occurred in the second year of the 111th Olympiad (335-34 B.C.).

35 DL V. 4 relates that 'when he [*scil.*, Aristotle] thought that he had stayed long enough with Alexander, he departed for Athens.' Similar views can be found in *VM* 24; *VV* 23; *VL* 24; *I VA* 10; *II VA* 19; 24-5; *IV VA* 6; 22-3. Although these *Vitae* state that Alexander's departure for Asia was the prime reason for Aristotle's return to Athens, they also imply that he wanted to return there in order to dedicate himself to the further study or to the teaching of philosophy. See, for instance, I. Düring, *Aristotle in the Ancient Biographical Tradition* (Acta Universitatis Gothoburgensis, vol. 63, no. 2, Göteborg, 1957), p. 460. The story, found in *VM* 18, *VV* 18 and *VL* 24, namely, that after the death of Speusippus (in 339-38 B.C.), the Academy recalled Aristotle and asked him to run the school together with Xenocrates, is probably a later encomiastic invention, as is the report that, after the death of Plato, Speusippus himself tried to bring back Aristotle. See also *II VS* 4.

36 Plutarch, *Alexander* 8.

37 Dionysius of Halicarnassus, *loc. cit.*, note 34.

38 See Chapter XI.

39 Prompted by wishful thinking, in 335 B.C. Demosthenes actually produced a man who allegedly had witnessed the death of Alexander. The same Demosthenes assured the Athenians that they had nothing to fear from so young and inexperienced a boy as Alexander. See Chapter XI, note 12.

40 See *I VA* 9; *IV VA* 16. Similarly, *II VA* 36 and *IV VA* 25. DL V. 26, lists letters of Aristotle to Philip, Alexander, Antipater (in nine books), Mentor, Olympias, Hephaestion and others. See also *VH* 10 (no. 137); *VM* 16; 27; *VV* 16; *VL* 16.

41 *IV VA* 15; Eusebius, *op. cit.*, XV. 2. 11.

42 *II VA* 28; *I VA* 7–8; *IV VA* 15; *VM* 15; 23; *VV* 21; *VL* 15; 23; 49.

43 *IV VA* 16; 17–18; *II VA* 20; *VM* 16; *VL* 16.

44 *IV VA* 16; *II VA* 25; *VM* 16; 20; *VL* 16; 20; DL V. 2. *IV VA* 12 relates that Aristotle 'tried his hand at governing cities' (was engaged in politics) until he reached the age of thirty.

45 *IV VA* 17–18; *I VA* 11; *II VA* 25; *VM* 20; *VL* 20.

46 *IV VA* 17–18.

47 It will be noted that the text found in Usaibia (*IV VA* 17–18) follows rather closely the traditional pattern and style of Greek honorific decrees or inscriptions. This fact in itself lends some support to the assumption that the whole report of Usaibia may be based on historical truth. See A.-H. Chroust, 'Aristotle returns to Athens in the year 335 B.C.,' *Laval Théologique et Philosophique*, vol. 23, no. 2 (1967), pp. 244–54, and Chapter XI, especially notes 30–2, and the corresponding texts, as well as the discussion of this problem in the text of Chapter XI, after note 33. See also E. Drerup, 'Ein attisches Proxeniendekret für Aristoteles,' *Mittheilungen des Kaiserlichen Deutschen Archeologischen Instituts*, vol. 23 (Athens, 1898), pp. 369–81.

48 See A.-H. Chroust (see note 47) and Chapter XI.

49 See A.-H. Chroust (see note 13) and Chapter XII.

50 DL V. 5–6.

51 Athenaeus, *op. cit.*, XV. 696A. *VM* 41, *VV* 19, *VL* 43, *II VA* 20, and *IV VA* 7, report that Eurymedon had charged Aristotle with impiety, but they do not base this indictment on the allegedly sacrilegious hymn or paean in honor of Hermias, or on the honorific inscription at Delphi commemorating Hermias. Neither the *VM*, nor the *VV*, nor the *VL* mentions the indictment of Aristotle. They merely relate that 'the Athenians turned against him [*scil.*, Aristotle].' *VM* 41; *VV* 19; *VL* 43. *VH* 6, on the other hand, explicitly cites the hymn or paean. See also note 52.

52 Athenaeus, *op. cit.*, XV. 696A–696E (frag. 675, Rose). See also Chapter XII, notes 3–7, and the corresponding text; DL V. 7–8; Lucian, *Eunuchus* 9 (frag. 675, Rose); Himerius, *Oratio* VI. 6–7. Athenaeus' source is probably Hermippus. See Athenaeus, *op. cit.*, XV. 696EF. For the hymn or paean, see also Areius Didymus, *op. cit.*, col. 6, 22 ff.

53 *II VA* 20-1.

54 *IV VA* 7-10.

55 See also Origen, *Contra Celsum* I. 380 (Migne, vol. II, p. 781b).

56 This particular account recasts some of the events which, according to the testimony of Plato, Xenophon and others, allegedly transpired during the indictment and trial of Socrates in the year 399 B.C.

57 *II VA* 20.

58 *II VA* 21.

59 *IV VA* 8-9 in substance restates *II VA* 21, adding, however, an important bit of information: apparently no one interfered with Aristotle's voluntary departure from Athens. See also Eusebius, *op. cit.*, XV. 2. 8, and note 81.

60 See A.-H. Chroust (see note 17), pp. 164 ff.; 189 ff.

61 The story that Aristotle composed a speech in his defense (DL V. 9, quoting Favorinus) is probably spurious. This is stressed in *IV VA* 10. See also Athenaeus, *op. cit.*, 697AB; Aelian, *Varia Historia* VIII. 12; Origen, *loc. cit.*, note 55; VH 10 (no. 189), where a *Defense Against the Charge of Impiety, Addressed to Eurymedon*, is listed among the spurious works of Aristotle. But, like in the case of Socrates, there might have existed a *Defense* (or *Apology*) *of Aristotle*, composed by some unknown author or authors.

62 *IV VA* 8-9. See also note 59. Apparently, Aristotle was also permitted, or somehow managed, to take with him all his moveable possessions, which must have been considerable, as well as his many servants. See notes 82-4. Accordingly, his departure from Athens in 323 B.C. must have been a rather leisurely affair.

63 In the case of Socrates, too, the Athenians seem to have hoped that he would leave the city voluntarily, and thus relieve them of the unpleasant and always risky task of a formal trial. It is also believed that after the trial the Athenians would have preferred to see Socrates escape from prison and flee to some other city, thus relieving them of the unpleasant duty of executing him. This is indicated by the Platonic *Crito*, unfortunately not a very reliable source.

64 *II VA* 20.

65 Eurymedon, we are told, was the highest religious official connected with the Eleusian mysteries. From this it might be inferred that some of the charges brought against Aristotle in 323 B.C. were, in some way, also related to the story that, according to Lycon Pythagoraeus, Aristotle had sacrificed to his wife, Pythias, after her death, 'as the Athenians sacrifice to the Eleusian Demeter' (Eusebius, *op. cit.* XV. 2. 8); or, according to the author of *Aristippus or On the Luxury of the Ancients*, that he had done so while Pythias was still alive (DL V. 4). Hence, Aristotle would have been guilty of blasphemy. However, neither Lycon nor the author of the *Aristippus* are reliable reporters, although they are dedicated detractors of Aristotle.

66 See, for instance, *VM* 20; *VL* 20; *I VA* 25; *IV VA* 17-18.

67 See *VM* 12; 42; *VV* 6; *VL* 12. These reports stress the fact that Aristotle

was an 'alien' (ξένος, *extraneus*) in Athens and hence lived there by mere sufferance, having no power or influence whatever.

68 This fact is stressed many times not only by Aristotle's biographers, but also by a number of ancient historians and authors, such as Plutarch, Pliny, Aelian, Quintilian, Dio Chrysostom, Curtius Rufus, Arrian and many others. In his last will and testament, which was drafted probably in 323–22 B.C., Aristotle named Antipater his chief executor or administrator. See DL V. 11; 13, and the corresponding provisions in the Arabic versions of this will. See also note 85.

69 Eusebius, *op. cit.*, XV. 2. 11 (Aristocles) maintains that Aristotle was envied and hated [by the Athenians?] because of 'his friendship with kings.' This remark may refer to Aristotle's close connections with King Philip, Alexander, and with Antipater and Hermias.

70 Demochares, the nephew of Demosthenes, in 306 B.C. justified (and supported) the decree of Sophocles (DL V. 38) which called for the expulsion of all foreign, 'subversive' or philo-Macedonian philosophers. At the same time, Demochares denounced Aristotle in particular. He alleged that Aristotle had sent many letters (intelligence reports?) to Antipater (DL V. 27, no. 144, mentions nine 'books' of letters addressed by Aristotle to Antipater), that some of these letters had been intercepted by the Athenians, and that the content of these letters was detrimental to the (political?) interests of Athens. See note 16 and notes 72 and 87.

71 Antipater had been denounced to Alexander by Olympias, the mother of Alexander, who charged Antipater with disloyalty and with conspiring against the king. Alexander, who had become increasingly suspicious of his own lieutenants and whose temper and general disposition was steadily worsening during the last years of his life, saw himself surrounded and betrayed by a host of alleged conspirators and enemies.

72 It is possible that in his *Oration Against the Philosophers*, Demochares also revived, and magnified, some of the accusations made against Aristotle by the anti-Macedonian faction in Athens in the year 323 B.C., and probably during the years 335–34 to 323 B.C. See notes 16, 70, and 87.

73 *IV VA* 17–21. See also Chapter XI.

74 It has already been pointed out that in its technical phraseology the honorific inscription mentioned in *IV VA* 18–19 is very close to the traditional wording of Athenian decrees of *proxenia*. See note 47 and the corresponding text; Chapter XI.

75 *IV VA* 20.

76 Together with other prominent anti-Macedonian leaders in Athens, Himeraeus was executed by Antipater after the battle of Crannon and the re-occupation of Athens by the Macedonians in the fall of 322 B.C. See Plutarch, *Demosthenes* 28.

77 DL V. 5–6; Athenaeus, *op. cit.*, XV. 696A ff.; VH 6; Areius Didymus (see note 24), col. 6, 18 ff.; 6, 36 ff.

78 This seems to be implied in *II VS* 3.

79 *II VA* 20; *IV VA* 7. We may add also the story, widely circulated in Athens, that Aristotle had allegedly sacrificed to his wife, Pythias, as the Athenians sacrificed to the Eleusian Demeter. See note 65.

80 It could possibly be argued that Aristotle, being a philosopher, under the circumstances should have acted as Socrates had acted in 399 B.C. and hence should have faced his enemies and accusers in open court rather than run away. Such an argument, to be sure, is without merit. Socrates was an Athenian as well as a citizen of Athens, while Aristotle was a Macedonian and an alien who, as he himself admitted, had no legal standing in Athens. See notes 16 and 67. Moreover, as a 'political agent' of Macedonia he most certainly had no cause for making a heroic stand in the name of philosophy in an Athenian court. See also Chapter XIV, note 28.

81 *IV VA* 8. See also Eusebius, *op. cit.*, XV. 2. 8, and note 59.

82 DL V. 11–16.

83 For a detailed discussion of the Arabic version of Aristotle's last will and testament, see A.-H. Chroust, 'A brief analysis of the *Vita Aristotelis* of Diogenes Laertius (DL V. 11–16),' *Antiquité Classique*, vol. 34, fasc. 1 (1965), pp. 126–8; A.-H. Chroust, 'Aristotle's last will and testament,' *Wiener Studien*, vol. 80 (Neue Folge, vol. I, 1967), pp. 90–114; A.-H. Chroust, 'Estate planning in Hellenic antiquity: the last will and testament of Aristotle,' *Notre Dame Lawyer*, vol. 45, no. 4 (1970), pp. 629–62; Chapter XV.

84 Eusebius, *op. cit.*, XV. 2. 6–8. See also DL V. 16, and note 62.

85 DL V. 11; V. 13, and the corresponding provisions in the Arabic version of Aristotle's will. See also note 68.

86 DL V. 27 (no. 144) refers to 'nine books of letters addressed to Antipater.'

87 Eusebius, *op. cit.*, XV. 2. 6. See also notes 16, 70, and 72.

88 See Plato (?), *Sixth Epistle, passim*; A.-H. Chroust, 'Plato's Academy: the first organized school of political science in antiquity,' *Review of Politics*, vol. 29 (1967), pp. 25–40.

89 See notes 20–30 and the corresponding text. Undoubtedly, while residing with Hermias (for whom he had much admiration), Aristotle encouraged and supported a pro-Macedonian and anti-Persian (and, perhaps, anti-Athenian) policy on the part of Hermias. K. J. Beloch, *Griechische Geschichte*, vol. II, part 1 (Berlin-Leipzig, 1922), p. 527, note 3, remarks that Aristotle might have been Philip's political agent in Atarneus. W. Jaeger, *Aristotle: Fundamentals of the History of His Development* (Oxford, 1948), pp. 120–1, suggests the possibility that Aristotle was a political agent representing Macedonian interests in Atarneus. It is also reasonable to assume that upon his return to Macedonia in 343–42 B.C. Aristotle continued to recommend Hermias to Philip as a useful and reliable ally. See D. E. W. Wormell (see note 24), *passim*.

90 See Areius Didymus, *op. cit.*, col. 6, 50 ff.

91 See Arrian II. 14. 2. See also note 32 and the corresponding text.

92 See Areius Didymus, *op. cit.*, col. 6, 13 ff.

93 See also Demosthenes, *Fourth Philippic* (*Oratio* X) 32, and note 27.

94 Areius Didymus, *op. cit.*, col. 6, 50 ff.

95 See, for instance, Aristotle, *Nicomachean Ethics* 1149 a 10; *Politics* 1255a 3 ff.

96 See, for instance, *VM* 15-16; 20; *VV* 15; *VL* 15-16; 20; *I VA* 8; *II VA* 27-8; *IV VA* 15-16. The additional evidence may be found in Plutarch, *Alexander*, *passim*; Plutarch, *Adversus Coloten* 32-3 (*Moralia* 1126DE); Plutarch, *Ne Suaviter Quidem Vivi Posse Secundum Epicurum* 15 (*Moralia* 1097B); Diodorus Siculus XVI. 52. 9; Valerius Maximus V. 6. 5; Pliny, *Hist. Nat.*, VII. 109; Dio Chrysostom, *Oratio* II. 79, and *Oratio* XLVII. 8; Aelian, *Varia Historia* III. 17; etc.

97 Aristotle might have learned the art of 'practical politics' in Plato's Academy, which was certainly a hotbed of political intrigues and schemings. See A.-H. Chroust (see note 88). And he most certainly learned a great deal of *Realpolitik* from Philip of Macedonia and Hermias of Atarneus.

98 See, however, Chapter X.

99 Plutarch, *Alexander* 8.

100 When Philip married Cleopatra, Attalus (the uncle of Cleopatra), presumably at the instigation of Philip, expressed the hope that Cleopatra would present the king with a legitimate son and heir. See Plutarch, *Alexander* 9.

101 See, for instance, *VM* 15; *VL* 15.

102 See notes 32-3. There exists a further explanation for Philip's desertion of Hermias. In a letter addressed to Philip, usually dated between 343 and 341 B.C., Theopompus, the rabid detractor of Hermias, pointed out that the latter had a very bad reputation among the Greeks for being a treacherous and untrustworthy scoundrel. See Areius Didymus, *op. cit.*, col. 5, 21 ff. It is possible that Philip paid heed to Theopompus' incriminations of Hermias. See also D. E. W. Wormell (see note 24), p. 71. Theopompus, a Chian, harbored an unrelenting hatred for Hermias (and, incidentally, for Aristotle, the friend and kinsman of Hermias) probably for the following reason: Eubulus, the 'predecessor' of Hermias, had wrested Atarneus from the control of Chios; and Hermias had failed (or refused) to support the oligarchic faction on the island of Chios, to which Theopompus and his father belonged, against the Chian democrats. The resulting victory of the democrats over the oligarchs forced Theopompus and his father, Damasistratus, to go into exile, something for which the former never forgave Hermias.

103 It is certainly significant that Chalcis, a town on the island of Euboea and the place to which Aristotle retired in the year 323 B.C., was at the time philo-Macedonian. Admittedly, he had a house in Chalcis (which he had inherited from his maternal ancestors), but he also possessed a house in Stagira (which he had inherited from his father). Stagira, we know, had been rebuilt by King Philip (or Alexander). Chalcis, however, was much closer to Athens than Stagira. This fact might support the assumption that after his flight from Athens in 323 B.C., Aristotle still entertained hopes of returning there once more. See Chapter XII, note 60.

104 See notes 40–8.

105 I. Düring, *Aristotle in the Ancient Biographical Tradition*, Acta Universitatis Gothoburgensis, vol. 63, no. 2 (Göteborg, 1957), *passim*, as well as some other scholars at times are inclined to disregard or 'play down' these reports as mere fabrications invented by some encomiastic biographers of Aristotle.

106 According to Dio Chrysostom, *Oratio* XLVII. 8–10, Aristotle maintained in his old age that his only truly meritorious achievements had been his political and diplomatic activities which, among other beneficial results, had led to the restoration of Stagira.

107 See, in general, A.-H. Chroust (see note 88), *passim*.

CHAPTER XIV   THE MYTH OF ARISTOTLE'S SUICIDE

* In a different form, this chapter was first published in *Modern Schoolman*, vol. 44, no. 2 (1967), pp. 177–8.

1 DL V. 6.

2 *VH* 6–7.

3 See *Frag. Hist. Graec.* (Jacoby) 77, F. 1. See also F. Jacoby, *Frag. Hist. Graec.* (Berlin, 1926), part II C, p. 131; part III B, p. 483.

4 Eumelus also claims that Aristotle joined Plato and the Academy only at the age of thirty. DL V. 6. The Syriac and Arabic *Vitae Aristotelis* likewise mention a tradition according to which Aristotle turned to philosophy only at the age of thirty. *I VS* 6; *I VA* 6; *IV VA* 12. See also *VM* 11; *VL* 11. The story that Aristotle turned to philosophy only at the age of thirty (*VM* 11 claims that he did so at the age of forty) contains the nasty implication that he was a 'slow learner.' It might originally go back to Epicurus or the Epicureans, the implacable and tireless detractors of Aristotle, who insisted that in his youth Aristotle was a dissipated person who turned to philosophy only after having failed in everything else. See Eusebius, *Praeparatio Evangelica* XV. 2. 1 (Epicurus); XV. 2. 7 (Cephisodorus); DL X. 8; Athenaeus, *Deipnosophistae* VIII. 352D ff.; Aelian, *Varia Historia* V. 9; Philodemus, *De Rhetorica: Volumina Rhetorica*, vol. II, pp. 50 ff. (ed. S. Sudhaus), col. 48, 36–57, 45. See also Chapter VIII, notes 2, 8, 13.

5 See A.-H. Chroust, 'Aristotle's Flight from Athens in the Year 323 B.C.,' *Historia*, vol. 15, no. 2 (1966), pp. 185–92, and Chapter XII. See also Chapter XIII, which attempts to show that the political situation in Athens in the year 323 B.C. compelled Aristotle to leave the city. All the *Vitae Aristotelis* agree that Aristotle fled to Chalcis. See Eusebius, *op. cit.*, XV. 2. 8–9; Strabo X. 1. 11; Justin Martyr, *Cohortatio ad Graecos* 34B (Migne VI. 305).

6 *II VS* 7.

7 *II VA* 21–2. See also Eustathius, *Dionysius Periegetes* (*Geographi Minores*, ed. Bernardy), p. 189. Al-Mubashir or, more likely, his source may have had in mind the Περὶ τῆς ἀναβάσεως τοῦ Νείλου (see *VH* 10, no. 159;

Ptolemy (-el-Garib), no. 25; frags 246–48, Rose) or, perhaps, the Περὶ τῆς λίθου (DL V. 26, no. 125; VH 10, no. 117).

8 Justin Martyr (see note 5); Gregory of Nazianzus, *Oratio* IV. 72 (Migne, vol. 35, p. 597a); Procopius VIII. 6. 20. See also Aelian, *op. cit.*, IX. 23. Mediaeval authors seem to know that Aristotle drowned himself in the Euripus exclaiming: '*Quia non possum capere te, capias me,*' or '*Quoniam Aristoteles Euripum minime cepit, Aristotelem Euripus habeat.*' This would indicate that the story of Aristotle's alleged suicide persisted into the Middle Ages.

9 DL I. 95 (Periander), and DL V. 78 (Demetrius of Phaleron). See also notes 12–14.

10 DL II. 111–12.

11 Pseudo-Plutarch, *Vita Homeri* 4; Heraclitus of Ephesus, frag. 56 (Diels-Kranz). This passage has also been recognized as a fragment of Aristotle's lost work *On Poets*. See frag. 76, Rose; frag. 8, Ross. It relates that Homer once overheard some fishermen saying that 'what we have caught we do not have, and what we did not catch, we have.' The fishermen were referring to lice, but Homer, believing that they were talking about fish, failed to grasp the meaning of this statement.

12 DL II. 142. See also DL II. 13, where we are told that Anaxagoras, being unable to brook the indignity of being jailed, took his own life.

13 DL IV. 3.

14 DL VI. 100. It will be noted that DL II. 142, DL V. 78 and DL VI. 100 are based on Hermippus. For additional material, see W. Hertz, *Gesammelte Abhandlungen* (Stuttgart-Berlin, 1905), pp. 350–62.

15 The story of Aristotle's alleged suicide can also be found in Suda, 'article' Aristotle.

16 Censorinus, *De Die Natali* XIV. 16.

17 See DL V. 10 (Apollodorus): '[Aristotle] retired to Chalcis and . . . died there a natural death.' *VM* 43 and *VL* 46 simply report that 'he died' in Chalcis.

18 Censorinus (see note 16) refers to Aristotle's *naturalis stomachi infirmitas*, as well as to his other physical infirmities. See also DL V. 16, where we are told that Aristotle placed a skin filled with warm oil on his stomach, presumably in order to alleviate pains caused by his stomach ailment. Lycon Pythagoraeus, according to DL V. 16 and Eusebius, *op. cit.*, XV. 2. 8, related that Aristotle bathed in warm oil (and afterwards sold the oil). See also Aelian, *op. cit.*, IX. 23; Gellius, *Attic Nights* XIII. 5; Valerius Maximus V. 6. ext. 5; Dionysius of Halicarnassus, *I Epistola ad Ammaeum* 5. *IV VA* 11 relates that 'when Aristotle arrived at his home [in Chalcis] he stayed there until he died.' This might possibly imply that he was already a sick man when he went to Chalcis. Gellius, *loc. cit.*, states that at the time he went to Chalcis he was '*corpore aegro affectoque ac spe vitae tenui. . . .*'

19 *I VA* 15.

20 *II VA* 23.

21 *IV VA* 11.

22 *I VS* 5.

23 *II VS* 7.

24 *II VA* 23.

25 DL V. 6.

26 DL V. 8.

27 See, for instance, *IV VA* 8–9, where we are informed that when Aristotle learned about his indictment by Eurymedon, 'he departed from Athens . . . before any official action was taken against him. No one did him any harm prior to his departure.' Eusebius, *op. cit.*, XV. 2. 8, relates that when Aristotle 'was starting out for Chalcis, the custom-house officials found in the vessel seventy-five brass plates.' DL V. 16 narrates that after Aristotle's death in Chalcis a large number of plates belonging to him were found among his possessions. Aristotle's last will and testament likewise bears out the fact that he died a wealthy man. See Chapter XV, *passim*.

28 In *Nicomachean Ethics* 1116 a 13 ff.; 1138 a 3 ff.; 1166b 12 ff, and in *Eudemian Ethics* 1229 b 32 ff., Aristotle condemns suicide. Plato, *Laws* 873C, on the other hand, recommends suicide under certain circumstances. The Cynics outright recommended (and frequently practiced) suicide (see DL IV. 3; VI. 18; VI. 24; VI. 77; VI. 86; VI. 95; Aelian, *op. cit.*, VIII. 14; XII. 11; Athenaeus, *op. cit.*, IV. 157B), as did the Stoics. See K. A. Geiger, *Der Selbstmord im Klassischen Altertum* (Augsburg, 1888), *passim*.

29 *VM* 41; *VV* 19; *VL* 43; Elias, *Comment. in Porphyrii Isagogen at in Aristotelis Categorias, CIAG*, vol. XVIII, part 1 (ed. A. Busse, Berlin, 1900), p. 123, lines 15 ff.; Aelian, *op. cit.*, III. 36; Origen, *Contra Celsum* I. 380 (Migne, P.G., vol. II, p. 781A).

30 DL V. 8.

31 A similarly confusing story can be found in DL II. 101. Here we are told that Euryclides, the hierophant, was found guilty of disclosing the Eleusian mysteries to the uninitiated. 'Yet he would hardly have escaped from being brought before the Areopagus if Demetrius of Phaleron had not interceded on his behalf. Amphicrates, in his *On Illustrious Men*, relates that he was condemned [by the Areopagus] to drink the hemlock.'

32 This 'riddle of the Euripus' is also mentioned in Livy XXVIII. 6; Cicero, *De Natura Deorum* III. 10. 24; Lucan, *Pharsalia* V. 235; and others. Aristotle refers to the Euripus in *Meteorologica* 366 a 22 ff., and in *Historia Animalium* 547 a 6.

33 See note 8.

34 It will be noted, however, that *I VS* 8 reports that at the time of his death Aristotle was 67 years old; *I VA* 15, that he was 66 years old; and *II VA* 23; *III VA* and *IV VA* 11, that he was 68 years old. It is commonly believed that Aristotle died at the age of 62, that is, in his 63rd year. He died during the first half of Philocles' archonship, in the third year of the 114th Olympiad, a short time before Demosthenes committed suicide. Philocles entered office early in July of 322 B.C., and Demosthenes, according to

Plutarch, *Demosthenes* 30, took his own life on the sixteenth of Pyanepsion, that is, 14 October 322 B.C. Accordingly, it is safe to assume that Aristotle died (a natural death) in the late summer or early fall of 322 B.C.

CHAPTER XV   ARISTOTLE'S LAST WILL AND TESTAMENT

* In a different, much shorter and less adequate form, this chapter was first published in *Wiener Studien*, vol. 80 (Alte Folge), vol. I (Neue Folge), pp. 90–114. Some of the legal or technical aspects discussed in this chapter were also analyzed, under the title of 'Estate planning in Hellenic antiquity: the last will and testament of Aristotle,' in *Notre Dame Lawyer*, vol. 45, no. 4 (1970), pp. 629–62.

1 See Chapter IV, notes 1–6, and the corresponding text. See also I. Düring, *Aristotle in the Ancient Biographical Tradition* (Acta Universitatis Gothoburgensis, vol. 63, no. 2, Göteborg, 1957), pp. 183–246, especially, pp. 219–20; M. Plezia, *Aristotelis Epistolarum Fragmenta cum Testamento* (Academia Scientiarum Polona, fasc. III, Warsaw, 1961); J. Bidez, *Un Singulier Naufrage Littéraire dans l'Antiquité: A la Recherche des Épaves de l'Aristote Perdu* (Brussels, 1943), pp. 57 ff.

2 This view is based on the fact that in DL V. 64 we are told that the will of Straton of Lampsacus had been preserved in the *Collection [of the Wills of the Peripatetic Scholarchs]* of Ariston of Ceos, who is credited with having recorded, collected and transmitted not only the will of Aristotle, but also that of Theophrastus (DL V. 51–7), Straton of Lampsacus (DL V. 61–4) and Lycon (DL V. 69–74). In his will Lycon mentions Ariston of Ceos as one of the persons who witnessed his will (DL V. 74). Lycon also enumerates Ariston among the men whom he charges with carrying on the work of the Peripatus (DL V. 70). See p. 184, and Athenaeus, *Deipnosophistae* XIII. 589C.

3 *VM* 43; *VL* 46. See also *I VA* 19; *III VA*; *IV VA* (at the end); Elias (*olim* David), *Comment. in Porphyrii Isagogen et in Aristotelis Categorias, CIAG*, vol. XVIII, part 1 (ed. A. Busse, Berlin, 1900), p. 107, line 11. Usaibia, it will be noted, starts his *Vita Aristotelis* with the following introductory remark: 'Thus speaks Ptolemy [-el-Garib] in his book addressed to Gallus on the life and history of Aristotle, his last will, and the list of his famous writings.' About the Syriac and Arabic biographers of Aristotle, see also A.-H. Chroust, 'A brief summary of the Syriac and Arabic *Vitae Aristotelis*,' *Acta Orientalia*, vol. 29, nos 1–2 (1965), pp. 23–47, and Chapter IV.

4 See A. Baumstark, *Syrisch-Arabische Biographien des Aristotles* (Leipzig, 1900), p. 35.

5 An attempt to reconstruct the general arrangement and main content of Ptolemy's lost *Vita Aristotelis* has been made by I. Düring (see note 1), pp. 472–4; and by A.-H. Chroust, 'A brief account of the traditional *Vitae Aristotelis*,' *Revue des Études Grecques*, vol. 76, nos 364–5 (1964), pp. 50–69, especially pp. 61–9, and Chapter I.

6 DL V. 64; Strabo XIII. 1. 54. See also note 2.

7 DL V. 52: 'And the whole library [of the school] I leave and bequeath to Neleus.' See also Athenaeus, *Deipnosophistae* I. 3A; Strabo XIII. 1. 54. Theophrastus, it must be borne in mind, expected that Neleus of Scepsis would succeed him in the scholarchate of the Peripatus. When Neleus failed to be 'elected' scholarch, he went back to Scepsis in the Troad, taking with him the library which contained the 'intramural' compositions or treatises of Aristotle as well as those of Theophrastus and other early Peripatetics. This incident also explains why the doctrinal treatises of Aristotle and those of other Peripatetics were lost for some time. See A.-H. Chroust, 'The Miraculous Disappearance and Recovery of the *Corpus Aristotelicum*,' *Classica et Mediaevalia*, vol. 23, nos 1–2 (1962), pp. 50–67. It also explains why some doubts exist as to the authenticity of the extant *Corpus Aristotelicum*. See the corresponding remarks in the Preface.

8 DL V. 51–7.

9 *Ibid.*, V. 61–4.

10 *Ibid.*, V. 69–74.

11 See A.-H. Chroust (see note 7), pp. 50–1.

12 See A.-H. Chroust, 'Aristotle's Flight from Athens in the Year 323 B.C.,' *Historia*, vol. 15, no. 2 (1966), pp. 185–192, and Chapter XII.

13 This is borne out by the remark of Usaibia (*IV VA* 9), who maintains that when Aristotle fled from Athens in the year 323 B.C., no one interfered with his voluntary departure. See also Eusebius, *Praeparatio Evangelica* XV. 2. 8–9; DL V. 16; etc. Tradition has it that before he left Athens, Aristotle gave his library to Theophrastus. See Athenaeus (see note 7).

14 *II VA* 33–4. See also *VM* 43–4; *VL* 46–7; *I VS* 11; *IV VA* 35.

15 See, for instance, Isaeus, *Oratio* III (In *re* Estate of Pyrrhus) 59.

16 See Demosthenes, *Oratio* XLIV ([Aristodemus] versus Leochares, In *re* Estate of Archiades) 19.

17 Isaeus (see note 15), 4–43.

18 Demosthenes (see note 16, at 22); Demosthenes, *Oratio* XLIII ([Sositheus] versus Marcatatus, In *re* Estate of Hagias) 51; Isaeus, *Oratio* VIII (In *re* Estate of Ciron) 31; Isaeus, *Oratio* X (Against Xenaenetus, In *re* Estate of Aristarchus) 5. 12; Hyperides, frag. 8 (ed. Loeb).

19 Demosthenes, *Oratio* XLVI (II [Apollodorus] versus Stephanus, Charged with Perjury) 20; Isaeus, *Oratio* VIII. 31; Isaeus, *Oratio* X. 5. 12; Hyperides, frag. 39 (ed. Loeb).

20 Isaeus, *Oratio* III. 50–51. The legal right of the ultimate taker as against the adopted son was called κληρονομία ἁπάντων πάππων.

21 Thucydides V. 88. 2; V. 6. 1; V. 18.

22 Dionysius of Halicarnassus, *I Epistola ad Ammaeum* 5.

23 It has been suggested that Stagira was founded in the thirty-first Olympiad (656–52 B.C.).

24 One of our main sources or chief authorities for Athenian testamentary

law are the forensic speeches of Isaeus. Isaeus himself was a native of Chalcis and, like Aristotle, a 'resident alien' in Athens. Since Isaeus composed many forensic speeches dealing with matters and issues arising from the problems connected with testamentary and intestate succession, it is not likely that there existed a great divergence between the law of succession prevailing in Athens during the latter part of the fourth century B.C. and the law of succession prevailing in Chalcis or, for that matter, in any city which formerly had been a member of the Delian League or which had been settled by Athens.

25 For a discussion of the many and involved problems inherent in Aristotle's last will and testament, see G. Bruns, 'Die Testamente der griechischen Philosophen,' *Zeitschrift der Savigny-Stiftung für Rechtsgeschichte: Romanistische Abteilung*, vol. I (Weimar, 1880), pp. 11–23; A. Hug, 'Zu den Testamenten der Griechischen Philosophen,' *Universität Zürich: Festschrift zur Begrüssung der Versammlung Deutscher Philologen und Schulmänner* (Zürich, 1887), pp. 1–21; M. Plezia, 'Testament Platonia i Arystotelesa,' *Meander*, vol. II (1947), pp. 215–24. Some of these discussions and analyses disagree with the statements made by the present author. For additional information, see J. H. Lipsius, *Das Attische Recht und Rechtsverfahren* (Leipzig, 1905); J. Beauchet, *Histoire du Droit Privé de la Republique Athénienne* (Paris, 1897); J. W. Jones, *The Law and Legal Theory of the Greeks* (Oxford, 1956), especially pp. 189–97, and the literature cited there; A. Kränzlein, *Eigentum und Besitz im Griechischen Recht des Fünften und Vierten Jahrhunderts v. Chr.* (Berliner Juristische Abhandlungen, vol. 8, 1963), pp. 94 ff.; W. Erdmann, *Die Ehe im Alten Griechenland* (1934); H. Wolff, 'Die Grundlagen des griechischen Eherechts,' *Tijdschrift voor Rechtsgeschiedenis*, vol. 22 (1952), pp. 9 ff.; H. Wolff, 'Marriage Law and Family in Ancient Athens,' *Traditio*, vol. 2 (1944), pp. 63 ff.

26 See, for instance, DL V. 51 (the will of Theophrastus). This will is also discussed by G. Bruns (see note 25), pp. 23–36.

27 See DL V. 51; DL V. 61 (the will of Straton of Lampsacus). See G. Bruns (see note 25), pp. 36–41.

28 See Demosthenes, *Oratio* XLVI. 14.

29 See note 27 and DL V. 69 (the will of Lycon). See also G. Bruns (see note 25), pp. 41–6; Demosthenes, *Oratio* XLV. 18–20.

30 *II VA* 34.

31 See, for instance, *VM* 42; *VV* 20; *VL* 44. DL V. 27 (no. 144) lists no less than nine 'books' of letters which Aristotle addressed (or is said to have addressed) to Antipater. See also *VM* 23; *VV* 21; *VL* 23; M. Plezia (see note 1). It is interesting to note that some of Aristotle's political enemies in Athens were executed by Antipater after the battle of Crannon and the retaking of Athens in 322 B.C., which brought to an end the so-called Lamian War. See also *IV VA* 20.

32 See also No. IX, pp. 205–6, and, especially, note 96. Under the terms of Aristotle's will, Antipater's position was apparently akin to that of the Roman *tutor honoris causa datus*, as contrasted by the ordinary *tutor gerens*.

33 See, in general, A.-H. Chroust, 'The Genealogy of Aristotle,' *Classical Folia*, vol. 19, no. 2 (1966), pp. 139–46, and Chapter V. See also H. Berve, *Das Alexanderreich* (Munich, 1926), pp. 275–6.

34 See text, pp. 209–13, No. XV (Arabic version). This seems to be the crux of the whole will. If Nicomachus is indeed the universal heir or legatee—at the time of Aristotle's death, he was still 'very young' (see note 35)—the legal position of Nicanor may be described as follows: as the nearest grown male agnate or male kin of Aristotle, he is under a duty to take care of Aristotle's two minor children. At the same time, he has a right not only to claim Pythias in marriage and with her the estate of Aristotle or, at least, Pythias' share or 'future interest'—since Nicomachus is only an adopted son (adopted during the lifetime of Aristotle) he has merely a life estate which at his death would return to Pythias (or to her male children by Nicanor)—but also to become the guardian of Nicomachus as well as the administrator of Nicomachus' life estate (or life interest) until the latter comes of age. In this sense Nicanor may also be called 'interim heir designate.' As such he was granted certain temporary powers as well as privileges (and had certain fiduciary duties) as regards Aristotle's estate in general and Nicomachus' life interest in particular. Since the expected male offsprings of Nicanor and Pythias were the ultimate takers, Nicanor could not dispose of the estate *mortis causa*.

35 *II VA* 33. Eusebius, *op. cit.*, XV. 2. 15, relates that Nicomachus died 'in the war' a mere lad. This statement would find support in the will of Theophrastus, drawn probably in 287–86 B.C., where the testator instructs his trustees to see to it that a memorial statue of Nicomachus is completed. See DL V. 52. DL V. 39 also reports that 'Aristippus, in the fourth book of his *On the Luxury of the Ancients*, asserts that he [*scil.*, Theophrastus] was enamored of Aristotle's son Nicomachus, although he was Nicomachus' teacher.'

36 See also text, p. 203, No. VI.

37 The decree of *proxenia* bestowed upon Nicanor by the city of Ephesus (for some meritorious deeds he had performed for the Ephesians), however, calls him 'the [adopted] son of Aristotle' (Νικάνορι Ἀριστοτέλεος Σταγε[ιρίτηι]). See also note 33. This is, however, not supported by the provisions found in Aristotle's last will and testament, which seem to contradict the assumption that at one time Aristotle had adopted Nicanor. It will be noted, however, that under Athenian law wills and adoptions, either posthumous or *inter vivos*, had certain characteristics in common.

38 See also text, pp. 203–4 and 209–13, Nos VII and XV.

39 Under the terms of the Synedrion of Corinth, Alexander had no authority to dictate to the Confederates in matters concerning the management of their internal affairs. But only two states, Athens and Aetolia—which were prepared to resist Alexander—objected to this order. They objected primarily because if this edict were enforced, they would lose some of their ill-gotten gains: the Athenians would have to return their former lands to the Samians, and the Athenian settlers on Samos would have to relinquish

the island. The Aetolians had taken over Oeneida and driven out the rightful Acarnanian owners. They, too, would have to return to the Acarnanians their former possessions. See Diodorus Siculus XVIII. 8. 4-7.

40 See Dinarchus, *Adversus Demosthenem* 81. 103; Diodorus Siculus XVIII. 8. 4; Aristotle (?), *Rhetorica ad Alexandrum* 1421 a 38; Curtius Rufus X. 2; H. Berve (see note 33), pp. 276-7. Apparently there was no objection to Alexander's demand for divine honors.

41 See R. Heberdey, *Festschrift für Theodor Gomperz* (Vienna, 1902), pp. 412-16. See also note 37. It appears that Nicanor was rather active, both as a politician and soldier, in the service of Alexander and in that of some of the Diodochi. This might be inferred from a number of references to him by ancient orators and historians. See, for instance, Hyperides I. 14; I. 18. 9 ff.; Dinarchus (see note 40), I. 169. 175; Plutarch, *Phocion* 31 ff.; Diodorus Siculus XVII. 109, *et passim*; XVIII. 64; XVIII. 68; XVIII. 72. 3 ff.; XVIII. 72. 7 ff.; XVIII. 75. 1; Polyaenus IV. 11. 2. See also J. Beloch, *Griechische Geschichte*, vol. III, part 1 (Strasbourg, 1904), p. 106; pp. 108-9; vol. III, part 2, pp. 192-3; p. 384.

42 See also Chapter VI. Should the statement about Nicanor's absence actually refer to the deeds he performed for Alexander rather than for Cassander, then Aristotle's will must have been drawn before 13 June 323 B.C., the date on which Alexander died in Babylon. If this is so, then the will was drawn in Athens rather than in Chalcis. It was the sudden death of Alexander which subsequently caused Aristotle to leave Athens rather hurriedly and to retire to Chalcis in the summer of 323 B.C. See Chapter XII.

43 See *II VA* 34. It will be noted that in the last will and testament of Theophrastus, Hipparchus is mentioned among the members of the Peripatetic community. See DL V. 53; V. 54.

44 Suda, 'article' Hipparchus, calls Hipparchus a 'relative' of Aristotle. Under Athenian law, the appointment of an executor or trustee was not restricted to a kinsman of the testator. In order to prevent fraud or depletion of the estate by the executor or trustee, the latter, especially if he was not a kinsman of the testator, frequently received a generous bequest. Moreover, the testator, in order to prevent abuse, often attempted to create ties of kinship between himself and the executor or trustee by affiancing the executor to the testator's wife or daughter.

45 See also No. IX, text, pp. 186-7 and 205-7.

46 See Sextus Empiricus, *Adversus Mathematicos* I. 258.

47 DL V. 39. In his will, Theophrastus stipulates that a memorial statue of Nicomachus be erected in the Peripatus. DL V. 52. See also note 35 and note 147.

48 This seems to be the obvious meaning of Nos III-IX. G. Bruns (see note 25), pp. 19-23, gives a different interpretation, as does O. Schulthess, *Vormundschaft nach Attischem Recht* (Freiburg i. Br., 1886), pp. 60-1.

49 See also No. X, text, pp. 187, 207-8 (Arabic version), where we are told of

the loyalty and devotion with which Herpyllis had served Aristotle. This would clearly indicate that she was his (or Pythias') maid-servant.

50 See Eusebius, *op. cit.*, XV. 2. 15. This story would conflict with the report that Aristotle married Pythias, the daughter (?) or sister (?) or niece (whom he later adopted) of Hermias of Atarneus, unless Pythias was also the concubine of Hermias. Pythias bore Aristotle a daughter, also named Pythias. Naturally, it might be possible that Pythias, the mother, died soon after marrying Aristotle (and after giving birth to her child), that is, while Aristotle was still in Assos and near Hermias; and that after her death Aristotle took up with Herpyllis, whom he could not, or would not, marry because she had been Hermias' concubine (?). But if Pythias died while Aristotle was still with Hermias (348–47 to 345 B.C.), then her daughter Pythias would have been at least twenty-two years old at the time Aristotle made his last will, something which No. IV ('when the girl [Pythias] shall be grown up') expressly contradicts. In any event, Aristotle's daughter Pythias was not yet fourteen years old at the time Aristotle drafted his will (probably in 323–22 B.C.) and hence must have been born after 341–40 B.C., that is, after Hermias of Atarneus had been captured and executed by the Persians.

51 DL V. 1; *VH* 4. See also Athenaeus, *Deipnosophistae* XIII. 589C.

52 Eusebius, *op. cit.*, XV. 2. 15. See also *Frag. Hist. Graec.* (Jacoby) 566, F 157.

53 See also note 101.

54 DL V. 3.

55 Eusebius, *op. cit.*, XV. 2. 14–15.

56 Eusebius, *loc. cit.*

57 See No. XXIV, text, p. 217.

58 See also note 151; Eusebius, *op. cit.*, XV. 2. 5; XV. 2. 12; XV. 2. 14–15.

59 Under Athenian law, an adopted son could inherit intestate only if he had been adopted during the lifetime of the deceased. Testamentary adoption was possible but would not have this effect.

60 See Nos X–XIV, text, pp. 207–9.

61 DL V. 1.

62 No. XI, text, p. 208.

63 *VH* 4.

64 See, for instance, Athenaeus (see note 51); Eusebius, *op. cit.*, XV. 2. 15; Timaeus, in *Frag. Hist. Graec.* (Jacoby) 566, F. 157.

65 Demosthenes, *Oratio* XLVI. 22; Isaeus, *Oratio* VII. 30–1; *Oratio* X. 12–13. It might be interesting to note that, in *Laws* 924D ff., Plato advances similar views. But he insists that this rule should not be rigidly enforced, and that the law, like a good father, should in such a case take into account disparity of age as well as defects of mind or body.

66 Demosthenes, *Oratio* XLVI. 20.

67 See Diodorus Siculus XVIII. 75. 1; Polyaenus IV. 11. 2. See also notes 37 and 41.

68 Sextus Empiricus, *Adversus Mathematicos* I. 258.

69 DL V. 53 (the testament of Theophrastus).

70 DL V. 53 (the testament of Theophrastus).

71 *Ibid.*

72 See also No. IV, text, pp. 200–2.

73 Nicomachus was taught by Theophrastus (DL V. 38–9) and died a young soldier 'in the war.' See Eusebius, *op. cit.*, XV. 2. 15; Suda, 'article' Nicomachus. This Nicomachus apparently was a never-do-well. See also *Gnomologium Vaticanum* (ed. L. Sternbach, Berlin, 1963), no. 330, p. 130; Chapter V at the end; notes 35 and 122.

74 Some of the modern interpreters of Aristotle's testament (see note 25) consider this instrument primarily an appointment of Nicanor as the guardian of Aristotle's two minor children. This view, which seems to have been fostered by the text transmitted by Diogenes Laertius, is not entirely correct. It must also be borne in mind that the text of Diogenes Laertius is only an abridgement and, perhaps, a badly garbled version of the original document.

75 See also note 37. This passage probably signifies that, as the 'interim heir designate,' Nicanor, at least for the time being, had the temporary rights and duties of an older brother (and father) and, it may be assumed, acted as a sort of guardian of the two minor children.

76 See also No. III, text, pp. 195–200.

77 See note 67.

78 It appears that these 'other trustees (or executors),' namely, Timarchus, Hipparchus and Dioteles, as well as Antipater and Theophrastus, had been appointed in the event Nicanor should prove to be unable 'to take over.' See No. III, text, pp. 195–200.

79 See Demosthenes, *Oratio* XLVI. 20.

80 See Demosthenes, *Oratio* XLIV. 65–8; *Oratio* XLVI. 14.

81 See note 34 and the corresponding text, and No. XV, text, pp. 209–13.

82 See note 37.

83 See also note 67 and No. IV, text, pp. 200–2.

84 Sextus Empiricus, *Adversus Mathematicos* I. 258, and No. IV, text, pp. 200–2.

85 *I VA* 16.

86 This, then would imply that Arimneste, the (older ?) sister of Aristotle, had been married three (?) times: to Demotinus or Callisthenes, the father of Hero (the mother of the historian Callisthenes); to the father of Theophrastus; and to Proxenus, the father of Nicanor.

87 *II VA* 32.

88 *IV VA* 34.

89 DL V. 53.

90 See note 68.

91 DL V. 52.

92 DL V. 52. Theophrastus may have acquired this property or house from Aristotle. It might be the house mentioned in Aristotle's will (DL V. 14). See No. XIII, text, pp. 208–9.

93 DL V. 39.

94 Theophrastus also composed a *Callisthenes or On Bereavement* (DL V. 44). This work was probably a 'memorial' or *consolatio mortis* dedicated to the memory of Callisthenes, the historian, who had been foully murdered by Alexander in 327 B.C. This, then, might possibly be an additional indication that Theophrastus was a relative both of Callisthenes and Aristotle.

95 DL V. 53. For a detailed genealogy of Aristotle, see A.-H. Chroust (see note 32) and Chapter V; A.-H. Chroust, 'Aristotle and Callisthenes of Olynthus,' *Classical Folia*, vol. 20, no. 1 (1966), pp. 32–41, and Chapter VI.

96 It has already been pointed out that on account of his high position as well as his power, Antipater was appointed by Aristotle a kind of *tutor honoris causa datus*, primarily to see to it that the provisions of Aristotle's last will and testament would be carried out. See note 32 and the corresponding text.

97 Theophrastus, it must be presumed, did so after the death of Nicanor in the year 317 B.C.

98 Under Athenian law, some of the duties of a guardian seem to have been the following: he could make certain transactions regarding the estate which were deemed necessary in order to conserve the estate, or carry on an enterprise that had already existed at the time of the testator's death. But he had no right to devise or alienate land holdings.

99 Under Athenian law, the testator could make some limited bequests to persons other than his natural male heirs. It will be noted (see p. 208) that Aristotle does not, and could not, bequeath to Herpyllis one of his two houses (in Stagira and in Chalcis). Legally he could not alienate this kind of property through a bequest, but merely stipulate that she may have temporary use (life use) of one of these two houses. See here also Isaeus, *Oratio* IX. 12.

100 'My maid-servant Herpyllis,' a passage which is omitted by Diogenes Laertius. See note 49.

101 See DL V. 1 (Timaeus); *VH* 4. This is also confirmed by Athenaeus (see note 51): 'As for Aristotle of Stagira, did he not beget Nicomachus from the courtesan (concubine) Herpyllis and live with her until his death? So says Hermippus in his first book of his work *On Aristotle*, adding that she received fitting provisions by the terms of the philosopher's last will and testament.' Eusebius, *op. cit.*, XV. 2. 15 (Aristocles), claims, however, that 'Aristotle married Herpyllis of Stagira.' The dispositive provisions found in Nos X–XIV, it will be noted, are in themselves not entirely inconsistent with the assumption that, after all, Herpyllis at one time became Aristotle's legitimate wife. And it was not unusual that in his will the husband gave his surviving wife in marriage to a kinsman or friend. See also notes 51–2.

102 This seems to be indicated by the remark found in DL V. 16, where we are informed that Aristotle 'placed a skin of warm oil on his stomach,' presumably to alleviate pain, and that 'he bathed in warm oil.' *Ibid.*; Eusebius, *op. cit.*, XV. 2. 8. See also Aelian, *Varia Historia* IX. 23; Gellius, *Attic Nights* XIII. 5; Valerius Maximus V. 6, ext. 5; Dionysius of Halicarnassus, *I Epistola ad Ammaeum* 5; Censorinus, *De Die Natali* XIV. 16;

VH 8; DL V. 10; A.-H. Chroust, 'The Myth of Aristotle's Suicide,' *Modern Schoolman*, vol. 44, no. 2 (1967), pp. 177–8, and Chapter XIV.

103 Athenaeus (see note 51).

104 See Demosthenes, *Oratio* LIX (*Against Neaera*) 52; Isaeus, *Oratio* III. 35.

105 Like the provision in No. XIV, this passage seems to indicate that Herpyllis was never Aristotle's lawful wedded wife, and that she was only his 'maid-servant.' See, however, note 101 and Eusebius, *op. cit.*, XV. 2. 15. However, it was not unusual for a husband to given his surviving wife in marriage to a kinsman or friend.

106 We do not know whether Herpyllis married after the death of Aristotle.

107 So far as we know, the Roman *talentum maximum* never exceeded 120 *librae*. Hence, the reference to 125 *librae* might be a scribal error.

108 Such generous provisions for loyal and valued servants were not uncommon in antiquity. It has already been pointed out that Aristotle could not, and did not, outright bequeath one of his two houses to Herpyllis. Under Athenian law, he could not alienate this kind of property in a will, although he could grant more limited interests, or make some limited bequests, such as a life estate or life use, to persons other than his male heirs. See also note 92

109 Phaestis' ancestors originally came from Chalcis on the island of Euboea. See Dionysius of Halicarnassus, *I Epistola ad Ammaeum* 5.

110 See Eusebius, *op. cit.*, XV. 2. 15. This might also have been one of the reasons why Aristotle stipulates in his will that Herpyllis could live in his ancestral (paternal) house in Stagira, if she should choose to do so.

111 Aristotle's paternal ancestors originally came from the island of Andros. Thucydides IV. 88, calls Stagira a colony of Andros. See also Strabo VIII. frag. 35; Chapter V.

112 The rebuilding of Stagira by King Philip or Alexander, which has been questioned by some scholars, is attested by *VM* 17; *VL* 17; *I VA* 13; *II VA* 27; *IV VA* 25; Pliny, *Hist. Nat.* VII. 109; Dio Chrysostom, *Oratio* II. 79, and *Oratio* XLVII. 9; Aelian, *Varia Historia* III. 17; XII. 54; Diodorus Siculus XVI. 52. 9; Valerius Maximus V. 6, ext. 5; Plutarch, *Ne Suaviter Quidem Vivi Posse Secundum Epicurum* 15 (*Moralia* 1097B); Plutarch, *Adversus Coloten* 32 (*Moralia* 1126C). See also O. Gigon, *Vita Aristotelis Marciana* (Berlin, 1962), pp. 56–7.

113 The will of Theophrastus, for instance, contains a similar provision. There the testator stipulates that of his 'household articles so much shall be given to Pompylus, as the executors think to be proper,' because 'Pompylus . . . [has] long been emancipated and [has] done me much service.' DL V. 54–5. Since Theophrastus was something of a 'lawyer'— the catalogue of his writings preserved by Diogenes Laertius mentions several treatises on law—his will is of great interest from a legal and technical point of view.

114 It is held, however, that adoption as such could not be used to legitimize an illegitimate son. See Isaeus, *Oratio* XII (*ex rel. Euphiletus*) 2–3.

115 Under Athenian law, properly adopted or legitimized sons had the same right to intestate succession as had legitimate sons, provided the adoption or legitimation had taken place during the lifetime of the adoptive parent. See notes 15–16, and the corresponding text. But an adopted son could not devise or alienate the estate he had inherited, either by adopting someone else or by a formal will. If he should die without male issue, as Nicomachus apparently did, the estate went as if he had never been adopted —in the case of Nicomachus, to the male children of Pythias. See Demosthenes, *Oratio* XLIV. 65–8; Demosthenes, *Oratio* XLVI. 14.

116 See note 114.

117 Since at the time of his death, Aristotle apparently had no estate in Athens—something which may be inferred from his will which makes no reference whatever to Athens—Athenian legal policy regarding the legal status of a male offspring of a legally unrecognized union (concubinage) between two aliens, after all, may not have affected Nicomachus' claim against his father's estate. More than that: the omission of any reference to Athens or to any real estate there also seems to dispose of the traditional and still widely held view that Aristotle ever owned a 'school' of his own (consisting of distinct grounds, buildings, a 'garden' and a common library) in Athens, allegedly founded between 335–34 and 323 B.C., that is, a school in the physical as well as legal sense of the term, which was on an equal footing with the Platonic Academy. It also may vitiate the traditional opinion that Aristotle was the first scholarch of this 'school,' although it does not deny that he probably inaugurated a new and very fruitful philosophic trend. While the preserved wills of Theophrastus, Straton of Lampsacus and Lycon, all of them scholarchs of the Peripatus, are replete with provisions and directives regarding the 'school' and the 'school property,' the last will and testament of Aristotle contains no such provisions and directives. This omission probably constitutes the most important and most far-reaching aspect of Aristotle's will in that it decisively affects our whole conception of the history of Greek philosophy. As such it might compel historians of ancient philosophy to revise and, in all likelihood, discard the thesis that Aristotle owned a physically or materially as well as legally distinct 'school' of his own in Athens, over which he presided. R. A. Gauthier, *Aristote: Éthique à Nicomaque*, vol. I, part 1 (Louvain-Paris, 1970), p. 43, note 107, however, does not accept this argument. He argues as follows: although it is true that Athenian law did deny *metics* the right of acquiring real property in Athens or Attica, in practice this interdict was frequently ignored or simply circumvented in that the *metic* acquired this real property by making use of a 'front man' or by using a pseudonym. Accordingly, we may surmise that Aristotle, too, managed to circumvent these legal restrictions and acquire a house or 'garden.' Gauthier also maintains that DL V. 39, where we are informed that Theophrastus 'is said to have become the owner of a garden of his own after Aristotle's death, thanks to the intervention of Demetrius

of Phaleron,' in itself does not prove that Aristotle did not have his own distinct κῆπος. Gauthier bases his view on DL V. 36, where we are informed that when Aristotle 'withdrew to Chalcis, he [*scil.*, Theophrastus] took over the school himself, in the 114th Olympiad [in 323 B.C.]. See here also J. Pečirka, *The Formula for the Grant of Enktesis in Attic Inscriptions* (Acta Universitatis Carolinae Philosophica et Historica, vol. XV, Prague, 1966), *passim*. Gauthier, whose matchless scholarship cannot be contested, seems to overlook, however, that the text of DL V. 36 does not necessarily imply that the 'taking over of the school' by Theophrastus was tantamount to a conveyance of title to a building. It is possible, however, that at one time Aristotle may have leased such a building in Athens, and that on his departure from Athens in 323 B.C. he transferred this lease to Theophrastus. While the thesis advanced by Gauthier certainly has much merit, there still remain a number of fairly weighty arguments against his otherwise persuasive reasoning: unlike the wills of the other Peripatetic scholarchs, the will of Aristotle makes no reference whatever to any property, real or personal, or to any 'school' in a legalistic or physical sense, in Athens. Naturally, one might interpose here that on the eve of his departure for Chalcis in 323 B.C., Aristotle, who is said to have donated his library (the 'library of the school'?) to Theophrastus, may also have handed over or donated the 'physical plant' of the 'school' to Theophrastus. Such an argument, however, is faced by a further legal difficulty: since Aristotle had a daughter (about to be married to her cousin, Nicanor) and an adopted or legitimized son, Nicomachus, under Athenian law he could not have alienated so valuable a piece of property by donating it to Theophrastus, thus depriving his descendants (through his daughter) of their rightful claim to this property. This leaves a further possibility: Aristotle simply sold the 'school property' to Theophrastus, perhaps by resorting to a 'token sale.' However, we have no evidence whatever in support of such an assumption. One final remark: Theophrastus might have been a remote (agnatic?) relative of Aristotle. See notes 85-95 and the corresponding text. Aristotle gave or sold him the 'school property' on the condition that at some later time he would marry his daughter, Pythias, and thus keep the property within agnatic lines. But the will of Aristotle mentions Nicanor rather than Theophrastus as the prospective husband of Pythias. Theophrastus is mentioned in the will as a possible administrator or executor of the will (and of the estate), and as a possible husband of Pythias in the case Nicanor should die prematurely, that is, before having married Pythias.

118 See note 128.

119 This seems to follow from Nos V–VII (Nicanor), and from No. VIII (Theophrastus).

120 See here also the comments to No. III, text, pp. 195–200, at the end.

121 This is the view held by some scholars.

122 See also the comments to No. III, text, pp. 195–200. *Gnomologium Vaticanum,*

no. 330, p. 130 (ed. L. Sternbach, Berlin, 1963), relates that as a student, Nicomachus displayed little or no interest in his philosophic studies. His teacher, Theophrastus, attempted to spur on the indifferent student by reminding him that he, Nicomachus, was not only the heir to his father's (Aristotle's) estate, but also the successor to his father's intellectual work and philosophic achievements. This remark, if historical, would indicate that Nicomachus did in fact inherit Aristotle's estate. Since Nicanor died without any male issue by Pythias, it is quite likely that, for the time being, Aristotle's whole estate went to Nicomachus. It is also possible that Nicomachus subsequently squandered his father's estate. This might be inferred from the following: when Epicurus (and other detractors of Aristotle) claims that in his youth Aristotle squandered his patrimony, he might have in mind Nicomachus rather than Aristotle. See Eusebius, *op. cit.*, XV. 2. 1; DL X. 8; Athenaeus, *Deipnosophistae* VIII. 354C; Philodemus, *De Rhetorica: Volumina Rhetorica*, vol. II (ed. S. Sudhaus, Leipzig, 1896), col. XLIX, 37 (p. 52, Sudhaus). See also Chapter V at the end, and notes 35 and 73.

123 Some of these problems have been discussed by G. Bruns (see note 21), pp. 11–23; A. Hug (see note 21), pp. 1–21; M. Plezia (see note 25), pp. 215–24; O. Schulthess (see note 48), pp. 60–1.

124 See, for instance, Demosthenes, *Oratio* XLVI. 14–15.

125 See No. XIII.

126 See Nos XVII–XXI.

127 See Nos V–VII (Nicanor), and No. VIII (Theophrastus).

128 In Athens, an illegitimate son lost his right to succession in 403–2 B.C. See Demosthenes, *Oratio* XLIII; Isaeus, *Oratio* VI (*In re Estate of Philectemon*) 47.

129 Demosthenes, *Oratio* XLVI. 18.

130 Failure on the part of the freedman (or freedwoman) to comply with the conditions attached to his manumission might result in his being reduced once again to the status of a slave. By the same token, full freedom, as a rule, was not granted until all the conditions attached to the manumission had been met.

131 Pliny, *Hist. Nat.* VIII. 16. 44, for instance, relates that King Philip and Alexander gave generous financial support to Aristotle's scholarly and scientific investigations. Lycon Pythagoraeus, according to Eusebius, *op. cit.*, XV. 2.8–9, refers to Aristotle's wealth, as does Seneca, *Dialogus* VI. 27. See also Aelian, *Varia Historia* IV. 19; Athenaeus, *op. cit.*, IX. 398E; DL V. 16; Gellius, *Attic Nights* III. 17.

132 Ancient testators not infrequently emancipated their elderly and deserving slaves. In some instances, they also rewarded them with small gifts or repaid their loyal services with small bequests.

133 As to the meaning of this phrase, see No. XI. Here, again, Aristotle seems to be concerned with having everything done in a proper and dignified manner, thereby upholding his own standards and reputation, as well as the reputation of his family and household.

134 These differences in the texts may, after all, reflect an inaccurate translation on the part of the Arabic (or Syriac) biographers, or on the part of their immediate source, or perhaps the product of Diogenes Laertius' deliberate abridgment.

135 The particular phrasing of this passage seems to exclude the assumption, however, that Myrmex was a (illegitimate?) son of Herpyllis (and Aristotle?). Assuming that Myrmex was a slave of Aristotle, something which is by no means certain, then it should be borne in mind that under Athenian law a slave, as a rule, was incapable of acquiring property for himself. But it was frequently in the interest of the master to leave to his slave at least part of what he had acquired. The latter might use his earnings to buy his freedom.

136 Some scholars are of the opinion that the name should be rendered as 'Thale' rather than 'Thales,' and that Thale was a maid-servant.

137 The implication seems to be that Thales (or Thale) was an elderly person who had faithfully served Aristotle and his family over a long period of time.

138 See also No. XVIII, p. 214.

139 It seems unlikely that the divergent Arabic text is the result of a later interpolation.

140 A similar stipulation can be found in the will of Theophrastus, DL V. 55. Here Manes and Callias are promised their 'freedom on the condition that they would stay four additional years in the "garden" [scil., with the Peripatus and with the property belonging to the Peripatetic community] and work together, and that their conduct be free of blame.'

141 Lycon stipulates in his will that Agathon should be emancipated after two years, while Ophelio and Posidonius should be freed after four years of further service. DL V. 73. See also note 140.

142 See DL V. 55 (will of Theophrastus); DL V. 63 (will of Straton of Lampsacus); DL V. 72–3 (will of Lycon). In his will (DL V. 55), Theophrastus explicitly stipulates that the slave Euboeus 'must be sold.' Euboeus apparently had been a poor or disloyal servant. In Politics 1330 a 33, Aristotle maintains that it might be 'expedient that liberty should always be held out [to slaves] as the reward of their services.'

143 Theophrastus directs in his will (DL V. 51) that a bust of Aristotle, which apparently had been damaged (during the siege of Athens by Demetrius Poliorcetes in 296–94 B.C., or during the anti-Macedonian uprising in Athens in 289–87 B.C.—see Plutarch, Demetrius 33–4; 46; Pausanias I. 25. 2; I. 25. 8; I. 25. 26), should be replaced (repaired?) and set up in the sanctuary of the Peripatus. In his will (DL V. 64) Straton of Lampsacus directs Arcesilaus, Olympichus and Lycon (the last two were executors of Straton's will) to take care of his—Straton's—monument. In his will (DL V. 71), Lycon directs that 'proper commemorative rites' in his honor be instituted by his heirs, and that a statue be erected in his memory.

144 Dionysius of Halicarnassus, I Epistola ad Ammaeum 5.

145 See also *VM* 3; *VV* 2; *VL* 3; *IV VA* 3.

146 *VM* 3; *VV* 2; *VL* 3.

147 About Arimnestus, see Chapter V. In his will Theophrastus stipulates that 'the life-size statue of Nicomachus [the son of Aristotle and Herpyllis] should be completed . . . [since] the price agreed upon for the making of the statue had been paid to Praxiteles. The rest of the cost should be defrayed [from the trust funds at the disposal of Hipparchus].' See DL V. 52. The 'trust funds' mentioned in this connection are also to be 'applied to complete the rebuilding of the Museum.' See DL V. 51. The sculptor referred to by Theophrastus is Praxiteles the Younger. The provision mentioned in DL V. 52 is also indicative of the fact that at the time Theophrastus made his will (he died in 287–86 B.C.) Nicomachus was already dead.

148 See Pliny, *Hist. Nat.* XXXV. 106.

149 According to a tradition distinctly hostile to Aristotle, the latter is said to have sacrificed to his wife Pythias on the occasion of her death in the same manner 'as the Athenians sacrifice to Demeter of Eleusis.' See Eusebius, *op. cit.*, XV. 2. 8 (Lycon Pythagoraeus). It is not impossible that the slanderous story related by Lycon is simply a perversion of the stipulation contained in No. XXIII, as well as a transfer from Phaestis (Aristotle's mother) to Pythias (Aristotle's wife).

150 *I VS* 10 relates that upon the death of Aristotle, the grateful people of Stagira, in order to honor him and to show their gratitude for what he had done for his native city (he was instrumental in having Stagira rebuilt, see note 112), brought his remains to Stagira. This story, with further elaborations, additions and embellishments, is repeated in *II VA* 25–30, *III VA* and *IV VA* 30–1. See also *VM* 17–18; *VL* 17; 19; Chapter IV, notes 76–7, and the corresponding text. We possess no other evidence, however, in support of this attractive story. We do not know when and where Pythias, the wife of Aristotle, died. It is possible that she died in Macedonia, that is, before Aristotle returned to Athens in 335–34 B.C. Hence, it is possible that she was laid to rest in Stagira. Since, however, Stagira might have been rebuilt only after Pythias' death, her remains might have been transferred from her original resting place to Stagira at some later date.

151 This would dispel some of the unpleasant stories about the marriage of Aristotle and Pythias which a slanderous tradition, hostile to Aristotle and Pythias, had invented and circulated in order to malign and embarrass Pythias, the 'barbarian,' and Aristotle. See note 50.

152 See, in general, A.-H. Chroust, 'Aristotle's religious convictions,' *Divus Thomas*, vol. 69, fasc. 1 (1966), pp. 91–7, and Chapter XVI.

153 See note 146, and the corresponding text.

154 According to Plato, *Phaedo* 118A, Socrates' last words were: 'Crito, I owe a cock to Asclepius. Will you see to it that this debt is paid?'

155 See No. III, text, pp. 195–200.

156 See No. XV, pp. 209–13 (the Arabic version).

157 See No. XIII, pp. 208–9, especially note 112.

158 See No. XXVI, p. 218.

159 See note 131.

160 Strabo XIII. 1. 54.

161 See, for instance, *I VA* 16; *II VA* 32; *IV VA* 34.

162 See DL V. 39.

163 See note 117.

164 See also W. Jaeger, *Aristotle: Fundamentals of the History of His Development* (Oxford, 1948), pp. 320–1.

CHAPTER XVI   ARISTOTLE'S RELIGIOUS CONVICTIONS

* In an essentially different form, this chapter was first published in *Divus Thomas*, vol. 69, fasc. 1 (1966), pp. 91–7.

1 Demetrius, *De Elocutione* 144 (frag. 668, Rose). In *Metaphysics* 982 b 17, Aristotle admits: 'A man who is puzzled and wonders thinks himself ignorant. Hence, even the lover of myths is in a sense a lover of wisdom, for the myth is made up of wonders.' Μυθολογεῖν, a term used here by Aristotle, may mean (1) to tell mystic tales (see Plato, *Republic* 392B; Plato, *Gorgias* 493D); (2) to tell something in the form of a mystic tale (see Plato, *Republic* 378C); (3) to interpret mystic tales; (4) to invent or fabricate fancy tales (see Plato, *Republic* 379A); (5) to tell stories, to be fond of story-telling or to be talkative; and (6) to be concerned with, or love, myths.

2 Seneca, *Quaestiones Naturales* VII. 30 (frag. 14, Rose; frag. 14, Walzer; frag. 14, Ross; frag. 19, Untersteiner). Similar views were expressed by Cicero, *De Finibus* IV. 5. 11, a passage which might contain an echo of Aristotle's religious position. See also Dio Chrysostom, *Oratio* XII. 29 ff.

3 See also W. Jaeger, Aristotle: *Fundamentals of the History of his Development* (Oxford, 1948), p. 160. The notion that the whole visible universe is a sacred temple was further elaborated by the Stoics (Cleanthes). It is also reflected in some of the writings of Philo of Alexandria and in those of certain Neo-Platonists.

4 Plutarch, *De Tranquillitate Animi* 6 (*Moralia* 477C-F—frag. 14, Ross; frag. 19, Untersteiner).

5 See E. Bignone, *L'Aristotele Perduto e la Formazione Filosofica di Epicuro* (Florence, 1936), vol. I, p. 74.

6 Synesius, *Dion [of Prusa]* 10. 48A (frag. 15, Rose; frag. 15, Walzer; frag. 15, Ross; frag. 20, Untersteiner). This fragment is generally credited to Aristotle's On Philosophy. *Ibid.*, 10. 47D ff., Synesius maintains: 'Those, however, who have taken the other road [*scil.*, the road of faith] ... do not appear to have taken just one single road.... Their mode of deportment is akin to an exultation similar to a Bacchian frenzy ... and they travel beyond the confines of reason without having made use of reason.

As a matter of fact, the experience of the holy or divine is never under the constraint of reason or, perhaps, achieved by way of an intellectual progress.' See frag. 20, Untersteiner.

7 Psellus, *Schol. ad Ioh. Climacum* (Cat. des Manusc. Alchim. Grecs, ed. J. Bidez, Paris, 1928) 6. 171 (frag. 15, Walzer; frag. 15, Ross; frag. 20, Untersteiner).

8 Aristotle, *Eudemian Ethics* 1248 a 30 ff.

9 See also Plato, *Epistle* VII 341CD.

10 See J. Croissant, *Aristote et les Mystères* (Paris, 1932), pp. 152–53.

11 See here also Cicero, *Tuscul. Disput.* I. 27. 67. This passage contains an echo of Aristotle's 'mystical' views.

12 Simplicus, *Comment. in Arist. De Caelo*, CIAG, vol. VII (ed. J. Heiberg, 1894), p. 485, lines 19–22 (frag. 49, Rose; frag. 1, Walzer; frag. 1, Ross). DL V. 22 (no. 14) and *VH* 10 (no. 9), list an *On Prayer* in one book. *VL* 52 concludes by citing this passage: '*Quod enim intellegat aliquid et super intellectum et super substantiam, Aristoteles manifestus est apud finem libri de oratione plane dicens quod deus aut intellectus est aut aliquid ultra intellectum.*' It might be interesting to compare this Aristotelian passage with St John IV: 24: 'God is a Spirit ($\pi\nu\epsilon\hat{v}\mu\alpha$); and they that worship Him must worship Him in spirit and in truth.' See also A.-H. Chroust, 'A note on some of the minor lost works of the young Aristotle,' *Tijdschrift voor Filosofie*, vol. 27 (1965), pp. 310–19, and Vol. II, Chapter II, notes 7–22, and the corresponding text.

13 A similar view can be found in Aristotle's lost *On Philosophy*. See Cicero, *De Natura Deorum* I. 13. 33 (frag. 26, Rose; frag. 26, Walzer; frag. 26, Ross; frag. 39, Untersteiner): 'Now he [*scil.*, Aristotle] ascribes all divinity to Mind....' See also Aristotle, *Metaphysics* 1072 b 14 ff. (according to W. Jaeger, part of the *Urmetaphysik*); 1074 b 34 (where God is called $\nu\acute{o}\eta\sigma\iota\varsigma$ $\nu o\acute{\eta}\sigma\epsilon\omega\varsigma$); Aristotle, *De Generatione Animalium* 736 b 27–8; Aristotle, *Protrepticus* (Iamblichus, *Protrepticus*, p. 48, lines 16–21, ed. Pistelli—frag. 61, Rose; frag. 10c, Walzer; frag. 10c, Ross; frag. 110, Düring; frag. 106, Chroust). See further A.-H. Chroust, 'The concept of God in Aristotle's lost dialogue *On Philosophy* (Cicero, *De Natura Deorum* I. 13. 33),' *Emerita*, vol. 33, fasc. 2 (1965), pp. 205–28, and Vol. II, Chapter XIV, as well as this chapter.

14 See also Aristotle, *Metaphysics* 1072 b 14–29; 1074 b 15–1075 a 11. In Aristotle, *Eudemian Ethics* 1248 a 23 ff., it will be noted, God is still the main theme. Moral action is man's striving towards, and communion with, God. There is a 'principle' beyond which there is no further principle. 'As in the universe, so also in the soul, God moves everything. [Hence,] the starting point of reasoning is not reason itself, but something greater than reasoning. But what could be greater than even rational knowledge or the pure intellect than God?'

15 See note 13 and the text.

16 In *Republic* 509B, Plato insists that 'the Good is not only the author or

cause of man's knowledge of all things known, but also the author or cause of their existence. And yet this Good is no ordinary being, but rather something that is far beyond being. . . .'

17 Essentially the same notion can be found in Plato, *Republic* 613 AB.

18 Aristotle, *De Virtutibus et Vitiis* 1250 b 18 ff.

19 Aristotle, *Eudemian Ethics* 1249 b 13 ff.

20 Plato, *Laws* 966A ff. See also *ibid.*, 893A ff.; 896C ff.

21 Sextus Empiricus, *Adversus Mathematicos* IX. 23 (*Adversus Physicos* I. 23— frag. 10, Rose; frag. 12a, Walzer; frag. 12a, Ross; frag. 14, Untersteiner). This fragment, like the fragments referred to in notes 22 and 23, is commonly ascribed to Aristotle's *On Philosophy*. We shall not discuss here the several attempts on the part of Aristotle to prove the existence of God with the help of the visible and orderly universe (the cosmological proof for the existence of God). See A.-H. Chroust, 'A Cosmological Proof for the Existence of God in Aristotle's Lost Dialogue *On Philosophy*,' *New Scholasticism*, vol. 40, no. 4 (1966), pp. 447–63, and vol. II, Chapter XIII.

22 Sextus Empiricus, *Adversus Mathematicos* IX. 26–7 (*Adversus Physicos* I. 26–7—frag. 11, Rose; frag. 12b, Walzer; frag. 12b, Ross; frag. 26, Untersteiner). See here also Cicero, *De Natura Deorum* II. 37. 95–6 (frag. 12, Rose; frag. 13, Walzer; frag. 13, Ross; frag. 18, Untersteiner); Philo of Alexandria, *Legum Allegoriarum Libri Tres* III. 32. 97–9 (frag. 12, Rose; frag. 13, Walzer; frag. 13, Ross; frag. 15, Untersteiner); Philo of Alexandria, *De Praemiis et Poenis* VII. 41–3 (frag. 13, Walzer; frag. 13, Ross; frag. 16, Untersteiner); and Philo of Alexandria, *De Specialibus Legibus* I. 34. 185–36. 194 (frag. 13, Walzer; frag. 13, Ross; frag. 16, Untersteiner). It might be appropriate to cite here Philo, *Legum Allegoriarum Libri Tres* III. 32. 97–9: 'The earliest thinkers inquired as to how we came to recognize the divine. Later, the most excellent philosophers said that it was from the world and its parts and the powers inherent in these that we came to comprehend their cause. If one saw a house carefully constructed . . . he would gain an idea of the architect, since he would reflect that the house could not have been completed without the art of a craftsman. And so too with a city, a ship or any structure small or great. So also if one comes into this world as into a vast house or city, and sees the heavens revolving and containing all things within them, planets and fixed stars moving uniformly in an orderly and harmonious fashion for the good of the whole, the earth occupying the central region, streams of water and air in between, living beings also, mortal as well as immortal, varieties of plants and crops—if he should perceive all this he will surely reason that these things have not come about without perfect skill, but that there both was and is an architect of this universe, namely, God.' This passage is commonly regarded as a fragment of Aristotle's *On Philosophy*. See also Cicero, *De Natura Deorum* II. 37. 95–6, which is likewise considered a fragment of the Aristotelian *On Philosophy*: 'Great was the saying of Aristotle: "Suppose there were men who had lived always underground

... [and] had never gone above ground. ... Suppose that then, at some time, the jaws of the earth opened, and they were able to escape and make their way from those hidden dwellings into the regions which we inhabit. When they suddenly saw the earth and the seas and the skies, when they realized the grandeur of the clouds and the power of the winds, when they saw the sun and learned its grandeur and beauty as well as its power shown in its filling the sky with light and making day—when, again, night darkened the lands and they saw the whole sky spangled and adorned with stars, and the varying phases of the moon as it waxes and wanes, and the risings and settings of all these celestial bodies, their courses settled and immutable in all eternity—when they saw all these things, most certainly they would have come to the conclusion both that there are gods and that these great and magnificent works are the works of gods." Thus far Aristotle.'

23 Philo of Alexandria, *De Aeternitate Mundi* III. 10 (frag. 18, Rose; frag. 18, Walzer; frag. 18, Ross; frag. 21, Untersteiner). Philo (and Aristotle) declared the visible and harmonious universe imperishable because it is the perfect handiwork of the perfect Creator Who in His perfection cannot create anything defective and, hence, perishable. See also *ibid.*, VII. 34 (frag. 20, Rose; frag. 19b, Walzer; frag. 19b, Ross; frag. 28, Untersteiner); VIII. 39–43 (frag. 21, Rose; frag. 19c, Walzer; frag. 19c, Ross; frag. 17, Untersteiner). Now we may also understand why Philo (and Aristotle) called the visible and harmonious universe the 'visible God.' See *ibid.*, III. 10 (frag. 18, Rose; frag. 18, Walzer; frag. 18, Ross; frag. 21, Untersteiner), and V. 20 (frag. 19, Rose; frag. 19a, Walzer; frag. 19a, Ross; frag. 29, Untersteiner). When Philo (and Aristotle) maintained that the visible and harmonious universe or the 'visible God' is ungenerated and imperishable, we must assume that for Aristotle this visible and harmonious universe or the 'visible God' is without a definite beginning, although it is still the perfect handiwork of the 'invisible God' or pure νοῦς. This view, which most eloquently proclaims a *creatio ab aeterno* rather than a *creatio in tempore*—which, in other words, insists on the co-eternity of God and the universe while maintaining that the universe is the creation of God—would also resolve some of the problems raised by Plato's creationist thesis (in the *Timaeus*) as well as by Aristotle's assertion that God is the cause of the cosmic order and cosmic orderliness. See Cicero, *De Natura Deorum* II. 37. 95–6 (frag. 12, Rose; frag. 13, Walzer; frag. 13, Ross; frag. 18, Untersteiner); Cicero, *Lucullus* XXXVIII. 119 (frag. 22, Rose; frag. 20, Walzer; frag. 20, Ross; frag. 22, Untersteiner). In other words, the 'visible God' or universe has not come about *in tempore*, but is Himself *ab aeternitate*, though dependent on the 'invisible God' or pure νοῦς. (There exists a remote similarity between these views of Aristotle and the relationship of God the Father to God the Son in the Trinitarian doctrine of the Christian tradition. One might even go so far as to maintain that in his notion of the 'visible God' Who exists *ab*

aeterno, Aristotle comes rather close to the concept of Incarnation of the Son of God.) The Creator or pure *νοῦς,* Who is responsible for the *creatio ab aeterno* of the 'visible God,' is not perchance the Platonic Demiurge of the *Timaeus,* but rather the 'cosmic soul' of Plato's *Laws* (897B) which with Aristotle becomes the 'invisible (Supreme) God' or pure *νοῦς.* See Vol. II, Chapters XIII and XIV.

24 See note 21.

25 Aristotle, *Metaphysics* 982 b 28 ff.

26 Aristotle, *Nicomachean Ethics* 1177 b 31 ff. The passages from *Metaphysics* 982 b 28 ff. and *Nicomachean Ethics* 1177 b 31 ff., seem to echo *Epinomis* 988A: 'Let none of the Greeks fear that it is not right for mortal men to preoccupy themselves with divine matters. They must hold an entirely opposite view.' W. Jaeger (see note 3), p. 164, points out that among the ancient Greeks, religious speculation of any kind was traditionally frowned upon. The Greeks held to the view that a knowledge of the divine is a thing that must forever remain unattainable to mortal man. See, for instance, Epicharmus, frag. 20 (Diels-Kranz); Euripides, *Bacchae* 395; 427 ff. For additional information, see Vol. II, Chapter II, notes 7–22, and the corresponding text.

27 The notion expressed here by Aristotle may be a faint echo of Plato's doctrine of the ὁμοίωσις θεῷ, the 'becoming like God.' See, for instance, Plato, *Theaetetus* 176AB; Plato, *Republic* 613AB.

28 Aristotle, *De Caelo* 284 b 3 ff.

29 A faint echo of this notion might be detected in Aristoxenus, frag. 31, Mueller, which some people have credited to Aristotle's lost dialogue *On Philosophy.* According to Aristoxenus, Socrates once met an Indian (Zoroastrian?—see DL II. 45, who relates that Socrates once met a magician from Syria; and A.-H. Chroust, 'Aristotle and the "Philosophies of the East,"' *Review of Metaphysics,* vol. 18, no. 3 [1965], pp. 372–80, and vol. II, Chapter XVI) who asked him about his particular philosophy. When Socrates replied that he was attempting to 'know himself,' the Indian pointed out to him that it was impossible to know oneself unless and until one knew God. See also Aristotle, *Eudemian Ethics* 1249 b 13 ff., quoted in the text to note 18; Plato (?), *I Alcibiades* 132E ff., where we are informed that this 'know thyself' can be fully achieved only in and through the self-contemplation of the intellect whenever the latter is mirrored in the knowledge of God (or God's existence). Similar notions can also be found in the *Epinomis, passim.*

30 Aristotle, *Nicomachean Ethics* 1153 b 32.

31 Iamblichus, *Protrepticus,* p. 48, line 16 (ed. Pistelli—frag. 61, Rose; frag. 10c, Walzer; frag. 10c, Ross; frag. 110, Düring; frag. 106, Chroust). See also note 13 and the corresponding text. Aristotle, *loc. cit.,* continues by pointing out that 'this being so, we ought either to pursue philosophy and philosophic wisdom or bid farewell to life and depart from this world, because all other things seem to be utter nonsense and hopeless

folly.' The notion that the soul is 'the divine in us' can also be found in Aristotle, *Nicomachean Ethics* 1177 b 31 ff., quoted in the text to note 26.

32 See note 12.

33 Aristotle, *De Caelo* 270 b 6 ff.

34 See note 1.

35 See, in general, J. W. Verdenius, 'Traditional and Personal Elements in Aristotle's Religion,' *Phronesis*, vol. 5, no. 1 (1960), pp. 56–70. For his discussion, Verdenius relies almost entirely on the doctrinal treatises credited to Aristotle.

36 Aristotle, *Metaphysics* 982 b 12 ff. See also Plato, *Theaetetus* 155D: 'For wonder is the feeling of a philosopher, and philosophy begins in wonder.'

37 The assertion that philosophy starts in wonder might also explain why in the *Protrepticus* (Iamblichus, *Protrepticus*, p. 53, lines 15 ff., Pistelli; frag. 58, Rose; frag. 12, Walzer; frag. 12, Ross; frag. 44, Düring; frag. 42, Chroust; and *ibid.*, p. 4, lines 15 ff.; see also Iamblichus, *De Vita Pythagorica* XII, p. 31, lines 20 ff., ed. Deubner), Aristotle recommends the impassionate (and reverent) contemplation of the universe. Contemplation of the divine universe in itself is worship of the Divine dwelling within as well as above the visible universe. This being so, man is born into this magnificent universe, into this most sacred temple of God (see note 4), primarily for the purpose of thoughtful contemplation. And thoughtful contemplation is the most exalted form of prayer. See also vol. II, Chapter II, notes 7–22, and the corresponding text; A.-H. Chroust, 'Comments on Aristotle's *On Prayer*,' *New Scholasticism*, vol. 46 (1972), pp. 308–30.

CHAPTER XVII ARISTOTLE'S 'SELF-PORTRAYAL'

* In a different and shorter form, this chapter was first published in *Laval Théologique et Philosophique*, vol. 21, no. 2 (1965), pp. 161–74.

1 See chapters I–IV, *supra*. To cite a few examples: *VM* 15–16, *VV* 15–16, *VL* 15–16 and *IV VA* 16; and 24, relate that Aristotle 'practiced goodness with zest,' and that he devoted himself to the promotion of universal happiness among men; *VM* 31–4; *VV* 24 and *VL* 33–4, cite some of Aristotle's 'guiding maxims'; *VM* 16, *VV* 16, *VL* 16–17, *I VA* 12, *II VA* 25 and *IV VA* 24 report that he had an abiding interest in the promotion of public welfare and in the wellbeing of the commonwealth and commonweal; and *I VA* 12, *II VA* 26 and *IV VA* 24 maintain that he supported the feeble, helped maidens to get married, protected orphans, assisted those who were eager to learn, and obtained alms for the poor. These last statements indicate that the Arabic biographers of Aristotle imputed to him the practice of the typical 'duties of mercy' demanded of a faithful Muslim. The one *Vita Aristotelis* which, in the main, is not blatantly encomiastic is the *Vita Aristotelis Hesychii*. The *Vita Aristotelis* of Diogenes Laertius (DL V. 1–16), on the other hand, combines both encomiastic and derogatory statements about Aristotle.

2 It is assumed here that the extant (or traditional) *Corpus Aristotelicum* contains, at least in part, the authentic writings of Aristotle. This assumption, however, still lacks complete confirmation. It would be outside the limited scope of this investigation to discuss whether and to what extent the traditional *Corpus Aristotelicum* also contains some of the writings of the Early Peripatus, including those of Theophrastus; and whether it might not be preferable to call the *Corpus Aristotelicum* more appropriately *Corpus Scriptorum Peripateticorum Veterum*. See Preface.

3 *Rhetoric* 1355 a 16. Similarly, *Metaphysics* 980 a 21; 993 b 21.

4 *Nicomachean Ethics* 1096 a 16. See also the famous dictum ascribed to Aristotle by his biographers: '*Amicus quidem Socrates, sed magis amica veritas.*' *VL* 28. See *ibid.*: '*De Socrate quidem parum est curandum, de veritate vero multum.*' See also *VV* 9; *VM* 28; 33; *VL* 33; note 86.

5 *Rhetoric* 1355 a 21; 1356 a 1 ff., Aristotle insists that truth itself is the most persuasive force.

6 *De Generatione Animalium* 760 a 30.

7 *De Caelo* 279 b 18.

8 *De Generatione et Corruptione* 325 a 18. See also *Physics* 252 a 23; *De Caelo* 293 a 25; 308 b 13.

9 Iamblichus, *Protrepticus*, p. 40, line 1 (Pistelli). This passage has been identified as a fragment of Aristotle's *Protrepticus*. See frag. 52, Rose; frag. 5, Walzer; frag. 5, Ross; frag. 40, Düring; frag. 38, Chroust.

10 *Topics* 105 a 7.

11 Plutarch, *De Virtute Morali* 7 (*Moralia* 447F ff.).

12 *Nicomachean Ethics* 1109 a 35. See also *ibid.*, 1113 b 3 ff., where Aristotle admits that evil acts may become responsible for good acts.

13 *Ibid.*, 1109 a 29.

14 *Ibid.*, 1110 a 24.

15 Iamblichus, *Protrepticus* (Pistelli) 46, 22 ff. (frag. 55, Rose; frag. 9, Walzer; frag. 9, Ross; frag. 103, Düring; frag. 99, Chroust). See also *Magna Moralia* 1201 a 1 ff.; 1213 b 15 ff.; *Politics* 1252 b 30 ff.; 1342 a 19 ff.; *Eudemian Ethics* 1215 b 15 ff.; *Nicomachean Ethics* 1109 b 34 ff.; 1109 b 19 ff.

16 Sextus Empiricus, *Adversus Mathematicos* IX. 23 (*Adversus Physicos* I. 23—frag. 10, Rose; frag. 12a, Walzer; frag. 12a, Ross; frag. 14, Untersteiner). See also Aristotle, *Metaphysics* 982 b 12 ff.

17 Sextus Empiricus, *Adversus Mathematicos* IX. 26–7 (*Adversus Physicos* I. 26–7—frag. 11, Rose; frag. 12b, Walzer; frag. 12b, Ross; frag. 26, Untersteiner). See also Cicero, *De Natura Deorum* II 37. 95–6 (frag. 12, Rose; frag. 13, Walzer; frag. 13, Ross; frag. 18, Untersteiner); Philo of Alexandria, *Legum Allegoriarum Libri Tres* III. 32. 97–9 (frag. 12, Rose; frag. 13, Walzer; frag. 13, Ross; frag. 15, Untersteiner); Philo of Alexandria, *De Praemiis et Poenis* VII. 40–6 (frag. 13, Walzer; frag. 13, Ross; frag. 16, Untersteiner). See also A.-H. Chroust, 'A cosmological proof for the existence of God in Aristotle's lost dialogue *On Philosophy*,' *The New*

Scholasticism, vol. 40, no. 4 (1966), pp. 447-63, and vol. II, Chapter XIII; vol. II, Chapter XIV; vol. I, Chapter XVI.

18 Philo of Alexandria, *De Aeternitate Mundi* III. 10 (frag. 18, Rose; frag. 18, Walzer; frag. 18, Ross; frag. 21, Untersteiner).

19 Seneca, *Quaestiones Naturales* VII. 30 (frag. 14, Rose,; frag. 14, Walzer; frag. 14, Ross; frag. 19, Untersteiner). See also A.-H. Chroust, 'Aristotle's religious convictions,' *Divus Thomas*, vol. 69, no. 1 (1966), pp. 91-7, and Chapter XVI.

20 DL V. 22 (no. 14); *VH* 10 (no. 9); Simplicius, *Comment. in Aristotelis De Caelo, CIAG*, vol. VII (ed. J. Heiberg, Berlin, 1894), p. 485, lines 19-22 (frag. 42, Rose; frag. 1, Walzer; frag. 1, Ross). See also *VL* 52; Chapter XVI; vol. II, Chapter II, notes 7-22, and the corresponding text.

21 Simplicius, *loc. cit.* See John IV: 24: 'God is Spirit ($\pi\nu\epsilon\hat{\upsilon}\mu\alpha$); and they that worship Him must worship Him in spirit and in truth.' See also Chapter XVI.

22 Athenaeus, *Deipnosophistae* IV. 178E ff; XV. 674E ff. These passages are believed to be fragments of Aristotle's *Symposium*. See frags 100-101, Rose; frags 1-2, Ross. For this whole section, see A.-H. Chroust (see note 19); Chapter XVI; vol. II, Chapters II and XIII.

23 *Nicomachean Ethics* 1179 a 23 ff.

24 *Ibid.*, 1099 b 10 ff.

25 This is the meaning of *Politics* 1325 a 21.

26 *Ibid.*, 1325 a 32. See also *Nicomachean Ethics* 1098 a 17; 1098 b 30 ff.; 1099 a 26; 1102 a 10; 1169 a 28; 1176 b 2; 1177 a 10; *et passim*; *Metaphysics* 1072 b 27.

27 *Nicomachean Ethics* 1099 b 15.

28 Iamblichus, *Protrepticus* (Pistelli) 40, 6 (frag. 52, Rose; frag. 5, Walzer; frag. 5, Ross; frag. 53, Düring; frag. 50, Chroust). See also *Metaphysics*, 1072 b 27, where Aristotle emphasizes that true life is intellectual activity.

29 *Rhetoric* 1370 a 30 ff.

30 *Ibid.*, 1371 a 31 ff. See also Aristotle, *Eudemian Ethics* 1209 a 13 ff. Similar notions are to be found in Aristotle's *Protrepticus*. See, for instance, Iamblichus, *Protrepticus* (Pistelli) 57, 19-23 (frag. 14, Walzer; frag. 14, Ross; frag. 83, Düring; frag. 79, Chroust). Here we are informed that he who actively uses his mental endowments 'lives more' than he who merely possesses mental gifts. See also *Metaphysics* 982 b 12 ff.

31 *Nicomachean Ethics* 1177 a 24 ff.

32 *Rhetoric* 1410 b 10.

33 Iamblichus, *Protrepticus* (Pistelli) 59, 19-23 (frag. 14, Walzer; frag. 14, Ross; frag. 83, Düring; frag. 79, Chroust). See also note 30.

34 Iamblichus, *Protrepticus* (Pistelli) 57, 23-58, 3 (frag. 14, Walzer; frag. 14, Ross; frag. 84, Düring; frag. 80, Chroust).

35 *Ibid.*, 58, 10-14 (frag. 14, Walzer; frag. 14, Ross; frag. 86, Düring; frag. 82, Chroust).

36 *Ibid.*, 59, 3–7 (frag. 14, Walzer; frag. 14, Ross; frag. 90, Düring; frag. 86, Chroust). See also *ibid.*, 56, 22–57, 23 (frag. 14, Walzer; frag. 14, Ross; frags. 80–3, Düring; frags 76–9, Chroust); Aristotle, *Nicomachean Ethics* 1095 b 32 ff.; Aristotle, *Eudemian Ethics* 1216 a 3 ff.; *Magna Moralia* 1185 a 10 ff.; 1201 b 15 ff.

37 Iamblichus, *op. cit.*, 59, 10–12 (frag. 14, Walzer; frag. 14, Ross; frag. 91, Düring; frag. 87, Chroust).

38 *Nicomachean Ethics* 1099 a 10–17.

39 *Ibid.*, 1099 b 15–16.

40 Iamblichus, *op. cit.* 52, 1–5 (frag. 11, Walzer; frag. 11, Ross; frag. 17, Düring; frag. 18, Chroust). See also Aristotle, *Nicomachean Ethics* 1142 a 15 ff.; *Politics* 1334 b 14 ff.; 1334 b 32 ff.

41 *De Partibus Animalium* 644 b 22–645 a 4.

42 *Topics* 105 b 12–19.

43 See also Aristotle, *Physics* 194 b 19 ff.; *Metaphysics* 983 a 25; 993 b 23; 994 b 29; 1025 b 6; etc.

44 See also Aristotle, *De Anima* 402 a 1, where we are told that knowledge is honored for its own sake; and *Metaphysics* 980 a 21, where Aristotle maintains that knowledge is desired by all men.

45 The passage from the *Topics* should also explain why Aristotle became a 'collector of historical facts' —why, in other words, he compiled and organized data as well as the opinions of others. This is the starting point of the doxographical and biographical tradition, which contains the seeds of the later (Hellenistic) 'histories of philosophy,' encyclopaedias, *florilegia* and plain 'text books' or 'introductions' to a specific science.

46 *Posterior Analytics* 99 b 20 ff. See also *ibid.*, 71 b 7 ff.

47 *Ibid.*, 99 b 35 ff.; 100 b 3 ff.

48 *Nicomachean Ethics* 1140 b 31–1141 a 8.

49 *Ibid.*, 1100 b 30 ff.

50 *Ibid.*, 1173 a 4.

51 *Ibid.*, 1098 a 23–5.

52 *Metaphysics* 993 a 30 ff. See also *Meteorologica* 351 b 25.

53 *Politics* 1281 b 1 ff.

54 *Ibid.*, 1281 b 39 ff. See also *Topics* 151 b 12.

55 See *Nicomachean Ethics* 1098 b 9 ff.

56 *Ibid.*, 1098 b 27. See also *ibid.*, 1173 a 1.

57 *Rhetoric* 1355 a 15 ff. See also note 3.

58 *Eudemian Ethics* 1216 b 31.

59 This becomes evident, for instance, in *Metaphysics* 1074 b 10. Aristotle frequently refers to the views held by 'the men of old.'

60 *Rhetoric* 1387 a 16. In these last statements, Aristotle, at least by implication, also makes a fervent plea for historical studies, including the scholarly study of the history of philosophic thought.

61 *De Sophisticis Elenchis* 183 b 17–23.

62 *Topics* 151 b 12 ff.

63 *Meteorologica* 351 b 25-6.

64 *Politics* 1264 a 1-4.

65 *De Caelo* 270 b 19-21. Taken at face value, this statement, like the following statement (in note 66), seems to reiterate the Zoroastrian principle of the 'eternal return.' There can be no doubt that Aristotle was acquainted with Zoroastrian teachings. See A.-H. Chroust, 'Aristotle and the "Philosophies of the East,"' *Review of Metaphysics*, vol. 18, no. 3 (1965), pp. 572-80, and Vol. II, Chapter XVI. For the problem of the 'eternal return,' see also B. L. van der Waerden, 'Das Grosse Jahr und die Ewige Wiederkehr,' *Hermes*, vol. 80 (1952), pp. 129-55; C. Mugler, *Deux Thèmes de la Cosmologie Grecque: Devenir Cyclique et Pluralité des Mondes* (Paris, 1953), *passim*; W. J. W. Koster, *Le Mythe de Platon, de Zarathoustra et des Chaldéens* (Leiden, 1951), *passim*; P. Boyancé, *Études sur le Songe de Scipion* (Bordeaux-Paris, 1936), pp. 164 ff.; E. Effe. *Studien zur Kosmologie und Theologie der Aristotelischen Schrift Über die Philosophie* (Zetemata, Heft 50, Munich, 1970), pp. 64 ff.; J. M. Le Blond, *Logique et Méthode chez Aristote* (Paris, 1939), p. 262; W. J. Verdenius, 'Traditional and Personal Elements in Aristotle's Religion,' *Phronesis*, vol. 5 (1960), p. 57.

66 *Meteorologica* 339 b 29.

67 *Politics* 1329 b 25-7.

68 *Metaphysics* 1074 b 10. See also *De Sophisticis Elenchis* 183 b 17, quoted note 61. See notes 65-6.

69 *De Anima* 403 b 20 ff.

70 *Eudemian Ethics* 1216 b 32 ff.

71 *Politics* 1329 b 34 ff.

72 *Metaphysics* 993 b 11 ff. This passage not only testifies to Aristotle's generosity towards other philosophers, but also reiterates his basic belief that there is something good in everything. See notes 49 and 50.

73 *Politics* 1252 a 24-5.

74 *Rhetoric* 1355 a 18 ff. This passage may also contain a criticism of Isocrates and his type of rhetoric. See Chapter VIII, *passim*.

75 *De Caelo* 279 b 7 ff.

76 It has been suggested that in his later works, Aristotle abandoned the form of the dialogue and resorted to 'acroamatic reports' because he was less interested in moral edification, as was the case with Plato, than in intellectual training. Scientific training must include the experiences of the past. It must be systematic as well as inductive. This might explain why Aristotle's doctrinal treatises are composed in the form of 'prosaic lectures': they are lengthy 'monologues' of the philosopher Aristotle, uninterrupted by the objections of other discussants. The discussion of earlier philosophers, to be sure, is for Aristotle still a dialectical debate—in this sense he is always Plato's disciple—but this debate is merely preliminary to the 'prosaic work' of philosophy and hence no longer the whole or even the main issue.

77 See, for instance, *Physics* 187 a 12 ff.; *De Anima* 409 b 18 ff. This is also

evident from the manner in which Aristotle discusses other philosophers or philosophies in the *Metaphysics* as well as in his other treatises.

78 See *Metaphysics* 980 a 26; 981 b 13; 982 b 12 ff.

79 See, for instance, *Metaphysics* 983 b 20 ff.; *De Anima* 404 a 18 ff.; 405 a 19; 405 a 25; *Physics* 203 b 15 ff.

80 *Metaphysics* 986 b 27 ff.

81 *Ibid.*, 986 b 13 ff.

82 *Ibid.*, 983 b 2 ff.

83 *De Partibus Animalium* 645 a 8-23.

84 *De Caelo* 288 a 2. See also *Nicomachean Ethics* 1173 a 4.

85 See also Iamblichus, *Protrepticus* (Pistelli) 49, 3-52, 16 (frag. 11, Walzer; frag. 11, Ross; frags 11-21, Düring; frags 10-20, Chroust).

86 *VL* 28; 29; *VM* 33; *VV* 9. See also note 4.

87 Olympiodorus, *In Platonis Gorgiam* (ed. W. Norvin), p. 197. A 'fragment' of this Elegy, which was probably composed at the time Aristotle returned to Athens in 335-34 B.C., can be found in *VM* 26, *VV* 11 and *VL* 30. K. Gaiser, 'Die Elegie des Aristoteles auf Eudemos,' *Museum Helveticum*, vol. 23, fasc. 2 (1966), pp. 84-105, gives this Elegy a different interpretation, claiming that it was dedicated to the memory of Eudemus of Cyprus (who is also the 'addressee' of Aristotle's *Eudemus or On the Soul*), rather than composed in honor of Plato. See note 94.

88 *Nicomachean Ethics* 1096 a 12-17. See also notes 4 and 86. In *Nicomachean Ethics* 1155 a 5, Aristotle points out that no one would choose to live without friends, though he may possess all the goods of this earth.

89 *Ibid.*, 1164 b 2-6.

90 *Ibid.*, 1172 b 15-16.

91 *Politics* 1265 a 1-12.

92 This hymn, paean or eulogy can be found in DL V. 7-8; Athenaeus, *Deipnosophistae* XV. 696A ff.; Areius Didymus, *In Demosthenis Orationes Commenta* (ed. H. Diels and W. Schubart, Berlin, 1904), col. 6, 18 ff.

93 DL V. 6; Areius Didymus (see note 92).

94 See, for instance, *Topics* 116 b 37, *et passim*; *Nicomachean Ethics* 1126 b 21; 1155 a 3-32; 1155 b 17-1158 b 11; 1163 a 24 ff.; 1169 b 3 ff., *et passim*; *Eudemian Ethics* 1209 a 4 ff.; 1210 b 23-32; 1213 a 24; 1245 a 30; 1239 a 36 ff., *et passim*; *Politics* 1262 b 7, *et passim*; *Rhetoric* 1361 b 35-38, *et passim*. It should also be borne in mind that Aristotle 'dedicated' a dialogue, *Eudemus or On the Soul* (see note 87), to the memory of his friend Eudemus of Cyprus who had died in Sicily in 354-53 B.C. See A.-H. Chroust, '*Eudemus or On the Soul*: a lost dialogue of Aristotle on the immortality of the soul,' *Mnemosyne*, vol. 19 (series IV), fasc. 1 (1966), pp. 17-30, and vol. II, Chapter V. As regards Aristotle's lasting friendship with Antipater, see, for instance, frags. 663-74, Rose.

95 DL V. 11-16. A slightly different version of this testament can be found in the Arabic *Vitae Aristotelis* of An-Nadim, Al-Mubashir, and Usaibia. See A.-H. Chroust, 'Aristotle's Last Will and Testament,' *Wiener Studien*, vol. 80 (Neue Folge, no. 1, 1967), pp. 90-114, and Chapter XV.

96 DL V. 14.
97 *Ibid.*, V. 13.
98 *Ibid.*, V. 16.
99 *Ibid.*, V. 15.
100 *Ibid.*, V. 16.
101 Demetrius, *De Elocutione* 144 (frag. 668, Rose). There exists an undeniable affinity between this statement and Aristotle, *Metaphysics* 982 b 17: 'A man who is puzzled and wonders most certainly thinks himself ignorant. Hence, the lover of myths is in a sense a lover of wisdom (a philosopher), for the myths contain wonders.'
102 See, in general, A.-H. Chroust (see note 19), and Chapter XVI.
103 See W. Jaeger, *Aristotle: Fundamentals of the History of his Development* (Oxford, 1948), p. 321.
104 When about to die at the age of around 84, Theophrastus was asked by his disciples 'whether he had any last message for them. He made the following statement: "Nothing else but this. The many pleasures which life promises are but dreams. For when we are just beginning to live, we die. Nothing, therefore, is as unprofitable as the love of glory and fame. Farewell, and be happy. Either reject my teachings, which will demand of you an almost infinite amount of labor, or stand forth as the valiant champions of these teachings. In the latter case you might gain much acclaim. Life holds more disappointments than fulfillments. But, since I am no longer able to discuss what we ought to do, you must carry on the inquiry into right conduct." With these words, it is said, he breathed his last.' DL V. 40-1. These remarks, which could have been addressed to all thoughtful men in all ages and in every place, might well have been made also by Aristotle. They convey what, *mutatis mutandis*, seems to have been Aristotle's basic outlook on life as well as a summary of his personal experiences.
105 Aristotle, *Metaphysics* 982 b 12 ff.
106 For some recent attempts to sketch Aristotle's personality and character, see H. Jackson, 'Aristotle's lectureroom,' *Journal of Philology*, vol. 35 (1920), pp. 191–200; E. Barker, 'The life of Aristotle and the *Politics*,' *Classical Review*, vol. 45 (1931), pp. 162–72; P. Wilpert, 'Die wissenschaftliche Persönlichkeit des Aristoteles,' *Blätter für Deutsche Philosophie*, vol. 12 (1938), pp. 293–303; C. M. Bowra, 'Aristotle's hymn to virtue,' *Classical Quarterly*, vol. 32 (1938), pp. 182–9; R. McKeon, 'Plato and Aristotle as historians: a study of the method in the history of ideas,' *Ethics*, vol. 51 (1940–1), pp. 66–101; I. Düring, 'Aristotle the scholar,' *Arctos: Acta Philologica Fennica* (new series), vol. I (1954), pp. 66–77; M. Grene, *A Portrait of Aristotle* (Chicago, 1963), *passim*; J. M. Zemp, *Aristoteles in Selbstzeugnissen und Bilddokumenten* (Hamburg 1961); M. Plezia, 'The human face of Aristotle,' *Classica et Mediaevalia*, vol. 22 (1961), pp. 16–31.

CONCLUSION

1 See Chapter I.

2 See Chapter III.

3 Undoubtedly, Hermippus also cited some unfavorable and even derogatory reports about Aristotle. He did so in order to rebut these reports and, we may presume, in order to make his own account more persuasive and more readily believed. See also note 5, and the corresponding text.

4 See Chapters I and IV.

5 See Chapter I. See also note 3.

6 See Chapters I and IV.

7 See Chapter II.

8 See Chapter III.

9 See Chapter IV. See also Chapter XIII.

10 The chronology of the main events in Aristotle's life is probably the following: he was born during the first half of the first year of the 99th Olympiad, during the early part of the archonship of Diotrephes (384–83 B.C.), that is, between early July and early October of 384 B.C., and probably closer to July. He went to Athens during the first half of the second year of the 103rd Olympiad, during the early part of the archonship of Polycelus (367–66 B.C.), that is, in the (early?) summer of 367 B.C. It is possible, however, that he went there during the latter part of the first year of the 102nd Olympiad, during the latter part of the archonship of Nausigenes (368–67 B.C.), that is, in the late spring of 367. He fled from Athens for the first time during the first half of the first year of the 108th Olympiad, during the early part of the archonship of Theophilus (348–47 B.C.), that is, in the summer or early fall of 348 B.C. He went to Hermias of Atarneus during the second half of the first year of the 108th Olympiad, during the latter part of the archonship of Theophilus (348–47 B.C.), that is, in the spring of 347 B.C. He returned to Macedonia during the second year of the 109th Olympiad, during the archonship of Pythodorus (343–42 B.C.), but it is impossible to determine the exact time he did so. He returned to Athens during the first half of the second year of the 111th Olympiad, during the early part of the archonship of Evaenetus (335–34 B.C.), that is, in the fall (October–November?) of 335 B.C. He fled from Athens for the second time (and went to Chalcis) during the first half of the second year of the 114th Olympiad, during the early part of the archonship of Cephisodorus (323–22 B.C.), that is, in the summer (or early fall?) of 323 B.C. He died in Chalcis in his 63rd year in the first half of the third year of the 114th Olympiad, during the early part of the archonship of Philocles (322–21 B.C.), that is, between (late?) July and early October of 322 B.C., and probably closer to October and prior to the death of Demosthenes, who committed suicide 14 October 322 B.C. See Plutarch, *Demosthenes* 30.

11 See Chapter V.

12 See Chapter VI.
13 See Chapter VII.
14 See Chapter VIII.
15 See Chapters IX and XIII.
16 See Chapter XIII.
17 See Chapter X.
18 See Chapter XIII.
19 See Chapter XI.
20 See Chapters XII and XIII.
21 See Chapters XII and XIV.
22 See Chapter XV.
23 See Chapter XVI.
24 See Chapter XVII.
25 See Chapters XII and XIII.
26 Thanks to the efforts of Demetrius of Phaleron, the Peripatus acquired its own 'garden' during the scholarchate of Theophrastus, that is, some time after the death of Aristotle. See DL V. 39, and Chapter XV, note 117.
27 See A.-H. Chroust, 'Plato's Academy: the first organized school of political science in antiquity,' *Review of Politics*, vol. 29 (1967), pp. 25–40. See also Chapter XIII, note 107, and the corresponding text.

Index of Ancient Authors and Sources

Simple Arabic numbers refer to the text; small Roman numerals to the Preface. Roman numerals and Arabic numbers, when separated by a comma, refer to chapter and note. References to notes in the Preface are indicated as Pref., and Arabic numerals. Detailed references to Diogenes Laertius (DL), Hesychius of Miletus (*VH*), Hermippus of Smyrna, Ptolemy (el-Garib), the *Vita Aristotelis Marciana* (*VM*), the *Vita Aristotelis Vulgata* (*VV*), the *Vita Aristotelis Latina* (*VL*) and to the Syriac as well as Arabic *Vitae Aristotelis* (I *VS*, II *VS*, I *VA*, II *VA*, III *VA* and IV *VA*) are omitted.

Aelian
Varia Historia
(III. 17) I, 45; III, 142; IV, 74; VI, 29; XII, 46; XIII, 96; XV, 112
(III. 19) I, 33; I, 121; III, 24; III, 25; III, 40; III, 41; III, 64; IV, 46; V, 35; VI, 29; IX, 7; IX, 30
(III. 36) I, 53; II, 59; III, 189; III, 198; III, 200; XI, 29; XII, 18; XII, 35; XII, 59; XIV, 29
(III. 46) III, 144
(IV. 8) V, 10
(IV. 9) I, 26; I, 34; I, 35; I, 36; I, 121; III, 47; IV, 44; IV, 46; IV, 48; VII, 10; IX, 7; IX, 30; XIII, 13
(IV. 19) XV, 131
(V. 9) VII, 10; XIV, 4
(VIII. 12) XII, 20; XIII, 61
(VIII. 14) XIV, 28
(IX. 22) VII, 13
(IX. 23) I, 54; II, 47; III, 191; III, 206; XIV, 8; XIV, 18; XV, 102
(XII. 11) XIV, 28
(XII. 43) V, 10
(XII. 54) I, 45; III, 142; IV, 74; VI, 29; IX, 19; XV, 12
(XIV. 1) IV, 79; XI, 30; XII, 40

Aelius Aristides
Oratio
(XLVI 249. 10) I, 27; I, 35; I, 36; III, 40; III, 47; IV, 46; IX, 7; IX, 30
Aeschines
Contra Ctesiphontem
(156) XI, 14
(160) XI, 12
(239 ff.) XI, 14
Oratio
(II. 125) X, 32
Ambryon (Bryon, Bryson)
On Theocritus 27, 40
Ammianus Marcellinus
(XVIII. 3. 7) 83; V, 27; VI, 8; VI, 24; VI, 37
Ammonius
Comment. in Arist. Cat.
(1, 1 ff.) Intr., 1
(3, 8 ff.) III, 74
(6, 25 ff.) Intr., 2
Amphicrates
On Illustrious Men (DL II, 101) XIV, 31
Anaximenes (Anaxarchus?)
Rhetorica ad Alexandrum III, 3; III, 7; III, 172; VI, 42

Index of Modern Authors